DUALISMS:
THE AGONS OF THE MODERN WORLD

RICARDO J. QUINONES

Dualisms

The Agons of the Modern World

UNIVERSITY OF TORONTO PRESS
Toronto Buffalo London

© University of Toronto Press Incorporated 2007
Toronto Buffalo London
Printed in Canada

ISBN 978-0-8020-9763-7

Printed on acid-free paper

Library and Archives Canada Cataloguing in Publication

Quinones, Ricardo J.
Dualisms : the agons of the modern world / Ricardo J. Quinones.

ISBN 978-0-8020-9763-7

1. Literature – Philosophy.   2. Literature – History and criticism.
3. Humanities – Philosophy.   I. Title.

PN49.Q85 2007   801   C2007-903497-7

University of Toronto Press acknowledges the financial assistance to its
publishing program of the Canada Council for the Arts and the Ontario
Arts Council.

At all times we are either Esauites or Jacobites ... and even if ... our doctrine which is proper to the true Church were to triumph yet from our very midst would arise Papists and Turks who would sell title of the 'Church.' Thus the Anabaptists and Sacramentaries have arisen ... thus always Cain or Abel, Esau or Jacob.

Martin Luther, 'The Righteousness of God'

Contents

Preface

Presenting a new typology with a distinctive paradigm of development, *Dualisms* considers four different encounters from four different centuries: Erasmus and Luther, Voltaire and Rousseau, Turgenev and Dostoevsky, and Sartre and Camus. These four dualisms are important for what they are and what they represent; they are historically specific, psychologically far-reaching, and quite dramatic. They stand out as the major intellectual contests that create the modern era, the agons of our time. They turn the eternal dance of twos, the duet, into a duel where they represent not only themselves but also the deep divisions of their societies. They were the recognized centrepieces in their own times, and their actions and responses were anticipated, awaited, debated, scrutinized, perhaps celebrated, but finally, then and even now, thought to have been inevitable.

They were rivals in spirit as well as in thought, and therein lies their appeal. They brought to argument the force of personality, their different and representative sources of intellectual energy, their different fields of vision. In their exchanges they do not 'stick to the subject.' Their debates, while intellectually substantial, are more than that. They express two clashing forces of temperament, two ways of seeing and being, proof of which is that even in their afterlives they remain unreconciled and recurrent.

Evidence is mounting that we are in the midst of a revived interest in dualisms as represented by the complex interactions of prominent artists, writers, and philosophers. To the abundant field of Luther-Erasmus criticism, Fiorella de Michelis Pintacuda has contributed a superb study of their profound theological differences, *Tra Erasmo e Lutero* (2001). And more recently, following up on his *TLS* essay (22 September 2002), in *Camus and Sartre* (2004) Ronald Aronson gives an exemplary account of 'the twentieth century's most famous literary quarrel.' Appearing coincidentally with Aronson's book and marking the kind of renewal I am suggesting, is Ronald E. Santoni's *Sartre on Violence: Curiously Ambivalent* (2003), the second half of which, despite its title, is devoted to the famous confrontation between Sartre and Camus. Also in 2004, David Sprintzen and Adrian van den Hoven's *Sartre and Camus: A Historic Confrontation* provides a valuable documentary history of the quarrel accompanied by opposing essays. Much notice was given to *Wittgenstein's Poker* (2001) by David Edmonds and John Eidinow, which passes as a work of detection but is actually a more elevated account of the clash of two separate philosophical worlds, one of puzzles (Wittgenstein) and the other of problems (Popper). Rona Goffen's *Renaissance Rivals* (2002) revives the concept of the pagan agon to explain the spirit of competition that existed among eminent painters, and so, too, Harold Bloom's *Where Shall Wisdom Be Found?* (2004) is based upon contests, or agons, between rival figures in the quest for wisdom. Ever germane to our subject is Ann Hulbert's *Raising America* (2003), which relies on the rival educational theories of Locke and Rousseau, and, as Sue Halpern highlights in a review essay (2003), carries into the twentieth century new dualisms, such as the 'odd couples' of Holt and Hall, Watson and Gesell, and Spock and Bettelheim. One cannot ignore Norman Podhoretz's *Ex-Friends* (1999) or Rachel Cohen's *A Chance Meeting* (2004), each fascinatingly close to the arguments of this book. Judging by recent exhibitions, the art world's attention to dualisms has been growing at a hectic pace. My project, which has been a long time in the making, received its own welcomed surge by the success of the Matisse-Picasso show in Paris, London, and New York, notably abetted by Jack Flam's splendid story and brilliantly antedated by Yve-Alain Bois's *Matisse and Picasso* (2001). This exposition has been paralleled by another, that of Pissarro and Cezanne, once again heralding the collaborative functioning of artists, not artists in isolation but rather in association. These were followed in the summer of 2006 by Peter Paul Rubens and Jan Brueghel together at the Getty Museum in Los Angeles, and Bellini, Giorgione, and Titian at the National Gallery of Art in Washington DC.[1]

The time seems right to expand inquiry into the nature and function of dualisms at the highest level of encounter between pre-eminent figures, and in so doing, to lay open a new area of study, with its own concepts and avenues of approach. My account appropriately starts with the early modern and the first and the foremost dualism of Erasmus and Luther. Such historical positioning is not accidental; it arises out of the upsurge of radical Protestantism at first augmented and then contested by the expanding consciousness of the Renaissance. It was practically inevitable that the clash between two such as Luther and Erasmus should have occurred, the one requiring such totality of commitment in the exercise of conscience, and the other engaged in the play of consciousness upon the world's multiplicity – Matthew Arnold's 'Hebraism' and 'Hellenism.' What was not inevitable but just as remarkable was that the great dualisms that follow adhere not only in general but in many particulars to their founding pattern. There is a discernible persistence even within abundant historical change. On history's larger plane, the most radical change was the movement from the challenging demands of the Cross to those of Revolution. Yet it is clear that despite this earth-shattering alteration the dynamics of dualisms remained constant.

Such an enlarged historical and comparative scope carries us well beyond the storylines of the separate cross-rivalries. For instance, in regard to Erasmus and Luther, I have long felt the need to open discussion beyond the embattled, rival claims of historians and theologians. *Dualisms* has the capacity to universalize and intensify the terms of understanding, to bring such outstanding figures into a larger and ever ongoing, still-living intellectual conversation. As it moves back and forth between the individual pairs, it provides comparative illuminations; it also engages separate lines of affiliation from which observations can be drawn, principles deduced, and characteristics compared. Put more provocatively, it can make Luther the contemporary of Sartre and indeed, all the figures, in their vibrant engagements of debate, 'our contemporaries.'

In individuals and culture alike, dualisms perform a double duty: while predicated upon the passionate presence of individuals, their effect is stereoscopic.[2] One of their major contributions is to show the formation of ideas in association as creative exchange replaces the view of the artist in isolation. As is evident, revivals respond to needs, to hungers that seek to be satisfied. In intellectual life a relationship exists between wants and their satisfaction. What is largely wanting and sorely needed in contemporary intellectual life is the commitment to seasoned rational discourse. In the full presence of engagement, dualisms inspire argumentation at the highest level, especially when contentious. Conversely, a genuine dualism can never emerge where debate is hobbled and bold utterances are stifled. The score of recent and older works concerned with dualistic encounters might thus represent the beginning of a needed response to this malaise. Certainly, they make the argument for argument.

Although it would be impossible to omit from such a study any of the four primary pairs mentioned, there are of course other pairs. In providing a frame for the various dualisms my purpose is to invite such additions. While an emergent theme, dualisms is also an abiding one. It bears the shock and stamp of recognition. One can see portrayed in it a picture from one's own mind. It resonates. Once mentioned, its import becomes clear and one does not have to proceed far into the subject before auditors or readers begin calling up and compiling their own dualistic pairs. Think of the wealth of materials and insight that has already been derived from the Spanish-language literature of the past century alone: Unamuno and Ortega, Borges and Neruda, and most appropriately Octavio Paz and Carlos Fuentes. One could go on to English literature with similar productive results: Richardson and Fielding, Wordsworth and Coleridge or Wordsworth and Byron (now recognized to be of far greater future significance), and Carlyle and Mill. In German literature, Goethe and Schiller and Burckhardt and Nietzsche stand out.[3] They all participated in and addressed their own dualism. Expanding on his discussion of drama, the ever-quotable John Russell (1982) adds famous oppositions from other fields: 'What Poussin was to Rubens, what Brahms was to Wagner, what Turgenev was to Dostoevsky, Stanislavsky was to Meyerhold' (3–6). The topic is spacious, but for that very reason it requires solid terms of measurement, some reliable gauges for effective comparisons. It requires a more practicable theory of dualisms – one that derives from within the individual encounters, and by so doing produces its own formatting, principles, and formulations, such as are put forward in the introduction.

The ideas in this book have preoccupied me over several decades and were incubating even as other books were hatching. I do not regret the lengthy gestation, as the intervening projects turned out to be fruitful, and the thoughts themselves underwent revision and maturation, awaiting their own slow time. For instance, the first sentence of the book was to be 'This is a study of friends who became enemies.' But further inquiry showed dualisms to be quite different from the falling out of friends, as the introduction explains. Length of time and a deepening appreciation of the scope of the work allowed me to discover some of the more basic principles and formulations that attend these grand dualisms.

While the essential model and its stages of development were intact from the beginning, this is a story that bore surprises for even the author. All true scholarship is a journey of anticipation that ends in discovery. The chosen dualisms present no real difficulty: even that of Turgenev and Dostoevsky has finally met its well-merited acceptance, from Yuri

Nikolsky's study of 1921 to N.F. Budanova's exemplary *Dostoevsky and Turgenev: A Creative Dialogue* of 1987 (my translation), and brought to its dramatic culmination through the rare understanding of Joseph Frank in the last volume of his biography of Dostoevsky (2002). But what was left unattended, and what only recent studies by Aronson, Budanova, Henri Gouhier, Frank, Pintacuda, and others reveal is the extent and intricacy of their involvements, the effects they exerted one upon the other, and the remarkable principles their dualism revealed. What might appear to be a limitation turned out to be an invitation.

What I had only guessed at, however, were the historical alignments that emerged only in the course of the study. Althusser has called Sartre 'our Rousseau,' for his intransigence, for his refusal to be beholden. For two of his contemporaries, Belinsky and Strakhov, Dostoevsky was already 'their' Rousseau, and Coleridge makes astonishing comparisons between Luther and Rousseau. Consider, for example, one of the many brilliant aperçus of René Girard, who in his early essay brings together Rousseau and Dostoevsky: 'The lucidity of Dostoevsky the genius is not given but won through conquest; and we will comprehend that this conquest was not at all predetermined ... once we recognize that the work of Rousseau reflects, without ever completely revealing, obsessions quite similar to those of the Russian writer' (1997, 97). The word *obsessions* is quite correct, as is his emphasis on the nature of the writerly transformations undergone. As I went along, it became apparent that, beyond such appropriations, there was an entire field of bequests from each to the others, and even more crucial details of similarity, of emotional and intellectual solidarity, of in fact two lineages, two intellectual nations, that have come to constitute the most important intellectual contests in our tradition, the virtual agons of the modern era.

Confronting these very divergences amid continuities, family resemblances within difference brings the author to a dilemma, forces a choice of strategies, and that is whether the arrangement of the study be chronological or thematic. After much inner debate, I opted for the former. To start with, the chronological arrangement permits the fullest presentation of the give-and-take back and forth between the antagonists, the public agreements, the private reservations preceding the open clash. It allows one to trace their itineraries of encounter, and to decode the 'inter-responsiveness,' the private messages contained in their works that were frequently understood only by the combatants themselves. A corollary to such special understanding and insight is attentiveness. Despite much gainsaying, each member of the pair devoted extraordinary attention bordering on fixation to what his rival was doing. There was hardly an Erasmus letter from 1519 onward that did not contain some reference to Luther or Lutherans. For his part, in the minor revival of their controversy in 1534, it was clear that Luther was familiar with much of what Erasmus wrote. Secondly it has the advantages of entering into 'deep background,' by which some major, some under-appreciated or understudied works are critically re-evaluated and brought into the discussion as revelatory of the authors' habits of intellect. Such deep background further shows that such clashes, when they did unavoidably occur, should have come as no surprise. Their makings were already present had earlier works been read aright, where the cut of the mind was already discernible, the persistence of qualities apparent, particularly in the rhetorical persuasions employed. Lastly, in its extensiveness, the method adopted shows the complexity of their qualities and the changes brought about by their encounters. Then the remarkable transformations occur that it is the business of *Dualisms* to explore and explain.

Thus, without design, chapters 1, 2, 4, and 5 acquired a form of their own. The early sections discuss other influences, rival claimants and pretenders; since the value of such a work is incremental, these same sections also increasingly discuss the new intellectual plateaus and the differences and similarities within a line of affiliation. However, their major task is to suggest the affinities, the convergence of interests that brought the individuals together in the first place. Affinities brought them together, even as temperamental differences tore them apart. The middle sections are thus largely devoted to the developing careers, with critical evaluations and re-evaluations of some essential texts that reveal profound temperamental divergences. These works show more than the habits of the intellect; in their rhetorical characteristics they show the more enduring psychic formations awaiting their occasion to break out. The last sections of each of the four chapters present the denouement of open warfare, the primal clash, and in its ascendancy and appeal all the public attention it attracted.

Some cautions. This study does not offer the conciliatory resolutions of the ecumenicist – rupture is real and contention far-reaching; nor the approval nor condemnation that denominationalists require, for dualisms are formed in association, both in their prior affinities and later discord. It does not accord with the procedures of pathologists; for instance, of the troubled souls here encountered, all, despite their afflictions, underwent enormous intellectual development and even expansion of their thought, and enjoyed continuous creative activity. And all the authors with which I deal showed the presence of mind to translate the most abhorrent features of personality into the stuff of art. It was said of Dostoevsky that he was his own analyst and analysand. On notable occasions some were even able to exhibit great generosity toward their enemies. Another factor undermining the arguments of the pathological reductionists is the broad appeal and favour that works of even the 'sickliest' of writers found among an eagerly receptive readership. Most reluctantly, this study cannot adopt the quite valuable working methods of the historian, who is obliged to cover all the bases, to render the fullness of the time in all its macro- and micro-configurations, in all its multiform variety. Dualism is a dramatic concept, and so it requires salience. Thus it engages the prime combatants, attends to the duet, while the historian hears the voices of the chorus and the instruments of the orchestra. Of course, each can fortunately follow the same score, hear the same music, arrive at similar judgments. Thus remaining ever aware of the intricacies that constitute the histories of the times covered, I make use of the endnotes to modulate my main argument as well as to offer more extensive confirmations. While I devote space to under-appreciated works, I also avoid some major works that do not impinge on the topic. This could mean that I abuse the privileges of the literary critic and my fondness for texts by eliciting their qualities and submitting them to critical judgment. But my constant aim is to develop the manifestations of a concept in all its dramatic complexity. In so doing, I also avoid the temptations of the historian to rewrite history. Even so eminent a historian as Diarmaid MacCulloch can assert, 'In reality the worlds of humanism and scholasticism did not need to be in conflict' (2004, 86). In reality, they were.

D'autres langues, d'autres soins. The variety of languages essential to this study require different treatments. For two, Latin and Russian, I have resorted to standard English translations but always checked these renderings against the original. Occasionally I have modified the translation or inserted the original when the meaning is crucial. When the quotations are brief I give the German, French, and Italian versions in the original, followed by either the standard translation or, where no translation is otherwise available, my own. Lengthy quotations are offered solely in translation. In some cases, I have opted for texts that are readily available rather than for standardized versions.

Some pardonable inconsistencies. Occasionally where the sense is clear I leave some small expressions in the original, and at times I permit paraphrasing to do the work of translation. At other times, in order to preserve the flow of the narrative, I consign the original to the endnotes. But on all occasions I keep the references clear both as to the original and the translation.

I am most grateful for their very generous subventions toward publication on the parts of the Salvatori Center and the Gould Center, both of Claremont McKenna College and their very able directors Charles Kesler and Jonathan Petropoulos. Special thanks also go to Pamela Gann, President, Claremont McKenna College, for her generous support. The materials of this book were taught in courses at the Graduate Center, CUNY, at the University of Kansas, at Whittier College, and through the years at my home institution, Claremont McKenna College. Portions of the book were delivered as lectures at the University of Washington, Indiana University, the University of Kansas, Whittier College, several conferences hosted by the Consortium for Medieval and Early Modern Studies, hosted by Professor Nancy van Deusen, and the University of Georgia. My warm thanks for the kindnesses showed by my very generous hosts. Portions of this manuscript were read and corrected by Ed Haley, Nancy van Deusen, Ajno Paasonen, Mark Blitz, and particularly my valued colleague, Jay Martin, who gave large sections a very good scrubbing. I benefited from the technical assistance of my son, Sam Quinones, from my partner at the Gould Center, Richard Drake, and Mark Howard. Finally, this book would not have been completed without the loving encouragement and critical acumen of my wife, Roberta L. Johnson.

DUALISMS:
THE AGONS OF THE MODERN WORLD

Introduction

1. Two Intellectual Nations

They stand together and apart. They rule together and apart. They fall together and apart. And in some ways they are revived together and apart. As a kind of epitaph, this describes the course of the cross-rivalries, which I call dualisms, that prevailed between such pre-eminent figures as Luther and Erasmus, Voltaire and Rousseau, Turgenev and Dostoevsky, and Sartre and Camus. Although not exclusive to it, one of the persistent characteristics of modern Western culture – and more necessarily so since the Renaissance and Reformation – is the evident need to bring together pairs of authors, or other figures of the creative intellect, and to form linkages in association. The evidence is apparent – in their time as well as ours – of the figures included above, and others, like Brer Rabbit and Brer Fox: you can't have one without the other. The recurrent prominence of such dualisms, the dramatic and complex involvements of the cross-rivalries, and with it all, the surprising similarities in the historical lines of affiliation, provide the attraction and the substance of this study.

These clashes are at the forefront of intellectual combat because they lead us into the farthest reaches of the human personality and ask such questions as why one person is willing to go to the water's edge, in Erasmus's famous expression of defence, but then pull back, while the other is willing to plunge forward, with the sense that he is being swept along in the grips of a greater passion of belief. The former is not willing to relinquish his hold on consciousness or deliberate action, while the latter seems more able, after intense trauma, to heed the messages sent by what William James has called 'the deeper parts of our mental structures' (*The Varieties of Religious Experience* 241). The object of this study is not to compile biographies nor even less to reproduce the examination-worn requirements of 'compare and contrast,' but rather to explore the contradictions and contests, the enigmas of exchange, the damages and rewards when such radically different personages collide.

These exchanges are crucial for the questions they prompt and for the answers they provide. Why, for instance, could Erasmus never break with Mother Church and why finally had he to come out against Luther? What were the spiritual and emotional motives that impelled both Rousseau and Camus to separate themselves from the reigning ideologies of their times? Why is the dispute of a genuine dualism not between conservative and liberal but between rebel- or moderate-reformer and revolutionary? Why did the leading intellectuals of their day – Erasmus, Voltaire, and Turgenev – undergo such steep demotions in their literary reputations? Why could Sartre never complete the fourth volume of his remarkable series of novels? Why did radical Protestantism play such an abiding role in the resistance to the advanced states of European consciousness, and why in the twentieth century did rebellion seem to change camps? These are the issues that emerge in any engagement with genuine dualisms.

From the very outset I would like to remove any confusions that may exist between dualistic principles, that is, binary concepts in opposition as ways of understanding the world and human personality, and the dualisms that are the object of my study here, the almost literal duel between rival personages. There should be no argument between the two approaches since they differ in content and in the directions of their thought. A.O. Lovejoy captured a major trend of twentieth-century thought when he wrote *The Revolt against Dualism*. Mind versus matter, appearance versus reality, realism versus idealism, thought versus feeling, subjective versus objective, and finally monism versus dualism are the rival philosophical propositions that dualistic principles have typically maintained. Such philosophical principles have had their literary representations in Schiller's division of the world into realists and idealists and Turgenev's influential essay on the shared dominance of the Hamlet and Quixote types, and their critical expositions whereby Shakespeare's works were thought to have been dominated uniquely by time and Milton's with equal singularity by space, and even literary qualities in other works were divided, as in the original Garden, into male or female components. Such dualistic principles are too facile, too euphonious, too easy in themselves. And the proof is how readily they dissolve.

In reality each of the supposed pairs stands for unattainable polar outposts that exist only as abstractions, and is undone by the nature of experience, by the experience of Nature. Even Schiller and Turgenev acknowledged that – in their formal purity – such character types were non-existent and that in fact every person was in varying degrees a combination of the two. And in *Culture and Anarchy* (whose subtitle, *An Essay in Political and Social Criticism*, is too often ignored), Matthew Arnold argued against the preponderance of one element of his great dualistic principles, Hellenism and Hebraism, over the other, and in favour of an 'equipollency,' even anticipating a time when they would no longer be 'dissociated and rival' but rather a 'joint force' (155, 207). Consequently the end of such dualistic principles is loss of their sustaining oppositional powers, a blending into what we have come to call complementarities, supposed oppositions that actually comprise the horizon of the situation; banks of the same river, two sides of the same coin, they exist on a lexical axis of relationship. By the very breaching of their divide, dualistic principles or types cease to be. This is far from the case with the dualisms I have in mind. With Luther and Erasmus, Voltaire and Rousseau, Turgenev and Dostoevsky, and Sartre and Camus, despite their early intellectual comradeship, the importance of which this study emphasizes, their opposition did not dissolve or blend or become complementary, but rather in the historical substantiality of their own persons and beliefs stood in unflinching real-life and real-time antagonism. The twain they had come to be was not bridged but rather confirmed by the conditions of experience in which they found themselves.

At one level *Dualisms* is a study of difference – difference that is real and symbolic, radical and far-reaching. Whether we like it or not, difference will find its way, and not only will but *should* find its way and most energetically seek its expression. So it is in the four cross-rivalries of this study: their tangled fates and fortunes led to remarkable formulations and clarifications that involved not only themselves but their entire societies. They were cast together as pre-eminent figures in epochs of intellectual ferment and social change. Their disparate and yet conjoined voices brought heat but also light to the most fundamental divisions of their time. Polemos rules, but as Dostoevsky was fond of saying, polemics lead to clarification. Even Camus, responding without consternation to a particularly disputatious conference, in *Essais* agreed, 'c'est avec des différences qu'on crée un monde' (it's by difference that one creates a world) (738).

Dualisms attract our attention for many reasons, one of which is quite simply that they have, in Ronald Aronson's words, 'a riveting story' to tell, a story of provocation and response, of confrontation and development, of affinities and dispute, of grave misreadings and yet of uncomfortably accurate insight, of super-session and yet the achievement of parity by the very means of opposition (*Camus and Sartre* 3). Beyond such ample storied interest, dualisms attract because they present a new and dramatic paradigm of ideas in the process of formation, one that – by going beyond the valuable 'history of ideas' or the ideological – insists on the profound intervention of other characteristics involving emotions, feelings, and temperament, all those things that finally enter into the make-up of the fully developed and fully thinking human being. Personality inhabits philosophy; temperament drives ideology. But one does not live and work alone: there are intersection points with others, what contemporary psychoanalysts call 'intersubjectivity'; but whatever terms we employ, such interchange is constant, specific, and complex, indeed a mobility back and forth, that shows how ideas are approached, appropriated, and pushed forward, how they emerge from personal difference and conflict.

Inquiry must dispense with false dichotomies, with artificial categories, in fact, with the normal assumptions of typological criticisms. In scholarship devoted to any of the pairs, eventually the adventurous critic will conclude that two fundamental types are at issue, expressions of a 'perennial dichotomy,' or contest on the eternal plane of ideas.[1] But such typology neglects the transformational function of dualisms, the ways one figure impinges upon the other, bringing about for each a change in both personal thoughts and historical positions. Typology must move from stasis to history. Far from stationary, genuine dualisms enjoy an engagement over time, what I call an itinerary of encounter. They swam in the same pool; they emerged from the same cocoon. They thus require a dynamic representation of closely observed realities in their process of formation. Such encounters are more like a duel than a dance. They are storm warnings that call for drastic readjustments and deserve special names.

2. Names

Understanding that rubrics are only as good as the attributes they uncover, the conceptual byplay they generate – and that, even then, some are positively dis-informational – I would like to call one line of affiliation, that of Erasmus, Voltaire, Turgenev, and Camus, *writers of consciousness*. They are rebel reformers who adhere to deliberate reasoning in their stalwart defence of the constructive accomplishments of culture and civilization. They share an inveterate suspicion of spirit itself, whether it be the Holy Spirit, the *voix intérieure*, or other manifestations of deeper strivings. The other strain, that of Luther, Rousseau, Dostoevsky, and Sartre, I call *daemonic* (notably to be distinguished from the demonic-diabolic, although the diabolic is very active in the register of their mental landscape, just as it is largely absent from that of the writers of consciousness). These writers seem remarkably open to the pressures coming from the marginal areas of experience. While the writers of consciousness are devoted to well-being both for society and their own persons, the daemonic writers seem impetuous, tumultuous, driven by their need for justification to undergo more than one conversion. Obviously there is an entire panoply of qualities and characteristics that converge and congregate around these separate poles of the Western psyche. Even such advanced billing barely touches upon the full sweep of their interactions, the complexities of which can be better understood when I examine more closely the qualities of Erasmus, Voltaire, Turgenev, and Camus on one side of the divide, and those of Luther, Rousseau, Dostoevsky, and Sartre on the other.

In the construction of this divided typology, some remarkable pages from Ernst Cassirer's *The Question of Jean-Jacques Rousseau* provide helpful pointers. Fully acknowledging the reformist interests of the Encyclopedists and their pre-eminent ally, Voltaire, Cassirer nevertheless draws a clear line between their ameliorist thought and the more revolutionary reformations demanded by Rousseau:

> The thinkers of the Encyclopedist circle wanted to ameliorate and cure; but hardly one of them believed in the necessity for, nor possibility of, a radical transformation and reformation of state and society ... All these thinkers were convinced *eudaemonists*; they sought the happiness of men, and they agreed that this happiness could truly be promoted and secured only through slow, stubborn labor in single, groping experiments. (66)

Given this dimension of the liberal reformers, the contrast with Rousseau becomes all the more striking. For Cassirer, Rousseau was a man 'driven onward by an ethical imperative,' and 'it was not a matter of more or less but of either/or.' In fact, in the second part of the same essay, Cassirer refers to the 'daemonic' qualities of Rousseau, those qualities that set Diderot on edge, made him grind his teeth, and affirm that Rousseau filled him with the terrors of hell (70, 91).

Unlike that of writers of consciousness, the concept of the daemonic has easy access. I can invoke Morton W. Bloomfield's 'The Two Cognitive Dimensions of the Humanities,' an essay that gave more than nominal form to my thought when he wrote, 'The final end of scientific investigation in the humanities is to know everything; the final end of inner experience is to face the demonic' (263). In his *Irrational Man*, William Barrett called Sartre's sense of freedom 'demoniacal' (261). But one of the fullest meanings of the daemonic spirit is given by Karl Barth, who quite rightly places Rousseau in the 'Protestant tradition': 'Driven by a demoniac or foolish spirit arising out of some depth of his being which was at first inexplicable he [Rousseau] hurled his impeachment at society ... It was that the life of society, ruled as it was by this capacity for civilization and by this will for form, was no real human life at all ... but rather signified its complete perversion and destruction; that it was not the heaven it pretended and told itself it was, but a hell' (203–19). Stretched across so vast an emotional extent, between heaven and hell, between God and the devil, the daemonic is not only at odds with the achievements of European culture and civilization but frequently suffers from a torment within. The writers of consciousness, as eudaemonists, on the other hand, are committed to the well-being of their societies and to their personal peace and securities (however difficult the latter might be to attain).

Cassirer's notable contrasts were anticipated in Hegel's thought, which by virtue of its speculative genius and profound psychological insights raises the large questions that determined many of the paths of future scholarship. Hegel asks why the Reformation, so essential to the development of the modern world, did not occur in the Romance countries. While we can make some allowance for the persuasive power of simple political authority and other complications historical in nature – which Hegel in this contrast does not – still he contributes to our theme when he finally settles on 'the fundamental character of these nations.' Hegel alleges a 'disharmony,' an 'internal schism,' the product of the holding fast to an abstract principle, and, as counterpart to this, the absence of any 'totality of Spirit': 'There is not that meditative introversion of the soul upon itself; – in their inmost being they may be said to be alienated from themselves ... Their inmost being is not their own. They leave it as an alien and indifferent matter and are glad to have its concerns settled for it by another' (414–21). We can eschew the national stereotyping and still retain the helpful psychological insights. His comments of course reflect a northern Protestant light, one that beams on the subject and, while not providing fullest illumination, can still set a direction to thought.[2]

Culturally provocative, Hegel's remarks are also alert to an internal division in the writers of consciousness, as if they were not committing all of their guns. In the course of this study it will become apparent how their meditations seem external to the self. But the argument can be reformulated and two additional points made. First, each of the writers of consciousness, even when under fierce attack or simply confronting the ascendancy of the other figure, continued quite courageously to stick to his principles, to offer rational arguments that continue to stand up well to the light of reason and the vicissitudes of history. Second, while each of the figures may be charged (as Erasmus was and as Voltaire never could be) with lacking ego sufficiency, it is equally possible to argue that the writers of consciousness enjoyed an ego security that permitted them to function in a condition of contradiction. They may have had a larger and more plastic sense of self, or a more rooted scepticism, neither of which felt diminished in the face of only partial and competing truths. They may have possessed what Camus came to call an 'équilibre supérieur.' The issues are obviously complex and can be mediated only through the details of the individual cases, where other more practical bases for comparison present themselves.

3. Paradigms of Development

Within the divergent typologies there huddles a team of issues extending from the practical to the formative, waiting to break out. These are not simply intellectual contests but engage a large medley of related differences. In any paradigm of development, how can one ignore class background and all the attendant manners and mores? When one is addressing the quarrel of Voltaire and Rousseau, or Sartre and Camus, the differences in class and family situations are practically unbridgeable. Dostoevsky wrote of a sort of people different from those of Turgenev, who, like Tolstoy, depicted the world from the viewpoint of a representative of the landowner's class. Then there are 'career episodes,' the different ways by which the members of the pairs entered public life. Entrances of writers such as Luther, Rousseau, and Dostoevsky were marked by sudden breakthroughs, by works that surprised even themselves and took the newly aroused readership by storm. In fact, their entire careers were marked by tumultuousness, by abrupt changes and sudden transformations, even by conversions. While it is difficult to explain how and why conversion occurs or is required, all four of the figures of one historical alignment – Luther, Rousseau, Dostoevsky, and Sartre – underwent more than one conversion. The public careers of the other four are marked not by radical change but rather by gradual evolution, by enrichment, like slowly forming rings around a core, adding to the circumference but not altering the conformation.

The figures differ also in their receptions and readerly response. Were their works greeted with acclaim and approval or with dispute and contestation? Did they impose discomfort and spiritual challenge or comfort and accommodation? In placing them alongside each other, one is confronted with the crucial and incontestable critical fact of differing rhetorical persuasions. Finally, they differ in their *fortune*, their literary afterlives. It is regrettable that as one of Voltaire's editors lamented, '*Candide* excepté lit-on toujours Voltaire?' (Except for *Candide* does anyone still read Voltaire?) (Groos 1: v). As with Erasmus, Voltaire – the prince of letters in his day – and Turgenev may have survived only in a single work. This unfortunate fact, while possibly an expression of the waywardness of tastes and fashions, may be due to more enduring and intractable elements of their character and presentations.

In the dynamic involvements of Erasmus and Luther, Voltaire and Rousseau, Turgenev and Dostoevsky, Camus and Sartre, the tides do change but the resulting patterns and rhythms are stable and clear. However much the configurations alter and even trespass, clearly being part of a dualism is an inescapable and defining part of their intellectual positioning. Dualisms might not provide the whole story, but as Craig R. Thompson has argued in the introduction to his valuable modern edition and translation of Erasmus's *Colloquies*, they are a crucial part of the story (xx). No biography of either member of the pairs is complete without a full inquiry into the dualism. And when the lines of affiliation are added, it comes clear that dualisms may be treated as an intellectual concept, with an independent life of its own. It also yields insights, solves problems, and resolves paradoxes. Dualisms represent a living and lived engagement that brings together the personal and the intellectual and point a new way for understanding cultural formation.

Here I can provide a frame, a pattern of unfolding, one that houses dualisms in a reasonably coherent way. My format distinguishes greater dualisms from lesser ones; it provides lines of affiliation between respective members of the pairs. I aim to show that what might be termed idiosyncrasies in one writer are actually attributes in common and that even in different epochs with different starting intellectual baselines the same kinds of dualisms recur. More importantly I answer the question, why these?

These new typologies share a distinctive paradigm of development.

A. Each of the members of the pairs was a leader in the intellectual vanguard and reform movements of his day. As such, each was presumed to be a comrade-in-arms with the other, allied in the struggle against a very definite and in most cases powerful and extensive enemy. This means that each was endowed with the two great gifts that history can bestow. The first, one that generates the youthful verve and vigour of animated hostility, is the gift of opposition: they all started with enemies in common. All of the pairs found their origin in opposition to a well-entrenched and intellectually vulnerable enemy. But in their united undertakings they also advanced new ideas and new principles. Common projects as well as common enemies formed the bases of their affinities. Here the intellectual alliances are quite obvious: Erasmus and Luther joined in espousing the principle of Christian liberty; Voltaire and Rousseau were strong advocates of a rational theology that had its basis in a practical morality typical of the Enlightenment; Turgenev and Dostoevsky were members of the Western-inspired reform-minded intelligentsia seeking to change the nature of feudal Russia; Sartre and Camus were active members of the anti-Fascist Left participating in the Resistance and later sharing the hopes of great changes following the end of the Second World War. But perhaps the most astonishing indications of their shared universe of perception and belief were the early reviews each wrote of the other's first works before they even knew one another. These were the works that would eventually join them in an enduring fame.

Going beyond such dual gifts, they shared intellectual procedures. Erasmus and Luther existed in the renascent culture of authoritative citation – a formidable quotation could constitute evidence (albeit buttressed by reason). Both have been most accurately called 'biblical humanists,' eager to apply the tools of the new philology to an understanding of sacred texts, thus greatly contributing to the resurgence of a learned piety that accompanied the northern Renaissance. Rousseau and Voltaire both regarded the Reformers as their primitive forerunners, whose works were, however, never brought to completion, and felt it was incumbent upon them to perfect. In their roles as independent intellectuals, simple citation no longer carried the same weight as did the argumentative validity of thought. Rather than subscribing to the authority of the past, their focus was the present and personal taste and judgment. Voltaire concluded one of his most engaging poems with the affirmation, 'Le Paradis terrestre est où je suis' (The earthly paradise is where I am) (*Mélange* 206). Turgenev and Dostoevsky depicted the more complex dimensions of the Russian character and society through the creative syntheses that the novel afforded; by these means and by their mutual depictions of the new nihilism, by the very virtues of their dramatic 'presentness,' by their lively address as public intellectuals in a society where culture was inextricably bound up with politics, they both invited distaste and misunderstanding, although for very different reasons. Where Turgenev and Dostoevsky were addressing the questions of Russia's future, Camus and Sartre and other French intellectuals had to face the facts of living in a country that had been degraded politically. Their France was a France *sans lendemain* (without a tomorrow). Yet it was because of the unaccustomed political demotion that they were compelled to train their intelligence on the cognizance of the self. Their taste for lucidity found in common the world of the absurd. Consciousness, seeking value in a valueless world found access to revolt, and *la révolte* soon spread outward to the other, forming a common solidarity. Braced by their working faith in the fusing power of philosophy and art – a necessarily joined action that they fervently adopted and never relinquished – they each developed what was no longer a French but a European consciousness, and in the midst of France's political demotion, signalled the aspirant leadership of the French intellectual. At this point, however, the basis for difference also intervened.

The real nexus between the future rivals may be derived from this stage of formatting: a true dualism can occur only between those who are at the forefront of the intellectual world of their time, between those who are, in Ortega y Gasset's words, 'at the height of their times' (Quinones, *Mapping Literary Modernism* 118).[3] It does not occur between conservatives and liberals, but rather between those who possess a common vocabulary. As Arthur Koestler may have been the first to warn, the major debate of the second half of the twentieth century would be between communists and ex-communists, or mutatis mutandis, in a later time, between liberals and neo-cons. Sartre himself, not allergic to contention, adopts the same principle when he declares, 'Le véritable ennemi est toujours celui qui est le plus proche de vous' (The veritable enemy is always the one closest to you) (*Les écrits* 238). Isaiah Berlin, in his classic essay 'The Counter-Enlightenment,' confirms this judgment: 'Such opposition [that of the counter-Enlightenment] largely because of the absence of a common ground made little headway, save by stimulating regressive actions against the spreading of ideas regarded as dangerous to the authority of Church and of State' (243). This very point – the absence of a true interlocutor in the enemies of Enlightenment and the need for a common ground in language and interests – becomes abundantly clear when Jean-Jacques Rousseau opens his lengthy letter of defence to the archbishop of Paris with the same kind of recognition. The exchange is a classic confrontation in pristine form between Catholic and Protestant sensibilities, and yet it is not a major dualism, and Rousseau explains why this is so: 'Pourquoi faut-il, Monseigneur, que j'aye quelque chose a vous dire? Quelle langue commune pouvons-nous parler, comment pouvons-nous entendre et qu'y a-t-il entre vous et moi?' (Why is it necessary, Monsignor, that I should have something to say to you? What common language can we speak, how can we understand one another, and what is there really between us?) (*Œuvres complètes* 4: 927).[4] Despite his opposition to Voltaire, such a disclaimer could never be used in regard to that antagonist, because initially they did share a common ground in the interests of the Enlightenment. Rousseau's attacks were all the more challenging because they did not come from outside their shared premises, but from within their actual unfolding. For potent reasons, this is an 'in-house' quarrel. But this relationship contains a further cause for embitterment and strife. When attack is made from within the dualism, it is not directed against matters of debasement, or lesser accomplishments, but rather against the height of European attainments and consciousness of the time. It may even be directed against consciousness itself, now seen not to be authentic but rather an imitative contrivance. The very highest in the traditional sense of rational attainment can thus become the worst, and this reversal accounts for the turmoil and the fierceness of the estrangement. The challenge may well appear bewildering.

B. As with any alliance between talented individuals – those at the forefront of intellectual life – these genuine affinities existed along with suspicions and dislikes, small rifts that prefigured the larger fissures that were to occur. For instance, despite being heavily influenced by Erasmus's 1516 Greek edition and translation of the New Testament, Luther believed Erasmus weak on Paul's conception of original sin. Erasmus, for his part, despite defending Luther in a crucial white paper, found the German monk's arguments too abrasive and contentious. Voltaire thought Rousseau crazy, but he was 'our' crazy, a *fou de famille*, whom one protected. And Rousseau regretted that his one-time intellectual mentor should have succumbed to the reigning culture of accommodation. Turgenev privately and then quite openly satirized Dostoevsky's egomaniacal streak, while the latter, welcoming Turgenev's contribution to the debuting volume of his journal *Epocha*, privately found the piece 'fatuous.' Sartre always spoke condescendingly of Camus's preparation in philosophy, while Camus complained of Sartre's 'acidity' of tone. As Coleridge put it so pithily in regard to Erasmus and Luther, such utter unlikes cannot but end in dislikes (*Literary Remains* 4: 57). Lurking tensions always exist among colleagues who enjoy a pre-eminence, but as tensions turn into dualisms they are indicators of more basic fissures of temperament, what Schiller called 'inner[n] Gemütsform' (inner mental dispositions – Schiller, *Schriften* 4: 357; *Naïve and Sentimental Poetry* 176) – those tendencies of thought and character so ingrained in the human personality that they are thought to be irreducible. We remember William James's powerful assertion that 'the history of philosophy is to a great extent that of a certain clash of human temperaments' ('Present Dilemma' 19). Harboured dislikes can lead to strenuous intellectual challenge and genuine insight.

C. In time, by virtue of the personal encounters and the public debates in which the thinkers were engaged, an issue, or issues, emerges, an episode that is a shock to the system, revealing how different they really are in their mental dispositions, how they do signal two different worlds of thought and feeling, of fervour and presentation, of method and manner. Their presumed alliance may have been only that – a presumption that was brought together by circumstance and then brutally disrupted by circumstance. Quite obviously some serious misreadings had occurred, and this is true in all four dualisms as bitterness and disappointment are increased to the extent that the new antagonist seems to have become a changed man. But as any deeper reading will discover, this is not the case at all – the evidence of profound difference was available in the earlier works, disguised by the circumstances that had pitched them together, but also simply awaiting its moment. This brings us to the role of circumstance, whether it be the French Revolution or the Cold War. Clearly such pressures are instrumental, necessary but not sufficient, something more than only an occasion but also something less than a cause. Schiller is quite right to explain that the antagonism of the 'inner mental dispositions' is responsible for a division ('eine Trennung'), more severe than any fortuitous conflict of interests could ever produce ('als der zufällige Streit der Interesse je hervorbringen könnte') (Schiller, *Naïve and Sentimental Poetry* 176; *Schriften* 4: 357). Such external conflicts may serve to pinpoint, even direct, the dramatic ruptures that basic traits of personality provoke.

D. Not in spite of, but because of the pair's previously shared affinities, the eventually revealed divergence erupts into a kind of cosmic warfare, one that involves not only them but also their sharply divided partisans, who are only too eager to take sides. Debate becomes nuclear because this is a break from within a house, a clash of presumed allies who were at the forefront of intellectual advancement. Their debate is thus emergent and expansive and becomes the defining debate of their age and for successive ages as well. The shared affinities focus more narrowly, as in a circle, the spotlight on the principles and principals involved, leaving in lesser positions if not obscurity the non-combatants and non-essentials. The very principles of their agreement become the basis of schism. The argument also becomes transcendent when temperamental differences enter into and inform ideas, pushing each by means of their reciprocal engagement to the farthest reaches of their thought and endeavour.

Such formatting reveals the first principle: a genuine dualism can occur only between those who are at the forefront of intellectual developments in their day. It also brings out the closely related second principle: the connection between affinity and ultimate discord is not merely sequential but is necessary. A causal relationship exists between the two. This characteristic appears most clearly in the reactions of erstwhile friends to the apparent defections of Rousseau and Camus. Clearly the early and later *philosophes* had misread their men. Consequently, when Rousseau or Camus attacked the new Left with the same rigour with which they had denounced the old Right, such moral equivalency smacked of betrayal, and each was charged with being a renegade, a turncoat. The newly advanced opponent from within one's own camp induces a sense of betrayal and promotes a powerful onset of emotions – rancour, disbelief, and outrage – which lead to an explosion of animosity. What might have been a simple quarrel now becomes similar to a familial uproar, where pent-up emotions finally break out onto the surface. Without the prior sense of affinity – that presumed closeness of relationship – the outbreak of enmity could not have been as explosively revealing. A true contest of values is now on the table, as antagonists of equal talents and previously shared visions glare at each other.

Like twins themselves, their greatest influence is one upon the other. In dualisms, each writer feels the impact of the other – each is agonist and protagonist. And such influence yields extraordinary insight not only into the other, but also into themselves. Each member confronts an irreducible aspect of himself, what Shakespeare in *Antony and Cleopatra* (and here he is following Plutarch) refers to as the 'daemon,' the 'Genius' of the self (2.3.20). Character is reduced to so fundamental a quality that there is no room for further explanation or argument. Perhaps it is here – in such extraordinary personal clarity – that we find part of the appeal of dualisms. One of the major goals of a dualism is thus achieved, and the third principle derives from it, as difference is legitimized and a kind of parity attained. The contestants can thus face one another in their separate – and in this case equal – worlds of validated ideational difference. This ultimate line of defence provides more than a stalemate; it yields the validation that proceeds from such recognition and the justification that then promotes full intellectual involvement and debate. The participants were the first to recognize and to formulate their own dualism. This is the case even with Erasmus, when every bone in his body worked to discount the dualism into which he had entered, or as was the case with Voltaire, when he dismissed as worthy only of oblivion the combined warfare with Rousseau (which he waged with a particular meanness of spirit). But David Hume, while defending himself, saw in the combat of Voltaire and Rousseau something different: he saw a true dualism. He recognized that 'Voltaire and Rousseau were two noble gladiators who had entered the lists; the suppleness, grace and irony of the one contrasted with the vehemence and energy of the other' (Gouhier, *Rousseau et Voltaire* 111). Even in Hume's words we can see how the construction of a dualism with distinct but equally valued properties can validate the opposition itself. Moreover, the very differences of their characteristics brought out of their clash the greater divisions of the age.

The same can be said of Erasmus and Luther, our first and, for the modern world, the foremost and fullest dualism: 'Zwei Welten stehen gegeneinander, die das Gesicht der sich erneuernden Deutschland und grosser Teile Europas bestimmen sollten. Noch ahnt niemand den kommenden Konflikt, aber er ist unausweichlich.' This encompassing statement by Heinrich Bornkamm ('Erasmus und Luther' 38), one of the most insightful commentators on Luther from the past century, moves us more resolutely into our theme. Paraphrasing the German, Erasmus and Luther did represent two worlds in opposition; their conflict was about which should preside over the changing, self-renewing face of Germany and Western Christendom, and judging from the early years of 1514–17, no one yet suspected the coming conflict. Yet when it did come, it seemed unavoidable. Bornkamm's words suggest a more dynamic understanding than those of Hume, that within a field of encounter there is an itinerary of encounter, one that we are obliged to follow, working our way in and out of their thought of such great foes and more importantly observing the way in which the dualism emerges, with its shared affinities and fault lines, the way it exerts its own magnetic draw, until, as Bornkamm suggests, it is unavoidable.

The insightful Joseph Frank writes in similar fashion of the ways that Turgenev and Dostoevsky – and not others – came to represent the larger divisions of Russian culture, particularly when they made their appearances at the Pushkin festivities of 1880:

> Other writers also participated, but all eyes were fixed on Turgenev and Dostoevsky. Their juxtaposed presence on the stage brought together the opposing poles of Russian culture. As the writer B.M. Markevich put it, 'What is there in common, I asked myself ... between such an "incurable Westernizer," to use Turgenev's own words about himself, and that eternal seeker of the *genuine* Russian truth – whose name is Dostoevsky?' Both were competing, on those nominally apolitical occasions, for the minds and hearts of the public on whom would depend the future. (5: 415)

Such formulations call up borderline differences, which by their very closeness serve to mark boundaries. The first has to do with the falling-out of friends. Friends may become ex-friends, even enemies, brothers may become enemies, but these facts by themselves do not constitute a dualism. In fact, contrary to my earlier assumptions, they differ in their very bases. Even when made public, the disengagements and re-engagements of friends do not possess the full power of a great dualism, whose story is rather that of an intellectual alliance that turns out to be a misalliance. This is not the account of a love-affair manqué but rather of a collision course awaiting its moment. Certainly it tracks some of the elements of a quarrel – the bickering, the intrigues, the pettiness, the panderers. But when the two combatants are fully engaged, when Erasmus, for example, finally sets out after Luther, the age has met its match and recognizes itself in the contest. The duellists become the standard-bearers, behind whom followers gather, thus expanding the conflict that has become generalized and widespread. When friends break up, they adopt a policy of containment, trying to minimize disclosure, perhaps secreting away some hope for an eventual reconciliation.

Another reason for dislodging the two is that with friends a kind of parity has always existed; thus when a breach occurs – frequently because of some misunderstanding – it results in a great emotional disappointment, injured feelings. But, in time, better instincts prevail and original bonds are somewhat restored. Tolstoy and Turgenev were able to make up after a long period of bitter estrangement, the result of unthinking private exchanges. The same was true even of Sartre and Merleau-Ponty, when their dispute was based upon sharp intellectual differences. But things were different with Dostoevsky and Turgenev, or Voltaire and Rousseau, or Sartre and Camus; despite apparent similarities, they were never quite capable of papering over the differences in class, character, and thought. Nor was breach provoked by a thoughtless phrase, an outburst of sudden pique; with dualisms, difference is attained by a long and thoughtful process. Not by misunderstanding but by understanding one another all too well, they maintained their opposition. That is, with the one, parity is undone by a breach, while with dualisms, parity is attained by virtue of breach, as genuine difference is not only acknowledged but validated. And rather than leading to keen emotional distress, such recognition leads to greater intellectual formulations, confrontations with the issues that divide them.

Still, there is something dramatically fraternal in dualisms. The early bonding of shared affinities promotes the comradeship of brothers-in-arms. But this very closeness and its early attractions require an act of exorcism, if the younger, searching, budding talent is to come into his own measure of accomplishment. He requires the psychic expulsion of the brother – now become the dualistic antagonist – to bring out his own powers of expression and independence. Thus, it took many years before Rousseau was able to uphold his own end of the dualism and declare Voltaire to be his enemy. So, in all the others, a length of time was needed, producing an itinerary of encounter, before a true recognition of difference could be attained. Such affable, accomplished, skilled, and talented figures as Erasmus, Voltaire, and Turgenev had an allure, an attractive self-possession, so admired and close enough to be a kindred self that they posed a threat to the discovery of the true self. It is only through the tumultuous and even confused upsurge of his own emotions (as Barth so eloquently explains), of recollections of his former life, of needs that are being unfulfilled, in the basic recognition of difference that the initial bond is broken and is revealed to be an obstacle to full self-discovery. Impetuousness and discontent become instruments of liberation and lead to higher argument.

We all write for a variety of audiences, but we also write against faces in the mind, against figures leaning over our shoulders. Inter-textuality is private warfare. Almost obviously such remarks recall Harold Bloom's

The Anxiety of Influence, certainly one of the boldest and most compelling studies of the past thirty years.[5] Indeed, as he argues in terms most relevant for this study, the weak imitator seeks out continuities, he needs to be buttressed by the extensions of the past, while the strong or impulsive imitator triumphs by discontinuity and disruption, by a self-assertion that, while aggrandizing, becomes justified. These and other commonalities exist between the two kinds of studies, but their operational differences are more revealing. They both participate in *antithetical criticism*, that is a study of oppositional pairs or subjects. But where Bloom's study undertakes a *vertical poetics* between generations, the poetics of dualisms is lateral. This has several important consequences. In Bloom's vertical poetics the presence of a powerful predecessor is almost overwhelming, threatening to crush the latecomer, who by a series of manoeuvres, one of which is misprision (a kind of unconscious misreading or highly selective, even blind, insistence), manages to rescue and assert himself. But in the *lateral poetics* of dualisms, the two combatants understand one another all too well. In fact, as with the cryptophasia of twins, they can send signals that are understandable only to themselves, or to a limited group of initiates. They have the insight of suspicion; their quarrel is not only with outright assertion, but, such is the extent of their understanding, they are able to penetrate the more ulterior implications of their opponent's thoughts.

An even greater difference between my poetics and that of Bloom is that generational differences are soon elided. Erasmus was some seventeen years older than Luther (give some three years, if a later birth date is accepted), and Voltaire was some eighteen years older than Rousseau, but in the life of the dispute these differences soon disappear, as the very separateness of their intellectual positions introduces an equality of evaluation. One of the goals of a dualism is to legitimize difference, in fact to introduce equality where there is difference. Some anxieties of course persist in the dualistic disputes, but they are minor in regard to the material engagements of the larger debate, where the disputants address not only their own deepest resources but also those of major segments of society. Bloom's discourse is the stuff of high literature, where poet speaks to poet and where poem reads and is read by poem. Dualisms do not shy away from these reciprocal engagements, but transcend the purely (with no belittlement intended) literary by reaching out to and even mobilizing convictions and beliefs of many people. They bear the stamp of contemporaneity and the urgings of collective involvements.

Naturally it is not an easy matter – it is an ungracious task – to place such conflict and division on a historical pedestal. Yet there must be some reason why we are drawn to dualisms, just as we are drawn to tragedy. Dualisms offer no linear progression, or even a comforting dialectic resulting in some sort of synthesis, but rather a recurrence of opposition, a kind of intractability that stymies any sense of advancement. Dualisms speak to the nature of things, where history is not to be second-guessed, plumbed for the deeper drift of meaning in its anodyne processes, but rather as revealing dire contention. And if resolutions do occur, they continue not in a combined state of harmony but as separate lines of conduct, even in their historical afterlives still unreconciled.

Such formulations can be succinctly summarized and others added:

A. As the evidence of four centuries reveals, despite apparent resolutions and the attainment of new baselines and intellectual plateaus, there is always a *recurrence of dualisms*. Dispute always re-emerges; there is never a peace. Nor should there be, as William Blake well recognized, in his own dualistic constructions of Byron versus Wordsworth, and Chaucer versus Milton: 'These two classes of men are always upon earth and they should be enemies. Whoever seeks to reconcile them seeks to destroy existence' (McGann 46). Erasmian culture regained its influence at the end of the seventeenth century and formed the intellectual starting point for the *philosophes*, but this did not prevent the breaking out of animosity from within that same cultural formation. In fact, each new dispute begins on the same axis of relationship. And, we might add, while a culture might be profitably studied in its unifying features, it might be better understood by its internal divisions.

B. This contentious principle means that, at different historical epochs, variations on the same basic tensions may be replicated. This is even more surprising when we realize that another of the key features of any dualism is that, while being replicative, it is *non-imitative*. One can trace the steps of a mastering father figure, but such a procedure would be impossible with a dualism. As Coleridge was fond of saying, such dualisms must emerge from 'real resemblances' and not from 'intentional imitation.'[6] They could not possibly be arranged or staged but must arise from genuine forces in an at once unpredictable but still unavoidable conflict. Furthermore, one imitates what one desires; the traumatic nature of a dualism is far from desirable, hence inimitable. Painful truths are brandished and painful facts exposed, the contest of truth-telling so necessary that it is not hard to understand why great dualisms, while exemplary, are not subject to easy repetition.

C. The reappearance and nature of dualisms further argue, within admittedly limited conditions, against cultural deterioration or decline. The dualism of Sartre and Camus is just as pithy, pungent, and revealing as was that of Erasmus and Luther. Each requires and deserves our fullest involvement and attention. The historical conditions may have varied but there is still a frothy perseverance in dispute. As a sub-corollary, it should be noted that rarely are organic or seasonal metaphors appropriate when discussing the developments of human culture.

D. Such recurrences and renewals are the products of generational change. Each of the pairs in their affinities and differences appealed to a new generation with new interests, new ways of living, and new ways of responding to their experiences. Each of the two protagonists captivates a new generation because he captures its living reality, its language and gestures. One may of course deride the Parisian Left Bank café existentialists but they knew that when Camus wrote *The Myth of Sisyphus*, he was describing the parabola of their lives, the choices with which they were faced. Similarly, and at the same time, Sartre, according to Bernard-Henri Lévy, became at once a pattern and a patron, from whose works and conduct of life, young intellectuals imbibed a new way of regarding existence (20). And yet when we look back to Erasmus and Luther, and, for instance, the changes that Erasmus as a new enterprising humanist introduced into the university curriculum, we can observe a generational change just as pronounced as those that followed.

This paradigm of development and the accompanying principles and formulations help explain why these dualisms and not others were anticipated, even magnified in the intellectual imagination of the day. All the figures of this study had their significant exchanges with other figures, but it is this one that adheres and remains in the imagination. Perhaps the major reason for the distinctiveness of this kind of debate is its representativeness. In it, and through the great enmity aroused, issues are at once contained and released. Not only do they in their mutually related antagonisms comprehend the issues of their day, but they go beyond those historically conditioned issues and even beyond their own knowing and even telling to uncover matters that are emergent, far-reaching, symbolic, and radical. The most interesting proposition of my study might be this: these dualisms become so dominant, and eclipse others of their time, because they fully embody the particular paradigm of development that has been sketched out, but also because they expose and represent perennial tensions within Western culture and the Western psyche. These tensions have much to do with the complexities of Christianity,

for, as Hegel recognized, 'Christianity is an intrinsically spiritual principle and, as such, has a boundless elasticity' (407). Christianity can be a
principle of spiritual submission and humility, or, as in the thought of
Erasmus and Luther and Voltaire and Rousseau, a principle of liberation, of spiritual freedom. Even within this same grounding a division
can occur, as some will hear in Christianity a call to peace, accommodation, even expediency, while others will hear a summons to the most
severe of spiritual challenges, that terrifying economy where one is
called to abandon everything not essential to salvation. Christianity is
essentially dualistic. Christ's words are chilling and challenging: 'Think
not that I am come to send peace on earth; I came not to bring peace but
a sword. For I am come to set a man at variance with his father, and the
daughter against her mother ... And a man's foes shall be they of his own
household' (Matt. 10.34–5). These powerful words – anticipating the
perilous mission and the Cross – reveal the dualism within Christianity
itself, as they stand in opposition to the very announcements of peace
attending Christ's birth (Luke 2.14). Given their temperamental divergences, Erasmus and Luther were able to understand the meaning of
Christ's words in quite opposed ways.

1 Erasmus and Luther: First and Foremost, a Pattern Established

1. Public Intellectuals and Reform

For many reasons, the epochal encounter between Erasmus and Luther is the first and foremost dualism of the modern world.[1] It embodies the convergence and the eventual separation of the two most formative movements of our era, the Renaissance and the Reformation. We have lived and continue to live in the midst of their competing demands. In their own itinerary of encounter, Erasmus and Luther encapsulate both the early hopes of this dual resurgence and the consequences of their divorce. Their mutual involvements, their character and being, and all the signposts along the way arise out of their individual traits and yet become massively representative. These two pre-eminent intellectuals, starting with similar principles and procedures, spoke out on issues of broadly European concern. Jean-Paul Sartre, writing in admiration of the activism of the *philosophes*, linked them to their predecessors in the Reformation: 'Pour la première fois depuis la Réforme les intellectuels interviennent dans la vie publique' (For the first time since the Reformation, intellectuals intervene in public life) ('Qu'est-ce que la littérature?' 154).

Of course there had been public intellectuals before the Reformation, as the involvements of Dante and the Florentine civic humanists amply attest. And Dante even gave definition to the intellectual (or lay philosopher) as one who uses his technical philosophical training to address the pertinent issues of the day.[2] But with Erasmus and Luther, there are differences. They not only entered into public life, but public debate revolved around them. Their names became nouns and verbs. Erasmus was identifiable with Erasmianism and Luther with Lutheranism (to the distinct discomfort of each). And the question was circulating whether Erasmus Lutheranized, or whether Luther Erasmianized.

Their early reservations about one another and later hardly private expressions of difference culminated in a debate over a seemingly recondite topic: the freedom of the will; yet it was this topic, adroitly manoeuvred by Erasmus, that summarized the philosophical bases for much of their thought and feeling and was thus truly representative of the central issues that divided them and their time. Luther recognized this fact when he declared that, with his argument, Erasmus had grabbed him by the jugular. But Erasmus's provocation drove Luther to an expression of his greatest work, *De servo arbitrio* (On the Bondage of the Will). Pintacuda, whose brilliant study focuses on the many implications of this debate, emphasizes their theological divergences, in the conviction 'that they represent one of the most significant among the many fruitful [confrontations] out of which modern culture was in the process of constituting itself' (37).

The exchange of 1524–5 was emblematic because it showed the intervention of radical Protestantism into the full intellectual life of the West, and the measures undertaken by a supreme writer of consciousness to cope with the newly resurrected and powerful presence. Earlier nascent Reform had surfaced not only in the thought of John Wycliffe (ca. 1320–84) and Johan Hus (1370–1415), but as Erika Rummel has so lucidly demonstrated in that of many others as well, stretching from the intrepid Lorenzo Valla (ca. 1407–57), who showed that historical philology possessed a critical bent as well as a creative potential, to an immensely powerful patron, the Spanish Cardinal Ximenes de Cisneros (1436–1517) ('Voices of Reform' 64–9, 79–80). That is, there were numerous forerunners and contemporaries all anticipating and sharing in the actions of reform. But for many reasons these pre-reformational and even contemporary interventions did not have the same impact as did the dispute between Erasmus and Luther. For one, they may have lacked a 'ready audience' (MacCulloch 123), the emergence of a worldly, successful laity and an ample university-trained readership. Nor were the political configurations – so instrumental in Luther's success and protection – available. While not lacking opponents, they did not have a notable contestant of Erasmus's stature, for in most cases the divisions of the times were not as eloquently expressed and sharply embodied. Thus dualisms have their own accumulating powers. As in a painting, other figures were drawn around the central pair but all were pointing, leading to the dualism of Erasmus and Luther.

The primacy attributed to this later debate was abetted by another intrusion: the use of the new mechanical device of movable type, which permitted letters and their responses to be printed and disseminated quickly, voluminously, and widely. The winds of change were fanned by the increased rapidity, scope, and accuracy of communication. The printing press, which made the important tasks of finding, editing, and printing classical Christian and pagan texts all the easier and all the more urgent, thus advanced the causes of both Renaissance and Reformation. Luther's public posting of the Ninety-five Theses caused little stir, but once printed and distributed in the vernacular they created a sensation. And in the course of his life he became the 'most widely published author of his age.'[3] This extraordinary invention (Erasmus referred to it as a 'superhuman art') materially added to the intellectual temperature and metabolism of the time, as we shall further see in the exchanges between the partisans of Luther and those of Erasmus. Letters of the one or the other were quickly seized upon, printed, and disseminated, and became a quite profitable business. Such letters became the equivalent of articles in modern journals of opinion, or when printed in unauthorized pirated versions opened the field to the bloggers of the day. It is more than accidental that these polemics and the printing press came of age together.

2. The Gifts of History

Erasmus and Luther benefited from history's first gift of ready opposition. Although nearly a generation apart in chronological years, Erasmus (1466/69–1536) and Luther (1483–1546) were at one in their lifelong opposition to the training in scholastic philosophy that dominated the reigning universities of Paris, Louvain, and Cologne. They opposed its methods, its resources, and its goals. What had once been a flourishing and purposeful method had fallen into decadence, with its vaunted instruction in disputation, moved by probing questions pro and con (*sic* and *non*) intended to yield a great synthesis (or summa), seemed doomed in the eyes of Erasmus and a later generation to yield only quibbles over non-essential matters. They were high-powered technical machines that were only spinning their wheels. It was argued that they were too restricted in their resources, having lost contact with the textual and historical riches of the Gospels and of biblical study and the ripe teachings of the early church fathers. In a letter Erasmus exclaimed, 'What can Christ have in common with Aristotle?' (*Collected Works of Eras-*

mus [CWE] 3: 124). Luther bemoaned university education, in which Aristotle became of more consequence than Christ. For 1,200 years Christian doctrine seemed to get along well enough without Aristotle, then, some 300 years ago, he complained, with the reintroduction of Aristotle into Western philosophy, the simplicity of the Gospels was forsaken in the interests of high-sounding technical discourse. In *The Babylonian Captivity*, he laments the way the Mass has been taken captive, the holy communion divided into substances and accidents and finally transubstantiation, before lashing out, 'The Holy Spirit is greater than Aristotle' (*Works of Martin Luther [WML]* 2: 190–3). Both Erasmus and Luther are in strict accord in their very goals; the current university scholastics in their philosophical practice had become more and more distant from the living message of the Christian Gospels and even further from providing matters of use for the emerging laity. Erasmus and Luther were joined in a vibrant faith that the evangelical Gospels and the apostolic letters were living documents of practice and doctrine meant to be incorporated into the everyday lives of Christians.

They were perhaps even more opposed to the expanding authority of the church in such matters as ceremonials and 'works,' those human ordinances such as fasting, regulations concerning dress, indulgences, pilgrimages, private masses, and masses for the dead (and through the extent of their writings, the list of offences expands). After the bitter years of separation and conflict – the Great Schism – that marred and considerably weakened the fourteenth-century papacy, by the end of the fifteenth- and the early years of the sixteenth-century, the church became a unified and extensive power, capable of entering in all ways into the lives of ordinary people. In the time of Erasmus and Luther, it had become a well-tuned and highly organized financial enterprise and empire. For Erasmus and Luther, so many of the spiritual functions of the church seemed blurred by the prevalence of the profit motive, by commercialization. While Luther never ceased to object to the money factor, at the root of his objection to 'works' is a much more abiding suspicion of their motivation and efficacy. Along with Erasmus and Luther, their cohorts, their adherents, their disciples, a large number of seriously minded and well-schooled Christians were offended by the extensive overlay of ecclesiastical prescriptions governing daily practice that found no basis in holy scriptures.

As we shall see from one of Erasmus's many debates, there was some justification for this current practice and scholastic theology, in that by relying on their own intellectual resources and powers of reasoning their defenders were trying to answer for Christians questions that were left unanswered by the Bible itself and satisfy quite valid contemporary needs (*CWE* 3: 165). To their credit, they had the sense of an evolving Christianity. In fact, they felt that they were the 'moderns,' and were frequently so called by Erasmus and Luther. But Erasmus and Luther and their growing number of cohorts were not fundamentalists but rather firm believers in Paul's notion of Christian liberty, and again and again asserted that lay people were not children but adults who deserved to be treated as such. In this contest, the defenders of ecclesiastical practice and theological doctrine felt they were up to date, and Erasmus, Luther, and their kind were antiquarians relying solely on the authority of scripture. But Erasmus and Luther knew them not to be moderns, but only pseudo-moderns, misplaced near-moderns, who had strayed and were lacking not only in contemporary relevancy but also in original doctrine.

In addition, each deplored the expanding controls exerted by the mendicant friars and by monks over the troubled consciences of a susceptible people. Each vehemently objected to the growth of begging clergy who inundated the towns and villages, and they objected to the disputes for priority between and within the religious orders. Erasmus, in particular, made this the object of his biting satire in his *Colloquies*. But their arguments for change were even more substantive. While each began his career as an Augustinian canon (however, responding to the monastic calling in profoundly different ways), they both came to regard the monastic life as not, in Erasmus's decisive words, a special status of holiness but rather as a way of life among several that are open to pious Christians (*CWE* 3: 165). The life of a layman can be as holy as that of a monk. In the profound revolution that he brought to the bases of faith and the status of the Christian, Luther went even further and discounted the lives of the saints. Their own arduous and ascetic lives are no more saintly 'in God's eyes' and by the virtues of baptism than those of a farmer or a housewife undergoing his and her own daily Gethsemanes (2: 241).

Not only occasionally, but durably throughout their mature careers, Erasmus and Luther fought against these errors and abuses: such opposition gave mettle to their spirits and heat to their prose. In fact opposition to such abuses entered passionately and eloquently into their most important works. They opposed them for what they did and what they did not do. In their eyes, they served as masks of righteousness promoting a new kind of Phariseeism, a false confidence that prevented Christians from a true appropriation of their shared faith. The true message of Erasmus and Luther was a challenge to Christians to live their lives fully and sincerely. Of course, for the secularly minded and for the profane, this call to authentic belief was a difficult responsibility, a burden too onerous to bear. In this regard, the ministrations of the church, with its attendance from cradle to grave, offered a more comforting appeal.

That these three arguments of opposition joined Erasmus and Luther and their numerous and growing cohort groups receives telling evidence from a later dispute, a crucial one, since it was the first open break between Erasmus and the forces that Luther represented. Ulrich von Hutten, writing as an adulator who laments that his leader has defected from the great cause, must still pay tribute to the accomplishments of Erasmus, accomplishments that led the way for von Hutten and Luther (even implying that he preceded the great Reformation figure in his appreciation of Erasmus). How could Erasmus be thinking of attacking Luther in 1523, or at last be standing in the way, a ready source of appeal to his and their erstwhile foes?

> Was it not only a short time ago you aided us in putting the Roman Pontiff in his place, with a vengeful pen castigating Rome itself as a cesspool of depravity and crime? Did you not curse papal bulls and indulgences and damn ecclesiastical ceremonies? Was it not you who scourged the curial system and execrated canon law and pontifical pronouncements? In short, did you not flay the entire hypocritical structure of that estate? And now this same Erasmus has entered into alliance with the enemy. (Klawiter ¶33)

The last sentence of course sets the stage for the drama of this chapter, which is the apparent defection of Erasmus from the cause of which he was the nominal leader. Erasmus was not only a reformer, he was regarded as the leader in reform (Kohls, 'Erasme et la réforme' 839). The quotation indicates what joined the parties in opposition and in so doing it also helps provide the beginning of an answer to that essential problem. A simple comparison between von Hutten's inflamed rhetoric and the modulated aspects of Erasmus's prose, a prose that is subtle and elusive, reveals the answer to be that it was not the same person. Von Hutten had misread his Erasmus, whom he did not understand aright, or came to understand tragically only too late. As we shall observe in a later brief stylistic analysis of some of his major works, Erasmus could never lay claim to the kind of vehement expression that typifies von Hutten's accusation. While it is possible to exaggerate their importance, clearly distinctions of rhetoric mark a major divide between Erasmus and von Hutten, and even more so between Erasmus and Luther.

But history has a better gift than simple opposition, which by itself can run aground all too easily. The second and related gift of history was that both Erasmus and Luther emerged in the springtime of humanist endeavour; they had larger principles on which to base their opposition. We can refer to Coleridge's apt description of an age, 'restless from the first vernal influences of real knowledge.'[4] They had greater linguistic tools of philology at their disposal, as well as the humanistic emphasis on the persuasive power of rhetoric. They were motivated by a fervent dedication to the recovery of ancient texts, and by the critical energy needed to apply the message of those texts to contemporary practice. They were sustained in their endeavours by cohort groups of fellow believers, all contributing to a broader and more enduring sense of a movement (Augustijn, *Erasmus: His Life, Works, and Influence* 133).

The consciousness of Europe was expanding not only in regard to distant lands but also in regard to the territories of the mind. At the first level this movement was directed toward the recovery of classical texts and languages. We can reach back to the middle of the fourteenth century, to Petrarch (1304–74) and Giovanni Boccaccio (1313–75) – the first, a crucial figure, and the second not to be overlooked – to see this impulse in action, as they were the first Western intellectuals in a millennium to catch some glimpse of the richness of *The Odyssey*, albeit in a somewhat garbled translation. Petrarch was also quite proud of having found some texts of Plato, as yet unknown, but which he could not read. Showing the alliance between humanist endeavour and critical spirit, in the latter part of his career in several masterful invectives he also vehemently defended the interests of rhetoric against the more methodical presentations of scholastic philosophy.[5] By the turn of the fifteenth century Italian humanists, under the tutelage of Chrysolaris, began to achieve a mastery of Greek. In the latter part of the century, through the Platonic Academy of Florence, Marsilio Ficino was responsible for the translation into Latin of Plato's works. Such linguistic tools can also be used as weapons, as earlier Lorenzo Valla showed the potency of philology in proving that the so-called Donation of Constantine could not have been written when it was claimed to have been written, and provided important impetus to biblical studies by compiling a small collection (a *collatio*) of texts of the New Testament, comparing variant readings to the Vulgate offered by some Greek texts. Later, Erasmus not only published this effort but he also quoted from Valla's own defence of his procedures.

This same spirit of humanistic endeavour – the recovery of classical languages and texts with an attendant critical energy – was translated to the north, so that we can profitably speak of a northern Renaissance. While Erasmus may be considered, as he was by his contemporaries, the capstone of this historical transfer of humanism, by the time he came upon the scene there already existed expanding networks of humanists, with (to mention only the most central figures) Robert Gaguin in Paris (who will prove to be instrumental in the advancement of Erasmus's career), Jacques Lefèvre d'Étaples (ca. 1460–1536), Johann Reuchlin (1455–1522), both of whom anticipated Erasmus's work and between whom there existed a spirit of friendly competition.[6] When Erasmus went to England in 1499 (the first of six visits, one of which lasted – with interruptions – five years), he found there a resolute group of humanists (including John Colet and Thomas More) who astounded him with their learning as well as their Christian piety. Such cohort groups lent support as well as sustenance. In fact, revealing the cross-germination between More and Erasmus, in one of the controversies in which Erasmus was engaged, More himself assumed the charge of the second rebuttal.

With a renewed alacrity, Erasmus took over the beat first begun by Petrarch in the fourteenth century. From the early life of Erasmus by Beatus Rhenanus we can gain some insight into the excitement caused by the recovery of texts, their proper editing (based upon the collation of available texts), and then their publication. This activity possessed all the excitement of an important scientific discovery. A major effort throughout Erasmus's life was the careful publication (and republication) of the works of the church fathers, Ambrose, Jerome, and Augustine, as well as works of pagan classical authors. It was for this reason that he turned some of the major presses of the Continent, whether in Venice, Basel, or Paris, into his own ateliers, with busy apprentices and fellow scholars all buzzing with activity.

Clearly we are presented here with a major change in generational appeal that went well beyond the scholarly issues. Erasmus recounts how he would steal away his monastic hours in order to read the classical authors, an early example of the enterprise that would make him one of the greatest Latinists of his time. He was part of a cenacle of likely poets whose interest was high literature. Brecht assures us that Luther, too, 'had attained a noteworthy, broad acquaintance with classical authors.' While his later Christ-centred theology would allow little room for such writers, his understanding of the nature of the world, of fate and human destiny, took many pages from them.[7] Most importantly he too shared the great faith in the new philology's potential for granting access to the better meaning of essential Christian texts.

We are obviously dealing with new ideas and also with new motives, attitudes, and generational instincts. This transformation can be seen when the campaign to include the three languages (Latin, Greek, and Hebrew) in the university curriculum, even establishing separate colleges for their instruction, became something of a cultural war, which Erasmus waged successfully against the conservative theological faculty of Louvain (but with some residue of bitterness). And while Luther gave less prominence to such instruction for his university, throughout his works he makes constant reference not only to the correct philological resources, but even in some cases to Hebrew grammar. What is important in his case is the reservoir of reference and the willingness to make use of it as part of his intellectual endeavour. Moreover, knowledge of these languages brought one into a more direct, immediate contact with the purity of classical wisdom, whether that wisdom be pagan, or more importantly, Christian and scriptural. Hence both Erasmus and Luther shared in a basic turn of the Renaissance, a direction *ad fontes* to recapture the true sources of Western culture and Christian belief, both of which had been waylaid in the past 300 years by the intellectual hubris of scholastic philosophy (called sophist by both Erasmus and Luther). The bond uniting Erasmus and Luther was 'biblical humanism,' where the resources of the new awakening are utilized in more accurate understanding of scripture itself (Augustijn, *Erasmus: His Life* 133). From approximately 1512 onward, this was Luther's constant task, and it certainly accounts for Erasmus's discovery of his own vocation, which led in the opinion of many to his most influential achievement: his 1516 edition of the New Testament (containing for the first time a Greek text, a revised Latin translation, and annotations, accompanied by various prolegomena) and its subsequent revisions. During his period of confinement Luther used a later edition of Erasmus's work to create one of the monuments of German prose, his translation of the New Testament into simple, direct vernacular. According to Jean Hadot, despite all the criticisms directed against Erasmus's New Testament, some quite justified, it remained the received text until the mid-nineteenth century. Even by way of various publishing channels and accretions, Erasmus's 1536 edition formed the basis of another jewel of national prose: the 1611 Authorized version of the Church of England.

Two other major interests brought Erasmus and Luther together. The leap backwards is part of a larger impetus, one that seeks to expand the horizons of knowledge and the bases of learning, thus representing a great challenge to the existing institutional powers. But even more effectively the movement backward is a movement outward into the larger needs of a beckoning society. We can think of a line that, as it extends itself, bows outward in an inclusive arc. The movement back is thus a large step forward, a necessary act of replacement that carried the day. Erasmus and Luther, and their cohorts and disciples, represented a movement with good working tools, sound principles, and effective doctrine. Furthermore, the ethos of humanism, well beyond its philological conquests, included an undeniable critical and creative purpose, which meant going beyond the methods of the schools: it could also include the transcendence of its own most valued sources. Both Erasmus and More argued that just as Jerome corrected his predecessors, so Erasmus, in bringing out his edition of the New Testament, could feel free to correct that of Jerome (and here they were repeating an argument made by Valla almost a century earlier). The common thread through all of this endeavour, and the one that finally unites Erasmus and Luther, is the fundamental notion of Christian liberty, summarized in Jesus' own words, that the Sabbath is made for man, not man for the Sabbath. This becomes essential doctrine that extends to the larger Christian community: an adult laity, united in a common faith, is free to use its own discernment where many of the ordinances of the church are concerned. This belief united Erasmus and Luther, and, as we shall see, it is the principle over which they clashed.

These arguments should alert us to the fact that the great debate between Erasmus and Luther should not be highlighted as a clash between Renaissance and Reformation. There could not have been a Reformation without the recovery of and the insistence upon the importance of instruction in the three classical languages. Beyond their recovery, the developing critical sense that their philological uses engendered contributed materially to the sureness of conviction among reformers. Philology was evidence as formidable as DNA to modern forensic specialists. The crucial nature of these acquisitions is attested by the opposition it generated (as Erasmus's experience at Louvain abundantly reveals). In the northern Renaissance, at least, Renaissance and Reformation went hand in glove, forming the sense of a movement, with both Erasmus and Luther sharing much in common (Augustijn, *Erasmus: His Life* 132–5, 145). By thus dislodging argument from a strictly theological context, evidence is clear that the essential conflict and ultimate break occurred not between Renaissance and Reformation but from within their amalgamation – the contest was over the new face of Christianity, over its theory and practice, over its very spiritual metabolism and temperament.

The battle indeed was over the future, which makes the contest between the two formerly allied forces so intense. The long-awaited confrontation between Luther and Erasmus is so monumental because they had become the standard-bearers and representatives of these new forces in transition. Above the other disputes of the time, theirs emerges as paramount because it represents the major divergence over the right way for the Christianity of the future. Other controversies, whether Erasmus's with Maarten van Dorp or Luther's with Andreas von Karlstadt, shrink in importance as well as historical record because they do not bear the same significance.[8] They each chose at last to take on their grander opponent in a critical dispute. The epochal debate between Erasmus and Luther carries even further meaning, revealing it to be among the foremost dualisms of modem culture, not only because of its remarkable historical dimensions, but because, like the other dualisms of this study, it reaches down into a perennial psychic tension within Western culture itself, a tension that it both embodies and explores.

3. Two 'Moments': Erasmus

While the particular itinerary of encounter between Erasmus and Luther could constitute a real-life five-act drama, sharper focus can be had by turning to two distinct 'moments' in each of their careers. For Erasmus the first was from about 1496 to 1503, from the time he decided to continue his studies at the University of Paris until his time of liberation and self-justification. The second records the moment of great acclaim and triumph, the moment of Erasmian optimism (1514–17), before the Lutheran crisis, before the moment when he became entangled in the conflict between Luther and the papal defenders, before he himself became a contested figure, challenged from the religious Left and Right, wishing to maintain a position of strategic neutrality, but in fact having become by this time a figure too enormous for such a tactic. For Luther, our focus turns to his first conversion experience and its aftermath (1505–7) and then from the breakthrough work of the Ninety-five Theses, with its contemporaneous 'reformation experience,' to 1520 and the three major works. These historical 'moments' set the stage for the critical years of 1523–5 and the debate over the freedom or the enslavement of the will, a debate that resounds because it says so much about the thought of the time, because it was awaited with such expectation, and because it brings to the front so much of the essential natures of both Erasmus and Luther, summarizing so much of what they represent.

This arrangement leads to one interesting conclusion and helps us resolve the problem besetting Erasmus criticism. Without a doubt Luther is the more overwhelming presence. His profound learning, his conviction of spirit and of conscience, his willingness to be the spiritual voice of a people, and the sheer courage he exhibited in dismantling some long-surviving institutions of the church led him to defy the combined powers of pope and emperor. One can go on and on, and still not even touch the complexity of the man, the religious genius and the remarkable balance and ballast required to accomplish all that he did succeed in doing. Granted all this, and much more, still Erasmus is psychologically the more complex, the more intriguing personality, filled with contradictions of mind and of character, a man whose reputation exceeds him, a name to invoke rather than a presence to behold, a man who has had no need to be forgiven by history but one who runs the risk of being forgotten, despite the fact that he thought plausibly and wrote well. As the list of perplexing attributes grows, it is the very combination of weaknesses and strengths that preoccupies us.

This phenomenon is particularly apparent when one asks the two questions that must be asked, and have been asked in relation to Erasmus: why was he never able to break with the church, and why at the critical moment did he choose to enter into dispute with Luther himself? Or put another way, why was he never able to accept leadership in the movement of which he was the nominal leader? Why did he not comprehend the force of his own impact, instead insisting on deprecating if not belittling his own presence and contributions (unless they were criticized by someone else)?

The critical dispute about Erasmus's career (with Huizinga and Spitz on one side, and Augustijn and Schoeck on the other) are portraits from two different epochs – one before Luther and the other after.[9] Until the advent of Luther, Erasmus was the prince of humanists, the foremost biblical scholar of his day, the star of the German north (and the epithets accumulate). This is the result of his program by 1503 and the years of great acclaim and optimism of 1514–17. By the latter moment he was confident in himself and optimistic for his times. Although subject to some controversies, he dispatched his opponents, not only with skill, but with some ease, if not disdain. But when the more dominant spirit of Luther entered the scene, the very dualism itself induced in Erasmus a different set of qualities, those more suited to Huizinga's understanding, or even to Spitz's belief that the final denouement of Erasmus's life was one of tragic unfulfilment. The contest with Luther brought to the surface aspects of Erasmus's character that had been submerged. Whereas earlier he had come out into a clearing, justified and liberated in his life's work, now dismayingly he finds himself constrained and forced to encounter an aspect of himself that lacks the buoyancy and élan of his earlier spirit. Now he is moved by the need to bow before the ages, before the accumulated wisdom of historical consensus, all represented if not by the church actual then by the church universal. In fact, he is constrained to take issue with the presence of Spirit, itself, and this at length will be the point of another essential quarrel with Luther, and another area in which he seems to be backtracking.

Formerly he had been challenged on matters of biblical exegesis, on the ill effects of historical philology applied to long-held church readings, and on his reliance on the fine art of satire. In these contests his better qualities as a defender of culture and civilization, of learning and knowledge, were exhibited. Now from within the same structure of belief, and even of aspiration, the same convergence of interests willing to apply philology to sacred texts he encounters a different kind of foe, one who shares many of his premises and yet disagrees radically on matters of theology and is, moreover, in matters of temperament more forceful, one laying confident claim to the access of the Spirit. It is this debate that pushes him into adopting an aspect of himself that future generations will find unattractive. Yet despite the accusations of von Hutten, of Luther, and their followers through the centuries, we must not think of Erasmus as cowardly.[10] This engagement with Luther produces extraordinary expressions of self-encounter as he tries again and again to understand and justify what had happened. And he does not desist from making well-reasoned arguments against what he finds paradoxical, extravagant, or dangerous in Luther's writings. Unfortunately, the very nature of dualism consigns him to play a role that may scant his better qualities, but in so doing reveals equally true dimensions of his personality. But we must also add that the sorrows of Erasmus are not only of a personal regret but rather derive from the sad perspective of an entire movement gone astray; the tragic denouement involves not only his own person but also his hopes for his time, when ever so briefly he has seen open before him the great cultural flourishing of peace, piety, and learning.

The course of Erasmus's career up until the moment of triumph was marked by an unswerving dedication on his part to a pursuit of his vocation and a justification of his talents. Attempting to account for Erasmus's character, Augustijn finds it 'in his toughness, his undaunted tenacity, in spite of all obstacles, in holding to the goal he wanted to attain' (*Erasmus: His Life* 40). (See also Schoeck's splendid defences in 1: 260 and passim, particularly where he describes Erasmus's success in attaining his goal of being a free-standing intellectual.) Erasmus started out with several handicaps. He was left an impoverished orphan while still quite young. As he himself tells us in a letter of 1524, his father was prevented from marrying his mother (to whom he may have been betrothed). Being misinformed that the young woman was dead, he entered the priesthood, thus disabling any possibilities of marriage. At least this is the account Erasmus would have us believe.[11] Thus when he entered the monastery at Steyn, he entered not out of a sense of calling but rather from the self-serving suasions of his guardians and for reasons of penury, one of several early differences between himself and Luther. While each coincidentally entered the austere Augustinian Eremite order, Luther took to the monastic life like a fish to water, but Erasmus chafed at it, at its regimen of rules, its rote existence, its benumbing aura of ignorance and at its meagre diet. With his delicate physique, sensitive tastes, and above all interest in and responsiveness to great literature, it was quite predictably a life for which he was not meant. As a consequence, throughout his life he satirized (both pointedly and massively) the dourness of the monastic life, and also argued against making binding monastic vows when one was young and susceptible, and before one could be aware of one's character and interests.

While these two arguments would be constants in his letters and in his *Colloquies*, his greater need was to liberate himself from such a drastic misstep. But here, as would occur more than once in his life, someone recognized his obvious talents and plucked him out of the monastic life to which he never returned. Hendrik van Bergen, the archbishop of Cambrai and the most eminent churchman of Burgundy, took the talented young Latinist into his services soon after his ordination in 1492. Despite acquainting Erasmus with the elegancies of life, this appointment did not turn out to be as rewarding as had been expected. A much-anticipated journey to Italy, for which Erasmus may have been recruited, never materialized, and in 1496 Erasmus sought his leave to pursue his studies at the University of Paris (more likely attending lectures at the Collège de Montaigu). That he might have thought this to be palatable now seems strange, but what it certainly did provide was a patina of justification for delaying his return to the monastic life at Steyn.

At Paris, once again his own natural desires, tastes, and needs overtook his choice, as he experienced a quite visceral antipathy to the methods and the language of scholastic theology. Two letters – one from this period of his study to a former tutorial student and the second a few years later to John Colet – explain the abhorrence he felt at the current instruction in theology. The first, a humorous letter to Thomas Grey, indicates that the necessity of following the university lectures caused lapses in his correspondence. In mock wonderment he asks his former student to imagine that Erasmus has become a Scotist (that is, a latter-day follower of the theologian Duns Scotus). He tells the tale of the legendary sixth-century Epimenides, who, contemplating the terminology of the later scholastics ('instances,' 'quiddities,' and 'formal qualities'), fell into such a deep slumber that he awoke only after forty-seven years. After this long sleep Epimenides was just as dumbfounded and irrelevant to his day as the new Scotists – the belated Epimenides – were in Erasmus's time. He then asks his student to imagine him Erasmus – the emergent humanist – listening to a lecture:

> If only you could see your Erasmus sitting agape among those glorified Scotists, while 'Gryllard' lectures from a lofty throne. If you could but observe his furrowed brow, his uncomprehending look and worried expression, you would say it was another man. They say that the secrets of this branch of learning cannot be grasped by anyone who has anything to do with the Muses or the Graces; for this you must unlearn any literary lore you have put your hands on and vomit up any draught you have drunk from Helicon. So I am trying with might and main to say nothing in good Latin, or elegantly, or wittily, and I seem to be making progress; so there is some hope that, eventually, they will acknowledge me. (*CWE* 1: 136–8)

Beyond the criticism of the outmoded methods of the scholastics as reborn Epimenides or the absence of good Latin or even any hint of wit and liveliness, what emerges is the portrait that Erasmus paints of himself, his pose of bemused spectator, even of struggling humanist amidst the theologians. Already Erasmus was framing a self-image, that of a humanist (with some ambitions as a poet), or man of letters, one that he intentionally exploits to show the humour in the discrepancy of Erasmus residing among the scholastics.

Of course Erasmus would maintain that he was not opposed to theology; rather he sought its renewal. But this would come later, particularity beginning around the turn of the century and his friendship with John Colet, the man who would become dean of St Paul's. But there is an interesting and revealing connection between the budding humanist misplaced among the theologians of Paris and the man who after 1500 found his life's calling to be employing classical learning and letters for the betterment of Christian thought and practice. Like any young man of unrecognized talent, Erasmus poured out letters of flattery to the great and established figures of his time (this was a habit that he did not totally abandon even later in life). These letters are pleas for inclusion, a means of entering into discourse with the famous, and an act of self-registration, and they help us to understand the moving ambition of Erasmus's character. One such letter in high-cholesterol Latin was addressed to Robert Gaguin, then the leading humanist in Paris and a man of redoubtable merit. A frank, fellow Lowlands man, he could not tolerate the larding and let Erasmus know that such adulation is always suspect. While the duly chastised Erasmus responded with greater restraint, this did not prevent him from writing a letter in elegant Latin praising Gaguin's recent work, *De origine et gestis Francorum compendium*. The letter was of a type common among Renaissance humanists eager to persuade those in power that the great are in need of poets to immortalize their actions. Here Erasmus got lucky: the letter was inserted to fill a blank page at the end of Gaguin's volume. And once again his talents were recognized and he was rescued from an unhappy situation. This fortuitous publication quickly made him into a man of note and caught the eye of John Colet, so that when Erasmus went to England, his budding reputation as a classical humanist helped account for the warm welcome he received from the thriving circle of English humanists.

After years of struggle and even despair, Erasmus had at last found a group of learned men with whom he shared a likeness of mind. These were kindred spirits who provided him with the self-confirmation he sorely needed, the self-confirmation that comes from recognition. An elite circle of educated, literate men, possessed of wit and generosity of spirit always carried appeal for Erasmus. His greatest colloquy imaginatively realizes such a gathering.

Colet's influence was immediate and enormous, grounded as it was in their commonly held distaste for the practice of contemporary theology and the need to return to the original sources of Christianity (in Erasmus more so than in Colet, this backward track also led to the pagan classics as well). As an indication of the pending and open break with Luther, soon after the debacle at Worms, Erasmus described Colet's ideal Christian qualities, his clarity of thought, his lack of abrasiveness, and his clear control of Christian doctrine – an obvious counterpoint to the impression made by Luther. In fact, at the time of their first acquaintance, Colet had already been lecturing on Paul's epistles at Oxford for three years. In 1499, Erasmus wrote from Oxford, 'When you tell me that you dislike the modern class of theologians, who spend their lives in theological hair-splitting and sophistical quibbling, you have my emphatic agreement' (*CWE* 1: 203). He then proceeds to some well-recognized criticisms of the disparaged theological studies as he had experienced them at the Sorbonne. Their methods are historically 'isolated,' without reference to the purer springs of an earlier age; they seem to produce no valid results, or bear no fruit, except a keenness for disputation that soon reduces itself to such meaningless philosophical puzzles as whether God can bring himself to take the shape of the devil or of an ass. Far from bearing the fruits of wisdom, this practice renders theology, which ought to be the queen of the sciences, unattractive. Moreover, showing the humanist's abiding interest in the persuasive powers of rhetoric, he deplores the scholastic lack of eloquence, thus 'neither quickening their subject matter with vital sap nor breathing into it the breath of life (203).' A new generation with different emotional and intellectual needs has made its appearance on the historical scene. Under the influence, or rather confluence, of interests with Colet (and with More as well), Erasmus emerged as the most appealing speaker for this new generation, one who was seeking to appropriate the original texts of Christianity and by so doing to revivify its current thought and practice.

But before this could be done, Erasmus needed to bolster his resources. Because theology is the queen of the sciences, Erasmus felt obliged to decline Colet's invitation to lecture on the books of Moses, or on the 'eloquent stylist' Isaiah (*CWE* 1: 205). The reason was that he knew little Greek. Consequently when he left England he had two purposes in mind: to acquire a mastery of Greek and to find the financial means that would permit him the freedom to devote all of his resources to biblical and to classical studies. In accomplishing both, Erasmus showed that remarkable tenacity emphasized by both Augustijn and Schoeck.

Upon his return to the Continent, his letters of this period (particularly those to Jacob Batt, his friend at the court in Cambrai) are filled with the need for patronage and on fire with new projects: mastery of Greek, money to buy the complete works of Jerome, and finally the undertaking that brought him his first independent success, the *Adagia collectanea*, a collection of adages he had gleaned from his readings primarily in Latin (there were a small number of Greek adages as well) and was published in Paris in 1500. Although with his habitual tic of scholarly self-deprecation and self-defensiveness, he dismissed the work as hastily composed and assembled in but a few months, it brought him well-deserved recognition. His adages (818 in all) were not to be thought of as simple sayings or maxims, such as 'love conquers all,' but rather as pithy statements, with some metaphoric or even contradictory content, which are in need of explication.[12] As would be the case with many of Erasmus's projects, his interest in classical adages blossomed and grew to over three thousand entries in the edition of 1508, such was the amplitude brought him by his acquisition of Greek. It would continue to flourish in the grand edition of 1515, from which some of the commentaries became independent essays, published separately. Adding to the complexity of his character, Erasmus was a man of opinions, which continued to enter into his works, accounting (but not this alone) for the many enlargements and revisions they constantly underwent.

Not only did the mastery of Greek add to his scholarly productivity, it contributed to his critical awareness. In a letter of 1501 to Antoon van Bergen we can see that the work on the *Adages* helped cultivate in Erasmus a sense of the importance of historical philology. He writes that he has come to the conclusion (admittedly a belated one) that Latin scholarship, however well developed, is maimed and diminished by half without a knowledge of Greek (*CWE* 2: 25). Showing the direction of his interests, he then gives several quite cogent examples from the Old Testament where the meaning is impaired without a knowledge of the Greek upon which the Vulgate was based.

4. Arguments, Stylistic Tropes, and the Carousel of Erasmus's Mind

Huizinga has referred to Erasmus's natural reclusiveness and that paradoxically we best get to know him not through the invaluable correspondence but through the works where he reaches out to the larger society (Huizinga 115–16). If this is the case, then an examination of even minor or lesser works should reveal the intrinsic parts, the contours of Erasmus's mental landscape. They better than anything else will help explain the choices that he made, and in diachronic fashion show his affiliations with other writers of consciousness. They provide earlier, more fundamental grounds for understanding the opposition between himself and Luther.

This most difficult period in Erasmus's life, one in which he had to overcome the severe obstacles of obscurity, poverty, and the serious misstep of his early entrance into the monastic life, was somewhat alleviated with the publication in 1503 of his *Enchiridion militis Christiani* – a small dagger, or a manual to aid the Christian soldier (*CWE* 66).[13] The devil is still in the flesh and his defeat requires such militant weapons of protection.[14] As he did habitually with other of his works, Erasmus regarded this effort somewhat dismissively as a detour from his more serious commentary on Paul's epistles and other work on the church fathers. The *Enchiridion* caused no great stir until it was reprinted in 1518, in the full season of Luther's arrival, when discussions of indulgences, purgatory, and the papacy were rife, another indication of their joint appeal and common aim. Up until 1518 the work saw eight printings, but in the next ten years forty editions.

Despite some modern dismissals, the *Enchiridion* can lay claim to being a foundation work. Schoeck refers to it as a 'landmark' (2: 20). It completes the aspirations of earlier efforts (the yet unpublished *Antibarbari*) and it establishes the ground for *The Praise of Folly* and the *Colloquies*. In fact, it should be discussed in conjunction with these other two works, as first offering the full nature of his life and belief. While differing in method, they treat the same subjects. What the *Enchiridion* reveals by way of straightforward argument and exhortation, the *Colloquies* disclose by stylistic tropes, the habitual formulae and rhetorical means by which Erasmus shows the cut of his mind. *The Praise of Folly* shows Erasmus at his most gamesome, that his mind's plottings are like a carousel, where all points seem to be touched but none taken in hand, where satire is high and comedy low, where all is part of a game, drawing down the ire of both Catholic critics and Luther, for turning serious matters into follies, into a jest. Luther charged that his proteanism shelters a sceptic; one does not know where to pin him down. The charge of scepticism resurfaced in the great debate. But in these earlier works satire rests on a discernible moral base and even the carousel in its wild spinning has a central mechanism of control. These are provided by the *Enchiridion*.

Most if not all of Erasmus's philosophy of Christ can be derived from the *Enchiridion*, particularly from the so-called rule five, along with the adjoining rules, which escape from any regulatory status and become small essays in themselves. Further, it contains the essence of Erasmus's interpretive methods and provides the first full justification of his higher purpose in abandoning the monastic life, in pursuing the ways of the Christian intellectual. It is primarily a work of education, a manual in the ways of the Christian life, a short course, freed from scholastic terminology, for achieving the 'good life' of a Christian. We 'acquire virtue' by always aspiring to the best (*CWE* 66: 104–5). But such ethical provisions are founded on Erasmus's central devotion to Christ, his address to the adulthood of the believing Christian, and his advocacy of Christian liberty. He stands and writes as another Paul; as Paul embraced the Spirit over the law, so Erasmus invokes the Spirit against the reigning practices of his day. His opponents remain the same: the alienating effects of scholasticism, the burdensome emphasis on ceremonials and works, and the assumed spiritual superiority and authority of the monastic orders. These reliances are harmful as they induce a smug self-satisfaction and represent a detour from the full benefits and obligations of the Christian life. They keep the believer in a state of infancy, thus blocking access to the spiritual adulthood of Christian liberty that Paul so ardently advocates (78). Here Erasmus is not only admonishing the general run of humanity but rather the supposed leaders of the Christian community who have lost sight of the larger things in their prescriptive zeal for petty observances: 'If the salt has lost its flavor, what will the others be salted with?' (74).

We grow into adulthood by acquisition of the Spirit. But for Erasmus Spirit does not mean some overwhelming presence, an undeniable force, something that comes from the outside and inhabits and takes control of the person. Rather it is the acquisition of spiritual joy, the achieved possession of an inner state of calm, peace, and understanding. Spirit is a tutelary presence and reward of the twin strivings of faith and knowledge. Its place is not initiatory but terminal; it represents an attainment, the object of constant effort. If the devil is present every day, so is Christ with his means of deliverance. Our responsibility is the active daily imitation of superior models, of the saints, of Christ himself, as part of the constant striving for 'perfection.'

Yet despite the ardour of his faith and the fervour of his exposition, Erasmus shows himself to be an accommodator – a role that comes even clearer in the stylistic tropes of his *Colloquies*. Even here in 1501–3, before any hint of the major troubles to follow, Erasmus shows an essential trait of not being able totally to exclude. Augustijn writes that Erasmus 'shrinks' from any complete rejection of earthly things (*Erasmus: His Life* 47). His rhetoric is incorporative: the mandates of the church, honourable traditions, and pious customs are not to be rejected, as they are necessary for the weak and observed by the strong so as not to give offence. 'Corporeal works are not condemned, but those that are invisible are preferred' (*CWE* 66: 81). Is it simple backtracking, fear, a normal cautionary stance, a simple respect and toleration for the erring ways of humanity, or a common human sympathy that characterizes Erasmus's mentality? Most likely a mixture of all, but features so ingrained, so prevalent that they are identifiable long before the outbreak of hostilities with Luther. Christian liberty is a strenuous call to a genuine belief in spiritual principle, one that stems from conviction. Poor straying humanity – that is to say, everyone in his and her daily existence – seems ill-equipped to follow this extraordinary summons. Thus out of sympathy Erasmus resorts to arguments, employs locutions and interpretive methods that offer encouragement, even accommodation. He cannot resort to outright rejection but requires some bases of mitigation, and finally of inclusiveness.

A letter to Johan Poppenruyter of 1501 came to form part of the introduction and the conclusion of the work.[15] Poppenruyter himself was the intended beneficiary of Erasmus's Christian instruction. As an armaments provisioner for both emperors Maximilian and Charles V, he was understandably a worldly man and hence a source of concern to his wife, who prevailed upon Erasmus to compose the *Enchiridion* for his benefit. The second part of the letter sharpens Erasmus's intentions: he is afraid that in his besieged situation this prominent layman might fall victim to the wiles of that 'superstitious fraternity among the religious,' 'as if Christianity did not exist outside the monk's cowl' (*CWE* 66: 126, 127). He writes that it is their art 'to fill his mind with thorny problems and mere quibbles and thorny problems they bind him to some petty observances of human, not divine, origin.' The final message to this highly successful layman – the ever paramount object of Erasmus's teachings – is that 'being a monk is not a state of holiness but rather a way of life' (127).

The *Enchiridion* is as important for its method as for its message. The men of his world are too involved in the flesh and the letter – as antidote to each Erasmus recommends the spirit both as a hermeneutic and salve. People must learn to read the scriptures aright, the true sense of which will be of greater appeal to the worldly successful man. Erasmus espouses a qualified training and exposure in the pagan authors because there the attentive modern will learn how to read, read for the spiritual sense of the work, allegorically. If properly directed toward an immersion in the life and thought of Christ, such exposure may prove valuable in providing the right methods for understanding scripture. Thus, as Thomas More praised him for being a 'litteratus,' Erasmus extols the virtues of the literary critic, who draws out the larger more representative sense of the literal, who sees the parable in the mix. The manna of the Old Testament has its several meanings: because it falls from above, it is of divine origin; the fact that it is a small thing connotes the vast mysteries contained in the inadequacies of words; that it is white indicates the purity of Christ's teaching; the fact that it is hard indicates the difficulty of shedding the outer shell in order to penetrate to the inner core of Christian teaching (*CWE* 66: 32). One can well imagine what little appeal such instruction in the method of the literary critic held for the intended recipient.

The letter finally provides Erasmus's own understanding and clarification of his genuine motives throughout this trying period, starting with his departure from the monastery at Steyn, to his three-year stay at the court of the bishop of Cambrai, to his ill-advised studies in Paris, to his period of self-discovery and self-confirmation amidst the English humanists. Finally he makes a clear record and defence of the purposes that were driving him. He had always felt the need to justify himself against his critics at Steyn; now he feels he can do so fully and faithfully. When in his youth he embraced the finer literature of the ancients – 'not without much midnight labor' – this was not out of a desire for fame or self-gratification, but rather according to a 'long ago determined' program to use these classical ornaments to adorn the Lord's temple that had been desecrated by 'ignorance and barbarism.' He then goes on to employ a phrase that captures our attention. Such treasures 'can inspire even men of superior intellect' (et generosa ingenia) to love the scriptures (*CWE* 66: 127). There is that in the essence of Christianity, which can appeal to the intelligences (called 'noble' or 'lofty') of worldly successful men – not simpletons, not children. The language is astonishing: it is men of superior intellect, and presumably of worldly accomplishment, who have been alienated and are now in need of persuasion. These adults active in the world were to become Erasmus's intended audience throughout his life. As a Christian intellectual, Erasmus will always reach out to such people, eminent lay people who might have been put off by the apparent childishness of some religious practices and thought.

Erasmus's style and manner are accommodating, appeasing; it is a style that brings along and encourages with modest expectations in the daily grind of mortal existence. These aspects are even more pronounced in the *Colloquies*.[16] Despite the fact that the *Colloquies* were vastly enlarged after the first edition of 1518 – thus advanced in any itinerary of encounter between Erasmus and Luther – they are valuable historically and give ample indications of the habits of Erasmus's mind. Its typical tropes show (1) a sense of proportionate value, (2) a habit of reconsideration leading to a 'double rhythm' in his exposition, (3) a need for inclusiveness rather than rejection, and (4) a reliance on the balancing locutions such as 'although/yet,' or 'yes/but' rather than 'either/or.' Thus Erasmus represents only a modified challenge to the reader, who, chuckling over vices being satirized, can by laughter readily exclude himself from the portraiture. Satire is always weakened when the principle of personal exclusion may be invoked, a notorious escape hatch. The reader goes away reassured, comfortable in his capacities and not shaken in his hold on the world. At the same time, by the abundant use of irony, the author himself is protected. As Jacques Chomarat reminds us, 'Irony can also provide a screen of distance. Erasmus is a secret man; he hides himself' (2: 1165).

The *Colloquies* are prime instances of the self-transforming powers of Renaissance humanism. They began as simple linguistic formulae, whose intention was to give sample dialogues for instruction in Latin, that is, they were teaching devices, skits, playlets, introduced by Erasmus perhaps as early as 1497, when he needed to earn his bread as a tutor. They eventually grew into such large and masterful exchanges and dialogues as 'The Religious Feast' and 'The Fish Diet.' In their growth and development from formulae to dialogues they may be compared to Montaigne's *Essais*, which began as a simple collection of classical commentary on such subjects as death, friendship, and old age, but in time, fed by the expanding awareness of Montaigne's own reflections, evolved into one of the masterpieces of European literature.

The same grandeur cannot be attributed to the *Colloquies*. They suffer from limitations of subject matter and of presentation. They pleased many and pleased often, but they do not please greatly; their appeal has been more extensive than intensive (Huizinga 190). They undertake to expose the common superstitions of their time – all the aspects of a materialized religion accepted by the common people, and all the systems of worldliness of those who would exploit the popular beliefs. Accordingly the misguided worship of saints is satirized in 'The Shipwreck,' as is throughout the abused veneration of Christian relics. So too are held up to ridicule the avid pursuit of monetary gain on the part of the various religious orders and pilgrimage itself – all caught up in the hucksterism that has lost sight of true Christian belief. The *Colloquies* mount a withering satire of the professions of doctors, of the military, of the various religious orders themselves. But none of this ever rises to the stature of great literature. Dante's *Inferno* is a masterpiece because it does not pretend to be a satire of the professions, but rather an exploration of the anguish of great souls. Erasmus's *Colloquies* are marred by superficiality. Their disadvantage is their very plausibility. We muster a wry smile, a modest assent, but little more. There is little that he tells us that we do not already know. Erasmus never enters into the genuine human natures and needs of his antagonists – they remain cardboard figures, characterized by their limited, unworthy actions. Moreover, Erasmus writes as an intellectual expositor with points to make, not with stories to tell or characters to unfold. His *Colloquies* thus resemble (and suffer the same fate as) Voltaire's *contes philosophiques*, without Voltaire's cynicism or his larger acceptance of the rules of the game. But like Voltaire, he is undone by his own facility, and on the larger screen he is undone by his very success. His arguments have become commonplace and thus open to shrugged dismissal. The writer who commits himself to history, to its topicalities, as writers of consciousness have done, can be victimized by history's cruel service of unjust oblivion. It is the daemonic writer who penetrates the screens of history, who goes beyond himself and thus surpasses the narrow circle of his intent and that of his time.[17]

Erasmus's tendency to reconsideration is made manifest in the 'double rhythm' of the *Colloquies*. One exemplary instance occurs in 'A Pilgrimage for Religion's Sake' (1526), where visits to the shrines of Our Lady of Walsingham and St Thomas at Canterbury are recounted. Unlike Dante, unlike Chaucer, who regarded pilgrimage as the true spiritual metaphor for *homo viator*, but very much like Luther, Erasmus frequently argues against pilgrimage itself, reminding his readers that it is much better to remain at home and discharge one's responsibilities to family and neighbours than waste one's resources visiting other lands. On this issue there is no equivocation, but when it comes to 'ceremonials' or to the veneration of saints and the adoration of relics, Erasmus can be of two minds. The most notable example might be the pseudo-letter from Mary, which was attacked by the Sorbonne (this over Erasmus's objection that it was intended as a satire of Zwingliite iconoclasm). The first part of the letter abhors the misdirected use of prayer as extortion, whereby petitioners turn to the Virgin for all manner of worldly gain and assistance. As in 'The Shipwreck,' Erasmus deplores such error not only for its obvious recourse to bargaining, but mainly for the deflection it represents from a primary reliance on Christ. But in the latter part of the letter Erasmus stoutly defends the place of Mary in serious Christian belief. He deplores the neglect, abandonment, and desecration of her places of worship by some Protestant reformers. In his argument Erasmus yields to elegant sentiment, even to a kind of aesthetic appreciation. She, the Virgin Mother, cannot be ejected 'unless at the same time you eject my son whom I hold in my arms. From him I will not be parted. Either you expel him along with me, or you leave us both here, unless you prefer to have a church without Christ' (*Colloquies* 291). The argument, Erasmian in its frequency, is twofold: it is wrong to turn to Mary in lieu of turning to God or to Christ, but it is equally wrong to remove her from the hospices of Christian belief. This would be tantamount to truncating the Christian family. Do we hear in this plea the voice of the orphaned Erasmus, who requires a matrix view of human history and experience, and who has endured separation himself and thus does not wish it in the Holy Family? Recall Kierkegaard's comment that Luther invented a religion for the adult male!

'The Godly Feast,' or 'Convivium Religiosum' (1522), is in many ways most representative of Erasmus's ideal. It shows a gathering of laymen in an enclosed garden – an ideal seminar room for engagement in learned exposition. Here there is no contest, no controversy, but all harmony and glowing intelligence. Nothing is taken literally, but all given over to the higher spirit of interpretation. Signs betoken larger things, things larger signs. The cathedral has been brought into the villa, where an adept and informed laity expound spiritual matters. Representing *eudaemonism* – the commitment to well-being at its fullest – in opulent but not lavish surroundings, an intellectual elite expounds without intervening commentaries, essential texts of the Christian life. This is a classical convivium, a symposium, reminiscent of the philosophical dinners of the pagans with male companions engaging in pleasurable conversation. Looking forward, it anticipates another gathering of philosophical elite in quasi-religious draping, Voltaire's *Sermon des Cinquante*, the fuller comparison with which will be undertaken in the next chapter.

After first explaining the trilingual inscriptions (Latin, Greek, and Hebrew) on the gate, the chapel's altar, and the frescoes, the host directs his guests' attention to scripture. The first passage, taken from Proverbs (21.1–3), reads, 'The king's heart is in the hands of the Lord; He turns it withersoever He will (*Colloquies* 57). The first elucidation conveys the conservative nature of Erasmus's political thought, certainly not unexpected for any reader of *The Education of a Christian Prince*. Vile kings are seen as God's punishment on an unworthy people; given that, it is also true that 'none of their subjects has the authority to condemn them.' Erasmus's need for consensus leads to an acquiescence to authority.[18] But interpretation does not end there. Proceeding up the allegorical scale, the next reading replaces 'king' with the perfect Pauline man, free in his Christian liberty (58–9). And the third interpretation shifts to the level of ceremonials, which are not to be omitted but are 'displeasing to God if a person relies on such observances but neglects works of mercy when a brother's need calls for charity' (61). Ceremonial works are not offensive in themselves but may be so if created to the neglect of better works of charity.

Erasmus's adherence to the Pauline doctrine of Christian liberty validates his appeal to the adult consciousness that is able to dispense, or not dispense, with ecclesiastical ordinances, depending on their centrality or indifference, on whether they strengthen or scandalize one's neighbours. In a lengthy and telling passage, Chrysoglottus goes through the ready church ceremonials, showing their presence from cradle to grave – as it were, another progress through the Ages of Man. But such easy and accommodating ministrations, he fears, give a false assurance, as if one could be saved by such ceremonials alone. They become matters of custom, perfunctorily performed; and worse, when custom replaces conviction, they deflect from commitment to the fullness of Christian belief. Yet despite these misgivings, Chrysoglottus does not reject outright such ceremonials. Rather he employs another familiar Erasmian locution, the 'although/yet,' or 'yes/but' in reference to the final rite: 'Although these ceremonies, especially the ones sanctioned by ecclesiastical usage, are acceptable, yet there are other, more interior means of helping us to depart from this life with cheerfulness and Christian trust' (69).

Even more revealing is Erasmus's commentary on a dire-seeming passage from Matthew 6.24–5: 'No man can serve two masters.' This seems to cry out for heroic choice: 'Ye cannot serve God and Mammon.' Yet here also drastic division is interpreted less severely, as once again Erasmus through his interlocutor dislodges any dualism, any possibility of collision or combat. Here again the interpretive force of the quotation is dispersed, this time by subordination. The passage now means that one should put away anxiety over the morrow, which is valid enough, but the interpreter Timothy also prioritizes: Christ declares the first and foremost care, not the *sole* care ('non dicet solum quaerite') to be that of spreading the Gospel (73). Is it now a matter of priority, not of exclusivity.

By these and other means we can see that Erasmus is congenitally unfit to partake of any dualism. He constantly seeks to dissolve the dualism, adroitly to outmanoeuvre it. His purpose is not to disquiet or to disturb, or even to challenge, but rather to lend assurance. One comes away from his writings, as one does from those of other writers of consciousness, with no sense of being severely challenged in one's spiritual life, or of being called to a drastic choice where so much seems to hang in the balance. One is rather left with a sense of accommodation: we are all capable, we can all do well, if given time, education, example, and the growth of rational habit. No one is condemned, or if so, only for being – as in 'Charon, or Cyclops' – warmongers, destroyers of the peace, boozers, whore-masters, notorious types of public dereliction. In Erasmus, we experience no metaphysical malaise, no spiritual sense of not belonging, but rather every attempt to overcome abandonment.

Erasmus and Luther participated in a culture of authoritative citation, in the dedicated reacquisition of classical learning itself and its application primarily by means of philology to a new understanding of sacred texts. Where they differed was not in their means and procedures but in their essential theology, as Pintacuda has so valuably shown. But there are other divergences, divergences from within their very natures that helped determine their radical separation. For Luther, the text was there to be wrestled with alone; it was authoritative, and because of that, its understanding required full personal attention of faith and reason. The question remains, where and how does one find justification? For humanists such as Erasmus, the culture of citation meant continuity rather than rupture, participation rather than isolation. To walk in the steps of the ancients filled their being, but also instilled a dependence, a reliance on the statements of others. It is the participation in this roll-call of the great that provides legitimation, and not the strength coming from individual conviction. At times the early humanists such as Erasmus were bedazzled by the profusion of classical lore that fell within their sights. Its exhibition thus became a means of personal delectation and elevation far from the agon with the angel of the Lord.

The Praise of Folly became a world masterpiece for several reasons. One is its biting survey of the errors of the day, with an overview that is both comprehensive and specific. But as in all successful satire, clear aesthetic, moral, and religious standards are present to provide bases for judgment; the morale of the Christian life expounded in the *Enchiridion* is no different from what is said 'under the guise of play' in *The Praise of Folly*, as Erasmus himself tells us in his letter to Dorp (*CWE* 3: 115). It attains its high ranking because it is also a daring criticism of humanism itself, a critical confrontation with the 'expense of spirit' and the self-sacrifice that the tedious labours of the scholarly life require. Erasmus well knew the costs of his most notable endeavours, and *The Praise of Folly* is a frank admission of the hardships of these vicarious reliances. In the midst of the Renaissance, the high Renaissance, we have a humanist's voice, that of the leading humanist, already giving honest expression to the dangers implicit in following the steps of the ancients. Memory can be a curse, quotation an impediment, the coveted imitation a noose. The educated person is beset by timidity and modesty, while those of an uninhibited animal energy forge boldly ahead. Here Erasmus the humanist bravely recounts other failings – his inability to stand alone, to endure discontinuity. His lack of ego-concentration (Huizinga found Erasmus to be not 'self-sufficient') ties him to others, to quotations, to authorities (Huizinga 190). Erasmus strikes close to home and in so doing makes of *The Praise of Folly* a classic. The humanist experiences the extremes of alienation both within himself, his tragic delusions, and from the world, where his once vaunted learning has confronted the facts of history, of being useless, of being pushed to the side-lines of life. The vanities of the vain. And lastly, *The Praise of Folly* becomes a work of self-justification, and this by recognition of difference, of full understanding of the bi-polarity of a divided world, of the lack of comprehension existing between those who follow the letter and the flesh and those who look to the spiritual and the invisible rather than the corporeal and the visible.[19] Oddly enough, Erasmus's one work that has eluded historical oblivion has done so because in it he admits the 'great contrarity of opinion' between these two sorts of people (*Praise of Folly* 147), thus confronting a dualism that it was his purpose to avoid. Chomarat, throughout his invaluable work, refers to Erasmus's dualisms, between mind and body, spirit and flesh, the rational and the carnal, the interior and the exterior. And indeed these are the vertical levels within which his arguments take their place. But there is always intended a clear subordination, a hierarchy of values determined. The inferior is not quite disallowed if the superior is kept in sight. Here, though, in the final pages of *The Praise of Folly*, a different kind of dualism prevails, one more in keeping with the argument of this study. In reflecting on the 'great contrarity [dissensio] of opinion,' he is not prioritizing, but addressing the fact of two different modes of perceiving. The enduring substantiality of the opposition, its very fundamental presence serves as a guide to understanding why the twain will always be at odds, espousing different versions of life. But this also means that the 'folly' of the humanist is validated by the same principle of ideational difference.

5. Acclaim and Controversy

Erasmus's path, although not totally cleared, was now discernible. Ever the cosmopolitan (another crucial point of contrast with the more locally centred Luther), Erasmus only added to his stature by extended stays in Italy and England. If Erasmus had first been discovered in England, he was celebrated in Italy. One of the great (no longer rising, but established) stars of northern humanism, he came to the centre of Renaissance humanism and found himself in his element, feted and honoured as an equal in the great pursuits of humanistic culture. He became a close friend and later correspondent of several cardinals and during this visit may even have met the future Pope Leo X. It may plausibly be argued (although it is an argument that requires some qualification) that it was such close familiarity and even the greater appeal of acceptance in such courtly quarters that prevented Erasmus from ever breaking with the church. The long-desired doctorate in theology he quite easily acquired from the University of Torino, and he quickly established himself at the very capable Aldine press in Venice, where in 1508 he brought out the vastly expanded *Adagia chiliades* comprising now over three thousand entries, including the results of his intensive study of Greek. What had taken the Italian humanists generations to achieve, Erasmus, of course benefiting from their precedent labours, had done in a short span of five or more years. Throughout his much-travelled career Erasmus felt the need to locate himself wherever there was an active press, a thriving university, or a circle of friends. He was a citizen of the world, as he frequently declared, and his library was his home.

The publication of the massively enlarged edition of the *Adages* and *The Praise of Folly* brought Erasmus acclaim in his native land. He deserved all the accolades and epithets with which he was showered – the star of Germany, the German Socrates, and so on. When he left Louvain in September 1514 to make his journey up the Rhine to Basel and the very active printing house of Froben, it was like the triumphal return of a military victor. Erasmus had indeed become the prince of letters in his day – and in more ways than one. Letters were meant for distribution, the equivalent of journal articles, or – understandably where direct contact was infrequent – the source of valuable information. For this reason alone, Erasmus's letters are treasures. Friends and even prestigious colleagues vied to be recipients of Erasmus's letters, holding them up and showing them off as models of Latin elegance and style.

Through this world of eagerness and joy (if somewhat marked by naivety) Erasmus moved like a giant. But en route back to England he saw a copy of a letter sent from Louvain in September 1514; his own response was not made until his return from England in May 1515. In the midst of his triumph we glimpse the first signs of trouble. At the University of Louvain (and from among its most prominent faculty, that of theology) rumblings were beginning to be heard about the satiric portraits of theologians and monks in *The Praise of Folly*, and fearful anticipations about the forthcoming work on the New Testament. Unwilling to confront Erasmus directly, they found a willing catspaw in Maarten van

Dorp (twice in his response, Erasmus implies that Dorp was 'put up' to his letter as a kind of stalking horse) (*CWE* 3: 112, 126).[20]

This exchange indicates the pre-eminence of Erasmus, in that even prior to publication his interests and projects were sufficient to cause concern. Behind the amiable Dorp's letter hovered the conservative theologians of Louvain, whose own persistent grumblings would re-emerge in more troublesome times and reveal issues that finally would not go away. Furthermore it shows Erasmus at the height of his powers as he quite confidently and adroitly dismissed the objections of his opponents. But most importantly, Erasmus's responses show him to his greatest advantage as a defender of culture, civilization, and the simple human right to knowledge. While Dorp published his 'open letter,' Erasmus's response (enlarged) appropriately was reprinted as a second introduction, or even apologia in later editions of *The Praise of Folly*. And well it should have been, because it ranks as a classic in the liberal defence of humane studies and learning. It is comparable in its wit and high responsiveness to Voltaire's rejoinder to Rousseau's attacks on culture. In his response Erasmus assumes his greater role as defender of culture and civilization, of high wit and liveliness, in fact, of knowledge itself.

Dorp's charges are plentiful. (In summarizing them I shall be collating his first letter of 1514, to which Erasmus responded, as well as the somewhat neglected, more effective reply of August 1515 to Erasmus's response. The quadrangle will be completed with Thomas More's very able rebuttal of Dorp's second letter.) First, Dorp charges that Erasmus seems to be writing for a cohort group steeped in the humanities, and thus can afford to make fun of the theologians and monks. But the common people will not be able to make the distinctions between good and bad practitioners – the extensive bite of his satire will put all of the profession in jeopardy. He will run into even greater danger in printing the Greek text of the New Testament: this will represent a severe challenge to 'the purity of the faith' (*CWE* 3: 161), in that it will cast doubt upon language that the church has used for centuries: 'For it is not reasonable that the whole church, which has always used this [Jerome's] edition and still both approves and uses it, should for all these centuries have been wrong' (21). He further argues that some of the Greek manuscripts that Erasmus is using, being later than those of Ambrose, Augustine, and Jerome, are more corrupt than the Latin. He also defends the use of logic and of dialectic as being helpful in interpreting texts, and the modern theologians for attempting to resolve 'knotty problems' that literal or even allegorical readings (which he belittles) fail to address (165). The arguments are finally two: disturbance of the masses who will not be able to make proper distinctions between bad monks and friars, bad theologians and the professions as a whole; and even to print variant readings from the Greek would call into question the versions of the church that have been in use for centuries and that have acquired the authority of the ages. Such alterations in regard to scripture can only serve to undermine church authority.

Some of Erasmus's responses reprise his characteristic disingenuousness – he does not seem to fare well as an aggrieved apologist. In his many defences (including that of the *Colloquies*) he tiresomely maintained that because he names no names he does no harm, that clearly he could not be attacking any profession in its entirety. Admittedly Erasmus was subject to the delusion that he could strike and not draw blood, that he could attack and cause no harm (*CWE* 3: 114). It is not in such matters that his response to Dorp should be registered as a classic, but rather when he rises to the essential argument and for more than 125 lines of printed page he sets out after the theologians and, in marvellous invective that made his copious style the envy of many, he scores in detail the errors of their ways. Without any sense of retreat or inner compunctions, he defends wit and liveliness against dour defensiveness, the spirit of generous scholarly engagement and cooperation as against nit-picking over errors that are corrigible or at the worst minuscule. Throughout his career as a scholar this latter quality proved to be one of Erasmus's main attributes – the sheer selflessness with which he was willing to share ideas, to make corrections and revisions in his work, the modesty with which he acknowledged that he and his confreres were embarked on a scholarly journey for which it would be hazardous to lay down any final word. While exhibiting such deference, he can nevertheless vehemently attack the arrogance of ignorance, as he does in these culminating words:

> These are the men who condemn St Jerome as a schoolmaster. They are the men who conspire with such zeal against the humanities [in bonas litteras]. Their aim is to count for something in the council of the theologians, and they fear that if there is a renaissance [si renascantur bonae litterae] and if the world sees the error of its ways, it will become clear that they know nothing. (*CWE* 3: 122)

The allied response of Thomas More, almost certainly one to which Erasmus made his own contributions (Erasmus's second reply appears to have been lost and More's was published only posthumously), indicates that we are dealing with a cohort group that is part of a movement, hence the extraordinary confidence in response. In defending the use of the Greek language, they were defending the means of acquiring knowledge itself. In defending the corrections made by Jerome, they were defending the right of their generation to make contributions to knowledge. The argument is as old as Petrarch and as pertinent to the period we call the Renaissance: what Jerome did to received texts, they have the same right to do to the text received from Jerome (More 81–3). This helps explain the forward-moving impetus of the renascent thinkers.

More makes it plain that he and Erasmus are not attacking all theologians, only some, chiefly those whose highly tuned professional methodology pretends to be applicable to all conditions and situations. Thus the two kindred spirits are able to cite the many errors made by this ahistorical method, where philology, comparisons of texts, and basic historical understanding are absent (this is a quarrel that has occurred from time to time in our culture). But more than that, Erasmus and More are arguing for a renewal of theology, one that eschews trifling matters or quibbles and is in the quest of those things essential for salvation. In their neglect of scripture and the church fathers, the 'pseudo'-modern theologians do little to advance the faith of the people. In answer to Dorp's charge that Erasmus's brood of grammarians have similar failings and can be chastised on the same grounds, More mounts a spirited defence of his friend (at one point he does stress that Erasmus is in agreement with what he is writing [57]): Erasmus might use the necessary philological tools of the grammarian but that is not his goal. His role is really that of a 'litteratus,' or man of letters, an intellectual, 'whose area of study extends across every variety of literature,' and who has a 'general command of sound literature, which means sacred letters' (13, 15). In making his charge, Dorp has shown himself to be a poor reader of *The Praise of Folly*, whose great merit lies in that section where Erasmus satirizes those fellow humanists who remain solely grammarians, confining themselves to hair-pulling over accent marks.

The conservative theologians of Louvain may have been easy opponents (certainly at this early date Erasmus appeared to think so, although that opinion was bound to change). But in some ways they better foretold the future than did Erasmus. They saw into the contents of the box of which he was loosening the strings; they knew what it forebode. They understood the net effect of Erasmus's satires, and better than he they sensed the coming assault that he was blamed for initiating. This is why the accusation was frequently made (and not by conservative critics alone) that Erasmus laid the egg that Luther hatched. Such a charge always rankled Erasmus, particularly in the coming dire moments of threatening charges that carried with them some danger, and to anticipate, it may have been a need to protect himself from such charges that would later incline him to come out against Luther. Erasmus would always reply that the bird Luther hatched was one of a decidedly different feather. But his opponents could respond that Erasmus was trying to stop a snowballing effect after it had gathered momentum halfway down the hill.

They were right and wrong: right in their anticipations but wrong in their responses. Their resorting to threats, reprisals, banishments, and excommunication was futile because they were opposing a widespread movement of history, one that was based upon sturdy principles. The first is the natural human tendency to know, and to resist the imposition of blinders that would impede knowledge. The methods employed to stifle reform were consequently quite mistaken. Erasmus always deplored the recourse to charges of heresy, to excommunication, or worse, and encouraged the head-on engagement with new ideas. Like More he remained unshaken in his faith. Consequently one of the constant remedies Erasmus urged for the ills of the age was that new ideas be discussed and understood rather than rejected out of hand. Not all new practices are threats to the structure of the church, particularly when they are so well grounded in the solid understanding of scriptures and the interpretations of the church fathers (this was before 1520, and Luther's three major treatises). Reasonable people will accept some articles and reject others. Not all forces are irresistible: why make them so by putting up unmovable objects? Not only Christian humanism but a liberal humanism would require this. We can see why Erasmus shines so splendidly in his time and later as a beacon of rational sanity and intelligent discourse.

These were blissful days for Erasmus and all the more halcyon as they were short-lived. The window that opened for him, the moment of acclaim extended to an optimistic projection onto an entire epoch when peace and learning seemed to reign together (see the high hopefulness expressed in the letter to Pope Leo X in May 1515 – *CWE* 3: 99ff.). All these expectations came crashing down with the advent of Luther. Stirring as were the defences on the part of Erasmus and More of culture and civilization, and of a kind of fearless individual judgment, the controversy with the Louvain theologians through their *portavoce* Dorp was not a major dualism. Certainly with aplomb and even success as even

Dorp came to admit, they manhandled their opponents. The coming of Luther was a different matter, engaging Erasmus in an entirely different kind of debate, one from which he could not as easily extricate himself. The arguments coming from Louvain were directed against the new philology that, presenting variant readings, called into question the presumed long-standing practices of the church. Their arguments were based primarily on practical problems emerging from a new methodology. Luther shared with Erasmus the methods of this biblical humanism, but he differed on the more fundamental grounds of theology. This was a genuine dualism and it caught Erasmus off guard, ill-prepared, and very ill-suited. He was being outflanked by an opponent with whom he shared very similar ideas, one who – even as did his cohorts and disciples – attributed (with all their unspoken misgivings) a kind of spiritual fatherhood to Erasmus. Not obscurantists or obstructionists, they could not so easily be discounted, because they were enemies from within his own camp. The critic now found himself in the uncomfortable position of being criticized, the master of biting satire now found himself on the defensive, particularly with the attacks coming from among the younger intellectuals, with whom once Erasmus but now Luther seemed to enjoy great appeal. The writer who had come to represent the advanced stage of European consciousness in his time now found himself challenged by a daemonic writer who found such reliance on culture and civilization, on history itself, to be illusory, to be a fake. Erasmus was now summoned to a contest of the spirit, to accept a divorce from those great figures of history, those models and exemplars in proximity to whom, in association with whom he felt his own being enhanced. The orphan boy found himself challenged where he had discovered a community. Having endured one orphanhood in time, he was asked to endure a second, one that would negate his great efforts, the efforts of a lifetime. This was too much. As we mount up reasons, try to pluck out the heart of his mystery, this might be the most powerful one. Understandably enough, tragically enough, Erasmus here found himself to be wanting. At least, what is clear is that he no longer felt the same momentum in his stride, the same conviction in his tone. He had fallen into an abyss, and was brought to endure the trepidations of a very complex consciousness.

6. Luther's Calling

Despite these looming differences – and in piecemeal fashion I have begun indicating some of the larger temperamental differences that will eventually intrude and prevail in this dualism – the affinities between Erasmus and Luther are genuine, particularly their shared faith in the doctrine of Christian liberty (even including arguments on both their parts of a charitable expediency) and in the spiritual message they bore as to the living reality of the Gospels. They had enemies in common, whose continued presence only aggravated the difficulties between Erasmus and Luther, in particular constraining the former, perhaps even precipitating the public break. But the final debate occurred because resident tensions and temperamental differences were already in place between the two, and though submerged, were only awaiting their occasion to erupt.

I have already referred to some of their differences. One of the most prominent among the biographical is their reasons for entering into the Augustinian hermit order and their accommodation to life within that order. Erasmus, as it turns out, spent a good deal of his adult life in concentrated efforts to correct that first misstep. Luther, too, was called to a serious correction, but in a different manner and for different reasons. Where Erasmus's father was a priest of some literacy, whose early death from the plague (along with that of Erasmus's mother) left the young man with no apparent alternative except the monastery, Luther's father was all too present.[21] From peasant stock, he became a miner who through grit and intelligence came in time to own or lease several foundries. He had married well and was quite ambitious for his son Martin, charting for him a career in law. But all of this was undone by the famous episode of 1505. Returning to the University of Erfurt, Martin was caught in the midst of a violent thunderstorm, and in the grips of this terror, he vowed to join a monastery, if saved by St Anne (who as mother of Mary had acquired extraordinary stature and powers). Five days later he made good on his pledge, entering the Augustinian order at Erfurt. His father was angered and felt betrayed. Later at the time of Luther's first celebration of Mass (in 1507) he warned his son that, rather than a message from heaven, this intervention might have come from the devil (thus enunciating a fearful ambivalence that all daemonic writers experience).

Much has been and should be made of this early experience as revelatory of Luther's needs and character. Like any young religious genius, he was particularly sensitive to the presence and imminence of death (Brecht 1: 46). Moreover, lightning itself – with all of its crackling drama and drawn-out anticipation – seems to represent that sudden descent of a unavoidable calamity that from Petrarch to James Joyce brought fear and terror to the most imaginative sensibilities. Moreover, the episode reveals one of the foremost characteristics of the daemonic personality, the capacity for conversion. Such an experience points to a need to achieve unity, to overcome division by submission to an apparently greater power, a power that is external to the conscious will. The difference with Erasmus, so confined by the limits of consciousness, could not be greater. Erasmus represented the advanced stage of European consciousness in his time, while Luther was suspicious of consciousness, its traps, its lures, its self-flatteries and self-promotions. Luther's distrust of works derives from his uneasiness with the directives of deliberate consciousness.

To mark another difference, in Luther's case, the domineering presence of one father, the earthly father, and the tensions that such a presence produced, could be overcome only by intervention of the other Father into whose hands Luther consigned himself. The tension is great; one can think of St Francis and other figures of supremely quick religious genius who were able to abjure the intentions of one father only by acting on the message of the other. What is required is nothing less than the total alteration of action and belief in the full prostration of the self and its dominating intelligence.

On the road to Damascus things happen, but one must also be the person to whom things happen, that is, a person of so committed a seriousness that he is willing to follow the biddings of the message and undergo a massive change in the course of his life, a person willing to act and act suddenly, totally in accord with the message. This is why Luther was able to exclaim in the preface to his Latin writings, 'So great a Saul was I!' (*Selections* 4). Before his later conversion to a fierce anti-papalism, he had been just as strong a defender of the church. As with Paul's change from a passionate anti- to fervent pro-Christian belief, the same kineticism persists: 'I was so drunk, yes, submerged in the pope's dogmas, that I would have been ready to murder all, if I could have, or cooperate with the murderers of all who would take but a syllable from obedience to the pope' (4).

The burning bush is just the latest straw but it is so intense that it consumes everything around it. The moment emerges as paramount, not contingent; it holds eternity in its sway, as if all of life were being determined in that moment. Throughout his life Luther felt himself extraordinarily subject to such interventions, to the sense and to the need of being swept up, carried along, independently of his will, following a course he had not consciously intended, but one that may have been his ulterior purpose all along. His was a soul that required total commitment; he needed to 'mean it.' There was no room for postponement or delay, or the thought that tomorrow will qualify what today has wrought, that in the long drawn-out drain of contingency, of the day-to-day, things will not matter all that much. There was no faltering, no liquidation of conviction by means of temporal dispersion. In Luther's and Erasmus's different senses of time, their keenest drama was being played out. As the moment passes, the ironies of a complex consciousness enter, undoing what was thought to be most certain, exposing the weaknesses of the greatest enthusiasms. In his own self-reflexiveness Erasmus was most prone to recognize the fallacies of such enthusiasms – their momentary and fleeting natures. In fact his own gradualism in ethical improvement is dependent upon this non-imposing, more contingent sense of time. Nothing is ever final; sufficient to the day, or, as Woody Allen would say, comedy is tragedy plus time. There is always time to recover, to regroup, and to undo what has been done. Uniformity in the sequence of objects induces an equanimity in the subject.

From Luther's more daemonic character two additional features may be derived. He needed to be carried along into steps he had not intended. But to encounter the unexpected requires an openness to experience; whether innocent or wild-eyed, one must be willing to step forward to meet that which is advancing toward one. However one might cry out, a willingness must be there. Furthermore, such openness to the unexpected leads to a fuller rendering of experience, as one is carried beyond the limits laid down by the conscious will into larger unanticipated areas of awareness.

Throughout his life Luther was in need of justification.[22] Luther had an exasperated and excruciating determination to lead his life aright. As so frequently happens, the first sudden step of entering the monastic orders was a necessary one for Luther, but it was a misstep. It was right that he follow it, but still it was not right for him. His capacity for wholehearted change persisted. The events of 1517–21 represent a correction, albeit with the same premises in character: more than one conversion is required of the figure in need of conversion, and Luther was moved to a more massive change, beyond his willing, beyond his conscious intent.

Not only scholars but Luther himself had difficulty in explaining the unexpected success of the so-called Ninety-five Theses: 'I am at a loss to know why it is fated that these particular theses of mine, and no other, should have spread almost throughout the entire country.'[23] This surprised Luther even more, since his propositions were made public at the University of Wittenberg and intended for an academic discussion, with the usual procedure of thesis followed by the pros and cons of respective arguments. This debate never took place. The prodigious and even sensational effect was brought about by the theses' immediate printing, particularly in translation, and their distribution by students and colleagues. Catching Luther and many others by surprise, it could be called a technological revolution, but the greater power was in the text, in the power of the ideas. Luther goes on to explain in this same letter to Pope Leo X that he observed the protocols of academic debate, even extending to the language, and in providing these theses for academic discussion he was doing none other than many had done before him. More importantly, he had proposed other theses for debate; consequently he did not understand why these caused such consternation, since they were not unusual ('alienas'); that is, while not exactly commonplace, such arguments concerning indulgences and purgatory were not unknown (in fact, they were widely anticipated by forerunners to Reform, and heavily criticized in Luther's own time, even earlier by Luther himself).

Whatever his own protestations, the Ninety-five Theses plunged Luther into history. But his role and prominence, while unexpected, were not unprepared. Two lines of his career converge here: his public pronouncements and his spiritual preparation. Whatever might be said, it is unrewarding to draw too fine a line, particularly any chronological line, between them.

As a monk he was a great Saul, more intensely fulfilling the rules than the rules required. In the monastery he had found his calling, and quickly with his susceptible imagination readily outdid any requirements imposed – his own impositions were inevitably more rigorous. Luther's confessions were painful, legendary, at times lasting hours, as he agonized over minor, even imagined, infractions. Like other religious geniuses doomed to seeking a spiritual perfection and endowed with a remarkable sensitivity, Luther sought out and found a master equal to his own demands upon himself. If God is all-seeing, all-powerful, and all-demanding, ought one to give only three hours in prayer, why not four, why not five? Why not total devotion to appease the totalitarian nature of the demands?

Much later, in his response to Erasmus's *On the Freedom of the Will*, in a moment of self-revelation that enriches the fuller theological argument, Luther explains why he could not possibly survive under the notion that his own actions, his own works, secured his salvation. Even if there were no demons of deception to assail him, he was still in the grip of the unappeasable, and herein lay the great fallacy of consciousness and its adjutant works:

I should nevertheless labor under perpetual uncertainty and to fight as one beating the air, since even if I lived and worked to eternity my conscience would never be assured and certain as to how much it ought to do to appease God. For whatever might be accomplished there would always remain an anxious doubt whether it pleased God or whether he required something more as the experience of all self-justifiers proves, and as I myself learned to my bitter cost through so many years. But now since God has taken my salvation out of my hands and into his, making it depend on his choice and not mine and has promised to save me, not by my own work and exertion but by his grace and mercy, I am assured and certain both that he is faithful and will not lie to me. (Rupp and Watson, *Luther and Erasmus [LE]* 328–9)

Such masterful pages of self-revelation help explain the greatness of *On the Bondage of the Will*, so rooted as it in the most intense personal drama of Luther's own spiritual journey. It casts retrospective light back on the years of spiritual transformation, showing why the argument against the efficacy of 'works' and the spiritual reformation came from the same source. The nucleus of the Lutheran drama is contained in this passage.

His confessor, John Staupitz, the neglected mentor and overseer so essential to the development of any great man, advised Luther not to bother him with exasperating peccadilloes but to come back when he had committed a real sin. Staupitz also recognized the true subversiveness of Luther's hyper-scrupulosity, saying that God was not angry with him but that he, Luther, was angry with God. He saw into the agonized consciousness of this religious phenomenon that seemed so hell-bent on spiritual perfection, a perfection that only a divinity could match, but in contest with which failure was foredoomed. From out of this uneven match, where one's very own demanding spirit is the source of undoing, there must result either some radical change or despair.

Unlike his first conversion, it was not a sudden event that liberated him from this desperate situation of self-punishment but rather the steady experience of poring over the Gospels (an experience that later made Luther suspicious of 'glib' conversions, or of doctrines that are not the product of intense study – interesting complications to commonly received ideas about Luther). But this hard-won experience marks a turning point just as well, and even a more momentous change that altered the nature of Christianity in his day. Formerly he had lived as a sinner before God with an extremely troubled conscience (although his life as a monk was beyond reproach – a fact acknowledged even by his opponents, and always stressed by Erasmus). Confirming Staupitz's insight, he raged against God until he finally came to understand the passage from Romans: 'He who through faith is righteous shall live.' His own testimony is dramatic and prototypal: 'I felt that I was altogether born again and entered paradise itself through open gates. There a totally other face of the entire scripture showed itself to me (*Martin Luther: Selections* 11). In conversion terms, such change is totalizing: from despair to liberation, from sin to the open gates of paradise, where one can breathe again. The metabolism of Luther's personality is understandably drastic, at a basic level confronting either/or equations (and in this way so unlike the emotional world that Erasmus experienced). While directing his Ninety-five Theses to actual church ordinances, and what could be considered 'works,' his 'reformation experience' came from the scriptural texts themselves. But the changes correspond one to the other and are in fact synergistic, as his own comments make plain. They show the same character in action, one with the capacity, indeed the need, to enter into radical change, with the overwhelming sense that he is being impelled, swept along by irresistible forces.

The Ninety-five Theses have all the characteristics of a breakthrough work. They made of Luther a marked man, a man to be confronted and whose works call out to be contested. Unlike Erasmus, Luther was willing to answer the calling that he did not seek. He was a man swept along by events and hardened by them. They brought him a prominence he did not particularly welcome or anticipate. But they also unleashed a drive of extraordinary creativity, of feverish almost non-stop activity, leading to the three great works of 1520, and lasting for the purposes of this study at least through 1525 and the exposition *On the Bondage of the Will* in the debate with Erasmus. He was brought to complete the premises of this work, as he most volubly asserted in his dedicatory letter to Leo X that forms the preface to *The Freedom of a Christian*. The ill-guided and ill-advised challenges from Cajetan and Eck led him to initiate what was only implicit in the Ninety-five Theses, an attack on the theory and the practice of the papacy. Not only did he pursue his original ideas and objections to papal practices, but he developed them, expanded them, and in so doing transcended them. From his later fuller development, he looked back and tended to discount the arguments of the Ninety-five Theses. For instance, in his preface to the collected works (1545) he regretted that he conceded too much to the benevolence of the pope, wishing to distance him from the activities of his agents; and in the famous conclusion to *On the Bondage of the Will*, he congratulated Erasmus for avoiding the extraneous matters that were the concern of the posted theses. But as in all breakthrough works, there seemed to be an ulterior purpose governing direction that only latterly revealed itself. If early in his controversies Luther wished to separate himself from Johan Hus, the Czech reformer of the early fifteenth century, finally he was bound to acknowledge, 'We were all Hussites without knowing it' (Brecht, *Luther* 1: 332).

The Ninety-five Theses and *On the Bondage of the Will* are of a piece, showing the extraordinary growth of Luther's mind and of his religious conviction. In fact, despite the discounting, in the later debate Luther acknowledged that the conclusions of the 'enslaved will' necessarily grew out of the earlier work.

While we can appreciate the protocol of academic debate, with the simple offering of propositions for discussion, it is misguided to regard Luther's theses as harmless exercises, as think-tank cerebrations. The metaphor used to describe the theses as a spark setting off a wildfire is thus erroneous in two ways. Despite Luther's disclaimers that he got into the turmoil 'by accident and not by will or intention,' the force of his exposition is more than a spark. It is rather like sticks of dynamite. And the terrain was most receptive at his moment – more like an arsenal ready to be ignited, or so Luther himself explains, when he describes the fatigue of the 'Germans' at the exactions emanating from Rome. As the ecclesiastical practices were 'hateful to all,' the occasion was ready for Luther's words to find eager reception (*Martin Luther: Selections* 490). The time was right and so was the messenger, with his message that fell like hammer-blows, stated with an urgency, a directness that helped account for the attention that these and not other similar theses received.

From the start, after issuing an invitation to debate, Luther significantly gives his academic credentials (master of arts and sacred theology, and duly appointed lecturer on these subjects at the University of Wittenberg – thus one capable of entering into such disputation) (*Works* 1: 29ff.). He then launches into the heady waters of theological dispute over the very nature of repentance itself. Jesus' call to 'repent' cannot be understood, according to theses 1 and 2, as referring to actions undertaken, or works of confession and satisfaction, but rather must be understood as meaning that 'the entire life of believers is one of penitence.' Erasmus had already interpreted the crucial Greek phrase as not meaning 'poenitentiam agite,' to 'do penance,' but rather as 'poeniteat vos,' to 'repent' or 'be penitent.' This subtle change was adopted by Luther and by a host of younger reformers, the appeal being not to external actions but rather to the sincere, abiding internal Spirit.

Since this work is more often referred to than read, it is tempting to recapitulate its contents, but instead I shift to the dire warnings of its conclusion. In a staggering series of questions (which remind us that all questions are remarks, and in this case, thunderous ones), Luther challenges the financial requirements of the indulgence system. He repeats a traditional point (anticipated by Abelard in 1140) that if the pope has this power, why does he not liberate the souls in purgatory out of love rather than for the sake of money (#82). He goes on to ask, why does not the pope repay the money given as benefactions in anniversary masses for the dead, 'since it is wrong to pray for those whose souls are now redeemed' (#83)? How can an impious man redeem a deceased soul by the payment of money? Since the pope's income makes him the wealthiest of men, why does he not rebuild St Peter's out of his own resources rather than with the money of indigent believers? Finally in thesis 90 he concludes, 'These are the serious matters of conscience to the laity. To suppress them by force alone, and not to refute them by giving reasons, is to expose the church and people to the ridicule of their enemies, and to make Christian people unhappy.'

However intended, the Ninety-five Theses were far from an invitation to an academic conference. How else can their remarkable spread throughout Germany and the consternation they provoked in the Roman curia be explained? Most of the theses seem to settle rather than invite discussion. What should surprise us is not their effect, but rather Luther's own surprise. Perhaps signalling a necessary characteristic of the Christian 'pre-modern,' he was most reluctant to acknowledge his own active energies, as if he were a member of the chorus and not the leading agonist and protagonist. For the moment we find in Luther a reluctance to admit willed action, as if it were a violation of reverential submission. To be sure, no one could have anticipated the swirl of activity that finally led him to brand the papacy as the Antichrist, and to write the works of 1520; no one could have anticipated that this relatively unknown monk would successfully dissent from pope and emperor. One can see why Luther would attribute so much to inadvertence and, in his terminology, to the inscrutable divine will.

Luther became a marked man, but he did not shy away from that calling. The Ninety-five Theses led to a superhuman spate of creative activity. He attributed his own development to the ineptitude of the papal representatives: Sylvester Prierias, Cajetan (Tommaso de Vio) at the Augsburg

Diet in 1518, Johann Eck at Leipzig in 1519 – all argued that Luther's attacks on works undermined the supremacy of the papacy (*Martin Luther: Selections* 5–8, 48–51). Reluctantly, almost against his will, he was forced to acknowledge the rightness of their arguments, with the notable consequences that followed. He was no longer a reformer, but rather a revolutionary, one who attacked the very structure of the system in which he was involved. Indicating his own rightness for the times, Luther possessed what Ortega called a 'cabeza clara,' the kind of clarity required of all great individuals in times of turmoil. Luther not only had the keenness of intellect that drove to the heart of the issues, he also possessed the full purpose to do something about them. Luther had the focus of moral directness and the directness of moral focus. He became more and more willing to accept the leadership to which he was apparently called. He realized that he was at war not only with the practices of the church, or with all-too-human frailties, but rather with the very bases of the papacy and the Roman Church.

7. The Great Year

This leap accounts for the intellectual distance between the Ninety-five Theses and the *Address to the Christian Nobility of the German Nation, The Babylonian Captivity*, and *The Freedom of the Christian*. They constitute a tripartite body of work; as in a suite of music, one part is linked to and announces what follows. The continuity of Luther's thought derives from the Ninety-five Theses, but it also expands to other issues, touching many aspects of religious and social life. In the indulgences controversy Luther took pains to separate the papacy from the abuses, but in these new tracts Luther no longer makes this distinction. Rather he indicts the papacy itself, and in so doing a large part of the sacerdotal hierarchy of medieval Christendom. This would be the first prong of Luther's complex relationship with modernity. The second – the basic notion of Christian liberty – both stems from the first and sustains it. To each of these resources Luther brought modulation and acumen, a sense of principle as well as a balance – one might even say, balance because of principle – that made him the true instrument of change in his time.

These works are powerful because Luther wrote from the fullness of the moment, from a sensed urgency of time. His very first words in his *Address to the Christian Nobility* are, 'The time for silence is over, and the time for speech has come' (quoting Ecclesiastes), and near the end he repeats, 'I cannot but speak' (*Martin Luther: Selections* 415, 485). He attacks first the three walls that seem to preserve papal authority, then sets an agenda for Council action, before persuasively driving home twenty-seven points to improve the nature of the Christian state. They are strong words for good works to be undertaken by the German nobility. There are no quibbles, no masquerades: Luther accepts and endures the obligation the time has imposed. In the same letter of introduction he understands the difficulty of the position he has assumed (404). Habitually the daemonic writer who rides the wave of the moment is derided for his presumption: who is he in his bare singularity to go against the accumulated wisdom of the ages? At first Erasmus could master this indictment, but later in contest with Luther he wilted and curiously became the one to make the charge of presumption. Luther recognized this as the voice of temptation and was able to withstand it. Despite some trepidation, he would continue to speak from conscience and convictions, but there is more at work. As he plunges from point to point, one senses the unleashing of years of observation (among his many duties, he was also the well-travelled vicar-general of his order), of study, and of moral concern for the welfare of the local undervalued parish priest. Concerns that had accumulated over the years come tumbling out as Luther responded to the urgency of the calling. Although his mind was capable of great modulation and conciliation, he did not qualify. Instead where the papacy was the issue, he fired cannon shots. Now, all pilgrimages are totally without merit and should cease. Religious orders should undergo a drastic contraction in their numbers. It is not just the number of the points (imagine twenty-seven!) but their accumulated force and cogency, and controlling all, the power of the assumed authority. This is not just Martin Luther holding to his convictions; this is a Martin Luther who is speaking as the spiritual leader of a people. Such was the remarkable emergence brought about by the experience of the years from 1517 to 1520.

Luther first attacks what he terms the three walls that contain and support the abuses he later itemizes. They provide the protective premises, that there is a qualitative difference between the clerisy and the laity; that the church is the sole agent responsible for interpretation of scripture and that only the Roman Church can convoke a council. His counter-arguments are nothing short of revolutionary. Office is not determined by status but rather by function, hence the notion of the priesthood of every believer. The sacrament of baptism provides the foundation upon which this change is based. 'It is not the Pope but baptism that consecrates us all and makes us all priests. Those who exercise secular authority have been baptized like them and have the same faith and the same gospel. Therefore we must admit that they are priests and bishops' (408).

Without hesitation he moves forward with biblical citation and reason to attack the sacerdotal hierarchy, concluding, 'There is at bottom really no other difference between laymen, priests, princes, bishops, or in Romanist terminology, between religious and secular, than that of office or occupation and not that of Christian status' (409). While this means the 'priesthood of every believer,' it should not mislead us into thinking that as a consequence every believer can or should be a priest. In fact, Luther explicitly warns against such forward behaviour. Rather the 'priest' is a person with a special aptitude for learning and preaching, who is selected by the community to attend to their spiritual and administrative needs. Hence the priest is now a minister.

But the implications extend even further. This attack on the sacerdotal hierarchy of the Roman Church, while not amounting to the deposition of the papacy, still goes far in that direction. Luther's thought joins that of Machiavelli and Shakespeare in desacralizing the claims of long-standing institutions, those that had been thought to govern by 'divine right.' What Shakespeare in his complex second tetralogy, commencing with *Richard II*, would later do to the divine right of kings, Luther does to the papacy. He invokes the principle that nobody has the right to do wrong. Luther insists that the pope himself may be called to answer before the state's bar of justice: 'If a certain person were not to be penalized on the ground that he were superior to the rest, then no Christian may penalize his fellows' (412). The difference is apparent with Erasmus, who in his *Colloquies* and *The Education of a Christian Prince* finally urges acquiescence. 'God's is the quarrel,' is John of Gaunt's feeble and discredited response in Shakespeare's *Richard II*.

But opposition is just as effective as deposition, and by opposing the papacy Luther comes to an even more significant conclusion: the right of every seriously minded Christian to interpret scripture. The argument is more qualified in its force; he denies that the pope *alone* has the right to give the meaning of scripture. Here again, as he did so dutifully and carefully throughout his career and as his most serious contemporaries, including Erasmus, were also obliged to do, he sifts through the various aspects and meanings of the Holy Spirit, assessing the rightness of the claims to that power. He does not deny the papal possession of the Holy Spirit, simply that the papacy has a monopoly: 'You must acknowledge that there are good Christians among us who have the true faith, spirit,

understanding, word and mind of Christ' (414). From this acknowledgment, he proceeds to the argument of right. Joined by baptism, one gospel, and one faith, 'why then should we not be entitled to taste or test, to
judge what is right or wrong in the faith?' Quoting Paul, as he does
amply throughout his treatises, he reaffirms the underlying principle of
Christian liberty upon which all of his doctrinal challenges are based:
'We ought not to allow the spirit of liberty – to use St Paul's term – to be
frightened away by the pronouncements confabricated by the popes. We
ought to march boldly forward, and test everything the Romanists do or
leave undone' (414). Just as Balaam's ass spoke truth, so obscure people
might be better readers of the scriptures than the anointed.

Luther marched boldly forward through the accumulated mass of
twenty-seven points of argument. Many of the concerns are familiar
ones: masses, pilgrimages, monasteries, the newly minted special sites
designed to attract the pilgrimage trade. Instead, I shall highlight a few
proposals, particularly those that show the fullness and complexity of
Luther's mind, his power of thought, his capacity for modulation, his
reliance on scripture, and his concern for justice, honour, and individual
probity and integrity.

Luther shows the way to modernity through his insistence on the
rights of the individual conscience. These are matters between the individual soul and a personal God that are able to stand up well against all
the pressures and interventions of the outside world. Here I am not
referring to the macro-drama of Luther at Worms, but to the smaller dramas of which he was aware and whose great defender he became. Luther
was intensely aware that the common spiritual struggles were fought and
maintained locally, at home and in the individual soul. Celibacy is not a
condition ordered by Christ; in fact just the opposite is sanctioned by
Paul, who urged the 'bishop' (meaning priest) to care for his wife. At
ordination Luther urges the young man to make no vow to remain continent. The bolder among them may remind the bishop that he has no
authority to demand such a vow, or when they make their proviso,
'Quantum fragilitas humana permittet,' they should make it clearly
understood that 'non promitto castitatem' (449). Only the 'strength of
angels' and the 'heroism of heaven' can fulfil such a vow.

Luther strips away those injunctions of the church that enjoy no scriptural basis and works to install the ministry that God did institute, which
was 'intended to form a church by sermons and sacraments, namely pastors living among the people and keeping house as other people do'
(zeitlich zu halten). The structures of belief are brought back into touch

with the ways by which people regularly (*zeitlich*) lead their lives. Certainly Luther wrought great changes in the sacerdotal hierarchy and the sacramental functions of the church, but his greatest revolution might lie in these homely terms. He is insisting upon a new common order to existence, with no need for extravagant relocations or transformations. The fabulous lives of the saints, those superhuman exertions of asceticism are no longer considered exemplary. The struggles of conscience and the religious life occur daily. Stay home, take care of business. Such acceptance and appreciation of one's mortal station is one of the great and undervalued innovations of Luther's reformation, making him suspicious of glib spiritualists, of people who adopt outlandish garb. One lives as one ought in the normal conditions of being, even with a three-piece suit.

This also means that the model theory of education – so essential to Erasmus's spiritual pedagogy – must be scrapped. The exemplary lives of the saints, be they Bernard, Francis, or Dominic, come under a cloud of suspicion. For us, 'the number of saints is unknown'; only God knows who the saints are.[24] But there is another psychological reason. The fault lies in overly conscious contrivance. It is like Karlstadt adopting peasant garb in order to emphasize his simplicity. It is too easy, an insurance policy, an overt acquisition that smacks of deliberateness and that does nothing for faith, for the inner struggle that must be encountered in whatever age and by whatever manner of dress. For Luther the existential struggle means one must not only believe in Christ but one must be Christ, without knowing it, and only then after the fact, after Gethsemane, realize – apart from conscious imitation – that one has undergone his or her own agony. It is from such experience that one acquires understanding and faith. Luther believes this experience to be wanting in Erasmus. Erasmus is an ethicist, speaking to conscious efforts of public engagement; Luther is a metaphysician of the soul.

In all of this we sense Luther's great sympathy for the parish priest. Pastors are not separated from ordinary folk by some special aura of spiritual superiority. This means he needs a housekeeper, and to expect him not to yield to the temptations of the flesh 'is like bringing fire and straw together, and trying to forbid blaze and smoke' (450). As a man with pastoral responsibilities Luther is well aware of the difficulties confronting the parish priest, particularly one who has already fallen in 'disgrace.' His response represents one of the strongest moments of the *Address*, showing his sympathy with the weaknesses of the flesh, the power of individual conscience, and above all his role as a spiritual leader. He urges such couples to marry. In one of the more remarkable passages in the *Address*, one that moves forward into the ranks of modernity, Luther stoutly defends this 'illicit' conjugal union, on the basis of personal commitment and individual conscience. When both partners are so minded that they could live 'faithfully and permanently together in a regular conjugal union,' such people should keep their consciences undaunted, for they are married 'in God's eyes' (450). The modern world stands here in witness, not only in the challenges presented to the sacerdotal structures, but in the emergence of a new reliance on a kind of personal integrity (as distinguished from that murky term, 'individualism,' for after all, conscience is still invoked and justified by God's witness). A serious adult commitment has been entered into, and its endurance is pledged for as long as such things can endure, whether store-bought, church-sanctioned, or individually confirmed.

To regard such profound change as breakthroughs to the 'modern' is not to give Luther a patronizing pat on the back, but rather to acknowledge an important alteration in thought, one that took great courage as well as insight to proclaim (as he did), and one that found large public responsiveness. Something new and modern was introduced, and it did largely prevail. There is a newly acquired firmness in Luther's voice. He urges the chagrined couples to stand by their consciences. But even more crucially he places the stamp of his authority on their personal vows: 'Let him who has faith enough to make this venture, boldly follow my word: I shall not lead him astray.' Rather than as a commentator, he speaks as a person who assumes responsibility. Erasmus was unwilling to accept direction of the movement, but Luther's interests, insights, and capacities push him into the role of spiritual leader. 'I have not the power of a pope, but I have the power of a Christian to help and advise my neighbor to escape from his sins and temptations' (450). The urgency of the times, the corruption of practices, the singular sense of the rightness of his own convictions, born of anguish and of study, the heavy sense of common human weaknesses and universal sinfulness, have called up and brokered this new, powerful, and yet quite practical spiritual voice.

His appeal is to the legitimation of the adult conscience. Inwardly, spiritually we might all be sinners, all fall short of God's perfection, hence the inadequacy and illusion of justification by works. But publicly, in our words and actions, we are all bound by standards of probity, right dealing. In Luther's moral lexicon there are certain codes that may not be broken. These involve simple human honour and personal integrity.

He looks back in horror at the treatment of the martyred Johan Hus (#24, 465–70), whose pledge of safe conduct to the Council of Constance was later revoked on the grounds that one is not bound to honour a pledge given to a heretic. As a consequence, Hus was burned in 1415. Only an Antichrist could engage in such trickery, not men of honour. This reneging was 'contrary to God's commandment and gave the Hussites every cause for embitterment.' Finally, in dealing with the persistent differences between the Roman Church and the Czech followers of Hus, Luther urged conciliation. The greatest obstacle was the Hussite contention that in communion both bread and wine may be offered by the laity, but wine was denied by the Roman communion. Luther pleads for tolerance of each until some larger council can establish an agreement. This is just one of many examples indicating the capacity for modulation not only of argument but of spirit in this quite complex yet towering figure of change.

The three momentous treatises of 1520 in their abhorrence of 'works' – in the fuller meaning given that term by both Luther and Erasmus – derive from the Ninety-five Theses, but vastly expand upon and develop their core. While different from each other they are like a series of rooms, one connecting with the other. In fact, at the end of *The Address to the Christian Nobility*, he announces his forthcoming work, *The Babylonian Captivity*, but with such gumption and twitting language as to indicate he is in no doubt as to what its impact would be (after reading the attack on the sacramental system of the church, Erasmus declared the evil to be 'incurable') (*CWE* 8: 212). Taking aim at his disputants in debate, he observes that 'God has used them to compel me' to speak out. 'O well, I have a little song [*The Babylonian Captivity*] about Rome and about them. Their ears are itching for me to sing it to them, and to pitch the notes in a treble clef. Do you grasp my meaning, O worthy Rome?' (485).

At the beginning of *The Babylonian Captivity*, Luther traces his own journey. The indulgences controversy did not represent his full thought because at that time he was 'still entangled in the gross superstitions of a masterful Rome.' His 'theses' represented a kind of moderate position – this in the light of future stages of thought – 'as they received the approval of a very large number of people' (250). But now with several years' distance, and thanks again to his disputants (in this case, Piereias and certain unnamed friars), he was pushed to see that the indulgences did not deserve the academic forum he allowed, but instead were 'impositions ... to rob men of their money and their faith in God.'

The same capacity for retrospective survey takes over his attitudes toward the papacy. Once again out of the heated debate with Eck, Emser (importantly a professor at Erfurt when Luther was a student there and later secretary to Duke George of Saxony), and others, Luther was brought from a more conciliatory understanding of the powers of the Roman pope (he did concede authority over the living but not the dead), to the one he currently held, that the papacy is the source of all evil, the Antichrist, in fact the kingdom of Babylon itself.

What is remarkable here is that these reflections reveal a habit of mind given to a kind of mental topography. He knows where he stands and is able to calibrate the distance from where he stood. He well understood the dangers he faced, particularly when approaching the dragon's den, as he does in *The Babylonian Captivity*. Despite the firmness of conviction, gained from the fire of controversy, Luther is under no illusion as to the arduousness of his task in doing away with four of the seven sacraments as sacraments, and retaining only baptism, the Lord's Supper, and (although with some reservation) penance. Modern Lutherans quip that he retained two and a half sacraments. In a passage of sincere meditation, he reflects on the accumulated abuses. Centuries of ancient custom have made it a matter of ingrained habit, so that 'almost the whole form of church life' would have to be altered or done away with. 'Entirely different rites and ceremonies would have to be introduced, or reintroduced' – an important addition that is a reminder that his call is a call for a return to the simplicity of earlier times (271).

The staying power, the durability, and appeal of Luther's views may be attributed to their simplicity and consistency. The doctrine of works has placed Christian fellowship in prison, in another Babylonian captivity. Works have replaced faith as the cornerstone of Christian belief, where the proper ramifying order should be the word, rightly understood, leading to faith, yielding love, bearing works. Instead, works have been made into the primary expression of the Christian experience: this substitution results in Christians being taken 'into a miserable servitude by the Roman curia and the church has been robbed of all her liberty' (256). The treasures are the gifts of baptism (about which Luther speaks in the most endearing terms) and the Lord's Supper; they constitute the promise of recovery from sin and salvation, which is the basis of faith. This knowledge and this faith comprise the essence of Christian liberty, which has been foregone by the church's insistence on the administration of works. But these are rather inestimable gifts, not to be won by our striving – and we see how Luther's own personal struggles have broken through into the simplicity of doctrine, how temperament has entered into ideas.

The mass is not a 'work,' and its benefits are non-transferable. And while Luther's pastoral concerns are comforting, and he has a sense of a community that is attentive to the word as preached, and while he insists on good neighbourly acts of love, still at its core Christian liberty can be terrifying. Responsibilities of belief rest on the shoulders of each believer. 'The mass is divine promise which can benefit no one, intercede for no one, be communicated to no one, except only to the believer himself by the sole virtue of his faith' (283). The import of this message can be awesome: when Christ brings the sword we know what Luther understands by this (Erasmus gives it an entirely opposed spiritual reading in *The Praise of Folly* 133).[25] Despite Luther's sense of spiritual community, he also acknowledges the requirements of the Spirit, which insist that everyone stands alone, outside history, outside tradition, outside models and exemplars. 'Each one stands for himself where the divine promise is concerned ... Each must respond for himself, and bear his own burden' (283). The action is fundamentally simple: I cannot believe on behalf of another, or cause another to believe. We come here to the core of radical Protestantism and the line of sharpest demarcation between Luther and Erasmus, a line that grows deeper in the great debate. Erasmus, having endured one bereavement, needs the comfort of the church – to be sure, spiritually understood and somewhat distinct from its mundane manifestations – the panoply of the saints, but even more importantly he requires the achievements of the great, the sense of historical continuity, or the accumulated wisdom of the past in which he can now figure himself, and of which he is a part. Erasmus understood very well the challenge of Luther to all that he required and came to stand for and above all the terror that was represented by the responsibilities of spiritual aloneness.

The sequel that Luther promises at the end of *The Babylonian Captivity* is *The Freedom of a Christian*, a work of apparent conciliation and even something of an antidote to the severity of the pronouncements that preceded (*Martin Luther: Selections* 42–85). The Latin edition is introduced by a dedicatory letter to Pope Leo X, in which Luther stipulates two very stiff conditions for future harmony: that he never recant his previous statements and that he not be obliged to acknowledge any authority beyond that of individual conscience in interpreting scripture (in the body of the letter and in these two conditions he did exhibit strange notions of conciliation). In it Luther addresses an outstanding problem stemming from his suspicion of works. We can readily understand his denunciation of pilgrimages, of masses for the dead, and other such practices. He not only denounces them in themselves but also in regard to the other superior works of Christian charity – the neighbourly acts of love and kindness. The problem that resists this formulation is that, if works are to be condemned, what happens to these other 'good' works, and where do they stand in the Christian economy of the primacy of faith?

Luther's exposition, while well outlined, is not so much logical as it is spiritual, that is, speaking from the heart of religious experience. In essence, Luther discovers that even good works by themselves cannot sustain faith. This is a basic insight into human psychology and religious thought. First of all, there is the danger of doing a good deed for the wrong reasons (like the fourth unexpected tempter in T.S. Eliot's *Murder in the Cathedral*), and they are many: from self-satisfaction, to self-congratulation, to some animosity against one's marriage, against one's parents. The common suspicion of 'do-gooders' might lie here: their deeds are ostensibly good but their motives arouse suspicion and do not reassure; one is not in the presence of a person who inspires confidence but rather in the company of persons who, despite their actions, inspire mistrust. But there is another reason why for Luther good works must derive from faith – which in modern terms let us equate with the attainment of an emotionally integrated personality – and why good works cannot inspire or create faith. The reason is a lack of equanimity in the human personality, so that good deeds do not last, are not remembered, but evil deeds seem to thrive and stick to the soul and to the memory. By these strange economies humankind will always be sinful (just as with Freud it will always know guilt, thus disabling the benefits of civilization), finding neither Lethe nor Eunoe unless it experiences a redeeming basis in faith. For Luther, then, the law only condemns humankind to sin, revealing its incapacities and shortcomings. Only faith can transcend the law or fulfil the law; only faith can redeem humanity from its dire dilemma, where even its good works fall short and are condemned. The substances of culture and civilization, those worlds of public engagement, avail nothing unless the personality is intact. Things do not stand up well, and even personal accomplishments slip away into nothingness unless a withstanding and abiding faith inhabits one's being.

Once this faith is recovered, then by a natural emanation of love good deeds flow and are acceptable. This is the condition of Christian liberty, where one can will or not will, according to the circumstances, to observe ceremonies of the church. The Pauline doctrine of expediency, or appropriateness, is not employed by Erasmus alone, but is endorsed by Luther as well, each finding justification in Christian liberty. If doing otherwise might give unnecessary offence to one's neighbour, then one can comply with customary actions (such as Mary undergoing the rites of purification, or Paul advising Timothy to be circumcised), but when it is a matter of doctrinal dispute, Paul can urge Titus to resist. In fact, in this conciliatory work, Luther believes he is adopting a middle position. There are those he fears, who learning of the kingdom of faith, now believe that all things are permitted. Their freedom is not a real freedom because it consists in scoffing and finding fault: 'as if they were Christians because on stated days they do not fast or eat meat when others fast, or because they do not use the accustomed prayers, and with upturned nose scoff at the precepts of men, although they utterly disregard all else that pertains to the Christian religion.' In the balance sheet of errors they are enlisted with their exact opposites, 'who rely for their salvation solely on their reverent observation of ceremonies,' and use this as a means of salvation rather than a central faith (80). For Luther each lapses into a concern for trifling externals; neither penetrates to the essence of faith. Strangely enough, despite the coming dispute, on each of these points Luther and Erasmus remain in agreement.

8. The Gathering Heat of Argument

It is natural that dualisms should be dogged by ambivalence – even in the midst of apparent agreement and genuine affinities. This is true of all dualisms and is represented in classical fashion by that of Erasmus and Luther. We have already seen the reservations shared by Luther and his colleagues over Erasmus's commentaries on the New Testament, from which they profited and upon which they relied: Erasmus was weak on original sin. But private suspicions were held by Erasmus as well. While he always credited Luther's message, indicating that his cause was right, he suspected the messenger, the vehemence of his tone, the rhetorical extravagance of his views (although very early he did think that the messenger was the right one, and much later thought Luther was God's just punishment for the evil of the times). When it became clear that matters were getting out of hand, and he was going to be tarred with Luther's brush by conservative critics, Erasmus sought to distance himself from Luther's ideas; he adopted a stance of some neutrality, claiming only to have dipped into Luther's written works.[26] Despite this apparent neutrality he performed several very valuable services on behalf of Luther. They could be summarized as attacking Luther's attackers, and protecting the papacy from the pope's protectors. Three works, one opposing the 'Acts' of the University of Louvain against Luther, another, the *Axiomata*, hastily written for Duke Frederick, and the last, his general plan of arbitration, the *Consilium*, offer, as Martin Lowry has written, a 'coherent picture of Erasmus' last efforts to settle the religious problem according to the principles of reason and moderation' (*CWE* 71: 100). Erasmus understands that the attacks on Luther coming from the University of Louvain were in actuality attacks on his own program of humane studies (but in his *Acta*, he does stoop to outright and vicious anti-Semitic attacks against a former friend, Girolamo Aleandro). That this was and will be his main concern comes clear from the first of the *Axiomata*: 'The matter has sprung from a tainted source, the hatred of literature and the claim for spiritual domination.' Furthermore, Luther's ideas should not be condemned but should be subjected to debate. The *Axiomata* close with a marvellous insight: 'The world is thirsting for the gospel truth, and seems to be borne on its way by some supernatural desire' (*CWE* 71: 107). He understands that beyond his own reckoning and even rational expectations a movement is underway that is carrying the people of his time in its broader sweep. It was this advisory letter – at which Erasmus excelled – to the very powerful and astute duke that persuaded him to shelter Luther with his life-saving political protection.

If this brief was helpful, Erasmus's broader scheme for a council of arbitration proved to be too little too late. He urged that Charles V, the newly crowned Henry VIII, and the king of Hungary should each appoint a learned person, which committee would then read and judge Luther's works, weeding out what was dubious and preserving what was not harmful or even needful. This arbitration would be final, and if Luther refused to abide by their judgments he and his works would be subject to the required response. Notable is the absence of a papal representative, which sacrifice Erasmus somewhat naively asks the pontiff to make for his own benefit and the peace of Christendom (*CWE* 71: 108–12). The good offices came to naught not only because of the omission of the papacy but because Francis I had already invaded Spain and Henry VIII had already entered into public dispute with Luther.

It was not until after *The Babylonian Captivity*, the public burning of the papal bull, and Luther's defiant stand at the Diet of Worms in April 1521 that Erasmus's alienation from Luther began (Soward, *CWE* 71: xlvii). Within a month after the disaster at Worms, Erasmus wrote to Justus Jonas, a professor at Erfurt, 'who gave Luther steadfast support at Worms' (8: 201). A companion letter (225) followed with the famous mini-portraits of Colet and Jean Vitrier, as counters to Luther's style and message, and both were published by Froben within the year. Erasmus in the first letter condemns Luther's lack of political tact, an incapacity to win over his opponents by modifying his claims. Instead, although 'Luther's teaching is no different from that of other people' (a curious and intriguing insertion), he insists on the singularity of his views (205–6). Erasmus dismisses the arguments that Luther was compelled by his opponents to adopt a more polemical tone, adding that the opposition would have been better met with conciliation (206). But the gravamina of the letter are self-protection and complaint. Erasmus objects that Luther's disciples have been intercepting his private letters and publishing them to his harm. The goal of such provocateurs is to incite the authorities against Erasmus and by such means lure him into the evangelical fold. Then in a massive display of disingenuousness, he tries to separate his own positions on vows, pilgrimages, and confession – expressed 'before he even dreamed that a Luther would arise' – from the later arguments on such subjects made by Luther. He seems to be struck by advanced amnesia, as he writes that 'somewhere, maybe' (fortasse alicubi) – a phrasing he repeats – in the midst of his many works he held such opinions, as if they are not readily to be found in *The Enchiridion* and *The Praise of Folly*. In the midst of this backtracking there looms also the palinode (a tendency toward recantation that only increased as the heat of argument rose), 'Had I known that a generation such as this would appear, I should neither have written at all some things that I have written, or should have written them differently' (209). One can follow the first clause, but the second leaves one wondering how it could have been written in a less offensive or more accommodating manner. It was this combination of disingenuousness, backtracking, and recanting that drove Luther and his friends to exasperation, an exasperation that found its full expression in Luther's *On the Bondage of the Will.*

Prior to declaration of war Erasmus advanced several peace initiatives. In a major letter to Johan von Botzheim, written in January 1523 and published in April, Erasmus explains that he has two projects in mind: the first would be three dialogues and the second, more discreet, was evidently the plan advanced in the *Consilium* (*CWE* 9: 347, 349).[27] Neither of these proposals met with success; Erasmus himself had to abandon the notion of three dialogues because, as he explains in an addition to the letter in 1524, while the discontent of the 'opposite party' (Catholic) might have been anticipated, he did not foresee the even greater ferocity of the evangelicals, who refused to countenance any debate with Luther, particularly from Erasmus. Evidently one of the proposed dialogues did survive in altered form in the *Colloquies* as *Inquisitio de fide* (The Inquisition concerning Faith), published in 1524, which again in Erasmus's moderating tone shows little disagreement between Lutherans and Catholics on genuine articles of faith.

The tipping-point in the controversy may well have been the assaults on Erasmus's character from the parties favourable to Luther. The most potent of these analyses was the letter from Ulrich von Hutten, sparking a minor skirmish that anticipated the larger defining debate between Erasmus and Luther. From a letter written by Erasmus to Marcus Laurinus (February 1523), von Hutten understood that Erasmus intended to enter into open dispute with Luther. This larger issue is complicated by a felt personal injury. When von Hutten, quite seriously ill, came to Basel, Erasmus refused to see him, fearing the association might compromise him, as von Hutten was under an imperial ban. Thus not only as an adulator who sees his mentor defecting but also as something of a snubbed friend, von Hutten writes his important remonstration (*Expostulatio*) against Erasmus. Acknowledging Erasmus's role as the head of a movement, but dismayed at his apparent disavowal of the beliefs he once held, the letter significantly explores the causes underlying Erasmus's failure to come forward in this time of need, or at the very least remove himself from the conflict altogether. He proposes several answers, among them, envy and bribery (Klawiter ¶82–94). But such simple summary does little justice to pages of passionate complaint that von Hutten mounts against his fallen idol. Von Hutten writes as a representative of German knighthood, from the deepest sense of personal honour and as a steadfast warrior, who, like Shakespeare's Hotspur, cannot tolerate the vacillations and calculations of a 'vile politician.' Erasmus had been the leader, who inspired his followers, only to defect and leave them stranded. Now he is praising the conservative theologians whom he had reviled in private conversation, even ingratiating himself with the members of the Louvain faculty, whose names, except for Erasmus's attacks, would never have been known in Germany. Von Hutten's refrain throughout is to ask how this could be. How could you have done such a thing, you who at one time were our great leader, the one we followed, I even before Luther? The 'expostulations' indicate how well known and publicized were Erasmus's own reflections, the changes in his opinions, and the complaints against him.

Von Hutten raises issue after burning issue before finally coming to Erasmus's character, now marked as he sees it by a 'certain cowardice,' a Proteanism of personality, a refusal to be pinned down. Erasmus is ruled by a timidity 'which causes you at the slightest provocation to fear the worst and thus to despair, reducing to naught your confidence in the progress of our common cause' (Klawiter ¶45). Here von Hutten's fury does not contribute much to his psychological penetration of the complexities of an Erasmus. This tendency has hampered criticism of Erasmus, limiting it to the epithet 'Proteus,' that Luther would also use and that would endure through the centuries. More pointedly, von Hutten does go on to discuss Erasmus's need for approval, his fear not of receiving harm but of giving offence, and Erasmus's trait of desiring to please and be pleasing – not hard to comprehend in a one-time poor scholarship student.[28]

There is some poignancy in von Hutten's description of Erasmus's prospects (it anticipates Spitz's sense of the tragic denouement of Erasmus's career, even repeated by Augustijn as he follows the 'tragic moment' of Erasmus's 'shift,' or slippage, in his debates with Luther).[29] He will be rejected by both parties (a prediction that later events brought keenly home). His attempts at ingratiation will be met with suspicion (as indeed his works after his death were among the first placed on the Index of prohibited books). But the greater alienation will be from himself, from the Erasmus who once was. His books will be there as constant reminders of his changed positions, hence the greater confrontation will take place in his own mind.

Here von Hutten was sadly right, but he was wrong in several ways. He never properly understood Erasmus's character, which only Erasmus by the force of circumstances came to comprehend. Erasmus was never in fact 'with' the Lutherans; he always held something in reserve, and even, as the previous sections 3, 4, and 5 disclosed, had some intrinsic temperamental opposition to what Luther in his person and in his cause represented. Nor was Erasmus a coward – witness the ringing response he delivered to von Hutten's expostulations, the sponge (*Spongia*) he offers to wash the aspersions clean. But the intriguing question of Erasmus, the one to which everyone returns, was prompted by Erasmus himself. Inquiries are compounded by Erasmus's own self-defensiveness, the tedious need for self-exculpation on every detail. Erasmus was a man who needed to be right; perhaps this is why he sits in the centre, taking something from here and from there, criticizing here and there while remaining unscathed because uncommitted – a man, certainly not a coward Chomarat argues, who, perhaps failing to 'interiorize' the father, remains on the margins, preferring to be a spectator.[30] This is the Erasmus that von Hutten scores and that Luther despises.

His long-awaited 'attack' against Luther was certainly not cowardly, but it was Erasmian. Somewhere in the midst of his encounter with von Hutten, Erasmus decided on the nature of his response to Luther. Von Hutten's attack had broken the ice, but he was only giving expression to sentiments that Luther was making known, and this was that Erasmus stood in the way, that his part in the changeful drama was past. Like Moses he had brought them a necessary distance but could not complete the journey. But more gratingly, it was in spiritual matters that Erasmus no longer served as guide. In a letter of November 1523 Erasmus quotes Luther as writing that 'I [Erasmus] am like Moses and must be buried in the wilderness and that too much weight should not be given to Erasmus in spiritual matters' (*CWE* 10: 109–10). Then he adds, 'This sort of thing means war.' Clearly the gloves had come off. The same Mosaic references with their implications are quoted in a letter to Ulrich Zwingli at the very end of August (10: 83). And shortly thereafter (September 1523), in a brief note to Henry VIII, he advises the king that he 'has something on the stocks [molior aliquid] against the new doctrines.' Later he would send to Henry the first draft of *On the Freedom of the Will* (10: 201).

While the choice is very Erasmian and suited his political and intellectual needs in many ways, it was still surprising. In that important letter to Marcus Laurinus, that is, as late as February 1523, one would have thought the topic to be poison to Erasmus. In a lengthy passage of complaint he tries to deflect the more radical criticisms of his earlier views on free will, where he maintained that 'something is seated in our own will and endeavor ... No man is condemned except by his own fault.' Rather than a defence one hears the accent of bleating: why am I being criticized for expressing views that Origen and Jerome, in fact all the theologians – and he names seven of the most prominent – had already stated? Why should I be blamed, and moreover, why should these views that are at odds with those of Luther, simply by that fact be called 'Erasmian' (evidence once again of his reluctance to be known as the leader of a party, or to be part of a dualism, *CWE* 9: 398–9)? This is particularly the case when – once again the dismissive note – his comments on free will were made only in passing. Clearly something happened between January and February of 1523 and September of the same year that went beyond simple alienation and led toward outright confrontation.

If this was war, it was war conducted in an Erasmian manner, and that itself derived from the very topic chosen. This dispute was not about articles of faith (about which the *Inquisitio de fide* showed common agreement) but about such matters as 'whether confession was instituted by

Christ; whether the regulations of the bishops can bind under penalty of mortal sin; whether free will contributes anything to man's salvation; whether faith alone is good enough for salvation; whether any works of man can be called good' (Klawiter #308). From this and other passages it is clear why, despite the complaining expressed in the letter to Marcus Laurinus, Erasmus chose the topic of free will: it is one on which one may present various viewpoints, and yet it is anti-Lutheran.[31] The argument over free will, as Erasmus argues in *On the Freedom of the Will*, actually derives from the ancients, who were also perplexed by the conundrum of fate and free will. Erasmus sees no reason why the world should be torn apart by such paradoxical impositions – 'some of which by their very nature cannot be fully understood, others that can be argued for or against, and still others that, considering their importance, contribute little to the improvement of morals.' The essential ambiguity of the topic suited a mind adept in ambivalences, in balancing and weighing alternatives, in the rhetorical devices presented above in the discussion of the *Colloquies*.

All of these arguments emerge in *On the Freedom of the Will*, but the question remains why Erasmus chose to come out against Luther. As usual – Erasmus being who he was – there are a multitude of reasons. First, when after the fall of 1523 he decided to confront Luther, the material was ready to hand. The issue of free will complied with his strategic aims – one of which was not to give succour to the Pharisees. His 'attack' on the Lutheran belief in the enslaved will would provide the conservative theologians with no special ammunition. Moreover, throughout his life's work he had advocated education, reason, and habit as means of striving to improve the life of the Christian. His constant aim was ethical, but that would count for little if the individual believed there was no point in constantly striving to be better. In the first instalment of the *Hyperaspistes*, a response to Luther's *On the Bondage of the Will*, Erasmus indicates the lifelong consistency of his views. And he had become increasingly alienated from Luther, from the vehemence of his rhetoric and its abusiveness, from the paradoxical and extravagant nature of his thought, from the brutal consequences (he attributed with some exaggeration the Peasants' Revolt to Lutheran ideas – *CWE* 76: 114, 170) and the disintegrating effect of the proliferation of splinter groups within the Protestant movement itself. But mainly, as we have seen, it was Luther's statement that Erasmus was old hat, not to be followed in questions of the spirit, that brought about a declaration of war. There was also pressure and threats from the princes of the church and from secular rulers as well (76: 100–1), voices that one failed to heed at one's peril, and Erasmus was always quite aware of the peril (in the letter to Zwingli, he distressingly notes the recent burnings at the stake of two dissident monks, 10: 81). Perhaps the greatest pressure came from the conservative Catholic critics who insisted that Erasmus declare his position and dispel the innuendoes (fostered by both sides) that he was in fact a closet Lutheran.[32] In fact adding their princely exhortations to that of Henry VIII, three successive popes – Leo, Adrian, and Clement – all urged Erasmus to silence the innuendoes by championing the cause of traditional consensus against Lutheran innovations (the enticement of a bishopric was included).

The next two reasons are perhaps even more crucial. Erasmus himself was constrained to follow his own advice, advertised in much of his correspondence, and especially apparent in his *Consilium*, that a well-reasoned conciliatory argument, offered with a generosity of spirit and Christian kindness, would do more against the Lutheran cause than all the threats, excommunications, and banishments had by then accomplished. His *On the Freedom of the Will* was putting into practice what he had preached. Finally, there is the larger issue of the dualism itself: Erasmus could not *not* have responded to Luther. Why were they brought together, such apparent dissimilar forces and faces, their names brandished as standards to rally adherents? Augustijn happily provides one answer: 'The two men were closer to each other than they were willing or able to admit' (*Erasmus: His Life* 132). Affinities precipitate clash. There was a magnetic draw in their opposition; this was an unscheduled event that had to take place, where the defining differences would be established. They were the two stars of the German northern Renaissance, and as such they had to contend. 'Two stars keep not their motion in one sphere,' Prince Hal explains to Hotspur in *Henry IV, Part 1*, one of Shakespeare's more compelling dramas of drastic opposition. Their very situation, their adherents, and they themselves demanded it.

Erasmus himself acknowledges this to be the case when he laments Luther's aggressive response to *On the Freedom of the Will*. Luther is under attack in Germany, in England (from More and John Fisher, the bishop of Rochester), from quarters in France and in Italy, and even from within his own camp from Zwingli and others (over baptism and the Eucharist). 'This being so,' Erasmus can only express surprise at what '[Luther] had in mind in making no reply to the others and responding to my Diatribe' (*CWE* 76: 98). Surprise is magnified, considering the 'restraint' of Erasmus's arguments and, according to Luther, their obvious flimsiness (98).

Later Erasmus will utter the same complaint (247, 277) that while he treated Luther courteously and others vilified him, it was Erasmus who bore the brunt of attack. Erasmus constantly abjures the role of participant in a dualism, yet that is the role he was brought to fulfil, the arena that he chose to enter. As Erasmus himself explained, he wishes to strike and not draw blood, to hit and give no injury, and von Hutten refers to Erasmus's fear of giving offence. Luther of course will have none of it: his universe is antithetical and he measures the weight of his words and those of his antagonist all too well.

One could of course say that pre-eminence itself attracts, and that in responding to Erasmus, Luther was responding to the most advanced stage of European consciousness in his day. It is difficult to maintain that Luther did not take Erasmus seriously as an adversary. He was no easy target, but as it turns out he was the inevitable target. Lined up against the daemonic writer, the writer of consciousness is his most natural opponent, in fact, his facing alternative. Luther's own antithetical universe entertained this prospect far more easily than did Erasmus's, yet Erasmus was also drawn, despite his disavowals, to the conflict. He too felt the grander challenge of the great enmity and so was drawn willy-nilly into the dualism, with all the elements at work that elevate the plane of regard beyond the purely theological. The two poles of the Western mind clash: it was this that made the dualism sparkling, astonishing, drawing all the attention and continuing to do so. This was a contest between two legitimate claimants. When I say that the dualism itself exerted its charge, this is what I mean. Each chose the other because he represented the greatest threat to himself, to his thought, and to his hold on the future.

9. The Unending Debate

The ensuing debate became, for the reason I have indicated here and in the paradigm presented in the introduction, a defining debate of the age. It was an epochal encounter and the premier as well as the foremost dualism of the modern age. It was much anticipated, with adherents from all sides weighing in and urging on their standard-bearers, or, as was the case with Luther's followers, trying to dissuade Erasmus from openly breaking ranks. The issue itself was of major philosophical importance, such that Luther was able to congratulate Erasmus for not bothering him with such trifles (!) as 'the papacy, purgatory, indulgences and the like,' but instead driving right at a central point (*LE* 333). But it also reveals another basic difference: while Erasmus chose 'free will' because it was an issue about which reasonable people could reasonably agree or disagree, Luther would not accept such customary Erasmian sidestepping; he insists that what is at stake is a true understanding of the Christian life. While each, despite gainsayers, proved adept at debating the intricate Christian and philosophical issues in dispute, it is not because of these issues that the debate is important but rather for the challenge each issues to the other at the most basic level of belief and personality.

As Heinrich Bornkamm maintains, 'Both parties in the match gave their utmost. Their respective polemics rank among the greatest documents of intellectual history' (*Luther in Mid-Career*, 418). Because both parties gave their 'utmost' – their temperaments became part of their ideas, informed them, inhabited them – they became 'life-ideas' such as are crucial to any significant dualism. This is the dominant reason why their debate was a defining moment. The exchange represented a superb self-defence on the part of each, as each was able under the larger problem of free will to return to the matters and interests around which their lives and ideas had been formed. Despite Erasmus's caution that he will be the spirit above the dust, one who presents evidence from both sides rather than one who judges, his defence of free will amounts to nothing less than a defence of all that he has stood for and defended since the forging of his vocation at the turn of the century. Even more interestingly, given the dimensions of dualisms, where each partner to the dispute is endowed with extraordinary insight into the other, it is Luther who points this out. In enlisting the roll-call of the ancients (as we have already witnessed in the letter to Marcus Laurinus), the testimony of the ages and of historical consensus, Erasmus is standing solidly on the side of culture and civilization, on the accumulated wisdom of the past. From the argument of the *Enchiridion* to his critical exchange with Maarten van Dorp, Erasmus is a biblical humanist, a Christian intellectual, an ardent expounder of the philosophy of Christ, who cannot abandon the consensus compiled by the wisdom of the church (even given his condemnation of certain practices). This is the position he cannot break away from and the one that informs his *On the Freedom of the Will* and even more volubly his *Hyperaspistes*. It is also the position – and more – that Luther attacks when he declares so powerfully, 'The Church is hidden, the saints are unknown' (*LE* 158). Cut off from history that offers no reliable assurances, so impressed with human fallibility, Luther later asserts, 'It is not astonishing that in divine things men of outstanding talent through so many centuries have been blind' (166).

Not surprisingly Luther defended a 'servum arbitrium,' a will that is not the expression of a directed consciousness, the product of effort toward goals. Given the circumstances of his own development, he argued for a kind of necessity in human experience, the way things turn out beyond our calculations. His entire career from 1517 onwards (one might even say from 1505 onwards) had been unforeseen, swept along not by his own conscious efforts but by what he considered to be the divine will and the Holy Spirit. In *On the Bondage of the Will* it is to these forces in the prostration of the self that he commits himself. Such powerful personal commitment and accurate representation on each of their parts help explain why this debate is a defining one for the time, and why it stretches even beyond that time into the most obvious tensions within Western culture. A dualism enters us into the full complexities of history and historical understanding, but by its very nature it escapes history and confronts us with perennial questions of the human personality.

This confrontation helps account for the vehemence of Luther's response, when, as Erasmus correctly states, he (Erasmus) allows so little for the freedom of the will, only the narrowest of windows (90). Somewhere between initiating grace and the grace that completes an action, humankind can apply itself to be congruent with the actions of grace, or can turn away and abuse its gifts (as Dante describes Lucifer's response to his blessings, when he 'raises his eyebrows,' in a gesture of defiant haughtiness, *Inferno* 34.34–6). While not too far apart in their relative positions concerning free will – or so it might appear to the modern reader, but certainly not to their contemporaries for whom the smallest matters could have the gravest consequences – they are worlds apart when it comes to premises, implications, and the net effect of their arguments.

Erasmus shared in some of the revived optimism of the Renaissance (he also repeats some of the arguments of the earlier Schoolmen). The Fall was a terrible blow but it did not totally obliterate human resources: 'some spark of reason remains' (*CWE* 76: 290); 'not every human inclination is given over to flesh'; there is 'soul' and there is 'spirit by which we strive towards goodness' (76: 61); 'there are certain seeds of goodness planted in men's minds, with the help of which they can to some extent see and strive after the good' (76: 62). The God of our kind cannot be a tyrant but rather a loving father, which means there must be some consonance between the will of man and that of God. Our God cannot be an irrational God. Humankind occupies a distinct and special place in the plan of Creation; we are the new being, Paul's 'new creation.'

Once we look to these premises, we see that, despite the small window. allowed to free will, there exists an abyss between his thought and Luther's. As an ethicist, Erasmus deplores the deterministic implications of Luther's thought. The *Enchiridion* exhorts the human being to constant effort and striving, with the goal of becoming the perfect Christian. Luther nullifies Erasmian thought at its very base. He argues that the whole person is guilty before God, not merely the worse part but especially the best part (*LE* 276–7). Erasmus's dualistic thinking made distinctions between the baser drives and the higher reason, but for Luther the rational part of man – what Erasmus would consider the essentially human – is the most guilty, as it induces smugness and alienation from God. These 'higher' qualities promote an inveterate sense of merit, of cosmic belonging, of having a rightful place in God's providential plan, that prevent the rendering up of the self in the fear of God. And as it is with the individual, so it is with the group. Even the very best are corrupt. The most eminent of the classical philosophers and schools could not conceive of the coming of Christ.

Throughout, Erasmus adopts an intermediate position and Luther abominates the framing of the argument by such mediation. To insist on the limited but still effective congruence of the human will in applying itself to its own salvation in essence negates the importance of Christ.

Why and whence have we that intermediate and neutral thing, the power of free choice, which although it is not Christ or the way, the truth and the life, still must not be error, or a lie, or death? For unless everything said about Christ and grace were said antithetically, so as to set over against its opposite – what I ask you would be the point of all the discourses of the Apostles and of the Scriptures as a whole? They would all be in vain, because they would not insist on the absolute necessity of Christ, which is in fact their chief concern; and they would not do so because some intermediate thing would be found, which of itself would be neither evil nor good, neither Christ's nor Satan's, neither true nor false, neither alive nor dead. (*LE* 323)

The small window opened to free will and the premises upon which the doctrine rests would amount to a repudiation of the Christian message, which is based upon stark antitheses, not on any attempt to bring together, to effect a balance. Luther strikes at the very bases of Erasmus's thought and expectations. Throughout, Erasmus affects a moderating tone, as if he were a moderator and not a judge, an inquirer and not a dogmatist (*CWE* 76: 8, 147). His high reasonableness, his assumed objectivity, offends Luther to the core, as if this were a minor dispute over money or a high school debate during which one was free to argue either side of the issue. Luther comes crashing down on this very attitude of Erasmus, which provides palpable evidence that he has no true understanding of sin and death, of the agony and despair, the sense of worthlessness from which the only redemption is Christ.

Erasmus's dualisms are vertical, the higher against the lower, the spiritual against the carnal. Luther's dialectic is lateral. While the daemonic is not diabolic, it can certainly conscript that presence. The antithetical nature of scriptures, upon which Luther insists, rests upon the larger antithesis, that of God and the devil. For Luther there is no middle kingdom in the economy of salvation (and we are reminded of his earlier suspicion of purgatory). Heiko Oberman, whose appealing biographical study of Luther's life and work is subtitled *Man between God and the Devil*, wrote that if only we possessed *On the Bondage of the Will*, we could deduce 'the total scope' of Luther's theology, but that is because we would be getting Erasmus as well (Oberman 212). It was the very presence of Erasmus and what he represented, the positioning of his arguments, as well as the arguments themselves that drove Luther to the fullest exposition of his religious and philosophical thought. He is arguing against the spirit of moderation that barely conceals its willing accommodation with the enemy – its recanting on some of the basic principles of reform that it had once upheld – and against not only a style of writing, but a style of man who seems too complicated for his own good, who seems to say and unsay and to fail the muster of simple courage. Where von Hutten denounces Erasmus with the outraged passion of a disappointed lover, Luther mixes his vehemence with disdain.

Erasmus is seen to be a renegade, who, contrary to his expressed opinions in the controversy with Dorp, is now reluctant to air certain issues in public for fear of arousing the people, and who now believes it is better to keep to the accepted practices of the church and even disowns his previously held adherence to the principle of Christian liberty and the singular conviction instilled by the Holy Spirit. His has become a balancing act that relies on probabilities. In the balance, given the weights of the founders of the church, the consensus of history, and distinguished philosophers, it is more likely that they are right and that Luther, by himself, or with his divided cohorts, is wrong. Furthermore Erasmus adopts the tactic of Pauline expediency, which he acknowledges that Luther has already advocated. But it is one thing to be prudent in the time of Paul, for instance in not making fully manifest the divinity of Christ, and another to be so almost 1,500 years later in the time of the supreme papacy, with which Paul did not have to contend. But Luther will have none of these arguments. Erasmus not only revokes their once-shared notions of Christian liberty but also reinstates papal control. By such moderating restraints, Luther argues, 'you set up for us again the whole tyranny of Papal laws as being useful and salutary because by them the wickedness of the common people is restrained' (*LE* 127). Luther might here have issued a refrain of the civil rights movement of the 1960s: 'Go slow, means don't go.'

Whereas Erasmus now finds himself constrained by the force of external circumstances, the disintegration, and the tumult that he fears, Luther holds to his either/or position:

> Human statutes cannot be observed together with the word of God, because they bind consciences while the Word sets them free. The two are mutually incompatible as water and fire, unless the human statutes are kept freely, that is, as not being binding – a thing the Pope cannot and will not allow, unless he wants his kingdom ruined and brought to an end, since it is only maintained by the ensnaring and binding of consciences which the Gospel asserts to be free. (*LE* 127–33)

We can see why the discreet moderate reformist position, based as it is upon Erasmus's vaunted philosophy of Christ (which Luther shared) produces no change at all. It led to a knowing acquiescence to prevailing conditions, and finally placed all things in God's hands to punish a straying humankind or beneficently to grant them an undeserved reprieve. Erasmus's political conservatism, expressed in the *Education of a Christian Prince* and also advanced in 'A Religious Feast,' has overtaken his formerly held position of Christian liberty in matters of doctrine. For Luther, tumult and discord are not to be feared; rather, they are signs that true doctrine is shaking the world. His Christ brings a sword.

We can understand Luther's vehemence, but how are we to comprehend Erasmus's anger at Luther's response? We know he was notoriously thin-skinned, so Luther's invectives stung badly.[33] In addition, he witnessed the defeat of his own advice in the *Consilium*. He wrote in a such a 'temperate' style that Luther could not have wished for a more 'courteous disputation' (*CWE* 76: 101). Luther was not placated by a moderate tone, by the complexities of a philosophical position, by sheer reasonableness upon which Erasmus prided himself. Just the opposite: Luther found abhorrent this very superior tone of high reasonableness, this pre-

emption of a position that was automatically correct, of the appropriation of virtue, and of the balanced consensus of the *bien pensant*. But even
more: Luther has found him out, Luther has caught him out. Erasmus
had arranged a masked ball, a kind of convivium where agreeable people
could agreeably agree, and Luther has torn the mask away, has refused to
play the game. From his habitual mode of ironic deference, Erasmus was
struck by an opponent of simple earnestness. Some part of himself had
been uncovered. In protecting his flanks so assiduously, Erasmus
exposed himself to a frontal attack, and attack Luther did against Erasmus's avowed scepticism, his balancing act of arguments, his concession
to received opinion and common practice, and his need to delimit
debate so as not to arouse the people. But even more critically, Luther
has taken Erasmus's argument and elevated it onto the larger stage of
philosophical-religious dispute. Erasmus had inadvertently confirmed
the charge that he was wanting when it came to matters of the Spirit –
and Luther drives this point home with force and cogency.

There is one offending passage where Erasmus seems to be saying
much more than he intends and where he is undone by his own man-
nered coyness. He rightly explains that he has no temperament for outright assertion, as indeed his style is always indirect, circumspect, ironic,
and not made for the hand-to-hand combat such argument requires. He
recoils from conflict: 'And so [I] have always preferred sporting in the
spacious plains of the Muses to engaging in sword-play at close quarters'
(*CWE* 76: 7).[34] This he follows with a remarkably strange sentence that
Luther pounces on:

> And I take so little pleasure in assertion that I would gladly seek refuge in
> scepticism whenever this is allowed by the inviolable authority of Holy Scrip-
> ture and the Church's decrees; to these decrees I willingly submit my judg-
> ment in all things, whether I fully understand what the Church commands
> or not. (*CWE* 76: 7)

Luther can barely contain his outrage, calling Erasmus by his favourite
epithet, 'Proteus,' as one who writes of the inviolable authority of scripture and the hallowed decrees of the church, while at the same time
maintaining that if left to his own devices, he would be a sceptic. Several
paragraphs later, Luther intones, 'The Holy Spirit is no Skeptic' (*LE*
109). One does not know where to pin Erasmus down, for his words lead
to no effectual practice, as Luther judges in his vilification of Erasmus
throughout *Table Talk* and in an open letter of 1534.[35] But one thing

Luther does know: such words undermine the belief in Christian liberty, the concept that had formerly forged their putative alliance. 'What new religion, what new humility is this that you would deprive us by your own example of the powers of judging the decrees of men, and subject us in uncritical fashion to men? Where does the Scripture of God impose this on us?' (*LE* 108).

Erasmus's Proteanism that places the peace of the world above Christian truth relies upon his covert scepticism. His moderation relies upon a suspension of judgment in the face of the obscurities of life – and to Luther's irritation – of scripture itself. Luther then summarizes Erasmus's thought in way that reaches far into the future. For Erasmus, Christian truth is, according to Luther,

> no better than philosophical and human opinions, about which it is stupid to wrangle and contend since nothing comes of it but strife and the disturbance of outward peace. Things that are above us, you say, are no concern of ours. So with a view to ending our conflicts you come forward as a mediator, calling a halt to both sides, and trying to persuade us that we are flourishing our swords about things that are stupid and useless. (*LE* 109)

Luther is painting a near-perfect portrait of the system of ideas that triumphed in the Enlightenment, in the rational theology and natural religion of Voltaire and of Rousseau. It is for this reason that Erasmus's reputation revived at the end of the seventeenth century and thus came to form the intellectual baseline for that next great dualism (of course, this would be an Erasmus stripped of his message, the philosophy of Christ, and of his method, his hermeneutics of allegory and spiritual reading). Ironically enough the very turmoil that emerged from the conflict wrought by perfervid belief helped to ensure the triumph of Erasmus's ideas that had been so disparaged. This eventual triumph and restoration of his opinion Erasmus himself knew would come with time.

Luther is in effect calling Erasmus a sceptic, which in the lexicon of early-sixteenth-century theology is equivalent to calling him an atheist. The next paragraph ominously seems to imply as much (with the special insight that one party to the dualism has into the other, and with the cryptophasia that typifies the communication of twins): 'That is what your words seem to mean, and I think you understand, my dear Erasmus, what I am driving at' (*LE* 109). What is Luther driving at but the undeclared assertion that Erasmus so values the human over the divine that his allegiance to the divine is suspect, that he is not a true believer.

Erasmus's anger seems to stem from the fact that he went against his better nature. He has slipped on his own courtesy (throughout the defensive *Hyperaspistes*, Erasmus calls attention to the courteousness of his disputation). Undeniably Erasmus has wavered. His *On the Freedom of the Will* and the *Hyperaspistes* are models of how not to respond to radical discourse (as we shall see when we compare Voltaire's response to Rousseau). They lack confident humour but more importantly they lack a quiet passion of belief. A certain concision might have helped too. They are massively over-determined, as in two successive volumes, each longer than *On the Freedom of the Will* itself, he must counter Luther's arguments point by point, evidence of a damaging defensiveness (the very title *Hyperaspistes* invokes a 'shield').

Such defensiveness is not the most egregious of Erasmus's deficiencies in the debate. Erasmus even goes so far as to condone (if not justify) the papacy's betrayal of Hus. He thought less badly of Hus before he read his 'abusive' attacks on the pontiff – Hus thus anticipating Luther. As he did not know the responsible pope of that time, he cannot presume to judge him: 'They are my judges; I am not theirs' (*CWE* 76: 230). Such deference leads to the balancing act of probabilities that discounts Luther's individual voice. Who is Luther to go against the consensus of the leading figures of the church? If the saints are unknown and the church hidden, why should not the same cloud of unknowing hang over Luther's assertions as well? Should not the same scepticism calling for a suspension of judgment prevail? And then he concludes, in another strange Erasmian trope, 'I do not say these things as my sincere opinions, but rather to confute you' (76: 225, 231). The voices of the past are invoked as authorities to drown out the upstart singularity of this man of the present.

The writer of consciousness suffers from a deficit when bridled by the accusatorial power and spiritual energy of a daemonic writer. This restriction becomes particularly evident when we compare Erasmus's later interventions with those of the controversy with Dorp, or even more importantly with one of the several introductions to his 1516 edition of the New Testament, the aptly named *Paraclesis*. In fact, Luther remarks on the better sense shown in that work, marking the change in Erasmus's thought (*LE* 133).[36] In the *Paraclesis*, Erasmus reaches lyrical – even Wordsworthian – heights, particularly when he argues against the sacerdotal monopoly and insists on making the sacred texts available to everybody.[37] This was part of his original drive, shared with Luther, of not only going backward to the great books, but indeed extending the line outward to the laity as well, to the general public, to the unlearned, to ploughmen, to weavers, and to travellers who might ease their labours by singing passages from the Gospels. From the *Enchiridion* on he had maintained that, were the message of the Gospels to penetrate into everyday life, it would find acceptance among even the eminently placed, and the world would be better for it. Instead the predominance of the theologians and the dependence on ceremonials have chilled the ardour of Christian belief. No one, he fears, is familiar with the biblical texts. The theologians have overlaid them with commentaries, and ceremonials have pushed them out of sight. Erasmus's fear is a remarkable one: in the midst of the bulging triumph of Christianity, his society has become de-Christianized. In fact it threatens to become so by the very triumph of these false faces of Christianity. And it is the most intelligent, or the most worldly successful, who have become alienated. To this church in crisis, the avowed purpose of bringing the true Gospels back into touch with the people is the aim of the biblical humanism that had joined Erasmus and Luther. Indeed, in a moment of great prophecy, Erasmus accurately predicts 'that the first steps of the great theologians and the days to come will be in these authors of [Holy Scripture]' (Olin 105).

But in the debate with Luther he argues that to air such issues as free will in public could be damaging to the moral health of the populace. While the level of engagement differs – on the one hand, the availability of Gospel texts, and on the other a recondite seminar debate over thorny theological matters – still the turnabout is apparent. Indeed, we may ask why one should not lead to the other: if the ploughman were to hold the vernacular biblical texts in his hands, even in the midst of song, why would not or should not the same questions occur to him that surface in the debate between Erasmus and Luther? Why should he not be eligible to entertain the same resolutions? It appears once again that Erasmus is not willing to accept the consequences of his presuppositions.

But perhaps the greatest reversal from that of the glorious earlier epoch was in his retraction of the Holy Spirit. If ever there were an inspired work, one breathing the very fire of the Holy Spirit, it was the *Paraclesis*, written after Erasmus had finished his monumental work on the New Testament. It is an exhortation, a summons to attend to the Holy Spirit present in the Gospels. It is ready to hand, available to all, even more so than the doctrines of Aristotle or Averroes that seem to be commanding so much attention, and in comparison with which the 'philosophy of Christ' bears the plainer message, the handsomer truth (Olin 99). But when the bolder, more dominant presence of Luther came upon the scene, Erasmus withdrew into a narrower conception of himself. He sought some occult and irreducible aspect of his own personality, rooted in an inherent scepticism, and marked by caution, care, the desire for peace, and an unwillingness to combat. But he faltered most over the Holy Spirit. The presence of Luther's conviction confronted him with a personal lack. And this lack is most poignantly expressed in his long letter to Marcus Laurinus of early 1523. It is a passage that shows Erasmus's full eloquence, an eloquence that propels one forward (because of which I quote it in full):

> Anyone who cannot love Erasmus as a Christian, though a feeble one, must adopt towards him what attitude he pleases; I for my part cannot be different from what I really am. If Christ has given anyone a grander measure of the gifts of the Spirit, and he has the self-confidence, let him use them for Christ's glory. I feel happier meanwhile in following a humbler but a safer course. I cannot fail to abominate discord. I cannot fail to love peace and concord. I see the great obscurity there is even in the affairs of men; I see how much easier it is to rouse uproar than to pacify it, and I have learned how many are the tricks Satan can play. I would not dare trust my own spirit in everything; far less would I be able to give a reliable opinion on the spirit of other men. I could wish to see all men make a concerted effort to secure the victory of Christ and the establishment among all men of concord in the gospel, so that disorder might be ruled out in favor of sound reasoning, and measures might be taken to promote on the one side the authority of the priesthood and on the other the freedom of the people, whom the Lord Jesus wished to be free. Anyone embarked on this course can rely on me to the utmost of my power. But those who prefer to cause universal confusion will not have me, at any rate, as a leader or a colleague. They put forward as their excuse the working of the Spirit. Let them dance then among the prophets – and good luck to them – if they have been inspired by the Spirit of the Lord. That spirit of theirs has not yet seized on me; and when it does, they may well say, 'Is Saul also himself among the prophets?' (*CWE* 9: 400–1)

This long paragraph conveys the essence of Erasmus in all its varied strands and all its complexity – its moving in and out, to and fro, from a recognition of his own character determinism, to his quest for peace and disavowal of any approach of Spirit, to his appreciation of the darkened meanings in human affairs, let alone the divine; to his suspicion of his own claims on truth with what consequence for the claims of others, to his envy of those who claim the Spirit, and to his own not quite vanquished thought that his revilers might still yet see him, like Saul, become proverbial among the prophets. Rarely is there a passage of such full self-revelation and modest self-defence, such truth-telling. And then to invoke the story of Saul, searching for his father's asses, anointed with the Spirit and dancing among the prophets. There is pure poetry in the biblical invocation, but sadly not historical fact (some of the poetry might be missing as well, because there is no biblical reference to Saul's dancing; prophesying but not dancing). In fact, the story of Saul is another story of conversion – he became 'another man' by virtue of the Spirit – thus remaining more appropriate for Luther than for Erasmus. Erasmus, as we have shown, went on to defend his positions tirelessly and redundantly; for his part, Luther did not feel compelled to answer the two instalments of the *Hyperaspistes*, except for one apparently lost letter. In his quiet confidence, with the conviction of a victor he felt there was nothing more to be said. Nevertheless, as the flare-up of 1534 showed, Luther, evidencing the attentiveness that exists between rivals in a dualism, continued to read everything that Erasmus wrote (Brecht, *Luther* 3: 78).

By this time Luther had passed through the wars, standing up against pope and emperor (with a success that astonished even him). Erasmus, by choice and by predilection, remained a spectator. To Luther his arguments would always be 'academic.' It is one thing to believe in Christ, it is another to pass through that agony. This should serve as a constant motto for Luther's spiritual quest. As he himself tells us, it is not by thinking, reading, or speculating that a theologian is made, but by living, dying, and even by being damned. As the writer of consciousness would be quick to remind us, intensity, of course, does not mean rightness; nor conviction, correctness. But we come here to the greatest difference between the two types, as the daemonic must insist on the correlation of the inner experience to belief, while the figure of consciousness readily uses his intelligence as an instrument of observation, meaning that he is subject to multiple and complex stimuli and not to dramas of internal absorption. This difference might also help explain why the writer of consciousness experiences a sense of some deficit in conflict with the daemonic writer. But it is not all that simple, as Luther, to his credit, had the intellectual means and ballast to distinguish what he was doing from the proposals of his 'false brethren,' those who carried his primary doctrines to extremes (see Edwards). There was something within him – perhaps his activity within a workaday world of pastoral responsibilities – that prevented him from being self-destructive. Whatever the source,

Luther cast an enormous shadow over Erasmus by virtue of his stout insistence on the enfranchising effect of Christian liberty, his sense of the power of individual conscience, the sheer abundance of his intellectual output, the range of his development, and his evolution into the role as leader of a people. Erasmus was never able to free himself from Luther's ascendancy – despite his continuing the debate, or perhaps as evidenced by that very insistence.

Erasmus wrote *On the Freedom of the Will* because he had no choice (to paraphrase a quip by Isaac Bashevis Singer). It expressed a lifelong interest in human betterment, yet it did not represent the better part of Erasmus. Not the better part, but perhaps, as he was driven to confront the recesses of himself, the truer part. While we can dream about the Erasmus who might have been (thinking back to the halcyon years of 1514–17), and even speculate about what might have been had his moderate reformism won the day (which in the short run it rarely seems to do), many a student seems content with the Erasmus who was. He carried his work as far as he was able, and if we think back to the obstacles he needed to overcome, to the dedication he needed to forge his vocation, we see that this was quite far indeed. As always, Erasmus is the best interpreter of Erasmus: 'I have advanced as far as the shore; am I thought to contradict myself [the Latin *contrarius* better indicates his unwillingness to be part of any faction] if I am reluctant to plunge headlong into waves?' (*CWE* 10: 464). There is a profound cleavage between Erasmus and Luther, between the writer of consciousness and the daemonic, between the man who leads us to the water's edge and then recoils from the deep, and the leader of a people who like Luther escorts us out into the flood.

In subsequent years Erasmus continued his fight with integrity, perhaps not with all the weapons at his command, but with courage and the kind of rational intelligence that out of the contest itself gained new insight. In conclusion I indicate two such arguments that show the continuing resiliency of Erasmus's mind. In a letter from Basel in 1527 – the place and dating are important, as Basel was gradually becoming a Protestant stronghold, thus necessitating Erasmus's later removal to Freiburg, just as in 1521 he had separated himself from Louvain – Erasmus now regrets his earlier advocacy of Christian liberty: 'I am deeply grieved at having preached freedom of the spirit in earlier writing.' Luther had already anticipated this recantation in his response to *On the Freedom of the Will*. But from experience itself, Erasmus's arguments acquire a new density and texture (however present or implied they may have been in his earlier work). Where before, he had argued, it was permissible under certain conditions to forego compliance with man-made ordinances, now in the full fury of the Protestant onslaught, such refusals have become obligatory. He goes on, 'Now what kind of freedom is this: not to be able to say prayers, or to offer sacrifice, or to fast, or to abstain from meat?' (*Selected Letters* 204). In our development of his argument, he is saying that freedom involves a tension between opportunity and constraint: if constraint is removed, one does not arrive at freedom but at an absence of discretionary power. One arrives at a new kind of obligation, where one is required not to do certain things, and this can represent an equally great obstacle to Christian liberty. A new kind of requirement has intervened, the requirement of adversarial denial.

In January 1525, Erasmus wrote an advisory letter to the Council of Basel concerning three topics: censorship, the eating of meat, and the marriage of priests. In the first he develops a thought that had been gaining ground with him, and although implied in his earlier reservations, now acquires through the heat of debate and added experience a new argumentative force. Where good will is absent, or the spirit of benevolence, all restrictions, even the smallest, are bound to be thought oppressive. In this he hits upon what many perceive to be a fatal flaw in the 'protestant' consciousness, one responsible for its splintering effects, and that is a certain relentlessness in change.

> Human affairs will never be in such a happy condition that one will not have to overlook many things, no matter what changes are made. At present some people are displeased by everything – clerical garb, sacred chant, bells, images, the tonsure, anointings, regulations, ceremonies, even the sacramental rites and laws.

He then goes on to the crucial sentence: 'And there is no end to this; there is always something to replace the old complaint' (*Selected Letters* 185). A culture of complaint believes that history is symmetrical, that all complaints are equally justified because validation is enshrined in the spirit of protest itself. Erasmus argues that this culture never arrives at equilibrium, with a capacity to distinguish true grievances from petty ones. What Erasmus failed to realize and what Luther exemplified is that at certain moments it is possible to inaugurate great change while keeping a sense of balance. Many of the articles of change that Erasmus itemizes were ones that Luther also deplored, either as coming too quickly or as being ill-advised. But when it concerns the legitimacy of all the sacraments, there he drew a line. In short, Erasmus's arguments of equilibrium do not constitute any basis for historical change, even where there is a dire, justly determined, and widely supported need.

This brings us to the futile and revealing question as to who – Erasmus or Luther – was the more modern. It is futile because interpretations of what is 'modern' alter from epoch to epoch (recall that it was the scholastic theologians of the early sixteenth century who considered themselves modern and by their light Erasmus and Luther, walking in the steps of the ancients, were antiquarians). In later days of ecumenicism, Erasmus's star shines more brightly, but in times of radical theology, of hostility toward bourgeois humanism, Luther recovers his appeal. The question is also self-flattering, even presumptuous, yielding to the assumption that to be more modern is an unadulterated advantage. But the question is also revealing because it shows that each was modern and their debate was ongoing long after their deaths. They had entered into a contest over the future, and each turned a different face to the prospects of change in the Christian West. For the irenic premises of the Enlightenment, with the strong dose of scepticism and historical rationality, the thought and wit of Erasmus served as the new intellectual plateau. But can we at all understand the bases of the American Revolution without reference to the radical Protestantism initiated by Luther (not forgetting the phalanx of alliance with the second generation of Reformers, Calvin, and his followers)? I shall present a specific transfer of this moment in the works of Rousseau, but I can also turn to a line from the fourth stanza of the unofficial American anthem, 'The Battle Hymn of the Republic,' where the transposition is complete and unambiguous: 'As he [Christ] died to make men holy, let us die that all be free.' The enduring influence of Luther may be further grasped in the simple response of Carlos Fuentes, no stranger to dualisms, who, when asked to account for the differences between Mexico and the United States of America, replied with a single name: 'Martin Luther.' There will always be advocates for each, indicating that in exploring this premier dualism we are reaching down into an active polarity and tension within Western culture itself, the abiding quality of which is manifest in the other great pairs of this study. In the mid-eighteenth century, where the rumblings of other changes were beginning to be heard, the same emotive and intellectual positions that mutatis mutandis characterized the debate between Luther and Erasmus will once again be paramount in the epochal encounter between Voltaire and Rousseau.

2 Voltaire and Rousseau: Never a Peace

1. Three Phases

At long last in a famous letter of 1760, Rousseau found the means to unburden himself directly of his hostility towards Voltaire.[1] 'I do not like you at all,' he writes. 'In short, I hate you.' Such outspoken clarity does not come overnight. In fact, in Rousseau's case it came as the result of nearly thirty years of complex emotional involvement with the great figure of Voltaire, at one time his mentor in so many ways. While Theodore Besterman, among the most esteemed and creditable Voltaire scholars of the twentieth century, can claim that Rousseau's letter is the expression of someone who is 'mad' and on the 'edge of mental collapse' and that it defies comment, this indicates only that advocates are not made for dualisms (Besterman 415).[2] Far from defying comment, Rousseau's letter invites study. This is the nature of true dualisms: the story inheres in the unfolding relationship, in the encounters along a very tangled pathway. But even this does not suffice for the chemistry of their drama. In 1778 Voltaire was brought back to Paris, exulting one last time in the city of his greatest triumphs. He was, however, brought home to die. He did so on 30 May. Rousseau was noticeably shaken by the news. When surprise was expressed at his reaction, he explained some of the private feeling at the roots of any great dualism: 'C'est que mon existence était attachée à la sienne.' And that attachment meant that he too, ailing, would not tarry to follow in death the great man with whose life his own was so inextricably bound: 'Il est mort; je ne tarderai pas à le suivre' (Trousson, *Rousseau* 295). And he did succumb within five weeks, thus compounding the dualism, as their future centenaries were thus fortuitously celebrated together. Ceremoniously in death they were obliged to face each other.

From the first – and to the end – Voltaire remained for Rousseau the great playwright, whose *Alzire*, with its high display of virtue and moral sentiment in 1737, sent Rousseau into paroxysms of tears, and whose *Lettres philosophiques* (Letters on England) served as both model and inspiration for Rousseau's lifelong dedication to intellectual endeavour at the most uncompromising level (*Les confessions* 214/*The Confessions* 205).[3] What is laudable is that Rousseau never revoked his early estimation of these contributions. In fact, they tragically form the highwater mark from which Voltaire seems to have receded, the pristine bases in comparison with which the later Voltaire can know only decline. As von Hutten did with the fallen-away reputation of Erasmus, so Rousseau will bemoan the 'abdication' of his one-time leader.

Yet the storylines of the two dualisms differ. Whatever their private reservations, both Erasmus and Luther took great pains to avoid a public breach. Letters back and forth and even emissaries tried to emphasize their common ground and joint interests. This was because each, as well as his colleagues, recognized the earth-shaking consequences of the issues at stake: nothing less than the peace and unity of Christendom. Overt rupture was necessarily and willingly deferred by both parties until their separate ways became too visible and the strong compulsions from both sides became intolerable, at which point the rope that had been pulled too tightly snapped. While both Voltaire and Rousseau sensed with some foreboding the dark clouds on the French horizon, their dispute was not driven by immediate political consequences – that was far off in the future. Rather their differences involved morality, religion, and the nature of the universe, but all based upon personal matters of style, class, faith, and temperament. Their history was not one of a deferred but necessary conflict, but rather one of a long series of provocations and responses, at first covered with politeness and inordinate respect on Rousseau's part, and always with politesse, wit, and then with the cloak of anonymity on Voltaire's part. But everyone knew the issues involved, as Hume's description of the dualism makes plain, and as Coleridge would later confirm, their divisions expressed nothing less than the divided French culture and society of their time.[4]

Rather than moments or episodes, the itinerary of encounter shared by Rousseau and Voltaire may be drawn by three phases. Such phases register the evolution, even in some cases the radical changes of their thought, but always preserve the essential temperamental unity. Phases suggest a developmental constancy in the midst of periodic exchanges. Their thoughts may change but their modes and qualities, their methods and approaches are intimately tied up with their enduring and opposed temperaments. The first phase may be formed around Rousseau's two *Discours*, the tumult they aroused, and Voltaire's reasoned and witty response in a famous letter of 1755. The second phase records Rousseau's growing religious thought and his response to Voltaire's poem on the Lisbon earthquake. Both seem to have undergone considerable change at this point, with Rousseau reasserting his submerged but all-important religious beliefs, and Voltaire, the thoroughbred optimist, discovering the destructiveness of Nature. This phase is completed by what Rousseau considered to be Voltaire's response to his *Lettre à M. de Voltaire sur la Providence* (Letter to Voltaire on Providence), and that was *Candide*. There then follows in rapid succession and accompanying acclaim Rousseau's *Lettre à M. d'Alembert sur son article Genève* (Letter to M. d'Alembert), *Julie, ou La nouvelle Héloïse*, the first European bestseller, *Émile*, and *Le contrat social*. Precipitously and unaccountably, because of the last two works, Rousseau went from being the celebrated author, even cult figure, to being banished under penalty of arrest and to having his books confiscated and burned. Following 1762, during Rousseau's period of exile and persecution, Voltaire persisted in covertly attacking Rousseau. In fact they each resorted to disclosures about the other. But it was Voltaire's revelation among others in *Sentiment des citoyens* (What Citizens Think, 1764) that Rousseau had deposited his five children at a foundlings hospital that stirred Rousseau to his greatest work, *Les confessions*.

Quite obviously the formal nature of the breach coincided with Rousseau's growing fame and fortune. What began as a great differential in age and status achieved what all dualisms attain, and that is parity. An equivalency is established that marks an equality by virtue of difference. Voltaire in the superiority of his self-possession was late coming to such recognition. In fact he remained blinkered to the fact that in the new age he foretold, the reigning intellectual might be this upstart, outlandish Genevan, Jean-Jacques Rousseau. That is, up until 1760 he continued to harbour a patronizing attitude toward Rousseau. But following the letter of 1760, and the adverse effects on Voltaire's own play group caused by the *Letter to M. d'Alembert*, Rousseau succeeded to his regret in arousing what he had desired and that was the great man's attention. Finally he escaped Voltaire's disregard and came within his sights, and to

Voltaire's discredit, the barrage was merciless, as Voltaire kept up his fire throughout Rousseau's great troubles of banishment and exile.

2. Original Affinities

Points of contest reveal the several major intellectual affinities between Voltaire and Rousseau. Both were able and committed abettors of the great project of the *Encyclopédie*. Rousseau, as the resident self-taught musicologist, was a member of the 'first team.' Voltaire, for his part, showed a remarkable capacity to keep up with his younger allies – although he did not think that their massive *Encyclopédie* would bring about much change. As a consequence, his own *Dictionnaire philosophique* was *portatif*, or portable, more of a readily available digest. In addition, both Voltaire and Rousseau were beneficiaries and exponents of that modified scepticism that so typified the starting intellectual position of the Enlightenment.[5] This meant that they were strong opponents of any abstruse reasoning in metaphysics or theology and of any grand systematic thinking. The objects of their inquiry were principles of moral conduct and questions of philosophy or theology that come within the reach of reasonable thinkers (hence their scepticism can be called 'modified').

But their larger alliance is to be found in the enterprise of the Enlightenment, which was not only to continue but actually to bring to completion the religious changes begun by their forefathers in the Reformation. For both Voltaire and Rousseau, however, a double mix was obvious. Voltaire found Calvin, while having an enlightened mind, to be an 'atrocious soul,' and was pleased that no one read Luther, Calvin, or Zwingli anymore (Gouhier, *Rousseau et Voltaire* 110).[6] Rousseau found Calvin distasteful because he was a 'théologien,' which meant that despite his personal greatness he did not take disagreement lightly ('[il] s'indigne qu'on la lui dispute') (Rousseau, *Œuvres complètes* 3: 715). Yet he also saw in Calvin a remarkable political figure and 'founding father.' In each of their cases, both points need to be sustained: some personal revulsion along with intellectual continuation. We do not need to mention Rousseau's roots in Calvinist Geneva, but it is noteworthy that the early Arouets, Voltaire's ancestors, 'were indeed Protestants' (Besterman 215). Moreover when he constructed his temple at Ferney, he was pleased with the inscription, 'Deo erexit Voltaire,' pleased that is that there were no intermediaries (413).

Two works, Voltaire's *Sermon des cinquante* (Sermon for Fifty) and Rousseau's *Lettres écrites de la montagne* (Letters Written from the Mountain), show both their alliance and the reason for the break in the alliance. Each reveals not only enemies in common, but more importantly the status of religion and of Christianity in the developing age of the *philosophes*. And quite incidentally, the two works added practical aggravation to their already severe breach.

The *Sermon* is part of the growing Masonic appeal of the eighteenth century (one that in the forming American colonies also gave birth to another philosophical society, with a secret code and handshake, Phi Beta Kappa). Margaret Jacob argues for the centrality of Freemasonry to the development of European radicalism. While this broader thought did not enlist Voltaire's involvement, and whether he formally belonged to a Masonic lodge is in dispute, still he shared in the larger notion of a brotherhood, a kind of republic of lettered men, of philosophers (Jacob 263, 270).[7] The *Sermon* is a description and example of the regular Sunday meeting of fifty 'personnes' ('instruites, pieuses et raisonnables' – that is, an elite) in a city 'peuplée et commerçante' – important Voltairean additions, that is a well-populated, modern city, committed to commerce (*Mélanges* 251, passim). The meeting begins with a prayer to the universal God of all peoples, followed by a sermon in three parts. It brings to mind nothing so much as Erasmus's *Religious Feast*. A narrow circle of lay intellectuals gather to discuss or hear discussed matters of religious significance, in which a dinner is served, and as a salve to conscience a collection is made for the benefit of the poor. It does not dilute the comparison to say that the differences are equally remarkable. Where Erasmus resorts to allegory to accommodate difficult portions of the Old Testament, and thus in some way preserve integrity of belief for an emerging and secularly minded laity, Voltaire dispenses with that method altogether as he moves through the first two 'points' of the sermon, laying waste to the palpable inconsistencies of the 'Hebrew' text. He does insist on that designation, thus emphasizing its Oriental and sectarian character. Absurdity then produced audacity, as the books of the New Testament do not hesitate to make a God of a man who walked on earth and was crucified. Moreover all of the Gospels contradict one another in facts. Insult is added when believers were obliged to take the body of this newly minted God in a 'pasty,' which progresses through the digestive system. Such jejune literal-minded iconoclasm would be barely tolerable but for Voltaire's wit and skill. He is the master of withering paraphrase; with detailed knowledge of both, he ransacks the Old and the New Testaments for literal absurdities and he rocks the claims of either to be authoritative or appealing. But the air of mischief is rife, too.

Authorship of the *Sermon* he denied, instead attributing it to J.O. de La Mettrie who died in 1751 (this was a necessary tactic, as his Pléiade editors warn, the content of the *Sermon* would have landed the author, if known, in the Bastille, or worse) (1434n1). As Rousseau complains, Voltaire does not reason, he jests. But therein lies the secret of the delight we take in Voltaire's work: we delight in his evident delight. Such wild fun-making cannot help but be an intoxicant: we laugh and smile even where we might believe. But such lively tossing about can also have a reverse effect: because of our willingness to engage in the fun – because of the very allurements of Voltaire's wit – belief may also remain unshaken. Luther insisted that Erasmus can only flout and jest; he cannot confute. That is true, but great wit can induce and, even more, seduce.

But beyond desecration, Voltaire makes restitution, and thus allies himself with Rousseau: his goal is to save religion from the consequences of blind belief, which, once shaken, can result in total disbelief with predictably adverse social consequences. Here, particularly, he is continuing the work of his 'forefathers' in reformation.[8] The fruit of the tree of the Cross has not been edifying. But this 'yoke' was given a shaking and some reform achieved. Our 'pères' removed certain superstitions, such as beliefs in 'transsubstantiation, l'adoration des créatures et des os des morts, la confession auriculaire, les indulgences, les exorcismes, les faux miracles, et les images ridicules' (transubstantiation, the adoration of [saints] and the bones of the dead, aural confessions, indulgences, exorcism, false miracles, and ridiculous images) (269). But how they left the work 'imparfait!' Now the time is ripe to 'achever,' to complete the work, to destroy the idol, of which only a few fingers have been broken. There are large movements underway, Socinianism, a proto-Unitarianism in England, in Germany and in the provinces of France as another indication, all promoting the adoration of a single God of all the people. Here as elsewhere, to which Rousseau will add his voice, he contests in advance the view of the Grand Inquisitor, famously presented by Dostoevsky's Ivan, that the people need mystery. But the people are not so imbecilic. They will accept belief in a 'Dieu unique,' the God of Abraham and of Noah, the God whom the wise philosophers of antiquity addressed, and the same one received by the educated classes ('les lettrés') of China. This preservation of religious belief will have beneficial social consequences, because at the moment, a 'grand nombre d'esprits faibles' witnessing the ridicule under which the current practice of religion suffers, believe in no religion, and hence give themselves over to excess. Voltaire saves a remnant of religious belief as being necessary for social order, but more importantly he fears the dangerous spectre of nihilism, Voltaire's true enemy, and the consequence of the prevalence of false belief (268–70). The cause of his much-noted directness, of his delight in material objects and practical thought is this fear of nihilism that voids the world by means of theory and that yields only a fatalism, or a belief in the eminent disposability of all things.[9]

Several dialectics are at work here. The first is an axis of relationship between blind belief, which, once shaken, transmutes into its opposite, total disbelief, or atheism. People need some kind of 'brake' on their actions; consequently, Voltaire, as Pomeau argues persuasively, is a deist, asserting often his belief in a universal deity. Hence the second dialectic: if nihilism means the ultimate dissolution of all things, then maintaining the faith of a deist restores the validity of the things of this world, human events and humane sentiments. This is more than a simple need for social order; rather it upholds the reality of mind's relationship with things. Idealists get lost in their own ruminations, their own projections onto the world; the mind in order to be fertile needs objects, events that exist outside the human will. This is the ultimate coupling that explains the continuities in Voltaire's superficially changeful beliefs, that brings together both his mundane poems as well as the apparently 'pessimistic' poem on the Lisbon earthquake. It disallows any sense of profound rupture in his intellectual development.

Although dated as early as 1749, Voltaire's *Sermon* was first published in 1762. Rousseau's *Lettres écrites de la montagne* were written between the fall and spring of 1763–4 and come in the midst of the most turbulent period of his life. The smaller city of Geneva was deeply divided by the turmoil produced by Rousseau's 'Profession of Faith,' a prominent insertion in *Émile*, and by sections of the *Social Contract* concerning civil religion.[10] Within some nine days Geneva followed the lead of Paris in burning Rousseau's books and threatening their author with arrest. The procurer-general, Jean-Robert Tronchin, wrote a defence of the city's actions, called *Lettres écrites de la campagne*, to which Rousseau's letters were the appropriate response. Letter 1, in its calm, reasoned, and concessionary account of the dispute, should serve to discredit pathologists in search of his 'paranoia' (*Œuvres complètes* 3: 687). Letters 2 and 3 are masterpieces of intellectual power. In the former he gives the pastors of Geneva lessons in the essence of the Reformation. Where else does the genius of Protestantism lie, he argues, but in the issue that separated it from the Roman persuasion, and that was in the forthright defence of personal freedom of belief (3: 712ff.). He seems to understand his Protestant forefathers perfectly when he maintains, as Luther did, that 'they said that the sense of the Bible being intelligible and clear to everybody in what concerned salvation, each person was deemed competent to judge (juge compétent) matters of doctrine.' This being the case, how can they remain true to their very founding and condemn Rousseau's works without a hearing? This second letter is thus crucial in showing the direct connection between the defence of Christian liberty, derived from the sixteenth century, and the defence of civil liberty in the eighteenth century. This is particularly apposite because in Letter 3 he specifically attacks many of the roots of the faith that inspired his predecessors, particularly the beliefs in revelation and miracle. In this letter he shows the moral rather than the theological dimensions of his thought when he maintains that, even were there no miracles in the Gospels, the meaning and the importance of Jesus would remain valid.

In the Letter 5 he describes the situation of Christian belief that his 'Profession of Faith' in *Émile* addresses. His aim is to assist the clergy of Geneva, who, not being speculative theologians, devoted themselves to the interests of morality and the duties of men and citizens. The circumstances of the work might have foretold some success, because everywhere 'enlightened folk,' even illustrious magistrates, shared his thought. Religion discredited by philosophy had lost its ascendancy over the people. The church did everything to hurt its cause, and the entire edifice of Christian faith was perched ready for ruin. In addition, by sheer exhaustion theological dispute has lost its appeal, and indifference to what were formerly burning issues now reigns. The branches have been pruned, and starting with the bare trunk, the tree of religion is ready to reflourish. Then, as ever the visionary, Rousseau exclaims, 'What more propitious moment to solidly establish universal peace than this one where the suspended animosity of parties leaves everybody ready to listen to reason.'[11]

As with Voltaire, the purpose of a rational religion is to 'serve God, love one's neighbor, and obey the laws of the state' (*Mélange* 253). But there is a major difference, one that will emerge in the *Letter on Providence* addressed to Voltaire, and the coincidental (but published later) 'Profession of Faith.' More than a deist, Rousseau is a theist, one who allows even for the divinity of Christ. But the difference lies even more in the manner of exposition: with all the similarities of their religious origins and even their programs of belief, a fervour prevails in Rousseau's expositions – he is intent on 'professions' and later 'confessions' – and adheres to the personal conviction underlying Protestant belief, while Voltaire will maintain his distance, managing even when shaking the tree not quite to show his hand. Satire, Voltaire's forte, is not Rousseau's genre. How wrong William Blake was to join Rousseau with Voltaire in the business of mockery: 'Mock on, mock on, Voltaire, Rousseau.' Rather than the weapons of humorous (and lethal) paraphrase, he resorts to long, detailed reasoning – much of it brilliant, but still exhaustive. In his own way he was an ardent polemicist.

The exchange with the ministers of Geneva had more practical consequences contributing to the already damaged relationship between Voltaire and Rousseau. In Letter 5 Rousseau commits the unpardonable sin – he 'outs' Voltaire, by identifying him as the author of the *Sermon des cinquante*. Clearly, in the accommodating culture of the time – and it was most pleasurably that – anonymity or pseudo-anonymity established deniability. This was a practice appealing to authors as to authorities alike. It was a game with a wink, as knowledge was common concerning true authorship (see *Candide*). This was a manoeuvre at which Voltaire excelled, and in which his true gamesome mischievousness was apparent. Rousseau, on the other hand, trusting in the eventual triumph of justice, forthrightly appended his name to his works, adding proudly his birthright, 'citizen of Geneva.'[12] This of course left him open to the attacks and condemnation he suffered. In Letter 5 he asserts that others have written just as seriously in defence of reason and tolerance. Then in a near-perfect imitation he has Voltaire speaking in his own voice defend his method, which by way of pleasantries causes people to reason. Thus dramatized, Voltaire then refers to his own books, including the *Sermon* (799). It is an oblique insertion, but one that is dramatically flagrant nevertheless: Voltaire is identified as the author of the *Sermon*. This was too much. Not only was Rousseau a renegade, but he was now a traitor, even an informer ('délateur') who had 'formellement' declared Voltaire to be the author of a work that could only force the hand of the punishing authorities.

3. The Agonist of His Age

Because the next sections will be devoted to a reassessment of the virtues and qualities of Voltaire, some preliminary attention must be given to Rousseau, to those aspects of his personality that produced such dire contention. Rousseau's world is accusatorial, dramatic; he must establish himself by encounters.[13] The reason for such charged exploits is that he needs to remove from himself those figures who have exiled him from himself. These include the interlopers, the intruders in the temple of learning and of life, who are so lacking in the spirit that they do not even know what questions to ask and thus are unable to understand the answers (to paraphrase the venerable Louis Armstrong). From the very beginning, that breakthrough first *Discours*, his high-mindedness rejects those who fail the muster of election. It is as if he were writing his own Inferno (despite his own abhorrence of theological notions of hell and original sin), and dispatching those souls who hamper him, who cast a shadow over his own best efforts. They are aspects of himself that do not lead him to himself. This means that he lives in a world of dire exclusions, and not in a world of proportionate value. The daemonic writer requires the double, or alternative selves that must be expunged. He writes as a twosome, the notorious 'double optic' of his style.[14] Thus he is in need of conversion. Only this sense of being swept away, of being carried along, beyond his conscious efforts can yield that experience of 'atonement.' And while Rousseau had several such experiences – the famous inspiration on the way to Vincennes in 1749, and then six years later, the calmer spirit that overcame him upon his removal from Paris – one can wonder if in his constant need for self-justification, in the vacillations that came from such moral scrupulousness, he was ever able to arrive at any full equilibrium. His genius does not lie in stasis.

Rousseau was the tragic agonist of his age, with all the pains, trials, and contradictions that his role as first critic of the modern world required. Carrying to the next step Erasmus's complaint that Luther engaged in paradoxes and enigmas, Voltaire was right to exclaim in his *Lettre au Docteur Pansophe* (see below, 178–80), 'Vous êtes un homme inexplicable.' Exactly, and that is because contradiction partook of the role Rousseau assumed; it inheres in all he does. A playgoer who denounces the theatre; a non-dancer who advocates dance. These are but the minor revelations of a larger position. He lives and thrives in the world he denounces. This is the contradiction of his being, what Starobinski refers to as his 'predicament,' the cause of his 'anguish' (Starobinski 42–8).[15] And yet he senses and we sense that he is saying something that is important. Even where he is faulted he cannot be dismissed. Against the advancements of modern culture he is arguing for the lost part. Something has been lost. He senses it in himself, in his own partial truths. And it is this vague sentiment of distress that he will pursue until it yields itself up to great thoughts, great works. Perhaps this is simply a maudlin nostalgia, a recollection of the life he knew from his childhood in Geneva, a sense that there was more to life than was advanced by the *philosophes* – their new philosophy that calls all in doubt, that results only in an adversarial consciousness with little room for the development of positive sentiment and belief. Rousseau is wrong (the Geneva of memory long ceased to exist), perhaps deadly wrong, but he is also right. And that is why his cry is the first cry of an early critic of a modernizing society. He knows something is missing, and from first to last (and with palpable growing success) he tries to identify what that something is: a sense of public happiness, of community, a goal and direction for human society that does not lead to distraction, or worse.

What began as experiences of humiliation and injury was conveyed into stern and eloquent analytical thought that brought him head to head with his erstwhile companions and allies, the *philosophes*. This helps account for the furore of the dualism with Voltaire. The critics are being attacked, and this not from the Right, which could easily be dismissed, but from within their own ranks, from one who shared many of the premises of their thought. Those who were comfortable in attack now found themselves attacked, outflanked by a new opponent who caused some bewilderment. This explains the animosity aroused; a renegade has emerged from within their ranks, who spoke their language, who understood their interests, perhaps all too well. In a momentous encounter, Voltaire and Rousseau, as free-standing intellectuals, meet to contest the future directions of European culture.

Rousseau was a man of intensity, one requiring fullness and dependent upon radical changes and choices (this despite his professed love of peace). His language is evangelical, bespeaking reform, renunciation, and personal transformation. Like other daemonic writers, he writes breakthrough works, works of such challenging power and sensibility that they capture the imagination. As 'career episodes' they open the way to extraordinary development and expansion. As he pursues more deeply the meaning of his agony, the sense of his contradictions, his later works are even more interesting than his first. Normally, the opposed writer of consciousness knows no such changeful evolution and expansion. He hits his stride earlier and in the security of his ego holds to a constant frame and focus; there is widening circle around a nucleus of interest but no radical alterations. This is not quite the case with Voltaire, who miraculously enough, after the age of sixty, became more aroused and defiant. Yet this does not alter the dynamic differences in the encounters of the two types, nor in their readerly receptions. The daemonic writer such as Rousseau engages us in his arguments because they express the struggles of the psyche and of the self. Rousseau, although he lived and participated in the age of the dawning secular, still carried within himself the dynamics of a personal religious struggle. As Starobinski points out, Rousseau, who even as a child thought himself a 'preacher,' communicates the energy of accusation, challenging people to discard the Pharisee within, thus creating a sense of guilt and existential uneasiness (43). Not knowing himself that kind of ego-security, the capacity to bridge and contain contradictions by means of the plastic resources of the self, the daemonic writer appeals because he is willing to enter unknown territory. For instance, Rousseau, the autodidact, challenged the reigning specialists in all areas of knowledge, music, education, ethnology, philosophy, and theology. His was the new first word. This means he opened himself to experiences he did not know existed, thus writing beyond his conscious intent. Such qualities help account for the daemonic writers' endurance, explaining why they enjoy such fuller engagement in the future. For instance, the editors of the important journal of issues, *Daedalus*, at first thought to devote a volume to Voltaire and Rousseau, but as Stephen R. Grabaurd explains in his preface, that project was abandoned because Voltaire was 'principally a historical figure,' while Rousseau 'anticipated an agenda of moral, political, social and aesthetic concerns that remains preoccupying for those today' (v). Thus the remarkable volume of spring 1978 (one that might have jointly celebrated the centenary of the deaths of Voltaire and Rousseau) became 'Rousseau in Our Time.' Fortunately, throughout Europe valuable colloquia were held, which, not excluding Voltaire, contributed greatly to our understanding of each.[16]

4. Voltaire: From Mundanity to Cultural Greatness

In the introduction to his edition of Voltaire's *Le siècle de Louis XIV,* René Groos regrets that Voltaire is largely unread except for *Candide* (1: v). Not only are some of his other major works not read, unless by specialists, they are not even known: the works of high aspiration, his tragedies that made him more than the designated heir to Corneille and Racine, in fact, their rival; his poignant and still readable epic, *La Henriade;* his *Lettres philosophiques*; his lengthy discourses in verse (such as *Le mondain,* and its *Défense, Le poème sur le désastre de Lisbon*), his address to the Académie française on the occasion of his installation, his later *Lettre au Docteur Pansophe* (which, despite his persistent and usual disclaimers, could only have been written by Voltaire), and the over-arching *Siècle de*

Louis XIV, a masterpiece of historiography. Reasons for restoring these works are many (beyond the possibility that the voice of history may be the voice of idiocy, preserving facile works while expelling works of merit). Not only do these and such-like works help us partially recover the pre-eminence of Voltaire in his time, they help preserve his permanence. They reveal other larger qualities of Voltaire, some of which have been obscured by the dominance of *Candide*. As such, they show the bases for genuine affiliations with Erasmus (whom Voltaire adored, linking him appropriately with Lucian and Rabelais). And finally, it is by the resuscitation of such works that we come to understand the forces intellectual and biographical in the contest between Voltaire and Rousseau, understand them in their length and in their depth, how Rousseau 'explicitly' was responding to Voltaire not only in his *Letter on Providence*, but earlier in the first *Discours*, how, to borrow Henri Gouhier's valuable image, Voltaire became the constant mirror in Rousseau's mind through which he saw himself and against which he fashioned himself (*Rousseau et Voltaire* 45).

These same works also present a fuller picture of Voltaire, one going beyond that fostered by Rousseau, for whom Voltaire was a failed leader who had succumbed to the belittling common tendencies of his epoch. In order to restore that early Voltaire, Rousseau in his first *Discours* calls out to Voltaire (now significantly referred to by his family name, presumably more authentic, Arouet and not by his adopted name) as one of the first victims of the triumph of sociability and polite letters: 'Tell us, famed Arouet, how many manly and strong beauties you have sacrificed to our false delicacy, and how many great things the spirit of gallantry that is so prolific in small things has cost you?'[17] Such direct address, the only contemporary so named in the work, shows a marked departure for Rousseau; he is beginning to gain some cognizance of himself and he does so by marking his intellectual distance from Voltaire.

This is not a casual intrusion: Rousseau is using Voltaire's own principles against Voltaire. Both Voltaire himself and his Italian colleague, Algarotti, whose letters in Italian and in French form prefaces to *La mort de Cesar*, are clear that Voltaire is writing with a renewed and 'male' energy, focusing on larger public issues with great individuals and without the amatory interests that were in vogue. Voltaire's plays are intended to instil pity and fear, and imitating Shakespeare, share the English dramatist's seriousness without his ferocity and blood.[18] In fact, in another instance of using Voltaire against himself, in the offending *Letter to d'Alembert*, Rousseau would admit into Geneva plays of the sort that Voltaire wrote in the 1730s, *La mort de Cesar* and the first act of *Brutus* (*Lettre à M. d'Alembert sur son article Genève* 227).[19]

Quite obviously for Rousseau there are several Voltaires: the early and the late, the one he was bound to revere as intellectual leader, one whose own outspoken ways led to many run-ins with authorities, but one who has since abdicated. This study will credit the more persistent and enduring qualities of Voltaire. Like Erasmus he pursued his intellectual and artistic endeavours within notable constraints, yet within such constraints he was also a figure for change, albeit one of modulation and balance. This essential intellectual quality emerged early, and is even present in those works that Rousseau attempted to resurrect, works that one could call the direct product of Voltaire's two-year residence in England (1726–8). As was the case with Erasmus, Voltaire's contact with England was staggering. We are reminded that the writers of consciousness have been almost uniformly anglophile, while the daemonic writer is in varying degrees anglophobe (from Luther and Dostoevsky to Sartre, even eventually including Rousseau).

The cause of his removal from France may have been just as critical in his intellectual development as what it was found in England. Voltaire was something of a bourgeois-gentilhomme. He never relinquished his bourgeois origins, particularly in his appreciation for industry and commerce (so present in *Le siècle de Louis XIV*, his *Mondain* poems, and in *Idées républicaines*). But his pretensions (if that is what they were) to have penetrated the aristocracy by virtue of his wit, brilliance, and artistic success received a shock when he became engaged in a quarrel with the chevalier Gui Auguste de Rohan-Chabot. Insults were exchanged over lineage. When Voltaire was dining with the duc de Sully, he was 'called out' by Rohan, who directed some of his servants to administer a thrashing to Voltaire. Outraged, Voltaire found his way back to the duke, only to discover this nobleman unwilling to take the side of a bourgeois against a fellow aristocrat: the despotic binding of class prevailed against an obvious injustice, and the lesson was seared in Voltaire's mind. When Voltaire sought to avenge his honour by a duel, he was instead placed in the Bastille (for the second time) for daring to engage a chevalier. After his brief period of imprisonment, the authorities accepted Voltaire's offer to remove himself to England (Besterman 113–16).[20] This was more than a fortunate fall; as with Erasmus, it was nothing less than a moment of spiritual discovery. The England of Voltaire's sojourn had flourished in genius and become the England of Shakespeare, Bacon, Milton, Locke, and Newton (who died when Voltaire was in England in

1727), just to mention the most prominent, and while he was there, Swift published his *Gulliver's Travels* and Pope his *Dunciad*.

Voltaire thus became an anglophile the remainder of his life; but more than that he became the great spokesman on behalf of English culture and English liberties, the prime representative of a new literary cosmopolitanism and the defender of the widespread solidarity of a 'république littéraire.' But the fact is, given who he was, given his capacity for discernment and the exercise of critical judgment, he remained a Frenchman. That is, while admiring Shakespeare and Milton (he credits himself with some accuracy as being the one who introduced Shakespeare to France) he was well aware of their presumed defects, and of the need to retain the virtues of the French language and French style while incorporating some of the literary qualities of these English masters. That is, he remained what he always was, and that is a man of balanced judgment.[21]

Nevertheless the effect was staggering. He returned to France with a new sense of what constituted great drama, one that featured spectacle, 'grands sentiments,' and large political and philosophical issues. In this new course he went against the reigning influence of amatory interest, which, like Rousseau, he found 'effeminate.' But Voltaire did not take over English qualities wholesale. He still found Shakespeare (and Milton) defective and irregular; he was still the heir of Corneille and Racine. Consequently, he argues for the retention of *vers rimés* as being essential to the traditions and the genius of the French language and theatre. He continues to hold – with very good reason – to the unities of time, place, and above all action. The primary virtue of the last is that it simplifies and concentrates the unfolding of a grim fatalism, directing all events toward an unavoidable and overwhelming conclusion. Just as the action must avoid distraction and over-abundance, so too language must be simple and pure, without the excesses of Shakespearean imagery. Even here he does not exclude the interests of love – up until that time deemed the primary concern of the French theatre – provided that they contributed to dramatic tension and were part of the unfolding fatalism of the play. His essential capacity for selective judgment is most apparent here. 'To want to have love in all tragedies seems to me to be an effeminate taste, but to proscribe it entirely is an instance of a bad humor that is very unreasonable.'[22] The sentence itself is balanced in its clauses, and the main virtue lies in the selectivity of reasonableness that does not fall victim to any insistent or fixed 'humeur.'

Not only on aesthetic grounds, but philosophically, politically, this same virtue of discerning intelligence that is not hostage to any one way, that recognizes certain historical realities is clearly present in the two plays *Brutus* and *La mort de Cesar* that Rousseau valued but egregiously misread. As a true dramatist Voltaire displayed the tensions of ideas in conflict. In *Brutus*, Messala, the conspiring friend of Titus, Brutus's son and Rome's champion, argues persuasively for the possibility of an enlightened monarchy.

> Ce pouvoir souverain, que j'ai vu tour à tour
> Attirer de ce peuple et la haine et l'amour
> Qu'on craint en des États, et qu'ailleurs on désire,
> Est des gouvernements le meilleur ou le pire
> Affreux sous un tyran, divin sous un bon roi. (3.7.319–23)

> (Such sovereign power, which I have seen in turns either loved or hated by the people, which one fears in [great] States, but elsewhere one desires, can be either the best or the worst of governments, frightful under a tyrant but under a good king divine.)

One remarks that a king is divine not by right, but by goodness. But Rousseau responded to the first act, where Junius Brutus reminds his fellow Roman citizens of the high republican courage with which they chased the Tarquins out of Rome – sentiments that account for the enormous revival that the play enjoyed in the early days of the Revolution. Yet the play seems to favour the transcendence of ideology. Voltaire's dramatic goal is to touch the human heart, to create pity and fear, and this he does when Brutus in a moment of terror is compelled to sentence his own son to death.

An even greater play is *La mort de César*. While *Brutus* calls upon filicide, *La mort de César* invokes patricide (exploiting as its dramatic premise the myth that Brutus was actually Caesar's son). With writers of consciousness we are loath to enter into any probings of depth psychology; they themselves seem to promote such disinclination. As Besterman himself tells us, Voltaire was the least self-analytical of men, and even his 'autobiography,' bare bones as it is, is written in the third person (Besterman 621–80).[23] But patricide does appear extensively through his works and is crucial in his life. He did not bear much affection for his ill-tempered father (although he may have garnered some of his own irascibility from that source as well as his financial talents). In fact, he quite willingly let it be known that he was not the son of Arouet, but rather the product of a love-liaison between his mother and the duke de Roche-brune, a minor poet and librettist. He committed a further act of patricide when he changed his name to 'de Voltaire' – although the reason may have been to give greater expression to the sprightliness of his nature.[24] As a 'modern' he takes a knife to the supposed supremacy of past cultures. One does not beat up on one's nanny, but that does not mean one does not have the instinct to kill off one's father – even if it is not realized. The theme of patricide in Voltaire however only complies with half the requirements of myths of personal consciousness: it is extensive, but it is not intensive. It is not a pressing psychological concern for Voltaire. The real theme of *La mort de César* is not parricide and its tensions but rather one much closer to our subject and that is the conflict between a large-hearted, generous great man, able to live in the midst of complexity, and those who adhere to a rigid moral code of high principle.[25]

For example, elsewhere Voltaire bestows high praise on Cato, 'l'éternel honneur de Rome' (*Les œuvres complètes* 8: 72). But in *La mort de César,* 'Cato's inflexibility of character is presented as less than admirable and even more baleful in the form in which it has been transmitted to Brutus' (8: 72). I quote from the exemplary introduction to the play by J.D. Fletcher. Brutus now becomes an atavistic upholder of republican liberties that seem to have lost their usefulness and succumbs to a sense of justice that closes off his humane response: he is 'farouche,' wild, in his commitment. Again quoting Fletcher, '[Brutus] suffers from a serious deficiency of what Voltaire called in the "Discours préliminaire" to *Alzire* (a play roughly contemporaneous with *La mort de César*) "cette humanité qui doit être le premier caractère d'un être pensant"' (8: 73). Cesar, on the other hand, shows that suppleness of intelligence that understands and responds to prevailing conditions. He shows the quality that Voltaire admired in Henri IV, and that is magnanimity, a generosity of spirit. These several qualities appear when Cesar gives the right response to Brutus's arguments in act 3:

> Nos moeurs changent, Brutus; il faut changer nos lois.
> La liberté n'est plus que le droit de se nuire.
> Rome, qui détruit tout, semble enfin se détruire.
> ...
> Enfin depuis Sylla, nos antiques vertus,
> Les lois, Rome, l'État, sont des noms superflus.
> Dans nos temps corrompus, pleins de guerres civiles,

Tu parles comme au temps des Dèces, des Émiles.
Caton t'a trop séduit, mon cher fils, je pévois
Que ta triste vertu perdra l'État et toi. (3.4.184–96)

(The times ['moeurs'] change, Brutus, so must our laws. Our liberty is now
nothing more than the right to harm ourselves. Rome, which laid waste to
all, is now about to destroy itself. Ever since Sulla, our ancient virtues, the
laws, Rome, the State are empty words. In these times of corruption, filled
with civil wars, you speak as if you were back in the times of the Decennie, or
Aemilius. Cato has led you astray ['t'a trop séduit'], my dear son, and I foresee that your unfortunate ['triste'] virtue will mean the end of the State and
of you.)

The historical figure overshadowing all is still the great Henri IV; it
was not his bravery, his military skill, even his acknowledged magnanimity that saved France, but rather his capacity to adapt to the changing
times, and become Catholic, that is, to forgo principle for the sake of a
larger good. This quality is made heroic in Voltaire's early epic poem, *La
Henriade*.[26]

These arguments are crucial for this study because already we see in
Voltaire's thought the groundwork for the later antagonism. Voltaire did
not change; his arguments and sensibility remained constant. His com-
portment relies upon an instinctive humane reaction, a kind of brotherhood, one even more palpable and real than what was to be expressed in
the Masonic ideal of the *Sermon des cinquante*, one that found its direct
expression in his reaction to the Lisbon earthquake and his insistence on
a bond of humanity that all the great theodicies seemed to thwart. It
showed itself in his outrage at the injustices committed against Protestants such as Calas (in which agitation Rousseau, for his own reasons,
declined to take part).[27] The bases of his complaints against Rousseau
are also prefigured here. An insistence on principle violates two necessities of Voltaire's personal code: it may proceed from a rigid moral idealism that does not respond to the changing needs of the time and is thus
willing to place principle above the common bonds of an enlightened
humanity; but even more intimately, Rousseau in breaking ranks with his
former friends will be guilty of fratricide, and this for Voltaire will be a
violation of that humane sentiment that inhabits all great souls.

We should not be surprised at their differences. Voltaire and Rousseau
were of different times and places; in their familial backgrounds and cultural preparations they were already set far apart. Voltaire, born in 1694,

lived the first twenty-one years of his life under the declining reign of
Louis XIV. He was not only called to address the past century and its
monarch, but also to represent it in another age. Most of his early childhood was spent in a very comfortable ten-room apartment on Isle de la
Cité. His father was a state-appointee and member of the high professional class; he also accumulated a fortune in finance. Voltaire attended
the very best lycée, Louis-le-Grand, and later in life always expressed his
gratitude for the instruction he received. The Jesuits were learned and
accommodating, committed to preparing young Catholics for leadership in the modern world. From them he acquired his deep learning in
the Latin classics and, more importantly, an appreciation of great models, expressed with high feeling. One might also add that either he
imbibed or had ingrained a distaste for the rival wing of Catholicism, Jansenism. Most significantly his older brother attended a largely Jansenist
school, Saint-Magloire, and remained an ardent Jansenist throughout
his life. Voltaire had very little to do with his brother, and this is true of all
of the members of our dualisms (save one). This brotherly disaffection
may help explain the fact that Voltaire remained a devoted enemy of Jansenism throughout his life.[28] Jansenism and Jansenists, even including
the great Pascal, whom he admired on a separate account, were the true
bêtes noires whom he combated at every turn (including *Le mondain* and
its *Défense*). While he had enormous reservations about Richelieu and
Mazarin, he praised these steadfast cardinal-ministers for preventing the
Jansenists from converting France into their own kind of Puritan theoc-
racy, and more particularly from shutting down the theatres, as their distant Protestant cousins were able to do in England. One can gauge
against what deeply held concerns he worked, what sensitive nerves
Rousseau touched when he countered with his *Letter to M. d'Alembert*, urging Geneva to preserve its ban against public theatres.

Voltaire's taste for the theatre was developed at his school, where the
Jesuits were constantly putting on masques, interludes, and other entertainments. His own literary gifts were quickly recognized by his teachers,
and such was the status of Louis-le-Grand as a proving ground for young
writers, that Voltaire was also quickly adopted by writers of merit in his
day who groomed him for higher things. These new mentors happened
to be the most brilliant relics of the court of Louis XIV, otherwise
referred to as *libertins*. These wits and wags, many of them clergy, were
most irreverent, quite naturalistic, and hardly withdrawn from the pleasures of life. The high-spirited Arouet (he had not yet adopted the nom
de plume, the *nom d'esprit*, Voltaire) very easily mixed with them. At this

point his careful father made two mistakes that guaranteed his bright son's future development as a free-thinking devotee of pleasure and of the arts. First he removed him to Caen and then to Holland, where the impressionable young man was able to imbibe the advanced doctrines of religious freethinkers. When the exile was permitted to return to Paris, his father made his second mistake: he opened the ways for his son to secure a position as a lawyer with the high civil service. This only confirmed the young Voltaire in his already well-developed determination to become a writer.

There is an even more important habit of mind that we can associate with this period of Voltaire's development, one that brings him into strong contrast with Rousseau, so given to professions and confessions and addresses to himself. Voltaire found it unseemly to write in such a personal way about himself. From the *libertins* he acquired the habit of the witty riposte, the use of wit to master any social situation. This was a matter of manners but also of morals. No matter how awkward, difficult, or painful the situation, the expressions of wit – even when barbed with ridicule – preserved the facades of society and of social form. But one also reasserted and thus retained the supremacy of the self by not succumbing to personal complaint. Even his first exile (1716) and his first *embastillement* (1717) he met with good humour and equanimity. The witty rejoinder reinforced and reclaimed the order of society, unflappable, it reinstated personal control and well-being.

Voltaire was cultivated right out of school, and his first tragedy, *Oedipe*, was an instant success at the Théâtre français. 'Overnight he became what he was to remain for 60 years: the chief ornament of French letters' (Besterman 86).[29] The contrast with Rousseau is unavoidable, who did not write his first *Discours* until he was approaching forty, having drunk of all his humiliations and injuries, and even after he was celebrated, he still came under constant and unrelenting attack.

Voltaire's *Le mondain* has the difficult task of defending in poetic form the welcomed objects of his day, the goods coming from distant places, the high style of living, in fact, worldliness itself, and in so doing, praises this world, his world, the world of the 1730s in France, the product of the financial policies of Colbert from the previous century (*Mélanges* 203). Voltaire is the inveterate modern, so certain he is of himself, of his taste and values, and so suspicious of the supposed superiority of the past – this last assumption one he delights in puncturing in his *Essai sur les moeurs et l'esprit des nations.*

Because of Voltaire's directness and delight, the absence of any feigned abhorrence of modern times and of hypocrisy, despite their topics of daily life, *Le mondain* and its subsequent *Défense* are remarkably successful. Voltaire's poems participate in the over-cooked debate of ancients and moderns, even the revered notion of decline from some past golden age. But these are invoked in such a glancing way, so spliced with the abundance of his jaunty wit, that they do not become issues of dispute. 'Regrettera qui veut le bon vieux temps,' he poem begins, let those who wish regret the good old days, he (Voltaire) is quite happy that Mother Nature, knowing his own preference for elegance and luxury, has landed him in the present, the age of iron, the bottom rung so suitable to his impure ('immonde') heart. Always concerned to debunk Old Testament accounts (as in the *Sermon des cinquante* and elsewhere) Voltaire brings his readers into a realistic view of the Garden of Eden. Rather than a fleeting happy innocence – that is, a moral condition, which its brevity accentuates – Voltaire, looking back from the accomplishments of his day, can depict only the squalor of the first times, the splotched and broken skin, the matted hair, the stench. How could any pleasurable lovemaking occur in such unpleasant physical conditions. Without 'propreté,' without some cleanliness, love becomes only a shameful need: 'l'amour le plus heureux / n'est plus amour: c'est un besoin honteux.' Ever committed to the finer pleasures of life, Voltaire finds no reason to envy the diet of water, grains, and nuts, nor the after-dinner snooze on the hard earth. 'Voila l'état de la pure nature.' An advocate of the refinements of culture and civilization, Voltaire does not reject this simple nature, but rather elevates it by reason of taste and elegance. As with his French predecessors who gave to European culture the codes of courtly love, *l'amour courtoise*, he remains naturalistic, but with a naturalism that is heightened by a significant consciousness of elegant pleasure.

In the second part of the poem he retraces the 'normal' day of a gentleman, starting from his 'pleasure palace' with its paintings of 'doux' Corregio, whose works were noted for their 'sentiment,' of 'savant' Poussin, the sculpture of Bouchardon, and among many other exquisite objects, the Gobelins tapestries (under Louis XIV become a state industry). He goes to rendezvous in his chariot, a veritable house on wheels, a good recreational vehicle with excellent shock absorbers, he hoots at some opera (Voltaire made this less specific, eliminating his jeering at a play, *Jason*, by a noted opponent, Jean-Baptiste Rousseau). Not omitting any of the sensory details, he then dines on the finest cuisine ('Qu'un cuisinier est un mortel divin'). The modern celebrity of the great chef is already on record. This schedule of daily rounds arrives at its climax with a fetching image of the French spirit itself: the effervescence of champagne. This enticing and splendid image holds the poem together:

> Un vin d'Aï, dont la mousse pressée,
> De la bouteille avec force élancée,
> Comme un éclair fait voler le bouchon;
> Il part, on rit, il frappe le plafond.
> De ce vin frais l'écume pétillante
> De nos Français est l'image brillante. (*Mélanges*)

> (A wine of Ain [?], whose bubbling pressure with great force shoots the cork like a bolt from the bottle. It fires and we laugh as it hits the ceiling. The sparkling froth of this fresh wine is the brilliant image of French vivacity.)[30]

And one could add that it is the image of Voltaire himself, who at the time of *Oedipe* changed his name from that of Arouet, to the more genial, high-spirited one, Voltaire, indicating also something that springs and dances in the air (see n24).

We come here to one of Voltaire's more sterling qualities, that felt need for personal authority that manifests itself in the exercise of critical judgment. This defence of worldliness becomes a staunch defence of his time, indeed a defence of Voltaire in his time. One does not need to go in search of imaginary Ithacas, as Fénelon does in his long modernized epic, *Télémaque* (which on other occasions Voltaire praises), or look for the historical sites of the Garden of Eden. The famous closing line 'Le Paradis terrestre est oú je suis' is actually an emendation; in earlier editions he had written, 'Le Paradis terrestre est à Paris.' But the change is warranted because the defence of his time is an act of self-assertion. With all boldness and courage, he is self-assured enough to stand in the midst of history, in the midst of cosmic nothingness and assert that these things of our life are valid. While in *Candide* the vaunt will be considerably trimmed down, the same sense of belonging, of being immersed in the world, however drastically limited, will all the more necessarily persist.

Le mondain is directed against a 'pauvre docteur' who out of some fearfulness is a detractor of his time. This interlocutor is given even more pointed clarification in the *Défense*, a poem that followed within the year when Voltaire, fearing reprisals for the *Mondain*, had taken refuge in Holland (*Mélanges* 207). The newly emerging detractor is a Jansenist ('maître cafard,' 'pieux atrabilaire,' 'faux dévot') who from his pre-sumed and predestined place in paradise will enjoy watching Voltaire suffer in hell. In the meantime this critic enjoys the benefits of the indus-try and ingenuity of his day, the coffee from Arabia, porcelain from China, silver from Bolivia's rich reserves at Potosi. This leads to Voltaire's major argument, which is to show the connection between luxury and the circulation of wealth in a 'great state.' Acknowledging that luxury might lead to the ruin of a small state, for great ones it is the prime motor and indicator of health. These verses, including a lengthy enco-mium of the policies of Colbert, Louis XIV's chief minister, are closely related to *Le siècle de Louis XIV*, particularly chapter 30, where he dis-cusses the 'finances et règlements' of the previous regime.

The magnificence of the reign of Louis XIV, its control of industry, its development of agriculture and shipbuilding, its lavish public expendi-tures including the arts are wrongly seen to have caused the financial ruin of the state; in fact, they enrich the state: 'les dépenses qui encour-agent l'industrie enrichissent l'État' (Groos 2: 95). The human plague adding to the infirmities of nature, that causes the ruination of a king-dom, is war – *Candide* thus exists in anticipation. Luxury means the circu-lation of money and provides the possibility of working people through industry and intelligence to increase income and ascend the social lad-der. This is true in England as it is in France – and one notes beyond the common appeal of deism the importance attributed to economics, industry, and work that unites Voltaire to the England of his day (Ven-turi, *Italy and the Enlightenment* 8, 16–17). The controlling image in the *Défense* is that of waterfalls in a planned garden, where the overflow fills up the surrounding pools and irrigates the land.

> Le riche est né pour beaucoup dépenser
> Le pauvre est fait pour beaucoup amasser
> Dana ces jardin, regardez ces cascades ...
> Voyez ces flots, dont les nappes d'argent
> Vont inonder ce marbre blanchissant;
> Les humbles près s'abreuvent de cette onde;
> Le terre en est plus belle et plus féconde.
> Mais de ces eaux si la source tarit,
> L'herbe est séchée et la fleur se flétrit.
> Ainsi l'on voit en Angleterre, en France,
> Par cent canaux circuler l'abondance
> Le goût du luxe entre dans tous les rangs;

Le pauvre y vit des vanités des grands;
Et le travail, gagé par la mollesse.
S'ouvre à pas lents la route à la richesse. (*Mélanges*)

(The rich are born to spend while the workers are ready to acquire. Look at the cascading waters of these gardens ... See how these waves flood the marble with its silver fringes. The low-lying meadows drink up these waters and the fields are made beautiful and fertile. But should the source of these waters ever dry up, then the grass would wither and the flower fade. Thus one can see in England and in France abundance circulate by a hundred such channels. The taste for luxury works its way through all the ranks: the worker thrives through the vanities of the great and industry, paid for by indolence ['mollesse'], opens the way by slow steps to wealth.)[31]

One could of course call this 'trickle down' economics, but that would not be quite accurate. There is a rising and a falling in the activity of a great state, as the 'vanité' and 'mollesse' of the great contribute to the advancement of the ambitious artisans. Ever one to heed the processes of a society. Voltaire acknowledges some form of vice to be a force of social equalization.

Le monde comme il va, or Babouc's Vision, forms a natural bridge in Voltaire's development. Perhaps occurring as an idea in the midst of events of 1739, it was not published until 1748 (*Romans et contes* 39–54). Babouc is a mini-Candide, an innocent, but better yet an 'étranger' who is asked to judge from presumed impartiality the ways of an extremely complex and complicated society. That is, he is a moralist. *Le monde comme il va*, the way of the world (the title is a direct translation of William Congreve's play of that name), is the ingénue's introduction into how society functions, or how, in spite of all, it manages to function. Unlike the *Mondain*, the world is not a pleasure fair of enjoyment: battles are horrendous in their bloody costs, justice is bought and sold, women entertain their paramours openly (as do husbands), churchmen are in fiefdom to the grand lama (the pope). In short, corruption and abuse are what first meet the eye. But upon deeper examination, the necessary step of reconsideration, of second thought so essential to the writer of consciousness, Babouc learns that these same wars yielded great bravery, that the scions who occupied purchased judgeships rendered decisions based 'on the lights of reason,' rather than lawyerly briefs, that husbands and wives were affectionate friends, each eager to assist the other. The world is thus a disordered order, with the good and the bad inextricably mixed.

Babouc's advice is to let the world go on its ways, for if 'tout n'est pas bien, tout est passable.' For the salon-wise Voltaire, things, if not good, are still acceptable. I linger over this attractive *conte* for several reasons; its dubious morale could not last long either in Voltaire's canon or in that of the larger French society. The later Voltaire, and this is what is amazing, the Voltaire who would already have passed sixty years of age, no longer yields to the *laissez aller*, but rises up in vehement protest against injustices. Nor would it appear that such equilibrium can long exist in a society at large. Equilibrium is precarious and enjoys only a short life before the tensions it composes break out in renewed fury. Rather than a work of acceptance, *Le monde comme il va* is an unintended work of foreboding and unwitting anticipation of a time when the amenities of society will no longer support its deep-seated disorders.

Obviously Voltaire was a man of many facets, even contradictions, from the bon vivant of the *Mondain* poems, to the frank acceptance if not cynicism of *Le monde comme il va*, to the outburst of moral indignation in his own later years. But he never relinquished his own understanding of where to place what he was doing, that is, he was singularly gifted with the encompassing vision of proportionate value. From this perspective, *Le mondain* and its *Défense* are not deviations, because in Voltaire's estimation they are given only relative standing. Voltaire sent off his manuscript of *Le mondain* in 1736, writing that while Newton is the god to whom he makes his sacrifices, 'j'ai chapelles pour d'autre divinités subalternes. Voici *Le mondain*' (Gouhier, *Rousseau et Voltaire*). He recognizes that mundanity is a virtue, but only a subaltern one. Thus his movement from mundanity to cultural greatness is not a chronological development, diachronic, but rather is synchronic, as each is a coexisting compartment of value. Voltaire's works are marked, even typified, by this same capacity to render judgments according to a loose scale of ascendant value. Unfortunately, historical estimation did not follow this Voltairean prescription, losing sight of the great Voltaire, praised in his first *elogia*, and preserving the satiric Voltaire (see ch. 3, n4 below).

History is the natural space for Voltaire's judgments, where the true greatness of his mind and spirit is shown. *Le siècle de Louis XIV* is a masterpiece, a necessary supplement to the grim tableau offered in *Candide*. It obviously displays the scepticism of a man of the world (the earl of Chesterfield's great praise for the *Siècle*: 'written by a man of parts, for the use of men of parts') (Besterman 331), but also Voltaire's graduated scale of values, his appreciation of genuine accomplishments by individual talents and as represented by illustrious ages, and his melancholy pages, where he places himself and his contemporaries in the aftermath of a superior culture.

Voltaire's scepticism covers not only the natural vicissitudes of things but extends to human imperfections as well. While there are illustrious periods of human history, 'tous les siècles se ressemblent par les méchancetés des hommes' (all centuries are alike in human evil). Even in the great periods, the cultivation of the arts by 'citoyens paisibles' does not prevent princes from being tyrannical, the people from being seditious, and priests and monks from being shifty and underhanded ('remuants et fourbes') (Groos 1: 3). And yet, despite these thoughts, accepted as one would a regular item of trade, Voltaire does not succumb to the vanity of human wishes, which, as in Samuel Johnson's nearly contemporaneous poem, needs to be shored up by religious faith. Despite all of the human liabilities, certain ages have emerged where genuine human accomplishment stands recorded, ages where prince and philosopher, patron and artist, politics and culture have collaborated to fix moments of high attainment. For Voltaire these ages are Periclean Athens (extending to Alexander), the Rome of Caesar and Augustus, the Italy of the Medicis (particularly during the papacy of Leo X), and the century of Louis XIV, which supersedes the others by virtue of having brought to greater perfection the tools of human reason, 'in general' (Groos 1: 3). These periods rise to our attention because they shall either be ignored by Rousseau or be condemned as evidence of the pernicious effects culture has on the moral fibre and physical sinews of a people, undermining the courage and the faith contained in simplicity itself.

In the face of criticism, Voltaire insisted on naming the preceding 'century' after the monarch (although he does allow that it could also have been named 'le siècle des anglais') (2: 108). Although a lesser person than Henri IV, Louis XIV was for Voltaire the generative centre of the grandeur that was France in the second half of the seventeenth century. It was he who moved France to the centre of European war and diplomacy, who made France feared (although Voltaire will always see war as contributing to a country's ruin, and harbour a secret admiration for the republican virtues of the beleaguered Dutch). It was Louis XIV who, through his finance minister Colbert, put luxury into circulation by sponsoring agriculture and shipbuilding as well as other industries, and by constructing superb buildings and monuments paved the way for the ascension of the middle class to wealth. It was he who encouraged the development of French literary genius – most notably Molière and Racine. And it was by the means of his éclat and subventions that France exerted a magnetic attraction for many of the intellectual figures and talents of Europe. In his reign, France became the central power of Europe, his court the most imitated, and the French language the common currency among educated classes, extending to the courts of Prussia and of Russia. Louis XIV displayed grandeur – one of Voltaire's favourite words; he was the ruler whose every move was watched, discussed, and analysed.

If one looks where France was in 1635, where the century begins, and where it was in 1715, at Louis's death, one notices other advances that were most gratifying to the *philosophes*. In a note Voltaire reminds the reader that in 1609, 600 witches were condemned by the *parlement* of Bordeaux alone, and most of them were burned at the stake. One can question the figures, but the observation remains. Under Louis XIV the laws condemning witchcraft on the basis of simple accusation were changed. However great the persons of Henry IV and Louis XIII, under them France was still a backward country. After Louis XIV it was well on its way toward being an enlightened country, an argument taken up by modern commentators such as Venturi and Israel, who note the spreading effects of the new philosophies in their public acceptance (Groos 2: 110).[32]

As an avowed admirer of Colbert, Voltaire was taken with the economic consequences of regal splendour. But as with his relegation of *Le mondain* to a subaltern position, he did not lose sight of true value. All the glittering entertainments of the court amounted to no more than that: pleasures of the eye and the ear, the brilliance that passes quickly: 'ce qui n'est que pompe et magnificence passe en un jour.' But *Tartuffe* is a different story. The king was so enthralled by this masterpiece that he read and had performed the first three acts even before the entire play was finished. Moreover, he protected Molière (as he did Racine) from the 'faux dévots' who invoked hell and tried to move earth to have the play suppressed (1: 371). The great court festivals, when they include such masterpieces, 'laissent une éternelle mémoire.' Full appreciation of such works that remain in the 'eternal memory' are instances of Voltaire's capacity to transcend mundanity.

Whitehead called it the 'century of genius,' and so does Voltaire in his own way. But Voltaire praises advances along a large common front, extending to many disciplines of both science and culture. Despite all the wars and the different religions, there has emerged 'une république littéraire' in Europe. It happened 'insensiblement' with the exchanges of scientific experts and scholars moving from country to country; moreover, many new discoveries were made independently on several fronts – one clear sign of a sweeping intellectual movement (2: 145).[33] Voltaire obviously stresses the great intellectual alliance between the English and the French and the large expansion of knowledge into many quarters of society, only excluding 'le bas peuple.' The century rose in genius but the century also fell. The greater quality of Voltaire's masterwork emerges not only in his broad and detailed studies, in his great praise for the monuments of enduring value, but in the later chapters where he engages in more contemporaneous stock-taking, where he not only sees himself and his cohorts as living in a declined age, but attempts to account in a reasoned way for this falling-off. The *Siècle* achieves its intellectual honesty when Voltaire acknowledges that he is constrained to live in the aftermath of a greater period. This arch-modern admits to belatedness, but we have to understand why and in what measure, because normally he resists arguments of decline. In fact, he argues that so far has the modern philosophy of Locke surpassed the ancients that there is not one ancient philosophy that serves as instruction to the young people 'chez les nations éclairées' (2: 143). This survey of the sciences and the arts in Europe of the time of Louis XIV concludes in chapter 34 with the ringing assertion that, in the past century, enlightenment has surpassed that of all the preceding centuries: 'les hommes ont acquis plus de lumières, d'un bout de l'Europe à l'autre, que dans tous les ages précédents' (2: 146).

However, within limited circumstances and for specific reasons, Voltaire must admit to a decline in the culture of his time. This brings us to an astonishing fact, which is his next major affinity with Rousseau. Not only do they concur that they live in the time of the inheritors, in fact, of epigones, but Voltaire's description of the qualities of the literary culture of his time is the same as Rousseau's. They differ in assessment and in prescriptions for remediation; that is, the very bridges that might bring them together reveal the greater chasms of separation. Nothing could bring Voltaire and Rousseau closer than in their description of the reigning state of letters, yet nothing could show them farther apart. Voltaire evidences that calm spirit of observation, noting conditions, adducing causes; he is a man of his times, accepting his historical assignment. In Rousseau's analysis this same condition is an instance of moral corruption, and of a deep rot that infects the entire system, for which there is no remedy except drastic surgery, but surprisingly he is not always willing to apply it.

Voltaire does not resort to drastic explanations for either the emergence of a great culture or its decline. The attendant figure of any age of genius is decadence. But even that word is to harsh. 'Il ne s'éleva guère de grands génies depuis les beaux jours de ces artistes illustres; et à peu près vers le temps de la mort de Louis XIV, la nature sembla se reposer' (2: 129). Nature seemed to need a rest, a small break in its activities. This charming phrase is accompanied by analysis. He does believe in a certain progress in the arts, which is a long slow process, a 'tardive fécondité.' It takes a long time for the literary arts to develop because it takes time for the language and for taste to be 'purified.' Thus the 'renaissance des lettres' in sixteenth-century France – the period that we value much more highly than did Voltaire – is marked by naivety and serves only as an initial phase of improvement. After the preliminary steps have been taken, the right path blazed, there follows a rapid surge of development, attributable to the spirit of emulation and full public response and recognition. But once a certain level has been attained, the natural subject matter for great works is quickly exhausted. This is true in tragedy and in epic verse: 'Tout a ses bornes' (2: 130). Everything has its limits, and quite quickly high attainments become roadblocks, because notable subjects and language become commonplace, imitated, and overdone. Hence it is that the slowly built fecundity is followed by a 'longue stérilité': 'le génie n'a qu'un siècle, après il faut qu'il dégénère' (2: 136). After a century, at most, of original genius, degeneration sets in. One is then reduced to either imitating or going astray: 'On est réduit ou à imiter, ou à s'égarer.' Here he means great literature, that of Corneille, Racine, Molière, and Boileau. Historiography, because of its new subject matter, does not suffer, nor, oddly enough, does painting, whose subjects may be repeated, 'mais on ne serait pas reçu à traiter *Cinna, Andromaque, l'Art poétique, le Tartuffe*' (2: 131). One is no longer in a position to treat such grand subjects.

That one lives in a derivative culture, that one comes at the end of a great time, that one is 'post-,' is hard to recognize, harder to acknowledge. This must have been even more so for Voltaire, whose tragedies from *Oedipe* to *Alzire* and *Zaire*, won the day in France, and became constant productions of the Théâtre français. A serious consequence of cultural decline is the proliferation of epigones. Imitation is rife, whether knowing or unknowing: 'il est devenu si facile d'écrire des choses médiocres qu'on a été inondé de livres frivoles, et, ce qui est encore pis, de livres sérieux inutiles' (2: 130). Not only do frivolous works flood the market, but even 'serious' works seem to contribute little to the understanding – a certain indication of a culture in decline.

Voltaire, within his realistic acceptance of limits, still finds some compensation and does not reject 'cette littérature légère qui délasse toutes sortes d'esprits' (2: 132). Yet it is this 'recreational' literature that Rousseau excoriates in calling Voltaire back to Arouet in the first *Discours* but it is this literature, with this kind of language that Voltaire now regards as the contribution of French letters to European culture. 'L'esprit de société' is the natural portion of the French genius. And the French language is the perfect instrument to express with 'facilité,' 'netteté,' and 'délicatesse' all the interests of the 'conversation des honnêtes gens.'[34]

The long publication history of the *Siècle* makes it unlikely that Rousseau was responding to these notable chapters in the first *Discours*. But he had other materials to work with, such as the *Mondain* and its *Défense* and Voltaire's efforts to ensure his induction into the Académie française. After being turned down for a chair in 1732 and in 1743, Voltaire decided to apply more assiduous efforts towards his induction; in short he decided to give them what they wanted. It was this kind of activity that offended Rousseau, which he considered to be beneath the high standards established by the earlier Voltaire. Evidently Voltaire thought so himself. His own verse indicates that he undertook the necessary steps only with a minimum of good faith, and with much knowing humour.

> Mon Henri quatre et ma Zaire,
>   Et mon Américaine Alzire
> Ne m'ont valu jamais un seul regard du Roi;
> J'avais mille ennemies avec très peu de gloire.
> Les honneurs et les biens pleuvent sur moi
>   Pour une farce de la foire.

There exists a near-contemporary translation for this verse:

> Alzire, Zaire, Henry writ in vain,
> Not e'en a smile could from our Monarch gain;
> A thousand critics rose to blast my name,
> At last a farce has brought me wealth and fame. (Besterman 285, 640)

Indeed, at long last, because of a farce – presumably *La princesse de Navarre* (see Voltaire's account, Besterman 640) – royal recognition came Voltaire's way: he was named historiographer, which gave him some impetus toward completing *Le siècle*, Gentleman in Ordinary of the King's Chamber, and finally in 1746 admitted to the Académie française.

Voltaire, with his mobility of genius, may have adopted a mask to gain acceptance into the Académie, but his inaugural address is remarkable, nonetheless. As a man who respected the protocols of institutional authority and decorum, he begins by praising the man who founded the Académie (Cardinal Richelieu) and by honouring the deceased predecessor whose chair he is to occupy. But, as he himself tells us, the importance of the discourse lies in the ways he deviated from etiquette and made use of the opportunity to address his larger interests in the nature of the French literary language of his day (his innovative efforts were imitated by those who followed him).[35]

Voltaire examines the emergence of the French language in the preceding century. Clarifying notions already expressed, he observes that it was only with Corneille and the French theatre that their culture began to reach its heights. The arrival of French literature coincides with France's political expansion: 'c'est Corneille seul qui commença à faire respecter notre langue des étrangers, précisément dans le temps que le cardinal Richelieu commençait à faire respecter la couronne' (*Mélanges* 245).[36] Culture and politics came of age together, when what Corneille did for the language, Richelieu did for the crown: they earned the respect of foreign nations, which for Voltaire is always the mark of distinction. But Corneille only initiated the great advance; he was surpassed by Racine, who never declaimed, but spoke to the heart with greater truth and charm: 'jamais déclamateur, parlant au coeur avec plus de vérité et plus de charme' (245). Voltaire's great passion and his skill are shown in such masterful pages of historical survey. Under the guidance of a master poet and a discerning and judicious critical mind, these and all his other pages of historical survey are a constant delight to read and ponder.

Voltaire was capable of writing so broadly, so sympathetically, and with such modulated but clear understanding because he feels himself one with history. He himself has an unshakeable sense of being part of what he describes. Unlike Erasmus, who subordinates himself, Voltaire feels himself naturally allied with all those who are part of the grand republic of arts and letters. This is the broader sodality beyond the quasi-Masonic ideal of *Sermon des cinquante*. This is why he has no difficulty in soliciting admission to the Académie française, and therewith elevating its form of address. He so values the enterprise of learning that all those committed to knowledge – whatever their shortcomings – belong to a group, are part of a pre-existing spiritual academy, that heralded 'république littéraire.' Unlike Rousseau, he possessed this larger notion of collegiality and of being a participant in a notable endeavour. It is around such differences that the dualism of Voltaire and Rousseau begins to turn.

5. Rousseau's Breakthrough: The First *Discours*

Rousseau's prize-winning response to the question posed by the Academy of Dijon – whether the re-establishment of the arts and sciences has contributed to the purification of morals – has all the markings of a breakthrough work.[37] In 1749–50 it brought to the surface Rousseau's long-submerged and long-suffering talents and made him an author of note. It laid down the lines and the future directions of an extraordinary explosion of creativity that would last through 1762 and beyond. As with other such works, its author emphasizes its inadvertence, its quality of unsought inspiration. Despite the fact that it opened the way for all that followed, Rousseau will later tend to discount it, acknowledging its somewhat jumbled arguments. Nevertheless it met with an instant success, one that was unforeseen and unforeseeable – abundant testimony to the fact that at mid-century the tastes and needs of the educated French reading public were undergoing great changes. As Luther would ask, why this and why not other theses? Yet the very challenging nature of the arguments made their author a contested figure, one constantly obliged to answer outraged attacks. Because of this work Rousseau emerged from relative obscurity and became a figure of history. Unfortunately it meant he became something of a lightning rod, drawing all the simple-minded epithets and insults from the Left and the Right, as Raymond Trousson has so admirably shown in *Rousseau et sa fortune littéraire*. The title page indicates Rousseau's own awareness that the nature of his arguments will be given to much misunderstanding: 'Barbarus hic ego sum quia non intelligor illis.' He himself quite consciously underlines the challenging nature of his own enterprise: he is a barbarian here because they do not understand him. But he certainly could not have understood how far into the future the dispute would extend. He would become not the subject of understanding but an instrument, an appendage of partisanship, a pretext, and a target. It was not until the early twentieth century, with the establishment of the Société Jean-Jacques Rousseau, and its resultant scholarly *Annales* that a fuller understanding of Rousseau became possible (Trousson, *Rousseau* 114). He was not taken *hors de combat,* but the engagement emerged from a fuller understanding of who he was and what he wrote. The prayers attending his ill-fated *Dialogues* were answered better than he could have foreseen.

The first *Discours* is the key to the beginning but not to the completion of Rousseau's thought. For this we have to turn to the *Letter on Providence*, to the 'Profession of Faith' of the Savoyard vicar, and to the strangely tandem works *Émile* and *The Confessions*. They indeed take their origins from the first *Discours*, whose arguments will be repeated consistently, but in their development go well beyond the earlier work. This tells us that Rousseau's thought underwent great changes: the first *Discours* was only the beginning of a series of radical departures. As we, following Cassirer, search for the unity of Rousseau's work, we find it not in his developing thought, but rather in his temperament, that abiding and enduring element that finds unity in radical change. So it must be with this tumultuous soul, with his hypercritical moral consciousness, which is constantly in need of justification. Even the first *Discours* is more than a product of inspiration. In fact, it approaches the nature of a conversion, as Rousseau must begin to settle accounts both with his world and with himself. He is the Rousseau of Geneva, the citizen of a republic; his personal honour and that of those whom he represents now require bold and forthright statement, a coming out from under, a manifest declaration of who he is and what he represents. Other people may have made similar arguments, but only Rousseau made the charge so personal and so challenging.

As Henri Gouhier has amply shown, the figure of contention in the first *Discours* is Voltaire, and not only the Voltaire of the *Mondain* and its *Défense* – the proponent of luxury and opulence – but more broadly the Voltaire who praises the great coincidence of art and culture, who accepts the necessary gradations of proportionate value, who complied with the rituals necessary for induction into the Académie française, who accepts compromise and is willing to live amidst contradiction, and who finally comes to terms with the afterglow of French culture, the genius of which lay in sociability and in the pleasing arts of polite conversation (Gouhier, *Rousseau et Voltaire* 33–5, 40, 44–5). This larger figure of Voltaire needed to be drawn because it is this one in whom ego-security yields to facility that is most at odds with the ardent demands of Rousseau.

Up to a certain point, but only up to that point, Voltaire and Rousseau have a similar understanding of the nature of their times. In fact, like Voltaire Rousseau regards such sociability as the logical development of French culture since the Renaissance, which by a 'revolution' that restored 'common sense' saved Europe from the 'scientific jargon' of the scholastics, a 'learning' that was worse than ignorance. The 'renaissance des lettres' preceded that of thought, and this second stage was followed by the triumph of 'politesse.' By such gradations, 'the major advantage of commerce with the muses began to be felt, namely of rendering men more sociable by inspiring in them the desire to please one another with works worthy of their mutual approbation' (Gourevitch 6; 3: 6).[38] Indeed the great triumph of the French nation is this amiable politeness and cultivated manners, by which 'our century and our Nation shall surpass all times and all Peoples' (7; 3: 7).[39] But where Voltaire accepts this historical reality with reasoned justification and even some praise, Rousseau attacks. He describes it as a stage of degradation leading to moral decadence. Deploying one of his characteristic triple plays, he interjects a third leg by moving from art and thought to politesse to dissimulation. This is at once the trickiest of his manoeuvres and the most intriguing – the one to which his contemporaries will most respond. Not quite logical, his argument is still insightful; with the sensitivity of a novelist he leaps over strict causality. The intellectual structure is shaky, but the tone, the charge is resounding. He is not addressing individuals but the times and announcing that an entirely new culture is needed. People are living their lives all wrong. A false superficiality prevails without any expression of the true emotional needs of humanity.

Not only does Rousseau denounce the falsity of manners, he also attacks the conformity required. Masks of righteousness are gotten wholesale. In his thought other-directedness converges with mid-cult. The art of pleasing has been reduced to principles, with the consequence that 'a vile and deceiving uniformity prevails in our morals, and all minds seem to have been cast in the same mould; constantly politeness demands, propriety commands; constantly one follows custom, never one's own genius' (8; 3: 8).[40] Since everyone knows the right thing to think or to say, whether he actually knows it or means it, there is a mass of right-thinking individuals, who, separated from their slogans, would be incapable of reconstructing the substance of their thought. The real enemy of Rousseau is this social correctness. People who would have been members of the infamous *Ligue* in the sixteenth century are now all turned right-thinking *philosophes* (or put another way, people who worked for Goldwater in the 1960s are now turned multiculturalists).

Conformity rankles, but there is an even greater enemy, one that reveals the morale of this hard-headed Calvinist of sentiment. This is the facility of learning. With 'compilations' – what we would call handbooks or anthologies – it has all been made too easy. Rousseau, the autodidact, is arguing for strenuous self-effort, but more than that he is arguing against all the interlopers who have come into the temple of learning, the intruders in the arcanum. The 'compilateurs' have broken open the doors of learning 'and introduced into their sanctuary a populace unworthy of coming near it' (26; 3: 29). With culture made easy, people without a gift or a calling are lured away from the simpler trades that might have been their better vocations. While this might indicate that the notoriously democratic Rousseau is a cultural elitist (which he adamantly was), the two positions are not exclusive. It is not undemocratic to lament people pursuing careers for which they have no talent. The popularization of culture means that someone who would be a first-rate clothier (that is, a skilled artisan) is a bad versifier or worse geometrician. There is in nature a kind of destiny, and hence great men like Bacon, Descartes, and Newton had no need of mentors. It is only to a small number, those capable of following in the footsteps of these giants, to whom 'it belongs ... to raise monuments to the glory of the human mind' (27; 3: 29). He is not arguing against culture and true learning but rather against its misapplication; the lack of true self-assessment is the cultural malaise of the times.

But there is another argument: the mass inundation of popularized culture blocks the way to true merit. And here Rousseau's own driving needs for recognition emerge. The corruption of taste means that if some hardy souls refuse to submit to the demands of their times 'and to debase themselves by puerile productions,' too bad for them (20; 3: 21). He adds, would this statement were a prediction and not a report of fact. It is from Rousseau, from the unleashing of his deepest personal needs for acknowledgment of his talents that the first *Discours* emerges. This is why Henri Gouhier is correct in asserting that it represents something of a 'conversion' beyond inspiration. While the larger issue is societal, the plea is personal; the first *Discours* represents a self-encounter, an 'autoportrait,' as discovered through the mirror of Voltaire (*Rousseau et Voltaire* 44–5).

Two aspects of Rousseau's spiritual quest begin to emerge that will loom large in Voltaire's complaints against him. One is this need for self-discovery, or singularity, and the other is Rousseau's reliance on inspiration, the response to Spirit. It is for this reason that we can now return to the crucial event that preceded the first *Discours*, the famous episode on the way to visit Diderot imprisoned at Vincennes (jailed for his *Lettre sur les aveugles*). Walking the several miles from Paris to Vincennes, Rousseau happened to come across the announcement of a competition offered by the Academy of Dijon concerning the question whether the re-establishment of the sciences and the arts has purified morals. This incident was made famous by Rousseau's several accounts of it, in book 8 of *The*

Confessions, in his letters to Malesherbes, and in the second dialogue of *Rousseau juge de Jean-Jacques, dialogues*. While each of the three shows some differences, depending upon the time when they were written, they all share common ideas.

The account in book 8 of *The Confessions*, while later and not as full, is the better-known. Upon coming across the Academy's question, Rousseau tells us, '[Je] vis un autre univers et je devins un autre homme' (*Œuvres complètes* 1: 351). He saw another universe, and he became another man. He arrived at Vincennes in a state of near delirium, having retained from his experience only the final speech of Fabricius that he had composed on the spot. It was a clarifying experience. All of the 'petites passions' to which he had been prey were snuffed out by this fuller revelation of truth, liberty, and virtue. And even more significantly this outburst of creativity was able to sustain itself for four or five years 'at as high a degree as was ever experienced by any human being' (*The Confessions* 326–9; *Œuvres completes* 1: 349–52).[41] As he tells us in the second letter to Malesherbes of January 1762, this inspiration provided the consistent element in his thought, one that unites the first *Discours* with the second and with *Émile*: man is naturally good, and it is only through his social institutions that he becomes bad (*Œuvres completes* 1: 1136). Like many other of his summary sentences, so gripping in their succinctness, this too needs to be interpreted, and even qualified by the fuller context of his thought. But as for the generative value of this episode Rousseau was right on target. He was consumed by his response, he tells us, mulling over sentences even as he slept, and to guard against squandering the ideas that came in the night, as soon as he woke up, he would have his mother-in-law 'milk' him – to use Milton's phrase about the composition of *Paradise Lost*. Rousseau had experienced for the first time the ardour and the full commitment of creativity. Inexplicably the doors that had been closed suddenly opened, and all of his pent-up ideas and experiences came tumbling out.

The much earlier account of this experience in the second letter to Malesherbes is a fuller rendering. He provides important biographical information – his dissatisfaction with his life in society, his futile attempts to deliver himself from his social and intellectual attachments that seemed to prevent him from being himself – all those things that would indicate that his experience if less than a conversion was still in its personal transformations more than an inspiration. Unlike *The Confessions*, this earlier account paints in vivid detail all the physical changes this moment of illumination brought about in him. His mind was 'ébloui' by a thousand lights, by the crowd of ideas that converged. His body was torn by violent palpitations. He lost his breath and was forced to rest under an oak tree, where he hastily composed Fabricius's speech, the only remnant of this extraordinary experience. He was swept up and swept along. Again, he expresses its inadvertence: 'lorsque j'y pensais le moins, je devins auteur presque malgré moi' (*Œuvres complètes* 1: 1135–6). Without thinking about it, without warning, a life that he was avoiding, and yet one that he needed in order to find his own genius, his own guardian spirit, suddenly descended upon him. And yet it was also one that had been slowly building in him.

There was much provocation for the great insights that finally emerged in the first *Discours*. Breakthrough requires a build-up, and here such personal revolution has its source in humiliation and insult. Rousseau was a typical man from the provinces, an outsider, even a foreigner. Voltaire persisted in referring to him as 'demi-gaullois, demi-allemand.' In addition he was an autodidact, with all the over-eagerness and high-sounding pronouncements that put learning on display (no wonder Baron d'Holbach called him, as Rousseau himself tells us in *The Confessions*, book 8, the 'little pedant' [360; 1: 387]). His mind was aflood with ideas, with the net effect that he was never able to produce a good one when on call. Rousseau had no deliberative capacity; the mere thought of being obliged to do something, such as prepare remarks, filled him with such fearful anticipations that he invariably bungled. This is what happened when he was called to appear before the Genevan pastors at the time of his readmission to citizenship and church affiliation. His prepared answers became so jumbled that he was reduced to responding yes or no to their by-then leading questions. And he did not have presence of mind. The fear of failure, or rather the need for perfection, tied him up so that he could not respond when under obligation. One can see why he required inspiration, the force that took him out of himself, because in himself he was condemned to a hyper-self-consciousness. Later he would recognize that he was a man in need of liberty, in need of the freedom to follow his own thoughts as they occurred. Consequently he could not write the occasional piece in which he would be obliged to conform to a certain demand; nor could he pursue the career of writing as a profession. This too would place him under a burden that he could not endure. Thus he made his living as a copyist of music, where his thoughts were free to wander, and he always wrote as he tells us from 'persuasion' and not necessarily from talent.

Socially Rousseau also felt out of sorts. His bungled attempts at wit misfired terribly. This was particularly humiliating in a society that prided itself on its finely tuned phrases, its gambols of wit. Conversation, its pleasures, was the natural literary genre of the French people, as Voltaire tells us. Rousseau's contrast with Voltaire was all too evident: Voltaire never at a loss for words, Voltaire the adopted son of the *beaux esprits* of the court of Louis XIV. Rousseau's own maladroitness made him vulnerable, particularly given his own high vision and his developing awareness of his own gifts. He was a Quixote looking for romanesque adventure, a devotee of Plutarch, of republican liberty and classical virtue, living in the midst of the salon. Better than Quixote, he was something of a Prufrock, except that these biting insults and burns of ego turned into abiding works of literature. His intellectual illumination, which of necessity had to come in a sudden rush, as if beyond consciousness, persuaded him that the fault was not his but instead lay in his situation, that the demands of worldliness were at fault, demands that became matters of social correctness without any hint of substantial thought or genuine conviction. A weed is a flower in the wrong place.

Throughout this work – so difficult to summarize because it is so varied in its resources – Voltaire is a constant figure, explicitly where he is named, but implicitly as well. If Voltaire glorifies the four great cultures where politics and culture seemed to merge, Rousseau not only discounts these moments but also diminishes the very premises for their glorification. Sparta and the Persia he prefers over Athens; the Rome of the Empire was the beginning of the end; Italy under the Medicis experienced political subjugation at the moment of its cultural height. Examples from history abound, he believes, to prove that culture has undermined simple practical virtue, teaching sophisms and futile questioning rather than encouraging bravery and physical endurance, or valuing the simpler virtues of loyalty and love of the homeland. Culture breeds sophistry and sophistry erodes primary obligations.

Where Voltaire (and others) praises the value of luxury and the circulation of money and changes in status that it promotes – those things that are essential for the continuity of any large state – Rousseau attacks luxury as the beginning of corruption; it leads to the perversion of morals and finally to the degeneration of taste – another triple play of dubious causation.

These differences are indeed explicit, but the greatest division between the two occurs more in the larger moralities that they represent. Rousseau speaks from a kind of cultural Protestantism, the Calvinism of the heart. 'What good is it to seek our happiness in someone else's opinion if we can find it within ourselves?' (Gourevitch 27–8; Rousseau, *Œuvres complètes* 3: 30).[42] This voice of rugged independence, or rather this search for same, will be heard throughout his works, linking his Geneva of memory with the Sparta of legend, the artisanal class of the Geneva he remembered with the heroes of Plutarch whom he adored. And it is as a religious and political outsider, as a 'métèque,' that Rousseau will be attacked by conservative nationalist thinkers down to the twentieth century (Trousson, *Rousseau* 123–4). The 'sublime science' of such virtue is ready at hand, available to simple souls. 'Are not your principles engraved in all hearts and is it not enough in order to learn your laws to return into yourself and to listen to the voice of one's conscience in the silence of the passions?' (Gourevitch 28; Rousseau, *Œuvres complètes* 3: 30).[43] It is not only the tumultuousness of their beings and their careers, which made Luther and Rousseau lightning-rods for attacks, which made them brothers under the skin, but also this reliance on the independent voice of conscience available to all souls that brings them together in a firmer linkage. And just as this reliance on the strength of individual conscience separated Luther from Erasmus, so it separates to an equal degree Rousseau from Voltaire.

Of course Rousseau is partially right, or only partially wrong. His notorious triple plays revel in false accusation. Undeniable minor deviations become major in the energy of his charge, that is, parts come to equal the whole. He ignores the fuller historical conditioning and sense of proportionate value so essential to Voltaire's understanding, and it is not until much later that he addresses the question of what is to be done. His half-hearted self-justification in the 'Preface to Narcissus' is off-putting: since the times are so corrupt, he does not recommend the elimination of the theatre, because that at least prevents bad people from doing worse things; one does not pull out the knife of the wound for fear the patient will bleed to death, etc. (3: 102–4). It is not for such arguments that one reads Rousseau. Yet people did read him, according to Diderot's report of the small essay's sales. The problem is not Jean-Jacques Rousseau but rather his reception. This can be explained in two ways. First is the suitability of his arguments to the needs of a people desiring a revival of sentiment. Rousseau has put his finger on an important change in French society, where the predominance of a courtly culture was coming to a close. Voltaire was right: the culture of the late seventeenth century did emanate from the character of Louis XIV, and after his death it was able to survive for only another few decades. It is this culture that Voltaire represented so fully and that Rousseau challenges and in which he finds such fulsome response (particularly among the cultured classes of Paris and the court – those endowed with sensibility, precisely the ones that he admonishes).

The second cause lies in the nature of radical discourse, which benefits from the energy of accusation. This strikes at the comfortable reader's feeling of guilt, so ready to accept the charges that are being made, whether personal or societal. Moreover, these charges in their partial truths are sufficiently hard to dispute because they invoke an ideal against which the real must invariably fall short. In seeking means of response it is quite obvious that the writer of consciousness will always labour under a disadvantage – so powerful is the language of accusation; that is, unless one is a Voltaire who makes use of wit and its power to bring down to earth in homely language that which is on rhetorical flight, sensible arguments, and most importantly clear, heart-felt appeal to larger principles and causes.

In 1755, by somewhat indirect channels Voltaire received a copy of Rousseau's the second *Discours* (*Discours sur l'origine et les fondements de l'inégalité parmi les hommes*). In his letter of response (August 1755) Voltaire acknowledges receipt of the 'nouveau livre' – thus indicating his awareness of the first *Discours* and then proceeds to respond to both of them in his short letter, which nevertheless must be regarded as a classic in defence of learning and culture against the appeals of ignorance. While the first paragraph has in view the second *Discours* the remainder of the letter is directed against the arguments of the first *Discours*.[44] The opening sentence shows Voltaire at his satiric best: 'J'ai reçu, monsieur, votre nouveau livre contre le genre humain.' Succinctly he already demolishes Rousseau's 'new book against the human species.' He lampoons the paradoxical nature of Rousseau's argument, the learning, and the intelligence needed to defend ignorance: 'On n'a jamais tant employé d'esprit à vouloir nous rendre bêtes.' Never has so much intelligence been employed to make us stupid as animals. Reading your work, the letter continues, one is overcome with a desire to move on all fours. However, having lost that habit more than sixty years ago ... Nor can he make the move to the wilds of Canada, because his health requires the best medical help Europe can offer, and moreover Canada has been overtaken with the very wars that have bedevilled Europe. Such jaunty wit alters the format of debate, transferring it from the plane of subtle argumentation to the more down-to-earth and commonly recognized areas of regular human existence.

The next part of the letter engages in sensible argument, with the common 'yes/but' provision. Yes, and Voltaire recounts his own difficulties with the pirates, or brigands of the printing press, who, unable to hold to an honest trade, 'become brokers of literature, steal manuscripts, disfigure and sell them.' Even in another letter (12 August) Voltaire expresses some accord with Rousseau: 'I am beginning to believe that Rousseau could be right, and that there are people whom literatures makes more wicked than they would normally be' (*Correspondence* 16: 278). He even reminds Rousseau of his own participation in the more notable achievements of literature and thought, and their alliance against a common enemy: 'As soon as our friends began the *Dictionnaire encyclopédique*, those who dared compete with them called them deists, atheists, even jansenists.' Why would Rousseau wish to ally himself with their common name-calling enemies?

This is the 'yes' portion followed by the 'but.' Even allowing such concessions to Rousseau's complaints, are they the whole story or only a minor part in the life of civilization? Are they not only the thorns that must accompany any great flowering of letters, particularly when compared to the many ills that have flooded the earth and that ought to be the genuine targets of attack. 'Les grands crimes n'ont été commis que par de célèbres ignorants.' The Khan, the most celebrated of such criminals, did not know how to read. The real plague of mankind – and the eighteenth century bears abundant testimony to this argument, particularly at the time of its writing – is war, carried on by greed and pride. He slices at Rousseau's arguments of causality when he reminds him that Marot did not cause the St Bartholomew's Day massacre, and Corneille had nothing to do with the wars of the *Fronde*. Such sensible 'yes/but' arguments rarely win the day; they need to await their time – as did Erasmus's responses – when the heat has subsided and the smoke has cleared. They are arguments of a historically *longue durée*.

But Voltaire's arguments do not end with this concessionary mode. They rest on articles of faith that affirm and uphold and that are all the more reliable for their very simplicity: 'les lettres nourrissent l'âme, la rectifient, la consolent.' Good letters nourish the soul, that is they enliven it with a new energy; they correct it, providing matters for moral arbitration; and they bring solace. One could say more, but for Voltaire and his simple directness, this is quite good enough. In fact, bringing Rousseau back to himself, he reminds him of the contradiction in his position that Rousseau tried to face in the Preface to his *Narcissus*: 'elles font même votre gloire dans le temps que vous écrivez contre elles.' The very cause of good letters that he attacks is responsible for the glory

Rousseau has attained. Writing from Geneva, he concludes by inviting Rousseau to visit him in his native city, where the natural salubriousness will restore his health and presumably clear his head.

6. A Dualism Determined

The second major phase of involvement between Voltaire and Rousseau reveals more compelling differences between the writer of consciousness and the daemonic writer. We have already described how the daemonic writer surpasses himself; he writes better than he knows, because he did not know all that he intended. There are reasons for this. First, he feels himself out of place, whether physically or metaphysically. Second, he is constantly engaged in sharp inner debate, caused by an acute moral scrupulousness. Third and paradoxically, in works so concerned with the dimensions of the self, the daemonic writer seems to exceed the self, and that is because he is a visionary, bearing within himself more positive sentiments. It has been said that what we witness in Rousseau is the phenomenon of the Enlightenment engaging in a self-criticism and self-overcoming.[45] But there is also something unaccountable and distinct in the new vision that prompts Rousseau, and that is derived from his own personal make-up, from his responsiveness to his readings of Plutarch and the romances of his childhood. It is different from the Enlightenment because it is not the product of future projection, of that kind of utopianism, but rather the residue of remembrance. It emerges in the later writings, that is, it comes to consciousness in them, in *Émile*, in *The Confessions*, but it is already present in the *Letter to M. d'Alembert*, and is the unexpressed yet driving force in the earlier works. It is something that goes beyond the need for intellectual unity, or even for transparency. It is the infusion of an act of recollection into the structure of society and serves both as its goal and as its meaning. Memory contributes to the density and texture of existence. Jumping ahead to a concluding passage from *Émile*, we garner some sense of the vision that is prompting Rousseau.

Conjuring up the peace and harmony that will accompany the wedding of Émile and Sophie, Rousseau – like Gonzalo and Prospero in Shakespeare's *The Tempest*, like Yeats in a 'A Prayer for My Daughter' – envisions the newly-weds among a happy people:

I believe I see the people multiplying, the fields being fertilized, the earth taking on a new adornment. The crowd and the abundance transform work into festivals, and cries of joy and benediction arise from the games which center on the lovable couple who brought them back to life. The golden age had been treated as a chimera and it will always be one for anyone whose heart and taste have been spoiled. It is not even true that people regret the golden age, since those regrets are always shallow. What then would be required to give it new birth? One single and impossible thing: to love it. (*Émile* 474)[46]

One does not need at this point to contrast this 'vision' ('I believe I see ...') with the grimmer representations of reality at the end of Voltaire's *Candide*. Rousseau himself will record in the sequel to *Émile* what happens after ten years' marriage, when Sophie has been seduced by the corrupting influences of a large anonymous city (*Œuvres complètes* 4: 881). What is important is the animating vision of Rousseau: he moves backward into the future by means of the power of remembrance, the recollection of the past and mythic memory of a childhood he did not enjoy, of a father he did not fully know, and of a Geneva that rejected him.

Putting aside the inevitable contradictions and reservations, we can still relish the vision that motivates Rousseau. Within its boundaries is found the key to his agony and to his strength as a writer, to his necessary confrontations with the self. These are not things that come under the heading of 'influences'; they are part of a new and personal drive that does not spring from the Enlightenment, as a kind of Hegelian 'self-over-coming,' but is rather an expression of a new and personal positive sentiment that will enter into his criticisms of the *philosophes* and make his arguments so compelling.

The success of the first *Discours* began to alter the basis of complaint. He became more convinced of his own talent and more critical of those around him in whose company he suffered such crushing pain. If culture and civilization were the real culprits, then he himself was vindicated and his recourse was not only to write works of scathing criticism, but more importantly to get his life in order, to live his message. With heightened conventional – even religious – rhetoric, he writes in the 'Third Promenade' about his newly won commitment to renunciation, to divestment. 'Je quittai le monde et ses pompes ... Je renonçai à toutes parures.' As a matter of fact, he divested himself of his gold lace and white stockings, he wore a simple round wig and gave up his sword and his watch (this last a minimal subtraction for the person who could not respond on schedule).[47] Going beyond appearance, this act of renunciation extended to position. For a time he was a reasonably well-paid cashier to the tax collector for France. This post was something of a plum, but for which he was ill-equipped and ill-prepared. He quit this position in his new drive of moral reformation, and even more seriously (and hilariously) he made sure he did not secure a pension from the king. Pleading illness (partially true, for he was afflicted with a urinary problem that made continence an issue) but fearing more any obligation, he absented himself from an audience that would have practically guaranteed him a regular income.

This first moral reformation on Rousseau's part required a second. As with Luther, the first – although necessary – step was also something of a misstep. Rousseau was too intent on demonstrations of principle. Here we must keep in mind the new acclaim that Rousseau had gained because of the first *Discours*, and because of the success of his 'operetta' *Le devin de village*, the score of which was so resounding that even the king was heard singing it – badly. Rousseau, the arch critic of society, became much sought after, in fact lionized. To his later chagrin – and Rousseau in this period created much cause for remorse – he turned up at the opening night of *Devin* unshaved, arrogantly dishevelled. In fact, Rousseau had engineered an enormous personal transformation. Old friends had trouble recognizing the new Rousseau. From the timid, shame-faced person who was afraid to show up, let alone speak up in formal occasions, who was overwhelmed by his own social ineptitude, who was thrown off stride, unable to answer any challenging remark, and who would blush at the slightest attention from a woman in the salon, he had become the rage. The worm had turned, and when he did, he became a dragon. The one affectionately referred to as the 'Bear' – as in cuddly – overnight became the boor. Now 'audacieux, fier, intrépide,' he vented his fire on those who had once been so intimidating. 'J'écrasais leurs petits bons mots avec mes sentences, comme j'écraserais un insecte entre mes doigts' (I crushed their little witticisms with my pronouncements, as I might crush an insect between my fingers) (*Œuvres complètes* 1: 417; *The Confessions* 388). What a change, he himself exclaims, in his own belated surprise. The proverbial 'tout Paris' – radical chic to the end – repeated his sarcastic rejoinders. Rousseau, the admirer and student of Plutarch and classical culture, the autodidact devoted to great principles, now found his 'sentences,' his utterances of moral instruction, conquering the little witticisms of the *beaux esprits* before which he had formerly quailed.

This adopted role was one he tells us that lasted about six years, and yet it was not a role that he relished. Nothing could have been further from his true nature ('à mon naturel') (388; 1: 417). Although a necessary step it was still a misstep requiring further correction, a second conversion, which came about with his removal to the Hermitage. He marks the date 9 April 1756 with special emphasis when, after repeated exhortations, he was able to accept Mme d'Épinay's offer to live in the remodelled cottage some few miles outside of Paris. From this time he was able to date his 'entier renoncement au monde' (1: 1015). Only by such 'complete renunciation' did he come closest to his long-held goal of simplicity and independence, and above all, freedom to write and think in the solitude of nature. His Parisian friends – the 'false brethren' – hooted at this retirement, predicting that he would be scurrying back to the city in a matter of weeks. He actually lived there for about twenty months. This geographic removal was a spiritual one and it represented a break in the ranks that the *philosophes* were less able to tolerate than all his attacks. By his removal he was not only telling them that he did not need them, but that it was their presence and their ideas that prevented him from realizing his better nature. From the *Letter to Voltaire* on, his thought would show only increased alienation from that of the *philosophes*.

By the mid-1750s both Voltaire and Rousseau had acquired new philosophical identities (and in Rousseau's case, a new and radical change in his way of life), and as a consequence their dualism takes on a new turn of opposition. Here again provocation was provided by Voltaire. Not only did his presence in Geneva prevent Rousseau from relocating in his native city, but his *Poème sur le désastre de Lisbon* motivated Rousseau to a re-examination of his religious beliefs – resulting in a direct contrast with the new argument of Voltaire's poem.

This poem, more an outcry within poetic form, shows many of the positive qualities of the former adherent to what has been called the moderate Newtonian system of the universe (*Mélanges* 304ff.). We turn to this somewhat neglected poem (unfairly overshadowed by the more comprehensive *Candide*) because it begins to reveal his multi-layered disagreements with Rousseau but also because it shows the more enduring qualities of Voltaire – ardent, aroused, outraged – the extraordinary directness of his grasp of reality, and the genuine reasons for his opposition to systematic rationalism. It may have shattered his prior optimism about the providential direction of the universe, but it represented no change when we compare it with his earlier drama, *La mort de César*. The ideas may have changed but the unity of response remains. The same insistence on humane sentiment that prevails over philosophical principle present in the earlier work finds its direct expression here.[48]

The November 1755 earthquake in Lisbon and surrounding areas meant, according to Besterman, the death of Voltaire's optimism (365–74). It was the climax of a series of bitter experiences for Voltaire: the death of his long-time companion and intellectual compeer, Mme du Châtelet; his disillusionment at the court of Frederick of Prussia, who wasted no effort in communicating to Voltaire that while philosophers are paid to think, it was the monarch who had the power and authority to act (thus dashing Voltaire's notions of an enlightened monarchy); and the beginning of his twenty-eight-year semi-self-imposed exile from France and Paris. But it was the earthquake that brought a shock to his emotional and philosophical system, which, deriving from Newton, centred on the belief in the orderly nature of the universe, of Nature itself.

The real difficulty that the philosophical theodicies of the eighteenth century presented to Voltaire, and the target of his complaint, is the benign distance they place between actual events and human response. Consequently the major impetus of the poem is to bring about direct confrontation. Its addressees are called 'tranquilles spectateurs,' 'tristes calculateurs.' The admonition is clear: brought face to face with the actual disaster, with the protruding bodies amidst the rubble, can anyone in good conscience declare that 'tout est bien,' that this is the best of all possible worlds? The problem is not only philosophical systematizing but also the distancing that such a position requires. To pronounce such slogans of consolation over so horrible a tragedy would be even more of an outrage. The power of the poem derives from the immediacy of the invocation, and through it all the poetically controlled yet direct outburst of a true humanist.

The change the poem represents for himself and for his time is enormous. One of the clear motives of the Enlightenment was to banish tragedy from its awareness in art and in thought. The notion of foundation sacrifice as necessary to religion or to civilization was anathematized. But in Voltaire's poem the disaster of Lisbon brings tragedy back into human experience – he is now talking about blood gods, Typhon and Arimanus. Now, the reader is given to know, evil stalks the earth.

The picture – indeed the poem's impulse drives at a visualization of the disaster – brings to mind the final desolate atmosphere of *Hamlet*, where the young prince begins to acquire lessons in mortality. If a man fishes with the worm that has eaten of a king, and then eats the fish that has fed off the worm, then the conclusion is clear: 'a king may go a progress through the guts of a beggar.' The dust of Alexander, made into mud, may be used to caulk a barrel of beer. It is not too far a step from that to Voltaire's new ruminations on the progress of nature. The vulture devours its trembling victim, only to be attacked in its turn by the 'bec tranchant' of an eagle. Man kills the eagle with a firearm, by which he is killed in turn and then laid open to the depredations of the vulture. This is the cycle of nature, to which Voltaire now responds. The world is nothing but a recycled slaughterhouse and nature the empire of destruction ('de la destruction la nature est l'empire') (*Mélanges*, 306).

One by one Voltaire confronts and dismantles the arguments that would incorporate the disaster into some system of justification. Here the intensity of his poetic energy and even moral ferocity more than compensates for the over-familiarity of his arguments. First, the argument attributing events to God's ireful punishment of human waywardness is answered by noting that Lisbon was not more vicious than London or Paris, yet 'Lisbonne est abîmée et on danse à Paris' (Lisbon is destroyed while they are dancing in Paris). The argument of 'tout est bien' relies on the metaphor of a great chain of being as well as on the belief that every part of the world is necessary to the whole, in which case the earthquake of Lisbon and other disasters are part of a universal compensatory system. In a lengthy note of seven substantial paragraphs Voltaire disputes both of these contentions (*Mélanges* nn1441–2). The chain of being is dependent upon vaguely intuited connections between the various strata of existence ('une gradation suivie qui lie tous les êtres'). With some force Voltaire argues for ruptures in existence, there being no gradual easing off from one level to another. Instead there exists 'une distance immense' between various organisms, as there is between 'l'homme et la brute, entre l'homme et les substances supérieures.' Naturally then there is 'l'infini entre Dieu et toutes les substances.' God if he is not 'totally' other, is at least somewhat other, and has become a force of inscrutable power in a world suddenly become mysterious.[49]

Just as there are these extraordinary disjunctions in nature, so too there is no happy economy. Nature is notoriously sloppy, if not careless in its dispositions. 'Tous les corps ne sont pas nécessaires à l'ordre et à la conservation de l'univers, et tous les événements ne sont pas essentiels à la série des événements' (Not all bodies are necessary to the order and conservation of the universe and not every event is essential to any series of events) (n1442). Not only is Nature not precise, it is not regular. 'Il y a des événements qui ont des effets, et d'autres qui n'ont pas. Il en est de leur chaîne comme d'un arbre généalogique; on y voit des branches qui s'éteignent à la première génération, et d'autres qui continuent la race. Plusieurs événements restent sans filiation' (There are some events that have effects and others that don't have any at all. Their chain is similar to a genealogical tree, where one sees some branches that are extinguished in the first generation and others that continue the family line. Many events are left without connection) (n1442). This most eloquent passage certainly routes Voltaire along the way of Byron's great play, *Cain*, which invokes the geological theory of Baron Georges Cuvier as to the role of cataclysmic upheavals in the history of the earth, and leads to the vision of the world embraced by the natural selection of Charles Darwin and even to the pessimistic philosophy of Bertrand Russell's *A Free Man's Worship*.[50]

There are broken branches, unrealized dreams, dead ends in nature, early deaths, horrible events that disrupt any notions of continuity and regularity in Nature. All of this is powerfully stated and explored in verse and in notes. This is a Voltaire different from the hedonist who in the *Mondain* poems sang 'des doux plaisirs les séduisantes lois' – as he himself tells us at the conclusion of the poem. But even within this change there is an abiding Voltaire who remains, and this is the Voltaire who shuns hypocrisy, who demands a direct confrontation with what is. Not only does he call humankind back to the picture of the horror but he also insists on the rightness of his emotional response. In his way, Voltaire stands for human dignity and, even where that is overwhelmed, for the solidarity of human response; his readiness to embrace the particular leads to the reassertion of a human community. This is the larger alliance that is always at the heart of his endeavour, his mobilization against certain injustices. In fact, if we think back to the elegy for Adrienne Lecouvreur, the most famous actress of her day and for fifteen years a personal friend, whose eyes Voltaire closed in death, we see that in the midst of the philosophical shift, where providence no longer seems to be a benign entity, the personal qualities of Voltaire remain: his indignation, his tenderness, his pity.[51] And as he can cry out against the hardness of heart that buried her at night in an obscure corner on the then-outskirts of the city, so he can show the same indignation against the philosophies that would muffle the outrage of Lisbon. The abiding human connection, the similarity of tone between 1730 and 1756 remains. The perspective alters but the temperament abides – Voltaire's constant effort is to bring humanity back to itself.

7. Rousseau's Religious Genius: 'Un novateur contre les novateurs'

Rousseau's letter of rejoinder to the 'Poème sur les désastre de Lisbon,' his Savoyard vicar's 'Profession de foi' (an obvious but nevertheless well-integrated and justified insertion into *Émile*), and his *Lettre à M. d'Alembert sur son article Genève* may be considered together as a series because they notably exacerbated the relations between Voltaire and Rousseau – the last in fact exploding the delicate tension and because of its practical effects turning Voltaire into a determined if still covert enemy. These three works show the expansion of Rousseau's thought and style beyond the first two *Discours* and by these very developments set him more at odds with Voltaire.

In this period and within this line of thought Rousseau began to construct his religious thought. The *Letter to M. de Voltaire* launched the great series of religious works for which Rousseau felt that his time and posterity would be grateful, for which he would be regarded as the founder of a neo-Christianity:[52] not only the 'Profession of Faith,' but the two letters following his disgrace – the *Lettre à Christophe de Beaumont* and the *Lettres écrites de la montagne* (already discussed briefly) – his superb condensation of his religious thought in his *Lettre à M. de Franquières*, when in 1768–9, he attempts to pick up once again the line of his thought ('le fil des idées') that had almost been effaced, and then in the 'Third Promenade' recounting the several 'revolutions' in his thought, he blesses the providential design that amidst his troubles sustained him by means of his religious faith.

Rousseau received a copy of the printed version of Voltaire's poem. Although it came by indirect means, Rousseau correctly assumed it was sent by the author, and such a supposition placed him under an obligation to respond – Rousseau was never one to evade a moral obligation, especially one so egregiously self-imposed. One of the important nineteenth-century commentators, Gaston Maugras, sees jealousy in Rousseau's response, and the opportunity to inflict a mortal wound upon his antagonist. In his magisterial study, Henri Gouhier corrects this interpretation, finding rather that Voltaire's poem provided Rousseau with the opportunity, even the necessity, of 'fixing' his ideas about God, Providence, and human existence (Gouhier, *Rousseau et Voltaire* 77).[53] He argues that the letter to Voltaire is the first full statement by Rousseau on the nature of his beliefs, providing a bridge between the two *Discours* and the later works. The letter thus occupies a critical position in the development of Rousseau's thought. But Maugras is not totally wrong: how can we absent animus from the prescription? Voltaire shows a face and a figure too available for dispute, particularly on the part of a young, ambitious talent such as Rousseau, eager for recognition. The value of a dualism is that it insists upon both interpretations, not in the niggling sense of trying to reconcile differences, but in the far more accurate sense of accounting for the virtual dynamic of an intellectual relationship, where the personal and the philosophical, the temperamental and the ideological blend. The ad hominem belongs and is necessary to the contest of ideas; it should not be shamed out of existence.

Rousseau's letter is elegant in its style, sophisticated in its argumentation, strategically respectful, and also head-on in its confrontation with Voltaire. Voltaire is brother, even 'master' – one from whom Rousseau has learned so much; indeed he is still touched by the 'première lecture' of his works. He would rather be a Christian of Voltaire's school than that of the Sorbonne (Gourevitch, *Rousseau* 241; Rousseau, *Œuvres complètes* 4: 1070). And following Voltaire's example, one could not attack too strongly the 'superstition' that troubles a society nor respect too much the 'Religion' that sustains it (244; 4: 1072). Finally, all embellishments to one side, Rousseau shows the genuine capacity of a participant in a dualism to penetrate to the core of the argument: Voltaire's poem is depressing and opens the road to despair.

Continuing the arguments of the first two *Discours*, Rousseau remonstrates that the damage in Lisbon would have been minimal except for the fact that city-dwellers insist on constructing 'between ten and twenty thousand [?]' buildings that are six to seven stories high. Had they avoided such density, they could have simply walked way from the earthquake. To compound their difficulties, they returned to their ruined buildings in search of their 'goods' – their possessions. This turns out for Rousseau to have been a fatal attraction because such misguided value was responsible for their being trapped by aftershocks. Earthquakes have occurred in deserted areas, but they do not come in for consideration by the 'messieurs des villes' (an obvious dig), nor do they cause much damage, because the native inhabitants do not suffer from collapsing buildings around them and have only to pick themselves up and move on (as in the second *Discours* 234; 4: 1061–2).

Other arguments remind us that, like Voltaire and the other *philosophes*, Rousseau was not at all shy about entering into philosophic dispute concerning the nature of causation and the structure of the universe. Oddly enough, he comes down on the side of future science that will reveal connections yet unknown to his contemporaries. But the true gist of Rousseau's argument and of his complaint against Voltaire and the *philosophes* is that they are materialists and he is an advocate of moral suasion as predominant in the biological life cycle. That is, they are absolutists in areas of speculation where they should be modest and accepting, and rel-

ativists in matters of morality where they should be firmer, more heroic.
Here again he invokes exemplars from the classical past who were willing
to sacrifice themselves for the good of the whole, that is, he follows his
Plutarchan legacy. Codrus, Curtius, the Decii, the Philenes gave up their
lives in acts of supreme virtue in order to preserve their communities,
and just as they did on the great stages of history, so each individual is
obliged to do his own part for the good of the whole (240; 4: 1068). If life
is an 'état d'épreuves' – what Keats called a 'Vale of Soul-making' – then
virtue only arises out of contest with life's necessary hardships.

Rousseau's argument is supported by major contentions. The first
adds an article to the dispute: instead of saying, 'Tout est bien' (Everything is good), we should say, 'Le tout est bien' (The whole is good). This
change does not mean that bad things do not happen, even to good people; it reasserts human acceptance and endurance within a larger
schema. But even this is based upon a larger supposition, and that is of a
providential deity. Pope has the stick by the wrong end. One does not
prove the existence of God by Pope's arguments – here Voltaire with his
balance of evil would win the day – but rather one justifies Pope's 'system' by the existence of God (240; 4: 1068).[54] If there is a God, then all
one's troubles will be forgotten in the larger rewards of a providential
design. Rousseau, that avid reader of Plutarch, nourished on his heroic
tales of Greek and Roman character, cannot believe that such virtue
would be abandoned and left to perish.

As he goes on, Rousseau, particularly in the 'Profession of Faith,' will
make even more sophisticated his arguments on behalf of moral suasion,
heroic virtue, and those human activities that are separate from the biological life cycle of which they are a part. For the moment he does not
take us through his reasoned thought processes that support his conviction. Rather he resorts to scepticism, finding that in the debate over such
fundamental propositions, neither side has 'véritables idées' and that
while the theist founds his ideas on probabilities, the atheist 'moins pré-
cise encore' (even less precise) founds his on only the contrary possibilities (4: 1070; 242). Since neither side can reach a definitive conclusion,
Rousseau will therefore accept the argument that is more 'consolant' in
which 'mille sujets de préférence' bring the weight of hope to the balance ('l'équilibre') of reason. Thus his scepticism, by disarming his
opponents, begins as Cartesianism but reaches back beyond Descartes to
his own source in Montaigne, and ends up in an entirely different camp.
Making use of discursive reason, the off-setting functions of scepticism
(all of which will be more elaborated in the 'Profession of Faith'), Rous-

seau adds the personal equation: 'l'état de doute est un état trop violent pour mon âme' (the condition of doubt is a condition too violent for my soul) (4: 1070; 242). That is, like Luther, and unlike the writers of consciousness, he cannot arrive at an equilibrium by balancing contradictions. Here a distinction is made between large principles such as the nature of the Godhead, the origin and constitution of the universe, and practical matters of faith and conduct. To have doubts when it comes to the latter is too troubling to his nature. Instead he requires personal faith and conviction, these qualities that will set him off against Voltaire.

The editors of the unpublished works and correspondence of Rousseau (1861) inserted an important argument that Rousseau repeats in the 'Profession of Faith' and in the *Lettre à M. de Franquières*.[55] He contests the major argument of Diderot's *Pensées philosophiques*. This argument holds that, given an infinite number of chances (or throws of the dice), one can thus fortuitously produce the universe as we know it. Rousseau disputes this argument, as he implies that there is a fallacy in the word *infinite*, that it is a phrase that loads the dice. Not a phrase with a definite meaning, it is so elastic in its usage that all it can mean in this equation is 'long enough for the project to be accomplished.' Meaning long enough for what was needed to have happened to happen, the word *infinity* is only an assumption that implies the outcome. It thus involves in its premise that which was needed to be proved. This is like saying that a tossing about of letters an infinite number of times would eventually produce Voltaire's *Henriade* (on another occasion, not so solicitous of Voltaire's approval, he will substitute the *Aeneid*). Such arguments vitiate individual creative agency and substitute mathematical randomness for cosmic support (243; 4: 1071).

Rousseau has thus opened warfare with the *philosophes*, adopting their arguments (against superstition, for religious tolerance and liberty) while outflanking them when it comes to religious belief. He has pushed them into the dangerous corner of atheism, while using the methodological tools of scepticism, discursive reason, and strong personal conviction. But while it is Diderot's specific argument that he disputes, it is with Voltaire that he contends. As part of their trail of mutual provocations, Rousseau chooses the occasion of Voltaire's poem to establish his own religious beliefs; that is, he defines himself in opposition to Voltaire, and in so doing, himself constructs the dualism in which they are involved.

In the penultimate paragraph of the *Letter* Rousseau engages in personal reflection. That this comes from the side of Rousseau should not be surprising. The fact is that we know blessed little about Voltaire from

Voltaire himself, thus imposing distance between the personal self and its public revelations (his private correspondence is only a minor exception). This was the format of his culture, where such personal revelations could only be considered indulgent self-absorption making for social awkwardness. An enormous difference between the two men lies right here. It is not only that we know almost everything about Rousseau from Rousseau himself – in the letters to Malesherbes, a kind of preliminary run-up to the prodigious *Confessions*, the *Dialogues*, the *Reveries*, and many other works that are interlaced with personal concerns – but such avid self-consciousness and self-revelation were essential to his way of thinking and being. *The Confessions* were not only an occasional occurrence; they were the necessary manifestation of his life's purpose, its spiritual end point and goal. Consequently it is Rousseau and not Voltaire who personalizes debate, who must remark on the 'opposition bien singulière' in their respective conditions; Voltaire, possessed of glory, living in the bosom of abundance, assured of immortality in all its forms, having ready at hand the ablest medical attention, yet despite all of these blessings, Rousseau charges, 'vous ne trouvez pourtant que mal sur la terre' (you only find evil on the earth),[56] while Rousseau, even with the accumulating litany of his ills, finds that 'tout est bien' (one notices the absence of the required article). The difference is that while Voltaire is committed to enjoying himself (is Rousseau reverting to the Voltaire of *Le mondain*, which Voltaire has himself forsaken?), Rousseau lives in the hope that Voltaire has only somewhat unconvincingly expressed at the conclusion of this poem.

But Rousseau goes beyond the paradoxes deriving from their physical conditions to mark an even more important opposition: 'nos différentes manières de penser' (our different ways of thinking) (4: 1064; 236). Such differences help Rousseau understand why Voltaire's arguments could not possibly be convincing for a person of Rousseau's intellectual expectations. Between two thinkers of such 'avis contraire' (contrary opinion) what one takes for proven is for the other only a sophism. It is the younger, the more determined Rousseau who thus provides the temperamental basis for the dualism, and by such differentiation produces a kind of parity. The *Letter to Voltaire*, whatever its ostensible purposes, is for Rousseau an act of self-definition and, in opposition to that constant figure haunting his mind, a necessary act of self-validation.

From this period of retirement in Rousseau's life we can date the landmark works in his prolific career. In this period of enormous creative productivity Rousseau explores more deeply his religious thought, most significantly in the Savoyard vicar's 'Profession of Faith,'[57] which goes beyond the 'Letter to Voltaire' in several important ways. Rousseau involves us in the itinerary of his belief, the formation of his ideas. By revealing his intellectual processes in their stages of development, he persuades us of his sincerity, his transparency. In this case, he believes, genealogy is justifying. In giving his ideas a biographical context, by showing their stages of development, Rousseau is establishing a first line – but not the only line – of defence. A further requirement is the insistence on detailed inquiry. In the 'Profession of Faith' Rousseau mounts in even greater detail the philosophical reasons for the belief that was expressed earlier in the 'Letter' of 1756. This means that his opposition to the *philosophes* becomes even more evident. But perhaps the most important revelation is the most personal, where through his spokesman, the vicar, Rousseau already addresses a need that will become only greater, and that is the need to achieve some restoration, to make some restitution for the wound in his own life.

Once again the true starting point of his intellectual inquiry is scepticism. But this is a tactical first move, not a final resting place. Like Luther, he can attest that 'doubt about the things it is important for us to know is too violent a state for the human mind' (268; 4: 568). For Rousseau, in Cartesian fashion, his scepticism is a way of clearing the boards, of settling upon certain clear principles that he can sufficiently know. Starting with only what he can be sure of, Rousseau asserts that he lives in an external world that is the source of his sensations, but that as he can compare, judge, enumerate, and even be in error about the objects that convey the sensations, he knows that he is endowed with an active force of intellect (270–2; 4: 570–3). A fundamental principle of Rousseau's faith is thus established: he is separate from that of which he is a part. Transferred to the world at large this leads to the conclusion that an active force and will not present in material objects directs the course of the world order (273–5; 4: 576–8). This will is intelligence, and if we are not deaf to our own inner sentiment we must acknowledge that this intelligence is the supreme intelligence, which we call God. These arguments all lead to the major observation and principle of Rousseau's faith that man must endure a necessary freedom, one by which his true virtue is gained. If life is an 'état d'épreuves' then one is proved, or tested, by the way one contests hardships. On the one hand, if mankind is thus responsible, 'The evil that man does falls back on him without changing anything in the system of the world (281; 4: 587). 'Le tout est bien.' But this same principle can lead to extraordinary acts of heroic virtue, whereby mankind inspired by a superior virtue rises above the claims of self-interest. Unlike the attributes ascribed to mankind in the second *Discours*, in this larger emergence of Rousseau's thought, motives other than those of self-preservation or compassion emerge. There is innate in mankind that which seeks out the higher virtue: 'To prefer oneself to everything is an inclination natural to man ... nevertheless the first sentiment of justice is innate in the human heart' (279; 4: 598). Humanity is not simple but rather a double compound, and thus might be not only separate from the natural biological life cycle, but also divided from its own self-interest. There has been placed in humankind 'that morality that ennobles them.' Evil is not innate, or original in humankind, but rather occurs when the business of the world obscures the better tendencies of our natures, which is summed up in the concept of 'conscience.'

The issue is here complicated because, while 'innate,' this conscience still is in need of development, and even more curiously this conscience is developed only in relations with one's fellow humans. While in the second *Discours* such sociability is a liability, here it is a necessary milieu for the individual's moral progress. There is even a further step: humankind does not have an innate knowledge of the good, which is drawn out only by education and reason. But once we have been taught to know it, we cannot help but love it. This is the work of conscience and this is innate (290; 4: 600).

This then leads into a prose poem in praise of conscience:

> Conscience, conscience! Divine instinct, immortal and celestial voice, certain guide of a being that is ignorant and limited but intelligent and free; infallible judge of good and bad which makes man like unto God; it is you who makes the excellence of his nature and the morality of his actions. Without you I sense nothing in me that raises me above the beasts, other than the sad privilege of leading myself astray from error to error with the aid of an understanding without rule and a reason without principle.[58]

It is this final sentence that marks Rousseau's opposition to the *philosophes* and the self-corrective in his own life. Blinded by the errors that they denounce, they do not see the greater error in which they are involved. What conscience provides for Rousseau is a principle greater than self-interest and that is the principle of intellectual justice, for which the idea of a Godhead provides the objective support. This objective principle of truth in justice is what allows one to acknowledge that someone else's performance is better than one's own, or that there is a higher morality to which one's own personal interest must submit. Such is the 'morality in actions' that Rousseau's personal discovery of conscience permits.

While opposed to the *philosophes*, Rousseau's argumentative plan is very tactical. He must first advance against the sectarians, the religionists who would personally appropriate universal principle and thus make it a matter of exclusivity. Rousseau separates himself from such 'inspirés' – those who do not need to filter their faith by means of reason (300–1; 4: 614–17). In fact, his spirited assaults on revelation and miracle were so keen, Voltaire thought that the pages themselves should be bound in leather (Gouhier, *Rousseau et Voltaire* 188–9). Like Voltaire's, his greatest fear is nihilism, by which he means the reason that knows no bounds. Such nihilism is the logical outcome of a blind faith that knows no exceptions, that cannot tolerate a Christian liberty. Very early in his 'Profession' the vicar argues that the absence of a respect for Christian liberty – that is, the freedom to judge articles of faith from the position of a knowing and sympathetic adult consciousness – was an inducement to total disbelief: 'By being told, "believe everything" I was prevented from believing anything, and I no longer knew where to stop' (268; 4: 568). A rational discourse thus is necessary to counter the ill effects deriving from the absolutism of blind faith. What is remarkable is that both Voltaire and Rousseau foresaw and lamented the development of the thought that 'no longer knew where to stop.'

While tactically Rousseau seems committed to creating a balance between what he terms the 'faux dévots' and the *philosophes*, like all such attempts at equivalencies it is not fair game, because in writing against the *philosophes* he is much more harmful to his erstwhile friends, who would normally have expected his support. He was thus called a renegade, a Judas. But such a falling out does not account for the full acerbity of the dualism: this emerges when in his analyses Rousseau exposes the weaknesses of their positions. Their critical intelligence is purely adversarial and does not allow for the development of any positive sentiment. Only strong in attack, they are left somewhat uncomprehending when they themselves come under attack from one whose arguments are at least as advanced or as sophisticated as their own. The arch critic happy in exposing the errors of fanaticism or superstition now finds himself criticized and is nonplussed. 'Triumphant when they attack, they are without force in defending themselves.'[59] Indeed, clarifying the dualism into which he has entered, Rousseau occupies that unique position of being the 'novateur contre les novateurs,' – the new innovative critic of the innovators – and the 'rebelle aux nouveaux oracles.'[60] Like Camus some two centuries later he will be the heretic amidst the new orthodoxy. From this dramatic development and from the added intensity of the emotions there involved, we can see why the greater dualisms occur only between those who are at the forefront of intellectual opinion.

The division becomes most apparent when in the most remarkable pages of the entire 'Profession,' pages that drew down the ire of Voltaire, Rousseau relying on his own 'inner light,' the testimony of his feeling, states his preference for Christ over Socrates (307–8; 4: 625–7). As others have done, he construes two Socrates: the first who was a sophist and the second who redeemed his life by the glorious consciousness with which he went to his death. But even this second does not pass undiminished. While he may be thought to have invented morality, there were the great heroes before him who practised it: Aristides, Leonidas, and the example of Sparta itself. But the life and death of Christ was unique. Ignorant of the later researches that would reveal traditions upon which Christ relied and of which he might have been the product, Rousseau underscores the difference between the hero of Greek thought and Christ by maintaining that there was no precedent for the message of Christ. Perhaps even such later scholarly historical research would count little for Rousseau, whose major argument rests upon positive sentiment: when he reads the Gospels he is immensely moved by the sublimity of the message; personal acquiescence and response prevail. While he admires Socrates at the time of his death, 'philosophizing tranquilly among friends, ... the sweetest one could desire,' he is astounded by Jesus, who in the midst of the most horrifying tortures, insulted and jeered, still found it within himself to forgive (307–8; 4: 598). More than a personal identification intrudes here, as Rousseau is anticipating his own fate (although he was also known as 'another Socrates'), but even more he finds in the death of Christ the culmination of his praise of conscience – that part of the human that is so superior to simple survival must be divine. Just as conscience is called divine, so there must be a divinity in Christ. Where Erasmus could exclaim, 'Saint Socrates, pray for us,' thus ushering in the period of Socrates' mythic supremacy for Europe, Rousseau goes counter to that consciousness when in his most memorable utterance, he writes, 'If the life and death of Socrates are those of a wise man, the life and death of Jesus are those of a god.' To which Voltaire, in one of his furious marginalia could only respond, 'What do you know about the death of the gods?' (Gouhier, *Rousseau et Voltaire* 188). And the quarrel, potent in its times, thus finds its own schedule in history. Voltaire will know his followers among those who, like him, seek to confront existence directly, without pose, without embellishments, without sublimation or transcendence, to paraphrase Raymond Naves (78),[61] while Rousseau will surely have secured a place among those who seek to invest experience with more than a passing value.

The 'Profession' is an eminently relevant insertion in *Émile. Émile* is a book about correcting mis-education; the 'Profession' is an accounting by an outcast priest to a wayward youth (Rousseau himself). Given the modified scepticism, no religious belief can be fully ascertained: each has its failures as well as good points. The religion into which one was born is as good as anything going. In fact, Rousseau's own native Protestant faith 'of all religions on earth ... is the one with the purest morality and which is most satisfactory to reason.' Therefore, the advice is clear, given by Rousseau after the fall to the Rousseau before the fall: 'Go back to your own country, return to the religion of your father' (311; 4: 631). Such a return would serve as compensation for that notorious 'faute inconnue.' Through the vicar's words Rousseau is showing the need to overcome the rupture in his own life, for which he holds himself accountable even more than the *philosophes*. One could find evidence that his greatest betrayal was in being born, from the difficulties of which his mother died – a fact evidently his father never let him forget and also perhaps accounting for Rousseau's 'matrix' view of nature. But such causation can never be fully determined. What we can know is that his sense of betrayal – that somehow he had strayed and had abandoned his native land, and in his straying had let his own people down – motivates the dominant trend in Rousseau's thought, one that is even greater than the celebrated need for transparency, and that is his need for return, to recover a lost part of himself. The conversion to Catholicism on the part of a needy and susceptible youth is only minor in comparison with the guilt that he has abandoned the better part of himself. Even the affair of the stolen ribbon, which looms so large in *The Confessions*, and for which the scandal with David Hume was originally regarded as a fitting punishment (although later excised) pales in comparison. This is an act of betrayal, the division that requires atonement, so typical of the daemonic writers. Rousseau's intellectual pilgrimage abides in this need to find restoration, and the journeying is so intense, so self-consuming because it was this betrayal that had to be overcome, the sense that he himself was guilty. The larger workings of the educational tract *Émile* is counter-Rousseau, and the 'Profession' is an intervention before the fatal turn. Consequently they need to be read in conjunction with *The Confessions*, together representing the warfare in Rousseau's mind between what he was and had become, the indelible, ineluctable trail of his life, and the ways – productive, generative – that he would have wanted his life to be. Each is a classic because beyond their ostensible differences they represent Rousseau's need for a recovery from the deep wounding that he had incurred.

8. *Candide*: The Necessary Response

The story of Voltaire and Rousseau is one of provocation and response, of jab and counterpunch. The *Poème* prompted but did not necessitate the *Letter* of 1756 – it did push Rousseau on his way to fixing his thought. A copy of the *Letter* was placed in the hands of Voltaire, who replied with a note of politesse but without any genuine interest in a philosophical engagement. But later when it was remarked that Voltaire never responded, Rousseau, with the gifted insight of a combatant, replied that indeed he had. *Candide* was the answer to the implied question of Rousseau's *Letter*: if what you say is true, how are we to live? Voltaire's masterpiece is devoted to answering that question.

Yet Voltaire's *Candide* is a work that teeters on the brink of failure (*Candide, Les œuvres complètes*, vol. 48).[62] This is true of the first section, roughly the first fifteen chapters, for two reasons. One begins to tire of the seemingly unrelieved piling up of mayhem and injury, the rapid-fire violence that can be compared to a cartoon or local evening televised news-briefs. But there is another reason: when Candide begins to encounter the inadequacies of the Panglossian philosophy, the lesson is unidirectional and mono-vocal. It is furthermore uninteresting because Voltaire himself has lost interest in it as a subject. The better answer is not lengthy examples but rather that of the dervish who greets Pangloss's desire to 'reason' with him about first causes – all those impertinent philosophical issues about which Voltaire himself has grown impatient – by slamming the door in his face (73; 48: 257). The response is abrupt and direct rather than drawn out. In his *Dictionnaire philosophique* Voltaire terminates his discussion of the entry *Bien* (*Tout est*) with a similar curtness. For those who inquire with good faith, the question of good and evil remains a 'chaos indébrouillable.' Impossible to disentangle, it can be met only with the stamp with which Roman justices indicated their refusal to hear a case: N.L., or *non liquet*. It does not flow. It goes nowhere. It is not clear (*Philosophical Dictionary* 74; *Dictionnaire philosophique* 60).

The work pivots at Eldorado (ch. 17) and that is because Voltaire's style, so frequently described by the simplicity of its rapid summary, actually has need of an interlocutor. While it is Martin who later fills that role, at Eldorado the work veers and acquires the great interest it deserves because it is Voltaire who is the interlocutor, and whose presence is marked by the pleasures, values, and ideals represented. Continuing the Voltaire of the *Mondain* poems, all the carriages are good and the cuisine is superb. For the upholder of natural religion and rational theology, there is only one God (it is beyond comprehension that anyone would hold to more), there are no monks and everyone is a priest, and the only prayers are those of universal thanksgiving. For the progressive Voltaire, Eldorado is a centre of technology, with its own palace of science and industry. Eldorado is thus a rational rebuke to the experiences of the world: it is a model for reflection, but it is also the utopian place, 'where no one could possibly go.' Its primary saving grace is that it is inaccessible and thus cut off from any intercourse with other nations. It is spared the lures of expansionism and the threats of subjugation. It was formed when the Incas expanded, only to be overthrown in their turn by the Spaniards (*Candide* 36; *Les œuvres complètes* 48: 187). By staying at home (indeed by maintaining also a homogeneous population), Eldorado enjoyed the protection of inaccessibility (somewhat in the manner of Switzerland) and thus avoided the cut-throat politics and reciprocal violence that led to the deposition of the six monarchs encountered in chapter 26. It is too often unremarked that in the artistry of *Candide*, the deposed monarchs, victims of the perpetual strife that Voltaire has come to recognize as a rule of existence, are the real life story, the anti-myth for the ideal that Eldorado represents.

Candide presents a further possibility of bringing Erasmus and Voltaire together in their two works that seem to have survived historical oblivion. Just as Erasmus's ricocheting humour never seems to stop reverberating – much to the consternation of Luther, who particularly despised *The Praise of Folly* – so Voltaire is given over to multiple reconsiderations, and this is why the style of the first part, so unidirectional, requires interlocution. The fact is that after Eldorado no original statement is allowed to stand; everything is subject to multiple qualifications. This shows the complexity of consciousness that Voltaire shares with Erasmus. There is an even more striking similarity: each of their works that has survived with popular appeal is the work that fully contains its own dualism, the kind of antagonisms their authors were most eager to consign to oblivion.

Two episodes reveal these qualities. The first concerns the 'savant' at the salon where the game of faro is being played (let us remember that

Paris for Voltaire of *Candide* is a morass of trickery and corruption) (50–1; 48: 216–17). The savant voices Voltaire's own insights into the difficulties of writing great tragedy: how one needs to be a great poet without any of the personages in the play appearing to be poets; how one must be such a master of the harmony and purity of the language that the rhyme is never forced at the expense of the sense. But this noble (and Voltairean) discourse is followed by a whipsaw, where the hostess marquise informs Candide that the savant has written one tragedy that was hooted and one book that remained unsold. But this obvious indictment is followed by another discourse where the savant, now in unison with Martin, describes a world where everything goes cross-wise ('où tout va de travers'), and indeed he describes a world of eternal war, just the kind of world Eldorado was made to avoid.

The second and larger episode involves the Venetian nobleman, Pococuranté (ch. 25). Like the savant, he represents many – but not all – of Voltaire's views; his is an essay in self-presentation. Like Voltaire, his great virtue lies in the exercise of independent critical judgment and as a modernist his refusal to be cowed into a reverential attitude toward obvious classics. Homer's *Iliad* is thus marred by the lengthy battle scenes; and rightly he argues that one can read only books 2, 4, and 6 of the *Aeneid* (add to this judgment book 1, and it is unlikely that many a modern critic would disagree); his criticisms of *Paradise Lost* are those of Voltaire in *Le siècle de Louis XIV* – with some notable exceptions. Candide is obviously taken in by these qualities of superior critical judgment – so redolent of the high confidence shown by the great figures of the Enlightenment: 'que grand génie que ce Pococuranté! Rien ne peut lui plaire' (what a great genius this Pococuranté must be! Nothing can please him). This provides an obvious opening for the even higher critical judgment of Martin, who rebuts Candide: this means 'qu'il y a du plaisir à n'avoir pas de plaisir' (that there is pleasure in having no pleasure) (48: 236; 63).

These are among the memorable moments of Candide, where physical dismemberment is replaced by intellectual exchange, where the unidirectional debunking of Pangloss is replaced by the dual responses of Candide and Martin. Martin is the self-styled Manichaean, but his message can be one-sided as well; that is, he sees only evil, perniciousness, and perversity; in fact he sees the world as a battleground – the view Voltaire presented in his *Poème sur le désastre de Lisbon*. But he also operates with a critical intelligence that is always alert (as in the episode with Pococuranté above), and with a sangfroid of lowered expectations. His insight extends not only to perpetual war but also to the hazards of peace: 'l'homme était né pour vivre dans les convulsions de l'inquiétude, ou dans la léthargie de l'ennui.' Humankind is doomed to live in the convulsions of war or the lassitudes of peace, a judgment that Candide cannot support but about which he can offer no positive opinion – a notable suspension of judgment, which should tell us that this young hero is far from hapless (73; 48: 256).

That we turn to Candide at this point indicates that Martin has as much need of Candide as Candide has of him. Candide embodies the simple animal faith and active energy that are the necessary counter-points to Martin's scepticism. However grim, restrained, and resigned might be the conclusion of *Candide*, the work's higher appeal might be in the spirit of engagement that it represents. That is, like Erasmus in *The Praise of Folly*, Voltaire is enmeshed in his world. There is no quitting or getting out.

It does not denigrate the work to say that to understand Voltaire *Candide* must be supplemented, that is, the spirit that is present in Candide himself is represented more fully in other works and deeds of Voltaire. For instance, his pleasure palace, Les Délices, is a cut above the *métairie*, or small farm that seems to be the ultimate destination of the diminished survivors. One of the benefits Voltaire derived from his earlier two-year 'exile' in England was an appreciation for the value of commerce, an appreciation shown in his praise for the policies of Colbert in *Le siècle de Louis XIV*. Even the phrase 'Il faut cultiver notre jardin' is susceptible to larger adaptation. As recounted in *Pot-pourri*, a so-called relative was in need of labourers to harvest a crop, but the Catholic workers refused because it was a saint's day, Saint Barbara's (another of those 'poetical saints' whose reality Erasmus questioned), and preferred to spend their 'holy day' in the tavern (*Romans et contes* 14: 251–2). His relative then hires Lutherans who were willing to work, and thus saved the crop. Suit was brought, and while the case was being heard on appeal, Voltaire was brought to conclude, 'personne sûrement n'est plus persuadé que mon parent qu'il faut honorer les saints, mais il prétend aussi qu'il faut cultiver la terre' (surely no one was a greater believer than my relative that we have to honour the saints, but he also knows that we have to cultivate the earth). This phrase brings necessary augmentation to the conclud-ing line of *Candide*, indicating a much more forthright and even more expansive attitude toward life and work. The fuller meaning would seem to be that humans must be allowed to go about their productive labour without irrational impediments or interference. As many a critic has inferred, the way has thus been opened for the spread of human consciousness and enlightenment.

But even more than this, the capacity for wonder shown by Candide, while tempered by the restrictions of Martin, is never relinquished by Voltaire. Pococuranté's jaded cynicism and ennui, while containing the germ of Voltaire's critical independence, is not the full story. Voltaire's own criticisms of *Paradise Lost* are given in even fuller detail in *Le siècle de Louis XIV,* where Voltaire is quick to add that, while such bilious attacks quickly expire, the praise is never exhausted: 'Milton reste la gloire et l'admiration de l'Angleterre' (Milton remains the glory and admiration of England) (Groos 2: 140).[63]

9. Rousseau Out on a Limb

Only since the mid-1980s (not forgetting the two editions – one in English translation by Allan Bloom, 1960, and the other by Michael Launay, 1967), has Rousseau's *Lettre à M. d'Alembert* received the critical attention it deserves.[64] The *Letter* had immediate practical consequences, because it pinched Voltaire where he lived and enjoyed himself. He promoted lively theatrical productions in his re-established residences in and near Geneva, thus confirming for Rousseau his corrupting influence and his role as an interloper in Rousseau's home place. A notorious stranger has found his way into the family. Exacerbating existing tensions, the *Letter* finally caused Voltaire to change his stance of bemused toleration into one of hidden enmity. But the other reasons for fuller study is that the *Letter to d'Alembert* shows the advances in Rousseau's thought, bringing to the first *Discours* a much larger dimension of perception: he is no longer dealing with the epigones and other-directed followers and inheritors but rather with the originals, Racine and Molière, and the very nature and appeal of the theatre. The *Letter to d'Alembert* further shows Rousseau entering into the true nature of his genius, and this we find not so much in his argumentation itself as in the digressions, the footnotes, the asides, the bouts of self-confrontation and self-consciousness.

When d'Alembert contributed his article 'Genève' to the seventh volume of the *Encyclopédie* he inserted the suggestion that Geneva sponsor a public theatre. This itself was something of an intrusion, as Rousseau recognized, 'la question qu'il vous a plu d'agiter dans un article où elle était à mon avis tout à fait étrangère' (the question which you were pleased to debate in an article to which it was in my opinion entirely alien) (230;

123). But curiosity turns to animosity when he suspects rightly, as was implied by Diderot (*Confessions* 10: 494), that the true agitator behind the suggestion was Voltaire himself. Personal animus raises its head once again, and the Maugras-Gouhier argument may be repeated here, with similar conclusions. One thing is certain, that despite the response addressed to d'Alembert's article, it was the smiling face of Voltaire behind the arras that continued to haunt Rousseau's imagination.

The *Letter* may be termed a series of digressions in search of an argument, but the argument is there, well outlined and finely honed. Far from providing a general law for all situations, Rousseau insists upon the different needs inherent in the conditions of various cultures. Where the pleasures of the theatre might be a useful palliative in a large city, opulent and abounding in leisure, they could only be harmful for a small city, one that cannot afford the largesse of a monarchy but is instead dependent upon the industry and frugality of its inhabitants. But the value of the discourse is not in what Rousseau presents – as can be expected, the arguments were soon to be outmoded, as the Geneva of his imagination and ideal recollection was being transformed and would within a matter of a few years (1766) actually sponsor a state theatre. Rather, the value is what is represented, the deeper tissues of his thought, the reasons for the positions taken, what they reveal about Rousseau, his digressions, his awareness (as, for instance, his awareness that his rewritten version of *The Misanthrope* would bomb [105; 42], and that the moralizing comedy of his own day is so boring, one might as well go hear a sermon [112; 47]).

In the *Letter* Rousseau assumes his many functions: he is writing not only as a moralist, a man of rectitude ('droiture'), but as a sincere moralist, one who identifies himself with what he says. In addition, in Rousseau we see the alliance of protestantism with republican liberty, and in each case Rousseau is a defender – indeed a protector – of these virtues of his native city. With his habitual creative insight, he foresees small causes as leading to great effects. His imagination has gotten away from him perhaps, but in the process it yields forbidding insights, such as prevailed in the first *Discours*. Rousseau, self-taught and thus inclined to follow his ideas to their ends, was not one to fear going out on a limb.

And go out on a limb he does, not only in his frontal attacks on the two giants of French drama, Racine and Molière, but on what he descries as the feminization of French culture (not individual female writers), or the defence of Genevan all-male drinking clubs ('cercles'). But his very attacks or defences are instances of the possibility of rational discourse that he values and that he fears is being warped by the culture of the salon, by the token rules of tenderness and *esprit*. What we must recognize is that the sentimental Rousseau is an ardent defender of strong-minded, physically capable citizen-patriots, and in no way does he see the current culture of the theatre as contributing to these virtues. The theatre he does endorse is the Greek theatre, because its subject was 'national antiquities' – a theatre that depicted the growth and the defence of historical Greek institutions, heroes, and values (such as might be seen in Aeschylus's dramas). Likewise his native Geneva should present dramas extolling the defenders of their national liberty. This should tell us that the battle Rousseau is fighting is again not one between conservative churchmen and liberal reformers (although his arguments might be construed as giving aid to the former), but is instead a political-moral debate. And as Michel Launay reminds us, the kind of popular theatre that Rousseau advocated would find its own defenders in Bertolt Brecht and Jean Vilar in the twentieth century (*Lettre à M. D'Alembert* 28). Thoughts out of place in one season have their ways of return in another.

In the first *Discours* Rousseau attacked what could be called 'imitative repetition,' that culture of uniformity and facility where everybody knows the right thing to say because they have heard it said often enough. In the *Letter* these issues are magnified. Beyond all the practical problems, of cost, of interruption of work schedules, of a need for fashionable refinements in dress, Rousseau's objections to tragedy are principled. The experiences of theatre are part of a much larger cultural war. Catharsis is a means of sublimation by which we exit the theatre so contented that no real problems bother us. It produces only a 'sterile pity' and not the 'least act of humanity' (78; 24).' We give ourselves over to 'foreign amusements' (66; 16). The assemblage in a theatre is a moment of isolation and a self-forgetting, where we weep over fables. He would far prefer that we drew our pleasures and our duties from within ourselves (231; 124). In the theatre – like the actors themselves – we give ourselves over to someone else's life and thoughts. We are filled with quotations and all the imaginative consciousness that diverts us from an independent and direct confrontation with our own ethical lives. This too offends the deep and abiding protestantism of Rousseau's spirit. A sentence taken from the *Letter to Christophe de Beaumont* but that finds its presence throughout his works as spiritual guide is 'nul n'est exempt du premier devoir de l'homme: nul n'a droit de se fier au jugement d'autrui' (no one is exempt from the first duty of man: no one has the right to trust himself to the judgment of another). When Ernst Cassirer has recourse to this quotation, he follows it quite rightly with the summary judgment that 'there is no doubt that with these propositions Rousseau once more returned to the actual central principle of Protestantism' (117).

Given their differences, it is fitting that, for Voltaire, Molière's masterpiece is *Tartuffe*, which unmasks religious hypocrisy, particularly when it enters into social politics, while Rousseau would identify with and find Molière's genius in *The Misanthrope*. But Rousseau moves beyond the letter of the play, the requirements of explication, and disputes it philosophically. That is, as in the first *Discours*, he moves beyond what is being presented to what is being represented. He thus disputes the premises of the play: not only is the nature of the misanthrope mistaken but the dramatic fulcrum of the play is all wrong. Alceste, were he to be presented as a true misanthrope, would be an *honnête homme* – and here clearly Rousseau is mounting a personal and quite indulgent self-defence – and Philinte, far from being insulated as the play's *raisonneur*, would be cast as offering the mendacious advice of the man of the world. Rather than having Philinte preside, Rousseau casts him as a contestant, and in the dramatic, antithetical universe that Rousseau shares with Luther, the true contest is between Philinte and Alceste. As Erasmus's moderating intelligence was to Luther in their great debate, so Philinte's is to Rousseau: this is not moderation, but rather a careless scepticism, whose basis in self-regard is devoid of any instinct of the spirit.

> This Philinte is the wise man of the play: one of those decent members of high society whose maxims resemble so much those of knaves, one of those gentle, moderate people who always find that everything is fine because it is to their interest that nothing be better, who are always satisfied with everyone because they do not care about anyone; who, at a good dinner, assert that it is not true that the people are hungry; who with a well lined pocket find it quite disagreeable that some declaim in favor of the poor.[65]

One could go on quoting this impassioned paragraph where so much of Rousseau's personal animus and insight emerges. Such people of which Philinte is the representative can suffer all the degradations and assaults on human society from their own 'maison bien fermée' – perhaps thinking of the enclosed villa where Voltaire's elite can gather – all of this because 'Dieu les a douées d'une douceur très méritoire à supporter les malheurs d'autrui' (Given that God has endowed them with a most meritorious [gentleness] with which they are able to support the misfortunes of others) (100; 39). Leaping back in time, one can reread into this presumption of merit Luther's tirade against Erasmus, so self-satisfied in human merit and his own reasonableness, and moving forward find Luther's more violent invectives in the distaste Rousseau must experience with the virtuous pronouncements of the man of reason. The smug self-certainty, despite the veneer of deprecating modesty and consideration, the self-satisfaction so confident in its virtue is the true antagonist for Luther and Rousseau. The notion each rejects is that by a kind of conscious disengagement one can be a spirit above the dust and avoid the necessities of heroic choice.

In the course of the nineteenth century three great works of criticism, those of Baudelaire, Meredith, and Bergson, showed the social functions of comedy.[66] But even such potent and prevailing counter-arguments do not detract from the value of the *Letter*, from its deeper textures. Its first lesson resides in the call to more public-spirited forms of entertainment, that is, something closer to home, even expressive of the festival spirit itself. The true beauty of Rousseau's communal sense emerges when he calls for entertainments that are participatory, that engage everyone as equals, and these can even include competitive amateur sporting events just as much as festivals. What truly emerges is what may not inappropriately be called Rousseau's idealism, but it is more than that because, rooted in time and in history, the recollected past becomes part of the visionary future that has seen and foresees people bound in a community coming together to celebrate events of great public and national importance – a communion of equals joined together in a mutual engagement. Whatever one might say against some of the very long-range implications of Rousseau's political statements – and most of the accusations seem dubious – there is no question that in his sensibility and projections for humankind he is a democrat, and values the communal, the festival, where everyone may be a participant. How he would have enjoyed and commended the innumerable small-town, homespun Fourth of July celebrations, the flow of hundreds of children in their patriotically coloured bicycles, trikes, and even infant carriages.

Part of the deeper texture, where Rousseau seems to be in touch with his original sentiments, is of course the digressions, in which Launay has seen consisting the originality of the piece. Like Hamlet's soliloquies, they come to constitute the true body of the text. This is partly because they present a new quality of directness and personal recollection in

Rousseau's writing. He attributes it to his retirement from Paris and the absence from his mind of the false friends who had surrounded him. He refers to a new 'douceur d'âme' (*Confessions* 465; *Œuvres complètes* 1: 502), and that he had returned to his natural element. In Rousseau's *Letter* we find a new willingness to let himself go, to write not only from the necessity of responding to arguments but from the years of accumulated wisdom and insight. In more than one sense he had returned to his element and that was memory, but more than that, remembrance. Thinking of the Geneva of his past could not but evoke the lyricism of recollection. Once again espousing the ethos of return, he thinks of all the Genevans forced to leave their native land because of the unyielding hardness of the terrain, the difficulty of making a go of it. What would draw them back would not be imitation French theatre but rather the public events and festival spirit from their childhood in which they took genuine pleasure. Exile's return is always keen in Rousseau's mind.

So too he thinks back to the ways of his childhood, thus setting the stage for the motivating spirit of *Émile*. 'We were coarser in my time. The children, rustically raised, had no complexion to preserve and did not fear the injuries of the air to which they had been accustomed from an early date.'[67] The passage proceeds to praise and enjoy through memory the freedom of his youth.

But it is in the final footnote where Rousseau's mythic memory, personal recollection, and even perhaps the motivations for his specific recommendations all cohere. By now this passage has been quoted frequently and analyzed, but still it remains as an instance of Rousseau's recovery by means of memory of episodes in one's life, and of investing these episodes, simple though they may be, with greater significance. He was struck when young by the St Gervais district regiment, who, after their regular training, broke into companies for their meal. But then they began to dance – a long line of five or six hundred men in uniform holding hands, circling around the fountain, moving in and out to the beat of the drums and under torchlight. Rekindled in memory, this was something not banal. It was late, and the activity wakened their wives who, coming from their windows, joined their husbands in a show of stately sexuality. Children also woke up and descended to join their parents. Rousseau watched this scene with his father, who, embracing him with a surge of emotion that he continued to feel, urged him to love his people and their good ways. Memory is frequently imperfect, but the desire to create or recreate it is not: it bespeaks an abiding presence of value, and this is Rousseau's conclusion: 'Non, il n'y a de pure joie que la joie publique, et les vrais sentiments de la Nature ne règnent que sur le peuple' (No, the only pure joy is public joy and the true sentiments of nature only reign through the people). Indeed, Rousseau was a visionary, one guided by a positive sentiment that sought out in the mythic and remembered past the genuine springs of civic virtue.

10. *Émile*: A Reconstructed Rousseau

Émile has all the markings of a masterpiece (repeatedly in his *Confessions* Rousseau refers to it as his greatest work, obviously excepting the work in which the praise occurs).[68] First, as always, Rousseau is a keen observer of the manners and the morals of the people; second, he is a fount of ideas, indeed to such an extent that recommendation after recommendation (from abandoning the tight swaddling of infants or corseting for women, to urging mothers to breastfeed) were duly adopted by many people. Not only in later times, but in its time, the work had tremendous influence: Rousseau, although he would have here declined the honour, might have been considered the Dr Spock of his age. Trousson refers to the sway *Émile* held for educators from Pestalozzi and Frobel to Montessori (*Jean-Jacques Rousseau* 182).[69] While a treatise on education, *Émile* is also a work of moral philosophy and of social psychology, and here it can only be said that his supporting principles have proved to be sound ones. Education begins with the first sentiment of being; in fact, even before that, education begins with the first sensations and extends through the crucial decision of marriage. This is not education as an academic institution but rather mentorship through life's critical stages. In a very compelling phrase he tells us, 'This is the history of my species that I am writing' (*Émile* 416; *Œuvres complètes* 4: 777). With this phrasing, *Émile* takes its complementary place alongside *The Confessions*, the one devoted to the history of his species, the other to the history of his soul.

Émile has other unmistakable signs of a masterpiece: it brings together in formidable coalescence much of Rousseau's earlier writings. Yet it transcends these works by virtue of an even greater contradiction: Émile is a counter-Rousseau. Like other great educational tracts, it advocates the education its author did not receive; it is an attempt to correct his own mis-education. Thus it complies with and expresses the fundamental impulse of return. In this sense the vicar's advice fits perfectly into the meaning of *Émile*: stay within one's limits, avoid the disruptions of alienation and discontinuous change. There is a natural order to existence, and that educational program is the best that adheres to the various stages of the human life cycle. If in the first *Discours* the enemy was imitative repetition and in the *Letter to M. d'Alembert* a vicarious mode of existence, in *Émile* the similar opponent is imaginative consciousness, that kind of foreign mental intrusion that seems to rob the growing soul of its simplicity. Yet this is the Rousseau who feasted on Plutarch, who worshiped the romances and tales of adventure, one who became the Quixote of imaginative adventure, the Prufrock of the salon. In the creative tension formed by these several demands of his own self-awareness, we see that Rousseau forms a cultural bridge between the West's first exemplary novel by Cervantes and one of the first great American novels, *Huckleberry Finn*, where a similar contrast is at work between the native soul progressing simply without elaboration in full rapport with its environment and the person of imaginative consciousness (Tom) who intrudes with an interfering and out-of-place rearrangement of the order of things.

Émile has yet another characteristic of a masterpiece: it is filled with blemishes, but blemishes that are the product of its whole-hearted pursuit of an ideal and an idea. Despite its diffuseness deriving from a discursive randomness of tone and story, there is a felt urgency of concern in *Émile*. As with Luther and the other daemonic writers, Rousseau writes from a different temporal metabolism. Luther was able to say, 'The time for silence is over.' The direness of the times requires the responsibility of a personal intervention. In different, even less chaotic and threatening circumstances, Rousseau adopts the same procedures. What is read in *Émile*, he tells us in the preface will be attacked as a 'visionary's dreams,' but that is exactly the case and the source of the work's power. 'It is not on the basis of others' ideas that I write but on my own ... If I sometimes adopt an assertive tone it is not for the sake of making an impression upon the reader but for speaking to him as I think. Why should I propose as doubtful what I do not doubt at all? I say exactly what goes on in my mind' (34; 4: 242). There is no indulgence either in Rousseau or in Luther for halfway measures. What is merely feasible is not effective. Rousseau will dispense with the 'do-able,' about which no one needs instruction. He will follow the persuasions of his own experience and insights. In fact, Rousseau himself might be guilty of runaway causality, so large do apparently small things loom in his heightened sensibility. As the twig is bent ... So, if mothers assumed their natural role as breast-feeders, most of the problems of his society would be overcome. Such intellectual over-achieving – an instance of his 'rhetorical hyperbole'? –

can either be met with hilarity or regarded as one cause of Rousseau's unfortunate influence (as fully evidenced by Trousson, e.g., 100). But one thing is sure: behind Rousseau's thought is the powerful role of change in human affairs. These are the formidable circumstances against which a contemporary child is to be raised, the matters that must be considered. And yet his advice to the anxious parents, whether *haute bourgeoisie* or gentry is one of greater trust in the forces of nature. Rather than placed under the control of stern governing hands, let childhood be a time of gaiety, let childhood be returned to children in the natural order of things. His argument is that if one does not get the early stages of the human life cycle right, it is hard for the others to come to fullness. Thus attention, and here Erik Erikson would agree, must be given to the requirements of the phases in the human life cycle. Consequently *Émile* addresses two sorts of parents: those who must be freed from being overly protective, thus disabling the child and preventing it from encountering its own experiences and thus from being itself, and those – to be avoided as much as the concern that coddles, the hovering solicitude – whose stern regimen would seek to make a premature and thus aborted adult of the child.

Rousseau's constant advice is the counsel of freedom. Just as he feels swaddling thwarts natural movements, so the over-solicitousness of parents prevents genuine experience – the real teacher in Rousseau's guardianship. Let children be children, let them be imps of mischief, rascals at heart – there is a better chance that they will grow up to be true adults. Above all, in restoring childhood to children, let them enjoy happiness. Given the prevalence of mortality, why should they be deprived of the few years of joy that may be theirs? Fearfulness prevents them from gaining their own rights, and sternness deprives them of enjoying the brief life that, given the human condition, might be theirs.

There is not only the constant threat of infant mortality, but there is also the impending convulsion of the social institutions. For this reason, the children of the gentry should especially be made to learn a trade. Here is Rousseau the son of a Genevan artisan speaking, but even more potently the Rousseau who anticipates not only the normal vicissitudes of life but revolution itself, and this he makes abundantly clear: 'You trust in the present order of society without thinking that this order is subject to inevitable revolutions, and it is impossible for you to foresee or prevent the one which may affect your children. The noble become commoners, the rich become poor, the monarch becomes subject. Are the blows of fate so rare that you can count on being exempted from them?'[70] This warning catches the traditional *de casibus* strain, but Rousseau's prescience extends much farther, as the next sentence and its notation make clear: 'We are approaching a state of crisis and the age of revolutions.' The note goes on, 'I hold it to be impossible that the great monarchies of Europe still have long to last.' Even this could be taken as a reference to natural mutability, the decline that normally follows a period of splendour. But then he adds ominously and not too cryptically, 'I have reasons more particular than this maxim for my opinion, but it is unseasonable to tell them, and everyone sees them only too well' (194; 4: 468). For one accustomed to delivering thoughts out of season, such a precaution on Rousseau's part can point only to the immediate prospect of profound political change.

Rousseau is famous for denying original perversities in human nature, but this does not mean that there may not develop perversities of our own making. The first of these in children, born of their weakened condition, is that of wilfulness. The first order for the new governor is to control this imperiousness, and he deploys many devices. But his main ally is 'things,' the physical reality of which serves to modify the will, to instruct the young master that there exists something outside of his will that he cannot control. From this instruction he learns one of the premier laws of Rousseau's philosophy, present in the *Letter to Voltaire*, and this is the capacity to endure the hard laws of necessity. Moreover, from such direct contact with things he is responsive to his own experience. Experience is the master-teacher: from it one acquires absorptive knowledge rather than abstract knowledge; what one learns indeed becomes part of oneself. One sees it clearly and simply. It is also active knowledge: there is less chance for a discrepancy between what one thinks and what one does. When at one point Rousseau lifts his pen to exclaim, 'Things, things!' there are several reasons for doing so (85, 91; 4: 311, 320). One is the experiential quality necessary to education. He desires the fresh contact of original response, because what one gains thereby one truly knows. But the final product of this education is the materially and intellectually self-sufficient adult, one who is capable of using critical judgment, which for Rousseau results in the final desideratum, and that is freedom.

In his advice to return childhood to children, Rousseau, as he did in the first *Discours*, writes counter to one of the main achievements of the Renaissance, and that was the conquest of time. From Petrarch and his Italian followers in the fifteenth century, to Erasmus and his disciple in these matters, Rabelais, an important principle necessary to any educational program is the proper and even militant use of time. One must be systematic, not only marshalling time but organizing it in such a way that not one minute of the day is lost. Such was the combined force of energetic appeal and systematic planning that the new humanism brought to the slumbering giants of learning.[71] In this one cannot say that Rousseau's counter-force was revolutionary in its effects, but his advice did give expression to one of the first voices of protest and did promote effectual modification. No, says Rousseau, his young pupil should have no consciousness of time because he is immersed in it fully, naively: 'The happy child enjoys time without being its slave. He profits from it, but he does not know its value' (187; 4: 459). To those who complain that his pupil wastes his time in doing nothing, Rousseau responds, 'What? Is it nothing to be happy? Is it nothing to jump, play, and run all day? He will never be so busy in his life' (107; 4: 343–4). Full enjoyment of the moment brings to the young child the best benefits of his time of life; and such moments will provide for him happy recollection in his later years.

It might appear that I am engaged in writing a prelude to Wordsworth's *Prelude*, and so it is. Attention to the stages of life, childhood as a period of wild abandon, the cultivation of a wise passivity – all will later meet with Wordsworthian endorsement, but none of these is as important as the power of recollection that through a 'natural piety' attaches one age to another, bringing a continuity, a cohesion where there had been disruption or fragmentation.

The independent experience of childhood provides the material where memory is sustained, and with memory a sense of the self: 'Memory extends the sentiment of identity to all moments of his existence' (La mémoire étend le sentiment d'identité sur tous les moments de son existence) (78; 4: 301). In one of his many digressions, Rousseau recalls a brief idyllic moment when he lived with his cousins in the country and enjoyed the company of a boyhood friend. This was perhaps the sole occasion where he had the taste of the kind of childhood he envisioned for Émile. But what is important is the way this experience is introduced and the obvious delight Rousseau takes in such a backward trek in time:

'There comes a stage in life beyond which, in progressing one retrogresses ['on rétrograde en avançant']. I feel I have reached this stage. I am beginning again, so to speak another career. The emptiness of ripe age, which has made itself felt in me, retraces for me the steps of the sweet time of an earlier age. In getting old, I become young again, and I recall more gladly what I did at ten than at thirty' (135; 4: 385). It should be noted that here I use Bloom's translation rather than that of the

Everyman *Émile*, because the latter in being colloquially freer displaces some crucial terms from Rousseau's original. The first is the verb 'rétrograder,' which figures significantly in Rousseau's thought, as he states quite vehemently that we cannot 'rétrograder' or regress to a state of nature, but that we can 'rétrograder' or recover what was most native to the past of an individual. The other instance is the avoidance in the Everyman edition of the phrase 'le vuide' or the emptiness of age. As the *Reveries* tell us, Rousseau was most vulnerable to these feelings of 'emptiness.' It is as a counter to this sense of 'vastation' that 'affective memory' shores up human experience and provides some substance from within the human life cycle. If we are reduced, he tells us, to seeing a man as he is, or picturing him as he will be in old age, this thought of decline ruins our pleasure. The only pleasure comes 'when the memory of his deeds leads us to look back over his life and his youth is renewed in our eyes' (C'est quand la mémoire de ses actions nous fait rétrograder sur sa vie et le rajeunit pour ainsi dire à nos yeux) (158; 4: 418). From within the human life cycle we are capable of experiencing something other than degradation or annihilation and that is a kind of comforting integration. But there are prerequisites for this acquisition: a childhood that was lived plentifully, a communion with one's own interior life, and a willingness to accept fully the necessities of life. Existence in time may be only a progressive frittering away of life's opportunities – the greatest betrayal – but it is also open to yielding an enduring sense of quiet gratification. This freedom to be one's own is Rousseau's way of investing the natural world with a more than ordinary significance and joining the stages of life by a 'natural piety.' And this might be Rousseau's greatest Romantic legacy. Nowhere in the directness of Voltaire's encounter with experience do we find the same instinct for personal enrichment.

At this point we return to that beautiful book by Georges Poulet, *Studies in Human Time*, which in its profound historical and philosophical argument explains how the dire condition in the Christian theology of salvation, so fully comprehended and expressed by Luther, was superseded in the Enlightenment by the development of 'affective memory.'[72] While I abridge his fully documented arguments, for Poulet the Reformers had an absolute distrust of the natural man. 'Original sin had from the first robbed the creature of all ... power over his individual continuance; and further it had rendered the creative act itself insufficient to establish within the fallen being a true nature and a true duration' (11). While Poulet is following Calvin more than Luther, we have already observed Luther's great dissatisfaction with not only ceremonial works but with works themselves. This is part of that strange human economy where good works do not last whereas bad works stack up in the storehouse of memory. Given such disequilibrium, works cannot thus sustain faith; rather faith is required to sustain works. Poulet confirms this when he writes, 'The justified cannot help but feel that his existence is that of a being which can only fall into the abyss, unless God renews for each new instant the operation of the moment before' (12). The relevancy this reading has for Luther's thought is apparent, as the processes of time themselves can produce no relief but instead purvey feelings of guilt and insufficiency.

As man needs to be plucked from the abyss in the Reformers' thought, so Rousseau needs to be saved from 'emptiness.' This quotient is active in each, and shows Rousseau's proximity to Luther's and Reformist spiritual dynamics. But the means are quite different. While Poulet traces in the course of the Enlightenment many factors responsible for this new 'affective memory' by which the past and the present are brought together, primacy is attributed to Rousseau: 'By means of those abrupt returns of which Rousseau was the first to discover the enchantment and the value, all at once the mind is able to feel an entire past born within itself. This past, together with the whole train of its emotions, surges up in the moment and endows it with a life that is not momentary' (27). Completing the comparison with Luther, both affinity and difference emerge. On the one hand, Rousseau harbours a similar suspicion of the contrivances of consciousness; but on the other, he introduces a new element – affective memory – that gives to existence a density, that out of nature itself provides a comforting consistency to the individual life.

In book 5, *Émile* elevates itself. In the marriage of Émile with Sophie we must once again invoke the by-now famous 'double optics' necessary for a true understanding of Rousseau's genius. Here once again Rousseau presents a counter-self, the self he did not have, the being his life's course did no permit him to become, one different from himself but that he cherished nonetheless. The book raises itself by magnificent self-address to its own propositions. Like Dante, like Milton in their small prologues to select cantos and books, Rousseau writes a second preface. This is the only book on education, he tells us, that 'addresses the most important and most difficult part of the whole education – the crisis that serves as passage from childhood to man's estate' (*Émile* 416; *Œuvres complètes* 4: 777). And that part is marriage. The final justification of any educational system is its preparation for the most critical choice, the choice of a marriage partner. In this final instalment Rousseau shows the way to the Great Tradition of the English novel, to Jane Austen, Dickens's *Hard Times*, and D.H. Lawrence. By culminating his work in the crucial act of the life process, marriage, he is choosing a subject ignored by 'educationists'; he is writing as a philosophical educator. He anticipates the criticism that the novelist and cultural theorist have replaced the educator. He will be accused of having written a romance, a novel. A fair romance it is indeed, he answers, the romance of human nature. 'C'est un assez beau roman que celui de la nature humaine' (416; 4: 777). Then in an even more compelling phrase he tells us, this is the history of my species that I am writing. 'Mon espèce' – far from the drawing room, the university lecture halls, other treatises on education, Rousseau shows his great capacity to extend his thought because he is sensitive to the fullest demands of life's decisions in the natural order of things.

In fact, virtue might be said to reside in nativity. By making one's peace, by settling one's accounts with the place where one was born, one acquires true virtue. This was Rousseau's constant need, in fact one driving him to a reordering of his own life's path in the formation of Émile. But Émile is a projection, a personal utopia, that is a nobody. His Émile would never come to write the books that Rousseau did, would never experience the woundings that enter into the makings of great art. So it is fitting that finally Rousseau does not renounce on himself, but accepts his lot. 'There are circumstances in which a man can be more useful to his fellow citizens outside of his fatherland than if he were living in its bosom. Then he ought to listen only to his zeal and endure his exile without grumbling ['sans murmure']. Such exile is one of his duties' (474; 4: 858).

11. Voltaire on Attack

In the meantime, following the consequences of the *Letter to M. d'Alembert*, the hostile letter of 1760, and Rousseau's extraordinary growth in stature, acclaim, and following, Voltaire's animosity became all the more trenchant. Somewhat surprisingly, in the midst of Rousseau's undeserved troubles Voltaire did not intervene but instead heaped fat on the fire, only adding to the difficulties that hounded the unsuspecting, vulnerable, and hypersensitive Rousseau. One could well subject to analysis 'le cas' Rousseau, but that should not leave without scrutiny 'le cas' Voltaire, and his unrelenting attacks. Sadly these very assaults appeared in the midst of Voltaire's most enterprising work, where his speculative genius as well as the foundations of his thought are in evidence.[73]

Erasmus and Voltaire represent different stages in the development of humanism. Erasmus's *Adages* were intended to be a compendium of classical lore, serving the enrichment of contemporary style. But always Erasmus fits the role of the scholar, collecting, collating, correcting, and groaning under the interminableness of the task, of history itself, the story that never ends. By the time of Voltaire, humanism's relation to history has passed into a far more critical and independent phase. While Besterman can rightly state that 'one is struck by Voltaire's high standards of accuracy,' and 'when it comes to objective facts Voltaire can seldom be faulted,' still one never hears from Voltaire the groans of laborious scholarship that one hears from Erasmus (482).

There are reasons for this absence: history is Voltaire's métier, it is his storehouse, his schoolhouse, his staging ground, his field of inquiry, his plane of regard. But this is history critically scrutinized, stalked, and culled for principles favourable to conduct. Raymond Naves succinctly summarizes Voltaire's historical humanism: the same historical figures whom as a modernist Voltaire can disdain, as a moralist he can make the object of his study, drawing from their actions the principles that enter into his great compilations of the 'manners and the spirit' of peoples. He adds, Voltaire's meditations always end in the values and understanding of the present (158). Voltaire scrutinizes history not as a detached scholar but as an engaged man of the world.

Voltaire began the project for a philosophical dictionary in 1752 and continued to work on it from its first publication in 1764, *Dictionnaire philosophique portatif,* until the appearance of new alphabetical topics in *Questions sur l'encyclopédie* of 1770–2. Rather than what we would consider a dictionary, it is more in tune with his *Lettres philosophiques* or his *Essais sur les moeurs et l'esprit des nations.* It might well be regarded as essays in alphabetical order. Despite its several versions, it is the early title that catches its purpose: *portatif*; it was meant to be portable, conveniently at the use of the general reader. With a succinct accumulation of a variety of historical examples and anecdotes, with pungent summary, the *Dictionnaire* provides matter for reflection. Like Erasmus's *Enchiridion*, it was meant as a handbook, a brief manual for instruction, and like the *Adages* it was intended for casual reading, providing the wisdom, judgments, or simple information one can carry with one.

Despite his 'gay wisdom' in the Nietzschean sense, Voltaire, who learned from his hard experience of his earlier years (his numerous disenchantments with possible patrons, his breaks with allies, his enforced exiles for imprudent remarks or works that outraged the authorities, not to mention his two sojourns in the Bastille), is very self-protective. He did not append his own name, thus allowing ready disavowal, a favour of which authorities were by no means unappreciative. He at times gives spurious attribution (such as crediting 'transubstantiation' to a 'M. Guillaume, protestant minister'), thus giving the impression that the dictionary is a collective enterprise. But there is more than self-protection in Voltaire's double game: such procedures and awareness form a genuine part of the cut of his mind. Most notably is this apparent in his entry 'Contradiction' and those that immediately follow, where he shows by the piling up of succinct instances that the inclination toward irony and paradox, the capacity to abide within contradiction and contrast, are hallmarks of his genius. In his republic of moral reflection, contradiction and inconsistency are the unwritten rules of the land. 'The more we see of the world, the more we see it abounding in contradiction and inconsistency' (Dugdale 1: 333). To wish for regularity would be like wishing rivers to run straight, for the mountains and the valleys to become as one. Only in games are lined rules observed. 'In the meantime irregularity is part of our nature. Our social world is like the natural world, rude and unshapely' (333). This is true of peoples, of princes, of institutions, and of men of letters. Montesquieu, who disparaged the Académie française for the vapid panegyrics of its members, was nevertheless inducted into that august body and praised for his skill in 'drawing likenesses' (332–3). Voltaire goes on, 'Men are everywhere inconsistent alike. They have made laws by piecemeal, as breaches are repaired in walls' (333). We are back in the late 1740s, the worlds of *Babouc* or *Memnon*: just as it would be folly to wish that nature functioned in a straight manner, it would be still greater folly to expect from man the 'perfection of wisdom.' Nevertheless, there is a 'principle of preservation,' a muddling through that works (333). Things might be irrational but not for that unreasonable.

In the judgment of human affairs he substitutes the principle of contrast for that of contradiction (1: 284–6). This opens the way to the exercise of critical judgment, the capacity to appreciate contrasts within the individual and even extending to revered works of art. All greatness comes to us marred. Alexander, Caesar, Mahomet, and Cromwell were men of enormous accomplishment but were variously disfigured by murder, debauchery, imposture, or fanaticism. Voltaire has the capacity to accept the combination of genius with what might be considered something more than blemishes. His sense of human history and the human personality is not made for Puritans or generalists, either of the old or the new schools. Perhaps more importantly he has the confident capacity of overarching critical judgment and the sense of proportionate value. These are some of the qualities that made him the premier critic of his day. The excellent critic does not contradict himself when he praises or blames the same author, be it Dante, Shakespeare, Pascal, or Corneille. It is the author who contradicts himself by not writing all of a piece. Sometimes even the great nod, thus requiring from the critic the application of attentive contrasting judgments.

Voltaire was able to hold to a solid core of values. We see this tenacity first in the directness of his confrontation with the earthquake of Lisbon. But even more, he is affronted by the injustices that offend rational dignity and intellectual honour. The maimed funeral rites for the great actress Mlle Lecouvreur would provoke in him a lifelong anger. His greater enemy is certainty, the zealot's unwillingness to entertain other probabilities. This leads to torture, and under that entry, he lists the victims of such barbaric treatment, who after their horrible deaths were found by evidence to be innocent. These form the roll-call of the great causes (Calas, Sirven) that he undertook either to spare the one or later to vindicate their reputations.

Voltaire had a great respect for industry and commerce. Who is more valuable: the courtier who gives himself airs and plays the lackey in the antechamber of the great, or the merchant who enriches his country? Under the topic 'Liberty of Conscience' (which he alleges to be a direct translation from a German source) he values the manufacturing resources of an Anabaptist, and the commerce of the English exchange where men of all religious persuasions can come together peacefully to carry on business (1: 324–5).

It is thus that throughout his work Voltaire shows great curiosity in and respect for the moral fortitude and the simplicity of the ways of the Quakers. The first four of the *Lettres philosophiques* are devoted to them, as is a lengthy section of the *Dictionnaire*. So intrigued is he that many of their ways and beliefs found themselves reproduced in Eldorado. As a young bourgeois gentilhomme in semi-exile in England he was naturally bemused by their 'tutoyant' speech, by their dress, and their refusal to remove their hats. In the *Letters* he is quite naturally suspicious of their 'inspiration,' as he was also of Socrates' *daimon*. He argues that one does not reason with an 'enthusiast.' But he was also extremely taken with the quiet simplicity of their practice and their return to the ways of early Christianity.

Seeking refuge from the religious and civil wars that wasted Great Brit-

ain (an instinct similar to what accounted for the beginning of Eldorado), William Penn established 'the primitive Church' in America.
While he was obliged to assert that in matters of doctrine and ceremony
the Quakers were in error (such lip-service is always recognizable in Voltaire and rarely persuasive), his admiration for what Penn was able to
accomplish shines through in every paragraph. Primary among the
achievements were complete civil liberty and religious freedom. Such
grounding is responsible, Voltaire believes, for the enormous flourishing
of Pennsylvania from a community of 500 at the time of Penn to the
then-current population of over 300,000. While half of the population
remains Quaker, twenty different religions comprise the other half. Philadelphia is a model for a flourishing modern city, prosperous in its
industry, based upon civic and religious freedom. Voltaire transcends
himself when he compares the Anglo-Saxon north to the Hispanic south
of the Americas; by their general imitation of Pennsylvania, in the colonies at large 'no one is molested in his creed' (1: 296–7). 'It is this which
has rendered the English power in America equal to that of Spain: 'If any
method could be devised to enervate the English colonies it would be to
establish in them the Inquisition' (297).

There is an even more staggering projection. Under the entry 'Climate' he works to show that the changes of empire and intellect have little to do with climate, and that government and religion count even
more in the establishment of a flourishing polity. His doctrine of universal change governing all things leads to another startling conclusion concerning the Americas: 'Perhaps the Americans will in some future period
cross the seas to instruct Europeans in the arts' (311).

The values of Voltaire shine in these passages with all their foresight
and historical judgment, but when it comes to his obsession with Rousseau these virtues are somewhat tarnished. In the *Lettres sur la nouvelle
Héloïse*, in the *Lettre au Doctor Pansophe,* and in his *Sentiment des citoyens,*
Voltaire would not let up in his attacks, denying authorship but rarely
succeeding in concealing his hand. They at times show him at his satiri-
cal best and his personal worst – his unrelenting attacks against Rousseau
– and in *Sentiment des citoyens* they have the unintended consequence of
provoking Rousseau one last time, and this into the composition of his
masterpiece, *The Confessions.*

Lettres sur la nouvelle Héloïse allegedly written by the Marquis de Ximenes
were so obviously written by Voltaire himself that even Ximenes later
admitted to having had his hand in only a small portion of the first letter
(*Mélanges* 395–409). Because of their nit-picking over small points of lan-

guage, their evident class prejudice and xenophobia, the letters back-
fired, even drawing the disapproval of Voltaire's friends, d'Alembert
among them. In his *Idées républicaines* (1768), written allegedly by a Swiss
citizen after Rousseau's *Social Contract* had been consigned to the flames
there, we witness a much better Voltaire, one of discernment and complexity who uses specific historical examples to derail large generalities.
This is once again the Voltaire of classical liberalism who, as in the *Mondain*'s defence, supported the presence of opulence as a way of contributing to the circulation of wealth. Particularly in large states, the
willingness of the rich to spend opens the way for the poor (here he
means the artisans and trades people) to prosper (508–9). On the whole,
the fortunes of small republics seem to be happier, but even here at times
the dread 'fureur de commander' takes possession and precedence, and
by this malady of human nature (it is 'la passion dominante') the small
republic seems to be more vulnerable than the large. Beyond his analysis,
what is truly Voltairean emerges in the remedy: with him, as with Erasmus,
this can occur only through the use of reason and the passage of time.
Reason will eventually be heard when the passions have subsided; then
opposing arguments will be more willing to relax the stubbornness of
their positions – 'mais il faut du temps' (510). It takes time. Clearly here
the sanity of both Erasmus and Voltaire emerges: their arena is not only
history but also historical time, through which slowly, after the conflict
and the explosions, a kind of compromise or consolidation may emerge.
It is a conditional world view, a diminished world view, and one that has
seen its triumphs from time to time, but which also does little to stem or
even to comprehend the onrushing historical cataclysms of revolution.

The *Lettre au Doctor Pansophe* (who is directly addressed throughout as
Jean-Jacques) should be much better known (*Mélanges* 831–9).[74] It is a
masterpiece of polemical satire and makes clear that, despite his public
disclaimers, Voltaire seems to have read every word of Rousseau – the
major works, the prefaces, the letters. In fact, even his marginal commentaries are themselves scholarly troves. The *Letter* is a model of Voltairean style: the sheer verve of the writing astounds the reader; the
sentences are hammer blows of directness, almost as if they were copied
down as spoken. The *Letter* is a survey of Rousseau's works to date, and
Voltaire's criticisms remain as they were from the beginning, but given a
new point and sharpness. It better than any other helps us to understand
the principles that Rousseau seems to have violated and the reasons for
Voltaire's persistent acerbity toward his one-time ally. Voltaire is out of
patience with Rousseau's defence of ignorance, the strain he sees perme-

ating his works from the first *Discours* onward. It becomes clearer and
clearer that if Rousseau sees·Voltaire as a corrupting interloper in the
familial confines of Geneva, Voltaire now sees Rousseau as traitor to all
that a modernizing, enlightened Europe has come to represent, all the
combined accomplishments since the Renaissance (which was the starting point for Rousseau's sense of the moral decline that accompanies the
advancement of the arts). If Rousseau wishes to return to the time of
Pope Gregory, he would be signing his own death warrant. Rousseau in
attacking the *philosophes* is biting the hand that feeds him: 'C'est à la philosophie que vous devez votre salut et vous l'assassinez' (You owe your
whole well-being to philosophy and yet you assassinate it) (833). Voltaire
stands out as a clear defender of the development of modern culture:
'Nous ne sommes plus esclaves de ces tyrans spirituels et temporels qui
désolaient toute l'Europe; la vie est plus douce, les coeurs plus humaines
et les États plus tranquilles' (We are no longer slaves of the spiritual and
earthly tyrants who used to desolate all of Europe; the life is sweeter, the
mores are more humane and the [countries] more at ease) (833). It
would take a man of Voltaire's certitude, of his confidence in his own
critical judgment, of indeed confidence of where and when he is standing to make so forthright a defence of the values of the culture of his day,
making use of satire and outright expressions of passionate (if modulated) defence to withstand the energy of accusation.

But there is more than this in his exasperation with Rousseau. Behind
this betrayal of the·intellectual brotherhood, of the common enterprise
of the 'république littéraire' there are two other more fundamental complaints that in their expression unite Voltaire and Erasmus. The first is
the charge of singularity. Just as Luther had to withstand the question
'Who are you to go against the combined wisdom of the ages?' so Rousseau had to endure the charge of being out of step, of breaking ranks,
and of flying in the face of the proprieties of dress and behaviour and
thought. Thus Voltaire instructs Rousseau that, were he a better person,
'[il] pourrait cependant apprendre que le vrai mérite ne consiste pas à
être singulier, mais à être raisonnable' (he would know that true merit
consists not in being singular, but in being reasonable) (836). The
charge also measures the distance travelled from the time of Erasmus to
that of Voltaire: Erasmus was defending the wisdom of the ages embodied in the structures and teachings of the church; for Voltaire, Rousseau's
need for singularity is a violation of the social code of reasonableness.

But Rousseau is moving to a different music. His singularity is the consequence of heeding the promptings of the Spirit, of the 'sentiment

intérieur.' We come to the spiritual divide that separates the writer of consciousness from the daemonic, the character of good sense and practical wisdom, who comprehends the complexities of his historical conditioning, from the person who follows some inner compulsion, some voice of mysterious yet palpable design. Where Erasmus could feel only misgivings that he was 'not yet' endowed with the light of the Spirit and did not find martyrdom for Luther's cause to be truly suitable to his nature, Voltaire, with his typical pointed satire, undoes the pretensions of such 'illumination.' Voltaire allies Rousseau with the English Quakers and evangelists, who are equally obedient servants 'à cette voix divine, qui parle si haut dans les coeurs des illuminés, et que personne n'entend' (to this divine voice which speaks so loudly in the hearts of the illuminated ones and that no one else seems to hear) (837). In an age of faith the more tender-hearted Erasmus falters in the absence of the Spirit; in an age of Thought, Voltaire can securely lampoon this divine voice, that speaks so loudly in the hearts of the 'illuminated,' and evidently to them alone.

12. The Wages of Persecution: *The Confessions*

But the story does not end here, if it ever ends. There is one last bit of provocation and response, but it is one that results in Rousseau's masterpiece, *The Confessions*. In his *Sentiment des citoyens* Voltaire makes three accusations, two of which were blatantly false, but with the third he landed a bitter blow concerning the placement of Rousseau's five children. Curiously enough, at first blush, Rousseau denied this charge, but then he recovered his strength and manifested his genius, by turning this charge along with many others unknown into the most important work of the eighteenth century, *The Confessions*. Showing his own myopia to matters large, Rousseau continued to believe that the *Sentiment* was written by one J. Vernes, despite apparently everybody else's knowledge that it came from the pen of Voltaire.

Rousseau's *Confessions* is another masterpiece for many reasons, not the least of which being that it is the only readable tragedy of the eighteenth-century. Despite his best intentions, despite his passivity, even his natural pacifism, Rousseau could not help but be the Alceste whom he so defended, and in whose defence he was showing the way to the tragedy he deplored. He became the Christ whose death agony was vindicating, and even his contemporaries referred to him as the Socrates condemned to drink the hemlock. Rousseau was the agonist of his age, the one made to bear the blow, 'le coeur sans défense.' Despite his abhorrence of Voltaire's depiction of the world as ruled by some hangmen gods, Rousseau was their victim. This was part of his daemonic nature: others may have written of the same issues, but when Rousseau wrote, clamour arose and the fire was drawn down. He was the one who, by the quality of his writing, by its implied or overt accusations, made people pay attention. Not a gladiator by nature, he nevertheless always seems to have entered the arena. Unlike Luther, he was mainly devoid of external supports. Luther enjoyed the invaluable political protection of Duke Frederick, the militant backing of the young German intellectuals, the new recruits from the recently formed universities. He was also a nativist upbraiding the extortions of a foreign power. In all of these areas Rousseau was so very different. He was a foreigner, an outsider who lacked true political resources. His cause was not against a foreign power but rather against the enemy within. Like Hamlet, he tried his friends among the elite and found them all running for cover in his hour of need. This is the tragic story told by *The Confessions.*

Of course this monumental work is startling for its revelations. The early books are structured around painful disclosures, which loom as obstacles to be overcome, and when they are cleared it is as if the author himself breathes a new life – that is, enjoying the cleansing of confession. It is due to the major accusation that he had abandoned his five children and the wreckage following the interdiction of his books and his own enforced escape that *The Confessions* emerge. With a burst of creative energy Rousseau outbid his accusers and surmounted his ruin. They succeeded in pushing him to where he had always wanted to be, where his life-direction and need for justification seem to have positioned him, and that is toward ultimate intimate revelation. If Voltaire has been called the 'least self-analytical of men' (Besterman), Rousseau is among the most self-absorbed and self-observant. He had for some time, he tells us in book 10, been urged by his publisher to write his memoirs. But if such a life were of no account by virtue of public accomplishments, it could make a contribution in its revelations, and this could be accomplished by adhering to the conviction that there was no human heart, however pure, that did not conceal some odious vice. Anyone can take pride in outstanding vices; he will, however, tell of acts that are shameful.

Memory is his natural but recently acquired ambience (distinguishable from Voltaire's attention to history). Anticipated fears fill him with fright and confusion; those frights that have happened he endures with a stoic acceptance and an application of reason. Similarly, because of the full openness of his personality, he cannot respond with a ready quip, or capture the essence of a new and immediate event. Upon first meeting, people think him sluggish, boring. It is only afterwards – emotion recollected in tranquillity – that he can reconstitute the event in all of its peculiarities. This explains why *The Confessions* is not an outpouring but rather an ingathering, why it is a masterful book of analysis as well as revelation.

Going beyond the devastating charge of having abandoned his five children, Rousseau takes us into the 'labyrinthe obscur et fangeux' (obscure and murky labyrinth) of his painful revelations that are 'ridicule et honteux' (both ridiculous and shameful) (*Œuvres complètes* 1: 18; *The Confessions* 29). The first is the moment of sexual arousal caused by Mlle Lambercier's spankings. When she becomes aware of his excitation – he evidently managed an erection – she removed him from the bed he had shared with her and thenceforth treated him as a 'grand garçon,' a big boy. For our age of progressive sexual promulgations, where what was once challenging has become domesticated, there is little that is shocking in this episode. Yet it retains its interest because Rousseau uses it to reveal an essential trait of his character: it becomes more than a confession as Rousseau discloses his constant desire to prostrate himself before women, his need to have them more in imagination than in reality – as well as his life-long propensity for masturbation.

This is the first of the three hurdles to be gotten over. The other two are the disgraceful episodes of placing the blame for the ribbon that he stole on the maid-servant and boldly facing her down in the interview with the lord of the house, and the abandonment of his travelling companion, Le Maître, who suffered a kind of epileptic fit in Lyons. Both of these episodes had dire consequences for their victims: in the first the maid-servant was fired, with only the bleakest of prospects facing her, and in the second Le Maître lost all of his valuable musical compositions. These latter two are ugly episodes, but neither is so ugly as Rousseau's first attempts to justify them. In the case of the stolen ribbon and false accusation, it was not the punishment he feared so much as the disgrace before the gathering; and in the second, he rationalized that there was little he could do to be of use. But in moments of reconsideration Rousseau realizes that these are insufficient explanations, and that indeed he has himself been injured by these wrongs that will always make his conscience wince.[75]

Telling of them here is a form of expiation. In the exposition of the vicar of Savoyard we alluded to the 'faute inconnue,' the act of betrayal. It is not so much in the events themselves that this characterization comes true but rather in the revelation of a soul so much in need of justification, of expiation, one who senses that indeed he has been and is being punished for these faults committed long ago. Guilt is the wound he was born to bear.

Such shameful revelations, as Thomas McFarland has argued, help to account for the book's appeal and greatness. But these are not the only reasons. The book reveals the full flowering of Rousseau's meditative and reflective intelligence, his analyses of culture and of character, both of himself and of others. Even the excruciating moments show the full power of his expanding film of consciousness, in fact, his taste for the comic, which falls under the title of his 'folies romanesques.' *The Confessions* tell us the ways by which Rousseau in his life was a counter-Émile; that Émile was an idealized creation of a naive prototype, different from his creator who brought to event and environment ideas and responses that were excessive or inappropriate. There are several variations of such 'folie romanesque,' but the most prominent of course have to do with women. Rousseau was always captivated by the charm and beauty, even the inaccessibility, of women – but always genteel women (the most notorious exception being his long-time companion and eventual spouse, Thérèse Levasseur). Descriptions of these encounters form many of the most fascinating episodes of *The Confessions*, where Rousseau blends the deliciousness of the moment with a sense of its ridiculousness, and always with close observation and astute character analysis.

The episode with Mme Basile in book 2 shows all of these tendencies coming together (78–9; 1: 75–7). One day he follows her up to her room, the door to which is left open, and Rousseau – without her knowing – enters. Spying her at her embroidery, with a flower in her well-brushed hair, with her creamy-coloured neck bent slightly in a coquettish manner, he falls to his knees and spreads out his arms as a votary. Here the perspective changes, as she catches sight of him through a mirror, and with an imperious movement of her hand, but without turning her head, gestures to him to move to a mat at her feet. Rousseau cries out and jumps to follow her command. Despite his extreme agitation he attempted nothing further, both remaining in their positions, as in a 'tableau vivante' (which Rousseau is quite consciously adopting). Both 'ridicule et délicieux,' this situation would have remained but for the arrival of the maid servant. Quickly they scramble to rearrange their positions, not before Rousseau delivers two burning kisses to Mme Basile's outstretched hand, which she reciprocates by pressing her hand hard against his lips. For Rousseau this moment of exquisite unfulfilled romance was superior to any number of times he may have 'possessed' a woman. It was illicit, secretive, adventurous; she, while virtuous, was succumbing to her natural instincts, and while bold, still retained a natural modesty and reticence.

As he later concludes, 'My lack of success with women has always come from loving them too much.' While lauding the purity, the sincerity of his own intentions, he has certainly lost sight of the womanhood of the object of his affection. As the Venetian courtesan counselled him, after a botched effort, 'Zanetto: studia la matematica e lascia le donne' (Johnny, stick to mathematics and leave the women alone) (302; 1: 322).

But his interest was always women, their strengths, their weaknesses, their insights, their foibles. Well might he then remonstrate against the feminization of culture. The countess de Vercellis, a spirited and educated woman, who was suffering from breast cancer, took in Rousseau to be a kind of secretary, writing letters that she dictated. While admiring her qualities he was put off by the directness of her questioning; she was much too sharp to inspire confidence. Rather than reciprocal exchange of intimacy (which Rousseau tells us was his heart's desire), her wish to show herself intelligent only provoked standoffishness and diffidence in response. But she died nobly, 'like a philosopher.' In her death agony she managed a jest. Having let out a loud fart, 'Good, she said turning over, a women who can fart is not dead.' And with a final stroke of the brush that bestows a fuller dimension onto this portrait, Rousseau concludes tragically, 'Those were the last words she spoke' (85–6; 1: 83).

This is a book where the genre of 'characters' abounds in wise and judicious assessments of the principal traits of people. Like Voltaire he was not interested in minutiae but rather in the springs of character and conduct. *The Confessions* is a book filled with such studies, always wise, always fair-minded, yet fully delineated. Among the most pressing and powerful is that of Mme de Warens, his adopted 'maman,' who brought Rousseau by some calculation into a ménage à trois, in which all three seemed to enjoy a life of somewhat happy coexistence. Like most of Rousseau's presentations, she is a person of contradictions between her tastes and her background, between her heart's directions and her misguided principles.

Mme de Warens's beliefs were moderately Protestant, but, as Rousseau writes, 'This did not hinder her knowledge of good literature, or prevent her from discussing it most intelligently' (111; 1: 111). In this she was like Rousseau himself, who fully appreciated that his works were not well received in the provinces or even in the Geneva of blessed memory, where he had hoped for a good hearing. Instead, he was esteemed in Paris and in the ambience of the Court, where 'delicate sensibility' reigns. From this he infers that the French still possess – whatever their failings – the capacity to exercise benevolent imagination, the tempered tendency to indulge the heart's affections. People of such delicacy possess what Rousseau calls a 'sixth sense' and that is a 'moral sensibility.' Hence it is that, despite Rousseau's comments that a shoemaker is superior to a poet, the inevitable draw of great literature prevails over political program – one among the many complexities that associate him with the later Sartre.

As with her literary tastes, Mme de Warens has even greater personal contradictions: she was sensitive but at the same time cold, with a strange passivity in her nature that allowed her to be untouched by her doings (190–2; 1: 197–9). This quality Rousseau attributes to a deceitful moral philosophy instilled in her by her first seducer. He corrupted her with philosophical sophistries, one of which being that sex itself was of little importance, provided that there was due concealment and at least no scandal. So Mme de Warens could move from lover to lover or have several lovers contemporaneously without any compunctions. 'She could not imagine that so much importance could be attached to something that held none for her' (190; 1: 198). By these means she attracted men to herself, usually less fortunate men, such as the young Jean-Jacques. But the false principles could not totally corrupt the premises of her heart. Again and again, throughout this work, we confront this division in Rousseau's characterization of people: they might act on false principles, even do bad things, but their actions do not touch their buried inward integrity and the purity of the heart's intentions. Benevolent imagination, a tempered optimistic intelligence seems to prevail in his estimations. People might be misled but not totally corrupted – the springs of conscience can still be stirred. In fact Mme de Warens's own easy-going temperament quite early disabused Rousseau of his fears of hell. It was her own presence along with the beliefs and fortunes of fathers Gaime and Gatier that went into the making of the teachings and the career of the vicar of Savoy. In fact, the closest she could come to any sense of damnation was a vague notion of purgatory, where the iniquitous spend some time before being saved. But Rousseau's tempered benevolence does not exist with blinders: he then adds, 'It must be admitted that the wicked are always a considerable embarrassment in this world and in the next' (218; 1: 229). Together they read LaBruyère, whom she preferred to LaRochefoucauld, whom Rousseau then proceeds to classify as a 'gloomy and depressing author, especially when one is young and does not care to see man as he is' (111; 1: 112). This highly conscious Rousseau, whose value extends through the length of this classic, should command more of our attention.

The Confessions begins as the story of an unpromising hero (early prognostics about his future fortunes were all unflattering). So we must read his earlier misadventures, his own descriptions of his fumbling character and all the humiliations he endured from the later viewpoint of a person who, despite the harpies of dire prediction, managed to achieve extraordinary acclaim. We must then imagine the great Rousseau, in fact, even stand in his place as he reads of his youthful errors. To an intimate circle of invited guests he did manage three readings of *The Confessions* before this activity was curtailed by the police under the fretful instigation of Diderot and Mme d'Épinay. But at such readings his presence is its own palinode, lending an undeniable comic effect to his self-presentation. But there are two turns to the story, two reversals. He also stands before us as not only as the unpromising hero who has overcome the worst expectations but as an Oedipus at Colonus who has been scarred by the gods, by fate, and his own doing, whose story is of two turns, the second leading to catastrophe. Yet this voice must be heard as well and this presence felt. We must be like his first auditors at his short-lived readings who can only shudder in silence at what he wrought and was brought to endure.[76]

3 Passages of History: From Mundanity to Philosophy

Exemplary and influential contributions have given dualisms a changeful history of their own. But it was at the turn of the eighteenth century that dualisms acquired an urgency of form and focus. Reasons for this new leverage are clear. One is the convergence of the divisive issues of religion and revolution. In the intense debates, charges and counter-charges filled the air, as matters became more heated – and lethal. While opposition was rife, needing no added incentive, standing behind the divisions was the ready-made dualism, already canonical, between Voltaire and Rousseau. Although at first they were jointly celebrated as harbingers of revolution, in time their true differences were discerned. They provided patterns of thought for the explosive disputes of the times. Soon other dualisms were added to the roster, in fact, going back to Dante and Petrarch, and Luther and Erasmus. Dualistic ways of thinking became a dominant feature of nineteenth-century thought.

Yet the paramount work in presenting character dualities is Plutarch's *Lives of the Eminent Greeks and Romans.* The comparison of things Greek and Roman, beginning with those made between Homer and Vergil, was practically in-born and present to any historical imagination, from Vergil himself (*Aeneid* 6) down to the famous canto 26 of Dante's *Inferno*, where the freebooting spirit of Ulysses is surpassed by the more earth-bound Roman virtues and transcendent Christian ones. Plutarch's work experienced a powerful re-emergence in the sixteenth century with the celebrated and much-used translation by Jacques Amyot, which was in turn englished by Sir Thomas North. Each translation exerted an enormous influence in its native language upon two of the most original thinkers of the time, Michel de Montaigne and Shakespeare. The great respond to the great – although in different ways. For Shakespeare, the experience of Plutarch represented an opening out into a broader historical world but, in addition, Shakespeare intensified his dramaturgical display of dualistic characters (Hal-Hotspur, Hamlet-Fortinbras) with the intriguing idea, potent in both *Antony and Cleopatra* and *Macbeth*, of how the presence of one character overshadows the genius or charisma of another. For Montaigne the influence, while equally liberating, was somewhat different. Despite Montaigne's willingness to entertain and speculate about the most bizarre happenings described by Plutarch, what he esteemed was the easy familiarity of Plutarch's style, and moreover, his capacity to describe his illustrious characters not only when they are on the lofty stage of history but in their 'naturel,' in their everyday dress. He also engaged in dualistic comparisons, bringing together Seneca and Plutarch, or, as was popular, Alexander and Caesar, where he was able to indulge his favourite pastime, the exercise of thoughtful judgment. He does not write as a scholar or as a disputant but rather as one who dips and chooses, who takes what is pertinent to his thought, and arrives at considerations open to being repeated in intelligent society.

In his own *Ritratti e Vite letterarie*, presented at the end of the eighteenth century but not published posthumously until 1816,[1] Antonino Valsecchi (1708–91) worked from a different translation of Plutarch's *Lives*, that of the eminent classicist André Dacier. Dacier also translated Aristotle's *Poetics* and Sophocles' *Oedipus Tyrannus*, thus exerting a complex influence on Voltaire's his first successful tragedy, *Oedipe* (Voltaire did not completely accept Dacier's advice on the inclusion of a Greek chorus). In his translation of Plutarch, Dacier lamented that his eminent model's comparisons of illustrious lives had not been imitated by his own compatriots, who failed notably by not bringing to the fore similar comparisons between 'eroi francesi e i personaggi illustri di altre nazione' (the heroes of France and illustrious people of other nations) (12), and thus bringing to judgment their respective 'valori.' Better informed, Valsecchi, who has been quoting Dacier, points out that such comparisons and judgments had indeed already been rendered by Varillas in his confrontations of Charles V and Francis I, and of Louis XI and King Ferdinand, the *rey catolico*; by Saint-Évremond in comparing Alexander and Caesar, the Prince de Condé and the Maréchal Turenne (prime combatants in the wars of the seventeenth century), as well as Corneille and Racine; by Rapin in bringing together Homer and Vergil and Thucydides and Titus Livy; and by Abbot Ricard in comparing two cardinals: Richelieu with the eminent Spanish humanist cleric, Ximenez (13). His own examples indicate that through the seventeenth and eighteenth centuries, in the wake of Plutarch, such confrontations were attractive and well known.

Two strands of Plutarch thrived. One was heroic, present in Shakespeare and Rousseau and even extending to the French Revolution; the other more homely, worldly, deriving from Montaigne, and represented by Saint-Évremond and ultimately Voltaire. For several reasons, of the comparisons listed by Valsecchi those of Saint-Évremond (1618–1703) most attract our attention. In the middle of the seventeenth century he was still using Amyot's translation (although augmented by several commentaries of which he seemed to be unaware); moreover, by his frequent reliance on Montaigne, a continued presence in all aspects of French thought, he represented and carried forward the literary values of mundanity, the culture of worldliness.

As his young and pleasant companion, Pierre Silvestre, reminds us in his brief exposition of the prominent moments and characteristics of Saint-Évremond (which fortunately is reprinted at the beginning of the most recent edition of his prose works), Saint-Évremond writes as a man of the world ('homme du monde'), and as such, he is concerned with what even became a literary genre, the so-called character ('caractère') (xxi, xl). This lends itself to the desired end, the exercise of judgment ('jugement'), those things that in 'conversation' 'honnêtes gens' or pleasantly reasonable people can discuss with an agreeable wit. The emphasis is on portable knowledge, those things – pre-eminent events and their causes, witty responses – that one can carry away, and that enter into and become part of one's life and activities. In fact, Saint-Évremond's comparison of Alexander and Caesar grew out of his frequent conversations with the Prince de Condé, who is apparently the 'vous' addressed in the small essay itself.

When comparing Caesar and Alexander he begins, naturally enough, with their affinities before proceeding to their differences (200). He compares Seneca and Plutarch (as did Montaigne, *Essais* 2: 10) and finds that where Seneca is severe, Plutarch is more amenable, able to 'insinue doucement la vertu, et veut rendre la sagesse familière dans le plaisir même' (insinuate virtue sweetly and to make wisdom comfortable even in the midst of pleasure) (159). By his gathering of the 'sayings' ('dicts') of his characters Plutarch shows how sensitive he was to 'conversation' – thus adding to the fullest pleasure of the man of the world. Yet there are deficiencies, such as Plutarch's interest in the *daimon* of Socrates, which impulsion of spirit Saint-Évremond admits, eludes him completely, as it did Montaigne (160–1). Also revealing some of the growing refinement of taste, Saint-Évremond regrets the lack of 'délicatesse' – attributing it perhaps to the grossness of the times, or to the possibility that Plutarch's own taste was not fully 'exquis.' This means that he was not able to treat matters of 'esprit' either ingeniously or delicately ('il n'a rien d'ingénieux ou délicat') (161).

Saint-Évremond provides a lexicon for one aspect of the coming century's literary and moral values, and thus calls up the character of Voltaire, who also writes as a man of the world, a man of parts writing for other men of parts, interested in knowledge that is portable, digestible. This includes his own impatience with Socrates' *daimon*, the kind of spirit that, Voltaire complains to Rousseau, no one other than the 'illuminés' has ever seen or heard. Between Montaigne and Voltaire, Saint-Évremond is an important link in the culture of mundanity. But the genius of Voltaire also lies in the way he transcends mere mundanity; he does not disown it but demotes it to a subordinate position in the great kingdom of genius. The contrast with Saint-Évremond thus serves the added purpose of establishing Voltaire's true complexity.[2]

Spurred on by the challenge of Dacier, working under the enormous influence of Plutarch, and having to draw on the still-living and growing example of the conflict between Voltaire and Rousseau, it was Valsecchi who first brings out the major interests of dualistic comparisons. He writes not as a man of letters but as a professor of philosophy, in fact, as an ardent Catholic apologist, who has already defended orthodoxy against the combined onslaught of freethinkers such as Hobbes and Spinoza, continued by Pierre Bayle, and finding its new centre in Voltaire and Rousseau. Valsecchi, however, writes with both hands. While making it clear that he is writing (and has written) to denounce their impieties, he describes their outstanding qualities so well that it is hard to imagine any reader not wishing to turn to their works.

Plutarch's *Lives* are not true dualisms, but rather imaginative comparisons called forth by some resemblances between prominent Greek and Roman figures who had no real interactions. However much we might pursue the convergence of minds and interests, parallel lives – like parallel lines – never cross or meet. But with Voltaire and Rousseau it was different; this was a dualism in one's own time, before one's very eyes. They were the most illustrious thinkers of their time, conjoined by many qualities, including 'friendship,' and so linked they pass inseparably into the future. Valsecchi notes their affinities, even their 'career episodes,' before developing their outstanding differences. He, unlike the man of letters, is not afraid to dirty his hands with a discussion of actual texts.

Their one fundamental link is their mutual contribution to 'impiety,' the demon shaking altar and throne, and menacing the texture of society. But given this indictment, which Valsecchi pursues vociferously, his account of their respective qualities is remarkably accurate, and in Rousseau's case, at least, more to the point than many modern versions.

For Valsecchi, Rousseau, whose 'ritratto' he undertakes first, was above all a 'ragionatore,' 'un uomo razionale,' thus emphasizing the rational and rationalizing aspects of Rousseau's thought. He proceeds further, describing both Rousseau's personal qualities and those of his writing. The citizen of Geneva was endowed with a 'spirito penetrante, una immaginazione feconda, una memoria copiosa, ma singolarmente una eloquenza robusta, seducente, dominatrice' (a penetrating mind, a fertile imagination, a copious memory, but above all an eloquence that was robust, seductive, and dominating) (14). Rousseau augmented these natural gifts by his early and sedulous readings of the classical authors, primarily Plutarch, who remained his favourite, because of his high style and fondness for heroic action – qualities so different from those admired by Montaigne and Saint-Évremond. But Rousseau was handicapped by his 'orgoglio intestino' (his inborn pride) and set on the wrong track by his reformist religious origins in Geneva, both of which led to a 'disprezzo,' or disdain, for any earthly authority (hardly the case if we recall only the *Social Contract*) and the latter leaving interpretation of scriptures to the individual judgment. The consequence of this freedom was that Rousseau moved on the open seas without any moral compass, without any recognizable confines ('che privi son di confini') (15); such criticism will be heard again.

As for Rousseau's works, Valsecchi praises the *Lettres écrites de la montagne*, for there Rousseau reminds the ministers of Geneva that in banning his books and proscribing his person they are violating their own founding principles. He also values the *Lettre à M. d'Alembert sur le spectacle*, until recently the most understudied of Rousseau's works, and quite obviously relishes the *Lettre à M. de Voltaire sur la Providence* – although he disputes the main notion that Providence can be justified only if the totality of the universe is considered and not by individual cases ('the very hairs of your head are all numbered' – Matthew 10.39). He has no use for the two *Discourses*, seeing them as injurious to human society and civilization, and a violation of common sense. He quotes fully from Voltaire's witty rejoinder, and points out the contradiction that did not escape notice even by Rousseau himself, that while Rousseau condemned the arts, he nevertheless went on to write his *Nouvelle Héloïse*.

Clearly Valsecchi knows his Rousseau and is spurred on to pit him and his personal qualities against Voltaire. His 'ritratto' of Voltaire begins with the repeated praise of Plutarch and the value to be gained from comparing the lives of the two most celebrated writers of 'his' century. Setting them together in the 'veraci colori di carattere' (true colours of [their] character) (37) not only brings their distinguishing features into prominence but in so doing provides a better basis for comparison. As he does with Rousseau, Valsecchi praises Voltaire's natural gifts: 'una immaginazione viva, e brillante, una memoria vasta e fedele, un orecchio armonio, e delicato, unito ad uno stile rapido,leggero, soave formarono ... le corde della sua cetera' (a lively imagination, even brilliant, a copious and accurate memory, a harmonious and delicate ear united with a style that was crisp, to the point, and smooth all came together to form the strings of his lyre) (39). His gift was that of poetry, while Rousseau's was that of reasoning. But rather than tragic or epic, his poetic vein was better suited – and in this Voltaire suited the taste of the day – to 'poesie leggere e pezzi fuggitivi' (light poetry and fugitive pieces) – such as constituted his *Mélanges.* Even in his most voluminous works, as in his several histories, Voltaire is nothing more than an epigrammist, content to cull clever sayings, the ordinary jousting tools of the man of the world, titbits from various hands that one can repeat on occasion. But this judgment does not come close to accounting for the genius of *Le siècle de Louis XIV.*

Finally in the third part, or 'parallelo,' he enters the direct comparison of the two, the 'confronto di loro ingegni' (the confrontation of their talents) (70). The two most famous authors of the eighteenth century stand in stark contrast: 'Dotato era dalla natura Voltaire d'una talento brillante veloce, e quale appunto chiedevasi per un poeta. L'altro fornito fu d'un talento grave, meditative, o penetrante quale conveniva ad un sumblimo ragionatore' (Voltaire was endowed by Nature with a brilliant quick talent, which was called for in a poet. The other was provided with a grave, meditative, and probing nature, one that suited a sublime thinker) (70). Even in 'career episodes' they differed notably: Voltaire achieved a tumultuous success with his *Oedipe* when still in his twenties, while Rousseau was close to forty before he attracted attention with his first *Discourse.* As in their lives, so in their afterlives they will pass onto posterity conjoined. Yet their claim will be similar to that of the second-century heresiarchs Celsius and Lucian, whose anti-religious tracts only served to stir defenders of the faith. While the latter might be true, at least at the time of the first centenary of their deaths, Voltaire and

Rousseau have stood their ground stoutly and conjoined and did not require heresiologists to make them known.

Despite this bit of self-serving wishful thinking, Valsecchi does provide us with one of the most serious dualistic studies of the eighteenth century. Although pervasively influenced by Plutarch, it surpasses 'parallel lives' by providing a living bridge to the complex thought of the age in its two most diverse yet representative figures. Combative, its very animus serves as recognition of the pre-eminence of Voltaire and Rousseau in the coming engagements of the nineteenth century. Unfortunately, Valsecchi's useful formulation of a more complex and complete dualism remained largely unknown and without influence. Thus Friedrich von Schiller's celebrated essay, *Über naïve und sentimentalische Dichtung* (Naïve and Sentimental Poetry), became the pivotal effort after Plutarch. Schiller's thought differs even more profoundly from that of Plutarch, at least when compared with the latter's involvement with the culture of worldliness that Rousseau, on the other side of the Plutarchan divide, so bitterly resented. Schiller's dualistic principles do not derive from random reflections, from the casual bringing together of illustrious figures as a basis for reflection, but rather describe a philosophical divide so profound, one that the *homme du monde* cannot possibly encompass, but in which he must become one of the contestants himself. He becomes a figure in the drama from which he thought himself set apart by virtue of thought, place, and position – by the exercise of judgment and his role as a *raisonneur*. He becomes part of a typology that is itself contested; the spirit above the dust becomes enmeshed. What Luther did to Erasmus, what Rousseau to Philinthe of *Le misanthrope*, Schiller does to worldliness. By their very nature, dualisms thus stagger and jar any presumed security of opinion. There is a difference in method as well. Parallel lives are there for amiable conversation between men of the world. Schiller's thoughts on the nature of the divide and its effects show the feebleness – or at least the one-sidedness – of that amiability. His thought is not for the man of the world but rather for the student of philosophy. Schiller has elevated the plane of regard; he raised it but also deepened it, to show the material effects in thought and in action of the manifest differences of representative types in a culture.

If the pivotal work in any historical survey of lateral poetics is Schiller's *Naïve and Sentimental Poetry*, oddly enough this value is not derived from the main body of the text, where he describes the two major alternatives of modern literature, but rather in the conclusion when he abstracts from the poetic presentations of the naive and the sentimental two enduring human personality types: the realist and the idealist. Certain key phrases indicate that Schiller might be recapitulating the debate between Voltaire and Rousseau. But there is an even greater confirmation of our subject. The essay grew in an important respect out of Schiller's relationship with Goethe – the Olympian, unflappable Goethe. It was an expression of self-defence, thus corroborating our theory, in which by establishing his own unbridgeable antitheses, Schiller was thus able to justify himself. In an excellent introduction to his translation of the essay, Julius A. Elias writes, 'The validity of each type is established independently of the other, and thus Schiller is emancipated from Goethe.' But conveying the genuine insight that attends any dualism, Goethe, despite his apparent distance, knew that Schiller wrote the essay 'to defend himself against me' (10).

Thus his essay looks backward to the century's most formidable dualism and grows out of Schiller's own trials, but it also looks forward and establishes the pattern for many of the dualities of nineteenth-century thought. Think, for example, of such engaging testimony as Matthew Arnold's Hebraism and Hellenism, Nietzsche's Apollonian and Dionysian, and even Turgenev's Hamlet and Don Quixote, and extending to the psychological types of introverted and extroverted, or tough and tender, and to the even later hedgehog and the fox, or paleface and redskin.[3] While ideally the drive of such dualistic principles seems to be toward a desired merger of qualities, nevertheless, they do retain a power of formulation that captures the imagination in registering the major forces of an age, or in indicating a fissure in society that is entrenched and extensive.

The temperamental divergence between realist and idealist is so radical, Schiller argues, as to affect all future thought – thus anticipating the coming clashes of the nineteenth century. This antagonism – because the divergence is so radically based upon 'inner mental disposition' (inner[n] Gemütsform) – is the cause of a division worse than any 'fortuitous clash of interests' (zufällige Streit der Interessen) could ever provoke and results in the dilemma that no work of poetry or of philosophy, no representation of the spirit can decisively satisfy one group without for that very reason bringing upon itself the condemnation of the other (*Naïve and Sentimental Poetry* 176; *Schriften* 4: 357–8). The intellectual chasm between intellectual groups based on this 'innern Gemütsform' thus becomes irreducible, literally fundamental, closing off any possibilities of reconciliation. The direness of the prognosis should not be overlooked. It means there is a temperamental factor, a human factor that is always responsible for conflict.

Schiller's commentary is useful, not because of the rubrics he employs – they are of the sort that we have referred to as disinformational – but rather because of the brilliant analyses and running comparisons they generate. His detailed contrasts are illustrative, paradigmatic, and provocative, both for what they say and do not say, for what they point to and imply, for what they do not cover but finally and inevitably push us toward. They invite us to take liberties, to maul and even to plunder, to amplify and by wilful substitution to alter. His discussion performs the function of any great text.

There can be no mistaking the direct meaning of Schiller's thought, for the contrast between the types is luminously introduced. The realist, when abstracted from the naive, depends theoretically upon the 'sober spirit of observation' and the uniform and regular testimony of the senses (ein nuchtern[er] Beobachtungsgeist und eine feste Anhänglichkeit an das gleichförmige Zeugnis der Sinne) and thus exhibits practically a resigned submission to an external necessity in the principles of antecedence, succession and causation in Nature – 'an accession to what is and what must be' (eine resignierte Unterwerfung unter die Notwendigkeit ... der Natur: eine Ergebung also in das was ist und was sein muss') (177; 4: 358 and passim). As there is a uniformity in the passing objects, so there is an equanimity in the observer. The realist, moreover, enjoys a sense of personal security, a contentment, that prompts him to place primary value on the peace and well-being ('Wohlstand') of humankind. From these premises there follow many truly engaging and useful insights.

The idealist, for his part, is not restrained by the external – the conditioned – but by his own restless spirit of speculation he is driven on to the urgent demands of the unconditioned ('das Unbedingte'), which then result in a moral rigorism that is willing to sacrifice simple well-being and peace as justifiable goals of human existence (180; 4: 358). One can discern the thought of Cassirer concerning the eudaemonism of Voltaire and the ethical reformation of Rousseau as having its roots here in Schiller's contrast. The idealist does not ask what a particular thing is good for ('wozu eine Sache gut sei') but rather whether it is good in itself ('ob sie gut sei'), according to the unconstrained rule of ideal reason and of what ought to be in the determinations of his own spirit (182; 4: 362–3).

While abstract, Schiller's discussion of the interaction of these two types permits a very rewarding and exciting intellectual drama, as each of the two cannot accept the findings or presuppositions of the other, yet they seem drawn together, caught in a mortal engagement across a deep divide (182; 4: 362). Schiller's formulations are dramatic as well as para-digmatic; they establish the useful terms and dimensions of the problem. They are provocative, opening up larger fields of speculation. We gain some needed amplification by conflating 'Nature' in some ways with 'History.' Schiller's conception of Nature does involve succession: for the realist 'nothing arises out of itself, everything springs out of the anteced-ent moment to give rise to the following one' (nichts springt aus sich selbst, alles nur aus dem vorhergehenden Moment, um zu einem fol-genden zu führen) (178; 4: 359). Schiller's 'realist,' and all of the related figures I call writers of consciousness, are responsive to the multiple and complex constraints of history, but they are even more obliged to remain within those constraints, to seek out continuity, even accommodation with the complex pressures that are brought to bear. Clearly, and here we move beyond Schiller's type, the writer of consciousness can embrace the movement of history and its traditions because of his firm belief that he is part of that line of connection: he has a sense of belonging. He par-ticipates in these continuities; they draw him up, they elevate him. These writers are convinced they can balance – even contain – various contend-ing elements because they sit securely in the middle, and thus while incorporating seemingly contradictory positions, they themselves remain unscathed by error. By seeking out the middle they even create the extremes.

Schiller's description of the idealist may be transferred to the dae-monic writer. If the realist calmly and with a sense of balanced equanim-ity submits to physical necessity, the idealist needs to be transported beyond himself, he needs to transcend his daily self: 'he must for the moment exalt his nature, for he can do nothing unless he is enthused. But then of course he can do all the more, and his behaviour will mani-fest a character of loftiness and grandeur that one looks for in vain in the actions of the realist' (er muss augenblicklich seine Natur exaltieren, und er vermag nichts, als insofern er begeistert ist. Alsdann freilich ver-mag er auch desto mehr, und sein Betragen wird einem Charakter von Hoheit und Grösse zeigen, den man in den Handlungen des Realisten vergeblich sucht) (181; 4: 362). There are convergences, if not complete coverage, between the larger needs of the idealist and the conversion experience of the daemonic. Schiller only intimates the prior period of disquiet and disharmony, and the following period of great creativity. But in the midst of their dramas the idealist and the daemonic both feel the need to be swept up, swept along by a greater upheaval. The dae-monic figure cannot live amidst partial truths and contradictory positions; nor is he willing to accept compromise. Such contradiction within the self is overcome by the experience of conversion (whether this be in religious or psycho-personal terms). While the realist seems stable within a system of relational constraints, the idealist, like the daemonic, is restless or has no sense of being comfortably at home. His lifelong being is in need of justification. Thus he suffers from a larger dissatisfaction that requires some transcendence that carries him along. The idealist, like the daemonic personality, requires these larger gestures of submission, of abnegation of the self, which in turn results in the strengthening of the self in ways not previously expected. The realist, like the writer of consciousness, lives in the pursuit of well-being, both for his inner peace and the concord of his world. The daemonic figure, like the idealist, experiences unrest and inner division rather than equanimity. He requires some transforming experience, in his need for which he is willing to expose both himself and his world to tumult and danger.

Well-being, 'Wohlstand,' or Cassirer's 'eudaemonism' versus some inner striving on the part of the daemonic are the facing alternatives of this new typology, which bear some resemblances to Voltaire and Rousseau. In the various facets of human experience, the realist advocates and works to bring about pleasure, happiness, well-being (183; 4: 365). The idealist does not seem to have this capacity, mainly because the demands upon himself and others are boundless. He is overcome by dissension within himself and with others (18; 4: 363). Rousseau seems to fit this description, as well as Schiller's notion that the idealist is so concerned with the larger picture that he misses the plain fact coming towards one – an omission so tragically real in Rousseau's fate. Equally certain is Voltaire's presence, when Schiller writes that for the realist the world is a well-planned garden; in contrast with the idealist, he feels at home in his place, the world is his (183; 4: 363). And both larger types come to mind when Schiller describes their attitudes toward each other: the writer of consciousness accuses the daemonic of indulging in fanaticism, wilfulness, and extravagant eccentricities (184; 4: 364), while the daemonic figure, like the idealist, will accuse his opposite of smallness, pettiness, the lack of a larger understanding. Having a more limited conception of human possibility, the realist will be more forgiving, while the idealist will be outraged at infractions against the larger good. His ambience is thus accusation. The one abides in a culture of limitation; the other in one of potentiality.

It is true that in Schiller's felicitous phrase the realist has the capacity to make the moment his friend (183–4; 4: 363), perhaps because all moments are uniformly alike and extended through time. Yes, he makes them friends, but not great friends. The writer of consciousness enjoys an ego-security, thus he thrives within a known and limited system, but does little to extend the limits of the possible (184; 4: 363). Supported by the topical relatedness of history, by its subjects and messages that are available, he turns out to be its victim (I transfer Schiller's implied thought into the conditions of this study). There is some hazard in ministering too closely to the superficial ills of an age, of becoming masters of public engagement and practical morality. History can be a cruel and merciless mistress. Many of the works of the writer of consciousness, while enjoying immense popularity in their day and accounting for his enormous stature, are maintained in a later age only by their 'historical' importance. Paradoxically, the daemonic writer, by insisting upon more than the facile topics of contemporary abuse, by plunging more deeply into the recesses of his own psyche, will – because of that ahistoricity – know a more compelling success. He will be called upon to write better than he knows, to exceed the limits of his conscious control, while the writer of consciousness will rarely exceed the boundaries of his intent. He is aware that what he is proposing is a more restricted view of the human personality, or its potential, and perhaps even of his own better nature. It is as if a full mobilization of his own resources is never quite possible, as if he suspects his own energies and as a consequence is limited to second thoughts, to halfway measures, to reconsideration, to partial truths and 'yes/but' locutions. While an abiding part of his nature, such circumspection comes even more into evidence when he meets the daemonic writer head on. One of the recurring features of this study is the investigation of the various strategies – some quite successful, some not – by which the writer of consciousness responds to radical discourse.[4]

While acknowledging the critical contributions of Schiller, benefiting from them, and even redeploying them, we are obliged to move beyond his nomenclature and even in some respectful ways his analyses. Coleridge knew this and did so, although not with acknowledgment. Coleridge, that audacious mind, rightly called by Alfred Harbage 'our' greatest Shakespearean critic, is important for many reasons.[5] First, judging from internal evidence, it is likely that he knew Schiller's essay; second, observing the preceding three centuries, he quite rightly selects the two dominant dualisms, those of Erasmus and Luther and Voltaire and Rousseau. Next, where Schiller fully analyses the interplay between representative types, Coleridge dramatizes, personalizes, and historicizes the dualisms. He names names and places them in their historical conditions. And not only does he make comparisons within the pairs, the two by twos, advancing on Noah's ark, the pas de deux, the 'dance of death,' he quite adroitly draws out the historical affiliations between the respective members of the various pairs. Enlisting more than a single dualism almost naturally inclines one to establish alignments.

Coleridge is the first to construct true dualisms, and he does so by means of his extraordinary historical and literary imagination and insight. He provides intellectual guidelines when he distinguishes the 'analogies of nature' from 'the masquerade figures of cunning and vanity' (*The Friend* 1: 130). By this he means that such true dualisms do not persist by virtue of influence or imitation but by genuine tensions and force of thought within distinct and different historical epochs. They are lodged and find their beings in the issues of a particular time and thus are truly non-imitative.

He proceeds by means of a musical analogy (but his epigraph, a quotation from the *Musophilus* of the regrettably neglected Samuel Daniel, provides literary justification as well: 'O blessed Letters! that combine in one / All ages past, and make one live with all'). From music he takes the concept of recognition (out of which in our time Edmund Wilson made the phrase, 'the shock of recognition'). Just as in music, where we can recognize similarities and echoes between various compositions, so in history 'the events and characters of one age ... recall those of another.' But there is more: 'The variety by which each is individualized not only gives a charm and poignancy to the resemblance, but likewise renders the whole more intelligible' (130). Within the different historical conditions an individuality is achieved that not only makes the resemblance more prepossessing but by virtue of the possible comparisons makes each of the parts more significant. Illumination is reciprocal between the larger and the smaller and is retrospective as well as prospective. One can move back and forth between the various contributions, drawing out otherwise occluded elements, and even using the larger principles derived from such comparisons to further decipher the independent, individualized parts.

More specific to our purpose he asserts, setting aside approval or disapproval (and his own are clearly pronounced) as well as the 'altered drapery and costume' of different historical periods, 'I have myself ... derived the deepest interest from the comparison of men, whose characters at the first view appear widely dissimilar' (130). He then strikes home when he declares that he has 'repeatedly found that the idea of Voltaire and Rousseau ... recall in a similar cluster and connection that of

Erasmus and Luther' (131). In remarkably subtle criticism he then proceeds to explore the similarities between Erasmus and Voltaire (the first
of whom he revered, while the latter he abhorred). They were alike in
their *effects* (which extended throughout Europe), in their *circumstances*
(both lived in ages of hope and promise, however much he approved of
that of Erasmus, 'restless from the first vernal influences of real knowledge,' and disapproved of that of Voltaire, also restless but with the 'hectic of an imagined superiority') (132), and in their *instruments* (those of
'wit and amusive erudition'). Then as in a soliloquy of Hamlet (he did
own up to having a 'smack' of Hamlet in him) he comes full circle by
concluding that the two men were 'essentially different' (Richards 426).

However, it will be one of the purposes of this and a future study to
explore more fully the affiliations between Erasmus and Voltaire – and
there are many that Coleridge ignores – as well as those with the other
writers of consciousness. There is some point to this endeavour: habitually critics have been willing to follow the connecting lines on only one
side of these great dualisms, those of Luther and Rousseau, but not
much farther beyond. In 1995 two books appeared that follow this line:
Thomas McFarland's *Romanticism and the Heritage of Rousseau* and Dennis
Porter's *Rousseau's Legacy*. The latter, while tracing Rousseau's legacy and
'powerful influence' (which are uncontested) makes the point that 'one
cannot speak in the same way of Voltaire's nineteenth- and twentieth-
century legacy' (12). If the dualisms I study here have any enduring
value and appeal – in the Coleridgean sense of genuine resemblances,
that is, those that emerge from the radical natures of their characters
and reciprocal involvements, their 'cluster and connection' – then there
are discernible markings, resemblances of thought, style, intellectual
positioning, habits of mind and character that need to be clarified and
pursued, not only in the one line of descent, the daemonic, but the
other as well, who defend their own positions in the enduring contest of
the two intellectual nations. In fact, Bruce Mansfield can authoritatively
assert in *Phoenix of His Age* that 'the comparison between Erasmus and
Voltaire has been a common-place since the nineteenth century,' and
gives large credit to Coleridge for this fact (18).

In his engagement with Luther and Rousseau, Coleridge shows his
mettle, indeed his own genius. This is Coleridge at his intellectually most
daring, attempting not a simple pas de deux, but rather a high-flying
jeté. Intimating the sheer outlandishness of the suggestion, nevertheless
he proceeds to draw the necessary lines of affiliation between the two,
between the 'heroic' Luther and the 'crazy' Rousseau, in the latter

description engaging in a necessary bit of exaggeration for comparison's sake, but by which he also means 'complicated,' 'paradoxical' – torn between the 'stoic pride of his principles, yet the victim of morbid vanity in his feelings and conduct' – the contradictions Schiller had already noted in the idealist (*The Friend* 1: 132). Indeed, he feels he can make the comparison, because, like Schiller's idealist, 'each referred all things to his own ideal' (133). Yet Luther had the better circumstances; because of his reliance on the Bible 'he had derived his standard from a common measure already received by the good and the wise,' and this taught him that he shared great common interests with others, a means for moderating his feelings and strengthening his convictions (133). Luther was part of a movement with a widely shared intellectual resource – he had a great text – and was a participant at many levels of activity in a community. None of these opportunities of occasion were offered to Rousseau, who, attempting to steer by the compass of 'unaided reason,' could not see the currents that were leading him off course (according to Valsecchi as well).

Marvellous pages intervene where Coleridge traces the 'temptations' Luther had to endure in his beneficial sequestration in Wartburg castle. Then in the final lengthy paragraph he reaches his goal, which is one of a grand *translatio*. That is, Coleridge asks us to make a leap in historical imagination and conceive Luther as a citizen of Geneva: suppose the French language to have been his native tongue, his predecessors to have been the English deists, and his contemporaries Voltaire and the Encyclopedists, that is, take Luther's temperament and transpose it to the 'unspiritualized' age of the Enlightenment. He takes to task the full meaning of *mutatis mutandis*. Bearing in mind Rousseau's own temperamental qualities, he asks if Luther's 'impetuous temperament, his deep-working mind, his busy and vivid imagination' would not also have been a 'trouble' to him, as it was to Rousseau in the later period, particularly in that world where 'nothing was to be altered ... or to cease to be what had been,' where there was so little possibility of realizing 'his preconceptions of what ought to be' (*The Friend* 1: 143). This is powerful enough, but he then goes on to make good work of the same temperament operating in different ages. Luther's spiritual world embraced the heavenly as well as the earthly city. In the absence of the former and given his great concern for human betterment, would not, Coleridge asks, Luther's passion have 'found in the inequalities of mankind, in the oppression of governments and the miseries of the governed, an entire instead of a divided object?' Even more boldly he asks if a new social contract would not have replaced in this reborn Luther's mind 'the reign of Christ in the New Jerusalem.' 'Henceforward then, we will conceive his reason employed in building up anew the edifice of the earthly society.' This should remind us that such rhetorical questioning should never become too specific, because the first response is, 'How can we ever know?' Yet there are trailways of surmise. For instance, at the time of the uprising of the peasants in 1524–5, Luther at first condemned the tyranny of the lords as well as the menacing actions of the peasants. But when the peasants increased their violent behaviour, sacking, pillaging, engaging in acts of iconoclasm, Luther in some notorious statements called down upon them the full and heavy power of authority. Luther held to the thesis of the 'two governments,' that of God and that of man. He suspected that religious enthusiasts (his enemies) were fomenting the rebellion, an unwarranted interference in the life of the polity. But he also believed that people were wayward, perverse, and given to violation unless curbed by the law. Granted these fundamental distinctions in Luther's thought it is hard to imagine his ever promoting the New Jerusalem among humankind. Nevertheless it is not so strange a thought. There is an extraordinary connection – which the chapter on Voltaire and Rousseau delineated, and which both Hegel and Sartre formulate – between the Reformation and the Enlightenment. Quoting from Rousseau's *Lettres écrites de la montagne*, I was able to establish a specific transfer of authority from Christian liberty to political liberty, a transfer very similar to the one Coleridge imagines. Primarily, though, we can relish Coleridge's insistence on the temperamental affinities, that same sense of restlessness, of homelessness in matters of the spirit, yet one that resists and detests as vile mere compromise, and finally one that arrives at an intransigence that is boldly assertive and unyielding in matters of importance for these representatives of a radical protestantism. This is the larger configuration emerging from Coleridge's great tableau. But perhaps for Coleridge, as for us, the greater similarity consists in the major dualism in which each of them takes part: 'In the relation too which their writings bore to those of Erasmus and Voltaire, and the way the latter cooperate with them to the same general end, each finding its own class of Admirers and Proselytes, the parallel is complete' (133).

Giosue Carducci (1835–1907), the Italian poet and intellectual, who was professor of literature from 1860 at the University of Bologna, adds considerable texture to these historical considerations. Carducci expands these issues in an essay, 'Della Varia Fortuna di Dante,' and then in a newspaper account of his lecture, which he in all likelihood provided or at least edited. Students of Italian literature are well aware of the tensions experienced by Petrarch, who came into maturity after Dante's death, and was obliged to assert himself against such prodigious influence.[6] Out of this vertical duality Carducci adds to the historical filiations that Coleridge adumbrates, but unlike Coleridge he draws a significant line of connection between Petrarch, Erasmus, and Voltaire: they are the three great legislators of 'la civiltà europea' from three illustrious centuries (249). Carducci, a figure of the Italian Risorgimento aflame with the rhetoric of liberation, makes of Petrarch, as many will do after him, the great fashioner of the Renaissance, and then in a substantial leap adds Erasmus from the sixteenth-century Reformation and Voltaire from the eighteenth-century Enlightenment, as leaders of the three critical phases that liberated the West from medieval culture. He sees the three figures as representing the advanced stages of European thought and consciousness in their time and as the leaders of a progressive unfolding of a culture of enlightenment so bound up with the essence of European civilization. But the newspaper account does not refer to the complications brought about by their involvement in a critical dualism. In his public lecture he completes the comparison, speculating whether the relationship of Dante to Petrarch might not find its equal in that of Luther to Erasmus and that of Rousseau to Voltaire. Between these two lines there exists an 'antipatia di natura' (250). Here we come to a division in Carducci's thought, one dictated by the nature of dualisms. If there is an antipathy of nature (or natures) between the members of the various pairs, there must be an antipathy in nature, which throws a check into the progress of civilization. The daemonic figure wars with the advanced stages of European thought, but so does the very nature of dualistic thought itself, as it concentrates attention on conflict and division. Thus even Schiller at the beginning of the section where he outlines the two personality types must bemoan the presence of such an antagonism in the midst of a century that is civilizing itself ('in einem sich kultivierenden Jahrhundert') (176; 357).

For Carducci, then, Dante, Luther, and Rousseau are the great rebels of their century, while their respective counterparts are 'in fondo conservatori' (250). Such is the transformative power of a dualism that once-heralded 'legislators' of the progressive liberation of European culture are now deemed conservative. This is not quite the case, as all of the writers of consciousness remained 'liberal' or reformist throughout their careers.

They simply did not and could not make the same personal choices or have the same dominant aspects of personality as did their rivals, only in relation to whom do they appear to be conservative. But Carducci does understand the sense of diminishment, retrievable from Schiller's essay, when he writes that they did have 'nel loro segreto un po' paura' of their more dominant opponents (250). While noting this 'fear' he neverthe-less credits the bravery of Petrarch's defensive response, calling it 'chi-ara, nobile, dignitosa' (251).

Carducci's terms of understanding are thus quite valuable, because they bring us into the personality of a writer like Petrarch, who feels in a self-conscious way that he is being over-shadowed, but still manages to defend his views in a very courageous manner. This is a characteristic of all of the writers of consciousness, and one of the reasons the dynamic of their dualisms remains so intriguing. Carducci's thought is equally important for the ideological construct he brings to the history of dual-istic formulations. Yes, the three – Petrarch, Erasmus, and Voltaire – were at the forefront of progressive European culture, but when they encoun-tered their gigantic foes, who were more 'rebellious' by temperament, their work appears more conservative. Their foes were opposed to the most advanced stages of European thought in their time, and the very effects produced by such antagonists and the continuing presence of such dualistic antagonism seem to strike at the heart of the developing culture of Enlightenment and even overwhelm its leading proponents. In this address to the politics of culture, Carducci's thought may take us even farther in the understanding of the complex roles of dualisms than do those of either Schiller or Coleridge.

4 Turgenev and Dostoevsky: 'What Is There in Common?'

> It is possible for you to reach [the mysteries of the kingdom], but you will grieve a great deal.
>
> – *The Gospel of Judas*

1. Separate Accounts

Unlike those of the first two dualisms of this study, the conflict between Turgenev and Dostoevsky was aggravated by personal contact where apparent friendship concealed a deep antipathy. 'They met them on the day of their success,' when, in the mid-1840s, as budding talents and rising stars, they gathered in the brilliant circle of Vissarion Belinsky (1811–48). While there were other candidates, it was upon Turgenev and Dostoevsky that the burden and the challenge of a true dualism descended, as personal antagonism soon led to a rupture and intellectual dissent. Reconciliation followed in the early 1860s, only to be broken once again and permanently by a celebrated clash of personality and ideology in Baden-Baden in 1867. Events orchestrated a grand finale to their itinerary of encounter when, a decade later, Turgenev made a triumphant return to Russia in a time of increased fear and perplexity. He returned as a voice of enlightened moderation, and what he represented and what he was were enthusiastically welcomed. In the meantime, of course, Dostoevsky had enjoyed his own return. Moreover, even those who disagreed with some of his political statements in the *Diary of a Writer* and *Demons* were enthralled by the voice of this man, the man who had almost literally come back from the dead, a Dante who had passed through his hell. This was a man who had been scarred by his commitments, who earned his face and his voice. Clearly the stage was set, and it was upon various public occasions that the two met to express, for all, the opposing ways of Russian thought and the country's future. At their first joint appearance in 1879 for the benefit of a literary fund, other speakers participated, but as Frank adroitly observes, 'All eyes were fixed on Turgenev and Dostoevsky.' Dualisms will exert their sway. 'Their juxtaposed presence on the stage brought together the opposing poles of Russian culture.' Frank then quotes B.M. Markevich's words, given in the introduction, questioning what commonality could exist between such an 'incurable Westernizer' as Turgenev, and Dostoevsky, the seeker after the 'genuine Russian soul,' before concluding with that intuitive understanding of the nature of dualisms: 'Both were competing, on those nominally apolitical occasions, for the minds and hearts of the public on whom would depend the future' (5: 415). It is almost as if Erasmus and Luther were to come together in 1526, or 1530, and present themselves and their own divided positions to a troubled and vociferous audience.

Their series of public appearances would reach its dramatic culmination at the celebrated unveiling of the Pushkin statue in Moscow, June 1880. 'What seemed to be a purely cultural event thus took on ... an important social-political subtext. On a more personal level, this subtext was dramatized by the culmination of the ideological duel that Turgenev and Dostoevsky had been carrying on ever since the mid-1860s' (5: 497–8). But in the introduction to his useful collection of essays concerning Dostoevsky, Robert Louis Jackson deplores this dualism, regarding it as only an expression of a competitive see-saw mentality: 'It is the unhealthy Russian custom to praise one writer at the expense of another' (2). Such a 'custom' is not unique to Russian culture (Unamuno is famous for having said that the sickness of *hispanidad*, which he abhorred, was that when praising one writer the speaker is actually wishing to dispraise another.) A Russian critic, D. Golsuorsi, puts it more luminously: it appeared in the literary world of the time that one light could not be lit before the other was extinguished (Budanova 5). But rather than being thus discounted, such a dualism should be appreciated for what it represents. First, among other reasons, it is an expression of ideological ferment at an important moment of cultural change and crisis. Second, in Dostoevsky's words, polemics lead to clarification, an expansive opening up of the issues involved. Difference, at such a level of encounter, requires expression. Given the volubility of their natures, suppression is not an option. Nor is silence to be sought, among neither the combatants nor their adherents, particularly when, as Bornkamm so perceptively remarked in regard to Luther and Erasmus, the debate itself was unavoidable.

But there are other reasons for not deploring the division between the two. In the close confines of Russian culture of the time, 'inter-responsiveness' was rampant, and in the case of Turgenev and Dostoevsky, the capacity to push the other to the farthest reaches of his thought and self-revelation. Therefore, while this might be in part 'the history of an enmity' (as Yuri Nikolsky has called it in the first full monograph on the rivalry of Turgenev and Dostoevsky in 1921), it is equally well understood by N.F. Budanova (1987) as a 'creative dialogue' (tvorchesky dialog); moreover, because of its deeply rooted nature, like the others in this study it could be called 'unending' (nezaversheny), that is, prominent in its own day and continuing down to ours. One thinks one is back in the same Maugras-Gouhier debate over Voltaire and Rousseau, trying to separate the interfacing between ideology and temperament, rather than seeing their coefficiency. Far from being a 'tragedy' to be lamented, the division is rather a highly informative mutual exchange that, while giving off plenty of heat, provides more than its share of illumination.

Yet Dostoevsky, to be sure, had other great enmities. Quite early he was naturally inflated by Belinsky's raptures over *Poor Folk*, only to be abruptly demoted when *The Double* was too much for that eminent critic's newly adopted code of social relevancy.[1] There were even more serious ideological and religious differences: Belinsky had become a socialist and thus was swept up in the notion that environment underpins all social behaviour, and thus excuses all crime (an adjoining remarkable entry in *The Diary of a Writer [DW]*, 'Milieu' shows Dostoevsky's most sophisticated thoughts on this matter).[2] Being a socialist, he was an incumbent atheist, and would shock Dostoevsky (apparently almost into tears) by his onslaughts on Christian belief. Christ, had he lived in their day, Belinsky was fond of asserting, would be a nobody. Belinksy died from consumption not long after these bitter exchanges, so while there was confrontation there could be no itinerary of encounter. Moreover, Dostoevsky always harboured a secret fondness for Belinsky's enthusiasms (ever changing though they might be), and the fact that when he spoke he did not speak to show off.

Even more importantly, Belinsky was at the centre of the emergence of a remarkable phalanx of Russian writers in the 1840s. Great literature requires great criticism. In February 1877, Dostoevsky takes pride in recalling that emergence. Far from being a period of stagnation, he explains, 'In the course of the last forty years there appeared the last works of Pushkin; Gogol came and went; we had Lermontov, Ostrovsky, Turgenev, Goncharov and at least ten or more other most talented creative writers who made their appearances ... It may be positively asserted that in so short a period, never, in any literature, did there appear so many gifted writers as in Russia – and without interruption' (583). And the listing is even more impressive in that it omits to name Dostoevsky himself and Tolstoy. Other than his neglect of the Elizabethans, we can largely agree with Dostoevsky's assessments. Dostoevsky values Belinsky, whatever their disagreements, because he showed the role that 'the business of criticism' must play if there is to be such an astonishing florescence. Although in his annual surveys of 1846 and 1847 Belinsky turned away from his earlier premature enthusiasm for Dostoevsky, it is his larger role in the formation of the new Russian literature that Dostoevsky could not forget, despite later bitter comments. Although Dostoevsky could not continue a real dialogue with Belinsky, he could carry on an imaginary one, and as Berdyaev so rightly confirms, he did so most dramatically in Ivan Karamazov and his prose-poem of the Grand Inquisitor.

Perhaps it is even odder that Nikolai Chernyshevsky (1822–89) does not assume any major part in a dualism with Dostoevsky. After all, he did write *What Is to Be Done*, the bible of revolutionary nihilism in the 1860s. This was the work that Joseph Frank has shown in a critical tour de force to be satirized in *Notes from Underground* (Frank 3: 310–47). Chernyshevsky (like the youthfully deceased Dobrolyubov) was a seminarian who had defected – confirming what both Voltaire and Rousseau had earlier maintained: in their rejection of a simplistic orthodoxy, people do not know where to stop. From one extreme, the same kineticism jumps to the other. Dostoevsky himself recognized this development, when he wrote that seminarians become 'most vicious atheists not to mention blasphemers. Nobody knows how to blaspheme so thoroughly and so skilfully as a seminarian' (Frank 5: 473). And yet, as Dostoevsky acknowledged, there is something in the Russian character that gives birth to such whole-heartedness. Personally Dostoevsky felt no antipathy for Chernyshevsky; in fact, he (unlike Herzen, who found him insolent and argumentative) was fond of him. 'For my part I liked Chernyshevsky's appearance and manners' (*DW* 23). This is just another episode to remind us of the temperamental bases to all dualisms. Unlikes lead to dislikes – and Turgenev and Dostoevsky were most unlike in ways superficial and profound – and dislikes soon yield intellectual dissensions; in fact, they open the doors to much larger argumentative distaste. The itinerary of their encounter is complex and brings together temperament, background, mannerisms, notions about art, thoughts about nation, and which way a nation undergoing profound changes – a nation deeply divided – should face, and about the nature of consciousness itself, the difference between conscious thoughts and lived thoughts. In short, they represent the fullest dimensions of what we have been following in the careers of the writers of consciousness and the daemonic.

A major figure of encounter is, of course, Tolstoy. The relationship between Turgenev and Dostoevsky is quite different from that between Tolstoy and Turgenev – a classic case of a dispute between friends. After a breach of some seventeen years, due to a 'misunderstanding,' they were able to patch things up, despite the fact that the 'intellectual' divide was just as sharp as – and in fact was quite similar to – what divided Turgenev from Dostoevsky. In a letter of 1876, Turgenev deplores the serial continuation of *Anna Karenina* (he had not yet read the concluding section): 'However great Tolstoy's talent may be, he cannot get out of the Moscow bog into which he has crawled. Orthodoxy, the nobility, Slavophilism ... the hatred of everything foreign, sour cabbage soup and a lack of soap' (*Turgenev's Letters* 220). Writing in 1882, he continues in the same vein, apropos of Tolstoy's *Confessions*: 'It is based upon false premises and leads ultimately to the most melancholy denial of any real living, human life ... It's also in its way a form of nihilism.' Then, like Voltaire taking to task Rousseau, he adds, 'And it amazes me how Tolstoy, who denies among other things, Art, surrounds himself with artists.' Despite these objections to Tolstoy's turn of career, he goes on to assert that Tolstoy is 'the most remarkable man living in Russian today' (287). While one may discuss the differences between Dostoevsky and Tolstoy, even their natural rivalry, between them there existed no grand enmity.[3] In *The Diary of a Writer* Dostoevsky makes it abundantly clear that, while Tolstoy is the historian of a particular class of Russians, he also expresses the fuller dimensions of the Russian people in their religious attitudes toward guilt and evil. There are strange exemptions in the unfolding of a dualism. The falling out of friends can result in reconciliation, whereas in a true dualism opposition is 'unending.'

2. Displacement, New Intellectual Plateaus, and Recurrence

There are other identifications in the cross-rivalry, the first perhaps more in tune with Jackson's complaint: quite early, remarkably early, Turgenev, following in his historical afterlife the route of the other two writers of consciousness, Erasmus and Voltaire, found himself displaced. This is made quite clear in V.V. Rozanov's comparison between the two, where already by 1894 Turgenev is assigned a role amounting to one of only historical importance. His characters 'responded to the interests of the moment, were understood in their time and now have left behind an exclusively aesthetic, artistic attractiveness. We like them as living images, but we find nothing left to puzzle out in them. It is quite the opposite with Dostoevsky. The anxieties and doubts that flood his works are our anxieties and doubts, and they will remain so for all time.'[4] This supersession is attributed to the tumultuousness of the times that would seek its corresponding and more enduring dramatic portrayal in the works of Dostoevsky. Our purpose is not to discount one author at the expense of the other, but rather to register a historical fact that seems to adhere to dualisms; one of the two suffers some diminution in the comparison, although the changed intellectual atmosphere and needs of the late nineteenth and early twentieth centuries obviously enter into the equation.

In her admirable collection, *The Essential Turgenev*, Elizabeth Cheresh Allen addresses this displacement as the essential question. Rightly she allies Dostoevsky and Tolstoy and opposes them in contemporary reputation and later fortunes to those of Turgenev. Professor Cheresh Allen aptly quotes Osip Mandelstam, who, like Rozanov, points to the changing tumultuousness of the times. 'In my youth, I already knew that the tranquil world of Turgenev was gone, never to be recovered.' Professor Cherish Allen then continues, 'And so Turgenev's reputation went into eclipse – even while Dostoevsky's and Tolstoy's were rising – because Turgenev's works were inextricably bound to a bygone era, irrelevant to the complexities of the twentieth century, and of interest predominantly to students of nineteenth-century social and literary life' (xiii). Turgenev became a victim of history, trapped by his very topicality, while Dostoevsky, following his own inner compulsions, left a far more enduring record. Attention to dualisms indicates that Rozanov's and Mandelstam's historically based hypothesis needs to be supplemented, as we follow other reasons – at least through our time – for the staying power and appeal of the daemonic writer. And it should not be forgotten that, as with Erasmus and Voltaire, Turgenev's own display of courage and reasonableness is not to be so easily vanquished, or that even Dostoevsky – when he dismisses such masterpieces as Turgenev's *Phantoms* – cannot help but admit its genius, that even the sun has spots.

Yet participation in a dualism can have unanticipated benefits. Dmitri Merezhkovsky, in 1914, where he establishes Turgenev as possessing the 'genius of right measure,' also acknowledges the decline in his reputation. 'Turgenev, they say, is outmoded. The two gigantic caryatids of Russian literature – Tolstoy and Dostoevsky – have really overshadowed Turgenev for us. Forever? For long?' Then he adds a particularly pregnant possibility: 'Aren't we fated to return to him through them?' (Jackson, 'The Root and the Flower' 163). This possibility takes on reality in the nature of the dualistic involvement, seen not as a see-saw, but as a noble engagement. The very entanglement with Dostoevsky does help to restore in a critical fashion the genuine merits of Turgenev, just as other forgotten portions of Erasmus and Voltaire were retrieved by their reciprocal involvements. They are restored and revived by the very dualism that seemed to diminish them.

Cassirer remarked that the dualistic tensions between Erasmus and Luther were played out again – in altered circumstances – in the controversy separating Voltaire and Rousseau. In similar fashion this latter dualism continues to cast its shadow over the Turgenev and Dostoevsky divide, permeating their attitudes and those of their characters – in contest or in approval – in so many direct as well as indirect ways. The Enlightenment provided the new intellectual plateau and baseline for the Russian writers. In *The Diary of a Writer* when Dostoevsky wishes to summarize, as in a shorthand, the significance of the Enlightenment, he does so by simply coupling the names of Voltaire and Rousseau. Their dualism continued into the nineteenth century, in part reflecting the different social classes and conditions to which each belonged, but also carrying with it profound philosophical and religious issues.

Such influence was far from monolithic, indeed quite complex in many surprising ways. Turgenev, like Tolstoy, was a member of the landed gentry. Under the influence of Voltaire, neither received what could be called an orthodox religious upbringing. In *Virgin Soil*, when Turgenev, with his fetching depiction of the customary way of life of Fomushka and Femichka, steps back into eighteenth century, in some ways his natural habitat, he quite naturally invokes Voltaire in describing the couple's hostility to religion. Voltaire had himself become synonymous with irreligion. Dostoevsky's family, on the other hand, was devoutly if conventionally Christian, and this early experience, only reinforced by the later events of Dostoevsky's life, entered him into severe contention not only with Turgenev, but also with Belinksy, and the emerging radical intelligentsia of the 1860s. The search for full belief represented a driving force of his later life and set him off defensively from those who rejected Christianity outright. Moreover, because he was a member of the landed gentry, the touch of condescension, as Dostoevsky argued, was never absent from Turgenev's approach to the common people. But in his novels,

Rudin and *Nest of Gentry*, as well as in his correspondence, Turgenev frequently urges fuller acquaintance with the character and habits of the Russian people. And in *Virgin Soil*, he will even tragically depict the outright failure of such a 'back to the people' movement.

As in so many matters, Turgenev was ambivalent if not vacillating. For instance, there is some disagreement about whether he had acquired an early familiarity with the prior classics of Russian literature. But in a letter to Khmyrov, where he lists numerically the major events of his life, he writes, 'My knowledge of Russian literature began with the *Rossiyada*, which a valet of my mother read to me in secret.' This touch of old Russia was read secretly, presumably away from the ever-vigilant eye of his mother, who made quite sure that he studied French and German ('from an early age') and English ('from the age of fourteen') (*Turgenev's Letters* 153). His apparent distance from the serfs did not prevent him from fathering a daughter with a serving girl in his mother's house, nor the absence of his own religious upbringing prevent him from insisting that this daughter, whom he disliked but cared for dutifully, should receive religious instruction from the priest at the Russian embassy in Paris. Despite these early ambivalences and even contradictions, in later life his own ideas hardened, particularly when in contest with Dostoevsky he came to see little of value in Russian culture and attributes. Even when the nature of the argument shifts to readership and appeal, the substance remains the same. Turgenev himself tells us, 'I never wrote for the common people ... I wrote for the class of people to which I belonged' (Shapiro 188). When, in his decisive speech concerning Pushkin in 1880, he attributed the same interest to that monumental poet, declaring moreover that Pushkin was never appreciated by the common people but only by a literary elite, this only drew down the ire of Dostoevsky, who saw in Pushkin an expression of the essential genius of the Russian people.

This quite obvious difference in background brought with it a difference in mannerisms – although it extends far beyond that. Voltaire was the master of conversation; he valued this form of social intercourse and thought it to be the natural genius of the French of his time. His own works leave the impression of a man talking. In his writing, his life, and thought Voltaire was a social being, for whom style itself was more than an aspect of thought: style, as an expression of taste, was an end in itself. We are well aware of Rousseau's social misfortunes. The pattern persists: while Turgenev was noted for the affability of his conversation and grace and elegance of his social manners, Dostoevsky was frequently morose and taciturn, breaking forth only at unlikely moments in volcanic anger or long pent-up expositions. Along with other personal traits, he dramatizes quite effectively this particular lack of sociability, the incapacity for small talk, the chit-chat of social grace in the character of Prince Myshkin. Totally misunderstanding the nature of the people with whom he was involved, in the memorable last party scene of *The Idiot*, where the so-called cream of Russian society was gathered, the prince is overflowing with benevolent feelings (which the narrator quickly gives us to understand are quite misplaced). He stumbles to correct himself when he seems to imply that the social lion with whom he is conversing could not possibly be the relative of his own 'magnanimous' benefactor (*The Idiot* 582). And quite unintentionally but then purposively he breaks out into a lengthy and frankly inspired attack on the Western Catholic church, which fully anticipates Ivan's prose poem of the Grand Inquisitor. Like Rousseau's, the prince's gaucheries are expressions of a concealed higher virtue. Not suited for small talk, he immediately establishes terms and insights of philosophical intimacy. Like Rousseau, he sees beneath the surfaces into the higher qualities and better purposes lodged in the hearts of people. All his outpourings are both highly attractive and at times exasperatingly maladroit.

Quite obviously, in regard to these prodigious predecessors, attitudes must be complex. For instance, Dostoevsky admired *Candide*, as the narrator reflects in *Demons*, presumably for its debunking of naive philosophical systems. Yet he also took umbrage at Voltaire's jejune iconoclasm, which betrayed a limitation of its own in keeping to a literal understanding of the Bible. Voltaire the mocker is mocked for attacking the popular image of the devil with horns and tail while being oblivious to his metaphoric significance as a spiritual principle. Moreover, Voltaire is identified as the prime source of irreligion in the culture of the Russian landowners. Dostoevsky's attitudes toward Rousseau are of a similar complexity, but even more crucial. In *Demons*, Rousseau is coarsely linked with the reformers who would, in the manner of Proudhon, prescribe phalansteries of social engineering. Yet when it comes to the confessional mode, his penetration into Dostoevsky's thought is remarkable. In fact, in two notable confessions, that of the parlour game initiated by Ferdischenko in *The Idiot*, and in a far grander way, that of Stavrogin in *Demons*, the episode of casting blame on a vulnerable young woman in the household is repeated (and in Stavrogin's case, Rousseau's penchant for masturbation). The young Prince Sergei Sokolsky in *The Adolescent* has similarly blamed an orderly, from which misdeed he redeems himself by an open confession. Quite obviously this episode from Rousseau's *Confessions* entered deeply into Dostoevsky's fictional repertoire. But when Stepan Trofimovitch completes his own pilgrimage, and on the verge of death makes his own literal *profession de foi*, it also derives from Rousseau: if there is a God, then I am immortal. A God of immense goodness would not consign the human soul to nothingness. While this is more of a plea, or a prayer, than the rational demonstration that Rousseau organizes in the Savoyard vicar's profession of faith, still it shows two things: the prevalence of Rousseau's religious idealism among the Russian intellectuals of the 1840s, and the fact that Rousseau was more correct than he was given credit for, when he declared himself the founder of a 'neo-christianisme' for the coming century.

Right from the start Dostoevsky was compared in unflattering terms with the personality of Rousseau of *The Confessions*. Belinsky, turning from an over-zealous advocate of *Poor Folk* (primarily because he saw in it a confirmation of his ever-changing critical tenets – now, social relevancy), wrote, 'Of Rousseau I have only read *The Confessions* and judging by it ... I have conceived a profound dislike of that gentleman. He is so much like Dostoevsky who is profoundly convinced that all of mankind envies and persecutes him' (Frank 1: 181). Much later Nikolay Strakhov, a rather dubious friend, wrote to Tolstoy, 'I cannot consider Dostoevsky either a good or a happy man. He was spiteful, envious, dissolute and spent all his life in a state of agitation that made him appear pitiful and would have made him appear ridiculous if he had not at the same time been so spiteful and so intelligent. Like Rousseau, he considered himself the best and the happiest of men' (Miller 98–9).[5]

Despite the aspersions cast by Belinsky upon the personality revealed by Rousseau in his *Confessions*, it remained the legacy-book of the nineteenth-century novel. In her insightful study, Professor Miller attests, 'Rousseau's *Confessions* provided the model for this genre throughout the nineteenth century' (95), and not only for this genre, might we add, but for the confessional mode itself, affecting even the quite different Turgenev, who could not escape a self-absorption that his predecessors in this study so adamantly avoided. If there is a difference between self-analysis and self-indulgence, then like Voltaire there was very limited self-exposure in Turgenev's correspondence. As Professor Cheresh Allen, remarks, 'It is the absence of extended self-exposure that makes them so Turgenevan,' and rarely in his letters, despite their descriptions of personal experiences, does Turgenev use such practices 'as pretexts to engage in elaborate self-analysis' (xxxiii). And yet, even here, true as the assertion is, there lies complexity. To be sure, like those of Erasmus and Voltaire, his brief autobiography is written in the third person (and that may have been the requirement of the particular form). But in an important letter to Ivan Goncharov (1812–91), who had accused him of stealing his ideas, Turgenev, like Erasmus, addresses rooted and irreducible aspects of his personality. He is a writer and must go on writing, but he cannot continue the sketches that brought him his first fame. He does not allow that his characters are 'complete or strong, or that I have penetrated life to any depth or described its many facets ... There will be deficiencies and patently obvious gaps ... He who wants a novel in the epic sense must not look to me ... Take me as I am or don't take me at all. But don't ask me to change' (*Turgenev's Letters* 75–6).

Naturally enough, Dostoevsky himself was ambivalent about 'confessions.' He was obviously attracted to the resources provided by confession. The second part of *Notes from Underground* was at first called a confession, as was the first part of *Crime and Punishment.* In *The Idiot* Ippolit's 'explanation' is actually a confession that misfires. One can indeed ask where in Dostoevsky one does not meet some form of the confession, this partly because he was aware of its deficiencies, of its 'cheating' tendencies as well as its possibilities of greater psychic exploration. The mode itself seemed to invite 'over-going,' as in the *petit-jeux* of parlour games where one was supposed to outdo the others in revelations. As indicated above, Ferdyschenko's own account is purloined from the infamous episode in *The Confessions* of the stolen ribbon. This same episode apparently appealed to Dostoevsky, as he makes use of it at least three times. In the same novel, Totsky's account, though, brims with self-satisfaction, as he, horrified at his haranguing of a dying woman, out of guilt becomes a great benefactor. Not only does confessing betray such indulgence in self-gratification or self-justification (as was the case with Rousseau, in part), finally it reeks of a 'literariness,' of which Dostoevsky was duly suspicious. Stavrogin's lamentably censored confession is criticized by Father Tikhon as being too well crafted, exposing the author to the unendurable reaction of ridicule. Going even further, the underground man in his own exasperated self-consciousness anticipates the charges made against his supposed self-revelations: 'There's some truth in you, too, but not chastity; out of the pettiest vanity you bring your truth out into the open, into the marketplace, and you shame it' (*Notes from Underground* 27). The accurate self-condemnation is enough to indicate some of the many uses Dostoevsky made of the confessional mode. It permitted him to enter into the most profound inner recesses of his characters – to create his amplest metaphor, that of the 'underground' itself – and to develop his taste for the fantastic, even the hallucinogenic. That is, it brought his presentation beyond single-minded sincerity (although always valuing the sincere or 'chaste' confession that was accompanied by true contrition and sorrow – by the simple recognition that a wrong had been committed) and enabled him to present his characters as indeed 'double.' In such confessions, the 'I' is always observing the 'I,' thus presenting a conundrum from which Dostoevsky sought to break out, and from which some of his most interesting characters never succeed in freeing themselves.

Despite his varied and complex attitudes toward the uses of the confession, Dostoevsky certainly valued it for the possibilities it offered of describing the double nature of humans, the double itself. As René Girard remarks, 'The theme of the double is present in all the works of Dostoevsky in the most diverse and sometimes most hidden forms' (Girard 35). But even here in this division between inherent complexity and the need for unity, he is in fuller emulation of Rousseau, who, in the *dédoublement* of his own personality, persisted in addressing in various works the eternal Tom Sawyer and Huckleberry Finn, the Don Quixote and Sancho Panza of his divided temperament, while ever intent to present to the public the true Jean-Jacques. Yet while Rousseau was deeply aware of the folly of imaginative consciousness, it was Dostoevsky who travelled the horrors of a falsely based being. The difference, while most complex in its causes, is partially summed up by Dostoevsky himself, who has Golyadkin of *The Double* reflect, 'Tender words aren't popular any more, in our industrial age. Jean-Jacques Rousseau's times are past' ('The Double' 135). But perhaps it is the words of Golyadkin's manservant, the obstreperous Petrashka, who comes closer to accounting for the new sense that Dostoevsky brings to the double: 'Nice people live honestly. Nice people don't live falsely and don't have doubles ... they don't have doubles ever. They aren't an insult to God and to honest men' (88).

Some features already observable in the youthful Dostoevsky reveal even better bases of comparison, such that not only link Dostoevsky with Rousseau, but with Luther as well. Like Luther, and other writers of a religious or artistic genius, Dostoevsky had a precocious presentiment of the imminence of death and dying (a sense that was only exacerbated by his increasingly frequent epileptic attacks). Throughout his life he had a preternatural fear of being buried alive, urging his friends to delay interment until it was certain he was dead. He experienced moments of 'mystic terror,' recorded in fiction and through conversation, already originating in the moments of his literary disappointments: 'It often seemed to me that I was dying, and the truth is – real death came and then went away again' (Frank 1: 167). This characteristic meant that, like the others, Dostoevsky had a tendency to see and to describe things *in extremis*, to write with a sense of urgency and to register and to respond to the apocalyptic. This is more than a matter of style alone; philosophically and emotionally he was aware of and responded to last days and final things. 'There is an urge for the extreme, for the fainting sensation of approaching an abyss, and half-leaning over it – to peep into the bottomless pit, and, in some rare cases, to throw oneself into it head-forward as in a frenzy' (*DW* 35). It is such a characteristic that Dostoevsky sees as rampant in his society; and, when Prince Myshkin recoils in horror at the portrait of Nastasya Filipovna, it is precisely this trait in her character that he perceives. But it is this same capacity for excess that Dostoevsky finds in himself. His letters are filled with such rebukes: 'Worst of all is that my nature is base and too passionate: everywhere and in everything I go to the limit, all my life I have been crossing the line' (Terras 40). But this expression of self-rebuke becomes the basis of creativity, as he must confront not only this part of his own character but, when projected onto the national screen, of the Russian character as well. We must recall that even Father Zosima, when a young cadet, was most 'impressionable' and thus likely to adopt the worst traits of his group. But beyond such heedlessness there is a more ingrained part of human nature, which finally he confronts in the sensuality of *all* the Karamazovs, and that might simply be called willingness, a willingness to engage life in all of its ways – as the father and the three sons most fully together and separately represent. But sensuality is only one aspect of an undertaking spirit that typifies Dostoevsky's most engaging characters.

Also like Luther and Rousseau, Dostoevsky had that unusual capacity for full identification with what he was reading, whether it be the native classics of Russian literature, Sir Walter Scott, or the gothic novel. He became what he read and was endowed with what could be called ultimate seriousness (notwithstanding his own skill at satire). His lifetime pursuit of faith and conviction led him, as it did the other two, to a distaste for those who were 'neither hot nor cold.' Later, even those who disagreed with him acknowledged the strength of his commitments. This was particularly true after the serial publication of *The Diary of a Writer* and *The Brothers Karamazov*, when he became a quasi-religious cult figure. The readerly effect was prodigious, appealing to auditors and readers alike, as if his own voice of faith and conviction allowed them to transcend their own egos, to be uplifted out of themselves, and for the moment be transformed into the spiritual beings they always wanted to be. None of the writers of consciousness possessed this power, and probably none desired to possess it.

Dostoevsky quite early showed an openness to experience. This propensity first comes into view in the summers spent at the newly purchased family estate at Darovoe. There he participated fully in the active peasant life, a trait that helped him considerably when he was imprisoned – the majority of his fellow convicts being former serfs. If not allowed to participate fully, he gradually penetrated their lives, bringing a sympathetic understanding to their strengths, their glaring weaknesses, and their lots. While Rousseau knew that his works were appreciated only by those of a more cultivated sensibility, and he himself also favoured the genteel, he still advocated for his alter ego Émile the rough and ready company found in rustic life, and particularly enjoyed hearing the raucous voices of children at play outside his study window. In the period of his beneficial sequestration, Luther devoted his time to translating the New Testament into the sturdy German prose of use for the common people. In all three, this 'popular' openness had other reaches as well: it indicates a capacity for self-transformation that leads to further revelations. Most of Dostoevsky's major efforts (*The Brothers Karamazov* is a notable exception) underwent enormous changes and modifications in the course of their development, as if some ulterior purpose were manifesting itself and the work could not rest until that ultimate purpose had been attained. But in order for this to happen, an openness is required, a kind of listening post, that is not eager to foreclose on events, but is willing to let them unfold in their own direction beyond conscious direction. Here, as Rousseau differed from Voltaire, and Luther from Erasmus, so Dostoevsky differs from Turgenev, who always seemed to write from within the highly planned and conscious boundaries of his artistic intent (although his acknowledged masterpiece, *Fathers and Children*, did undergo substantial revisions, but not radical change).

These are the preoccupations already present in the young Dostoevsky. But when he matured, or came into public renown, other features of temperament emerged that linked him even more closely with Rousseau. Like Rousseau, he felt himself to be something of a foreign presence, with a great imbalance existing between his social being and his inner life, his sense of himself, his fantasies, but also his higher vision. But in his acute self-awareness, this discrepancy and the reasons for it did not escape his own attention: it became the basis of his creative insight, the material he had to accost and wrench into shape. His letters, particularly those to his brother Mikhail are filled with expostulations about the abysmal nature of his character. Like Rousseau, he had the need of a second conversion, as the first, brought about by the success of *Poor Folk*, only unleashed the demons that he had been harbouring. Dostoevsky's 'second conversion' was brought about under much more traumatic circumstances, beginning with the excruciating moment when he fully expected to be executed. He turned to Nikolai Speshnev, later the model for Stavrogin, and whispered in French that 'they would be together in Christ' (nous serons avec le Christ), to which Speshnev responded with stoic hauteur, 'only a handful of dust' (un peu de poussière) (Frank 2: 58). But this event of closeness to death, his time in the Siberian penal colony (where his main reading seemed to be the New Testament), followed by his military conscription produced 'a regeneration of [his] convictions' (2: 31). For neither Rousseau nor Dostoevsky was this a bolt out of the blue, rather a slow gestation, as Dostoevsky himself tells us, an act of recovery that did produce a new intensity, a greater power and singleness of purpose, a renewed force and focus of conviction.

By their enemies you shall know them. Rousseau and Dostoevsky, as did Luther, warred with the advanced stages of the European consciousness of their times. And the word *consciousness* should be underscored, because of its several possible implications. On the one hand, compatible with the uses and habits of the writers of consciousness, it means that intelligence that reflects upon and takes into its focus the variety and multiplicity of the world; on the other hand, it can represent a divided, self-reflecting mentality, that has been penetrated by an alien idea or group of ideas that set it at odds with itself. This is the antagonistic use of consciousness adopted by the daemonic writers; all three – Luther, Rousseau, and Dostoevsky – had a deep suspicion of the contrivances of consciousness, that which seemed to alienate the individual from his better resources or his more authentic self. In Luther's own bitter struggles he could find no consolation in the models of the saints, in any kind of conscious imitation that brought a false assurance and confidence to the struggle for salvation; Rousseau rejected the play-acting of forms, the imitative consciousness, and the vicarious identities provided by the social world of the salon, the world of the theatre and misguided educational norms of the day. Dostoevsky added to this the foreign grafts brought to his native stock, all producing a hypertrophied self-consciousness, the profound schism existing between one's regular existence and fantasy life. This is the malady of the underground man, anticipated without full success in *The Double*, where bureaucratic oppressiveness is responsible for the split identity. It is brought to the fore in the excruciating clarity and the ironic style that unite *Winter Notes on Summer Impressions*, *Notes from Underground*, and *Crime and Punishment* before reaching its height of achievement in *Demons*. But whatever its causes, be they fantasy rising up against oppression, foreign ideas, pride, aimlessness, or arrogance, the malady is the same: a division in the mind and spirit. The underground man himself called it a lack of 'chastity,' that is a lack of simple directness and forthrightness, an intrusion of self-consciousness that reminds us that the double is the original serpent. The double is, make no mistake, the devil.

Dostoevsky was repulsed by false consciousness. Just as Luther mocked Karlstadt's adopting peasant garb – this was just as much a reliance on external forms as were the Catholic ceremonies – so Dostoevsky mocks the imitation of peasant life, all that which seems to stem from a misguided constraint: 'It is not necessary to conceive the giving away of property as a *binding* condition, since in the matter of love *constraint* resembles a uniform, fidelity to the letter. The conviction that one has complied with the letter leads to haughtiness, formalism and indolence' (*DW* 622). These sentences are remarkable because, despite his dislike for Luther's Protestantism, the essential spiritual component of that early master's thought is there, particularly in the consequences of adherence to the letter. External manifestations are not part of the principles of love: 'Don't follow the example of certain dreamers, who straightway get hold of a wheelbarrow and say, "I am not a nobleman – I want to work as a peasant." The wheelbarrow, too, is a uniform.' Like Luther, he urges the conscientious person to follow the calling that seems most consonant with his talents and desires: 'If you feel that you will be useful to everybody in the capacity of a scientist, matriculate in a university and obtain some means therefore.' There is no sanctity in peasant life if it derives from an intellectual contagion and becomes the socially acceptable 'thing to do.' Instead, like Luther, he urges one to stay at home (in the figurative sense), to be what one is, and to try to make oneself useful in that way. But there are deeper principles underlying this modest advice: 'Neither the giving away of property, nor the wearing of a peasant coat are obligatory; all this is mere letter and formality: *only your resolution to do everything for the sake of active love*, everything within the limits of your possibility, everything which you sincerely believe possible for yourself – is obligatory and important' (*DW* 622). These crucial passages link Dostoevsky with Luther (and with Rousseau as well, despite his adoption of 'Armenian' garb) because it cuts through ideological differences and brings us into contact with the driving spirit of the daemonic. The principle is that of 'active love,' which dispenses with false and even fake allurements, intellectual signs of affiliation that are only disfigurements of the genuine possibilities open to a person. What is also apparent is its eminent and thoughtful practicability: don't try to be someone else. Such intellectual transformations are too frequently short-lived because they are not solidly allied with actual possibilities. They simply represent a false compliance with fantasy ideas in the air, which themselves become part of a uniformed acceptance. What is remarkable and what joins all three is this combination of an active love that rejects the socially correct ideas around one while at the same time recommending simpler and truer means for finding one's way.

Rousseau and Dostoevsky have another trait in common, which does not show up on the schedule of ideas: they were most subject to being misunderstood, and given the obvious complexity of their thought, it is also easy to understand why. But there are other reasons as well. Because of his attack on the *philosophes*, Rousseau was thought to be a reactionary (a radical reactionary, he was), but this is to overlook his great affinities with the *philosophes* in his emphasis on natural religion, rational theology, his dismissal of any need for revelation or miracle. The dispute would have been less acerbic had Rousseau been a simple conservative rather than one who knew and who had mastered the arguments of the *philosophes*. So, too, Dostoevsky's position as a moderate reformer has been overlooked. He campaigned for the abolition of serfdom; he was a lifelong opponent of censorship and suppression; he loathed injustice and brutality in any form. His position in the major dispute begins with his full understanding of the thought of the radicals. He was able to describe them from the inside, with full power of identification, because he had been one, and moreover he never quite reneged on the openness and the generosity with which they pursued their misguided goals. The fact that they are not idlers and leg-swingers in the cafes, but young people who have imbibed the most advanced ideas from the West makes them all the more dangerous and tragic (as he tells us in 'One of the Contemporaneous Falsehoods' – *DW* 142–54). Consequently he leaves the door of the future hope open for Raskolnikov, and even – although more problematically – for Ivan. He was such a dominant and stalwart opponent, because like Rousseau, he had been one of them. The very rub of their closeness brought about the burn of hostility: having been one, he felt he had been there before them and had indeed paid the price; while ignorant of his own complex evolution, they simply perceived in him the voice of reaction. At times he explodes in exasperation. 'These block-heads have never dreamed of a denial of God which has the power that I put into the "Inquisitor" and the preceding chapter, to which *the whole novel* is the response. I certainly do not believe in God like some fool (fanatic). And these people wanted to teach me and laughed at my back-wardness! Why their stupid nature never even dreamed of such power of denial as I have passed through. And they want to enlighten me!' (Frank 5: 713). The table is set for misunderstanding. Ignorant of the complex-ity of his own evolution, they identify him with the ultra-reactionaries, while he feels not only that he has been in their position as radical reformer, but that he has indeed passed beyond them. They see him as abetting the enemy; he wants credit for the road travelled.

But there is an even more intriguing similarity: both Rousseau and Dostoevsky, fuelled by guilt, were driven by the impulse of return. We observe this most clearly in the Savoyard vicar's final words to the young Rousseau, uncovering in the author himself the essential need to make restitution, to return to the ways of life, to the people, and to the instincts that he had betrayed. This must be seen as one of Dostoevsky's own dom-inant instincts, the recovery of which accounts for his discontent with the St Petersburg radicals. They were the true demons blocking his path, and as a consequence they, too, must be exorcized. It is this impulse that is at the heart of Raskolnikov's own intellectual perversion. He must even go so far as to overstep the mark in order to achieve his more ulterior aims. This is not a utilitarian argument, but rather one of profound psy-chology, emanating as always in Dostoevsky (one of Louis Breger's keen insights) from his most personal experience. Like Rousseau, like Raskolnikov, Dostoevsky had strayed, and now he must restore himself by returning to his native instincts and his own people. Return and restitu-tion become the basis of conversion as well as antipathy to those who would hamper his way.

Profound religious and philosophical issues deriving from the eigh-teenth century continue into the nineteenth-century dialogue. Like Vol-taire and Rousseau, Dostoevsky and Turgenev were consumed by the debate over the nature of Nature, and Dostoevsky shared with the first two the keen awareness of the tendency toward disbelief that seemed to attend an unthinking attachment to a blind orthodoxy. Dostoevsky is convinced that the cause of nihilism is most rampant among ex-seminar-ians, that is, among those who from total belief are shocked into total dis-belief. Radomsky, who appears, despite his levity, to be among the few clear-headed individuals in *The Idiot*, holds forth on this process. The product is not a Russian liberal, he affirms, but an un-Russian liberal, one who develops a purely adversarial consciousness and a hatred of all things Russian. For whatever reasons, the new Russian remains inveterately 'anti' (371). Radomsky turns to Myshkin for support, and indeed the prince does provide it, affirming that the cases Radomsky adduces are not individual, but representative. Anecdotage is illustrative; the journalism of the day is productive. Thus, while working abroad in the years preceding the completion of *The Idiot*, Dostoevsky was an avid reader of all the Russian newspapers. News provides the collectibles that would later be transmuted into representative elements of his fiction. The prince supports Radomsky's arguments, even adding the crucial fillip that the differences between criminals in the past and the nihilists of his era is that the latter-day perpetrators have acquired a rationale and a justification – they are in possession of arguments indicating that their criminal acts are justified (374). Prince Myshkin will later indicate that the growth of disbelief is driven by a larger thirst for righteousness and true belief, which, once again anticipating Ivan's arguments, are frustrated by the power of the ecclesiastical imperialism of the Roman church, which is responsible, he argues, for the growth of disbelief.

There is yet another point of contact – the detail of the devil. Here the unreliable and unsavoury Lebedev dismisses Voltaire's materialistic and iconoclastic interpretation as being superficial. He is following Radomsky's argument that the principle of self-preservation is not sufficient to explain human conduct. Rather than introducing arguments of altruism, Radomksy introduces another principle, anticipating Freud and reaching back to *Othello* (which play by Shakespeare has an unexpected presence in *The Idiot*), and that is self-destruction, the death wish. Lebedev explains this principle, and in so doing, places Dostoevsky's dualistic universe in line with that of the other daemonic writers: 'The law of destruction and the law of self-preservation are equally strong in humanity. The devil holds equal dominion over humanity until a date in the far-off future still unknown to us' (412). As with Luther, he perceives humankind as caught in the struggle between God and the devil, or more inherently, between two impulses that dominate. In *The Idiot* it is the self-destructive impulse that triumphs, as it does in *Othello*.

While acknowledging these remarkable similarities that the fuller discussion of dualisms leads us to, still great differences exist. Despite some sense of an all-encompassing possibility of final Christian forgiveness, Dostoevsky recognized as Rousseau never was quite able to – and this comes clear in his Siberian prison experience – that unregeneracy can rule in some human hearts. He had heard murderers relate, as if still savouring the act, the killing of children. After one particularly outrageous episode recorded in *The Diary of a Writer*, Dostoevsky concludes, 'I simply wish to note the bestial degree which insensibility may reach in man' (*DW* 39). But there is an even greater difference, and this brings us to *The Eternal Husband* (1870), where Velchaninov finally uncovers the perversity of the human soul, the way idealism, altruism, can be converted into sadism, and all this from a subornation of Romantic idealism and noble principles of self-sacrifice, which finally turn on their own possessor (Breger). Speaking of the bizarre and dangerous conduct of Trusotsky, the man with whose wife he had had an affair some nine years in the past, Velchaninov now sees clearly into his twisted nature:

> And how he enjoyed playing the fool, didn't he like it? ... wasn't he pleased too when he made me kiss him? Only he didn't know then whether he would end by embracing me or by murdering me. Of course, it's turned out that the best thing was to do both. A most natural solution. Yes, indeed, Nature dislikes monstrosities and destroys them with natural solutions. The most monstrous monster is the monster with noble feelings ... Nature is not a tender mother, but a stepmother to the monster. Nature gives birth to the deformed, but instead of pitying him she punishes him, and with good reason. Even decent people have to pay for embraces and tears of forgiveness nowadays, to say nothing of men like you and me. (*Great Short Works* 652).

Dostoevsky is the great discoverer of perversity, where 'noble feelings' ricochet against their possessor. As René Girard remarks, 'Rousseau never wrote the equivalent of *The Eternal Husband*' (97). But his insights extend even farther. Dostoevsky was a bad Romantic, not from a deficiency, but rather from a superabundance of Romantic sentiment (98). As we have already learned from Luther, superabundance may be a form of subversion, an ulterior way of undoing, when more normal ways of protest prove to be too difficult. It is not through simple virtue, but rather through the intolerable excess of virtue that truths are painfully discovered and changes made. The discovery of perversity is at the root of Dostoevsky's liberation from Romantic idealism, and his chief difference with Rousseau.

3. Success and Its Consequences

Their days as members of the Belinsky circle were days of hope and ambition. Turgenev was a budding poet, a métier he soon changed to that of prose, without entirely giving up his licence. Dostoevsky had recently liberated himself from the Academy of Engineers and was ready to fulfil his literary dreams in the exciting city of St Petersburg. These were salad days, when dreams were alive and energies high. And above all, the talent, the talent was prodigious, making of those who gathered around Belinsky a virtual Pleiad. High art and culture – inspired by Schiller and German idealism – were the adventures of the day, and for Dostoevsky, where the demands of art were the concern, to the end of his days. He began modestly enough, even translating Balzac's *Père Goriot*, a work not unrelated to his first and astonishing success, the epistolary novel *Poor Folk*. The work became a critical success, ringingly endorsed by the great Belinsky himself, who adopted Dostoevsky as his own *trouvaille*. In marvellous pages of reminiscence, Dostoevsky tells us how, encouraged by his friend Grigorovich, he had left the manuscript of *Poor Folk* with the poet Nekrasov, filled with trepidation and fearing that it would be ridiculed by the 'party' of Belinsky. Typically enough, and this is both a record of and a source for the literary greatness of the period, he and a friend spent the night reading Gogol's *Dead Souls* together. As Dostoevsky remarks, 'In those days it used to be this way among young men.' Two or three of them would get together and read a work of Gogol – perhaps lasting all night. 'Then among the youth there were many who, as it were, were penetrated with something, and were awaiting something' (*DW* 584–5). Greatness was in the air, as a promise, as a pledge to these young talents so committed to literature. And the pledge was realized when both Grigorovich and Nekrasov returned to Dostoevsky's flat in a state of ecstasy at what he had wrought. They had thought to read some ten pages but proceeded to devour the entire short novel. Then, overcome with enthusiasm, despite the lateness of the hour ('What is sleep, this is more important than sleep'), they roused Dostoevsky, and in typical fashion, proceeded to discuss all that mattered the most: poetry and truth. Nekrasov then brought the novel to Belinsky's attention, who was enthusiastic for the right reasons. The scenes he praised were those that should still be praised: the interview with 'their excellency' the director of the firm, the attempt to kiss his hand, the lost button. These entranced Belinksy and seemed to take him out of his aesthetic of social relevancy: 'This is more than compassion for this unfortunate – this is horror, horror!' Critics can reasonably expound, but artists in one stroke, one image can clarify, he explains. 'This is the truth of art' (*DW* 587). And he welcomed a new star into his constellation.

As it was the age of enthusiastic endorsements and fervent embraces, part of the pleasure of extending praise was what it offered in self-recognition. Dostoevsky was quite enamoured of Turgenev – his elegance, his aristocratic manners, all those qualities that would later gall. He wrote to his brother Mikhail that Turgenev, recently returned from Paris, 'attached himself to me at first sight with such devotion that Belinsky explains it by saying that he has fallen in love with me. And what a man, brother! I have all but fallen in love with him myself! A poet, an aristocrat, talented, handsome, rich, intelligent, well-educated and twenty-five years old. And, to conclude, a noble character, infinitely direct and open, formed in a good school' (Frank 1: 162). But these days could not last, literary resentment and envy being what they are. On the one hand, Dostoevsky mistook Turgenev's easy affability for genuine friendship, but more importantly his early heady success revealed Dostoevsky's own demons, a kind of egomania that quickly turned his success into the object of satire. Turgenev evidently tormented him, with thinly veiled accounts that could only be degrading to Dostoevsky. False rumours spread (which were long dying) that he wanted his novel printed with borders; however, he did insist that it be printed either first or last in the volume. Memoirists relate how Dostoevsky was baited and taunted by his more worldly fellow writers, culminating in the satiric poem 'The Knight of the Rueful Countenance,' written by Turgenev and the talented poet Nikolai Nekrasov (1821–78).

When Dostoevsky published *The Double*, Belinsky had a change of heart, fearing that his over-praise of *Poor Folk* was now made apparent in the fantastic lunacy of the second work. Given this critical turnaround and the satiric mockery heaped upon him, Dostoevsky had had enough of this coterie and vowed never to see that bunch of 'scoundrels' again. We should not ignore how essential and necessary this break was: it determined Dostoevsky on his own path, a path he could have discovered only by separating himself from the Belinsky group and keeping to his own ways that *The Double* had marked out for him.

For different reasons, the two early pre-Siberian works continue to live. The first, *Poor Folk*, has been underrated by contemporary criticism, although Joseph Frank goes far in establishing its importance (82, 98). While Belinsky praised it because it complied with his new advocacy of the 'social novel,' we can see that the eminent critic also recognized the 'horror' of the situation in which Devushkin found himself. This 'gentle heart' shows generosity, true affection, and even the simple and moving identification with the kind of literature – for example, Pushkin's *Stationmaster* – that Dostoevsky himself truly valued. Despite his naivety, even his subverted masochism in doing the shopping for Varvara's wedding trousseau, for which she was made responsible, he raises his voice in protest against the inequities of life: 'Why is it that a good person lives in desolation, while happiness comes to another unasked?' (*Poor Folk* 99). Such questioning – here merely bathetic – persists and will persist in Dostoevsky's mentality, showing his undying sympathy for the insulted and the injured. And clearly, consistently, among Dostoevsky's most sympathetic portrayals is the plight of impoverished young women, who cannot seem to escape the 'for sale' sign that their poor fortune has hung around their necks. Thus, Varvara must finally forsake the deepest solicitude and concern of Devushkin and marry the arrogant, commandeering, yet prosperous man, who had previously violated her. His name is Bykov, suggestive in Russian of 'bull,' while Devushkin's name conjures up the Russian name for a young maiden, *devushka*.

Perhaps not a masterpiece, *Poor Folk* is still a major first work – in fact, like Rousseau's first *Discourse*, a breakthrough work. It brought to his unacknowledged talent the recognition and the acclaim that he fervently sought. And while it does not appear to be a work of inadvertence, it did catch on with critics with the suddenness of wildfire (although the lack of popular acceptance was not as gratifying). It further opened the way for Dostoevsky's future growth as a novelist, prefiguring his immense skill and artistry. It also had that other effect, similar to what happened to Rousseau after the clamour of his early successes: it showed his own egomania, and not only that, but after the silently endured humiliations, an instinct to have his own vengeance. If *Poor Folk* was more than an expression of inspiration – bringing with it a change of personality – it showed the need for yet another conversion, a second conversion, where Dostoevsky in the full powers of his own self-awareness would undergo a more determined regeneration of his convictions.

Most critics have noticed the not-too-buried similarities between the characters Devushkin and Golyadkin of *The Double* – both are minor civil servants, meaning the former at times shows the potential for contriving a fanciful being.[6] But his own simple honesty, his 'chastity,' restrains him. Golyadkin's more aspiring temperament results in a split consciousness that gives rise to the double. For Belinksy, the differences was too much: in the one the force of circumstances tramples over two people, while the other enters into the most obscure and morose features of the human temperament. And yet this became one of the more abiding themes of Dostoevsky's fuller fiction. Whether inspired by the oppressiveness of bureaucratic life, where the underdog rises up in his imagination to become the overdog, or by the infectious prevailing intellectual wind coming from the West and their theories of an overman, to whom all is possible, *The Double* leads the way to *Notes from Underground, Crime and Punishment,* and *The Brothers Karamazov,* it is a work of flawed imaginative genius, that in its day beyond his personal troubles contributed to Dostoevsky's premature literary demise. His was a talent that had failed to live up to its promise, or so it was thought.

The work was associated with Dostoevsky's own maligned character, representing thereby a failure on the part of his critics to realize that one of the signs of literary genius is this very capacity to translate the most offensive personal tribulations – which ordinary people suppress – into objective works of art. *The Double* is an amazing work for its sheer inventiveness, where for page after page we are introduced to new features, new conjectures, new vacillations, and new escapades. In this sense the critics were quite wrong. They also lacked two viewpoints that history would provide: the changes that Dostoevsky brought to the work in the revised version that we read (where all the picaresque chapter titles are eliminated – although it retained something of the mock-heroic style, 'the adventures of our hero'), and the enormous presence its subject matter had in the development of Dostoevsky's larger and more important later fiction. But aesthetically they may have been right: the work, despite its inventiveness, is tedious and suffers from a mixture of forms: the mock-heroic and psychological horror. It is further flawed in that Golyadkin's double assumes an objective character seen and honoured by others.

The real division occurs between Golyadkin's conception of himself as living in a world of benign amiability, of graceful acceptance, where he can show the generosity of his nature, and the world he does live in of office intrigue and deep-seated guilt and shame. The first is a dream world, superficial, while the other is just under the surface waiting to break out, as it does in the person of the double. I quote at length:

Sometimes he would dream that he was in the splendid company of people celebrated for their breeding and wit. He, too, distinguished himself for his amiability and wit, and everyone too to liking him – even certain of his enemies who were present – and this pleased him greatly. Everyone gave him precedence, and at last he had the agreeable experience of overhearing the host speak flatteringly of him to one of the guests whom he had drawn aside. And all of a sudden, for no apparent reason, a person notorious for his evil intentions and brutish impulses in the shape of Golyadkin junior appeared, and by so doing demolished in one fell swoop all the glory and triumph of Golyadkin senior, eclipsing him, dragging him into the mire and clearly demonstrating that Golyadkin senior, the real Golyadkin, was not real at all but a fraud. (*The Double* 94)

This remarkable passage goes a long way to explain the real nature of Golyadkin's double: as an alter ego, he is the sum of his progenitor's worst fears. That is, all of Golyadkin's dreams of affability, of easy success in a well-ordered universe, are transferred to him, while the horrors and fears, the paranoid suspicions lurking just under the skin, are allowed to emerge and settle on his original. Hence, little by little we are given to understand a long-standing guilt about a dubious relationship with a former landlady; in addition, snide allusions about office promotions come back to haunt him, and all his persecution manias emerge, his sense of conspiracies and foul treatment. But what this means is the annihilation of his persona – the double arises immediately after he is literally thrown out of the party that he had crashed – the reduction of himself to his worst sense of himself, a withering denial of who he is. This is an outright assault on being, and we are even farther from the Rousseauistic vision of the universe, but not perhaps the very events of his later life and their terrible psychic toll. The revelation of this ever-present capacity for psychic disorder in the midst of apparent order, this reduction of life to its most horrific dimensions, to imaginings that are ever-present but subdued, is the greatest achievement and purpose of *The Double,* and reminiscent of some of Shakespeare's most interesting plays: *The Comedy of Errors, A Midsummer Night's Dream, Twelfth Night, Othello, The Winter's Tale.* While such tensions were the source of Dostoevsky's great creativity, we can well understand why he would explain to his ever-loyal brother Mikhail that he needed a greater harmonization between his social being and his own inner self. This search for the ever-elusive unity of being would mark an even greater phase of creativity, the result of the needed 'second' conversion.

4. Turgenev between Hamlet and Quixote

The story of Dostoevsky's arrest, imprisonment, torturous expectation of imminent execution, years in a penal colony, and then the less arduous restraint as a military conscript are all well known. But in the critical environment of St Petersburg, the points on his badge of honour had already been tarnished. While he languished, or struggled to survive, his young contemporaries forged ahead, chief among whom was Turgenev. In his 'career episodes' Turgenev shows an entirely different itinerary from that of Dostoevsky, one not unlike that of Erasmus and Voltaire. This does not mean that there were not changes. After his aborted efforts as a poet, it was only when he published the first of *Sketches from a Sportsman's Album*, 'Khor and Khalinych,' that he received the notice he required and pursued his true vocation as a writer.[7] But even here he went beyond the 'sketches' (although making additions as late as 1872–4), to become (and remained for some time) the first and the prime Russian novelist of contemporaneous European reputation.

Sketches from a Sportsman's Album sparkles with its lively depictions of the character types of Russian provincial life, with all the particularities of their mannerisms and their dress caught with a painterly eye, and all their usages of language, from intonation to idiom, from the pretentious to the simple, reproduced with a dramatist's ear. It is unquestionably a work of some genius. In fact, the translation 'sketches' is itself something of a misnomer. While indeed some of the accounts are simple sketches, for instance, 'Two Landowners,' others are great stories, such as 'Hamlet of the Shchigrovsky District,' or the much later 'The End of Chertopkhanov,' with a full spread of lives and records in between. The topics and characters have a similar range, from the boastful and the foppish, to the diligent and the artful.

Satire is rife in *Sketches from a Sportsman's Album*, where Turgenev reveals his early taste for piling up devastating details, particularly of gatherings at a party. He is the master of accumulated details of dress, of gesture, and of speech, but also of the single addition revealing more genuine purpose. Chertopkhanov, a furious, neglectful, mad, and yet generous landowner had saved the hapless Nedropyushkin from social humiliation and had acquired thereby a lifelong loyal devotee. But as Nedropyushkin approaches his own end, a death that is flatly forbidden by Chertopkhanov, his dutiful follower can only mutter the words, broken and pathetic, 'I have always obeyed you.' To which the narrator adds, 'However that did not prevent him from dying the very same day, without even waiting for the arrival of the local doctor who, at the sight of his barely cold corpse, could do no more in tearful acknowledgment of the transitoriness of all earthly things than order himself "a glass of vodka and some salted fish"' (325–6).

But the *Sketches* do more than abound in satire; they are tragicomic tales of abandonment and decline, whether of villages or of individuals, and of forlornness in love; in fact, there are no portraits of a happy sustaining love – if we except the story of Radilov who, without notice, abandons all to run off with his deceased wife's sister. It is only by such purposeful escape that one seems to survive the death throes of entire areas. Yet one of the remarkable interests of the *Sketches* is the religious stoicism with which the Russians meet their ends, capped by the late addition, 'Living Relic,' but summarized by the final line of 'Death': 'Yes, Russians surprise one when it comes to dying' (230).

Remarkably enough, these 'scenes' from rural life were written largely between 1847 and 1851 when Turgenev was living abroad – hence accounting for the suffusion of recollection that enriches the lush descriptions of natural settings, as in 'Beshin Meadow.' The storytelling device of the avid hunter who is a local landowner also permits free and casual access; he is an interloper who is nevertheless respected, and as a sportsman he is accepted, provided with straw bedding and ready, if guarded, speech. He is something of an ideal means for entering into and acquiring all of the tools for narration.

Yet it is somewhat off the mark to credit him (or Turgenev) with being an 'uncommitted observer.'[8] The direct intervention of the narrator, complaining of the neglectful conditions of serf life, is a case in point. Turgenev was part of an entire intellectual generation – one including Dostoevsky – in his opposition to serfdom. The *Sketches* are filled with accounts of the destitute ways by which the serfs are compelled to exist. To be sure, such descriptions are kept within the requirements of the story, but selection of material is in itself an act of commitment. And there is no mistaking the prevalence of the injustices of serfdom, where entire villages are 'inherited' and then abandoned, and people compelled to scrape by in sub-poverty conditions, drinking the 'muddy waters' of their existence; where wealth is counted by the number of serfs one owned, and Shakespeare's words of lordly despotism stand ready for paraphrase: 'as they are mine, so I may dispose of them.' Summarily, in 'Two Landowners,' when a landowner responds to direct criticism by saying he represents the old ways – 'If you're the master, you're the master, and if you're a peasant, you're a peasant' – the narrator can only conclude with agreement but also with greater irony, 'It goes without saying that such a lucid and convincing argument was unanswerable' (189).

Nor were the censorious authorities impressed with Turgenev's lack of commitment. When published together in 1852, *The Sketches* earned the author a month-long stay in prison, followed by a lengthy 'rustication' at his family estate, from which he was permitted to return to Moscow only in 1854. Turgenev himself was sensitive to these conditions: 'Two Land-owners' and 'The Bailiff' did not appear in *The Contemporary* and were published only in the fuller volume of 1852. The latter is the only story that bears a telling place and date of composition: 'Salzbrunn, in Silesia / July, 1847.' This is quite significant in several ways, given that the story was completed before that date, but at the time Belinsky was conva-lescing in Salzbrunn, and that is the date appended to his famous letter to Gogol, where he denounces the once-thought opponent of the regime of Nicholas I for his new reversal and adherence to religion and the tsar. Turgenev's biographer, Leonard Schapiro, is quite certain 'that [Turgenev] would not have approved of the violent tone of Belinsky's "Letter" to a writer whom he considered, along with Pushkin and Lerm-ontov, to be the greatest of his generation' (Schapiro 59). But Richard Freeborn, with perhaps greater literary sensitivity, sees much more in the coincidence of dates: 'Turgenev was in Salzbrunn during part of Belin-sky's convalescence, and the latter's plea for justice in Russian social and political life, as expressed in the "Letter to Gogol," became Turgenev's sole religious and political credo.' There is then a point to the append-ages of place and date to 'The Bailiff,' which 'with its exquisitely savage portrait of the foppish tyrant Penochkin and its equally acute study of his bailiff, contains by far the most outspoken attack on the exploitations of the peasantry' (*Sketches* 8).

It is the second part of the phrase that should draw special attention. Turgenev was an observer; his writing thrives on the details of observa-tion, whether of nature or of people, and these are details of description that follow one after the other, sequentially, consecutively, connectedly. And it is at this point that we come to a strange paradox in Turgenev's role as a 'realist.' The very piling up of details in description, while pro-ductive of variety, can also quite readily become the basis of despair, of depression, as if the mere listing soon becomes pointless, as if there were no compelling or coherent purpose. These remarkable stories thus indi-cate an enduring part of Turgenev's psyche: the world seems to slip through his fingers. This phenomenon is most apparent in two stories, 'Pyotr Petrovich Karataev' and 'Hamlet of the Shchigrovsky District,' which are further joined by Turgenev's intimate knowledge of Shakes-peare, and his fascination, as was that of the nineteenth century, with the character of Hamlet. Like the one that follows, 'The Meeting,' 'Karataev' is a tragic story of lost love and consequently of forlornness, of lostness itself. Karataev had managed to fall in love with a serving girl, and against her mistress's wishes (who had him in her sights for one of her relatives) steals her off to live with him; in a wild and reckless sled ride she passes her former mistress, is recognized, and is forced to give herself up. Years later, the narrator encounters Karataev in Moscow, where he is living his life downward, but as a theatre-goer, filled with quotations from Shakespeare, all referring to women in *Hamlet*: Ophelia, Gertrude, and Hecuba. 'The past is a foreign country,' Karataev confides. One shouldn't go there again. As in so many of Turgenev's stories, the ending is one of facing up to desolation, both for the character in question and the narrator, who concludes, despite his expressed wishes, 'I had to leave Moscow and I never saw Pyotr Petrovich Karataev again' (*Sketches* 264).

This tendency will only become more reinforced in later years, both in correspondence and in his published writing. There is a waning in his sense of life, and a personal inability to take hold. He is too much the observer both practically and philosophically. In his emotional life, there is some question whether his love affair with Pauline Viardot was ever consummated. In a letter of 1877, he copies out a melancholy portion of his diary: 'In my soul it's darker than a dark night ... It's as if the grave were hurrying to devour me: the days fly past like some mere moment, empty, aimless and colorless' (*The Essential Turgenev* 818). Where the sequence of events was once the basis of variety and of satire, now the mere sequence is without point or purpose. And this coincides with his often quoted prose poem 'Nature,' where Nature indicates her capacity for universal destruction, without regard to 'goodness, reason or justice.' The 'universal mother' has menacing eyes and an 'iron voice': 'I know neither good nor evil ... Reason is not a law to me ... I have given you life, and I will take it away and give it to others, to worms or to people' (882).

But it was not always this way. If there is desolation in the *Sketches* there are also forthright characters such as farmer Ovsyanikov and the obstreperous, bull-headed, but generous Chertopkhanov, who stands up against cruelty and injustice. If on the one hand, we have already in the *Sketches* ample representation of Hamlet, we are also given the figure of greater faith, which is to say that the later classic essay 'Hamlet and Don Quixote' is already present to his imagination. Not only is Turgenev part of a great dualism, he also incorporates dualistic principles into his thinking. Spurred on by the continued relevancy of Voltaire and Rousseau, by the influential character types of Schiller, the nineteenth century was the supreme age of dualistic projections. And Turgenev not only learned them, he taught them, making them a part of his style and thought. The very first entry in *Sketches* is 'Khor and Khalinych,' which begins with this elementary division: 'Whoever has happened to travel from Bolkhov

County into Zhizdra region will no doubt have been struck by the sharp differences between the people in the Orel province and those in Kaluga' (*Sketches* 15). And the sharply drawn differences between the two main characters derive from this preliminary bifurcation. In their differences, though, they are separate but equal. This is not the case when we come to contrast between the Hamlet character, a figure of egotism, self-questioning, and doubt that leads to self-ridicule, and the massive figure of Chertopkhanov, who both in the early instalment and the later addition, 'The End of Chertopkhanov' (1874), is a character of drive and faith and justice, a Quixote-type character whom Turgenev admired both before the classic essay and after its well-received and influential appearance. Like other writers of consciousness, Turgenev was able to live in contradiction, in fact to preside over such division.

Already in 'Chertopkhanov and Nedopyushkin' Turgenev is struck by difference; the two characters are so unlike. 'What could have bound by bonds of indissoluble friendship such evidently different human beings?' (304). And we are immediately led into 'sketches' of the two personalities. To that of Nedopyushkin is added some reflection on the role of Nature, which 'in its indifference and perhaps in a spirit of mockery, endows people with different abilities and aptitudes without taking into account their position in society and their financial means' (308). Nedopyushkin was led into a life of buffoonery: 'In his time he served to assuage the ponderous whims and the drowsy and malicious boredom of an idle nobility' (309). On the other hand, Chertopkhanov, while a madcap, had a magnanimous soul: 'He couldn't abide any injustice or persecution and was a tower of strength in standing up for the peasants' (308). While not a knight-errant, a Quixote in search of righting wrongs, he knew them when he came upon them. Thus he saved Nedopyushkin from a some cruel taunting, and earned his lifelong loyalty: 'The weak, soft and not entirely spotless Tikhon prostrated himself in the dust before the fearless and unselfish Panteley' (313).

The sketch remains a sketch, but the sequel, written years later, is a masterful story, 'The End of Chertopkhanov.' All the vital things in life that he had embraced and admired seem to abandon him. The gypsy lover Masha runs off, not, as he believes, to a dashing young military captain, but simply out of the need for greater excitement. His friend, against his wishes, dies, but given to grand gestures, Chertopkhanov orders a monument for his grave. Instead of an angel in prayer, he acquires a quite curvaceous and naked Flora. Such turnabouts could be called the products of self-delusion (and that would be harsh), but they are also the results of an energetic, if misguided, generosity and magnanimity. The two seem inseparable in this Russian Quixote. As revealed in *A Sportsman's Sketches*, the dualistic principle of Hamlet and Quixote is already a part of his growing imagination, but so are other areas of response: Nature as an enormous, blind, threatening force, the waning of life, the faltering in love – all of these issues will become only more palpable in his series of novels that followed.

5. Turgenev's Major Novels: Culture and Criticism

When Dostoevsky returned in 1860 from his imprisonment and his military conscription, the world had changed. Since the death of Nicholas I in 1855, a period of liberalization had begun, witnessed by the fact that, prior to 1860, 150 new journals and newspapers had appeared. The time that passed also allowed him to patch things up with Turgenev, as more and more of their affinities became apparent. They both lived in and described with consummate artistry the emergence of Russian self-consciousness. A distinctive accomplishment for each was to present and then pass beyond the idealists of the 1840s, the 'non-productive' cultural intellectual heroes reared on German idealism. That is, in each of the works of their major development, characters are presented with a cultural-political importance. Each felt Russia was on the verge or on the eve. But of what? Turgenev, once hopeful, as in *On the Eve* and even in *Fathers and Children*, became in the late 1870s and early 1880s, more gloomy; Dostoevsky was always of two minds: the Russia of the nihilists was doomed, while the Russia offered by its native people, bearing the message of Christ, had a full and messianic mission of hope and prayer. But both brooded over immense future happenings that would come out of the East. They were both committed to understanding the nature of the Russian character. This concern had cost them dearly, as each was imprisoned for such attentiveness. In the very letter to Pauline Viardot, where he describes, among other things, the not altogether unpleasant confinement, Turgenev also expresses the wish 'to continue [his] studies of the Russian people, the strangest and most astonishing people in the world' (*Essential Turgenev* 153). This thought is given an ideological bent in *Rudin*, when Lezhnev tries to explain the title-bearer's failures: 'Rudin's misfortune is that he doesn't know Russia – and that's a great misfortune to be sure. Russia can do without each of us, but none of us can do without it' (286).

This statement becomes increasingly ironic, because it is precisely over

Turgenev's condemnation of almost everything Russian that he and Dostoevsky renewed their former animosity. And other differences are not too far from the surface. In the very same letter of avowed purpose, Turgenev cannot elude the elegiac tone: 'My life is finished; the charm in it is gone.' And the similar metaphor of living among the remnants, chewing brown bread, or as in other passages, drinking the dregs, is invoked (153). That is, even where there are similarities, they serve only to bring out and underscore the differences. When Dostoevsky returned from his much more onerous incarceration, he possessed the 'vitality of a cat'; he found his own convictions regenerated, and he threw himself into the intellectual life that became freer and more invigorated under the more liberal Alexander II.

Despite the valetudinarian affect of Turgenev, the time after prison and his return marked his true emergence. Not only did he forge ahead, one can say he leapt forward. Despite the undeniable excellence of *A Sportsman's Sketches*, *Rudin* is a different matter. It represents a new development in Turgenev's consciousness and begins the run of six major novels extending to 1875 and *Virgin Soil*, a development that will itself experience some change in scope with *On the Eve* and *Fathers and Children*. Turgenev has been credited, and rightly so, with renewing the cultural link with Pushkin's *Eugene Onegin*, as well as presenting the so-called superfluous man. But, as did Dostoevsky, he went beyond that defunct character to portray, beginning with Insarov in *On the Eve*, a new kind of political character, one that would provoke a storm of controversy, pro and contra, in the perfervid cultural atmosphere of Russia of the time. *Rudin* initiates this new start and development. It is a reflection of Turgenev's maturing skills as historian, as clinician of the Russian character (which is to say, his own). It continues the delineations of the 'superfluous man,' the Hamlet-like character already present in 'Hamlet of the Shchigorsky District,' in *Diary of a Superfluous Man*, in the smaller epistolary novella, *A Correspondence*, but all cast onto a broader intellectual and historical tableau. He shows himself the master of social interchange, including biting satire, and most importantly in all three works, he, while ostensibly detailing the life crises of a superfluous man, is most certainly and most avidly devoted to the description of the superior character, determination, and adamant will of young women, in contrast with which the weakness of the men is exposed. While presentation and estimation will vary, Turgenev's novels, beginning with *Rudin*, will invariably have these components: a cultural-intellectual infusion, a detailed depiction of the gatherings of the landed gentry, a powerful female force and love interest, and a decisive and defining moment where love is garnered or dispersed.

Rudin is placed in an intellectual and historical context. In fact, some of its most memorable passages are recollections of the enthusiastic student life, the eagerness for ideas, the hours spent in long discussion throughout the night. Tea and ideas, tea and ideas, and while they consumed the former, they were consumed by the latter. We can gather up some of the ecstatic moments from Lezhnev's recounting of the university days with Rudin (and here in the early part of the novel he has no intention of being complimentary), a description even more valuable for its cameo appearance of Belinksy as Pokorskii. They were young, enthusiastic, and eager for the power of ideas. They were 'poets in their youth.' This was a stage in their lives that Dostoevsky describes in the tumultuous response of his friends after their reading of *Poor Folk*. In this group, Rudin, although inferior in Leshnev's estimation to Pokorskii, shone because he had the capacity to make the 'fascinating, magnificent concepts, but fragmentary, isolated ones' come together into a system (240–1). When he enters the novel he does so with a similar mark of triumph, eagerly adopted by the culturally avid Daria Alexandra. The novel's development consists of a progressive stripping away of Rudin's pre-eminence. He totally captivates Natalia, Daria's daughter, who, by the fervour of his words, becomes a burgeoning woman, willing to make a full commitment to Rudin. But her mother will have none of it, and at the moment of decision, instead of manly defiance, Rudin succumbs to the mother's prohibition, a faltering that simply crushes Natalia, who would have been willing to risk all in her devotion to this man who had stirred her so much. Her staunch womanly forthrightness contrasts with the weaker will of the male. Rudin is undone; his high lofty words prove to be empty, and as we meet him in successive episodes he seems to sink even lower, except in the 'second epilogue,' added in 1860, where he perishes alone atop the barricades in Paris in the doomed uprising of 1848, shot down by a French soldier who mistakenly believes he is a 'Polonais.' Delusion and mistake continue to haunt Turgenev's Quixote-type characters.

But oddly enough, as in the course of the novel his fortunes sag, estimations of his character rise. The same Lezhnev, who saw through Rudin's weaknesses, later comes to his defence. Bridging the difference between words and actions, he now reassures the sunken Rudin that 'a kind word is also a deed' (300). But Rudin is already caught in a downward spiral. Turgenev, like Dostoevsky, here addresses the hazards of noble sentiments, the dangers of youth caught in the supremacy of words and then obliged to live out the consequences of their earlier decisions. They are young intellectuals doomed by life, by history, by nature, but mainly by the intoxicating authority of words and ideas. When in their youthful ascendancy they showed unmistakable signs of imagined superiority over their more practically minded compeers, this was only a hubris that would reap its own revenges.

Lezhnev attributes this to a feature of his temperament, which becomes his fate. An overflowing of generous ideas is tragically undone by life and history. Rudin is not a phlegmatic type, one who seeks out his own space, his own contentment, his own identity, and thus is able to secure his own singular happiness. As Lezhnev later explains in a chance meeting with Rudin, where their altered fortunes are all too readily apparent, 'It's not a worm, not a spirit of idle restlessness – the fire of the love of truth burns inside you, and clearly, in spite of all your difficulties, it burns more intensely inside you than it does inside many people who don't consider themselves egoists ... I, for one, would have managed to silence that worm in me long ago, and would have reconciled myself to everything, whereas you haven't even been embittered by it' (301).

While Lezhnev attempts by the spirit of understanding to bridge the gap between the idealist and the realist, in these early depictions of the superfluous man and the creative tensions they pose in Turgenev's artistry, the task is too difficult. The realist seems to imbibe too freely of the spirit of resignation (confused as reconciliation), and this primarily among the women, who seem to accept the second best, what their early world of amorous daring had no eyes for. Perhaps this is maturity, but it is also a comedown, and for the reader, a letdown. As on the one side, the spirit of realism tends toward resignation, so on the other the spirit of idealism succumbs to the ever-present Turgenevan elegiac mood. For Rudin, in his final meeting with Lezhnev, 'there's no fuel left in the lamp ... the lamp itself is broken and the wick's barely smoldering' (300–1). And these, his own self-indulgent words, echo sentiments that Turgenev himself will often repeat. The novel suffers from the failure of energy, as neither of the divergent characters seems able to sustain the opposing poles of the dialectic. Moreover, truths are told rather than dramatized. Clearly Turgenev's novelistic course will show further development, but along the lines that have already been set. But what he did set in order, and this quite clearly in his understanding of the 'superfluous man,' was the failure of a class, a class that because of serfdom was reduced to being negligent *rentiers*, passed over by time and events. The superfluous man is their totem and tombstone.

More can be said of the high artistry of Turgenev's novelistic world. He is the master of social interchange, particularly in larger gatherings where various voices and attitudes are entered and heard. Frequently social satire is sharply in evidence, as in the culture-vulture salonière, eager to show her importance by the attraction of acolytes, or in the local cynics and wags, filled with a misogynistic bug and who thereby sting for their supper. The smallest items of dress, demeanour, and voice are all significantly etched in, even shadowed. Turgenev is the master of the small tell-all detail. As I have heard John Updike stress, novelists of mundanity require precision, and Turgenev, like the other writers of consciousness, is above all a creature of mundanity. But in the midst of this narrow and limited exposure, life-altering decisions are made or forsaken. Turgenev is a devoted portrayer of the tragedies and failures of love, of love betrayed, of love sacrificed, but always of love ever so close, but ever so firmly out of reach. And then again, above and beyond the distraught humans pounded into submissiveness, there is the sense of the unity of nature, at once overwhelming and consoling – the bad stepmother and the true mother – interjected like the trailing sound of a flute, a fluttering yet distant commentary upon human involvements. The commentary seems to suggest that it all matters but little. This might be another reason why his work seems to shrink when contrasted with the new energy and massive scope brought to his polyphonic novel by Dostoevsky's more radical conjectures about religion, philosophy, and politics. One wishes to say there is an 'ordinariness' in Turgenev's world, where relationships once intense, simply grow distant, take separate paths, and are rarely if ever resumed. We are left with an impression of passingness, as if we, like the characters are simply passing through. In Dostoevsky issues take hold, have an urgency, while in Turgenev they seem to be pushed to the side.

But there in another quality that must be emphasized. Turgenev is the primary author of characters in search of freedom, freedom from family, from social ambience, from environment. It is the same quest that permeates Erasmus's search for intellectual independence or Voltaire's various removals from the overbearing pressures of French or Prussian royalty, his retirement to the borderlands of Switzerland with enough capital resources accumulated to live the life he chose to live. Perhaps because in Turgenev's fiction this quest is so involved with love it is a doomed quest, but never a futile one. The true genius of his cosmopolitanism lies in this pursuit of freedom, and he shows this quality primarily in his female characters, who are ever in search of something better, and that something better is individual freedom, the right to choose one's life's path, to elude the nets with which society enmeshes one. It is at this point that Turgenev is indubitably most modern. All of this is patently clear from the novels, but the correspondence lends the added confirmation of the letter, where he lays out his own credo. Asked to describe his personal philosophy of life, Turgenev writes in a letter from Paris in 1875, 'I am indifferent to everything supernatural; I do not believe in absolutes or any systems; most of all I love freedom ... Everything human is dear to me. Slavophile doctrines, like all orthodoxies, are alien to me' (*Essential Turgenev* 812).

While Turgenev never reneged on these basic principles (in fact, he held to them staunchly, presenting in his novels, and defending them against Herzen, Tolstoy, and particularly Dostoevsky), nevertheless there are tensions and contradictions in his work, those made clear in the classic essay 'Hamlet and Quixote.' In Turgenev the dichotomy is rampant, extending throughout his works. For him Quixote is not a comic character, as he was to the Spaniards of the seventeenth century. Something had intervened, most prominently, as Eric Ziolkowski argues, this was German Romanticism, where Quixote comes to represents all the strengths and weaknesses of idealism, in fact, eventually becoming in Dostoevsky's hands, a holy fool (99, 110–12, and ff.). For Turgenev, this aspect is absent, but what is present is the sense of absolute, single-minded commitment to some ideal, some truth outside of oneself. The self is as it were absorbed, forgotten in commitment. This quality is particularly strong in the female heroes, in Parianaa of *Virgin Soil* and Elena of *On the Eve*. They are in fact given over to self-sacrifice, with the willingness to forsake all, and to run off. The Hamlet character, on the other hand, can never abandon the self; beset by the spirit of consciousness he never can believe, or his belief is not quite whole, undermined by self-questioning doubts as to his own worthiness, a lurking suspicion of his weakness. In this internal division, his consciousness mines a self-defeat, the logical outcome of which is suicide. Hence the fullest representation of this type is Nezhdanov in *Virgin Soil*, certainly one of the most believable and gripping figures in all of Turgenev's work. He represents the fullest portrait of the Hamlet type, the character Turgenev comprehends and with whom he sympathizes. Because of the Hamlet of his own mind, Turgenev can never quite emulate the Quixote he reluctantly admires.

On this dualistic principle many variations are played. This is eminently true in an undervalued novel, which is clearly one of his best, *On the Eve*, situated midway between *Rudin* and *Fathers and Children* both in character and theme. It brings to bear all of Turgenev's novelistic virtues, his great attention to social detail (frequently satiric); it literally is transfigured with magnificent natural descriptions, but it even more enters into the complexities of character, and unlike *Rudin*, contains ample sustaining poles of energy, that of indomitable will, and that of those resigned to live in the ordinary world of little or no passionate commitment. Moreover, it begins to approach *Fathers and Children* by suggesting for the first time the conflict as being generational. While possessing familiar novelistic components, *On the Eve* represents the supersession of the superfluous man by a new political man, one in keeping with the coming intellectual tide of the 1860s, who is not a figure from the landed gentry, but rather one 'without rank,' a *raznochinets*.

Ralph E. Matlaw has rightly remarked that 'the sense of social responsibility, political commitment, and moral vision that informs Russian literature is in large part the product of a critical tradition established in the middle third of the nineteenth century' (Matlaw viii). The fervour and the pressure of the times brought together artist and critic in a remarkable –and perhaps unique – cultural exchange of opinion. If the critical attention, elevated to a high level of public awareness, had demonstrable effect upon the artist (*Fathers and Children* would be a case in point), the obverse is also true, as the power of higher literature produced in the critics a greater profundity, aesthetic consciousness, eloquence, insight. and even sense of fairness. Such at least was the effect of Turgenev's two novels, *On the Eve* and *Fathers and Children* on two of the foremost critics of the new radical generation, Nikolai Dobrolyubov (1836–61) and Dmitri Pisarev (1840–68). Almost everything else that they wrote could come under the heading of sociological philistinism, but when they wrote of Turgenev's novels they surpassed themselves and some of their convictions. They saw themselves and their conditions correctly mirrored in Turgenev's works, and thus by experience and intelligent attention they were able not only to see the text (which they read quite closely) but also into it and through it into what it forebode about Russian society. The powers of insightful self-identification in the presence of high artistry gave to their Turgenevan criticism a sense of importance and powerful purpose. Sadly, a lamentable feature of the society of the time is young death. Dobrolyubov died at the age of twenty-five and Pisarev at twenty-eight.

The best summary and fullest understanding of Turgenev's development and cultural importance occurs in Dobrolyubov's underappreciated 'When Will the Real Day Come?' Here occurs that rare event of a true fit between a novel, Turgenev's *On the Eve*, and a critical essay, almost as if in the course of Turgenev's itinerary this is the work for which Dobrolyubov had been waiting. Dobrolyubov's essay has been discounted as being 'sociological,' as eschewing the 'aesthetic' features of a work, but such a demotion is misinformed and unwarranted. In fact, Dobrolyubov treats literature as the highest form of cultural awareness. There is no shorting of Turgenev's text; rather, Dobrolyubov shows an unerring eye in focusing on its key elements, elements that he elevates by showing their supreme relevancy, their representativeness, for the changing nature of Russian society.

Dobrolyubov is as clear as to his methodologies as he is perceptive in his aesthetic insights. He tells us in a clear statement of methodology that he is not concerned with Turgenev's intentions but rather with the actual tale as it is told, and as it may be read. Long before D.H. Lawrence, he anticipated that author's famous dictum: trust the novel, not the novelist – the novelist is a liar. Or, more politely, the novel as the bright book of life frequently surpasses or subverts conscious intent.

The true and genuinely talented artist, one like Turgenev, renders the 'essential features' of his society. And here the criterion of the author's talent will be 'the breadth of his conception of life, the degree to which the images he has created are permanent and comprehensive.' Well could he have been describing Dante or Shakespeare. But he also understands Turgenev's more limited gifts: they are not of the 'titanic' kind, and he does not possess a 'turbulent and impulsive power' (179), thus making the kind of distinction that Carducci at about the same time was making in Italy, when he contrasted the powers of Dante, Luther, and Rousseau with those of Petrarch, Erasmus, and Voltaire. But it is the absence of these very qualities that have helped make Turgenev so successful, his every word so eagerly awaited. His very vacillations, his ambivalences are those of his society. 'Thus we may boldly assert that if Mr Turgenev touches upon any subject in a story of his ... it can be taken as a guarantee that this question is rising, or soon will arise, in the mind of the educated section of society' (180). But there is more than this in Turgenev's appeal: he succeeds in capturing the essential trauma of Russian society: 'He started out from the sphere of lofty ideas and theoretical strivings and proceeded to introduce these ideas and strivings into banal reality, which had digressed very much from them. The hero's preparations for the struggle, his sufferings, his eagerness to see the triumph of his principles, and his fall in the face of the overwhelming power of human banality have usually been the centers of interest in Mr. Turgenev's stories' (180). And while this formula does not account for all of Turgenev's work, it certainly goes far in comprehending the dominant developments and the quite interesting public appeal of *Rudin* and *The Nest of Gentry*.

Much to the displeasure of the new radical activist generation, the Russian public (for reasons that Pisarev will later explain) seem to sop up stories of submission and sacrifice. Turgenev's hero is undone by a failure of resolve, by failing to respond to the personal integrity and the more dominant will of the woman to whom he is attracted. But it is this inevitable tone of self-sacrifice and even doom that caught the reading public's fancy. Dobrolyubov notes all of this, which is why he emphasizes the fundamental importance of *On the Eve*. In Turgenev's evolving typology it represents a radical change. Thus at the centre of the novel, he quite accurately places the young woman Elena. Imprisoned by her condition within a family that does not know what to make of her, she is the maiden enclosed in the castle waiting for the true knight to liberate her. The situation of nineteenth-century Russian society and her own youth and dependence do not provide the means for self-liberation. Alienated from her family, she gives expression to her obscure needs in petty gestures of goodwill to all suffering creatures large and small. But this is not sufficient, and her life does not know fulfilment. Dobrolyubov insists on Turgenev's instinctual rightness in thus making her portrait incomplete, as one befitting her situation.

As in classical story, fairy tale, and Shakespeare, three contestants vie for her release. They are the artist Shubin, the prospective scholar Bersenev, and the Bulgarian revolutionary Insarov (there is actually a fourth, but his figure is not crucial). It is Elena herself who is initially drawn to and then dismisses the first two. Here Dobrolyubov gives the closest attention to the text. In that he is and will prove to be an artist of some merit, Shubin is not a frivolous character; he is rather too given over to self-amusement and can never even take himself too seriously. He protests to Elena that his repentance is sincere. But she responds that even his tears, his repentances, are too consciously observed – they amuse him. To which Dobrolyubov adds, noting the insufficiency of the highly conscious artist as a suitable character type, 'Shubin shudders as he heard this simple verdict, which must indeed have stabbed deeply into his heart' (194). Thereafter Elena had no eyes for this suitor.

The artist as highly developed self-consciousness holds no appeal for her, cannot be a source of liberation from her physical and psychological captivity. But neither can the scholar, imbued with the spirit of self-abnegation. Unlike Shubin, Bersenev is notably sincere, generous, and self-sacrificing. In a crucial exchange with Shubin, he accepts that 'the entire mission of our lives is to make ourselves Number Two' (195). That is, he is perfectly suited to the life of scholarship, as his subsequent volumes drearily attest, absorbed only with other people's activities, and thereby taking no risk of personal statement of belief or action. In a crucial diary entry, despite her sincere admiration for Bersenev's personal qualities, Elena cannot help but compare him to Insarov: 'Andrei Petrovich [Bersenev] may be more learned than he [Insarov] but I don't know why it is – *he looks so small in his presence*' (200). All that this entry implies does not escape Dobrolyubov's keen attentiveness.

But why Insarov, a Bulgarian? Why not a Russian? Turgenev himself might have answered as Joyce did when asked why Leopold Bloom was a Jew: 'Because he was.' Indeed the germ of the story – and even a bit more with a Bulgarian hero – was provided for Turgenev by his close friend Karatyaev. Dying before he could finish the story himself, he bequeathed it to Turgenev. But Dobrolyubov provides many more compelling reasons why this kind of character could not be a Russian. One is Russia's political situation – it is not enslaved by a foreign oppressor. Given this absence of external invasion, and the presence of laws, high ideals are reduced to effecting minor rectifications (225). Then the entire educational system, while endowing students with a love of justice, also induces a respect for their elders and a dutifulness, if not docility (hence the submissiveness of Rudin and Lavretsky). These arguments of explanation are among the most interesting because obviously they form a personal testimony, clearly deriving from Dobrolyubov's own experience and that of his cohorts – the very psychology against which he is at war. Despite the presence of the high ideals of the 1840s, such ideals are bound to end in passivity and reduce their protagonists to apathy. One is born not to rebel but to submit. It should also be apparent that his description of the lawfulness and justice of the Russian social institutions is entirely ironic. The ideals of the 1840s have not failed; they have succeeded only too well and have permeated all of educated society. They have taken on the allure of social and political correctness – everybody knows what is the right thing to say. The problem is to do what is right. And here the character of Insarov is instructive.

Insarov is totally committed to an ideal – to be sure it is a straightforward one, even obvious, the liberation of one's country from a foreign oppressor, Bulgaria from Turkish domination. This is somewhat different, Dobrolyubov knows, from the situation when the enemy is internal, in one's household. Nevertheless Insarov forms an ideal because he is willing to subordinate all actions to the larger goal. Despite the fact that his parents were killed by the Turks, he is not driven by vengeance. That would be too personal and individual – an example of what might happen in Russia. Insarov has his eyes on the big picture – just what is not possible in Russia, where only minor remediations are permitted. And in pursuit of his larger goals, he divests himself of personal ego – it does not matter whether he is Number One or Number Two. Consumed by dedication to a principle, he is unlike the contemporary Russian, Dobrolyubov tells us, who 'will always remain timid and dual-minded' (209). It is by this larger and active idealism, idealism with a true project and goal, that Elena is swept away, and thus dismisses what Russia has to offer. She has finally found a man who complements her own needs and suppressed energies. Her personal freedom is thus compliant with full dedication to some higher purpose.

But it also involves much more, and that for Turgenev is a sense of personal integrity, the clear sense and declaration of individual responsibility. And when he makes such a declaration, Insarov speaks with the voice of a leader. Rather than quailing before Elena's strong love and the opposition of her family, he declares that she is his wife, 'before man and God.' The phrase is an unexpected one. Closely resembling the personal commitment of Mariann and Nezhdanov in *Virgin Soil*, it returns us to the voice of another leader, Martin Luther, who affirmed that in the justness of their commitment and conscience a priest and his woman are united before man and God. This is a counter-historical since it represents the remarkable intrusion of the Reformation into Russian social life. Insarov's declaration stands out because, while truly committed to the national stage of political liberation, on the personal level, available to everyone, he represents that forthrightness of conscience that Luther was among the boldest to introduce to the modern world.

For Dobrolyubov, Insarov is another hero for his time, not the superfluous or unwanted hero, but rather one who spurns petty grievances and whose program is systemic, one who will – and the phrase is fearsome – 'take an axe to the root of the tree.' Dostoevsky with his sense of reality will show more fully what it means to take up the axe, while Turgenev, with his typical vacillations, one that however showed his knack for capturing the temper of the times – his 'presentness' – will next create a Russian Insarov, and that is Bazarov in *Fathers and Children*.

Given the sharply divided state of Russian culture at the time, split between generations and as well as ideologies, a time still 'on the eve,' when great change was looming. Turgenev's *Fathers and Children* was born for controversy, and Turgenev himself bound to be misunderstood (but for reasons that differed from those that made Dostoevsky misunderstood). Like Erasmus, whose character and fate he resembles more and more, his complex artistic vision was attacked from both sides. The Right felt that he had brought about an 'apotheosis' of the new radical generation, and moreover baptized it with a name that caught on, 'nihilist,' while the Left felt he had come upon a catchword and in the character of Bazarov lampooned Chernyshevsky (some of whose inane views are indeed reproduced) and taken out his resentment on Dobrolyubov (some of whose better arguments he had indeed adopted). But there is a difference in the cause of the divided opinion that Erasmus and Turgenev suffered. Erasmus was writing as a mediator, as one who advocated the spirit of reconciliation, who sought out a common ground upon which 'reasonable' people could agree (or disagree). The opposing fires that Turgenev suffered could not be attributed to 'indecisiveness' or 'hesitancy,' or even to the spirit of reconciliation, but rather to a higher sense of artistry, the felt need for truthfulness to life, an obedience to the promptings of genius that overtake one in the creation of complex character. Like a magpie, he stores up from here and from there, episodes, incidents, phrasings, all going into and filling out the design of character, creating the ambiguities that elude even the author's intent. The book itself is alive.

The multiple attacks from both sides of divided opinion prompted a stirring response on Turgenev's part, his 'A Propos of Fathers and Sons' published in 1869. There he lets it be known, as if by this time there were any doubt, that he is 'an inveterate Westerner.' Yet, despite this allegiance, he is able to put these sentiments (duly vulgarized) into the mouth of an unattractive character, Panshin, who is appropriately crushed by the Slavophil Lavretsky in *Nest of Gentry*. Why? His first argument is that 'in this given case ... life happened to be like that' (*Literary Reminiscences* 196). But there is more: 'a truthfulness that is inexorable in relation to one's own feelings' (202). There are aspects of the self that demand a hearing, adding richness and delight and above all avoiding the restrictions and boredom of a sermonizing predictability. The horns of this dilemma fully trapped Rousseau, who realized that his moralized *Misanthrope* would be a flop. But there is more, and Turgenev quotes a Russian proverb to the effect that learning is not only light, it is freedom (202). Breaking out of the polemically constrained camps of his day, Turgenev stands eminently, as do some of his characters, for artistic freedom, the freedom to astound, to create.

But it is also not surprising, however disappointing, that later in 1874–6, when as a result of long absences abroad he felt that he was losing his grasp of Russian society, Turgenev, also in the manner of Erasmus, recanted. He now admits that despite his abiding sympathy for the character of Bazarov, in his use of the term *nihilist*, he did provide a catchword for his enemies on the Right. Unwittingly he had brought aid and comfort to the enemy. The writer should have made a sacrifice to the citizen. 'Therefore I consider fair both the alienation of the youth from me and all sorts of reproaches heaped upon me. The problem [the social and political issues] was more important than artistic truth' (Matlaw 192). Just like conversion for the daemonic writer, recantation – the correlative recourse of the writer of consciousness – does not come out of the blue; the premises must have been there from the beginning. While we have no doubts about his Western political views, in the contrast between the 'wild' and the 'tame,' between the extraordinary and those who remain within the rhythms of nature, his true sympathies, despite his protestations and ambivalences, may have been with the tame and orderly all the while.

Obviously the sensational character of *Fathers and Children* is Bazarov, one who represents a new message from a new generation, a Russian Insarov, in fact one called for by Dobrolyubov in his classic essay. Of the elder generation he is unsparing: he questions everything and submits to nothing. There is, even as the characters make plain, something wild about him. And this was Turgenev's intention: 'I dreamt of a figure that was gloomy, wild, huge, half gown out of the ground, powerful, sardonic, honest – and doomed to destruction nevertheless – since it nevertheless still stands only at the threshold of the future' (186). Bazarov is what Turgenev termed a 'negator,' and because of that he operates on the first phase of rectification, misunderstood and victimized by the very problematic position he occupies. In but a few years, Nietzsche would say the same about his hero – dead on the barricades of change since he was in the vanguard of the opening charge.[9] Bazarov is not Rudin, whose death represents the last gasp of the generation of the 1840s; rather he is a new man, come with a different message, not one of high idealism but one of ruthless dedication to practical usefulness. It seems one cannot escape the presence of Dobrolyubov's essay in Bazarov's character, as well as the personal qualities of many of the new young men, whom Turgenev knew: 'All the real *negators* I have known, without exception (Belinsky, Bakunin, Herzen, Dobrolyubov, Speshnev, et al.) came from comparatively good and honest parents. A great idea is contained therein: it removes from the *men of action*, the negators, any suspicion of personal dissatisfaction, personal irritation. They go their way simply because they are more sensitive to the demands of national life' (185–6). The calling is similar to what Dobrolyubov admired in Insarov – a larger, systemic concern. Turgenev admires, is attached to, his Bazarov, but he is not like him. Rather he associates himself with the fathers, with Nikolai, and it is this very division in himself that accounts for the fury the book aroused and for the conflict of meanings it holds for us.

The character of Bazarov presents obvious problems, one of them being that we actually never see his 'greatness.' His revolutionary fierceness turns out to be merely rudeness. His materialist philosophy, copied from Chernyshevsky, is at best jejune (66). Turgenev does not share Bazarov's opinions about art – that Pushkin is Romantic rubbish, and that Raphael should be dumped. But this is merely the silly thought to which social progressives, believing they are advocates for the people, occasionally resort. Nor do his acolytes reflect well on the master. Sitnikov believes that to show contempt is a sign of intelligence and one way to make an impression. Even Arkady, the eager disciple, feels that they are a 'force' that is numerically large throughout Russia but also willing to use force – which sentiment would hardly meet with Turgenev's approval. While Bazarov can emerge victorious over the generation of Nikolai and Pavel, it is also clear that Turgenev's intentions are not always fulfilled, mainly because they are themselves ambiguous.

Such ambiguity reveals itself when we come to the main interest of the novel, and that is love – always decisive in Turgenev's oeuvre. Here we reach back to another prototype: Bazarov is an Alceste from Molière's *Misanthrope*. In a letter to his editor, Katkov, prior to publication, he asserts that 'Bazarov himself is empty and barren. Perhaps my view of Russia is more misanthropic than you suppose: in my mind he is the real hero of our time. A fine hero and a fine time you'll say. But that's how it is' (182). Empty and barren – harsh words and hardly justified. Yet, in love, there is a shortage in Bazarov. It comes from a failure to believe in and make consultation with the self, with one's feelings, with one's recollections and memory. Despite the completeness of his dedication Bazarov seems to exist at one level only. At his parents' home, trying to fall off to sleep, he could not: 'With wide open eyes he stared vindictively into the darkness; the memories of childhood had no power over him' (96). The brief phrase is jolting and shows the continued presence of Rousseau, not the fomenter of rebellion but the one who encourages affective memory, consultation with the self. Turgenev has Katya and Arkady divide humankind into the wild (Bazarov) and the tame (themselves). But there is another division between those who restrict themselves, are one-sided, and those who seek out their true feelings. The brutal satire of the female intellectual Kukshina might be justified by her total neglect of her own emotional life – she is a walking bibliography, peregrinating from one intellectual fad and subject to the next. Sitnikov is of the same ilk, only more mendacious. This brings us to the bitter experience that kept Bazarov awake: his declaration of his love for Odintsova, which she had obviously encouraged but was incapable of accepting. The declaration is almost torn from him, grimly vindictive. But unlike Alceste in love with Célimène, this represents more than the normal and humorous contradictions of character. Bazarov, who demoted love to a simple physiological process – all psychology is physiology – and could be quite coarse in his overall judgments about sex, is thrown tumultuously into a passion against which he is fighting. He unveils his soul to a woman who cannot tolerate having her life upset or penetrated by any form of disorder. She represents the sad effects of having been made beautiful 'overmuch,' as Yeats expressed his fears in 'A Prayer for My Daughter' for such,

> Consider beauty a sufficient end,
> Lose natural kindness and maybe
> The heart-revealing intimacy
> That chooses right, and never find a friend.

The real division in the book is between those who have the 'heart-revealing intimacy' 'the natural kindness' that allows them to choose right – they achieve a kind of personal integrity by virtue of consultation with their true feelings. Thus the aborted relationship between the two grander personalities, Bazarov and Odinstova, must be contrasted with the fulfilled one between Katya and Arkady. Little by little Arkady came to realize that the person whose company he enjoyed and felt most comfortable with was Katya, and not her more imposing sister. His natural instincts, or his awareness of his natural feelings in the matter, led him that way. One might say the same between his father Nikolai, and his mistress Fenichka, who had already born him a son. The magic circle closes, and the outsiders are the great ones – Bazarov, Odintsova, and Pavel Petrovich, although he does encourage his brother to marry Fenichka. Turgenev in his comments would insist that he wrote his novel 'as directed against the nobility as the leading class. Look at Nikolai Petrovich, Pavel Petrovich, Arkady. Weakness and languor, or limitations'

(185). But he could also write a short time earlier, 'Do I want to abuse Bazarov or extol him? I do not know that myself, since I don't know whether I love him or hate him' (184). How to reconcile these differences, except to say that Turgenev as an artist was truthful to the complexity of his emotions, his insights, and the many voices he contained. Such multiplicity represents the triumph of the novel. But here perhaps another interpretation might be offered: the distinction in Turgenev on the one side between his political views, as an arch-Westernizer who wished to see the aristocratic classes stripped of their privileges, to see Russia modernized along with his admiration for those willing to undergo the agony of effecting such change, and, on the other, his personal qualities, more elegant, reserved, aesthetic, even ironic. From this conflict we get the makings of a true novelist.

The beauty of Pisarev's essay 'Bazarov,' besides its sharp awareness of the text, is the intellectual and social background it provides and the understanding of Turgenev's attitudes to his work – it is almost as if he had been privy to opinions expressed by Turgenev in his correspondence (195–218). Through life experience and broad intellectual sympathy and understanding, like Dobrolyubov, he sees into and through the text: 'We see what shines through and not just what the author wants to show us or prove' (196). He writes as an engaged intellectual, for whom Bazarov is 'one of us.' And yet he approves of Turgenev's mixed portrayal, valuing its accuracy to the realities of the times. Bazarov is a true type because he is shown with all his deficiencies, and not idealized as one of Pisarev's colleagues would have drawn him. Here he strikes a chord of unanimity with Dostoevsky: 'If Bazarovism is a disease, then it is a disease of our time' (199). It is like cholera, but with the exception that it infects only the most high-minded, the most generous, and the most capable among the Russian young people. The 'real day' has not come, but when it does, it will look back upon the Bazarov's as forerunners of a better future. Pisarev, and those like him, looking back from the future upon this character, will see in him one of their prototypes; Turgenev is looking at him from the past. Yet because Turgenev is an 'honorable man and a true artist' (217), he could not bring himself to debase Bazarov. He can depict his deficiencies – and here Pisarev admits that these deficiencies are real – but he must also be in awe somehow of Bazarov's intellectual strength and commitment, the ways in which he towers over his alternatives – and here he might have been quoting Turgenev himself.

Pisarev sees accurately into the author and his chief creation. If this is not 'aesthetic' criticism, then we have devalued that term. Turgenev's nature is 'soft and loving, striving for faith and sympathy.' Then in a summary statement, with which any full reading of Turgenev must agree, he adds that 'he must become reconciled with existence' (202). While believing that Turgenev 'shrinks from the slightest contact with the bouquet of Bazarovism' (203), he nevertheless acknowledges that the portrait of the new intellectual hero is acutely insightful. With his philosophical materialism Bazarov is too one-sided. This Pisarev understands as deriving from his poverty as a university student and the nature of his studies – medicine and natural science. Pisarev, who wrote 'The Destruction of Aesthetics,' deplores the lack of aesthetic appreciation in Bazarov, and his 'intellectual despotism.' And moreover he sees this as an intellectual failing of his generation. 'This arrogance is generally a characteristic of us' (205). But it is also a necessity of the time: tired of the heady Hegelian phrases, his contemporaries have gone to the other extreme; the dialectic has provoked the new realists into the opposite error, that of denying 'simple feelings,' and aesthetic pleasures, 'like the enjoyment of music.' 'There is no great harm in this extremity, but it will not hurt to point it out, and to call it ludicrous is not to join ranks with the obscurantists and old romantics' (206). And thus by a truly insightful and revealing reading, Pisarev goes far to reconcile his generation with *Fathers and Children*. Not only does he understand the work in all of its larger implications, he also understands the nature of Turgenev's true artistry and his voice as being among the finest of the older generation. He credits both the artist and his creation, placing each in the larger historic frame from which they derived. Both are in a way victims of a national malaise, and like Dostoevsky, he understands that it is an infection that afflicts the best.

In a letter that has now been lost, Dostoevsky wrote to Turgenev praising *Fathers and Children*. But we gain some inkling of the letter's contents from Turgenev's response, where there and elsewhere he praises Dostoevsky as one of the two critics who understood that his Bazarov was a tragic hero (182). This was more than an exchange of politeness. We probably do not need Dostoevsky's letter. In *Winter Notes on Summer Impressions* (1863) he makes quite clear where the novel stands in his own assessment. Mocking the smug self-satisfaction of the Europeanized Russian progressive, he protests the lashing that Turgenev has received for daring to refuse that serene acceptance of their ideal and instead presenting the complex character of Bazarov. 'Well, he caught it for Bazarov, that sad, troubled Bazarov (the sign of a great heart), in spite of all his nihilism. We even lashed out at him for Kukshina, for that progressive louse whom Turgenev combed out of Russian reality to show us, and we even added that he was going against the emancipation of women' (*Winter Notes on Summer Impressions* 21).

From a review-essay written by Strakhov for Dostoevsky's journal *Vremya*, we can imagine some affinity between his views and those of Dostoevsky concerning the young radical intelligentsia (reprinted in Turgenev, *Fathers and Sons* 218ff.). Strakhov's review appeared just a few months (April 1862) after the publication of *Fathers and Children*, thus following shortly after Pisarev's own essay, to which it refers and with which it in large part agrees, thus effecting a remarkable confluence of acute criticism, talented writers, and a superior work of literature.

Both critics invoke the prehistory of the novel – university life in St Petersburg, where those of Bazarov's nature and background had already been penetrated by their studies of medicine and natural sciences. When they return home they are different people – the university experience having brought about a breach between their thought and their lives. Strakhov emphasizes that Bazarov's education did not occur by a gradual accumulation but rather by a sharp break (222). He thus falls victim to the 'deadening influence of theory.' His force of character, combined with this intellectual armoury, makes him the first 'strong character' in Russian literature. He is in the line of the other Russian intellectual heroes – and he mentions Onegin, Pechorin, Rudin, and Lavretsky, but Bazarov completes their beings by his need for action. Strakhov admires Turgenev's creation of a titanic force, of a superior being, but one who is, as Pisarev indicates, lamentably one-sided and thus not fully representative. The matrix of the novel contradicts his own theories: he falls in love with Odinstova, he makes a spontaneous pass at Fenichka, he fights a duel. Indeed he is an Alceste. But there is more to his destined doom, and that lies in the contradiction between his theory and his human needs, but also between his theory and the flow of life in which he is involved, 'Turgenev's reconciliation with existence.' The phrases are vague, but Strakhov indicates their meanings when he writes, 'Those who think that for a supposed condemnation of Bazarov the author contrasts to him one of his characters, say Pavel Petrovich, or Arkady, or Odintsova, are terribly wrong. All these characters are insignificant in comparison to Bazarov. And yet their life, the human element in their feelings is not insignificant' (227). Both Pisarev and Strakhov, writers from different camps, not only recognize the greatness of the novel, but actually agree on its reasons.

It is thus no accident that the battle over *Fathers and Children* produced a temporary rapprochement in the attenuated friendship of Turgenev and Dostoevsky. But the point remains that when Dostoevksy came to write his version of a provincial student who suffers his own breach between theory and the life he had known, who does not gain the benefits of a gradual accumulation of opinion, but rather the bone-scraping irritant of sudden change in life and thought, Dostoevsky in *Crime and Punishment* will follow to a more dramatic consummation and greater reconciliation his own Bazarov. Dostoevsky's genius resides in the triumph of accumulating thought, in the strong ideas that he pursued and developed until their full realization. The sheer moral energy and the far-reaching social implications of the ideas at work make of *Crime and Punishment* a revealing response to *Fathers and Children*.

6. The Enlarged Scope of Ideas

Like a man returning from war, Dostoevsky came home from prison with much to do. For ten years he had been on the sidelines, he who had once been the rising star of a remarkable Pléiad. His own avowed 'cat-like vitality' threw him into various activities, this at a time of extraordinary social and political change in Russia. He founded with his brother Mikhail the journal *Vremya*, which became a booming success, and was eager to make a big splash again as an author. This he did with the work Tolstoy considered his greatest, *The House of the Dead*, thus continuing the genre of the prison memoir, soon to become all-too-common in the annals of twentieth-century literature.

Oddly enough, given Dostoevsky's later reputation as a reactionary, a reputation this work should go far in dispelling, *The House of the Dead* enjoyed great success as an effort of social reform. The Russian educated public was horrified at its revelations – particularly the birch floggings, which were lethal, and the senseless bureaucratic rigidities to which the ill were subjected. But the greatness of *The House of the Dead* has to do with Dostoevsky's personal qualities, particularly his openness, his unblinkered awareness of and responsiveness to the 'phenomena of nature.' These qualities might be attributed to what Nicolas Berdyaev, that most lucid analyst of the Russian character, referred to as its 'paganism' (8). In that the scope of what was human was immeasurably broader and deeper Dostoevsky, was even more Terentian than Turgenev. In the noxious communal life of the prison, all the particularities and differences of character are noted. Dostoevsky is responsive to all the various peoples that make up the far-flung Russian empire, particularly extending admiration to the Muslims and, as do all the prisoners, a begrudging and bemused respect for the Jew Ismay, who holds so resolutely to his own religious practices (although he is slurred with being 'of course' a moneylender, as well as the killer of Christ). And there are taboos. Dostoevsky acquired first-hand experience about the unregeneracy in some souls. Child-murderers were quickly silenced in their attempts to retell their heinous acts. This was anathema. In such tight quarters, fierce hostilities were always at the ready, but they rarely led to blows. Instead the men engaged in operatic duets of mutual vilification, feats of Falstaffian proportions in which they took great pride and went away with their egos salvaged. Their virtuosity in the vernacular would even outdo David Mamet. They were obviously alarmed by outright excesses of prison brutality and other injustices on the part of authorities, but were equally ashamed by any over-eagerness to please on the part of officials. From those who were joined by a common fate, this was met with scorn as it indicated someone who had not accepted his station.

Openness leads to revelation, to life lived at the extremes. The bathhouse scene praised by Turgenev and others describes the tumult of a hundred convicts hunched over one another in very narrow quarters, spewing and mewling, taking in the hot steam and alternately dousing themselves with hot or cold water. But the most interesting scenes showed some of the better instincts of the men, their instinctual remembrances of a better life, and here Dostoevsky's appreciation of the fullness of life is most in evidence. Come the Christmas season and cognizance is apparent, even among the most hardened, that they are participating in a noumenal event. 'Respect for the solemn feast even acquired a certain ritual majesty among the convicts' (166). 'They all knew that it was a day of great importance, a religious holiday of the greatest magnitude' (169). Consequently, those accustomed to pass one another in grim silence, now offered earnest greetings and well wishes. It is as if they all sensed the presence of an earlier world with all its possibilities still intact. This is Dostoevsky's interpretation: 'In addition to his inborn sense of reverence for the great day, each convict had the feeling that by observing the feast he was in some way coming into contact with the whole world, that consequently he was not quite an outcast, a lost man, a severed limb, and that as it was in the world of men, so it was in prison' (166). To be sure, reversion occurs, and the joviality soon turns to drink, drunkenness, and stupefaction – from which the Muslims sitting outside the barracks absent themselves, muttering in their language that it is all bad, and the Jew Ismay turns away to his own religious practices.

But with the Easter season it was different, and again men who had committed hórrible crimes show a reverence for the meaning of life conveyed in the religious ceremony, but without the flagrant abuse and disturbing aftermath. One begins to witness a coalescence of cares on Dostoevsky's part: the first lies in the fulfilments offered by the seasonal rituals of the Christian calendar – obviously a recollection of his own youth and family traditions, and the other is his awareness of the prisoners' altered behaviour. However buried and tarnished, there still exists in them remnants of the earlier hope. We acquire a different picture of Dostoevsky himself from this work, where he presents the religious, the aesthetic, the importance of the sense of human worth still alive in the hearts of such hardened criminals, and does so not as a sentimental reformer of the 1840s, but as one of the condemned himself, who is able to see into the heart of unregeneracy, but is also able to pierce even more deeply into the profound mysteries of human needs and desires.

Prison time brought about in Dostoevsky a return to the traditions and beliefs of his early family life, but it also led to new discoveries. One such discovery that would form the substance of all his future faith and works is the human need for freedom. His differs from Turgenev's notion of freedom, which is premised on a rational faith in the capacity of humans to live the life of their choice. It harkens to the civilized being. With Dostoevsky, in entirely different circumstances, this new conception lies in the indomitable urge to be somebody, to express one's worth as a person. Of course, in prison it is the stuff dreams are made on, and Dostoevsky avers that convicts are great dreamers. Nevertheless he sees through the most convulsive and paradoxical behaviour into genuine motivation. Thus a prisoner will work months on good behaviour, even amass a sum of money, only to blow it all in a bout of drunkenness and brawling, almost certain to be punished with a severe flogging and added prison time. Dostoevsky does not look upon this as would a bluestocking, but sees underneath such behaviour a misguided but unquenchable desire to be free, to have one's own will, to express one's rightness as an individual. In *The House of the Dead* – and the title becomes increasingly ironic – Dostoevsky shows his fascination with the varieties of human existence, with the codes of human existence established even in the midst of the most dehumanizing conditions, with the ways humans will take to express their individuality, their need for freedom. Dostoevsky's thoughts about the Russian peasant and about the relationship of the intellectual to the peasant undergo a radical transformation. Rather than being the educators, it turns out the intellectuals have a lot to learn. All that is required is a relinquishment of the ego in the openness to revelation. In short, what is required is some sort of conversion experience. While the observing intellect does not abscond, still a form of submission is required, the kind of conversion and submission that the writer of consciousness, despite his manipulation of alternative ways of seeing, cannot endure.

The House of the Dead possesses that magical quality of readability. Intellectually, despite their generic differences, it is already on the way to Dostoevsky's next two tandem works, *Winter Notes on Summer Impressions* (strangely undervalued) and the true breakthrough work, *Notes from Underground*. *Winter Notes on Summer Impressions* is the strange and wonderful product of Dostoevsky's first travels abroad. It might better be entitled *A Russian Abroad*, or *Russians Not at Home*, because indeed its true subject is the absurd, or so Dostoevsky thought, and slavish imitation of things European on the part of the progressive, up-to-date Russians. The work utilizes the 'inverted irony' made more famous in *Notes from Underground* but is remarkable for its allusiveness, the metaphoric personal freedom of a true literary genius. Here if anywhere we find Dostoevsky in close company with Luther and Rousseau. Foremost among their traits in common is their united opposition to the advanced stages of European consciousness: they were beset with the problem of arguing against virtue, of defending the indefensible. Dostoevsky differs from Rousseau particularly in his rhetoric – Rousseau's is simple and direct; he believes in the native simplicity of the common virtues. So does Dostoevsky, but his rhetoric is far from simple. He must begin by disqualifying himself as any kind of travel authority; the tone is self-deprecating, even jeering. He belittles himself in order to disarm his opponents. In a chapter that Dostoevsky termed 'superfluous,' he appears to be defending the older Russian ways – including the foul practice of wife-beating. But having established this offensive action, he wonders in what ways the progressive Europeanized Russians are superior. They are simply creatures of fashion, imitating everything that comes from Europe and calling barbaric everything that seems native Russian. One practice is that of the matchmaker, who, drunk in a cab (the cabby is also intoxicated), drives through the town displaying the panties of the woman who has just enjoyed the first night of her marriage. Newspapers deride this practice as a barbaric remnant of worse times. But, Dostoevsky argues, in what way is this practice inferior to the latest custom brought from Europe of women padding their garments in appropriate places (imitated by young girls) (22)? The one at least has the virtue of primitive zestfulness, of having the smack of reality. Russians in their imitative consciousness are like lost dogs in search of their masters. Moreover, in their smug satisfaction – like Kukshina due to change when the intellectual fashions change – they lack everything that is primary, urgent, heart-felt. It does no good to exchange one set of 'abominable' prejudices for another – except that in the latter change there is an unmistakable tone of swagger, as if one were assured of certainties. Such inverted argumentation is always dangerous: it degenerates into questions as to which is worse. Dostoevsky argues that this imitative consciousness is the product of gullibility born of idleness, then advances his more positive formulae for true remediation: 'Nature is needed first of all, then science, then an independent, native, unconstrained life then a faith in one's own national strength' (23).

Dostoevsky is shooting from behind dodges, but little by little he begins to approach his true target, and this is the basis of life in the West, the highest attainments of French and English life. He will not accuse European consciousness at its worst – the imitative consciousness of the impressionable Russian is simply his premise – but rather at the acclaimed height of its accomplishments, and in so doing he follows Luther as well as Rousseau. Not by having read books and come with preconceptions, but rather instinctively by experience and observation, Dostoevsky formulated an enduring critique of the bourgeoisie and the aspirations of socialism, all based upon the triumph of reason and virtue. Dostoevsky was an inveterate streetwalker, and through all hours of the night he saw with Disraeli that the English were indeed two nations. London, that teeming colossal city, is one from which the masses have seceded, 'slunk into weekend drunken torpor, hidden away in their underground.'[10] He anticipates by shrewd insight what H.G. Wells was to confirm in *The Time Machine*, the existence of two societies, the Eloi, aboveground, who live in dread of the Morlocks, underground. Dostoevsky's tone is apocalyptic: 'These millions of people abandoned and driven away from the human feast, shoving and crowding each other in the underground darkness into which they have been thrown by their older brothers, gropingly knock at any gate' (39). Speaking with the insight of last days, or the first days of brotherly love turned into the last days of cannibalism he too raises the cry of the long-oppressed: 'Looking upon these pariahs of society you feel that yet for a long time the prophecy will not come true for them, that for a long time yet they will not be given palm leaves and white garments and that for a long time to come they will appeal to the throne of the Most High, "How long, O Lord?"' (39).

Paris is different; while both worship Baal, the Londoners manage to disregard the inequity, and in Paris they disguise it behind an exalted manner – a veneer of noble demeanour, of protestations of virtue, and of high-sounding eloquence. But there is an insecurity in the bourgeoisie. Since their motive is security, their ethos is standstill. They have achieved the level of their attainment. They have no new worlds to conquer and yet must always be doing for fear of slipping. And yet there is also a smugness, a self-contentment, as if they were quite sure of success in this world and salvation in the next. It is as if they have an ontological right to possession, *mon arbre, mon herbe*, my newspaper, my coffee. How alien this sense of possession is to the daemonic writer, so aware of his own dispossession, of contingency, and how close the description is to that of Sartre's in *La Nausée*, where sacred *devoir*, which the social leaders shoulder so manfully, bestows those inalienable *droits*, which they enjoy so dutifully. But there is more in anticipation: just as Dostoevsky's description of the underclass in London anticipates H.G. Wells, so here his sense of the stagnation of the bourgeoisie anticipates similar analyses of Ortega, Virginia Woolf, Thomas Mann, and D.H. Lawrence and helps explain the great esteem enjoyed by Dostoevsky among the later modernists.[11] Of course Dostoevsky rigorously underestimated the capacity of Western bourgeois societies to transform themselves. The apocalyptic fosters its own blindness.

Dostoevsky had the unenviable task of arguing against an optimistic rationalism. He speaks as a novelist from the broad human experience of lived ideas and is tired of the blackboard schema of juvenile projections that are simply undone by the realities of the human condition and human history. There are conditions of reality that cannot be contrived, that if not innate are at least bred in the bone. Western society is too individualistic to truly embrace socialism. All attempts at liberty, equality, and brotherhood must fail because there is no adequate grounding for these possibilities in the conditions of society. For these reasons the bourgeoisie repeatedly repulsed the socialists, who are now reduced to replacing their present goals with future projections. And it is for the sake of this future utopia that present sacrifices must be made. Although not quite explicit, it is more than implicit in this work, that socialism – already compulsory in its regimentation – must become coercive, as certainly comes clear in *Demons*. Future prospects are invoked to justify all actions in the present. And that instinct for freedom, which showed itself so undying, even among the most resigned lot of prisoners, is forced to submit. Dostoevsky, become more fully aware of the coercive nature of this bartering of the present, here repeats the dread fourth term to the triadic slogan of the French Revolution: '*liberté, égalité, fraternité – ou la mort*'

(50–2). We know the genuine meaning of this addition, but it bears a more menacing implication, not self-sacrifice in the struggle to make these values prevail, but death to whomever should fail to comply. '*Sois mon frère, ou je te tue.*'

Notes from Underground is a true tandem piece to *Winter Notes*. But one can also say that it utilizes and completes all the major developments in Dostoevsky's thought and artistry. It bears the jarring disharmony and the confessional mode of *The Double*; in fact, one of Dostoevsky's earliest notions was to refer to it as a 'confession.' Bakhtin is in certain respects right to leap directly from the earlier work to *Notes from Underground*; while this manoeuvre creates some difficulties, it does emphasize the common problem of the confessional mode, and that is its infinite regress. These and such-like terms have been used by excellent commentators to show how Dostoevsky, while revelling in the confessional mode, also showed the shortcomings of this complex consciousness; there is no place to stop in this infinite self-questioning, with mirror on mirror mirrored being all the show. Moreover, like Golyadkin, the underground man is also a minor civil servant, thus compensating for his submissive position with protests of imaginary magnification. Despite the fact that in its day *The Double* was vilified, Dostoevsky, while concurring with the judgment as to the artistic performance, felt that he was onto something. In a *Writer's Diary* entry of November 1877 he revisits both the time and the milieu of *The Double*, concurring with the aesthetic judgments of the Belinksy circle while defending his conception: 'The tale of mine did not turn out well at all, but the idea behind it was quite lucid, and I never expressed anything in my writing more serious' (*DW* 883). What it permitted was the telling of 'terrible truths,' that kind of horror before 'the horror,' a penetration to the heart of darkness without the journey, without the violence, but with an equally powerful unmasking of the false semblance of 'noble sentiments.'

But *Notes from Underground* also contains the vital interests of *The House of the Dead* and *Winter Notes*. What this means is that Dostoevsky's artistry, his concern with the Mittyesque dreams of a low ranking civil servant have been enriched by his developing social, political, and religious thought. Indeed it is the combination of all of these qualities that makes the underground man into a representative figure, as Dostoevsky alerts us in a footnote right from the start. There should be no mistaking the meaning: the book contains the portrait of a generation. Such a type not only 'may, but actually must exist in our society, considering the general circumstances under which our society was formed ... He is a representative of the current generation' (3n1). Undervalued and misunderstood in its time, *Notes from Underground* has truly provided one of the profound metaphors of modern literature – the underground man himself. Dostoevsky has found what every novelist desires and that is a spokesman, an unreliable one, paradoxical, narcissistic, one who in his own 'inertia of consciousness' reveals the consequences of the radical ideas. His tone of defensive self-mockery, or 'inverted irony,' derives from the underground man's attack on virtue. How does one argue against virtue? Quite obviously one adopts the self-strangling tone of the underground man. But what if 'virtue' is based upon the wrong set of facts, if it makes future projections that we have no way of knowing whether they can be realized, or if realizable if they are desirable when they should appear; or if they entail inevitable counter-results such as the revenge and rebellion of the psyche in acts of subversion, such as Dostoevsky witnessed in the urges for freedom in prison? It is quite clear that we should not prefer the way of life of the underground man, but that does not mean that his criticisms are invalid.

Against this lamentable infringement Dostoevsky raises several flags – that is, the narrator might not know the way out of the labyrinth of his divided consciousness, but the author has some sense of direction. First is the idea of 'freedom,' the instinct for which is so brilliantly captured in *The House of the Dead*, then the ideal of brotherhood so bravely described and offered as a true ideal – one absent from Western individualism – in *Winter Notes*, and finally the foundation of these in Dostoevsky's most personally embraced philosophy of Christ.

The new progressive agenda entails social organization moving from the top down, planning without any cognizance of local requirements, thought without history, the elevation of the environment as all-important in shaping change, and the establishment of a rational self-interest as the new basis for social action. Western ideas have infiltrated the Russian intelligentsia of the 1860s, in whatever modified form, and have disturbed the consciousness of the most eager, the most naive, the most generous. This new direction of Dostoevsky's thought was excised by the censors (and we are reminded of Dostoevsky's longstanding dislike of censorship and suppression rather than allowing the free discussion of ideas). The underground man himself acknowledges not only his own incompleteness, but also his own awareness that he is in search of a fuller existence. 'I know that it is not the underground that is better, but something different, altogether different, something that I long for, but I'll never be able to find' (26). Inexplicably the censors removed what that something was, namely 'the necessity of faith and Christ' (as we learn from a letter by Dostoevsky) (26, 94). Why the censors behaved as they did is one of the more spectacular enigmas of literary history. It is far from my intention to attribute aesthetic designs to the censors, but however wrong they were politically, their actions may have had a desirable effect. Despite his extraordinary insights, the underground man must remain underground, he must remain a victim of the inertia of consciousness, of his own inability to transform his own doubleness as both critic and victim. To remove him from this inverted and perverse dialectic would betray the logic of the story. It would also subvert the magnificent paragraph that follows, where the underground man, in the fullest expression of his consciousness, imagines the more accurate criticisms that are directed against him: 'Perhaps you really have suffered, but you don't respect your own suffering. There's some truth in you too, but no chastity; out of the pettiest vanity you bring your truth out into the open, into the market-place, and you shame it ... and without a pure heart there can be no full, genuine consciousness' (27). After this retort one can well see why the excluded material was unnecessary; one can also see why Camus's *La chute* is both a commentary and continuation of *Notes from Underground*. This look ahead is endorsed by Richard H. Weisberg, who includes Rousseau as well: 'In a deliberate parody of Rousseau's diarists, and presaging that of Camus' Clamence, Dostoevsky's protagonist reveals his lack of genuine self-analysis' (191). Or, we might add, the kind of analysis upon which he is willing to act.

7. Dissension and Its Causes

This is the period of brief and tenuous rapprochement between Turgenev and Dostoevsky. Beyond the more obvious social get-togethers and the exchange of correspondence, we can discern more critical intellectual affinities. Robert Louis Jackson indicates what these might be: 'The Underground Man ... remains a skeptic and a prisoner of the "underground." But insofar as his skepticism is directed against a rationalism that is devoid of spirituality, or life, it serves the higher truth in which he is unable to believe. In all of this he bears a certain resemblance to Turgenev's Hamlet-type ... in his irony, in the nature of his contradictions and in his uncontrolled instinct for negation, he is linked genetically with Turgenev's Hamlet-type' (*The Art of Dostoevsky*, repr., *Notes from Underground* 185n5). Indeed, both Turgenev and Dostoevsky depicted the crisis of self-consciousness that beset the Russian intellectual

(Mochulsky 329). They both showed the excruciating divisions victimizing those who were most eager and searching (we must not forget that the underground man was in quest of true companionship, unfortunately seeking it among his boorish ex-schoolmates, over whom his intellectual superiority is all too evident). Yet this very proximity also reveals the profound differences that separate the two. Beginning with *Crime and Punishment* Dostoevsky will depict and seek to escape the tangle of contradiction. Soon the differences between Dostoevsky and Turgenev would break out with a renewed hostility. Turgenev, whatever his artistic complexities, would remain an inveterate Westernizer, while the underlying drives and ideas of Dostoevsky's work would reveal a totally opposite orientation. Leonard Schapiro, Turgenev's biographer, has referred to this division as a 'perennial dichotomy' (215), but this phrase, while accurate, does not go far enough in describing the manifold differences between Dostoevsky, the visionary idealist, and Turgenev, the brilliant realist, the objective observer, the observer of objects, the deeply moving portrayer of the anguish and tensions of love. It is in the context of such rival forces that the itinerary of encounter between Dostoevsky and Turgenev takes its shape.

Even in the midst of apparently thriving harmony, among genuine antagonists there exists a lurking suspicion or dislike, This is the case in every dualism of this study; an antipathy is there waiting its moment to break out. Existing affinities prove to be a slender reed when compared with personal antipathy and larger philosophical and religious differences. Following the much-appreciated defence of *Fathers and Children*, Turgenev and Dostoevsky were on friendlier terms. Dostoevsky and his brother eagerly solicited a contribution by Turgenev to their periodical, *Vremya*, and when that was mysteriously and obtusely closed down by the censors, succeeded in printing *Phantoms* in their new journal, *Epocha*. After having paid lip-service to its quality, Dostoevsky thought differently upon publication: 'In my opinion there is a good deal of rubbish in it; something rotten, morbid, senile, disbelief out of impotence, in a word, all of Turgenev and his convictions, but the poetry compensated for a good deal' (Frank 3: 294). Even a later short story is referred to in private as 'vapid' (4: 352).

The interfacing between personal antipathy and difference of belief is hard to separate. Finally, Dostoevsky must avow that he dislikes the man, personally and in his aristocratic mannerisms: for instance, the way Turgenev would lean forward to kiss a friend, only to turn the cheek (the mannerism that would add to the satiric portrait of Karmazinov in

Demons). All of this comes out into the clear in their celebrated and notorious exchange in Baden-Baden after the publication of *Smoke*. Mochulsky summarizes quite concisely the cause of the revived antagonism: 'Dostoevsky accused Turgenev of atheism, hatred for Russia and worship of the West' (326–9). In his much more detailed account of this famous episode, Joseph Frank sifts through all the contending evidence, before reaching the conclusion that indeed Turgenev did become extremely agitated, particularly when Dostoevsky with some xenophobic stupidity denounced the Germans. Turgenev averred that he in fact belonged more to Germany than to Russia, as it were renouncing his own nativity and even discounting Russian accomplishments.

First, *Smoke*. 'In conflict with the author of *Smoke*, Dostoevsky's world-outlook was crystallized' (Mochulsky 327). It is time for a re-evaluation of the canon of Turgenev's novels. Works such as *On the Eve* and *Smoke* must begin to share the pre-eminence of *Fathers and Children*, without of course demoting that accomplishment. So, too, the remarkable qualities of Turgenev as a novelist must rival his 'political message.' His capacity for detailed description of social exchanges, the apparent 'objectivity' of his observations – by which I mean his keen interests in objects themselves and for what they show – is paralleled only by Tolstoy. By this virtue he is well set apart from Dostoevsky, who, as a visionary idealist, invests all things with the higher significance and drive of his inner purpose. Even more central is Turgenev's description of the tensions of love. From the effect that dazzling beauty – again described in detail – has upon a lover, to the anguish the lover undergoes, and finally the bitter lessons when grim necessity rolls over the affections, love is his great subject. There is nothing quite like the descriptions of Litvinov's turmoil when he goes to greet his fiancée Tatyana after having won back the love of the long-absent Irina. The reader is enthralled not only by his inner tension but also by the calm if distressed recognition on Tatyana's part that something has irremediably changed, and she suspects the cause. Nothing in Dostoevsky's descriptions of love can equal these moments of acute embarrassment and shame.

For Dostoevsky, given his capacity to plunge to the heart, the gist of the matter, the 'meaning' of *Smoke* lies in Potugin's tirades against Russia and his defence of Europe and of civilization. These political criticisms coincided with that personal quarrel that broke out when the two met in Baden-Baden (there was also the minor irritant of Dostoevsky's alleged unpaid debt). Potugin's argument, put simply, is that the Russians lack due diligence. They are overwhelmed by theories that are ill-digested.

How often in both Turgenev and Dostoevsky the metaphor of digestion is appropriately used to describe how poorly Russians fare with foreign ideas. But with Turgenev the fault lies not in the ideas – primarily those coming from the West – but with the Russian incapacity to implement them fully. They know step one, conception, and they leap dream-wise to step five, ideal realization, without bothering to master steps two, three, and four. This means they are never finishers but must always be jumping from new enthusiasm to new enthusiasm. While Dostoevsky can bemoan the gullibility of the Russian intellectual – he places greater blame on the nature of the ideas being imported. The menu is too rich, too extreme, and is itself the cause of intellectual reflux.

Potugin's greatest attack is directed against the so-called accomplishments of Russian culture. While the Russians will seek, like a *nouveau arriviste*, to claim credit for being the first to have done something, or as being the best, actually their results are mediocre. He comes to the statement that infuriated nationalists. Unlike Dostoevsky, he has nothing but praise for the exhibition of the Crystal Palace, a monument to accomplishments of human ingenuity. But what was Russia's contribution to this achievement? 'If it were decreed that some nation or other should disappear from the face of the earth, and with it everything that nation had invented should disappear from the Crystal Palace, our dear mother, Holy Russia, could go hide herself in the lower regions without disarranging a single nail in the place; everything would remain undisturbed where it is; for even the samovar, the wooden bast shoes, the yoke-bridle and the knout – these our famous products – were not invented by us' (102).

Conflict is immediate with Dostoevsky, who had an entirely different conception of the Crystal Palace and all that it represented, and who acquired from his prison experience a changed attitude toward the potentialities of the Russian people, one not involving technological inventiveness and gadgetry. This conflict becomes even more manifest when Potugin indicates the genuine substance of his position, that he is an advocate of civilization and culture and that these in their advanced stages are represented by Europe and not by Russia, in such defence aligning Turgenev with the other writers of consciousness. Potugin declares with some finality, 'Yes, yes, I am a Westerner, I am devoted to Europe. That is to say, speaking more accurately, I am devoted to culture ... and to civilization – yes, yes that is a better word – and I love it with all my heart and believe in it, and have no other belief, and never shall have' (35).

Dostoevsky regarded Potugin's speeches as the gist of the novel's anti-Russian tendency, and indeed Turgenev is free-handed in satirizing both the bureaucratic Russian establishment and their group assembled in Baden-Baden as well as the flittering and feeble-minded enthusiasts of Young Russia. But here Dostoevsky's personal vision may have led him astray as to the nature of Turgenev's true interests. To be sure, there is always an ambivalence in Turgenev's works between the political significance, the representative types, and the interests of love. But there is something else in Turgenev that Dostoevsky misses and that is the extra dimension, the layers of awareness present in every great artist, the capacity to go beyond the material at hand, even to jostle the reader with the unexpected. After his lengthy tirade concerning the inadequacies of Russian contributions to culture and civilization, Poutgin realizes that Litvinov had not been listening at all. 'Litvinov started. He had not in fact heard what Potugin was saying; he kept thinking, persistently thinking of Irina, of his last interview with her' (107).

Such a misapprehension does not dislodge the dualism, it reinforces it. It shows the differences between them to be two-tiered, that beyond the political and ideological there are other factors of personality and attitude that are crucial to an understanding of a genuine dualism. Turgenev has convictions, but without engagement. Dostoevsky's own beliefs have been seared into his heart by the most desperate of circumstances. Turgenev is literally an 'object' observer, things are observed in their simplicity of being; with Dostoevsky things are part of larger processes of spiritual significance. Even love is complicated and while revealing is subordinate to the larger spiritual meaning. For Turgenev, to be reconciled to existence means the loss of great passions, a settling in, if not a settling down. But this brings us to the title of the novel, *Smoke*. Behind the veneer of civilization, the lining up of objects, Turgenev is most vulnerable to the sense of vacuity, of the passingness of all things. Existence itself is passingness.

On the long and bitter train ride home to Russia, Litvinov observes the smoke and the steam drifting by. Despite their changing shape and form, he is overwhelmed by their monotony. The thought leads him to similar reflection on the recent events, the Russians from both camps, even the love affair. '"Smoke, smoke," he repeated several times, and suddenly it all seemed smoke to him, everything, his own life, Russian life – everything human, especially everything Russian. All smoke and steam, he thought; all seems for ever changing, on all sides new forms, phantoms flying after phantoms, while in reality it is all the same and the same again; everything hurrying and flying toward something, and everything vanishing without a trace, attaining to nothing' (195). This is an acute attack of the elegiac and valetudinarian mode that is an essential part of Turgenev's mentality. But there is more to it than that: civilization itself, that bulwark against nothingness, can itself provide only markers in the sand, and even its varied objects in succession soon provide only a succession of objects, undifferentiated and monotone. The despair to which Litvinov succumbs is only the scepticism that hangs over all of Turgenev's attachments, the nemesis itself that civilization breeds, when it becomes mere linearity, without shaping spirit, without faith of character. This same reflection leads to the self-indulgent pathos of the 'I' that Dostoevsky satirized so effectively in *Demons*. This is quite different from the austere and yet serene philosophical reflections of Ecclesiastes, but rather indicative of the self-absorption of the Romantic observer observing his own sensitivity. Perhaps in the novel Turgenev is characterizing what he would consider Russian attributes; it was the nature of Russian life and character that he himself lived and knew that led him by way of Litvinov to yield to the haunting spectre of nothingness. When Luther accused Erasmus of an inherent scepticism, it was not so much on individual points of doctrine but rather the scepticism that yields to a larger demon of despair that haunts civilization, a larger kind of nihilism, that he sensed and against which he himself contended. The conclusion to *Smoke* may have the appearance of being hastily arranged and easily come upon, but given Turgenev's sense of the Russian character as he himself knew it and lived it, its final recourse to small steps has its point and is far from banal. Perhaps in a larger sense we begin to comprehend why Turgenev, like the other writers of consciousness, was anglophile.

8. The Great Emergence

Dostoevsky was hostage to fortune; his life has the elements of a saga. From the tarnished star of Belinsky's Pleiad, he was brought to endure the unendurable – four years as a convict in conditions much worse than those he portrayed in *The House of the Dead*. He returned to the newly energized and liberalized world of cultured Petersburg with the vitality of a cat but with the fortunes of Job. He succeeded in making the splash he wanted with his prison memoir, and with his beloved brother Mikhail produced a journal of some notice, *Vremya*. But tragedy struck again: the journal was closed down, his brother Mikhail died suddenly and his wife died slowly. One can say of him as of King Lear, 'He hath but usurped his life.' And yet he had another quality comparable to that of Lear: indomitability. He wrote the tandem works *Winter Notes on Summer Impressions* and *Notes from Underground*, each of which bore the new elements that went into the composition of his first major work, *Crime and Punishment* (indicating their ongoing but latent tensions, the first half of which Turgenev praised but the second half detested).

We are well past the stage where it is necessary to defend Dostoevsky's artistry, the holdover from the conception of him as a 'firebrand,' or even as possessing titanic powers (which rarely yield further analysis). Any attentive reading of part 1 should satisfy the most astringent demands for artistic coherence and anticipation: almost all the themes of the novel are there prepared for the reader. What notebooks for *Crime and Punishment* reveal is the extent of revisions the novel underwent. Where Turgenev, yielding reluctantly to editorial pressures, makes local adjustments in his works, Dostoevsky is given to wholesale changes. This capacity for total transformation (with some reincorporation) is part of the openness of Dostoevsky's personality, his willingness to risk, to venture. Here he started with the most important, and that is voice, as he changed the novel from a first person 'confessional' novella, to the large-scale descriptive novel. In his narrative he is able thus to capture Raskolnikov's turmoiled vacillations and the development of his own psychology as well as the thoughts and attitudes of other characters, and a better delineation of events. The novel, particularly part 1, still contains remnants of the confessional mode that so appealed to Dostoevsky, as Raskolnikov undergoes intense inner debate over his plot.

Like Turgenev's, Dostoevsky's work is imbued with that quality of 'presentness.' Moreover they both benefited from the inter-responsiveness, the cross-fertilization of radical criticism and creative fiction (in both friendly and hostile takeovers). But there is a difference that leads on to an even greater variance. At first we can call it Dostoevsky's power of identification. While Pisarev (somewhat unfairly) can say that Turegenv 'shrank from the bouquet of Bazarovism,' the story of *Crime and Punishment* with its various guises and voices is Dostoevsky's own story: that somehow through break-up and even collapse, through a misdirected failure, one can achieve a higher resolution. With this realization we begin to approach the superior claims of *Crime and Punishment*, the reasons why it emerges from 'presentness' to become, moulded by the fullest conceptions of art and artistry, a work of universal attention.

Fathers and Children is a remarkable novel but *Crime and Punishment* is a world classic, first because it presents in its main character a man of a special calling. Like Dante's *Commedia*, like Shakespeare's *Hamlet*, *Crime and Punishment* is not about Everyman, but rather a story about an especially endowed hero who is obliged, and in Raskolnikov's case one could even say self-obligated, to undergo an agony. The agony is a mark of his distinction as is his tendency to misdirection. Superior native capacities run the greatest risk of going astray. Such is the case when Beatrice rebukes Dante in *Purgatorio* 30.115–29: 'This man in his early life was such potentially that every right disposition would have come to marvellous proof in him; but so much more noxious and wild the ground becomes, with bad seed and untilled, as it has more strength of soil.' And in *Henry IV, Part 2*, the anguished and dying Henry IV provides some excuse for Prince Hal: 'Most subject is the fattest soil to weeds' (4.4.54). But with Raskolnikov there is more than this, a more ulterior drive, perhaps closer to that of Hamlet. Returning once again in the epilogue to his Siberian experience, Dostoevsky himself reflects on his chosen hero: 'What should he strive for? To live in order to exist? But he had been ready a thousand times before to sacrifice his existence for an idea, a hope, even for a fancy. Mere existence had always meant little to him; he had always desired more. Perhaps it was just because of the strength of his desires that he considered himself a man to whom more was permitted than to other men' (520). As with Hamlet there is a mystery to be unravelled, a mystery marked by presentiments, undeclared purpose, and ulterior motive.

With these cautions in mind we turn to the second great difference from Turgenev and that is the large moral questions, perhaps the most fundamental moral questions, that this novel addresses. Not only through the extraordinary personality of Raskolnikov but by virtue of the profundity of the moral issues it evokes, *Crime and Punishment* has a perennial value. Dostoevsky's immersion in his times, his understanding of the moral issues involved, takes him out of his time. These are genuine moral dilemmas that Dostoevsky explores and makes the soul and substance of not only *Crime and Punishment* but all his major novels. The issue with which he grapples is what I have in other occasions termed 'foundation sacrifice,' the notion that at the origin of every great culture, Hebrew, Roman, Christian, a crime occurred, a 'dark event,' that requires justification or denunciation.[12] Augustine and Dante, under different historical circumstances, will link Cain and Abel with Romulus and Remus to indicate that recourse to foundation sacrifice entails an inevitable taint not only on existence but on culture and civilization itself: we exist by virtue of the sacrifice of the brother, of the other. But there are other voices – voices that eventually were among those heard by Raskolnikov – contending that in certain circumstances one can enter into ambiguous circumstances, evil itself, if the larger good of the state requires it. The much-abused Italian Niccolo Machiavelli has no use for the unarmed prophet, but neither does he praise the armed butcher. There seems to be a middle ground, where a just consideration for the existence of the community depends upon a heinous act. This is the role of the 'sacred executioner.' This same vision was adopted by Shakespeare in his justification of the deposition of Richard II, and his eventual while complex legitimation of Bolingbroke's act of rebellion. The issues are obviously complicated. One character from *Crime and Punishment*, Luzhin, at one base level represents the commonsensical version of English utilitarianism, where one not only may but *should* sacrifice the lesser for the good of the greater number. However, this is only the socially acceptable version of Raskolnikov's more daring argument that certain individuals have the moral right to overstep the bounds of morality, to go beyond good and evil by virtue of the superiority of their individual being and their goals.[13] To this endeavour he enlists the names of Solon, Lycurgus, Mohammed, and Napoleon. The utilitarian argument has been elevated into the 'great man' argument, but in principle they are the same: where expedient, the sacrifice of the lesser is not only warranted but morally justified. Showing the powerful resources of his own mental awareness, those of an 'ideal visionary' but could also be called eschatological, the capacity to carry a thought to its farthest reaches, Dostoevsky grabs hold of Benthamite utilitarianism, the Bazarovism of Pisarev's brilliant article, and plunges to the core of the moral question: can foundation sacrifice become a rule for existence, can the actions of great leaders in constrained situations that may promote the welfare of the state become in the hands of everybody (or anybody) a justification for similar acts of murder? The question for the individual remains: what is the higher principle, what the genuine motivation, what the necessity, and what the higher good? At what point and according to what end are violence and murder (and by extension revolution) justified? Raskolnikov overhears the student conversation that eerily captures his own thoughts, but he does not heed the second part, where the student refuses to be the one to put such a theory into practice. Woe to him who causes scandal. *Crime and Punishment* is the first of the four great novels because it is on the way to illuminating the question that Shigalyovism in *Demons* and Ivan's legend of the Grand Inquisitor will extend and explore. There are many points of difference between Turgenev and

Dostoevsky, but it is by the sheer scope of Dostoevsky's moral canvas that the wide diversion between their perspectives is revealed. They differ not only in the scope, but in the road travelled, the way Dostoevsky works to develop his thought, before discovering his great principles and premises. In Dostoevsky we are witness to the sheer triumph of achieving thought.

The 'theory' of the great man to whom everything is permitted seems to be the motivating one of the novel. But as Porfiry explains in the crucial encounter in book 6, the encounter that is the stepping stone to understanding Raskolnikov's later conversion and provides Dostoevsky's essential premise of development through suffering, it is not even an original one. It is expounded by the students in the bar, it is given vulgar form (exposed by Rasklonikov) in Luzhin's mimicry of Benthamite utilitarianism, it is explained (and also exposed) by Porfiry himself as he resumes the contents of the article 'On Crime,' written by the twenty-three-year-old ex–law student, it is denied mockingly by Svidrigaylov, and Raskolnikov himself discussed it with Mrs Sarnitsaya's daughter, and both Dunya and Sonya debate it. Moreover, there is some question whether Raskolnikov believes it. He holds to it as a matter of pride, but does he believe it? Despite its prominence, the 'great man' theory does not go far in explaining either the novel or even Raskolnikov's motivations. It is too present, too evident for this novel that bears the significant markings of 'ulteriority.'

There are different and more important plot lines: one is Raskolnikov's repeated and yet put-off efforts to confess, his need to confess; the other is the constant use of parallelisms, that is the reflection of Raskolnikov's actual motives and personality as seen in the mirror of others (sometimes distorted). There is a mystery here, and these two plot lines help us uncover the nature of that mystery. They also bring together as in a common link Raskolnikov's relationship to others and to a particular historical reality, thus adding further credence to his final restoration.

Like a gambler Dostoevsky is a man of extremes: all or nothing, destiny is met by the turn of a card or of a corner. Consequently he takes issues to their farthest point. As the insightful Porfiry explains, while the theory is not original, still this is a 'contemporary' case. 'There are bookish dreams here, and a heart troubled by theories; there is resolution evident here, for the first step, but resolution of a special kind – a resolve like that of a man falling from a precipice or flinging himself off a tower; this is the work of a man carried along into crime, as it were, by some outside force' (437). He distinguishes between the irresolution of Raskolni-

Turgenev and Dostoevsky 271

kov and the resolve of a hardened criminal who is sure of himself. This is a quite different case, where the 'criminal' is in the hands of outer forces and inner drives that he does not quite comprehend but that will force their way into the open. This is a story of several resolves, the one external, by committing the crime to prove himself adequate to his theory, but the other to reveal himself, to find out what the forces are that drive him. It is for this reason that the first plot line of the novel is not the gradual exfoliation of Raskolnikov's theory, that becomes too well known by several of the characters. Rather it is the line of confession that, however repugnant to his pride, represents an expression of Raskolnikov's moral conscience. He initiates several movements in this direction only to have his intentions prevented and thus deferred. But Porfiry understands and can wait: he knows that 'his man' will come of his own accord, that he will need to confess.

We begin to perceive the true issues behind Raskolnikov's agony: he is a proud man who has a need to assume a burden. Hence the strange business where he seriously intended to marry Mrs Sarnitsaya's malformed, simple daughter. Whence comes this need to assume a burden, this need to expiate some guilt, some *faute inconnue*? Raskolnikov observes the same grim determination, the need for self-sacrifice in his sister Dunya's ill-matched marriage with Luzhin. What is driving these Raskolnikov children – each strikingly handsome, higher-minded, even arrogant – to sacrifice themselves, because clearly in Dunya's actions Raskolnikov sees the prototype of his own? Is there some need to atone? Or is it something else, the realization that one cannot be whole, cannot come to fuller realization until one has been broken. *Crime and Punishment* is a novel that abounds in such ulteriority, and while it shows Raskolnikov's need to unburden himself by confessing, his greater need is to undergo suffering. Only from this can the greater reconciliation occur. The story, come to be understood in the magnanimous exposition of Porfiry, is ultimately Dostoevsky's own, but elevated to the plane of world consciousness.

Despite the heinousness of his deed, Dostoevsky, in his larger scheme, must avoid portraying Raskolnikov as a villain. Raskolnikov has all the traits Pisarev indicated in his remarkable essay on *Fathers and Children*: an impoverished university student who experiences a 'breach' of alienation – the story is familiar with the onset of universal higher education – yet with admirable qualities. Raskolnikov has a keen moral sensitivity, as when he staves off the respectable gentleman's predatory intentions on the drunken girl, or when he leaves his last kopecks for Marmeladov's family. Razumikhin, always willing to play the Horatio to Raskolnikov's Hamlet, remarks that Raskolnikov was always the smartest of their set. Like a would-be Titan, although he is no giant, he is destined to fail in his extravagant project. For one, even in his guilt he shows some hubris. He experiences a surge of insufferable invincibility and superiority when he practically admits to Zametov that he is the killer; he even retraces for him the actual steps in hiding the stolen goods. Pride in guilt is one way of demonstrating superiority: at least he attempted something that was better than those who were neither 'hot nor cold.' And Raskolnikov, like a character in a tragedy, is willing to assume the burden, to enter into the action and to pay the price. He is not fit for the chorus. His guilt is a mark of distinction, a requirement of his soul. And because it leads to the ultimate atonement, Dostoevsky's hero must endure great suffering. The novel's title does not mean punishment to fit the crime, but rather crime in order to draw down punishment. Finally, by virtue of guilt, the division of his consciousness, the breach in his being, can be overcome, an 'at-onement' can be attained.

Another consistent plot feature is the 'parallelisms.' The relevancy of Marmeladov is apparent. Mikolka, whose 'confession' almost clears Raskolnikov, is a schismatic with a similar need to confess, to find himself unworthy, and by imagining crime to attain suffering. Porfiry in his final analysis affirms that Mikolka was right after all. But the two major instances are Dunya and Svidrigaylov. Raskolnikov's sister is made of the same stuff as her brother – and thus the three are conjoined, as Svidrigaylov recognizes a potential kindred spirit in Raskolnikov and is captivated by the fiery independence and character of Dunya. To him, she is like an early Christian martyr, who, in effect smiling through her agony, 'brought it on herself.' 'She is the kind of person who hungers and thirsts to be tortured for somebody, and if she does not achieve her martyrdom is quite capable of jumping out of a window' (456). Again Porfiry uses similar terms of suffering through a martyrdom to describe Raskolnikov (441). And indeed Dunya is the one who counsels her brother to advance toward his punishment, 'for surely,' by so doing he is half atoning for his crime (498).

By far the greatest parallel and most significant is with Svidrigaylov, who bids fair to dominate the second half of the novel. His introduction is a colossal use of the double: as physically attracted as he is to Dunya, he is intellectually attracted to her brother. Part 5 ends with the ominous voice, 'You shall see that it is [still – the Russian includes the word 'escho'] possible to live with me' (419), a phrasing heard once before when Othello, in a kind of black mass, wedded himself to Iago ('You are my own forever'). Indeed Svidrigaylov knows of and expounds Raskolnikov's theory of the 'great man' to whom all things are possible – by his own telling he does not believe a word of it. Yet he recognizes in Raskolnikov the touches of greatness. In his final suicidal meanderings he reflects, 'What a rascal that Raskolnikov is, though. He has brought a lot on himself. He may becomes a great rogue in time, when the nonsense has left him, but now he wants to live too much. In that particular people like him are wretches' (485). The thoughts deserve some glossing. Like his sister he brings a great deal upon himself – he seeks out the burden of suffering. Yet in his willingness to enter into action, to assume the burden, he has the potentiality to become as great 'rogue' as Svidrigaylov himself, once he has shed the nonsense of his theories. His problem is that he loves life too much. And with these words Svidrigaylov intimates his own malady and Raskolnikov's still-saving grace. Nevertheless, the proclivity toward Svidrigaylov, marked by their 'chance' meetings that are far from accidental, is that they both possess a high degree of cynical intelligence. Svidrigaylov, as in a distorted mirror, could represent Raskolnikov's own future – there is enough to join them. Once disabused of his nonsensical theories and even his love of life, what is open to Raskolnikov's future is Svidrigaylov's present: boredom alleviated only by sexual adventure, or as it is called 'debauchery.' Sex is the last frontier for defeated dreams. Svidrigaylov's last hold on life is cut when Dunya resists his calculated advances – and the truth is he probably does love her. His horrid dream of a five-year-old child ogling him and attempting to allure him as would a prostitute is the final picture of corruption that he cannot countenance. His suicide is a moral act to avoid the prospects that the dream foretold. By his suicide he shows that he knows where to stop. As Camus would later explain, suicide is better than nihilism: with suicide one kills the self but spares the other.

The epilogue – and this seems to be in the nature of such things – has its detractors and defenders. While it may appear too sudden to be convincing, there are several suggestions in the novel that the way may be open for Raskolnikov's own regeneration by means of the agony undergone. The decisive judgment is rendered by Porfiry, who, by reason of experience and maturity, oversees the fuller development of the plot. In a remarkable admission, he sees into the difference between himself and Raskolnikov. 'Who am I?' he asks. 'A man, perhaps, of feeling and sympathy, of some knowledge perhaps, but no longer capable of further development. But you – that's another matter; the life God destines for you lies before you (but who knows, perhaps with you too it will pass away like a puff of smoke and nothing will come of it). Well, what of it, if you are to pass into a different category of men? With your heart, you will not pine for comfort. What will it matter if nobody sees you perhaps for a very long time? It is not time that matters, but you yourself. Become a sun and everybody will see you' (441). Porifiry is far from a mediocre 'ordinary' man; instead, he is a man whose life knows no further development (a 'pokonchenny chelovek,' in fact 'completely' come as far as he can). The emphasis on his having reached the limit of his development suggests the opposite possibilities in the future for Raskolnikov, whose superior qualities still shine through and are perhaps made even more visible by his own misdirection. This very prediction both lays hold of the epilogue and transcends it, because it is not only Raskolnikov's life that is being discussed, but Dostoevsky's own lived faith and life experience as well. Raskolnikov's recovery – pitched to a higher level by means of the Fall – tells the story of Dostoevsky's own regeneration and conversion. But in his fiction Dostoevsky could only point to the fuller picture of regeneration. Despite the intention stated in the epilogue that such a story was the matter for another tale, he never quite succeeded in that project. And this is the amazing paradox, that the true story of his life's own regeneration he was never able to complete in the dramatically mythopoetic novels he wrote. The farthest he was able to go was to suggest the germ of redemption in the better instincts of his misguided heroes. The sensed triumph in the daring and courage with which he faced the intellectual turmoil of Russian society of his time was to remain his own. Yet he strove again and again to suggest that grander myth of misdirected superior energy and talent courting its own abyss, needing to assume a burden, to walk the edge, and yet to see in this misdirection the seeds of a greater reformation of character, born of suffering that leads the way to understanding. It is the struggle itself that is Dostoevsky's story to tell.

Following the self-acknowledged failure of the belaboured *The Idiot*, Dostoevsky, still living in Dresden, abandoned his project for the life of a Great Sinner, and began, spurred on by the events of the notorious Nechaev affair, what would become to some minds his greatest novel, *Demons*. This work shows the features that we have highlighted in the Russian culture of the time, the sense of 'presentness,' the inter-responsiveness, and above all, in Dostoevsky's case, the powers of transformation. If *The Idiot* shows the stains of perspiration, *Demons* shows the signs of inspiration. It underwent its own profound transformations. Begun as a pamphlet attacking the nihilists, in a matter of months it became the novel we know. The story of the nihilists and the Nechaev circle and his murder of Ivanov became the story of Stavrogin, where Dostoevsky reveals his remarkable ability – I would consider it Dantesque – to take contemporary figures and transform them into representative and universal types. Creation becomes an act of discovery in process.

There is not only a world of difference between *Demons* and *The Idiot*, but worlds. Dostoevsky had recovered from the clear failure of that precedent work: he now had something to work with. Rather than sporadic episodes, he had a plot structure, one that permitted the full development of character. To be sure, there are stirring episodes – the Fête, the murder of Shatov, the suicide of Kirillov, the killing of Liza – but these all cohere in a marvellous symphonic relationship. Even more importantly there are the memorable characters (how many of the characters of *The Idiot* do we actually remember?). In *Demons* we recall 'minor characters' in all their distinctness: Shatov, Kirillov, Marya, Varvra, Youlia, and others. Just think of the major characters, the Iago-like Pytor, his father, Stepan, the faded idealist of the 1840s, Karmazinov-Turgenev, and above all, Stavrogin. What is remarkable is not only the clarity of their characterization, but their necessary relationship one to the other, and each to all. They are all connected; it is as if Dostoevsky poured all his thought, feeling, and accumulated experience into the creation of these characters, who fit so congruently into the simplicity of the plot structure. And unlike *The Idiot*, where ideas are expounded in what only appear to be revealing parts, purple patches, here the ideas are fully expressive of the nature of the characters, who stride from his pages, as do characters from Dante's *Inferno*, into representative history. While heroes of their time, they also become archetypes: Pytor recalling not only Mephistopheles, but the too infrequently remembered Iago, and Stavrogin bearing comparison with Milton's Satan. But as with those of Dante and Shakespeare, Dostoevsky's characters have become types in their own right, figures of reference in the repertoire of modern myth.

There are many chairs at the table of *Demons*. For the purposes of this study, three characters assume prominent positions: Stepan, Karmazinov, and Stavrogin. *Demons* is another story of fathers and children, that of liberal fathers and radical sons. It confronts the agonizing question played out in history before and after, why between these generations there should exist warfare and not respect, rupture and not support. It invokes the family dynamic portrayed so vividly in *King Lear* by the generational conflict between the new intellectual Edmund and the fuzzy, guilty, and yet good-hearted Gloucester.

Stepan Verkhovensky – Turgenev's heroes grown old, as Maikov remarked (Frank 4: 453) – is a virtual amalgam of many figures whose past and present relations with Dostoevsky find here their composite fruition. He is Belinsky; he is Herzen, who died while Dostoevsky was in the midst of writing the novel; he is the historian Timofei Granovsky (1813–55); and not far from the mix and open for inclusion would be Turgenev – did not Dostoevsky reserve a special more prominent role for him as Karmazinov? In the character of Stepan, Dostoevsky represents his fullest confrontation with the generation of the 1840s, the most formative in his own development. As his own thoughts and experiences developed, he became more hostile, even bitter toward this generation of liberal reformers. While Stepan comes from such an amalgam, he is his own character as well: feckless, vain, lacking serious conformation, and most important, guilty. At the same time, Dostoevsky's portrayal is amiable and ultimately forgiving because, independent of his character deficiencies, Stepan continues to hold onto three convictions: the early socialism (Chistianized or not of the 1830s and the 1840s), the high Schilleresque sense of the importance of the aesthetic in the formation of a country, and, despite his evident glee in being reputed the village atheist, his final religious conversion. Moreover, it is left to Stepan to apply the lessons of the two main leitmotifs of the novel, the message to the angel of the church of Laodicea and the parable of the swine.

Following Karmazinov's disastrous farewell address, Stepan rises to uphold noble sentiments – this in the midst of an increasingly unruly crowd, with its share of provocateurs, with their catcalls and heckling. Disorder is about to break out completely when, at fever pitch, Stepan proclaims the supremacy of Shakespeare and Raphael because they help define the ideal of that culture, its ends, its goals. 'I proclaim that Shakespeare and Raphael are higher than the emancipation of the serfs, higher than nationality, higher than socialism, higher than the younger generation, higher than almost all mankind, because they are already the fruit, the real fruit of all mankind' (485). Obviously his claims are excessive, prodded into hysterical ranting by the disturbances that engulf him. But his own larger grief is undermined by guilt. It was left to a seminarian to bellow out that Fedka, the shadowy figure and eventual murderer, was sent to the army fifteen years in the past by Stepan to pay off a debt in cards (487). Stepan, like Gloucester, is personally undone by what he has spawned, by what he has engendered.

Broken and splintered from his group, he takes at last to the natural calling of the liberal idealist, like that of Rudin himself, a wandering pilgrimage. More and more enfeebled, almost at wit's end, he is comforted by a Christian evangelical, with whom he finds his last refuge and, in part, redemption. At this point, his 'companion' of some twenty years, at least the person with whom he has achieved a history, Varvara, finally catches up with him. The scene is remarkable, as she cannot subdue her wrath, her impatience, or her love, as she realizes that they who had lived a casual comedy for so many years must now encounter finality. Nor does she let him forget the matter of the cigar. Sometimes a cigar is more than a cigar, and so it was in their one moment of prospective romance, where her femininity was all yielding, and he faltered. Later she comes upon him smoking a cigar, representing his own self-involvement and self-enclosure, indeed his own 'idealism' that refuses to confront the other realistically, and hisses the wrathful words, 'I will never forgive you for that' (19). She does forgive but she does not forget, and even in his moment of agony – as one of the great expressions of Dostoevsky's creative freedom – she reminds him of the cigar (659). But this, as it turns out, is only a remnant covering her grief that this man of her life's history is about to die.

In the midst of his agony he asks his now faithful friend and companion Sofya Matveevna to open the Bible at random (she had previously read from the Sermon on the Mount). She opens fortuitously to the passage from Revelation (3.14–17), where those who are neither hot nor cold are spewed from the mouth, are cast out – indeed as Dante places them in Inferno 3, as not even worthy to enter hell (653). This very passage was also part of Stavrogin's confession. We must recall that while the biological father of Pyotr, Stepan was also the spiritual father of Nikolay Stavrogin, Varvara's son. Their kinship, or rather Stepan's unenviable tutorship, is here established.

But in the same episode he also applies the lesson of the swine, and here his 'other' son is involved. He asks Sofya to read the passage from Luke 8.32–6 (which the narrator somewhat strangely reminds us forms the epigraph to his 'chronicle'). We recall that both Dobrolubov and Pisarev referred to some mass contagion that has taken possession of a country, as well as Raskolnikov's dream in the epilogue of the epidemic sweeping over Europe out of Asia. Again the daemonic writer makes use of the demonic to give expression to the mass delusion, to the control of false ideas, and the sway of false gods. Dante, among the greatest of the daemonic writers, could explain the presence of such false delusion only by the domination of the satanic. In the evangelistic account, Jesus transfers the demons of the possessed man into the swine, who rush to their destruction and are drowned. The townspeople find the formerly possessed man healed and sitting at the feet of Jesus. Stepan makes the application of this story – one not without its strange aspect – to Russia and to his own and his son's generation. The demons have already entered the swine: 'It is us, us and them, and Petrusha ... *et les autres avec lui*, and I, perhaps, first, at the head, and we will rush, insane and raging, from the cliff down into the sea [lake?]. And all will be drowned, and good riddance to us, because that's the most we're fit for. But the sick man will be healed "and sit at the feet of Jesus"' (654–5). Like Gloucester, he can cry out, 'I had no way; I stumbled when I saw.'

Once a playful, attention-getting, conforming atheist, in his final days he experiences a spiritual recovery. Confronted now with his own mortality, he refuses to believe that his life and his consciousness will come to nothingness. A just creator would not permit that. The argument – here it is more of a plea, a prayer – reaffirms the position Rousseau established in the Profession de foi of the Savoyard vicar: if there is a God, then I am immortal. 'Voilà ma profession de foi' (663). Despite all Stepan's faults of character – and they are not trivial – Dostoevsky must acknowledge that at the heart of the generation under which he was formed, and of whose faults he became only too glaringly aware, lay a substantial faith, a faith that may be traced back beyond its origin in Schiller's idealism, to the complex beliefs of Jean-Jacques Rousseau. Dostoevsky's confrontations with Rousseau here reach their fullest expression.

Such absolution granted to Stepan is not accorded to Karmazinov-Turgenev. From the earliest turn of the satiric 'Knight of the Rueful Countenance,' through *Smoke* and the blow-up at Baden-Baden, through his contempt for Turgenev's Western ideas and his aristocratic mannerism, to his disdain for Turgenev's self-indulgence, his private misgivings about 'Phantoms,' his scorn for 'Enough,' and his shocked reaction at Turgenev's insistent self-regard in 'The Execution of Troppman,' Dostoevsky had quite obviously built up a schedule of recrimination, one that found its fullest and most brilliant presentation here in *Demons*. Karmazinov gives forth a sentimental farewell effusion in the midst of a rowdy, brawling crowd, representing for Dostoevsky some of the raw disorder that had become the new realities of Russian life. But to remain there would be to miss some of the even more devastating presentations of Turgenev throughout the novel.

The narrator-chronicler (who is quite obviously much more than that, even entering into the action) has his own revealing run-in with Karmazinov, an encounter where much of Dostoevsky's pent-up hostility toward

Turgenev is let loose. Anticipating the somewhat skewed coming judgment of history, the narrator describes Karmazinov as a 'written-out' talent, and a minor one at that, whose public hold was only fleeting and
who does not realize that he has outlived his day. A listing of disparage-
ments follows. He realizes that Karmazinov's front of charm and affability is only a mannerism that can quickly be discarded by change of scene
or the entrance of a more prestigious person. 'It was said of Karmazinov
that he valued his connections with influential people and with higher
society almost more than his own soul' (85). Then, in a thinly veiled
exposition of 'The Death of Troppman,' he recounts a magazine article
where the 'great man' described the wreck of a steamer, and the efforts
made to save the survivors and to retrieve the drowned. But the account
is deflected by Karmazinov's self-regard, his insistence on calling attention to his own dismay at what he witnessed. In postmodern fashion he
casts his own aghast and lamenting reactions as central to the drama
being described (84–5). To be sure, as the catastrophe of the Fête makes
plain, this may be just criticism of Turgenev's penchant for self-indulgence, the self-invoking elegiac quality that has already been exposed.
But insofar as this satire relates to 'The Death of Troppman,' it borders
on calumny, where indeed the reaction of the onlooker must be central
to the account, particularly of a guillotinement (witness how often
Camus describes his father's own reaction to such an event). If one
wishes to register one's objection to public execution, one wonders how
best to do so if not by a personal expression of the emotions aroused.

But this travesty is redeemed by what follows, as even the put-off narrator cannot help fawning over the 'great man.' The byplay is enormous, as
Karmazinov is himself aware of the narrator's over-eagerness to be pleasing, and to his own disgust the narrator is aware of Karmazinov's awareness. The clear obsequiousness is compounded when Karmazinov drops
a satchel he is carrying, and the esteemed narrator hastens to retrieve it,
only to be waved off by the seigneurial author. But the servile intent of
the gesture was clearly apparent, which obliges the narrator to realize
that he had made a fool of himself (86–7). Perhaps one source of Dostoevsky's rankling discontent with Turgenev might be discernible here, as
he himself tells us how early in his career he was so eager to please the
aristocratic and self-assured Turgenev.

The piece that has attracted most attention is Karmazinov's ill-fated
and ill-timed final farewell, *Merci*. In the earlier encounter with Stepan
before the aspiring social lionesses, the narrator unmasks the 'puffed up
creature,' who, it is announced, will bid his adieu and, as is fitting for 'us

great men,' will find his final resting place in Germany (454). Praised for being the accurate portrayer of the mores and thoughts of contemporary Russia, he pretends to be dismissive, as if he were simply yielding to the persistent demands of his compatriots. One should bear in mind that satire, at its most brilliant, has never been accused of being fair-minded. As we have already remarked, insofar as it is intended to indict Turgenev's self-regarding egotism as revealed in 'The Execution of Troppman,' it borders on travesty. Moreover, if it refers to his 'A Propos of *Fathers and Children*,' it neglects Turgenev's defence of artistic freedom, the capacity, the need of a creative artist to display the most disabling aspects of himself, even to have dearly held beliefs uttered by unsavoury characters. It is a defence, with which Dostoevsky's own achievement is a perfect example, of multi-layered consciousness in the aesthetic event. Even in reference to 'Enough,' it ignores that this is a piece of creative fiction, the final testimony of a 'dead artist.' There the description of Nature as an overwhelming beast that reduces all to nothingness, even the highest achievements of humankind, is well in accord with a consistent feature of Turgenev's though – the elegiac mode of decline and passingness. But it is the spirit of superior-minded, self-regarding, condescending pathos that Dostoevsky wishes to capture, and he does so most effectively. The presentation is enlivened by the narrator's commentary that reduces all to blather and by the rowdiness of the crowd, whose brazen hostility Karmazinov did not expect and cannot comprehend. In Germany, Dostoevsky ventures, Turgenev has not caught the ill wind blowing through Russia. The speech ends in a fiasco. Here the warfare between the two is no longer covert and cold but rather heats up and breaks out into the open. The dualism, if not fully acknowledged by the public heretofore, now receives its deliberate status in the public mind, and prepares the way for the great debate of the early 1880s.

But as others have reminded us, the parodistic exposure does not settle the accounts between them. Once again, Budanova is right in urging us to look beyond the personal pique at Turgenev's mannerisms to the more abiding ideological quarrel between them. The arguments of Potugin in *Smoke*, the heated declarations of Turgenev in their personal encounter in Baden-Baden, even the apparent recantation in 'A Propos of *Fathers and Children*' here resurface, and Turgenev as Karmazinov is shown not only to be an arch-Westerner but as an outright careerist who has kowtowed to the younger generation of nihilists out of a fear of being passed by, of not keeping up to date. In this sense Dolinin is right: Pyotr Verkhovensky is the biological son of Stepan but he is the spiritual heir of Karmazinov (Frank 4: 462–3). This comes out both by blunt statement and dramatic encounter.

The narrator has his own understanding as to why Karmazinov, so new to town, should so quickly visit Pyotr (thus stunning the father): 'In courting the nihilist, Mr Karmazinov certainly had in mind his relations with the progressive young men of both capitals. The great man trembled morbidly before the newest revolutionary young men, and, imagining in his ignorance that the keys to the Russian future were in their hands, sucked up to them humiliatingly, the more so since they paid no attention to him' (213). Here Dostoevsky has his narrator speak in his own voice, calling attention in vulgar terms to the vices of the careerist.

As pressing for this study is, the now openly declared warfare with Turgenev in the portraiture of Karmazinov, even more dominant and prepossessing, is the character of Stavrogin. It is confirmed in the author's note to himself: 'Everything is contained in Stavrogin's character.' And then underlined, 'Stavrogin is everything' (Mochulsky 432). Joseph Frank concludes that 'the capstone of Dostoevsky's intricate thematic construction in [Demons] is the character of Stavrogin' (4: 465). But Stavrogin did not emerge whole from Dostoevsky's imagination. Like the novel itself, in fact with the novel, his character underwent its own profound transformations, once again revealing that total openness to new illumination that is so characteristic of Dostoevsky's daemonic imagination – his willingness to let his material lead him, or, to put it another way, to heed his own ulterior intentions. In earlier versions Stavrogin has a much more complex role to play, including one 'where he discloses the nihilists' conspiracy, uncovers the murderers, establishes peace in the disordered city' (Mochulsky 431). He in fact becomes the bearer of the new Russian orthodoxy, issuing forth as the saviour of the world. Still he hangs himself at Skvoreshniki. Such a discrepancy is too extreme, and Dostoevsky was obviously right in focusing on the blighted nature of Stavrogin's character. Mochulsky seems to regret this crucial elision: 'All the author's original plans were upset. The diabolically fascinating figure of Stavrogin appeared, matured, and "declared its own will"; it "captivated" the writer, mocked his good intentions, and subverted his theological designs' (432).

Despite these critical regrets, Dostoevsky succeeded in creating one of the great characters of Western literature, and he does so out of absence, complicity by way of omission, and fundamental disappointment. Stavrogin is the circumference that touches all points and is unmoved by any. Yet, as Conrad wrote that all Europe went into his making of Kurtz, so

Dostoevsky said of Stavrogin: he was the product of the Russian century. His ancestry goes back to the arrogant and destructive aristocrats portrayed by Pushkin and Lermontov; his more immediate intellectual and emotional parentage belongs to the Romantic idealist of the 1840s, Stepan, who would awaken his charge in the middle of the night and subject him to tender weeping. He has been rightly linked to Lucifer in Byron's *Cain*, with that frightful luminescence. But his closest prototype, one with whose grandeur and intellectual weakness he bears the greatest resemblance, is the father of all of these types, Milton's Satan. Stavrogin suffers from willed consciousness, literal idealism without a genuine ideal. He believes – tinges of modern gnosticism? – that his actions have no real bearing in consequences, and can laugh to scorn any semblance of an external reality or moral truth. Indeed, like Milton's Satan, he believes that the mind is its own place and can make a heaven of hell, a hell of heaven. Out of the plastic resources of his own personal superior consciousness he can spurn the consequences of his actions. Like Milton, however, Dostoevsky is a moral realist. And as Satan, despite his intellectual armoury, comes to realize, 'Myself am hell,' so Stavrogin confesses, 'I can never lose my mind.' His consciousness is his own satanic punishment.

Stavrogin proceeds by complicitous abstention. He has given birth to Shatov and to Kirillov, but he cannot share either the pan-Slavic universalism of the one, or the Man-god theology of the other. He is besieged and beseeched by Pyotr to become the tsarevitch, the necessary crown to their revolutionary movement, the kind of figure required by the people who need legend and mystery and myth. Anticipating the Grand Inquisitor, he would be part of the small group who would lead the hordes in their slavery of equality. The people still need their prince. But with the same sneering smile with which he dismisses any commitment, he acquiesces in Fedka's murder of Lebyadkin and of his wife, Marya.

Stavrogin is something of a blend of Raskolnikov and Svidridaylov. Like the former, he has a need to assume a burden; hence as an outrageous joke he marries the lame and eccentric Marya. He differs from Raskolnikov in that the young student would have married Mrs Stashanya's daughter out of kindness – he did have forthright and honest discussions with her, not withholding presentation of his 'theory.' Women are Stavrogin's undoing, and he is theirs, indications that willed consciousness and bodily reality might be different things. Marya utterly denounces him, at first to his bemused sarcasm, but then to his intense irritation when her utterances begin to strike home. He is not the falcon of her dreams, but rather a disappointing owl – a figure of totally mental desire. He is not a prince, but rather the pretender, the notorious Grishka Otrepev (277–8). Cassandra-like, she is prophetic in her idiocy, foretelling the doom that awaits her, and not sparing Stavrogin.

Even more point to Marya's disappointment is provided by the misadventure with Lisa. She too is swept up by love for the dashing promise of Stavrogin. But their one night together ends in disgust and, as the enterprising Pyror insinuates, a 'fiasco' (530). Women are the real touchstones to Stavrogin's infirmity, to his belief that consciously directed will can be the master in all situations. Yet, showing his capacity to captivate and destroy, he did impregnate Shatov's wife and has Darya willing to follow him to the ends of the earth.

The critical point in his journey is the episode called 'At Tikhon's,' containing the notorious 'confession,' which episode was censored by the watchful officials of Dostoevsky's day, primarily his editor, and which unaccountably even in our modern editions, continues to be printed as an appendix, rather than occupying its rightful dramatic place. In this episode, the dominating confession indicates Dostoevsky's own ambivalence toward that mode, its artfulness, its deliberate challenge, its want of true sincerity and repentance. But it also allows Dostoevsky to plunge even more deeply into the mysteries of human personality.

Like Raskolnikov, but without the same means at his disposal, Stavrogin (whose name suggests 'cross') is in search of a burden. As his mock marriage would indicate, he needs to hobble himself. But the corollary to this impulse is the contrary need for forgiveness; it is himself that he needs to forgive. And such humiliation of consciousness he cannot bear. This is the fateful insight of Bishop Tikhon. Stavrogin's apparent confession – the episodes of false accusation against an underling in the house (once again borrowed from Rousseau) and then his sexual assault on the young Matryosha (the kind of outrage even Svidrigaylov feared and abhorred), his indolent detachment while knowing she was about to kill herself – these events are more shocking than he realizes. While he is intent on issuing a challenge, in taking pride in guilt, his confession is more a statement of defiance than one of sincere repentance. He misunderstands his audience – they will not be moved by his revelations, but shaken into mockery and ridicule. His is not the way of true repentance, which can come about only by subordination of the ego to a true penitential discipline, something Stavrogin's adaptable consciousness will not permit him to do. Dostoevsky, as a daemonic writer, is justly at war with the advanced stages of European consciousness, but he is also at war with consciousness itself, not merely with its contrivances, but with its wily circumventions, with its lack of moral realism and with its want of conviction.

Dostoevsky outdistances Turgenev by the sheer scope of his arguments, by the issues contained, and by their future tragic and unfortunate accuracy. His great conceptual imagination inclines to first days and to last things and to the terror in between. Shigalyov's arguments and their glosses by Pytor can still send shivers through any cognizant reader. Of course, at the time Dostoevsky was relying on actual documents, but it was he who drew out their conclusions and consequences. As Marx would also do, Shigalyov rejects the idealistic projections of Plato, Rousseau, and others, and by the most careful and realistic analysis comes up with his famous paradox: 'Starting from unlimited freedom, I conclude with unlimited despotism' (402). Following Raskolnikov's similar division, and adding another stage in Dostoevsky's development toward the Grand Inquisitor episode, he divides mankind into two parts, one-tenth of the population having freedom and granted unlimited rights over the remaining nine-tenths. But this earthly paradise can reach its goal only if the hundred million are eliminated – a figure that even falls short of the numbers of the victims of twentieth-century despotic regimes, according to contemporary computations.[14] Shigalyov's theories are expounded in private by Pyotr, who at first displayed a mock indifference, but now in attendance on Stavrogin, proclaims Shigalyov a genius. 'He's got spying ... Each belongs to all, and all to each. They're all slaves and equal in their slavery ... Slaves must be equal: there has never yet been either freedom or equality without despotism, but within a herd there must be equality, and this is Shigalyovism' (417). But slaves must also possess obedience. In fact, again anticipating the Grand Inquisitor, he advocates a pope: 'The Pope on top, us around him, and under us – Shigalyovism.' Stavrogin, whom he is trying to woo with these grand schemes, considers it all madness. Pyotr also denounces it as book-learning: what he wants is immediate action, his small crews of terrorists, with the crown prince Stavrogin as the legend that will attract the people to their cause. His detailed description of the current state of corruption indicates that Russian society is not only due for a radical change but in dire need of it (420).

In the midst of such cataclysmic conceptions of final things and ultimate resolutions, in the chapter that should normally follow this one, 'At Tikhon's' completing the pursuit of Stavrogin in 'Ivan the Tsarevitch,' Stavrogin harkens back to the first days. He recalls Claude Lorrain's 'Acis and Galatea' and sees it as a picture of a golden age. 'Here European mankind remembered its cradle ... its earthly paradise. Here beautiful people lived' (702–3). When this chapter immediately follows the preceding two, the contrast is apparent between two visions, two earthly paradises, and the reason even for Stavrogin's complicity with Pytor is made clear. When this chapter is removed, the entire dramatic structure of contrasting visions is thwarted. Stavrogin, unlike Rousseau, cannot sustain this vision. The dark spider intervenes, the unwanted remembrance of his violation of Matryosha. His personal guilt, his lack of true self-forgiveness deprives him of the possibilities of happiness, and throws him into the complicitous if unspoken responsibility for the catastrophe that Pyotr engineers. The prince has gone wanting to the cads; the Golden Age has acceded to that of iron – the iron law of totalitarian discipline and outrage. The story itself is massive and overwhelming.

9. Thought Transformed

Despite its being a nominal but necessary 'prologue' to the future life of its hero, Alyosha, *The Brothers Karamazov* remains remarkable for its plenitude. By this I mean both plenty and ease – ease not in the sense of facility but rather in the full accumulation of resources. In this most synoptic of novels, Dostoevsky not only preserves his most persistent concerns but he elevates them, brings them to their fullest clarifications. Like Dante's *Commedia* it is a work to be read in process, but also retrospectively. From his release from prison onward, Dostoevsky's entire life's work was one of searching, unfolding thought. Not only are issues from earlier novels recuperated and taken up again, but characters are carried forward, and, as it were, clarified. Stavrogin steps forward and has his character replicated by Ivan and amplified in the latter's several crucial discourses, and the way each of them is both understood and answered by Father Zosima. There are other such instances: Ivan may also be understood in association with Raskolnikov, and obviously Alyosha completes the character of Myshkin, abandoning the social ineptitude, retaining the simplicity, even profundity of psychological insight, in fact, positioning himself for some unspecified role in the world, where his activist Karamazov nature would show itself. In his future fate, the thought apparently was that he would become a revolutionary, followed by regeneration, thus completing the development only adumbrated in the character of Raskolnikov. But absent the unwritten second part, Dostoevsky is certainly right in asserting that the nub of the novel takes place in books 5 and 6, 'Pro and Contra' and 'The Russian Monk,' to which should be added Ivan's encounter with his devil in book 11. Dostoevsky was among the few, last artistic geniuses and genuine intellectuals who could still convey the real possibilities of religious belief. Luther lived in an age of theological intensity; Rousseau founded a religious philosophy, while Dostoevsky defended a philosophy of religion. The living Christ, and all that it meant, was much more pertinent and necessary to his faith than even to Rousseau's.

This is time for a minor correction: Coleridge quite ingeniously displayed and discussed the two major dualisms of the preceding three centuries, those of Luther and Erasmus and Voltaire and Rousseau.[15] Actually his twosomes were threesomes. To each of the two he added the shadowy third, that is, the one who will more violently misapply the teachings of the two. Luther and Erasmus have their Thomas Munzer and Voltaire and Rousseau have their Robespierre. Dostoevsky also seems to understand this principle, that waiting in the wings is a much more violent force willing to put into action the words of the others. Both Stavrogin and Ivan exist in passive complicity with murder. In his presumed impunity Stavrogin can only haughtily laugh at the ex-convict Fedka (whose intentions he fully comprehends), while Ivan is nettled and even infuriated by the insinuating dandified manner of Smerdyakov, yet he obviously provides by his absence passive consent to his father's murder. Smerdyakov, who has picked up the hyper-literal Voltairean iconoclasm of his putative (but denied) father, Fyodor, also takes to heart Ivan's last and most pernicious principle that without God and immortality, all things are permitted.

The Brothers Karamazov in parable fashion summarizes the most momentous happenings of the nineteenth century: the death of the father, God the Father, the king as father, and the patriarchal father. It rests on the drama of the remaining brotherhood, as an ideal and as a consequence. In the midst of this great drama, the puzzling challenge is presented by Ivan's prose-poem, 'The Grand Inquisitor.' Dostoevsky had been building up to this dramatic episode from his first encounters with the West, with socialism, and with the Roman church in *Winter Notes*; Prince Myshkin adds his fulsome attack on French socialism as a product of the Roman discipline: one absolutism by kinetic transfer replacing the other. Shigalyovism and its glosses by Pytor help bring the picture to near completion. The Grand Inquisitor represents the challenge at the spiritual centre of the novel. Unfortunately when it was first presented in its periodical serial form it dismayed even Dostoevsky's allies, who felt that it was too strong an attack on religion, too formidable a presentation of atheism. Those who reprint it as a separate document today make the similar error. Dostoevsky consoled his colleagues by asking them to wait until they could read the episode in its context: the entire book, he declared, was a refutation of the prose-poem.

Ivan's rebellion leads to disastrous consequences; it is not with his premises that Dostoevsky disagrees, but rather with his conclusions. In Dostoevsky's mind, Ivan's error is the most dangerous of contemporary errors. 'All of socialism issued and started from a negation of the meaning of historical reality and arrived at a program of destruction and anarchism. My hero [Ivan] takes a theme which is *in my opinion* irrefutable – the senselessness of the suffering of children – and develops from it the absurdity of all historical reality' (Terras 38). His humanistic premise of revolt at the brutalities committed against the innocent, as well as his refusal to accept a universal world order, or eventual harmonization, as adequate compensation for the suffering of the innocent is laudable and even in both instances draws Alyosha's consent. But these same humanistic principles result in an anti-humanistic deduction that all things are thus permitted – somewhat paradoxically, because while he admits the existence of God (it is his world that he is rejecting) the latter conclusion rests upon a disbelief in God and immortality.

But this is the way it should be with Ivan, whose ambiguities and paradoxes mean that he lives in contest with his own disbelief. He is the victim of his own thought – the defeat of idealism by the forces of entropy. So his Grand Inquisitor prose-poem gives full range to his many personal contradictions. This defender of humanity ends up in league with its oppressor, and we are reminded of Shigalyov's astounding paradox. 'The Grand Inquisitor' provides the historical diagram for this perversion. Historically, and this is not mentioned enough, it is quite accurate. It does not begin with the Counter-Reformation and the autos-da-fé of Seville, but rather with the Protestant Reformation, when the advancement of the notion of Christian liberty appealed to an adult consciousness and sought to bring the individual into a more personal relationship with religious belief. Its message is one of freedom, but also one of struggle. Dostoevsky's own attitude toward Protestantism was complex, but is clarified once we distinguish between the original impulse and what he believed Protestantism had become. For him, Protestantism breathes the spirit of denial, it means the eventual subservience of religion to the state, and it ends up with the mentality of the shopkeeper and merchant. This is of course pure xenophobia. But in more than one way Dostoevsky may be linked with Luther. He clearly understood and appreciated the original motives of the Protestants. Writing of Pushkin's universality, of which much more will be said later, he praises that poet's capacity to enter into the very heart of that which he depicts: 'You seem to sense the spirit of the age of the Reformation; you begin to understand the militant fury of early Protestantism' (*DW* 978).

It is this religious fervour, seeking the return of a living Christ, that the Grand Inquisitor must quell. His argument, advocated by Shigalyov and extended in its practical applications by Pyotr Verkhovensky, is the division of humankind into an elite, the master class, and the underlings, the hundreds of millions who cannot tolerate the dreadful freedom of the adult consciousness, who come crawling back to the church in search of spiritual calm and ease of conscience, fearing what it is to be in the hands of a living God. While Ivan's understanding of history differs from that of the socialists, in the former, freedom will only cause the herd of humanity to nestle back into the bosom of Mother Church, while in the latter there is no need of a church. Dostoevsky links both together because in the end they each divide humanity into a master class and a slave class. That is, the unattended and under-studied third term of the Revolutionary triad, brotherhood, is forgotten, and this is the ideal around which Zosima's response resounds, and one that will finally be the term in Dostoevsky's proclamations of the bequest of the new Russian spirit, as a third force of pan-humanism.

But beyond this all-too-sad semi-truth – there are some elites that are representative, whose leading ideas the people understand and approve – there is another insight, one more appropriate for Ivan's bitter awareness, and that is that charismatic individuals, as did Luther, must encounter their own tragedy, the failure of the ordinary world to live up to the strenuous demands placed upon them; the way genius will be modified and diluted, struggle attenuated, great beginnings encounter their own dystrophy, utopias their own dystopia. As a failed and disappointed idealist, this is Ivan's story in the telling, his own tragedy, and the point where his similarity with Raskolnikov is most acute. Here is where the Grand Inquisitor picks up the pieces and becomes an overlord in the period of defeated expectations. Underneath the prose-poem from Seville this is the other lesson – his own – that Ivan explains.

We sometimes forget that after his temptations, when Christ began his own ministry, his first disciples were brothers, and his first preachments concerned brotherhood (see Matt. 4.16–21, 5.22). Before his encounter with Ivan, when Alyosha asks Smerdyakov if he knows of Dmitri's whereabouts, the upstart servant answers in Cain's words, 'Am I my brother's keeper,' only to have the same phrase repeated by Ivan when he asks that brother about the other.[16] Brotherhood is the missing term in the Grand Inquisitor's discourse and one of the central pillars of Dostoevsky's religious faith and hopes for humankind. After the recitation of the legend, Alyosha kisses Ivan, just as Christ kissed the Grand Inquisitor. This is more than a gesture of affection, it is a sign of brotherhood, of bringing the straying and troubled brother back into connection with humankind, with what Dostoevsky more generally calls 'historical reality,' the context of relationship.

But the figure standing over all and thus answering both Stavrogin and Ivan in their several ways is Father Zosima, who provides both intellectual and personal refutation of the previously advanced theories of Ivan and the challenges they represent. If Ivan is the Grand Inquisitor, in his assumption of the burden of the mystery, then Dostoevsky is Father Zosima in his story of regeneration. He begins with the story of the death of his own brother, and his manifest courage and recovered joy when confronting the termination of his life. It is Alyosha's face that serves as a remembrance and a prophecy – bringing to mind Zosima's own lost brother and showing the way to the future trials of the young hero. Father Zosima is strengthened by one of the several Rousseauian bequests (one that is absent in Bazarov as it is in Stavrogin) and that is remembrance. 'From the house of my childhood I have brought nothing but precious memories, for there are no memories more precious than those of early childhood in one's first home ... Indeed precious memories may remain even of a bad home, if only the heart knows how to find what is precious' (269). (We are mindful that in Dostoevsky's discourse on Pushkin it was Tatyana's childhood memories that established the connections in her life and the stability of her character.) Evidently he needed all of these resources, when as a cadet at Petersburg he displays that misguided and heedless enthusiasm that Dostoevsky finds at the heart of the Russian character. In adhering enthusiastically to the new values of the group, he was perhaps the worst because of his open willingness to assimilate their qualities: 'I was perhaps worse than the rest in that respect, for I was so much more impressionable than my companions' (274). In such overly eager compliance, he was ready to participate in a senseless duel, when he underwent his own conversion experience. He brutally beat his servant Afanasy, who endured the blows with a stoic stolidity, almost as if he were a steadfast soldier. This deterioration in his own character so disturbed Zosima that he began to come to his senses, to recover his better self. He behaves courageously in the duel, receiving the first grazing shot, and then declining to fire in turn, not in the disdainful provocative manner of Stavrogin but rather as an act of refusal. He forthwith resigns his commission and shortly after becomes a monk.

But this story of regeneration is followed closely by another one – a true and terrible confession to a horrible but unknown deed. The mysterious stranger who befriends Zosima after his own apparent 'disgrace' and who is most moved by his words bears a terrible burden, the secret of a murder committed long ago from which he escaped without any suspicion of his guilt. This is not an exceptional man, but he has absorbed Zosima's words of responsibility, of brotherhood, and of that 'Paradise [that] lies hidden within all of us' (282). An essential Rousseauistic faith here makes its reappearance. Finally he reveals to Zosima the fact that he had murdered a woman he loved but by whom he was spurned, and is now determined to make a full public confession. The difference between his trauma and its consequences for his family contrasts starkly with Stavrogin's glib admissions. The one knows what it is to be in the hands of a living God, and to endure the agony of a genuine spiritual transformation. Stavrogin, even after his 'confession,' remains Stavrogin; it costs him nothing. But for Mikhail it could cost everything. His wife and children will be destroyed and he will be obliged to part from them forever. Despite these consequences – and one notes there are no such consequences to Stavrogin's admission – under Zosima's urgings he does move forward and declares his guilt (not without a strange return where he fully intends to kill Zosima, as the only other person in possession of his secret). Admittedly there are some problems with the story – Mikhail does die conveniently, and his wife and children are spared disgrace because he is deemed to be insane. But the facile resolution should not blind us to the import of the story, that of an average man undergoing a profound spiritual crisis.

This is where Zosima's doctrine of brotherhood clashes most centrally with Ivan's Grand Inquisitor who separates humankind into the disabused leaders and the beguiled and easily led masses. While the Grand Inquisitor thought that he was coming to correct the improvident return of the living Christ as contained in the message of the Reformers, and that they were providing only for an authoritarian elite, in fact he misunderstands Protestantism and is refuted quite simply by the fact that Luther took the Latin Bible and, translating it into German, placed it on the table of many a household. So Zosima advises the beleaguered Russian priest to take the peasant into his cottage and read to him from the

Bible: 'Let him open that book and begin reading it without grand words or superciliousness, without condescension to them, but gently and kindly, being glad that he is reading to them and they are listening with attention, loving the words himself, only stopping from time to time to explain words that are not understood by the peasant' (272). They will respond to the richly varied stories of the Old Testament, with special emphasis on those of Jacob and Joseph and his brothers. Stories of such moral worth both inspire and are expressions of that 'active love' so valued by Dostoevsky (and by Luther, too, it might be added).[17]

In all ways this is Dostoevsky's own story, particularly, as he reminds us, his own story of regeneration of moral conviction during the time spent as a fellow convict. This is made clear in some of the lingering debates that followed the overwhelming success of his Pushkin speech, which enters into and is an integral part of the great coherence of Dostoevsky's fully achieved vision. Contact with the people, a genuine understanding of their virtues, of their respect for and submission to the noumenal, has not only generated a new appreciation in Dostoevsky but has effected a return, a return to his childhood beliefs. In response to a strong attack by Gradovsky, he reminds his readers of his prison experience, of his daily close contact in every way. 'I worked with them at real, backbreaking labor when others ... who were playing at liberalism and snickering about the People, and were concluding, in their lectures and their newspaper columns, that our People "bore the image and the stamp of the beast." So, don't tell me that I don't know the People! It was from them that I accepted Christ into my soul again, Christ whom I had still known as a child in my parents' home and whom I was about to lose, when I, in my turn, transformed myself into a "European liberal"' (DW 984). There could be no more explicit, succinct, and moving account of one of the primary theses of this study: that in their openness to experience and their popular trust and religious belief, Luther, Rousseau, and Dostoevsky all experienced a 'return,' a necessary regeneration that clearly set them at odds with the advanced stages of European consciousness.

The memorial meeting over Pushkin constitutes the grand finale of the long and twisted debate between Turgenev and Dostoevsky. Since Turgenev's return in 1879, they had met on several special occasions, where it was already apparent that despite the presence of other speakers it was these two who represented the two faces of Russia, two faces looking in different directions, the one facing westward to the offerings from Europe, culture, civilization, and civic order, and the other looking to the East, to Russia, to the capacities of the Russian people and their religious belief. Thus the long-delayed unveiling of the Pushkin statue turned out to be more than a simple ceremonial: it was Russia's confrontation with its future by means of their remarks over its greatest poet. Turgenev gave a remarkable speech, still eminently readable and just, subtle and sophisticated, bestowing the highest praises on Pushkin, but finally leaving the question open as to whether he was a truly 'national universal' poet or whether he was there to prepare the way for another who more fully deserved that crowning title.[18] Moreover, Pushkin was never a poet appreciated by the common people but taken to their hearts by only a cultured elite.

This gave Dostoevsky the opportunity to deliver one of his most astonishing speeches – a work of art in itself. Speaking directly, simply without dramatic exclamation, but from the soul of conviction and deep understanding – in fact, lifelong understanding of the role of Pushkin in Russian literary life and in his own development – he traces the phases of Pushkin's career, beginning with the aimless wanderings of the disillusioned and dispossessed aristocrats, such as Eugene Onegin.[19] For the creation of this rootless type who would soon have his successors in the Russian literary gallery, Pushkin deserves credit. Against this anti-hero he also created Tatyana, who represents the moral solidity of the Russian woman, moral and insightful. Despite her affectionate but apparently loveless marriage to a much older man, she refuses to be seduced by Onegin – once upon visiting his quarters she wonders if he is some kind of parody. But the culmination of the speech – and its stroke of genius – comes when he establishes Pushkin's pan-humanism. Throughout his career, Dostoevsky had been severely critical of the adaptability of the Russians, their impressionability, their open willingness to take over and absorb ideas from the West. They did not consume ideas, ideas consumed them. What was a hypothesis in Europe became axiomatic in Russia. The listing is extensive. But by his greatest insight into Pushkin and hence into the Russian character he transforms this glaring weakness into an abundant virtue. We are witness again to the accent of self-surmounting thought. It was this very derided Russian trait of assimilability that became the genius of Pushkin's last phase, where he was able to write not only in the manner but in the actual spirit of the other national types. Thus he caught hold of the true motives of the incipient Protestant Reformation. But on the larger stage of world history, this very quality of generosity of intellectual spirit becomes the basis of a pan-humanism: no longer pan-Slavism, or nationality elevated to the godhead, but rather a true generation of brotherhood, coming from an inner appreciation of the qualities of the other. Here if anywhere, Dostoevsky, always searching, at times failing, hits the right tone and the right argument. The reactions were astonishing, if not convulsive, and the triumph he had always sought was his. In the competitive judgments of the see-saw mentality, it was thought that Turgenev was vanquished. But Turgenev himself, showing the courage of his own conscious intelligence, was quite able to recover, later attributing Dostoevsky's success 'to a falseness that was extremely appealing to Russian self-love' (Frank 5: 530).

It is in the character of their writing that their differences are told. Despite their different masks, they bear similar reflections, similar traits, and similar contests, as do their predecessors in the fields of dualisms. Turgenev's novels – slender, exquisite, meticulously observed and composed, and always self-contained – did have broader repercussions in their day and created storms of controversy. But always there is ambivalence and finally acquiescence, acquiescence to a sense of passingness, which while descriptive of his class is amplified in his own personal reflections. Despite his advocacy of civilization and its accomplishments, he falls victim to the nothingness to which all-encompassing Nature seems to have consigned humankind.[20] Transformative, generative, Dostoevsky's works seem to exceed their bounds, as he follows to their end the thoughts that have *pursued* him. Rather than confined, he seems stretched between God and the devil, as was Luther and Rousseau. He speaks urgently of first days and final things. And yet he seems to take possession of being, as if God, in the words of Stepan and Rousseau, would not commit him to nothingness. In this enormous struggle, civilization's markers are too slender, too fragile. A faith and a commitment are required, and these two perspectives constitute the story of the tensions experienced by the psyche of the West.

5 Sartre and Camus: 'Revolt Changes Camps'

1. Preambles to the Review

The dramatic rupture between Jean-Paul Sartre and Albert Camus had its immediate origins in the most unlikely of places – a book review.[1] Francis Jeanson's adverse criticism of Camus's *L'homme révolté* appeared in the May 1952 issue of *Les temps modernes*. The August issue carried the combined weight of Camus's bitter response, Sartre's brutal attack, and Jeanson's rebuttal. While the debate attests to the intensity of Parisian intellectual life, especially in the contentious and divisive period of the postwar years, it also indicates that more is at work here, precisely what it has been the business of dualisms to uncover. Through this small opening rushed an avalanche of pent-up animosity, long-simmering disagreement, mutual accusation, and personal pride. Such close combat of these pre-eminent figures was devoured by the public at large. To be sure, there were other disputes in this period, those between Sartre and Merleau-Ponty, or between Sartre and Raymond Aron, but it was this open discord that became in the words of a recent commentator, 'the most important literary quarrel of the twentieth century' (Aronson, 'Camus vs. Sartre'), and according to Sartre's very able editors, 'un des grands moments de la vie intellectuelle française de l'après guerre' (one of the great moments of French intellectual life in the period after the war) (*Les écrits de Sartre* 251).

Never was there a pair so apparently similar in beliefs, in philosophical and literary positions, and yet so dissimilar in the more emotive reasons for their affinities. Together and independently they each addressed the century's greatest problems, one of which, among intellectuals, was the widening gap between aesthetic consciousness and civic involvement or, put more largely, the philosophical isolation of the individual along with the practical need for solitude set against an equally strong desire for community and solidarity. Camus and Sartre may be joined together in their early affinities because they both were stretched between these several demands. But what is even more intriguing and what brings them together is the fact that they both in their intellectual projects and practical efforts strenuously endeavoured to bridge this gap and to overcome this discrepancy, and it was this attempt that separated them from many of their predecessors. This effort was uppermost in their intellectual register. It joined them, but eventually it would be a cause of separation.

There was an even more basic affinity. Each was a successful novelist, playwright, and moral philosopher. They were linked in their common faith in the working cohesion between art and philosophy, between literature and metaphysics. The meeting place of these concerns was history, the history of their times, to the major questions of which each brought the full bearing of his knowledge and commitment.

From first to last, their mutual involvement was charged with strong intellectual exchanges. Strikingly enough, they each, independently and without personal acquaintance of the other, wrote reviews of the other's early works, reviews that while stern in some judgments still showed the remarkable insights that come only from interests in common. Their careers were marked by such inter-responsiveness, even extending after the debacle to their final words, *La chute* (*The Fall*) and *Les mots* (*Words*) – their final words but not their last words. Their first meeting was in 1943, when they were two obvious talents on the rise; by 1945 they were established stars, their names in conjunction (despite the fact that Sartre was some eight years older, born in 1905 and Camus in 1913, this difference in age was soon elided); by 1947, despite the beginning of the Cold War, there were more points of agreement than difference – quite curiously, as their divergences became more apparent, so did their affinities accrue – but there were always the lurking suspicions, the private mutterings, and the lack of ease in their relationship. But in 1951–2, what had been a long-time brewing boiled over into this most widely publicized clash. The split between the two was brutal and permanent, with no making up such as might occur in the disruption of a true friendship.

The itinerary of encounter shared by Sartre and Camus fits the classic format of the other grand dualisms, but one that is complicated by the fact that, unlike the others, following 1943 they enjoyed a tangled friendship, exchanging pleasantries (occasionally bawdy ones), changing partners, partying together, and even brawling. But as Sartre admits in his response to Camus's indignant letter to the 'director' of *Les temps modernes* it was not an 'easy friendship.' Simone de Beauvoir called it 'une amitié distante' (*La force des choses* 289).Their breach was not that of the falling-out of faithful friends (as we shall see when it is compared with Sartre's contemporaneous split with Merleau-Ponty), nor was it a love affair manqué, as so many tried to make of it. Again according to Simone de Beauvoir, it was one a long time coming. 'En vérité, si cette amitié a éclaté brutalement, c'est que depuis longtemps il n'en subsistait pas grand chose' (In truth, if this friendship exploded brutally, that is because for a long time there was not much left to it) (179). It was only 'the final moment of a long disagreement.' In fact, their 'friendship' was aggravated by periods of breach and sullen silence (126). She attributes this disagreement to the end of the common cause in the unifying moment of Resistance under the Occupation. But if the differences over the Cold War were the basis of the rupture, they were not the motivation. To her judgment she adds Sartre's later more personal assessment that, because of his prideful vulnerabilities, Camus was 'parfaitement insupportable' (280).

As in the other dualisms, there are pointers and markers along the way that indicate reservations and suspicions. Sartre sniped at Camus's lack of technical philosophy, and while publicly praising *La peste* (*The Plague*), derided it privately as he would later do openly. Such things will always occur, small indicators of lurking attitudes. But it is not only to these asides that we turn in order to understand dualisms. Our concern must be city centre – not a single road pointing to the crack-up but a convergence of well-trod pathways. It is the major works – and some under-appreciated 'minor' works bearing the fullest embodiment of their active awareness – that reveal the profound differences that underlie apparent affinities. Germaine Brée knew this when she wrote, 'Nothing is more illuminating than to put Sartre's *Roads to Freedom* alongside *The Plague*; his *Dirty Hands* and *The Devil and the Good Lord* beside *The Just Assassins*. The rift over *The Rebel* was in fact only the culmination of a deeper misunderstanding. The two men had been traveling for some time on a collision course' (224). True understanding requires such 'deep background' – going back beyond the moment of the clash to what showed the profound differences that were being overlooked or set aside but when properly recognized constituted a line of inevitability.

This procedure requires critical modifications as well. The middle sections of this chapter will take some pains to re-establish Sartre's reputation as a novelist. His success as a technical philosopher seemed to place some historians under the obligation of regarding his novelistic ventures as sheer dilettantism, a curious description of works that consumed years of his most devoted attention. His novels were philosophy in motion, thought in movement, with even his philosophy suffering refutation when put to the test by honest record of the vagaries of human existence. Camus, for his part, is considered even by defenders to have been only a 'dabbler' in philosophy.[2] The first error is that of refusing to acknowledge what both Sartre and Camus insisted on, and that is the necessary fusion of art and philosophy in twentieth-century writing. But the other misapprehension is even more serious. If Camus was a dabbler, he was a dabbler in the ways that Shakespeare or Wordsworth were dabblers. They did not need to explicate works, because they had appropriated them; that is, they understood them from the inside, both from the inside of the works, that is, their gist, their import, but more importantly from their own insides. These are works, for instance, that they could have written themselves – elective affinities, the shock of recognition, a mind finding itself and its beliefs presented by another. Hence they can quite easily pierce through to the essential concepts, fully understood. Such dabbling contains the insight of genius.

If dualisms and its 'deep background' require a meeting at 'city centre,' they also necessitate a recognition of 'home central,' all those areas of personal metabolism that were outlined in the introduction. Here Sartre and Camus differed most radically in family background, childhood experiences, and education, bringing to the fore those sentiments that determine the nature of the man. When Sartre wrote his great work, *Words*, the past was something to be disowned, a place where he was forced to become what he disliked, duplicitous, inhabited always by a wish to be other (despite his philosophical statements). Where he was an adult child and a self-accused impostor, Camus knew all the wild freedoms of street urchins, the eager games, the naked joys, the sheer freedom, but also the merciless teasing and name-calling of their hapless victims, the terror of the off-campus fist-fights. Where Sartre's family was quite comfortable in its means and conditions, Camus's was sub–working class. Where Sartre's family never mentioned God, neither did Camus's, but for different reasons. Sartre's represented the advanced liberal Protestantism of the late nineteenth century, one that in fact accomplished so much in educational and social reform, while Camus's family lived in the unawareness of the impoverished. Religion did not enter their lives, except as part of a civil formality requiring certification of birth and death. These were the ways of the poor, who in anonymous silence passively faced life's inevitabilities and death. They could afford no special condescension toward the Arabs because they were all in the same stew.

The differences and similarities between Sartre and Camus accumulate. Camus was a political activist from an early age. With some prompting and encouragement, he became a member of the Communist Party, which he felt represented the deep and abiding interests of the working class. Despite what might be said of his presentation of the anonymous Arabs in *L'étranger* (*The Stranger*), he militated for the improvement in the conditions of the indigenous peoples, and his early reportage on their deprivations in the Kybalie helped bring about some modest reforms. Later in life, when under fire from the far Left, he would point to his earlier commitments as certifications of his good faith, and that he hardly needed instruction or correction from those he regarded as Johnny-come-latelies. He was there early and strong before it had become fashionable, and argued that had his proposals for full citizenship been heeded, the troubles of the 1950s would have been avoided, as well as that much larger threatening spectre that he accurately predicted – Islamic fundamentalism.

Camus attempted to merge his commitment to art and social causes in the theatre, whose possibilities to both form and reflect a collective consciousness appealed to him greatly, as it would later to Sartre. He also valued it as a communal, cooperative enterprise. He worked indefatigably as director of the Théâtre du travail, in an attempt not only to highlight social causes but to entertain and engage the working man. When that theatre was shut down, he started another, Théâtre de l'équipe, in which he continued to put on adaptations, original plays, and his own productions. One, *Révolte dans les Asturies*, told of the miners' uprising in 1934, but at the time of its production had much more to do with the outbreak of the Spanish Civil War. The defeat of the Republicans was a smashing blow to Camus – a closet Spaniard – and he groaned at the decree of non-intervention on the part of the French government. All his life he spoke and worked diligently on behalf of the exiled Spanish Republicans, with whom he considered his relationship fraternal.

During the 1930s, Sartre, while politically aware, was more of a spectator at the tragic happenings of the times. He had little to say about Hitler – despite living a year in Berlin – and even his awareness of the issues of the Spanish Civil War did not lead him to active political involvement. He was driven to write, to construct his philosophy, to make of his mind the best instrument it could possibly be. Even as a student, Gerassi informs us, Sartre's interest was literature rather than politics. He was among the uncommitted (116–17, 139–40).

Both Camus and Sartre shared a taste for low life, for colourful language. They enjoyed observing the intrusion of the private into the public. This is one of the reasons Camus loved Italy, particularly Naples (or why Sartre took annual vacations in Rome), and never felt comfortable in the Germanic north. When Sartre searched for an apartment in Le Havre, at the time of his first teaching assignment, he fled in horror from a discreet bourgeois home with its covered furniture. Instead he sought refuge in a hotel in the seediest part of town. He thus put into practice his lifelong belief in contingency, in owning nothing, in not being beholden. Although, contrary to popular belief, Sartre did own an apartment, which after the death of his stepfather he shared with his mother (1945–62), his preferred mode of living was hotel flats and rented apartments and spent his time writing in cafés. He took his great principle of contingency to heart.

Most decidedly Camus did not fit the paradigm of the emergent French intellectual of the mid-1940s, of the years after the war. He was not a member of the 'class' born in 1905, did not go through the 'khagne' – those lessons at the best Parisian lycées that prepared one for the entrance examination to the École normale supérieure. But then all dualisms require a person who does not fit, who eludes the sociological and historical paradigms. Luther was an obscure German monk who, the Roman Curia thought, would come to his senses; Rousseau was 'demi-gaullois, demi-allemand,' another provincial without class come to the metropolitan city; and Dostoevsky was not, unlike Turgenev and Tolstoy, a member of the land-owning gentry. So, too, Camus does not fit, and his last work, *Le premier homme* (*The First Man*) will make eloquent record of this alienation.

2. Cameos in Triage

But lack of fit does not disqualify an eminence attained, nor should it be supplanted by those paradigms that do fit. Two works would push Camus aside, as if Sartre reigned alone in intellectual hegemony, while two others would have the essential quarrel and contention as being between Sartre and Merleau-Ponty, or Sartre and Raymond Aron. Randall Collins's prodigious effort, *The Sociology of Philosophies*, offers many arguments that coincide with those of this study: the emphasis on the creative potential of conflict, the need for cohort groups, intergenerational networking, etc.[3] He accurately describes the compact and competitive intellectual space in which the Parisian intellectuals of the 1930s and 1940s sought their ways (an arrangement Cohen-Solal independently advanced, when she writes that both Sartre and Camus dreamt of 'dominating the same intellectual territory' – 334). But, Collins argues, in such tight space there is room for only one to 'personify' the group. 'Sartre is the energy vortex of the group' (776). Indeed, Sartre, particularly after 1945, did become a standard-bearer, a 'chef d'école,' but there was a rival claimant who was making his own way to distinction. Here Collins dismisses Camus, referring to him as an amateur where Hegel is concerned (thus slighting, as will be common, Camus's capacities as a philosopher) and as one whose stylistic skills disguise the 'thinness of his argument' (781). But the evidence of the times and the evidence of other dualisms should indicate that it is not always the case, or even primarily the case, that out of the tightly wound intellectual competition only one should emerge. As debate is over the future and as it is likely that a society's vision is deeply divided, it is only natural that there should be several contenders.

Even more engaging than Collins's generalized theory is that presented in Bernard-Henri Lévy's complex, judicious, and yet scintillating work, *Le siècle de Sartre*. The century of Sartre? Yes, but far from a coronation, it is meant in an ambiguous sense. It was the century where the greatest philosopher, Heidegger – *sic* – was also a Nazi. Why not characterize the French century with similar ambiguity, when its greatest philosophical defender of liberty became something of a Maoist? For Lévy there were two Sartres, the first Sartre as well as the second, that is, the Sartre who underwent several conversions. There is the first Sartre of committed aesthetic isolation and detachment, followed by the Sartre who during the years of Occupation and postwar Liberation was the prince of the city, the pattern and the patron, showing the way to his cohorts and contemporaries, who were able to imbibe from his works 'his taste for breaking all the taboos and the conformities, his sense of thought and life as becoming one, the possibility of seeing – thanks to him – things, the world, and beings, as it were, for the first time' (20). This ascendancy, though regarded as diminished after 1968, nevertheless was continued in the line of French 'postmodern' philosophers – Deleuze, Derrida, Lacan, Foucault (that is, among those who sought to replace him and even attack him mockingly, as did Foucault): 'Sartre, even here, is at the origin of all the modern current of the dissolution of the subject and of the certitudes of humanism' (296), Sartre from beginning to end was the century's last totalizing intellectual. But in all of this there is a neglect of the other sustaining pole provided by the appeal of the life and the thoughts of Camus. Step by step, hand in hand he certainly enjoyed an equally large patronage. While the notion of two Sartres may be – and will be – contested, there was always one Camus. The same defiant clarity with which he combated the Nazis he employed against the Soviet system and would have worked in the same clandestinity in the event of any Soviet takeover, which as late as 1976 was still a concern of some intellectuals. As he did not live to see the emergence of the 'modern' *philosophes,* mentioned above, one will always regret missing what he would have said and wonder how he would have understood their presence. In the section where he actually compares Camus and Sartre, Lévy, despite his thoughtful presentation of the pros and cons of their debate, simplifies by regarding Camus as a thinker whose yes to the universe is an act of acquiescence, preferring by virtue of the freedom it implies, Sartre's no. He finally succumbs to the French penchant for the witty and paradoxical aphorism: better to be wrong with Sartre than right with Camus, thereby inadvertently reinstalling the dualism that his title and argument work to disallow (472–82). Put to the test, the aphorism is frivolous, because being wrong with Sartre would have meant the despoliation of Western Europe to supply the despotic and colonizing needs of the USSR, such as happened in the satellite states to the East. One would also be obliged to do without the benefits bestowed by the so-called formal virtues of bourgeois society, such as freedom of the press, freedom of expression, the uncontrolled franchise, habeas corpus, in short, the many liberties that have opened the way to some economic advancement for the working classes. To be sure, as a philosopher of freedom Sartre is, as Lévy maintains, 'precious' (360), but the century of Sartre? Surely Camus would have enjoyed a good chuckle at that, perhaps repeating his famous quip, 'killing two birds with one stone' (d'une pierre deux coups).

The years following the war may have been the Sartrean glory years, the beginning of the three decades of intellectual prominence, or another Thirty Years War, as it was marked by three ruptures of varying intensity.[4] Maurice Merleau-Ponty, Raymond Aron, and Camus stand like three figurines, three statuettes each casting their gaze on Sartre, each referring back to him, thereby establishing him as being central, but not uniquely so.

The conflict that emerged between Sartre and Camus may be distinguished from the quarrel between Sartre and Merleau-Ponty, which shows all the features of a misadventure between friends. For one, Sartre and Merleau-Ponty were of the same class, *petit bourgeois;* they were both *normaliens;* and they were both trained philosophers whose trajectories bore much in common, that is, their independent discoveries of phenomenology and of history. Their falling-out was largely due to a psychological mishap, a conspiracy of silence, out of fear of treading on their friendship. It began with Merleau-Ponty's declining to have his name printed on the masthead of the leading French intellectual *revue*, of which he was the de facto editor-in-chief. As Sartre was later to perceive, this facilitated an anticipated easy departure, should the occasion arise. And the occasion did arise both intellectually and officially in regard to *Les temps modernes*. Their paths did start and proceed in crossed directions. After the war, in *Humanism and Terror* (1947), Merleau-Ponty mounted a qualified defence of Marxism, maintaining that in the long run it held the greater promise of a classless society. Sartre, while holding to the never-relinquished idea that every anti-communist was a 'dog' (or at times a 'rat'), was not quite as willing to stake such a wager. In the early 1950s, they found themselves in reversed positions, Sartre arguing that one must side with the proletariat, and its sponsoring agencies, the Party and the USSR. Merleau-Ponty had in the meantime come to believe that Stalinism was merely imperialistic Bonapartism in new dress, the classless society had only given rise to a new class, and there were better prospects for reform by remaining within the parliamentary system of the West. But the break occurred by the circumstance that had brought them together: the directorship of *Les temps modernes*. Sartre, without consulting Merleau-Ponty, eliminated a heading caption in which the latter absented himself from the opinions of the following article. When Merleau-Ponty read the proof sheets he realized immediately what had happened and by telephone informed Sartre of his resignation. But their friendship was able to survive a three-year period of silence and alienation because neither was willing to make the break public (*Situations* 4: 189). Slowly and awkwardly their friendship resumed, but with the difference that now their disagreements were not left unspoken – in fact, Sartre called the break this 'meurtre purificateur.' But inglorious scandalous death intervened before full restoration could be achieved, leaving Sartre to write the third of his great monodies, the lengthy essay on Merleau-Ponty, which follows those on Camus and Paul Nizan, reprinted consecutively in *Situations IV*. To be sure, as he argued earlier against Heidegger, death cannot bestow meaning on life, but in these essays so infused with the death of friends, it can permeate thought, now become penitential, filled with remorse, regret, and bitterness – bitterness that finally this was a love affair manqué, that the revival of friendship, however desired, was denied, and that to the end, they remained 'des inconnus' – unknowables.[5]

Despite an undertow of philosophical differences in their earlier works, it was not until Sartre's *The Communists and Peace* and Merleau-Ponty's remarkably acute dissection of that piece that their differences entered into a very limited public awareness – nothing like a famous, press-arousing spat. But after their reconciliation in 1956, Merleau-Ponty in such works as 'The Philosophy of Existence' was able to speak of Sartre *vivant* with intimate and cordial generosity and with broad historical understanding. Their differences were muted because philosophically they were kindred spirits. When Sartre describes Merleau-Ponty's later philosophy, it is a portrait of himself and his thought in another. This similarity has been recognized, first perhaps implied by Simone de Beauvoir when she accused Merleau-Ponty of attacking a pseudo-Sartreanism, later confirmed by Monika Langer, who finds in both the same concern for exploring the field of intersubjectivity existing between subject and the other.[6] This is as much to show that whatever differences may have existed between Sartre and Merleau they never rose to the same level of open enmity and public debate that we find in true dualisms.

The quarrel between Sartre and Raymond Aron lies somewhere in between that of Sartre with Merleau-Ponty and that with Camus. They were both of the same age, were friends, and occupied the same intellectual terrain. Like Merleau-Ponty, they were both *normaliens*, in fact it was Aron who advised Sartre to 'give them what they want' after he had failed the written part of the *agrégation* in philosophy, with the well-noted success the second time. It was Aron who helped Sartre receive the fellowship for a year's stay in Germany and who indicated the philosophical possibilities of phenomenology. They were both overtaken by the need to enter into the history of their times, but it was here by the force of circumstance and the pressure of the times that their philosophical and political divergences became apparent. After a brief tenure on the original editorial board of *Les temps modernes*, Aron resigned his position and became a Gaullist. Two episodes intervened in 1947 and 1948, which solidified their divergences. The first occurred when Sartre felt Aron failed to come to his defence after Sartre's presence on a radio program of political discussion was cancelled, and the second when, after being attacked in *Les temps modernes*, Aron sped off another letter to 'Monsieur le directeur.' But well before this, both Aron and Sartre had known that their friendship could not survive their political differences. This quarrel, well recounted by Jean-Francois Sirinelli in his *Sartre et Aron, deux intellectuels dans le siècle*, anticipated the later break between Sartre and Camus, even serving as something of a preamble and blueprint for the later dispute. But here differences become apparent. Aron, while a potent figure, was still somewhat 'isolé' and merely a figure in the wings ('coulisses') of central stage (255). He was even, according to Sirinelli, still a 'hundred yards' below Camus in reputation, and his dispute did not engage the public attention as did that of Sartre and Camus (259). It lacked the intensity of involvement, and moreover the far-reaching consequences. The real quarrel was not between communist and Gaullist (here Sirinelli is right in stating that the Gaullistes had not attained the same intellectual force as had the Left), but rather between the progressively minded Camus and the revolutionary Sartre (251). To ignore this would be as if in the disputes of the sixteenth-century Reformation one were to disregard the role of Erasmus and concentrate on the disagreements of Rome and Luther, which the latter had already discounted. In the muster of dualisms, other matters intervene besides politics and historical circumstance. In the clench of their grappling, class, background, temperament, latent enmity, moral positioning, and personal outlook all hold their sway. But there is more and that is the felt sense of betrayal and necessary reprisals that emanate from a fight at such close quarters.

3. Readjustments

Despite this adherence to the general pattern of formatting, the dualism of Sartre and Camus requires some major readjustments. It is practically inevitable that in any historical depiction of dualisms some irregular shadings should emerge: dispersals and recombinations. Given the nature of the twentieth century, truly as Eric Hobsbawm has called it, *The Age of Extremes* (1994), or better yet, particularly for the writers here in mind, after one of his sections, 'The Age of Catastrophe,' where the two world wars were one Thirty Year War, and the members of that generation endured a peace that never was, expected alignments were modified, and even roles reversed. There is a greater tendency toward hybridity (see below, section 13), because new intellectual inheritances provide new baselines, that, combined with the crashing world events, provoke even more unusual turnabouts, affecting Sartre and Camus in their personal qualities, in their cross-rivalry and in their shifting placement in their historical alignments.

In the three preceding dualisms, it was the daemonic writer who was given to being misunderstood and who made himself the arch critic of the advanced stages of European consciousness. But in the past century it was Camus, the writer of consciousness, rightly compared by Sartre to the *moralistes* of the eighteenth century, and pre-eminently Voltaire, who is in need of explanation and who considers himself 'heretical,' writing against a new orthodoxy. By a strange twist, in his time 'moderation' has been banished to a disquieting silence. And against such estrangements of reason, of establishing limits, and of a sense of value, it is the voice of moderation that dares to protest.

But even here nuances must be established, distinctions made. Too often Camus is regarded as a 'satisfying' author, an author of accommodation, even guilty of the 'fatal flaw' of being a vacillator. Even worse, he has been caricatured as a conservative 'mollet et tiède.' Olivier Todd, who quotes this opinion (*Albert Camus: une vie* 757) goes far to correct this judgment; in fact, his entire book is devoted to demonstrating the contrary opinion (759), and particularly his Conclusion should be read for its judicious and quite accurate assessments. The prevailing opinion ignored Camus's position as a 'heterodox of the Left.' In fact, he always maintained that he was of the Left in many matters, both in spite of himself and in spite of the Left (746). Turning from declaration, to the evidence of his works, the view of Camus as staid defender of the established order ignores the role of violence in his work – his century's dubious bequest; his resorting to the logic of absurdity and his own inner strain and even bafflement, his own complex contradictions, and the felt necessity of contention that he harboured, all of those things that the tragically curtailed *The First Man* courageously makes clear. One of the several 'first men' is Cain, and indeed in the heat of the African summer violence broods and murder lashes out; a Spanish fatalism prevails amidst the inevitabilities that poverty must endure and the anonymity of the poor folk facing a silent oblivion. These are only a partial list of the many qualities that Camus in his appealing work (Todd rightly calls it 'bouleversante') tells us are part of his environment and his psyche, and by which we enter into the more authentic meaning of his works. In this he is most unlike Erasmus, who, one feels, constantly tries to find the acceptable middle, the balancing of opposed opinions that will bring about a reasonable conclusion and reconciliation. His is a balancing act that will appease all parties, one that seeks to avoid dread contentiousness. Camus, to the contrary, seeks out contention because the opposite and contending demands are part of his nature. He, another 'first man,' suffers the contradictions and divisions that classically beset a second-generation immigrant intellectual, uprooted in more than one way, never quite at home, alienated from the people and places back toward which his heart strives. Discord – creative tension – derives from a basic division in his nature, one that runs through all of his creative work, from *Caligula* to *The Fall*. Responding to an interviewer's question, he has provided summary expression, 'Mon coeur ne balance pas' (*Essais* 742). While in some works he does advocate a reconciliation of apparent opposites, this is usually accompanied by a strict understanding of their own powerful forces and their limitations when standing alone.

As he himself tells us, he is 'up to his neck' in the history of his times; yet his predominant moral and intellectual purpose is to stand out against history. Indeed, Sartre rightly quotes one of the perceptions then current 'with Camus, rebellion has changed camps' ('Réponse à Albert Camus,' *Les temps modernes*, August 1952, 340). That is, the writer of consciousness now has become the true rebel, representing the 'free left' against the 'progressive left' – by which latter phrase he means the Marxist-existential Left that Sartre had come to represent. In *L'homme révolté* (*The Rebel*) Camus announces, as this study has done all along, that the real contest is not between conservative and liberal, between bourgeois and progressive, but between rebel-reformer and revolutionary. Erasmus argued that he was not to be blamed for going to the water's edge and not plunging into the deep. His withholding he feels is temperamental, part of his character, a fault. He felt diminished in the contrast with Luther, so beholden to the demands of the Spirit. Camus argues, but now on moral, historical, and philosophical grounds, that such restraint is indeed necessary, even required. The antagonist here is not an absolute spiritual commitment required by devotion to the Cross but rather the logic of history represented by Revolution – against which Camus must extract the human element, have the courage to say no.

Sartre and Camus began with a baseline different from that of their immediate predecessors in the chain of dualisms. Turgenev and Dostoevsky came into maturity when the heady combination of German idealism and French socialism (and the lingering background figure of contention, Rousseau) snared the eager young Russian intellectuals of the 1840s. Their careers could in one way be regarded as a long process of transforming this early burden, but never abandoning it. Despite his relegation to the status of being a bypassed windbag, Rudin is still praised because his words are good; and Stephan Verkhovensky himself is transfigured in his last pilgrimage. The early bequest seems never totally foregone, and even if subdued it remains present in their sense of the future fullness. Their hopes are never depleted; they live on the verge of great events. Sartre and Camus begin with a different composure, a world where the future has been squeezed dry. Rather then the high-energy philosophy of hope and eagerness, they had thrust upon them the world as absurd, where lucidity and indifference were the required tools of survival.

As with Turgenev and Dostoevsky where one of the preceding pairs – Rousseau–exerted a formidable and complex influence and challenge, so with Sartre and Camus it was Dostoevsky who emerged to both bedazzle and inform. While several good monographs have been written on the 'challenge' of Dostoevsky for Camus, we have yet to see any similar work on Dostoevsky and Sartre. Distinct phases of Camus's involvement with Dostoevsky are brought out in Ray Davison's clear-sighted and intelligent *Camus: The Challenge of Dostoevsky*. From the first he was fascinated by Kirillov, the theoretician of suicide, but in his theatrical group's production of *The Brothers Karamazov* there was no doubt in Jean Grenier's mind but that Camus would assume the role of Ivan. Yet Dostoevsky as presented in *Le mythe de Sisyphe* (*The Myth of Sisyphus*), while possessing undeniable greatness, required the leap of faith, thus disqualifying his works as truly representative of the absurd. The crucial all-important next phase of Camus's involvement with Dostoevsky came when Ivan is perceived to be the harbinger of an age of political totalitarianism, and *The Possessed* becomes the key text in understanding the transformation of metaphysical rebellion into twentieth-century despotism. Yet even with his high praise of *The Possessed* (his adaptation, *Les possédés*, was his last dramatic production), Camus could not finally accept Dostoevsky's conditions for the re-establishment of a sensible society, which for the Russian idealist could come about only by means of a faith in Christ. Here, too, Camus differs, as not being a believing Christian ('Christ never set foot in the Algeria' is one of his notations to *The First Man* 299; there are other more direct disavowals) he sought the rectification of society's dangerous intellectual tendencies in the cultivation of a sense of limits. The finitism that Ortega lauded in the Mediterranean world – a pagan world – was also Camus's cautious antidote. Like Voltaire he valued knowing when to stop.

There can be no question of the role of Dostoevsky in the evolving thought and work of Camus. Yet this leaves us with a paradox: in almost every way, except conscious thought, Camus was different from Dostoevsky. His style is not turbulent, but rather restrained, even classical, as Sartre describes it, and spiritually marked by a need to seek out an 'équilibre supérieur,' even perhaps a creative surpassing of mere dualities (*Essais* 854).

Oddly enough it is Sartre, untouched by Dostoevsky's religious or political conclusions, who, while separate from him in temperament, carries the burden of the daemonic. In fact, Sartre did plan an exposition of Dostoevsky, one parallel to the actual volumes on Flaubert. Moreover, he carries on while changing the valuation of two of Dostoevsky's fundamental bequests. While Camus, like Dostoevsky, condemns Ivan's startling statement that if God is dead, all is permitted (for Dostoevsky, the baleful effects of this extreme proposition demonstrate the necessity of belief in God), Sartre in *L'être et le néant* (*Being and Nothingness*) accepts the validity of the statement as providing the basis for an existential ethics. And the final project of human endeavour is to become a god-man such as Kirillov dreamed, but without suicide. This is explained in greater detail in *Being and Nothingness*. Thus in Sartre's work as well there are altered intellectual engagements with Dostoevsky's presence. But what might appear contrary to fact is Sartre's companionship with Dostoevsky as a daemonic writer, as he himself in his personality always exuded a notable confidence and self-possession. While he did have some periods of depression, particularly in the 1930s, and did have a bad mescaline trip, still we have the sense that the inner meanings of the terms he uses, terms of anguish, forlornness, and despair, have not touched him, have not entered into him in the ways they did into Luther or Rousseau (as the painfully acute final revelations of *Words* make plain). But it was Sartre who felt the need for and underwent several 'conversions' – however much the term in his case will require some modification – and who in his style approached the hallucinogenic, with no sense of classical reserve, who more like Dostoevsky plumbed the 'underground' of the human psyche and in his greatest efforts, the under-appreciated *Chemins de la liberté* (*Roads to Freedom*) showed the fullness of his complex imagination and his own need to push to the limits, to exceed the limits in the daemonism of his characters. He always maintained that he preferred abundance in his writing. In coming to Sartre and Camus, the lines separating the writer of consciousness and the daemonic waver. But even here the case of Dostoevsky alerts us to the fact that beyond ideology there are temperamental factors, metabolisms of style that enter into and even seem more relevant and enduring than arguments of issue and ideology.

4. Camus in Triplicate

Albert Camus made his enormous entrance into French intellectual and social life with his so-called absurdist trilogy, *Caligula*, *The Stranger*, and *The Myth of Sisyphus*. He tended to work in triplicate. They show the unifying nature of Camus's work, as each could very well serve as commentary upon the other. They also show the enormous versatility of his genius, one that he shared with Sartre, as both made their ways as novelist, dramatist, and philosopher, or moral essayist. In fact, it was this combination of artistry with philosophical thought that accounted for the sensed freshness and newness of their writing, their boldness and confidence. This combination of qualities meant that their ideas are brought to life, and by such personal appropriation incite and capture a shared responsiveness in the lives and thought of their contemporaries. This is why, despite their being second-generation modernists, and thus follow many of the attitudes and ideas of the preceding grand masters of modernism, they have their own vitality and appeal. They also enjoyed such mutual success because they obviously spoke to the needs of a new generation, a generation determined to survive in the midst of the Occupation. But with Camus there was even more: an intense self-examination, a self-inscription, and a self-inculpation as he tried to comprehend the attitudes that made the disaster possible. Moreover a unifying feature of all three works is that the 'absurd' marks a commencement, not a finale, a point of departure and not an end point. But even as a starting point, the absurd was a necessary premise of negativity that would come to be part of all of his works – superseded, transformed, but never relinquished.

To counter the later picture of Camus as an accommodationist, one has only to regard the startlingly dramatic quality of his new typology. Caligula, Meursault, Don Juan, and Sisyphus are meant to challenge and to astound. While his Caligula is too philosophically pathetic to be a Richard III, like Shakespeare Camus makes his most dramatic appearance with the portrait of a tyrant, but here a tyrant with some, albeit small, justification. In Shakespeare's theatre it was sixty years of civil strife that produced the twisted tyrant, who made his way because – through the accumulated degenerative actions of previous decades of war – nobody was innocent, nobody could invoke justice, all were guilty. They were all in possession not of a philosophy of nihilism but of a morale of nihilism. In Camus's theatre this same nihilism becomes more like an intellectual inheritance, a cultural milieu, one that prevents anyone from saying no, cutting away any moral grounds for condemnation. He would later call it the 'tragedy of intelligence.'

Caligula is a mixture of Kirillov, Shigalyov, and even Ivan. His new brand of 'nihilism' makes innocent-seeming the nihilism of Bazarov. He is Bazarov as completed by Kurtz. The death of Caligula's sister-lover is not the argument but rather the catalyst for the terrible development of his thought. 'Les hommes meurent et ils ne sont pas heureux' (People die and they are not happy) (*Théâtre, récits, nouvelles* [*TRN*] 1.3). Except for its leaden – almost drugged – flatness, this would have been a platitude in the nineteenth century, but the point is the spread of actions that this absurdist principle allows. In a cosmic transaction, Caligula will now match the gods in their cruelty, in the hoax they play, as it were by 'compensation.' He sleeps little, thinks much, and will mirror the pettiness of his contemporaries as well as reveal their vileness. Neither love nor conquest enters into the bargain. He wishes, as does Kirillov, complete freedom, and exercising the fullness of his liberty by acts of murder and mayhem he will show men the way to be like the gods. This malformed thought like that of Shigalyov begins with absolute freedom and ends with absolute despotism – he is free to take any life, or any wife, at any time.

Caligula become diabolic has his own contemporary resonances, which are even more pertinent in the drama's first full production in 1945 than when it was written in 1938. The later date gave the spectators ample prospects from which to look back and speculate by what intellectual deficiencies Europe allowed itself to be downtrodden and destroyed by upstart thugs, against whom they were not only physically helpless but to a large degree intellectually incapacitated. This is the quandary of he play, one in which Camus, as he readily and frequently admitted, was involved, and from which his entire intellectual adventure was to liberate himself.

The dangerous problem of the play is that truly forthright and powerful responses are not present. The young stoic, Scipion, whose father Caligula had executed, absents himself from action because 'he is too much like Caligula: '(Son) malheur est de tout comprendre' ([His] misfortune is to understand too much) (*TRN* 4.1). He shares too much of Caligula's own attitudes. The lone intellectual adversary is Cherea, who is not in agreement with Caligula's absurdist philosophy that all things are of equivalent value: 'il y a des actions qui sont plus belles que d'autres' (there are some actions more beautiful than others) (3.6). Caligula presents him with the dire choices of any intellectual endeavour: either one must pay for it or forfeit it, either one must follow thought to its utmost logical deductions or forsake it in the interest of petty commonalities. But Cherea wishes to do neither; he wants to live and be happy, and equally, like Voltaire, he derides those who do not know where to stop, who pursue 'idées vagues' to the limit. It would appear that with Cherea's more modest assessments Caligula are hemmed in. But Camus, as a fully venturing dramatist, in a way even turns the tables on Cherea, when he is addressed by Helicon, a slave whom Caligula had freed. In one of the work's most splendid speeches, Helicon plays Rousseau to Cherea's Philinte. Cherea is 'un de ces gens' who represent virtue. Cherea now becomes the 'honnête homme,' who risks nothing, who does not suffer. He runs a 'shop of virtue,' but underneath his noble toga he conceals the heart of usury, with a subtle hand of economic jobbery. His virtue gives off a very stale odour (4.6). In the 1930s and later, bourgeois values had experienced difficulties in withstanding such drastic attacks of the aroused intellectual. At least, and it is much more than that, Helicon the enfranchised slave will know how to die with his master in another twilight of the gods.

Indeed in the conspiracy he is stabbed by an unknown hand, thus preceding his master in death. But it is the death of Caligula that brings down the curtain. In his death rattle he consigns himself to history, not the history of classical studies, but rather the enduring history of Camus's own times. His last words ring with historical veracity – especially in the first production after the war: 'je suis encore vivant' (I am still alive). Camus includes himself in the dangers Caligula presents to an intellectual audience, who cannot find the means in their culture or in themselves forthrightly to denounce evil.

The Myth of Sisyphus provides the connecting link between the three absurdist works. In fact, Camus and friends militated with Gallimard that the moral essay and *The Stranger* be published at the same time, as they were conceived contemporaneously. As it turned out, *The Stranger* was published in July 1942, while *The Myth* had to wait until 1943, for 'local' reasons (meaning that because of Kafka's Jewishness that chapter had to be excised and publication delayed). *The Myth* not only found but opened a responsiveness among the French of the Occupation. It is not a work of systematic philosophy but more like an essayistic moral adventure, with a code of conduct, a style of life, and a new typology. Where else is Don Juan accorded a place of honour, not the repentant lover terrified by the stone figure, but rather the serial lover who seeks no lasting attachment, who avoids any depth of feeling, and who believes that the only genuine love is 'passager et singulier' (*Essais* 155). This is a new mentality, a concession to a new sensibility, and moreover one that found its appeal in consciousness. My situation is absurd but by the exercise of lucidity I know it is absurd and thus I have in some ways surmounted my condition. For one, I recognize it, perhaps even laugh at it (as if by laughter one can surpass defeat). Like Sisyphus I am stronger than the rock, 'plus fort que [mon] rocher' (196), whether this be the rock of the stone avenger, the wall of the Occupation, or the final rock of the intractable human condition.

The power of *The Myth* does not lie in its philosophical premises or in any systematic thought. In cleaning the boards and starting from point zero, too often Camus's argumentation seems to come down from another century, from Descartes, as parlayed strangely enough by Rousseau. Does Camus ever prove why suicide is not tenable, except by the code of the one-time athlete that one must play by the rules of the game and accept the terms of engagement (156)? One can attempt to deduce a prevalent principle: suicide is invalid because it is an act of finality in a world of contingency. And indeed later Camus and Sartre will make plain similar formulations. No, *The Myth* is a book of conduct, addressing a style of life with new and interesting characters, including Don Juan, actors and actresses, and above all, the creative artist, all possessing a lucidity that allows them to persevere in darkness and defeat. They are all willing to accept his famous condition that 'Un destin n'est pas une punition' (A destiny is not a punishment) (156).

It is the very act of persevering consciousness that separates Camus from his 'existential' forefathers – Kierkegaard, Shestov, Jaspers, Heidegger, Husserl, and others – who, Camus complains, after determining the indecipherability of the world, make a leap of faith and fall back on an irrationality of ancient origins: 'Credo quia impossibile est,' or on a rational phenomenology that bestows depth significance on passing events or individual objects. They finally yield to nostalgia and establish an emotional bond with existence (119–46). But Camus the lucid absurdist will have none of this and remains within the grips of the irreconcilability between his desires and, given the nature of the universe, his ultimate fate.

This is not so much philosophy, technically understood, as a description of a style of life – perhaps a more profound philosophy. In any event it certainly succeeded in describing a mode of being not only for his generation but for generations to come. Mostly the thought derives from the kinds of characters presented. Don Juan lives without any sense of deep attachments, without remorse, and with even a touch of humour in the amorous adventures his code of conduct imposes. The next character is 'le comédien' – the actor and actress who make no distinction between appearance and reality, who live in a state of doubleness or dissimulation, and for whom there is no such thing as 'objective reality.' If later Sartre will be credited with anticipating the dissolution of the subject in post-structuralist philosophy, here it is evident that the thought is not alien to Camus either. Beyond good and evil, beyond reality and consequence actors hold to their role. One feels that Camus here anticipates much that will happen in the development of art and the artist, and in particular the cinema of Federico Fellini, where the game is all the play, and all is for the game. Camus looks backward to one of Voltaire's favourites, Adrienne Lecouvreur, both as an artist and as an object lesson. Voltaire excoriates her maimed burial rites, all hugger-mugger in the corner of the night. Camus praises her final defiance, her refusal to renege on her profession, thus forsaking the last rites of the church. This was her finest role, where the choice was between hell and her life's work – and by choosing the latter she accepted the former (162).

Sharing the attributes of all of the preceding characters is the creative artist, and especially the novelist, where the challenge to go astray is the greatest. The temptation lies in sending a message, in making a pronouncement, in providing a solution. Such a way out betrays the absurd and fails to recognize that art is both worthless and the most valuable image of human destiny. It takes us everywhere and goes nowhere. It is best when, like the statuary of a temple or a piece of music, it seems simply to describe, to limit itself to the image, apparently to impose nothing by way of reasoning. Yet its method is also that of thought ('penser'), and Camus lists the novelists from Balzac to Malraux and Kafka (178) who are philosophical novelists, who out of the integrity of their inner conviction, their honesty to themselves, actually create a universe.

The Myth and *The Stranger* are thus not only roughly contemporaneous in conception (the novel was in all likelihood conceived in 1937 and finished in May 1940, and the philosophical essay began to take shape between September and February 1940–1), they are also up to a certain point complementary. Upon due reconsideration André Malraux, a staunch supporter of Camus with the Gallimard press, recognized their interdependence: 'The link between *The Myth* and *The Stranger* has many more consequences than I supposed. The essay gives the other book its full meaning, and above all, changes what in the novel first seemed monotonous and impoverished into a positive austerity with a primitive force' (Todd, *Albert Camus: A Life* 133). Meursault steps forward as a new primitive Bazarov, but with his own brand of nihilism and without any social purpose, that is, as an exponent of the metaphysical absurd.

As a novelist Camus works under these dual exactions of fidelity to the task of an almost ascetic responsibility to a faithful and lucid exposition, as well as the belief in the necessary interfusion of art and philosophy, where metaphysical claims cannot be ignored. It is this combination of qualities that helped make *The Stranger* the world success it has remained. With an austere discipline announced in *The Myth of Sisyphus*, Camus describes the daily routine, the habitual life of Meursault's modest existence. He is definitely not a hero (nor is he intended to be), nor an anti-hero; rather he is a negative hero. His virtues are all negative: he does not lie, he does not affirm what is not true, and does not exaggerate what is unnecessary. His customary response of 'cela m'est égal' is kin to the 'whatever' culture that made this book among the most frequently read by American undergraduates.

But there is a difference between parts 1 and 2, the former written in the Hemingwayesque style that Camus did not truly admire. But even in part 1, there are events that intrude and disrupt the routinized existence, that prepare the revolt of consciousness that takes place in part 2. The first disruption is the telegram announcing his mother's death. To be sure, he seems more concerned about his boss's reaction, but still it is disconcerting, requiring some alteration in regularized existence. In this novel whose early style is itself telegrammic, marked by disjunction and the absence of coherence – a fitting parallel to the life of little connection – two episodes occur that are eventful in the sense of bearing significant connection. At the rest home, his mother had acquired a 'fellow,' a 'fiancé' as he is humorously referred to by the inhabitants. He doggedly follows her funeral cortege, lamely trying to keep up by taking short cuts where the road bends, with Meursault recalling the tears streaming down his face and caught in the wrinkles of his skin like so many puddles of rainwater. And the second is the war of engagement between Salamano and his crusted dog. Abusive, ill-tempered, he vilifies his only attachment, his history, as 'Salaud. Charogne.' Yet he himself is rendered inconsolable when his dog disappears, and Meursault can hear him weeping at night.

The nature of the narrative itself undergoes a change after Meursault shoots the anonymous Arab, who, possessing a knife, is still threatening and dangerous. The final sentences of part 1 announce a new wave of existence, a new door of destiny that has been opened, one that is leading out of the habitual to conscious revolt. 'J'ai compris que j'avais détruit l'équilibre du jour, le silence exceptionnel d'une plage ou j'avais été heureux' (I knew I had shattered the balance of the day, the exceptional calm of a beach where I had been happy).[7] The four pistol shots were like four knocks against the newly opening door of disaster. These final sentences of part 1 announce a new wave of existence, a new door of misfortune, to be sure, but also one leading to conscious revolt. The narrative rises to the symbolic, as Meursault becomes representative, the 'condamné' literally with his back against the wall. One could play on his name and say that, rather than 'mer' and 'sault,' Mersault is the name of the protagonist in Camus's first discarded novel, *La mort heureuse* – sea and sun, he becomes 'meurt' and sault,' one who by conscious revolt faces up to his destiny, his farcical death sentence that nevertheless brings him into consciousness of a universal destiny.

Camus is like a trotter horse that has broken pace between parts 1 and 2. A new element rushes in, a new perspective. Meursault remains the same passive, reactive character, but he is no longer unaffected. He would have willingly embraced Céleste after the latter's helpless but comradely testimony. That of his friends, Marie, Raymond, Salamano is equally useless in the face of the down-rushing rock of 'objectivity.' We should not forget that Camus had been a court reporter and had occasion to witness such miscarriages of justice. But the farcical absurdity of the trial brings Meursault face-to-face with the more fundamental absurdity of death itself. The final session with the chaplain causes the outburst that places Meursault in the midst of *The Myth*. This amounts not so much to a correction as it does to a recognition and even in some small measure to justification. Finally he comes into consciousness of who he is and experiences 'la révolte,' a cry of protest. The door that was knocked upon had opened to a great wind that had been blowing towards him (*TRN* 1210). And he recognizes that he, and the chaplain included, are all 'privileged,' privileged to be condemned. This recognition, this coming into consciousness, prompts a feeling of liberation, indeed a benign indifference. He finally understands why in her last years in the rest home his mother took a lover. The very approach of death bequeathed that capacity for freedom. He pounces on the chaplain and assures him that at least what he has known and experienced, be it as little as a lock of Marie's hair, has greater reality and certainty than the chaplain's unknown God. The meaning of *The Myth* emerges fully in these final pages. Indeed, already, to look forward and to encompass the unity behind Camus's intellectual evolution, 'la révolte' itself, that crucial turning point in his later thought, already is suggestive in the absurd universe of a kind of human solidarity, or if not that, at least a commonality.

Camus argues for a real unity in the work of any true artist. And in his work the unity derives from a tension, a bringing together of opposites, of 'déchirement,' or laceration, and plenitude. In his youth he knew such fullness of being, not hostility but rather a 'plenitude.' There then follows the famous 'Ensuite,' with ellipses indicating the tragic experiences of his century. 'But later ... ' (*Essais* 380). He entered the intellectual world of Caligula, but ten years later he discovered the 'oui,' the yes to experience and to human capacities to extract a moral from the limitations of history. But this response of 'yes' is valid only on the condition that it does not separate itself from the 'refus originel,' the primary refusal that presupposes an eternal struggle in the search for an equilibrium (1705). Camus's own words, his sense of his mission and his own personal artistry, show Bernard-Henri Lévy's characterization of Camus as being a voice of 'oui' as being too simplistic.

5. Worlds in Common

A remarkable example of the 'inter-responsiveness' typical of all four dualisms is the early reviews each wrote of the other's earliest works, works that were destined to make them world famous. In October 1938 and in March 1939, the young and quite confident provincial, Camus, reviewed respectively and respectfully *La nausée* (*Nausea*) and *Le mur* (*The Wall*) (*Essais* 1417–22). The first review shows his constant concern with the tensions of philosophy and art, that indeed, the twentieth-century novel, as *The Myth of Sisyphus* emphasizes, must involve the union of the two. His unhappiness, among several with *Nausea*, is that the equilibrium between the two is broken when the philosophy is like a sticker ('une étiquette') placed on the description of the action (1417). Each is quite valid in its turn, but the genuine conjunction is never achieved. The coda of praise marking Sartre as a novelist to keep one's eye on does not eliminate the criticisms. There are other criticisms: true absurdity does not emerge from misery alone, or anguish alone, but the combination of anguish and some form of human grandeur – it is this discrepancy that gives absurdity its bite and for Camus its true tragic sense of deception and disappointment (1418–19). Mere anguish alone is only half the picture. We remark here a prefiguration of an essential drive in Camus to separate himself from existentialism, which argument will have several variants. More markedly, he reminds us, as he will do throughout his works, that the absurd is a 'commencement,' not an end point (1419). And finally he finds Roquentin's deliverance by his determination to be a writer a kind of mockery of the desperation of his condition ('dérisoire' is the word used), failing to realize that while Sartre completed his task as a novelist, Roquentin never does!

Camus writes of the artist and the artistry of *The Wall* with such insight and prescience that one could readily believe that years in advance he had already known *Being and Nothingness,* or more precisely the 'obsessive qualities' of *Roads to Freedom.* Sartre, with a 'maîtrise profonde,' has described with lucidity the banal daily lives of creatures who by an excess of liberty – without any attachments – are victims of their own obsessions (1420). It is one of Sartre's qualities to take things to their limits. In fact 'c'est aux limites du coeur ou de l'instinct que M. Sartre trouve son inspiration' (it is at the limits of the heart and the instincts that M. Sartre finds his inspiration) (1420). More perceptively, Camus conjectures whether at times Sartre himself does not know where the path he has taken will lead (1421). Like any great artist – an idea to be presented in *The Myth of Sisyphus* – Sartre creates his own world, but here it is one that turns toward 'nothingness' and 'lucidity' (1422). The image of a human being sitting in the midst of the ruin of his life, attests to the 'grandeur et la vérité' of his work (1422), despite Sartre's taste for 'l'impuissance' (1420). While one might disagree here and there, particularly with the notion of 'liberté' as being in the possession of Sartre's characters – in some instances it is the illusion of freedom, while in fact they are all enmeshed – still Camus's insights are staggering and as such adhere to the participants in any grand dualism, and the reason is of course that they are shared insights, fraternal comprehensions of a universe in common. Remarkably he no longer complains of the lack of grandeur, but instead praises Sartre for the instinctive skill with which he traces obsession and perversity.

Sartre, with equal insight, praise as well as reservation, reviewed *The Stranger* when it appeared in 1943 (*Situations I* 92–112). The review shows Sartre's extraordinary brilliance as an essayist, his capacity for full immersion in a work and for full extraction. He most certainly does his homework, and this essay like many others is filled with exact notations. Where Camus's essays are finely pointed but generalized assessments, and concerned with the most striking qualities of an author and his work, Sartre enters into the project with both hands working. Appearing in 1943, the essay 'Explication de *L'étranger*' permits him to make the necessary comparison that Malraux had already made, urging joint publication: *The Stranger* and *The Myth of Sisyphus* are complementary texts. The essay offering a 'commentaire exact' of the novel (93), provides 'le théorie du roman absurde' (97). Then by virtue of a remarkable stylistic analysis, he shows the way the disjunctive style, the sentences without connectives, the lack of linguistic coherence not only reveal the passivity of Meursault's character but also the nature of the absurd universe. This analysis is extensive and profound and makes this essay still one of the very best ever written on *The Stranger.*

But there is more. Sartre takes on the canard that *The Stranger* is 'Kafka written by Hemingway,' only to argue that it is neither one nor the other (104–5). In Camus's work he cannot find Kafka, who is the novelist of the most extraordinary events described matter-of-factly, of the hovering sense of a transcendence that is indecipherable. For him the universe is alive with signs that we fail to comprehend – it is the 'otherwise' of the decor. But for Camus there is an absence of transcendence. Strategically, yes, Camus found it advantageous to adopt the Hemingwayesque style – especially in part 1, but even there occasional bursts of lyricism show the possibilities of a larger stylistic power. This deliberate borrowing of a foreign style serves its purpose, but Sartre concludes with remarkable prescience, 'Je doute qu'il s'en serve dans ses prochains ouvrage' (I doubt that he will make use of them in his coming works) (106). And indeed Camus not only eschewed the style of Hemingway, he also discounted it, just as Sartre was able to do after his first infatuation with the works of John Dos Passos.

The essay ends with an even more stunning comparison, indicating that Sartre is also aware of their profound differences: Camus's style is clear, precise, limited, Mediterranean, while his is prolix, abundant, even vertiginous. Camus harkens back to the classical French tradition; he is a *moraliste.* In fact, a Voltaire. Despite the work's relations with German existentialists and American novelists, *The Stranger* according to Sartre remains very close to a *conte* by Voltaire (112).

Thus concludes this extensive essay, accurate in its detailed analyses, subtle in its discriminations, and prophetic in its judgments and comparisons. Sartre, as an essayist, is a treasure; indeed it is one area – among others – where he truly excels. As with Camus, this is because he is both philosopher and novelist. His 'explication' of *The Stranger* is an essay into the absurd, the omnipresent term, the proper understanding of which joins him and Camus and separates them from other agonists. Yet Sartre's technical training at the École normale supérieure, indeed at the time of the writing his deep immersion in completing *Being and Nothingness,* introduced a tone of condescension toward the philosophical preparation of Camus. Thus he is able to make the famous swipe that Camus plays a cute game ('met quelque coquetterie') when he cites Jaspers, Heidegger, and Kierkegaard 'qu'il ne semble d'ailleurs pas toujours bien comprendre' (whom by the way he does not always seem to understand very well) (94). The sly 'by the way' is as stinging as the wicked judgment that Camus might not fully understand the philosophers he disputes. But with the exception of Heidegger, whom Sartre knew exceedingly well, there seems little difference in the final judgments both Camus and Sartre bring to those who seek a recourse from the absurd in some leap of faith.

This dangerous strain of condescension, one that will make its explosive reappearance in their great debate, Sartre repeats in another major essay, 'Un nouveau mystique,' which should rank as a philosophical masterpiece, but is strangely unquoted and unappreciated (*Situations I* 133–74). One could call it a short course for *Being and Nothingness* – and this itself should have made it avidly sought after. The essay is devoted to Georges Bataille, who seems to describe an absurdist universe, where in the dark night the soul discovers the possibility of God. In short, Sartre's criticism of the absence of lucidity – there is more – and the necessary leap of faith is not too different from Camus's more concise and more generalized criticisms of the 'existentials' in *The Myth*. He is about to use Camus to *correct* Bataille but even here cannot avoid a philosophical putdown: Camus has only a passing familiarity ('qui n'a fait qu'effleurer') with the phenomenologists, and his thought is more properly assigned to that of the traditional French *moralistes* (144). Such insult is impertinent, given the context, but it seems unavoidable that when Camus seems to strike near Sartre's base of expertise, that is Heideggerian ontology, he must issue a stay-away warning. Thus it is that in the midst of their first arrivals, as novelists, as philosophers, and as critics of note, a serious fault line is notable, one that would only grow. Soon they would become apparent friends, but for two such intimate intellectuals it is quite odd that a barrier existed – they never discussed ideas.

Two of their most potent affinities – their insistence that art and philosophy were necessarily joined activities and that each required the full engagement, the 'présence totale' of its creator – attest to their mutual triumphs and account for their dual emergence as the leading intellectuals of the postwar period (de Beauvoir, *La force des choses* 53). They also set them apart from much that was to follow. As Simone de Beauvoir knew, they had become 'les mandarins.' The title of her novel is ironic and while accurate also a bit misleading. Somewhat disingenuously she denies that her novel is a *roman à clef* – better she had said not *totally* one; nor a *roman à thèse* with a solution imposed and answers provided. And this also is only partially true. It is after all dedicated to Nelson Algren, the Chicago-based novelist, her love affair with whom the novel fictionally depicts, and Henri Perron, the Camus-type in the novel, a 'flawless' character – reminiscent of the 'belle âme' the Sartrean *famille* denounced – who perjures himself. There are many other points of recall. Indeed, as a novelist Simone de Beauvoir is a great memorialist. (For a just assessment of these issues, see Aronson, *Camus and Sartre* 178–82.) If not given over to a thesis, the novel does describe the predicament facing the new French mandarins. The unity produced by the Resistance had concealed the fact that the postwar period revealed with a stark bluntness: France, it is repeated often in the novel, had become a 'fifth-rate' power. And this larger political demotion (certainly underway since 1870) casts its pall over the intellectuals who found themselves displaced and helpless, floundering between aborted political movements. In this sense they were true mandarins, with assumed positions of intellectual authority but without any effectiveness.

But the very predicament her novel presents also contains but leaves unexplored the greater paradox, that it was because France was a defeated power, a fact she, Sartre, Camus, and their entourage understood, that they were not impotent intellectuals but rather vibrant and multi-talented thinkers who emerged as the consciences and consciousnesses of their generation.[8] Their very predicament became their lodestar – they were obliged to refigure their situation as not being one confined to the problems of France but rather as one evoking a broader European consciousness, to which their thought now found its address. As a political power France may have been demoted, but this very demotion provided the occasion for its leading intellectuals to become voices of a larger European – even world – consciousness. The fan of their concerns was opened to many more points on the compass. In fact at a notable conference of 1949, Sartre insists that French culture can persist only by being integrated into the 'grande culture européenne' (*Les écrits* 214–15).

In *The Mandarins* there is the even more ominous presentiment that as a class the literary intellectual is outmoded. This means that in the larger sense the role of the public intellectual will become extinct, as a new generation or generations will arise for whom literature itself will have little significance. The two are seen to be in tandem: the lack of faith in the validity of the literary imagination and the declined public voice of the creative intelligence. This breakdown will even find its expression in the *nouveau roman*, itself a product of the defeated country that France had become, with no sense of the human, or of the presence of the writer as engaged in the life of the times, in politics, in history (*La force des choses* 648–51). In their own self-demotion, the mandarins – and here the Koestler-type character is most vocal and most prophetic – sense a coming illiteracy, where no literary figure will have any public importance because nobody will be reading. Indeed, it is this larger prophecy, this larger motion that brings to completion the sense of terror and depletion that the novel exposes. Yet in the very extended time that was foretold, in the 1990s, we witnessed the remarkable dual re-emergence of both Sartre and Camus. This had less to do with the abundant availability of new biographical materials but was itself a political and cultural act, as if in the midst of the far greater engulfment of globalization, under Anglo-American hegemony, the French felt compelled to reach back to its two leading intellectuals (there were others, Raymond Aron among the most notable), to its last totalizing intellectuals, and in so doing revived once again this apparently perdurable dualism. But there was also a hunger, a hunger for works where philosophy and art and politics combine to create an excitement of thought and involvement.

6. Second-Generation Modernists: Emergence and Paradox

In addition to surmounting in their personal careers the fate of their nation, young Sartre and Camus were able to overcome another apparent obstacle. Both Sartre and Camus were second-generation modernists. On the one hand this means that their absurdist description of the world was hardly something new, that it had been uttered before, even in similar detail and consequence, by the giants of high modernism. Like their predecessors they experienced their fullest successes after a great war, but they also knew the Occupation, and this experience had a distinct effect on their separate developments, for the moment leading both out of their absurdist conceptions of the world into one of human solidarity. Here we must speak again not of posteriority or decline but rather of a remarkable emergence. It is something of a practical wonder that their works did not suffer from any sense of belatedness; instead they communicated a freshness of discovery in the fervour, imagination, and lucidity with which they faced the problems of their generation. They had something to say, and they said it with verve and confident thought. They emerged in their full status as public intellectuals, bringing their philosophical training and address to bear on the crucial questions of the moment. But their success was far from instantaneous.

For both Sartre and Camus the 1930s were trying times, trying and trying-out, testing times. Each had to endure serious setbacks and disappointments both professionally and personally. In Sartre's case, because the expectations were so much higher, these defeats could have been even more daunting. He flunked the written part of the *agrégation*, following which the family of the woman to whom he was attached broke off all their relations. He did not receive the teaching position he sought in Tokyo, instead accepting an assignment to a lycée in Le Havre. He laboured eight years over what was to become *La nausée*, only to have it rejected twice by Gallimard. This may have had something to do with the various titles: 'Factum on Contingency,' 'Essay: On the Loneliness of the Mind,' and various others, including 'Melancholia.' The work was given editorial approval only through the indirect intervention of one of Sartre's students, and the title we have itself bestowed by Gaston Gallimard. The work was baptized and Sartre was on his way. *La nausée* proved to be a work of both critical and commercial success.[9]

Camus's setbacks turned out to be 'saving' rejections. His chronic bouts with tuberculosis brought him face-to-face with the absurd, cut short his ability to play soccer, and eventually curtailed any strenuous physical exertion, but it also rendered him ineligible for a teaching position, which had he won might have produced a different Albert Camus. His marriage to Simone Hie was an outright disaster, as she was a confirmed drug addict, who, as Camus learned, was the lover of her doctor-provider. Quite fortunately he escaped that marriage. His third rejection was his expulsion from the Communist Party in Algiers, which worked only to preserve his artistic independence and his efforts on behalf of the indigenous Arab population.

Yet, despite these setbacks, each had going for him an indomitable faith in his own creative powers and genius, grand hopes for future success, and a lifelong dedication to the powers of art and thought. Throughout their travails they wrote non-stop and had countless projects. Even under the most adverse conditions, each, writers-born, never ceased creating. In Camus's case the feat was even more remarkable. He came from a family where the grandmother was illiterate, the mother semi-deaf and only minimally literate, the uncle almost mute and deaf, where there was no radio, no newspaper, and above all no discussion – matters seemed to be settled by the grandmother's fist – but more importantly no way to bring into expression matters of genuine concern, so it is one of the most remarkable occurrences of modern literature that Camus himself did not acquire the habit of silence, become like a rock (that is, become Meursault rather than explore the meaning of Meursault), and like the other taciturn, stoic, passive people he knew, face up to life's inevitabilities with a silent acquiescence. Because a death-like mutism and passivity haunted the people he knew, they needed the suppliant offerings of his voice to enter the land of the living.

Even from the start, not only France, but eventually the world responded to their new voices and their new ways of seeing. In their exemplary notations to the *Œuvres romanesques* of Sartre, Michel Contat and Michel Rybalka join *Nausea* with *The Stranger* as the 'contemporary work' that was 'the most studied ... the most abundantly commented upon ... and the most read by the public at large' (1668). Indeed, as their reciprocal reviews indicate, both works share many remarkable qualities – in fact, what they share is what made them remarkable. Both authors were motivated by the abiding and fervent desire to bring together art and philosophy. In this of course they participated in the higher sweep of modernism, whose concern was not to show people making their fortunes, or even their livelihoods, or showing maligned goodness redeemed, but rather to discover how to be. Questions of being, their presence to the world – that is, everyday life shot through with metaphysical concerns – preoccupied Sartre and Camus as it did their great predecessors. They both succeeded because for them philosophy was not an abstraction but something etched in daily living – all matters of things were subjects of philosophy – and thus fully appropriated and absorbed by the emotional life of their characters and themselves. Their own personal crises and faiths became the matter of their works.

Camus's review of *Nausea*, containing some severe strictures, drastically under-estimated Sartre's capacity to bring together artistry and philosophy. The final entries of the imaginary 'Journal' exhibit a remarkable historical, political, and philosophical coherence of artistic orchestration. In fact, there is a spiralling intensity of discovery from the museum visit, to the following spiritual crisis, to the fall from grace of the humanist, to the more primitive experience of the sea and the public garden, to the episode with Anny and his final determination to write a novel (earning Camus's derision).

There is a historicity to the sequence of scenes, as Contat and Rybalka adroitly point out. The enterprising industrialists of the nineteenth century are pictured in the museum. While the editors indicate that the Autodidact is a humanist of the nineteenth century, it would be more apt to regard him as a man of 'bonne volonté' of the period around World War I (*Œuvres romanesques* 189), and Anny is certainly the aesthetic female of the 1920s (*Œuvres* 160–82; *Nausea* 135–54), whose portraits D.H. Lawrence had drawn so carefully. She carries her world with her, in her need to safeguard her epiphanies, her 'moments parfaits,' but they seem to have abandoned her to a position far from hopeful. And Roquentin himself might well be regarded as the type of Malraux of the 1920s and 1930s (see *Œuvres romanesques* 1729) in constant quest of the 'adventures' that never quite arrive or hold together. Roquentin might be an anti-hero, but he is effectively employed by Sartre to demolish past responses, the older ways that no longer are ways out.

Even fine political threads are woven through the portraits in the museum, particularly that of Blévigne (109–10; 91–4). As a young student he was frightened enough by the uprising of the Communards to establish a society devoted to Order. He participated in the suppression of the striking ship-workers in 1898, and while the encomiastic cliché referred to him as a person of conciliation, he was, we are given to suspect, an anti-Dreyfusard. Sartre as well as Simone de Beauvoir may have at this time existed only in an 'esthétique d'opposition,' that is, while being aware, they were not politically active. Yet politics is inseparable from the anti-bourgeois revelations of his anti-hero and even more palpably present in the account given of one of the leaders of the community.

The first effect of Roquentin's visit to the museum and his denunciation of the city leaders is to renounce his work on Rollebon. But in the pages that follow (113–22; 94–103) we have in philosophical-dramatic terms the fullest expression of personal crisis. What is remarkable is the lyricism to which Camus responded, the accumulated flow of this account of his discovery of his nothingness, of his being extraneous, not 'unwanted' in the common English translation, but unnecessary. Yet in this being nowhere and nobody, he still retains a consciousness of his own existence. He can no longer hide his existence in that of his subject of research, who is even more distant, unknowable, and alien than himself.

The lengthy luncheon with the Autodidact follows (123–47; 103–26). Sartre thus takes issue with the two dominant currents of his culture: first, the successful leaders of the public world, filled with a confidence of their 'rights,' not only social, but cosmic, as if their being had metaphysical approval, who never arrive at the consciousness that they are *de trop*, extraneous to existence itself, that their removal would not matter at all (121; 101); second, the world of humanism, with its wilful determination to love, to seek out a communion of souls, but equally enjoys only a surface existence. Such humanists are in love with cardboard figures, with generalities that bear no individual face, no particulars (142; 120). They are blinded by their need to love – turning love into something vapid, abstract. They adhere to the well-rehearsed stages of life – and incidentally, in rejecting all the phases, Sartre duplicates those areas carefully omitted or disallowed by the high modernists[10] – but their beloved generalities do not survive close inspection.

The two encounters with the reigning ideologies, that of the founding fathers and that of the humanist, give way to lyrical philosophical passages of personal distress and discovery. The second, following that of the humanist, is even more aggravated by horror, showing Sartre's inclination to push things to their limits. Like Eliot, Woolf, and Lawrence, Sartre probes the depths of the sea, searches beyond the decor, and finds monstrous beings, no image reflecting either God's or a humanist's world.[11] The visit to the public garden is even more frightening, as he encounters once and for all the facts of existence, its profligacy and its nothingness. Existence defies all explication, even the word *absurdity* does not cover it. But for Antoine Roquentin it is not a word, but rather an existential experience, that comes unwanted, uncontrived, and always in capital letters: *Nausea*. It is a brusque invasion not open to deduction. You are the only thing you can know and your very being is non-essential. But even this fact of nothingness, this experience of contingency, cannot help but be there. And he himself in this very fact of contingency finds his own existence to be real, something that cannot be avoided. Even in his own gratuitousness he cannot but know that he exists, his new *cogito*.

After the encounter with the social giants of the public world (he emphasizes their short stature), he gives up on his biography of Rollebon; after his encounter with the humanist and the subsequent discoveries, he decides to leave Bouville (his decision is followed by the disappointing meeting with Anny, where Sartre is at his best in psychological description – 160–82; 134–54). His personal journey of philosophical discovery has been completed; it has penetrated, finally understood, to his bones. Naturally enough, French critics have likened his discoveries to Jansenism, and even Pascal, a Pascal without God, without transcendence. But there is another presence, much closer to his home, to his transformed liberal Protestant origins, and that is Luther. If Coleridge can bring Luther into the eighteenth century, providing him with the intellectual antecedents then prevailing, and thus compare him in his 'impetuous' character and his social concerns with Rousseau, then we can move Sartre back, with equal conviction to that great sixteenth-century forbear. This wayward son of liberal Protestantism in the primacy of his conviction is a true heir of the Protestant founder. In fact, in a 1960 interview he declared that he had always found a more receptive audience among Protestants because, unlike the Catholics, they were more ready to accept ideas like solitude and forlornness. And while, unlike Sartre, they were 'believers,' still they were in agreement with him when it came to man alone (*Écrits* 331–2).

But perhaps in reverse direction, his own dissection of existence might also help us penetrate farther in our understanding of Luther. When Sartre writes of the 'manque intolérable,' of the 'péché d'exister,' of the horrors of existence, they might in a larger anthropological sense add more weight and meaning to the sixteenth-century theologian's malaise. Emptiness exists; acts do not hold together. There can be no adventures. There is only yawning in the breast of the beast a sense of his own nullity. Is this too what Luther felt and knew? But Roquentin's most profound Lutheran moment comes when he punctuates his abandonment of his thesis on Rollebon with the striking phrase, 'Jamais un existant ne peut justifier l'existence d'un autre existant' (Never can one existent [be used to] justify the existence of another) (*Œuvres* 210; *Nausea* 178). The juxtaposition is staggering and reminds us that, as with Luther, the individual suffers the burden of a terrible freedom. There is no past, no history that can help, but only the pulp of one's own existence, which at times fills the mouth with bile, or Nausea. It is thus quite natural that Roquentin should renounce his Rollebon project after his visit to the museum, where Phariseeism reigns in the portraitures. The same smug confidence that Luther abhorred – the self-satisfaction of works – is what Sartre denounces. He sees humans in the grips of a far more important struggle of mind and spirit. To be sure, Luther, as Coleridge reminds us, did have an anchor, and that was scripture. That removed, Coleridge was able to translate Luther into the eighteenth century in the *social* programs and dreams of Rousseau. Sartre enters far more deeply into the skin of these two remarkable protestants.

His role as a teacher reveals another aspect of Sartre's spiritual closeness to Luther (with all due allowances made). This heir of generations of German pedagogues remained a teacher – but in his own non-conformist, anarchist ways. When asked to lecture on Prize Day – as it was incumbent on the newcomer professor – Sartre turned to the cinema, much to the consternation of the parents present. At the following year's event he turned up stone drunk. He abandoned the customary academic garb of coat and tie, and came to class dressed in a simple sweater, but immediately began lecturing, while sitting on his desk. Obviously he attracted his select band of devotees, his younger *famille,* as they would be called. But this was much more than student-mongering, or a need for disciples. It was an expression of a mode of being, a style of life that had spiritual roots. He believed that learning was a full-time practice and not to be confined to a classroom with a preceptor. There are no hallowed grounds nor special models, saints in imitation of whom we can find safety. Democratic openness and philosophical grounding suggest the further likeness with Luther: in the natural equality of spiritual being there can be no privileged positions.[12] Taking the notion of the priesthood of every believer even farther than did Luther, he believed that each individual was burdened with the responsibility to seek out the truth, student as well as teacher – there is no difference. All questers, all travelling in the dark.

7. The Sartrean Moment

These were the years of transformations and change. In the midst of the war and the Occupation, both Sartre and Camus did some of their greatest work. (They have been criticized for continuing to produce under the Nazi Occupation, but on this point see Bernard-Henri Lévy's cogent defence, 424–44.) Sartre, with the publication of *La nausée* in 1938 and *Le mur* in 1939, was already a famous writer when he was conscripted as a meteorologist. These months of dulled routine – the so-called phoney war – he spent writing. He wrote to live and lived to write, filling up notebook after notebook with his thoughts and completing the first volume of *Roads to Freedom*. With the collapse of France he became a prisoner of war, and this was an entirely new experience. He may have experienced his first conversion with the shock of the defeat but more importantly with the newly acquired sense of solidarity, of belonging that his being a fellow prisoner bestowed. Normally the term *conversion* is reserved for his commitment to the communism of a later period, but we know that with the daemonic writer there are frequently more than one. Sartre's first conversion was brought to settle the discord in his being between his need for involvement and his aesthetic distance. Now he was one of the many, looking disaster in the face, and confronting the unspeakable – he was a German prisoner of war. Other wars were not his war, but now his own life, his only life, was under the thumb of German masters. He wrote a play, *Bariona*, for Christmas season, 1940, that confirmed his new experience both personally and intellectually. He had written satiric skits in school and at the École, but this was as a cut-up, acting out. This new venture, ostensibly a Christmas drama, addressed the fellow prisoners with hope and encouragement, urging them to march against Herod and his mercenaries – read Nazi's and collaborators (Cohen-Solal 154–5). Bernard-Henri Lévy rightly sees the prison experience and the production of *Bariona* as a turning point in Sartre's career, the first visible signs of the emergence of the second Sartre (414).

Despite Sartre's own later hesitations and reservations (he refused to have the play performed and considered it too 'talky'), *Bariona* is surprisingly attractive.[13] It has clear biographical and intellectual implications. Personally it marks Sartre's finding of 'adherence' or belonging, and his discovery of the theatre as a collective experience. 'As I addressed my comrades across the footlights, speaking to them of their state as prisoners when I suddenly saw them so remarkably silent and attentive, I realized what theatre ought to be: a great collective, religious phenomenon ... a theatre of myths' (Cohen-Solal 155). The two realizations coalesce: a new sense of the solidarity brought about by a catastrophic experience and the power of the theatre to transfix people in the collective depiction of their condition.

Bariona represents several transpositions. Dramatically it transforms a Christian mystery into a play of existential appeal, and philosophically within Sartre's own development it marks a significant transition from the despair of *Nausea* to the more hopeful philosophy of *Being and Nothingness*, to the human capacity to transcend its condition.

Early Bariona enunciates his dire conception of human existence in a dark world: 'Chacun de nous est seul, dans le noir, et le silence est autour de nous, comme un mur ... le monde n'est qu'une chute interminable et molle, le monde n'est qu'une motte de terre qui n'en finit pas de tomber' (each one of us is alone in the dark, surrounded by silence that is like a wall ... the world is only a never-ending and tedious fall [molle], the world is only a mound of earth that never ends its falling). People are caught up and abandoned in this 'chute universelle.' They break apart, they are undone. Life is a defeat, and the greatest folly is to hope (*Théâtre complet* 1130). Out of this philosophy of despair he contrives the solution that the Jews confound the Romans and their imposed hardships by a program of racial suicide: they will no longer procreate. And when the news of the birth of the new Messiah arrives, he compounds this plan with a new plot to strangle the Christ child and thus eliminate this source of hope.

On the way to this assignation he meets one of the Magi, Balthazar, played by Sartre himself, who turns his philosophy of despair into a more explicitly existential philosophy of hopeful freedom. The birth of Christ, like the birth of all the other children to the mothers in pain, marks a new commencement after a dark night. The Christian birth thus represents all births, all future possibilities (1174). Formerly Bariona had lived like a rock, encased in his own present and disowning the future. The coming of Christ, with all of his suffering foretold, brings a new message of 'par-delà,' the human capacity to live 'ailleurs,' the freedom of consciousness to surmount its suffering by refusing to make it paramount but rather subordinate to one's own free choosing (1172–3). Consciousness itself involves the freedom to go beyond.

Bariona and his band of poorly equipped partisans resolve to head off Herod's soldiers – almost certainly a suicide mission – and thus give Mary and Joseph a chance to escape. In the midst of the war, Sartre has Bariona speak across the lights to the prisoners themselves, urging hope and even mobilization. The play is both charged and charming – charged with the hope communicated to his fellow prisoners of the eventual defeat of the Nazis, and charming in the subtle yet dramatically valid way the Christian message of hope is transformed into one of existential challenge. Not only is it a turning point, it actually dramatizes the tuning point in the character of Bariona. Without a doubt Sartre's personal need to break out of the aesthetic of isolation, to surmount a philosophy of pure despair, was given a major push by the communal experiences of war and imprisonment and the newly discovered possibilities of the theatre.

The Sartrean moment hit with a bang in 1945, the beginning of what Sirinelli has called the 'glory years,' the thirty-year reign of the intellectual engaged in philosophy. Up until then he had of course been a famous novelist, an active dramatist, but with the lecture 'Existentialism Is a Humanism' (its original title was posed as a question, 'Existentialisme est-il un humanisme?'), it became clear that he was a celebrity and existentialism a vogue. His lecture was delivered under packed and riotous conditions, and in his address it was clear that Sartre was speaking as the intellectual leader if not of a movement at least of a widely accepted (and contested) mode of thought. His speech addresses accusations directed against 'us.' The same year saw the publications of the first two volumes of *Roads to Freedom*, written much earlier during the time of the phoney war and the period of incarceration. At this same time Sartre founded *Les temps modernes*, with its Chaplinesque title soon to become the most important intellectual review in France. One could also say that the lecture served to reactivate interest in Sartre's major philosophical treatise, *Being and Nothingness*, which at the time of its appearance in 1943 attracted one review, but after the lecture became the subject of some sixteen reviews. Herein lies an anomaly. Perhaps because of its brevity, its evident need in a public lecture to aim for clarity, succinctness, condensation, its need to project a 'tough optimism' in a time of national rebuilding, the lecture does not bear the same kind of personal involvement as does *Being and Nothingness*. When in the lecture he refers to anguish, forlornness, and despair, they do not enter into the skin, but remain philosophical concepts, rather like labels on a bottle of pills. But in *Being and Nothingness* one senses the years of struggle it took to bring that major work to completion.

Camus's and Sartre's works found their time and they each other. The relationships between their works is uncanny, their mutual yet independent efforts only stressing the affinities of outlook and appeal. The very year in which they met (1943) Sartre devoted a twenty-page review to *The Myth of Sisyphus* (and *The Stranger*). *Being and Nothingness* appeared in the same year as did Camus's *Myth of Sisyphus*. But both works were years in the making, and their origins reach back into earlier times and earlier works. In fact, one could say that the same synergy that exists between *The Stranger* and *The Myth of Sisyphus* also occurs in the relationship of *Nausea* and other works and *Being and Nothingness*. Just as the philosophical endeavour bestows stature and sheds light on the fictional work, so there is a reverse direction, and discussions of bad faith, temporal plenitude, nausea itself, no exit, the chips are down make a marked and valuable reappearance in *Being and Nothingness*, enriching that work with its practical field of example. While both The *Myth of Sisyphus* and *Being and Nothingness* reach back to earlier periods in their writers' careers, they each found their moment in the time of the Occupation. Each bestows on consciousness an illuminating power that identifies, extracts, synthesizes, in fact provides the defining basis for the situation in which they are involved. Snow is flat blankness until one chooses to ski over it; a mountain is unsurpassable only if one chooses to climb it. Intentionality can transform the inert thing-in-itself into some reactive part of human willing. The thought is fruitful and leads to an essential ingredient of human freedom. Both Camus and Sartre shared the idea – whatever their differences in detail – that consciousness, by placing its conditions in relation to purpose, can in some way meet and even transcend its circumstances. The rock of being that God did not create, so paramount in *The Myth of Sisyphus*, finds its redoubtable presence in *Being and Nothingness* and is similarly contested by the power of consciousness to understand its situation.

Between Sartre and Camus mutual recognition abounds – Cohen-Solal is right to underscore a clear reciprocal relationship, even a kinship of sorts, the profound basis of the dualistic inter-responsiveness, of which they partook from first to last.[14] Their conclusions are similar but their methods vary drastically. Sartre was intent on a philosophical magnum opus, the object of his determined thought since the early 1930s. He was totally involved in providing a structure in being for actions and attitudes, and judging from his later work, his masterful essays, even the famous lecture itself – so confidently condensed – he did. One could thus understand the insulting reference to Camus's apparent lack of familiarity with the philosophers he discusses. But this is true of all dualisms: within the structure of sameness, there exists the worm of differences, one that continues to eat away.

Being and Nothingness is an essential text that stands like a mountain in the middle of Sartre's career. It is both cumulative and prospective:[15] it accumulates much of his previous interest expressed in his novels, stories, minor philosophical essays, and the contemporaneous dramas. It is his early summa. Once its completion and triumph were secured, it laid the way open to Sartre's future development. And in itself it is a masterful elaboration in daring formulations of ontological premises as they extend into many facets of human life. One of the proofs of its success is the way that many of its basic ideas about human freedom, choice and responsibility, intentionality and consciousness have become so commonplace in our day. One can hardly see a film, read a novel, or witness a drama without experiencing some aspect of the Sartrean 'reality' therapy.

My purpose is not to render a full exposition of this magnum opus, but rather to give a general understanding of its intent, and then to isolate key concepts, such as bad faith, temporality, and death, to note the difference within similarity from the work and intentions of Camus, and finally to show by way of his devastating critique of 'realism' why, if he is not fully daemonic, he is totally distinct from the realist's working cousins, the writers of consciousness. *Being and Nothingness* shows why there is some majesty in fully developed systematic thought. The sheer consistency of application to a variety of problems and issues, all deriving from firmly established essential principles, the accumulating powers of reference and conceptual byplay all go to make *Being and Nothingness* a work that needs to be encountered. Whatever revisions in thought or outright recantations the later Sartre brought to his work, they all derive from this incandescent work of technical philosophy.

For Sartre it is not time as much as temporality that provokes the anguish at the heart of human experience. Temporality is not a succession of instances. Rather it is an interconnected plenum of our being, the arena of our consciousness as involved with the world. It is only through time that we exist, but it is only through consciousness that temporality comes into being. By the very fact of being born, humankind is given to temporality – at birth we acquire a past. The past as past is inert, it is intransitive; it may be acted upon but it has lost operancy. It has the simple characteristic of being there. The present is presence unto – something, but by its very presence it reminds the 'for-itself' that it is not that thing, and thus cannot be stayed or held in possession. Consciousness as presence is thus forever slipping away, and the for-itself is always moving on. The future, like *mañana*, never comes – it is never the end point of a series of actions, but rather only one of a series of possibles. One does not have to search far for the memorable phrases that summarize this condition: 'Hence the anguish ... which springs from the fact that I am not that future which I have to be ... a being whose meaning is always problematic.' 'The future does not have to be.' Humankind 'comes into the world with a past.' 'The future is the continual possibilisation of the possibles – The meaning of the present for-itself insofar as this meaning is problematic and as such radically escapes the present for-itself.'

But this does not lead to disillusionment. The past may be acted upon, retrieved from inertia by my present awareness of myself, of the kind of person I wish myself to be. How one chooses to regard oneself can change the nature of the past, that is, can transform its intransitiveness into anticipations of the future. Events may lie inert or they can be generative. (Sartre's example is a veteran of the Napoleonic wars looking back on his past exploits with a renewed pride.) In this sense, both place and time are not locked but open to the ever-present freedom of design. This is the great Sartrean bequest: within admittedly extremely limited conditions one possesses the *liberté* ultimately derived from Descartes, and not only a *liberté* confined to freedom of thought and judgment but one that extends to proposed actions as well. Hence the importance of his great cycle of novels discussed in the next section. Whether we like it or not, we are condemned to be free, because freedom is intrinsic to individual consciousness. We cannot not choose.

In the section 'My Death' we witness Sartre's analytical tools at their sharpest. While his major work is normally consigned to being an offshoot of Heidegger's *Being and Time*, this reliance on intergenerational networking is much too simplistic, ignoring the many instances where Sartre disputes Heidegger, and none is more potent than this section on death. For Heidegger the encounter with one's own mortality convinces one of the finiteness of one's being, and thus brings a sense of one's individual uniqueness. No one can die for you. With *Sein-zu-Tode* – this being unto death – begins the recognition of the *Dasein*. Sartrean ontology quite skilfully disturbs this conception. In remarkable pages he turns this thought around in his mind. Death is not like the final chord of a musical piece, the resolution of a life; it is not the last clue that solves the mystery. It may be the finale but not the fulfilment. It is utterly alien to life, a total blankness, which in Sartre's ontology means we can no longer realize our possibilities in the world (687).

Death is even unlike the past, which, while intransitive, can be reactivated. Death is totally alien; it is the opposite of life and worse. A foreclosure sign has been taped to the door because in death our possibilities have been taken over by others. That which the for-itself determinedly avoided has been fixed by death; our being has been repossessed by the Other. In fact, it is the prey of the Other. This is one of the anguished and helpless realizations of the three characters in *Huis clos* (*No Exit*). Francis Jeanson in *Le problème morale et la pensée de Sartre*, a work that remains one of the best expositions of Sartre's philosophy in *Being and Nothingness*, provides brilliant pages on how the play exemplifies the Sartrean conviction of the inevitability of conflict in human affairs (264ff.). Without excluding this reading, there is another, equally pertinent, which clarifies the crucial phrase 'L'enfer c'est les autres.' Hell is other people. Of course, relationships are bound in mutual conflict, but the people in Sartre's hell are there not because they are dead but because they have let themselves be defined by others, and they have shut down their own future possibilities.

Death is the ultimate absurdity, and where he first invokes this phrase it is perhaps indicative that he also encounters the problem of suicide. Death can never give life its meaning (as in Heidegger); it is what removes all meaning from life. It closes the door on our temporality. The same with suicide: it requires a meaning that only the future can give to it; but as it is the last act of my life, it denies this future, which is nullified. Perhaps other solutions were possible, 'but since these solutions can be only my own projections, they can appear only if I live. Suicide is an absurdity which causes my life to be submerged in the absurd' (*Being and Nothingness* 691). Sartre here puts together more explicitly, more coherently an argument that one only senses in *The Myth of Sisyphus*, but which Camus will explain more fully in *The Rebel*, that suicide introduces finality in a world of contingency. In fact, the similarity between their two views is striking.

With yet another incisive argument Sartre disbands Heidegger's contention that in mortality we discover our finitude. This cannot be, Sartre argues: 'Death is a contingent fact which belongs to facticity; finitude is an ontological structure of the for-itself which determines freedom and exists only in and through the free project of the end which makes my being known to me.' In other words, human reality would remain finite even if it were immortal because 'it *makes* itself finite by choosing itself as human' (698). Freedom and finitude are one and the same.

These considerations, powerfully argued, bring us to a word that takes on an added dimension in Sartre's later publishing career: his collections of essays were called 'situations.' Humankind's relation to the world is described as being in situation. On pages 700–7, he describes fully the seven aspects of 'situation.' In fact, so remarkably clear is the exposition that it could very well be read as a synopsis of his entire argument. Putting an end to the dichotomies that he abandoned in the opening pages, he argues that he is neither subjectivist nor objectivist, neither an advocate of total freedom of the will nor a determinist, neither an idealist nor a realist. Such dualistic principles, as my introduction has argued, are divided only on the level of abstraction; in actuality they are bound together. Our perception is neither subjective nor objective; nor can these two polar terms be effectively joined by a copula. If they are brought together by an *and,* just as surely they can then be severed. Hence the resort to the awkward hyphen, and hyphenated expressions, to indicate the existence in relationship between humankind and objects. Like twins, like our past, they are joined at birth. The same with freedom: there is no freedom independent of constraint, no projection of ends independent of the objects that we seek to circumvent (or accept).

These are thoughts gone over again and again in the body of the text. I would, however, for purposes relevant to this study, isolate two ideas, ideas that enter intrinsically into the nature of the Sartrean thought and his character as well. Sartre is a perfect example of why the Schillerian term *idealist* cannot be applied to figures like Luther, Rousseau – and Sartre. They belong to and constitute in their varied ways the line of radical protestantism, the upsurge of which helped constitute the first dualism of this study. Consequently when Sartre writes, 'There is no privileged situation,' the thought leaps out at us because we have heard it before in Luther and in Rousseau (despite the latter's cosying up to the aristocracy, he always attempted to speak to them as equals, on matters of just and broadly human concern). All bear the burden equally, or are equally responsible for so doing. 'I am an existent in the midst of other existents.' No one can exist for me – except under the painful guise of 'bad faith.' It is even difficult to make comparative judgments between differ-ent situations – 'each person realizes only one situation – his own' (703).

Despite the difficulties presented by some of the consequences of his thought and its later development, one thing shines through with per-fect clarity, and that is the integrity of Sartre's life and thought. Such adherence to ideas in one's conduct differs from idealism, because it does not derive from an abstract ideal, but rather from a condition of existence, a situation. We do not possess, we do not belong. Contingency rules. These are bases of conduct different from those that govern Schiller's idealist. But more importantly, rather than moving beyond the conditions of being, his freedom is bound with condition. There is no such thing as the 'Unbedingte.'

If the 'vrai' cannot stand or be sought by itself, Sartre is not an idealist in the Schillerian sense of the term. But neither is he a realist. Some of his most insightful pages take to task the specifics of the realist's position, this with an understanding in details that would not take second place to Schiller's own. When Sartre dissects the 'esprit de sérieux,' the thought is exciting in its pointed cogency and is further justification of the elabo-rate principles he lays down in *Being and Nothingness.* One is tempted to quote entire swatches of Sartre's brilliant exposition of the qualities of the 'serious' person. 'The serious attitude involves starting from the world and attributing more reality to the world than to oneself. Thus all serious thought is thickened by the world; it coagulates; it is a dismissal of the human reality in favor of the world' (741). We then enter an area of thought that might explain the attitude of the writer of consciousness toward the daemonic. the fear that Carducci suspects, the veering away from one's better self or the contentment with a restricted self: 'It is obvi-ous that the serious at bottom is hiding from himself the consciousness of his freedom; he is in bad faith and his bad faith aims at presenting himself to his own eyes as a consequence; everything is a consequence for him, and there is never any beginning. That is why he is so concerned with the consequences of his acts.' The realist, or serious man, lives in sequence, an external sequence, which then produces consequences – to this limited world and to this view he is bound. In later pages Sartre goes even further. The serious type transfers 'the quality of "desirable" from the ontological structure of things to their simple material consti-tution.' To quote Schiller, the realist wants to know what things are good for (Sartre would never add, as would the idealist, that things are good or true in themselves; the very nature of 'situation' would preclude that).

To conceal the anguish that is at the heart of freedom, Sartre explains, '[The realist] makes himself such that he is waited for by all the tasks placed along his way. Objects are mute demands, and he is nothing in himself but the passive obedience to those demands.' One can think back to Erasmus's enshrinement of his subservient function as a scholar. But there is a type much closer to Sartre's own situation and that is the revolutionary. There is no doubt that in his depiction of Brunet, particularly in *La mort dans l'âme* (known variously in English by the same translator as *Troubled Sleep*, or *Iron in the Soul*) he is showing the Party member as 'serious,' that is, as eliminating all elements of human subjectivity. This tension between subjective consciousness and objective restrictions is constant to Sartre's make-up, and in his later revised thinking in the 1950s he will have an altered viewpoint about the relative weights of each, but the tension will persist.

From these considerations and others, two offensive types appear in the Sartrean roster: the exponents of bad faith and the scoundrels ('salauds'). The first works by inertia, the second by appropriation, yet they are joined here and elsewhere. The one seeks to disguise anguish, the other to bar contingency. The one succumbs to the 'regard' of the other, and becomes the objectified thing-in-itself that the Other establishes. Here 'regard' is seen to be the esteem or estimation of the other and represents Sartrean bad faith. This flaw may be linked to Rousseau's first *Discourse*, where the play-acting of social forms is condemned. With Rousseau it becomes a national contagion, but with Sartre it does not acquire such extent, as he limits it to the failure of independence on the part of individuals. The bad faith people are marked by cowardice, the scoundrels by arrogance (they appropriate their positions in the universe and the subordination of others by converting obligations into prerogatives), but they are both brought before the bar of severe spiritual justice by this fallen-away but representative heir of radical protestantism.

8. Sartre, a Major Novelist

If *Being and Nothingness* stands like a mountain in the middle of Sartre's career, the proof-text of his status as a major philosopher, his remarkable series of novels, *Roads to Freedom*, are the unacknowledged masterpiece, like family jewels rarely displayed, but when shown dazzle in their opulence. Frederick Copleston strove to rescue Sartre the philosopher from charges of dilettantism because he wrote plays and novels.[16] Our charge has been to show the interpenetration of the two, the mutually fructify-ing presence of philosophy and the creative arts in the works of both Sar-tre and Camus.

In Sartre's case one can observe almost immediately the preoccupation with novelistic technique, technique not simply as an adventure in sound, but rather as part of an integrated philosophy, reflective of value, evident in the various essays he wrote at the time about Faulkner, Dos Passos, and others (*Situations I* 7ff., 14ff.), but more importantly in the novels them-selves and the time of their writing, as they straddled the composition and publication of *Being and Nothingness*. Technique reveals morale, and this novelistic series is nothing if not an ethic and a metaphysic for his time. As in *Nausea*, there are elements of autobiography, intensely observed details, as well as lucid consciousness of what is being observed, but now an even more important ingredient, the intervention of historical posi-tioning. By its ever-increasing roster of interspersed and interacting char-acters, *Roads to Freedom* represents a prodigious novelistic advance beyond *Nausea*: Antoine Roquentin may be regarded as a single philosophical exponent, bringing to the discovery of contingency at times a lyricism and despair, but with the major novels one follows the tracks of many characters, with many perspectives and representations of reality.

Given Sartre's obsessive nature as a writer, this later grand series under-went major transformations. The overall title was first to be *Lucifer*, with serious mythical implications but still as a description of his time, where light comes from the Fall, where good comes from evil. The separate instalments had their own titles, 'La révolte,' 'Le serment.' Sartre, that is, had in mind a large series of novels from the beginning – probably some time after 1939. Yet in the actual composition Sartre lived through great moments of doubt and despair about the work before him. On several occasions he writes that he has brought an end to his first volume, only to return to it, remodel, refinish, add lengthy parts of explanation, and then to remove them later (*Œuvres romanesques*, 1894–1911). His correspon-dence from this time is that of an obsessed, relentless, restlessly daemonic writer. Bernard-Henri Lévy has written that if Sartre was a *drogué*, writing was his drug (326). Eventually, he found his topic and his subject, – lib-erty, or freedom itself. He found its location, history, its quest in the lives of the people of his time, and even more than that, the problem of the central consciousness of all three works, Mathieu, who seems to absent himself from history, yet all are by the force of circumstance gradually dragged into the grinding cogs of history: the Spanish Civil War, the

Munich pact, the terrible defeat, Occupation, and imprisonment.

> What are you thinking of? What thinking? What?
> I never know what you are thinking? Think.
> — T.S. Eliot, *The Waste Land*

One of Sartre's notable editors, Michel Contat, presents a paradox. The first instalment in the planned grand cycle is, as he states, 'moins originel' than *Nausea*, yet it represents a massive enlargement by way of character and theme over the first work (*Œuvres romanesques* 1894). This paradox can be explained by the several related demands made upon Sartre as thinker and novelist. As he tells us in the *Prière d'insérer* of the joint publication of *L'âge de raison* (*The Age of Reason*) and *Le sursis* (*The Reprieve*) in 1945, the first's more novelistic technique was adapted to conform to the 'marasme français' of the time, the years 1938–9, when they lived in the sluggish and cloistered moments of an illusory peace that was 'dérisoire' (1912). The traditional form corresponded to the moment. It met another exigency: a faithful depiction of Sartre's own doubts and dilemma in the person of Mathieu, who had failed to historicize himself: 'il ne s'historialise pas' (1909). This latter exigency also helps explain why in the later years (volume 3 appeared only in 1949) he was unable to bring to completion the full cycle: by that time he was a different person, with different perspectives, no longer lending themselves to the interpretations necessary for the years 1938–44. Sartre began by believing himself to be more of a *romancier* than a *philosophe*, but in later years (and letters confirm this) he felt he did not have the powers of invention of a novelist. This perception runs counter to his actual accomplishments, but he was invaded by a need for authenticity, which cut short his career as a novelist. Quite faithful to himself, he may have considered the autobiographical *Les mots* (*Words*) to have been the genuine completion of the contemplated cycle of works. It certainly wrote 'fin.' (His editors suggest that the rightful completion may have been *The Mandarins* – justice here being served because Sartre had given Simone de Beauvoir a 'blank check' to change and correct whatever she found faulty.)

While the actual writing of *Being and Nothingness* did not take place until late 1941 and October of 1942, a letter of 9 December 1939 could very well serve as a short course to that massive tome (*Œuvres romanesques*, 1897). In that letter, he begins by asserting that he has 'achevé [sa] morale.' Slim pickings as far as any offered comfort is concerned, it notably enters into the spiritual rapport of the subsequent novels. In fact, Mathieu in what Sartre calls his 'monologue' (and over which he laboured), more or less recounts the gist of the letter. About to flip a coin and have chance decide whether or not he marries Marcelle, whom he has impregnated, he experiences a sudden revulsion:

> 'No,' he thought, 'no, it isn't heads or tails. Whatever happens, it is by agency that everything must happen.' Even if he let himself be carried off, in helplessness and despair, even if he let himself be carried off like a sack of coal, he would have chosen his own damnation: he was free, free to behave like a fool or a machine, free to accept, free to refuse, free to equivocate; to marry, to give up the game, to drag this dead weight [boulet à pied] about with him for years to come. He could do what he likes, no one had the right to advise him, there would be no Good or Evil for him unless he brought them into being [s'il les inventait]. All around him things were gathered in a circle, expectant, impassive, and indicative of nothing. He was alone, enveloped in this monstrous silence, free and alone, without assistance and without excuse, condemned to decide without support from any quarter, condemned forever to be free. (*Œuvres romanesques* 664–5; *Age of Reason* 320)

Fortunately for the novel such confirmations are few. Sartre's great achievement in this work and those that follow lies in the way he opens himself up to the living reality and unreality of his philosophical prescriptions, which are met head on, and turned to ashes in the mouth. The fabled consciousness is merely exacerbated anguish, stifling boredom, as people of little consequence succeed in making a mash of their lives. Lucidity is shown to be a weapon of mutual antagonism, freedom a farce. Even the title, *The Age of Reason*, which becomes the final words of the work, is nothing more than a sardonic repulsion, as Mathieu realizes his life has been restored to its customary nothingness.

Throughout the series, Mathieu remains the central consciousness; rebel but not revolutionary, he stands between the extremes on the outermost circle of the novel, his brother Jacques and the Communist Party member, Brunet. In subsequent scenes – they are remarkably successful (see chap. 8) – he rejects the conditions under which his brother will give him (not loan) more than the money needed for Marcelle's abortion. His brother sowed his wild oats (the biographical accounting is particularly repellent) and then he settled down, having attained the age of reason. He would provide Mathieu with the necessary funding should he marry Marcelle and give up his anti-bourgeois habits. The novel then swings to the opposite mode, when Mathieu resists the invitation of his former friend, Brunet, to join the Communist Party and thus become a man of conviction. As indicated earlier, for Sartre Brunet as revolutionary incarnates 'l'esprit de sérieux.' His values, unlike those of a true existentialist, are transcendent. History has an absolute and commanding sense of demands. He is a man who requires conviction and thus who liberates himself from the anguish of conscious freedom with very little cost. Making these comments in an interview in 1945, but which jibe with the novel and with discussion of 'l'esprit de sérieux' in *Being and Nothingness*, Sartre shows the conflict between existentialism and the Communist Party.[17] He does allow that there is a way of militancy that is free, but it is not that of Brunet and the Party.

Yet to leave the novel here is hardly to touch its greatness. Camus was so right in claiming that one aspect of Sartre's qualities as a writer of fiction – and the stamp of his greatness – was to push things to their limits. The unruliness of life disrupts the polished declarations of philosophy. At the innermost circle of the novel, Mathieu lives amidst studies in advanced perversity. He is a man of the eighteenth century fallen into the world of *The Possessed*. He is Rousseau's antagonist, Philinthe, fallen into the dire twentieth century, and succumbs to the benumbing and devilish environment. The most remarkable parts of the novel show people in the grips of dimly understood passions, ulterior purposes that guide their steps beyond their knowing. The book is indeed harrowing as we follow the semi-crazed troubles of the Russian siblings, Boris and Ivitch, the one determined not to live past his youth and who is also a cool-handed thief, and his sister, with whom Mathieu believes himself to be in love, but who is also bent on a self-destructive program of drink and despair. They all gather at the dark chambers of the Sumatra, a kind of hellish den. Mathieu, caught up in their wild misfortunes, demonstrates to Ivitch his own gratuitousness by stabbing his hand, and twice returns to the apartment of Lola (believed dead) to first purloin Boris's 'incriminating' letters and then to steal the money needed for Marcelle's abortion. The situations are absurd, the conditions wildly frustrating, and the novelistic telling riveting.

But by far the most startling and spectacular character is Daniel. Here if anywhere the Luciferean tones of the first overall title are residual. He is the dark archangel. For him Mathieu is a Goethe in his Olympian imperturbability, to whose Abel he is willing to play Cain, anticipating the crucial chapter 'Cain' in the still-to-be-written *Saint-Genet*. Yet he too, while possessed, is not in full possession. We know that despite his adopted scorn for the homosexual crowd at the arcade, he will turn up at the address left by his boyish lover. His steps will simply direct him there. He engages in a friendly wrestling match with a young lover, which suddenly turns more violent than he intends when he realizes that Bobby is actually quite strong and might defeat him. Panicked at such a possible defeat, he has to call up all his strength to subdue his opponent. But the point is that Sartre enters the reader fully into the terror and needs of Daniel as a character, even his supposed superiority and the anxiously relieved joy he feels at his hard-earned victory. We follow his first attempt at suicide (castration), knowing it will not succeed. Finally, to gain advantage over the self-composed Mathieu, he returns the stolen money to Lola, just as she is about to bring charges against Boris for theft (she never quite believes, despite his protestations, that Mathieu was the culprit). Daniel saves Mathieu another way, as he has agreed to marry the sluggish Marcelle. Intending to shock, he further announces that he is a homosexual. The shock effect does not work. But what does work is his effacement of Mathieu, who realizes that, unlike himself, Daniel has acted in a way that is irrevocable. That is, he has acted. But this is a marriage made in hell; Mathieu further realizes that Daniel is undertaking this unwonted step in order to become a martyr, to punish himself. It is seen as a product of his unwillingness to accept his own homosexuality. When finally in his ruminations alone Mathieu realizes he has reverted – after his own delirium – to his customary absence, to his nothingness, we have full and personal understanding as to why W.H. Auden referred to the 1930s as a 'low, dishonest decade' (57).

> So here I am, in the middle way, having had twenty years –
> Twenty years largely wasted, the years of *l'entre deux guerres*
> – T.S. Eliot, 'East Coker'

For Sartre, the coming of war brought the first change of attitude, as France moved from a cloistered aesthetic individualism to a generalized mobilization. The frightened and frightening exigencies of this new call are fully represented in the pages of the second instalment, *Le sursis* (*The Reprieve*). The walls of the cloister came tumbling down, as he tells us in the *Prière d'insérer* (1911–12), as all of France is plunged into movement by a generalized alert, where all are being called: called up in several ways, to prepare for war and to give an accounting, to undergo their own individual agonies and to encounter a revelation of who and what they are. There are few books that can compare with Sartre's presentation of the multitude of ways of thinking about Hitler, Germany, France, and the coming of war, especially as the Munich conference is clearly depicted as a grandiose *duperie*. If *Age of Reason*, with its increase of characters and perspectives, represents a distinct advance over *Nausea*, *The Reprieve* represents an explosion of novelistic form, technique, and genius. It is a genuine masterpiece, abounding and astonishing in its inventiveness, its convergence of detailed individual perceptions, of a multitude of characters and episodes, all seamlessly woven together, all wanderers on the same frequency but different by the music they hear. It was originally to be entitled *Septembre*, and it does describe events from 23 September to 30 September 1938, where indeed all is held in suspense. Mobilization has been declared but now instead of a small nucleus of nine or ten characters – those that appeared in *Age of Reason* reappear – there are an additional eighteen characters whose fortunes become just as prominent, added thereto another thirty characters of historical importance and name. For such a new situation Sartre had recourse to a new novelistic technique: the cinematic montage of the 'big screen' and the simultaneity employed by such modernists as Virginia Woolf and John Dos Passos (whom he specifically credits – 1911–12).

While the Munich conferences (the mega-plane covering all) is underway, various governments and people are moved into activity, literally a nation on the move. But Sartre does not wish to emulate Zola (he tells us, 1912) and write of the large crowd, the nation, as a single entity; rather his genius is in giving to each one an individual signification and response, and individual discovery of being. Several elements coalesce here to make this an unquestionable masterpiece: the first is the Sartrean philosophy itself, whereby every existent is responsible for facing up to his own existence – the general mobilization makes it possible to trace the various reactions. The klaxon is general but the response is individualized and required. But in an equally active way the genius of Sartre coincides with what Ortega called 'perspectivismo.'[18] The variant individual readings and realizations have a philosophical relevancy – there is no privileged position, no outside onlooker, as all are called and called upon.

Mathieu remains something of the central consciousness. And it is he who adapts, who refuses to be duped, who recognizes the spuriousness of the peaceful existence between the wars. He had lived as if he had time on his hands, bountiful time, abundant time, where one can sleepwalk through one's life. His is the first awakening.

I had time enough. Time, peace – they were the same. And now the future
lies at my feet, dead. It was a spurious future, an imposture. He contemplated those twenty years, like an expanse of sunlit sea, and now he saw
them as they had been: a finite number of days compressed between two
high hopeless walls, a period duly catalogued with a prelude and an end,
which would figure in the history manuals under the heading: Between the
two wars. Twenty years: 1918–38. Only twenty years! Yesterday it had seemed
both a shorter and a longer period; and, indeed, no one would have
thought to compute it, since it had not ended. Now it had ended. A spurious future. All the experiences of the last twenty years had been spurious.
(*Œuvres romanesques* 807; *The Reprieve* 86)

Mathieu remains the man in the middle, between the 'realists' such as
brother Jacques, who, despite his somewhat intelligent understanding, is
a German sympathizer and a future Vichyist, and the General LaCaze, a
cocksure (*cazzo*), overbearing man who dominates his stepson Philippe,
and including even Gomez, fighting the war in Spain, but also, like Brunet, a man of limited perceptions, and the others, the victims. Just as
Czechoslovakia will be plundered, so are the women: Maud who sleeps
with the captain in order to procure better berthing for the all-female
orchestra; Ivitch, herself, who abhors the young man she sleeps with.
Boris, who in search of a valiant military death will later abandon the age-
ing Lola, and Daniel remains married to Marcelle, while silently admiring the young man in his ken. But so are other characters manhandled
and abused. Sartre depicts the travails of Gros-Louis, the illiterate shep-
herd, fallen upon and beaten by thugs whom he had befriended and
forced to wander aimlessly, not comprehending anything of the conscription that had uprooted him.

It is somewhat futile to attempt a full recapitulation, except to remark
on several of Sartre's abiding novelistic traits, generally assumable under
his talent for pushing things to their limits. First is his description of the
bed-bound Charles, who views everything from his horizontal position.
Being transferred by the likelihood of war to a safer location, he finds
himself in the awkward situation of having desperately to move his bow-
els. Constrained by the presence of a young woman, also bedridden, with
whom he has developed a cordial relationship, he manages to restrain
himself, only to hear her embarrassed defecation (958–9; 252–3). This
has been dismissed as 'potty talk,' but for Sartre it represents a gesture of
humanity, an attempt by Charles to overcome his painful subservience to
the 'verticals.' For him, the coming of peace or war has no meaning. The

urgent call they have answered is the only one they can know. Sartre will always be attracted by the presence of the body and bodily needs, the presence of physiology in the midst of psychology, for which he was abundantly attacked (*Les écrits* 241–2).

Others, like Maud's beau, Pierre, reveal cowardice, of which his girl-friend becomes aware with a subsequent abhorrence. How important is the issue of cowardice for Sartre under the conditions of wartime? He returns to it as a choice again and again: no one is born a hero or a coward. Humans choose themselves alone.[19] Without external reference, not humanism, not realism, not the 'sagesse commune,' or popular understanding, nothing external, but in one's own hands lies the determination of the self. Daniel for his part writes a lengthy letter to Mathieu, wherein he acknowledges their mutual dependency, following the revelation of the prior June. This letter could have been taken from *Being and Nothingness*, except that Daniel acknowledges his subservience to the 'look,' now the all-seeing eye of God. Strangely enough, Mathieu, as a new indication of his pending change, despises the letter, calls it trite, crumples it into a ball, and throws it out of the lowered window (1093–9; 402–8). Such lame paraphrase can only suggest the wide expanse existing between its blunt retelling and the highly attuned and mixed register of reflection and observation that attends each of these many characters whose minds seem to lie open in front of us. Sartre will insist that the criticisms of his novels stems not from the low-life depicted – its 'misérabilisme' – but rather from the lucidity with which self-observation is made, the consciousness of each pertaining to the situation, even when erroneous decisions are made or revealed. They are all swept up and engaged by the new dimension of crisis and war, but none so much as the young reader of Verlaine and Rimbaud, Philippe.

Philippe has been crushed by the overbearing 'realism' of his stern stepfather, General LaCaze, for whom he considers his mother to be nothing more than a hetaera. Under pacifist influences he refuses to observe the call to military duty. His most amazing adventure occurs when, alone in his shabby hotel room, he hears next door the sounds of lovemaking (896–905; 182–94). He brings his ear to the wall to listen to the gasps of ecstasy, as he did in his mother's house. Then not the unexpected but the expected happens. The reader anticipates with uneasy premonition and yet with heightened disbelief what he is going to do. Indeed, he does just that. He exits the room, knocks on the door, and proceeds to denounce the war. The two lovers, known already as Maurice and Zezette – Maurice is a committed proletariat, with distinct anti-Nazi sentiments – are shocked and bewildered. When Philippe suggests that he knows how to procure false identification papers, Maurice ends up slugging him, and the distraught adventures of Philippe are underway. He is threatened by a drunkard when he only begrudgingly toasts 'victory,' he is befriended and cared for by a black prostitute, who tries to 'devirginate' him, and finally he is beaten by a mob for yelling pacifist slogans. At this point Mathieu enters, showing unwonted vigour and capacity for authoritative action by claiming he is an officer of the law and dispersing the crowd. He then spends a happy night with Irene, an acquaintance of Philippe, while the young man finally ends up in jail. His stepfather when summoned wonders why the police did not administer the third degree – obviously approving such treatment.

Finally all, beginning with the Czechs, have to accept their imposed conditions. There is general hilarity in France that the 'peace' conference managed to avoid going to war over Czechoslovakia, but better heads among them – Gomez, the fighter in Spain, knows his cause is lost, and Birnenschatz, the wealthy Jewish businessman who had repulsed his co-religionists in need – feels ashamed. As the separate articles of the agreement are announced, they are spliced with such manifold reactions, including those of Ivitch pained by her enforced sexual act, and of Mathieu who refuses to be duped. Daladier returns home to cheering crowds, to whose mistaken frenzy he can only respond with 'Les cons,' a reference to the female sexual part, language of which Sartre knew him to be capable. War has not been granted a reprieve, only postponed if not in fact guaranteed. For a moment, a week, France was in literal suspension – the true meaning of 'sursis,' but meant philosophically as well as politically, as it is in such 'suspension' that choices are made and personality revealed as betrayal of the self or as its confirmation.

There should be more discussion and debate as to the relative superiority of Sartre as a novelist; after all, he did create remarkable series of works (the most brilliant being *The Reprieve*). The fact is that other interests intervened, external as well as internal, already discernible in the hiatus between the first two parts of the trilogy and the third instalment, which did not appear until 1949. But this brings us to his own development after the war. Sartre's true greatness as a novelist can lead only to speculation as to why he never completed the full cycle, stopping after the third volume, *Troubled Sleep*. It is the one question, the essential question, that brings us directly into contact with Sartre's postwar development, his own personal tensions and requirements, his second conversion, and most assuredly his relations with Camus.

9. Camus: A 'Cabeza clara'

What is really confused, intricate, is the concrete, vital reality, always a unique thing. The man who is capable of steering a clear course through it, who can perceive under the chaos presented by every vital situation the hidden anatomy of the movement, the man ... who does not lose himself in life, that is the man with the really clear head.

– Ortega y Gasset, *The Revolt of the Masses*

The re-emergence of *Caligula* is 1945 is an act of expiation for an entire generation, an admission of intellectual complicity. The work serving as a bridge between the composition of *Caligula* in 1938 and its stage reproduction in 1945 is *Lettres à un ami allemand* (*Letters to a German Friend*), the first two of which were written in 1943 and published clandestinely, the four in their entirety published together only later, after the Liberation (*Essais* 219–43). The letters show Camus's search for values, his need to retrieve some remnants of partial truths as against a total lie, some humane gesture as against murder and destruction.

The table was set by the First World War. France suffered 1.3 million deaths, leaving 600,000 widows and 700,000 orphans. Stalin is reported as having remarked that one death is a tragedy, but a million is only a statistic. As usual, such hard-headed cynicism has its momentary appeal, but is appallingly wrong. Who cannot be moved by such losses? These figures carry with them other casualties, of which Camus was well aware. Writing for *La Tunisie française* in 1941, Camus indicates some of them: 'la décadence européenne, les défaites de l'esprit, la montée des médiocrités, et l'absurdité des existences individuelles' (European decadence, the crushing of the spirit, the ascendancy of mediocrities, and the absurdity of individual lives) (*Essais* 1466). The Germans endured the same crisis, but they took a wrong turn, trusting in the reaches of a militaristic nationalism. Only France among the Continental powers resisted, if only for a time, the varied fascisms within and those that haunted its borders. But its sense of justice, Camus writes in the first letter, and its yearnings for peace ill prepared it for the coming war. But out of defeat and in clandestinity came the realization of why they were obliged to take up the sword, not the naked sword, but the sword girded with some sense of moral purpose. This is a nuance, Camus argues, but an important one (224).

What gives the letters their density of texture is Camus's hallmark of thoughtful complexity as well as his own record of self-incrimination. Both he and the Nazis had fallen victim to the 'tragédie d'intelligence'

(242) that left the way open to nihilism, not that of Bazarov but rather that of Ivan, according to whom everything is permitted (the concept of nihilism like that of humanism has its own changing denotations). Caligula was rampant, and Camus concedes that he, like his intellectual generation, had shared in this malady. 'Vous n'avez jamais cru au sens de ce monde et vous en avez tiré l'idée que tout était équivalent et que le bien et le mal définissait selon ce qu'on voulait' (You have never believed that the world made sense and you derived from that the notion that everything was of equal value and that good and evil depended only on what meaning you wished to give them) (240). Only to add, 'Et à la vérité, moi qui pensais comme vous ... ' (And in truth, I who thought like you ...). This is not only the world of Caligula, they are also the words of Caligula and help explain the verve that Camus was able to invest in that horrendous character of such dramatic force. But now Camus's task is different: the Nazis have forced the French to enter into history (241), to extract some sense from existence, to engage in an act of self-definition and retrieve some moral being. 'We' are not like 'you' becomes the defining moral refrain, one that was reduced to some silence when years later 'they' had become like 'them.'

In this sense the *Letters to a German Friend* mark the dramatic entrance of history and some morality into Camus's philosophy. He might not know Truth, but he does know truths, because he can detect and detest lies, and murder, rampage, the belief in force are lies. 'Voici notre force qui est de penser comme vous sur la profondeur du monde ... mais en même temps de avoir sauvé l'idée de l'homme au bout de ce désastre d'intelligence et d'en tirer l'infatigable courage des renaissances' (Our force is here to think like you about the [depths of being], but at the same time at the end of this disaster of intelligence to retrieve some idea of humanity and to draw from it the inexhaustible courage for rebirth) (243). He does not revoke his philosophy concerning the 'profondeur du monde,' his philosophy of the absurd, which he shares with the Germans but now he knows what must be saved. One could say that Camus is divided between Voltaire and German existentialism, between a philosophy that abhors nihilism and one that embraces it. Finally, like Voltaire, he speaks on behalf of a culture of Europe, its accomplishments and its bequests, as against a destructive nihilism. As usual his thought is nuanced, as he seeks out a 'juste équilibre' (237). The Nazis would have him choose Faust over Quixote, Siegfried over Hamlet, figures of force and will over characters of dreams and deliberation (the figures that Turgenev severed are here recombined), but Camus sees the need to fuse the divided pairs.

All things are not equivalent: moral discriminations can be made. In this sense the four letters represent crucial stepping stones along the way of Camus's own moral progress. And of course he is not writing only for himself but as the conscience of a nation, who itself is in need of rejuvenation, of rediscovery of its intrinsic moral roots that the direst of experiences was only too ready to reveal. Up against it, that nation saw into its errors. But for Camus the same standards of judgment that he had displayed in arguing against the Nazis will, with small modification, be used against the soon-to-be-dominant Marxist and Communist Left. In the midst of this change, he was one of the few who managed to keep what Ortega called a 'cabeza clara.'

It borders on calumny to accuse Camus of being a 'dabbler' in philosophy. The error seems to stem from the assumption that only technical or systematic philosophy is genuine thought. And indeed, such systematic thought as practised by Aquinas, or Descartes, or Hegel, or Heidegger, or Sartre is majestic and should not be discounted. The fault lies in the exclusionary term *only*, and the demotion of moral philosophy allied with a vivid literary imagination. One can turn to another work, *Ni victimes ni bourreaux* (*Neither Victims nor Executioners*) to recognize the fallacy of this restriction (*Essais* 331–52). In these small essays, first appearing in *Combat*, from 11 November through 30 November 1946, one can see the profundity of Camus's thinking, the clarity of his understanding of his actuality, but even more importantly his prescience. He fulfils Joyce's description of the true artist: he is the historian of the future.

Four selections from *Neither Victims nor Executioners* show Camus's astonishing anticipation of ideas that in some fifty years would become widely accepted, even popular. And this is because the germs of their growth lay already in the world that the end of World War II was developing. These momentous ideas are (1) fear as a technique, (2) the acceleration of historical change and its consequences, (3) the end of ideology, and (4) the clash of civilizations.

It is perhaps the first that needs greatest explication, because Camus is not simply writing of fear, fear of some horrendous happening, but rather of fear as a technique, that is a mechanism, an installation, a way of muzzling discourse. The method is that of stigmatization, of branding what is out of step with the dominant ideology. Unlike the 1930s when Left and Right went at it with full force and fury, much to the detriment of the struggling Third Republic, the period after the war witnessed the discrediting of the Right and the ascendancy to intellectual domination of the Left and the far Left. The taint of the Vichyist and the collaborators became an intellectual weapon of de-legitimization, to such an extent that Raymond Aron could be called a 'fascist,' and any attack on the Soviet Union regarded as aiding and abetting the enemy. This is the gag rule as a mechanism that Camus deplores. Any independent thought that questioned the role of violent revolution or the appeal of the USSR was quickly placed out of bounds ('insulté, trahi' – 334). It was thus out of fear that voices of dissent were silenced, and fear could justly be described as a 'technique,' that is as a social mechanism (332). Such a stifling atmosphere can only be offensive to a man like Camus, so given to intellectual justice, a man of exemplary reason, and a voice for rational discourse. The laudable victors in the Second World War in their turn became part of a non-violent but just as effective system of oppression. That is, they failed to evolve, they failed to use the same instruments that Camus applied in his previous *Letters* to the new situation they confronted. In the midst of changed circumstances Camus thought his way through to a position of extraordinary intellectual clarity.

We are always prepared to fight employing the methods and mentality of the previous war, but history has a way of outpacing thought. This truism rankled more in France after the crushing defeat of May 1940. Saying more than this, Camus insists that in our time the acceleration of history has sped up to a degree that was unknown in the past. Two new factors emerge here: the first is the nuclear age and the second is globalization. He does not use the latter phrase, but to the ordinary concepts of political transnationalism he adds economic factors. Borders are of little account. Coffee from Brazil is drunk in Europe, American manufactured parts are used in Siberia. Not only are national frontiers silly politically (his example is that separating France and Italy), they have been superseded economically. One singular consequence is that revolution is outmoded, *dépassé*. Violent revolution is a vestige from the past, where the relatively low number of casualties could in some small way justify the means. In the globalized world of the second half of the twentieth century, on whose verge he stands, in this interconnected bipolar world, revolution could not be isolated in one country and would accelerate to a nuclear catastrophe, the consequence of which could not possibly justify the means. (He was writing before the implosion of the USSR and the relatively peaceful liberation of its client states.) Marx's program for revolution is a thing of the past, an element of archaeology (however much Camus values Marxist analysis as a critical tool).

This leads to the third thought, the end of ideology ('la fin des idéologies' – 338), which Francis Fukayama in his widely misunderstood book has called *The End of History.* Absolute utopias, Camus argues, bear the means of their own undoing – they are too costly. Once again, ends do not justify means, hence they are undone by their own inner logic. The same intellectual procedures by which in *Letters to a German Friend* he was able to denounce a nihilism based upon power, a nihilism with no goal, now are utilized under different circumstances to refute Stalinist Marxism. The one was based upon Ivan's arguments that if there is no God then everything is permitted, and the other upon the adopted absolutism of the Hegelian processes of history (while giving them a meaning Hegel never intended). But there is another evolving characteristic at work and that is Camus's disenchantment with grandiosity, or any messianism. His realization that the genuine fallacy of both Right and Left is their willingness to go all the way, their pursuit of a thought to its absolute limits. The better utopia might be a more modest utopia. At least it will be less costly. One notes that throughout he does not forsake his position as man of the Left, as an aspirant for a lesser form of utopia, but even such modest criticism did not succeed in dampening the ire of the fully committed, which should tell us, as the argument of dualisms implies, that there is much more involved than surface appearances.

With far-reaching insight, Camus argues that even the pressing conflict between the United States and the USSR (certainly on everybody's mind) is on its way to becoming secondary. The 'choc d'empires' will be replaced by the far more dangerous 'choc des civilisations.' From his deep familiarity with the Muslim world, Camus had already experienced the spectre of Islamic fundamentalism – one of the reasons why later he would not favour Algerian independence. But the threat is even greater than that: 'Dans dix ans, dans cinquante ans, c'est le prééminence de la civilisation occidentale qui sera remise en question' (Within ten, fifty years it is the pre-eminence of Western civilization that will be called into question) (345). Such prophecy staggers one with its accuracy. Camus is the sort of thinker who, by his commitment to exemplary reason, is thought to be wrong in his time but usually turns out to be right.

The new detectable change in his thought is toward greater restraint, modesty, more limited solutions, more circumspect antidotes and responses. Indeed he has become the author of *The Plague* that Sartre with his usual acumen and understanding described so well in a *Vogue* article of 1945, where he makes Camus the representative figure of the new generation of writers in France, those who unlike their predecessors have entered into history, but who write with a clarity, modesty, and restraint.[20] Camus's great mentor Ortega y Gasset called for a return to the classical world of finitism, of limit, and of 'measure.' One could say that in the next three works (again in triplicate), *The Plague, Just Assassins*, and *The Rebel*, Camus follows in this very pathway cleared by Ortega. But his erstwhile allies felt this to be not a confirmation but a defection, particularly the last-named work, and this brought to the fore all the hidden animosities that are lurking in any dualism.

Like most of Camus's (and Sartre's) works, *The Plague* underwent a complex and lengthy birthing. The ideas perhaps occurring as early as 1939, Camus actually began writing in 1941, but the work was not finished until 1946 (and that 'difficilement' as its Pléiade editor, Roger Quilliot, reminds us – *TRN* 1935–43). War was declared in September 1939; France occupied in May 1940. *The Stranger* was completed in 1941, and published in 1942, followed by *The Myth of Sisyphus* in 1943. Such overlapping accounts for the several layers of the novel. Rather than only roughly determinate, the very first sentence in an earlier version is much more specific as to the time and events: 'en 1941, pendant la deuxième guerre mondiale' (in 1941, during the Second World War) (1943). Such phrasing was excised in the final version in the interests of mythic generality. While Camus's adopted style is that of an objective chronicler utilizing a descriptive astringency, the story is multi-layered, covering many aspects of experience, reflecting the times in which it was written. Yes, the plague is the Nazi Occupation, as he corrects Roland Barthes in an important letter of 1955 (*TRN* 1973–5). The novel reflects the point zero of absurdity that Camus had reached in both *The Stranger* and *The Myth of Sisyphus*, but it also represents an important advance beyond those positions (while still absorbing them). In the same letter he marks the difference between the two stages, from 'la révolte solitaire' to a community, to solidarity and participation. But despite the novel's evident 'advances,' his contemporaneous remarks concerning *The Stranger* and *The Plague* reveal how inextricably involved they are one with the other, and that the latter is just as much a picture of the absurd as is the former. The first chapter of the second book was printed under the Occupation in 1943, and it tells of exile and separation, of all being prisoners, of all being condemned. While not denying the historical, it rises to the universal, the second all-important wing of the mythic presentation. And thirdly, in perhaps its most appealing and honest parts, describing events similar to those experienced at the time of the Liberation, Camus writes at his most affective of the difficulties of return, of the strangeness of inevitably attending reunion, and even of its failures, and then with the reserve that marked his own silence on his own activities, the regret for all those who died silently and bravely and were never to come back. While this third and most appealing feature does not deny the advocacy of community and participation, it certainly introduces another sombre ghost-like figure, the figure of remorse and regret, and even better, affection for those who did not survive.

The recourse to myth and the somewhat strict adherence to the objective style of the chronicler permits all these layers to co-exist, not so much as intercalations but rather as currents and counter-currents, as waves and undertows. Its naturalistic description of the development of the plague, its technical language, the changing attitudes of the government and the populace are engrossing. It has a remarkable list of characters: the profiteer Cottard; Grand, the hermetic poet; Rambert, who protests that he 'belongs' to another city, that he has a true 'patrie' that is elsewhere and who refuses to accept the absurdity of the human condition where everybody is an exile; Paneloux, the priest whose second sermon reveals a theologian come to the either/or moment of crisis theology; Tarrou, the aspirant saint; and Rieux, himself, who is finally revealed to be the chronicler. What is remarkable is that whatever their eccentricities and errant ways, no one, not the ludicrous Grand, not the would-be escapee Rambert, not Paneloux, not even Cottard, who eventually goes mad, not the judge Othon, no one is finally rejected. All are brought back into the fold, all contribute and participate unto the death. In this Camus is most like Erasmus, with an inability to exclude, and most unlike Sartre, for whom human relations begin in conflict, and who finally divided the world in Manichean fashion.

Yet despite these qualities and its remarkable commercial success, both at its time of publication and its later 'pocketbook' reissuing, *The Plague* remains a work of mixed appeal and disappointment. It is oddly uncaptivating in both its medium and message. The novel has many virtues except the novelistic. Conor Cruise O'Brien refers to it as 'a sermon in the form of a fable' (49). Even Camus's biographer, Olivier Todd, refers to it as 'carré et didactique' (760). Its method of presentation is classical, with a series of characters from Grand, to Cottard, to Paneloux, to Tarrou who enter offering alternative solutions to a problem. Yet there is very little dramatic interaction between them; thus the novel is message-centred, deriving its meaning from declarations rather than from actions and interactions. But the fault is greater: being message-centred and too dependent upon outright declaration, it is too subservient to the author's will. It lacks the spiritual energy, the independent swell of incremental actions that both withstand and surpass the author's intentions. In this novel Camus did not write better than he knew; he knew all too well what he intended to say, and the novel is laboured because of that.

As for the message, it is a noble ethic that provides no solution. Small steps, modest day-to-day commitment is preferable to reigning dreams of grandiosity, but the plague of the Occupation was not defeated by small steps but rather by massive interventions and enormous sacrifices by the armies of the USA and the USSR. Moreover, the plague as pestilence was not removed from the West but by the remarkable discoveries and antidotes of medical research and science. Gaëtan Picon detects similar deficiencies when he writes of the 'modest means of response' that the novel seems to advocate (150–1). It is not only that the message of *The Plague* is over-determined, subject to simple declaration; it is too meagre, too unchallenging and lacking in the larger formulations that characterized *Neither Victims nor Executioners*. *The Plague* lacks the generative intellectual energy of this work, its prophetic genius. So too, compared to that much larger work, already underway at least in essay form, it lacks the insight and central urgency of *The Rebel*, where the general principles of a new plague are unmasked. Even Germaine Brée, Camus's most sympathetic (and insightful) critic, expresses some dissatisfaction when she suggests the novel only inadequately answers the questions it raises: 'The real question then lies beyond the book itself. The Oran plague leaves the real problem unsolved' (220).

The Plague will and should continue to be read: it attains some greatness in its depiction of the patient stoicism of Rieux's mother (Camus always found an anchor in reality in the memory of his own mother, repeated in the tolerance of Tarrou), and its general sense of affection that widens the circle of inclusion. It will also be read as a tribute to the dead, to those brave individuals who died courageously and silently in the Resistance. But its 'grand theme,' as Camus himself has told us, is 'separation,' a book of remorse and true understanding of the conditions of those who came back to disjointed relationships, to mediocre reunions, only to realize that the time of exile and separation is irreparable (*TRN* 1941, 1957). Later, historians were obliged to recognize what Camus knew at the moment, that the Liberation (which, going beyond the Occupation, became the eventual concourse of the novel) brought 'tears of joy and despair.' Under the inevitable pressures of human events and the frailties of humanity itself, love does not last. Romantic possession is overcast. And this brings us to the true theme of this work and future works as well: given the human condition, irreparable and sterile, the real need is for forgiveness.

While it requires being taken out of phase, *Le premier homme* (*The First Man*), Camus's last work, the one he was carrying with him when he died so tragically in the automobile accident and which was published posthumously, best enters into and explains this grand theme and much more besides. Among the many revealing notations appended to the novel, Camus informs us as to why his work is one of recovering the past, of redeeming it, of saving from the faceless silence of eternity the people he knew and loved. 'Rescue this poor family from the fate of the poor, which is to disappear from history without a trace. The Speechless Ones. They were and they are greater than I' (300). A double prong of affliction enters into Camus's enterprise. These people who he is intent on saving from nothingness will never be able to read or understand his work, except in the sense of his being the person who managed to escape, who 'made good.' The book is dedicated to his mother, who will never be able to read it, and written for a father who cannot. And to add to the pain, in order to write the books, he must alienate himself from that world (while it never leaves him). Camus faces the classic dilemma of the second-generation immigrant intellectual. Indeed, one can call *The First Man* an American novel. Alienation from all he holds dear is the price to be paid for his engaging in the works of rescue. He adds a note to himself on page 133, 'but are they after all aliens? (no, he was the a).' And as it were trying out a first line, 'I am going to tell the story of an alien' (304). But alienation carries with it the conviction of betrayal; recuperation of the past is not only a large-scale rescue work, it is in search of personal vindication, of forgiveness for what has he had to do, the path of his life, for which neither they nor he is responsible. He wishes to stand before them all and ask for mercy. 'No, I am not a good son: a good son is one who stays put. I've traveled far and wide, I've betrayed her with trivialities, with fame, a hundred women' (316). The most fixing figure in his family portraits is his mother, who quietly in her semi-deaf but observant world sits rocking by her window 'like an ignorant Myshkin. She does not know Christ's life, except on the cross. But who is closer to it?' (301). Behind the worlds that Meursault and Tarrou represent, it is not too difficult to discern the abiding figure of this mother, who has the dominant hold on Camus's imaginative and emotional life.

A father whom he never knew and whom he thinks he has abandoned (yet in this genealogical pilgrimage he is seeking out the traces of his life), a mother whom he has betrayed (here his notorious Don Juanism comes into play) – these sources of guilt swarm in his mind. The fortunate fall, or the ruinous success came about by his entrance to the lycée. The pathos of his early schooling, his adoption by his instructor M. Bernard (Louis Germain), his extra tutoring so that he and four of his classmates could pass the lycée entrance exam, their eagerness to learn, possessed of all the innocence of immigrant children, their proud acceptance of corporal punishment, all make of these pages what Todd must have had in mind when he called the unfinished novel staggering. Yet at the same time, the entrance into the lycée is a fatal choice of uprooting. When years later in 1945 Louis Germain calls on his favourite son in Paris, he is acknowledged as the man who has launched him in his career, and who took 'on himself alone the responsibility for uprooting him so that he could go on to still greater discoveries' (159).

The First Man is a tragically uncompleted novel of a life tragically cut short. One can say all one wants about the quality of life rather than the quantity of years, or that his tuberculosis precluded any lengthy life, but here is one reader who regrets enormously that the original plan of bringing *The First Man* up into the 1950s was never fully achieved. Sartre was right to lament that he would on every issue now only wonder what Camus would have thought. Unfinished as it is, *The First Man* reads remarkably well. It also has another great virtue that only the most penetrating works possess: it provokes recollection in the reader. This is journey of guilt and abandonment, of restoration and forgiveness that is a shared journey.

Camus has mapped out for us the logic and schematics of his works in triplicate. The three works under the rubric of the absurd lead into the next trio where 'la révolte' is dominant. And while he is keen to mark the intellectual advances that the one grouping makes over the other, he is also aware of their overlapping and interpenetration. He was the master of his own intertextuality, and for good reasons: like all great writers, Camus is his own best reader.

Among the second threesome of kindred works, *The Rebel*, Camus's own favourite, has all the qualities of a masterpiece (*Essais* 1629). It has aphoristic flair, with leaps of interpretative skill that validate the literary, moral, and philosophical imagination; it possesses the electric charge produced when art and culture, politics and philosophy are combined to address the realities of one's time. It has one further quality that makes it a chef-d'œuvre: it brings together and summarizes most of his previous works. Such masterful self-address accounts for the pleasure that Camus took in writing *The Rebel* (unlike the painstaking labour of *The Plague*).

Ease is cause of wonder. Earlier and later works are brought back or anticipated. The story as well as the moral of *Just Assassins* is rendered in the chapter 'Fastidious Assassins.' Tarrou's hatred of state-sponsored execution is found in the Marquis de Sade, and Camus's lifelong captivation by Ivan Karamazov is relived in this metaphysical rebel, who speaks to God as an equal, who does not deny God, but rather his creation, who returns his ticket if it means the death of an innocent child, but who, while condemning the executioner, is an accomplice to the murderer. Clamence is already present in the misguided century, 'the century of justice and ethics, in which every one indulges in self-recrimination,' the century 'where nothing is pure' (543; 135).

Yet the major engagement is with his own starting point, 'the error of a whole period of history' (419; 9), and what was for him presented by the major question of suicide in an absurd universe. Here he explains more fully than he did even in *The Myth of Sisyphus* why suicide is no solution, why the absurd is involved in an untenable contradiction but why, at one level, it is at least superior to the new logic of murder justified by the rationale of ideology. Ringing pronouncements are Camus's gift. He writes with the insight of an imaginative artist, not as a historian or a sociologist. He does not seek to cover all bases, but rather to analyse the dominant passion, the issue that is in play. And this he grabs by the jugular.

In the period between the wars, the revealing issue was suicide, but it was rejected as a non-solution. It represented a forfeit, a refusal to show up for the game, as he explains more fully here: 'The final conclusion of absurdist reasoning is ... the repudiation of suicide and the acceptance of the desperate encounter between human inquiry and the silence of the universe. Suicide would mean the end of this encounter, and absurdist reasoning considers that it could not consent to this without negating its own premises' (415; 6). Moreover, there is a discrepancy between suicide and the new logic of rational murder. Suicide kills oneself and spares the other; rational murder (except in the dubious case of the 'just assassins') kills the other and spares the self. The absurd universe suggests (as Meursault discovers) a commonality in the fate of the human condition. Absurdist thought cannot yield to absolute negation, and suicide cannot be its logical outcome. Therefore the first step of absurdity can only be that – a first step, a point of departure (417; 8).

If suicide does spare the other, because it too is nihilistic it has no intellectual grounds for doing so. This is accomplished by 'la révolte' – which I shall continue to use here rather than the translation 'rebellion,' because the French phrase implies more of an uprising of consciousness rather than a specific kind of action. In clear determined thought Camus explains why 'la révolte' provides what the world of absurdity cannot do, and that is a limit to human action; it is able to construct and construe a value in existence, a line beyond which humans should not pass. It reintroduces the 'ought' and 'ought not' into the lexicon of despair and nihilism. Here I argue that Camus's thought is more acute than Sartre's. While it is admirable that Sartre feels that every human action should be regarded as a potential model for all of humankind, this remains on the level of assertion and declaration rather than deriving from the logic of his thought; indeed, it does not seem to follow from his own premises of interpersonal conflict.[21] With Camus, however, there is a plausible logical consistency in his development and defence of the establishment of value, for oneself and for others.

When the slave says no, he reaches the limit of his endurance, beyond which he cannot go. This no is a simultaneous yes, that is a yes to a common code, a point of inviolability that remains good for himself as well as for others. This is a 'negative progressive,' not a dialectic but a no that progresses to an affirmation, or yes for humankind. There is a nature in himself that is shared by other human beings; its violation gives rise to protest, and in this protest there is recognition of a source of value, and that is intellectual justice. One knows when a wrong has been committed; consequently one has some inkling of the right; one can detect a lie, therefore one knows there are truths. This forms the basis of a new moral code of the 'negative progressive,' born out of 'la révolte' that escapes from the conundrum of the absurd and its ghost of nihilism:

> In the absurdist experience, suffering is individual. But from the moment when a movement of rebellion occurs, suffering is seen as a collective experience. Therefore the first progressive step for a mind overwhelmed by the strangeness of things is to realize that this feeling strangeness is shared with all men and that human reality, in its entirety, suffers from the distance that separates it from the rest of the universe. The malady experienced by a single man becomes a mass plague. In our daily trials rebellion plays the same role as does the 'cogito' in the realm of thought: it is the first piece of evidence. But this evidence liberates the individual from his solitude. It extends its first value to the whole human race. 'Je révolte, donc nous sommes' (I rebel, therefore we exist). (*Essais* 432; *The Rebel* 22)

This paragraph exquisitely condenses Camus's own evolution up to that point, from *The Stranger* to an understanding of *The Plague* on a more universal scale. It also disallows the charge of a 'rupture' existing between *The Myth of Sisyphus* and *The Rebel* brought by Roger Grenier.

Camus's large concerns are focused on the realities of his time, and the most prominent is nihilism. Nihilism establishes the morbid connection between rational historical terror and irrational historical terror; it joins Nazi and Stalin, concentration camps and gulags. After all, Caligula who is 'encore vivant,' can declare, 'I am the plague.' The material indifference, the lack of spiritual being, of guiding spirit, that was the malady joining Camus with the excesses of his time, is indeed such nihilism. If all things are of equal value and all are eminently disposable, what does it matter – except in the interests of statistics – if 10,000 or 10,000,000 beings are taken from the earth? The sands of the desert, the bottom of the sea can, like history, easily accommodate such losses. Cosmic despair joins with historical necessity to contrive the calculus of death. History itself can stifle any voice of protest or outrage. Camus reaches here his greatest measure as a moralist, yes, a Voltaire who similarly detected in the theodicies justifying the Lisbon earthquake a fatalism that smacked of nihilism. In such larger cosmic or historical perspectives nothing seems to rise up to the level of life-sustaining value.

Critics of *The Rebel* have been either blind or blindfolded. They miss the caveats and cautions, the statements of purpose that Camus has laid down indicating his intentions. 'The pages that follow,' he writes in his introduction, 'present certain historical data and a working hypothesis. This hypothesis is not the only one possible; moreover it is far from explaining everything.' He then prescribes his qualified intent: 'But it *partly* explains the direction in which our times are heading and almost entirely explains the excesses of our age. The astonishing history evoked here is the history of European pride' (420; 9–10). Despite the caveats, the boldness is apparent. Camus is at great pains to explain that he is not writing as a professional scholar. Nor does he, as worthy academic might do, try to give a full picture of an author's thought. For example, his descriptions of Rousseau and Hegel are limited to the uses to which their works have been put by later writers. Although Camus informs us in a footnote (523; 114) that Rousseau abhorred violence, Rousseau's 'general will' was exploited by Saint-Just as a means for quelling factionalism (disagreement?) and as an excuse for mass executions. The same applies to his reading of Hegel, who would have been mortified at the uses to which his own dialectical historicism had been put by the Hegelians of the Left. Such openly stated prescribed limitations, that this is a moral-philosophical essay, did not prevent criticisms that he avoids the socio-economic developments, the historical infrastructures, that his reading of particular authors (notably Marx) is one-sided.

Other criticisms of the work – that it found favour with the Right and that is was written in an elegant style – border on the ludicrous. He answered both of these objections with panache. The first went against Camus's sense of intellectual justice as well as the testimony of his senses and spirit of observation. 'On ne décide pas de la vérité d'une pensée selon qu'elle est à droite ou à gauche ... Si, enfin, la vérité me paraissait de la droite, j'y serais' (The truth of a statement does not depend on whether it is from the Left or the Right ... If finally the truth seemed to be coming from the Right, I would be with them) (Todd 562). The need for labels does not constitute access to truth.

When they touched on the elegance of his style, his critics troubled a sore point. While Camus boldly answered that his antagonists certainly did not mean to reserve style for the Right and that men of the Left were confined to 'gibberish and jargon' (563), obviously a greater sensitivity is involved here. As Roger Grenier, in certainly one of the more insightful books about Camus, reminds us, literature was for him the 'humble enfant de Belcourt, né dans une famille d'illettrés' (the poor kid from the Belcourt slums, born into a family of illiterates), a world of which he had always dreamed and one he had feared to be inaccessible. For him, Gide was the guardian of the 'jardin où j'aurais voulu vivre' (the garden where I always wanted to live) (9–10). To take away this garden was to take away his life, and would be, as it was for Erasmus, to consign him to a second orphanhood in time.

He was warned by both Jean Grenier and Albert Beguin that his work would make enemies (as he had anticipated – see Todd 544, 556). The book was embattled from the start – he had manhandled some sacred cows: the French Revolution and Saint-Just as being forerunners to Lenin, thus bringing together 1789 and 1917, and also implicating Rimbaud and the surrealists (leading to many counterblasts from Breton, with whom however he sought to patch things up). But it was mainly from the Left that the most enduring hostility derived and final rupture with Sartre took place.

That the attacks came vociferously from the Left was to be expected. *The Rebel* fell afoul the dogmatism of the bipolar intellectual stations. The argument runs something like this: if you attack those whom we support, you must be of the Right, and if you are of the Right you must be wrong. Then there was the 'technique of fear,' of which he wrote so perceptively, the very silence that it imposed certifying the hegemony of the Left. It would be awhile before the anti-Communist Left or others would remove the cloth over their eyes and have the courage to denounce, as

Camus was among the first to do, the totalitarianism of the Left. Todd reminds us that *The Rebel*, while contemporaneous with works of Orwell or Popper, was quite alone in France, antedating by four years Aron's *L'opium des intellectuels* and by many more J.-F. Revel's *La tentation totalitaire* (553). Camus had the courage to follow his own insights, a commitment to untrammelled rational discourse, and an openness to new realities. A fidelity to the testimony of his senses liberated him from the blinding *partis pris* and the demagoguery of epithets. Moreover, despite the warnings and his own anticipations, he had the courage to stand alone. As Ronald Aronson attests, in one of the fairest and most balanced discussions of *The Rebel*, 'He was willing to fly alone into the storm, indeed, to provoke a storm, in order to say what he regarded as true, in order to produce and legitimize the alternative that no one else was advocating. It was a strength that Sartre, for all his genius, lacked: the ability to stand alone politically' (125).

Greater reasons and hidden tensions, however, are at work within such dualisms. While Sartre may be compared to Rousseau in his intransigence and his refusal to be beholden, along with many other qualities, it was Camus who endured Rousseau's fate of being badly misunderstood and then even ostracized by the *bien-pensants* and others of his day. In both *Neither Victims nor Executioners* and *The Rebel* Camus makes it clear that he was opposed to the 'formal' virtue of bourgeois society, a virtue of form that conceals deep injustices and inequities. In the remarkable chapter 'State Terrorism and Irrational Terror,' he exposes the underlying, spiritual malaise of Fascism. In the next two chapters he performs the same service for Marxism-Leninism. This is quite similar to the Profession of Faith of the Savoyard vicar, where Rousseau's clear attack on the principles of revelation and miracle (so praised by Voltaire) is followed by a denunciation of the dogmatism of the *philosophes*. Camus's even-handedness establishes an equivalency where his erstwhile allies had expected a preference, and in the demands of the times, a choice. Such behaviour on the part of a presumed ally smacks of betrayal, and in fact, Camus, like Rousseau before him, was denounced as a renegade, as a defector.

This psychological motivation explains why, throughout this study, true warfare, a true dualism exists not between conservative and liberal but between those who had been in the vanguard and those who turned to criticize it, between rebel reformer and revolutionary. We can further see that the detractors had misread their man, they had the wrong expectations. What a full chronological study shows is that this was not a sudden turnaround: the bases were there all the while, even in *The Stranger.* Going back beyond that work, as *The First Man* explains, they were already present in the needs for restoration and recovery, which the alienated outsider experienced, and which made of Camus an even closer partner in tribulation with Rousseau. The very depth of the misunderstanding leads us to affirm that indeed we are dealing here with two kinds of temperaments, with two intellectual nations, whose clashes are imminent and eminent, whose differences can never be reconciled, but are simply waiting the occasion for the more fundamental causes of their rupture to break out.

10. Sartre of the Antinomies   ·

It was bound to happen, what with Sartre's notorious statement that only violence can bring an end to violence, his strongly determined antis: anti-bourgeois, anti-colonialism, anti-racism, anti-Anglo-Saxons, virulent anti-anti-communism, and breaking through all his inability to live in contradiction, his daemonic need for conversion. There are trajectories of the life and of the works. He himself indicates in *Words* what the climactic changes in his life were, adding dates to the historical compilation: the defeat of 1870–1, which the later young aspirant warrior was determined to avenge and from which he would bring back to his country its lost provinces and thereby attain his lasting imaginary glory; the death of his father, which ambiguously both liberated him and deprived him of the determined self that he had always wished to be, and that he always envied in others; the coddled childhood, and the painful humiliation of not being allowed into the other children's games in Luxembourg garden; the painful separation brought about by the remarriage of his mother; his difficult years as a student in La Rochelle and the damaging hurt to his pride when he found himself to be considered 'ugly'; the incarceration as a prisoner of war, where he acquired that sense of what he had never possessed, 'l'adhérence,' or a sense of belonging to a group of men; and in 1952 his break with Camus and the composition of *Communistes et la paix*, that is, as *Words* will tell us his decision to choose between *les mots* and *les choses*, to make the choice for political activism. But for the moment, despite the completed lines of his trajectory, the great Sartre was the Sartre of the antinomies, of the complex ambivalences, of the moral equivalencies. This Sartre is the great Sartre because it provides an embattled portrait of himself, in interview, essay, drama, and novel form, and is not a projection of whom he would have liked to have been, a Saint-Genet, outlaw, pederast, thief, a person who always seems to be one, always himself, a person who authenticates himself. Instead he writes as the bourgeois intellectual, torn by his own antinomies, but clear as to his purpose; he is the bourgeois intellectual, the writer of 1947 who takes history by the throat because history has forced itself upon him and his generation, and who must not choose his age, but choose himself within his age.

One obvious starting point in tracing Sartre's intellectual development might well be the lecture of 1945, published as *Existentialism Is a Humanism*. Equally well one might consider the contemporaneous (October 1945) 'Presentation' to the inaugural issue of *Les temps modernes*.[22] But both works shrink in comparison with the lengthy last section of *Qu'est-ce que la littérature?* (*What Is Literature?*) called 'Situation de l'écrivain en 1947' (The Situation of the Writer in 1947) and buttressed by the third section 'Pour qui écrit-on?' (For Whom Does One Write? – *Situations II* 202ff., 116ff.). These essays show the full complexity of Sartre's awareness, his far-reaching insight, his combined qualities of hard lucidity and passionate hope. They bring back into consideration his previous works; as it were, combining *Nausea* with *Being and Nothingness* and *The Reprieve*, these essays require many rereadings and are themselves provocations to meditation. In comparison to them, the lecture is a bald manifesto, its anguish, forlornness, and despair showing little personal involvement. In the later essays he removes these 'moments' from the show window and places them in the lived context of Resistance fighters, who are compelled to be their own witnesses and are forced to choose: 'l'angoisse commence pour un homme et le délaissement et les sueurs de sang, quand il ne peut avoir d'autre témoin que lui-même; c'est alors qu'il boit la calice jusqu'à la lie, c'est à dire qu'il éprouve jusqu'au bout sa condition de l'homme' (anguish and forlornness, even sweating blood, begins for a man when he stands alone as his sole witness; then he drinks the chalice to the dregs and feels to the limits his condition as a man) (250). The essay abounds in such profoundly felt moments that are real-life translations of the formulae of the lecture. Similarly, the 'Presentation' is a work of defiant, bristling militancy (Cohen-Solal has called the lecture a 'vulgarized abridgement' of *Being and Nothingness* and the introductory piece, a declaration of war – 285, 257). One has only to compare its understanding of the Enlightenment, a rather staid depiction of an unqualified belief in the universality of human nature, with the brilliant historical placement of the writers of the eighteenth century, with their new causes and hopes and actions, in

'For Whom Does One Write?' and the many (some eight in all) descriptions of the real services provided by the *philosophes* now become, as far as possible, Sartre's models and prototypes, whose successes he can only envy and try to emulate in conditions far from propitious.

These essays are Sartre in his grandest manner. Like Voltaire he is a superb literary historian, master of all he surveys: the three preceding centuries of French literature, the three preceding generations of the twentieth century, in the midst of which he locates himself and his cohort writers (including Camus) shaken out of their aesthetic torpor and solitude by the war, now compelled to enlist new forces in an attempt to show the way for the writer. But mainly it is about himself, his own needs for fullness of life, for a plenitude, the antinomy, which he must bear like a Cross, of being a bourgeois intellectual whose choices are complicated if not mutually cancelling. The essays have their curiosities and their dubious recommendations. For one they are class driven, fundamentally concerned with the consciousness of the writer in regard to the dominant class and ideology of his day. But this does not make them studies in sociology. The social conditions form only a segment of the circle, of which one needs to comprehend the circumference, the totality that literature represents, including history and metaphysics, the public and its myths. Literature is the main outline, the subject and indicator of 'l'Esprit,' the reflexive consciousness of an age. If the essay is a call to praxis it does not yet mean this in the fullest sense of militant action (that will come later) but rather as a call to consciousness of one's historical and existential situation. Its ends are literary, as the literary imagination is summoned to show its validity by both understanding and representing the synthetic unity of a culture. While coherent and cogent, its greatest strength as historical analysis lies in the large descriptive realities by which it comes to define a culture, their points on the compass, their ultimate satisfactions and the values upon which they rest. Its scope is thus large and comprehensive. But mainly it is an address to himself, the basis of his thinking, subsuming as in recollection his previous works, with their modes and their qualities.

Sartre's emergent heroes are the *philosophes* of the eighteenth century, although the very differences that exist between them and Sartre's generation provides a tragic lesson in historical situation. Like the clerks of the Middle Ages, the lay writers of the seventeenth century adhered to an accepted and constituted ideology. They were sustained by the twin pillars of the church and the monarch, and in their values looked to the past. But they wrote for a select group of similarly talented people: writers wrote for people who knew how to write.[23] They adopted the values of 'la société,' their reader the 'honnête homme,' their measure, nothing new but *lieux-communs*, and their badge, 'la politesse,' guided by taste. One was a member of a corporation, and literature was a 'greeting,' an act of mutual recognition ('reconnaissance') across the stage or the page.

With the writers of the mid-eighteenth century, things changed. The writer lived in a divided house, being of the bourgeoisie yet courting the aristocracy, which latter was only too ready to remind him of his place and return him to his station (the *bastonnade* or the *embastillements* of Voltaire). The collapse of the clerisy, the resort of the church to threats and fear, removed it from true debate: no longer containing a reference to freedom, it ceased to be at the forefront of expression (144). With the inefficacy of the director class, the new writer became the advocate of the rising class, the bourgeoisie, and its demands for enlarged political freedoms. Caught between the two, the new writer came into a cognizance of himself and of his autonomy: he discovered the world where he could be free, and that was in the world of mind and thought ('l'Esprit'). His adopted tools of critical analysis, that is, what Sartre calls 'négativité,' but he constructed thereby a model of 'l'homme universel' (148–9). For the first time a writerly class had the means to ally itself with an emerging class, and had its activities serve as a liberating force. His natural enemies, ready for the picking, were 'les institutions, les superstitions, les actes d'un gouvernement traditionnel' (the institutions, the superstitions, and the acts of traditional government) (153). The domain of the spirit, of rational understanding, was the present. This does not mean that they did not know history, or did not write about history (both Voltaire and Rousseau are sufficient witnesses to discredit this theory), but they judged things from the courageous possession of present values (153). The defence of the self in the presence of universal values would naturally enough lead to the defence of the political liberties that the bourgeoisie both needed and claimed. The *philosophes* were public intellectuals who spoke to the needs of the historical moment. They were not idealists, but if there were no other remedy except revolution, so it had to be. In fact, like Camus, but on different principles, Sartre sees the influence of Rousseau (granted 'de longue main,' or from some distance) reaching not only to the fall of the Bastille, but to the fourth of August, when the privileged legislators forsook many of their advantages.[24] One can, of course, criticize Sartre's formulations on several fronts. Such emphasis on alliance of writer with a class readership leaves out the intervention of other forces; it exaggerates homogeneity within an epoch – for instance, ignoring the adversarial position taken by Rousseau against Voltaire and the *philosophes*. But what it does present is supportable, usable, and illuminating.

The eighteenth century, in grand manner, became Sartre's 'paradis perdu' because the liberated class would soon become the oppressor in its turn (143). Cognizant and defender of formal liberties, it overlooked material liberties and thus turned its back on the rising proletariat. The nineteenth century thus witnessed the failure of society and writer alike. The bourgeoisie confined itself to the defence of the freedoms gained with the assistance of the intellectuals of the previous century. A culture of assimilation, it looked for coherence, obliterating class distinctions. One of its aims was to fashion a human face for its means, and in literature to show the rectification of moral and psychological misunderstanding by the just recognition of an abused goodness. But, as Thomas Mann so amply testified in his major novels, it failed to ask the 'Wozu?' question, 'To what end?' It was a culture of means, which it then brought together, or catalogued, in larger systems. Consequently it failed to develop that reflexive consciousness of itself, as did the writer, who was alienated from the culture upon which he was dependent. Nineteenth-century literature is thus devoid of that first step, the one that emerges from the depths by a metaphysical encounter with the depths. It fails to overstep its own humanistic and bourgeois constraints by a recognition of the irrational, the terrible, the separation of things and thoughts. Coherence theory had no place for the philosophy of existence. The world it perceived returned the human image. But in the absurd universe that Sartre construes to be the artist's necessary battle line, words and things are displaced: ideas are poor replacements for the irrational existence of things. Yet within this system of displacement there is the start of great liberty, not by transforming things into ideas about things, but showing Being as Being 'avec son opacité, et son coefficient d'adversité par la spontanéité indéfinie de l'Existence' (with its opacity, and its coefficient adversity by the indefinite spontaneity of existence) (159). *Nausea* is conjoined with *Being and Nothingness*, and both with future prospects when he goes on to add that 'Être,' or being, cannot be fully produced by thought, and this is because 'being' is penetrated by existence, 'c'est-à-dire par une liberté qui décide du sort même et du valeur de la pensée' (that is to say by a freedom which decides even the fate and value of a thought). For this reason, the true artist always has a sense of Evil ('le Mal'), which is not based upon misapprehension, as it is in the search for remediation and rectification (whether in Hugo or Dickens), but rather upon the 'l'irréductibilité du monde et de l'homme à la Pensée' (irreducibility of man and the world to Thought). Nor, as an endnote (198n3) reveals, does nineteenth-century fiction (and it is clear he is writing about French literature) confront the famous phrase of Ivan Karamazov, 'If God does not exist, then everything is permitted,' which Sartre claims is the terrible challenge that bourgeois society struggled to conceal in the 150 years of its reign.

While this dire news is the starting point, it is not the end point. Sartre's true aim is a sense of plenitude, of fullness, that it is the task of literature to convey. Here we can invoke as leading to this fullness of representation such phrases as praxis, situation, the need to historicize oneself. Sartre had a commanding need to enter into life, to know and relish its heights and depths, its fully human quality. The main fault of humanism is that it removes so many of the real and tactile dimensions in the name of an abstract benevolence. The literature of praxis is a literature of participation, moved by the festival spirit ('la fête'), even carnival. But in order to do this, the writer must realize that he is in situation, that he is located in a density of events and awarenesses, that he is part of his time. Sartre sees this possibility of fullness as being most available in a classless society, where the writer has the best opportunity, because of its supposed freedom and openness, of actually recovering what had been lost – a lost childhood, a lost adolescence – which he must now struggle to bring back. If Camus has his own personal myths of restitution for what he has left behind, of guilt and forgiveness, so Sartre has his: to immerse himself in all fullness into the life that was taken from him. The new literature that beckons is actually a 'reprise,' a taking back or recovery. 'Et il n'y a rien d'autre à spiritualiser, rien d'autre à reprendre que ce monde multicolore et concret, avec son lourdeur, son opacité, ses zones de généralité et son fourmillement d'anecdotes, et ce Mal invincible qui le ronge sans jamais pourvoir l'anéantir. L'écrivain le reprendra tel quel, tout cru, tout suant, tout puant, tout quotidien, pour le présenter à des libertés sur le fondement d'une liberté' (And there is nothing left to spiritualize, nothing left to take up again, except this multi-coloured and concrete world, with its heaviness, its opacity, its zones of general expression, and its swarm of anecdotes, and this invincible evil that eats at it without ever being able to annihilate it. The writer will take it back such as it is, all raw, all sweating, all stinking, all day-to-day, only to present it to those liberties on the basis of a more fundamental liberty) (195–6). In his need for recovery of what was lost, of what was shorn from him by the discreet, confined bourgeois society, he dreams of a society where people are free, where the artist is free to make his 'gift,' his offering in the spirit of festival. For this reason Sartre advocates a classless society, apparently confusing a literature of freedom of movement and entrance into life in all its complexities and configurations, that is a literature that moves between classes and things, with a classless society, where such movement has proved to be illusory, contradictory, and prohibited. In fact, the kind of fullness that he requires he already described in *Nausea* but it was excised because of its lyricism: 'Tout ce que les hommes font de nuit, je l'entends. J'entends le chasse d'eau des cabinets; j'entends, le samedi soir, les soupirs amoureux du couple irrégulier qui habite au 9, j'entends les trains qui sifflent, les musiques des cafés. Toute la rue passe par ma chambre et coule sur moi' (I hear everything that people do at night. I hear the flushing of the toilets; I hear on Saturday evenings, the amorous sighs of the transient couple who occupy room 9, I hear the whistling of the trains and the music of the cafes. The entire street passes through my room and flows over me) (1736).[25]

Continuing this need for plenitude, to be immersed in density of being, indeed showing this to be one of the more attractive parts of his personality, a democratic openness of being, is his preference for the audience of the cinema. Sartre and the cinema grew of age with the century. Unlike the theatre, which reflected the hierarchical and ceremonial orders of society, the crowd of the cinema existed *en masse*. The cinema brought people together in colour and confusion. The mixtures of people, the teeming crowds, gave him the same sense of danger, of nakedness, and of *l'adhérence*, the sense of being a participant in a communal experience that he would later feel only as a prisoner of war (*Words* 101).

A child enjoying the freedom of carnival, the festival spirit – such is the remedy to heal the wounds of a childhood regretted, to recover what has been lost. In another indication of the insight one bore to the other, Camus writes in his journal, this notation: 'Sartre or nostalgia for the universal idyll,' where the 'or' is in apposition and not an alternative (Aronson 98). In their mutual needs to overcome alienation, Camus sought to make restitution, even to seek forgiveness for leaving behind the people and the places, forgiveness for his success, and thus his work will always enshrine remarkable and staying memories, while Sartre will seek to recover what had been lost, but also to destroy what had waylaid him, the bourgeois *bonne conscience*, the class restrictions that had prevented him, the veils placed over most of existence, over existence itself: two opposing tendencies, but each bespeaking the same truth: how deep and even hidden are the psychological pressures that drive our intellectual thought, how far back they reach, how far forward they extend themselves.

Sartre primarily addresses people of 'good will,' solitary readers, who enjoy the communion of intellect, the meeting of like minds in the commerce of reading. Here in solitary reveries they enjoy the City of Ends, the eternal depictions of the human condition, the catharsis of tragedy. But oddly enough, like Rousseau, his Protestant forebear in the *Letter to d'Alembert*, Sartre does not find this sufficient. The capacity to lose oneself in the book comes to an end with the reading; there is no follow-through to political action. The City of Ends expropriates the City of Means. The comparison with Rousseau is apparent, deriving from a need for authenticity in each, a moral reach that can suffer no disjunction between aesthetic pleasure and personal conduct. The goal must be, without losing sight of the City of Ends, to *historicize* oneself, to render the same homage to one's actual conditions, as one is willing to pay to grand figures and themes. As with Luther and Rousseau, the matter is to bring the spirit into touch with what is one's own. Rousseau recommended popular festivals instead of plays, or plays that presented the struggles of Geneva to achieve its independence. The City of Ends, where contemplation is complete, must be brought home to the real city of their lives, where work still needs to be done.

But Sartre's work is complicated by class and situation. Bourgeois by class and committed to the liberties gained ('libertés politiques, *habeas corpus*, etc.' [298]; one can remark on how belittling is the perfunctory 'etc.'), he is nevertheless committed by his historical situation to join the efforts of the proletariat and produce a classless society – that is to administer the poisoned chalice to himself and his cohorts. This is the antinomy that 'The Situation of the Writer' bestrides, the two horses he must ride, that makes the remarkable essay the midpoint of Sartre's development. His is the position of the liberal who must apply an intellectual self-poisoning. Yet he acknowledges the necessity of maintaining both positions. 'En un mot, nous devons dans nos écrits militer en faveur de la liberté de la personne et de la révolution socialiste. On a souvent prétendu qu'elles n'étaient pas conciliables; c'est notre affaire to démontrer inlassablement qu'elles impliquent l'une l'autre' (In a word, in our writings we have to militate both in favour of personal liberty and a socialist revolution. It has often been claimed that they are not reconcilable; it's our business to demonstrate tirelessly that they are involved

one with the other) (298). The proletariat could disdain political liberties – they have other fish to fry ('chats à fouetter'); the bourgeoisie
restrict themselves to formal liberties, without regard to material ones.
But the Sartrean intellectual is 'double duty bound,' without relishing
the role of mediator, torn between the demands of each class, 'condam-
nés à subir comme une Passion cette double exigence' (condemned to
undergo as in a Passion this double exigency) (298).

But while full understanding and complexity of thought are not
absent, there are indications that this middling position of Sartre's midpoint essay could not be long maintained. A literature of praxis is one of
reflexive consciousness, where one understands the conditions of his
time, the governing myths. It is not yet a call for direct militant action, as
his ablest commentator, Simone de Beauvoir, points out, a synthesis
between his existential point of view and his need for direct involvement
(*La force des choses* 243). But if one adopts as one of its goals a program to
change history, then it is not too far a step from that to outright action.
Sartre's attitudes toward violence are ambivalent. His argument is twofold: violence is a dead end but also only violence can end violence. In
fact, in these crucial pages he seems to be explicitly responding to
Camus (as Aronson points out, 96–7). In *Neither Victims nor Executioners*
Camus deplores violence as a solution (but if we read *The Rebel* carefully,
it is clear that his attitude is not simplistic either), but, Sartre responds,
on the very next day *Combat* announced the beginning of the war in
Indochina. For Sartre the question comes down to which violence – that
of the colonial powers or that of the indigenous peoples? Either way we
are involved in a world of violence, and one is obliged to choose. Obviously, these thoughts about violence anticipate Sartre's later radicaliza-
tion, particularly in his defence of the revolutionary rights of the
colonized. Sartre of the antinomies cannot hold out long. For one, a daemonic character, that is a character of spiritual energy, who seeks authenticity and is subject to several conversions, cannot long survive in an
attitude of contradiction. He is in search of unity of being and action and
feels a compulsion to choose. The very language by which he describes
his 'doubles exigences' as an Agony he is condemned to endure indicates a need for atonement in the double bind of the Cross. Lastly is the
way he ties himself to the fortunes of the proletariat. When the war in
Korea broke out, the fear was widespread that the USSR, its divisions
poised just a few hours away (just two stages of the Tour de France, de
Gaulle graphically pointed out) would invade Europe. People, including
Camus, were urging Sartre to be prepared to flee. But his staunch reply

was that he would never fight against the proletariat. Eventually all three impulses will join together to render inevitable the clash with Camus. In particular, the last exchange indicated the difference of their future directions. When asked what he would do in the case of a Soviet invasion, Camus replied that he would behave as he had under the Nazi's, that is, enter into clandestine resistance. In describing this encounter, Simone de Beauvoir remarks, that they no longer felt free to discuss such matters with Camus: either by anger or by vehemence he let himself be carried away too quickly (*La force des choses* 250–1).

But for the moment all of Sartre's work represents the antinomy expressed in 'The Situation of the Writer in 1947.' One attraction of a classless society is that it would bring about a reconciliation between word and action, between lyrical description and objective testimony, between the divided consciousness of the bourgeois intellectual and the simple man of action, between Quixote and Hamlet. Yet it is the very presence of these antinomies that accounts for the value and appeal of his philosophical and literary essays, and above all his creative writing. It is as this period that Aronson sees Sartre at the peak of his powers (98). While he is torn between his bourgeois consciousness, his lack of acceptance by the truly committed proletariat, his own abhorrence of violence, and yet his fascination with and proclivity toward violence, this material dramatically rendered and magnified, incarnated in voices that speak to us, becomes the basis of his concluding third volume of *Roads to Freedom, La mort dans l'âme* (*Troubled Sleep*) and his two plays that dominated their respective theatrical seasons, *Les Mains Sales* (*Dirty Hands*), April 1948, and *Le Diable et le Bon Dieu* (*The Devil and the Good Lord*), June 1951.

The young Sartre, rejected by his playmates, is invaded by a 'wish to be,' a wish to be other, to be a man among men (Aronson 113), to enjoy the 'adherence' he knew as a fellow prisoner of war. This antinomy accounts for the dramatic qualities of *Dirty Hands*, where the bourgeois intellectual Hugo lives in awe of the person he is chosen to assassinate, the well-centred, psychologically solid, and independently minded Hoederer. He even secretly admires and envies the singularity of purpose of the two thugs, Slick and Georges, who are Hoederer's bodyguards. They might even be named Grunt and Oaf, as their sensibility rarely goes beyond their own epidermis. Hugo endures all the misfortunes of a derelict from his class. His idealism is a product of hatred of his upbringing, which, as Hoederer perceptively recognizes, is self-hatred (and of which Sartre will write more fully in *Words*). He seeks out his assignment from the Party in order to prove himself, which is itself false consciousness. His very idealism insists on a purity in action, which brings about his delay in carrying out the assassination. He refuses to enter into the direction of his life. He Hamletizes, and Philip Thody justly remarks on the presence of Hamlet in his character (92–3).[26] Hoederer, on the other hand, seems to be well-placed in his skin, with an acute intelligence and willingness to make pragmatic and strategic compromises. It is Hoederer whom Sartre acknowledges to be the hero of the play, and indeed 'the most sympathetically drawn character in the whole of Sartre's works' (Thody 93). It is he who signs off on the drama's message and indeed signals the emerging motives of Sartre's own evolution. Deploring the bourgeois intellectual's need for moral purity as an excuse for doing nothing, he, on the contrary, has 'dirty hands': 'Moi j'ai les main sales. Jusqu'aux coudes. Je les ai plongées dans la merde et dans le sang. Et puis après? Est-ce que tu t'imagines qu'on peut gouverner innocemment' (Right up to the elbows. I've plunged them in shit and blood. And what happens afterwards? Do you imagine that we can govern innocently?) (*Théâtre complet* 331). Hoederer expresses the Sartrean need to enter into the fullness of life, which the bourgeoisie has restricted. But as has already been in evidence, this need is mingled with political activism and is itself restricted to a classless society. Hoederer is clear about his goals – the elimination of a society based on class – and he will utilize any means to achieve that goal, even one of entering into a government with the conservative or liberal parties. Hugo deplores these means, but Hoederer declares that all means are good that are effective.

This debate about ends and means occasioned a curious exchange between Camus and Sartre.[27] In the midst of their cooling relationship, Camus sat in on a rehearsal of the play. Their pending split was already present in their differing interpretations. For Camus, who was writing *The Rebel* at this time, Hugo was the hero, since he refused to adopt all means, while Sartre sided with Hoederer, who obviously represented a station along the way of his own moral and political itinerary (Aronson 106). The differences were becoming clear, and even their more and more infrequent social get-togethers were flat, without their usual warmth.

If *Dirty Hands* prefigured the differences over means and ends, *The Devil and the Good Lord* made them all the more palpable. This play, much closer in time to the tumultuous split with Camus, was seen by Sartre as a sequel to the earlier play. Interestingly enough, it takes place in the early sixteenth century, at the time of Luther and the Peasants' Rebellion, that is, at the time when well before the *philosophes* there was an intellectual class working for change within the public world. The placement of the action is not accidental, nor is that of the main personage, Goetz – a man of contradictions, a daemonic character of extravagant wilfulness, in fact, a bastard child, with the imaginative consciousness that Sartre deplored in himself. Goetz is another portrait-on-the-way of Sartre, not as he was but as he would want to be, a man among men. Unfortunately the play is deplorable, riddled with metaphysical language, with bizarre actions (some public reaction, finding it 'execrable' seems justified, although despite ideologically based mixed reviews, it was a success – de Beauvoir, *La force des choses* 257). After giving up a siege by sheer gratuitousness and establishing a kind of communitarian settlement, Goetz realizes that his utopia was a dream, and worse, that it led to complete destruction. He consents reluctantly to become once again the leader of the peasant uprising. But first he must establish order by hanging deserters. In the final *coup de théâtre* he stabs a captain who refuses his orders. This drab sensationalism reminds us of young Christopher Marlowe's second part of *Tamburlaine* where the ascencionist figure so admired by the playwright stabs his own effeminate son. Those who are captivated by the play are normally those who are tracing Sartre's moral and political evolution (*La force des choses* 261). So capable a critic as Maurice Cranston calls it 'a work of the highest art' (109).[28] But in any dramaturgical evaluation, it is as if Shakespeare, after having written *Hamlet*, would then write *Titus Andronicus*, or even *Tamburlaine* part 2.

11. The Great Debate

Their itinerary of encounter shows that the dispute between Sartre and Camus was a long time coming. Adding a more combustible element to the charges and the counter-charges. keen intellectual affinities necessarily preceded the eventual break-up. Certainly in the pursuit of causes one can invoke the Cold War, but this, while more than the occasion, was less than the cause of the dispute. Other occasions would have presented themselves equally well: Indochina, Algeria. One can more subtly point to differing attitudes toward violence, and indeed there were strenuous disagreements over means and ends. Nevertheless, while Sartre disagreed vehemently with Merleau-Ponty, they still managed to *wish* to restore the tattered relationship. But between Sartre and Camus differences existed at a more fundamental level. What was there in common, one could ask, as Markevich did of Turgenev and Dostoevsky, between Camus the young provincial from Algiers for whom culture was an acquisition, and Sartre, the heir to an enlightened liberal protestantism for whom culture was a dispensation, but who was in quest of a modern Jansenism, lodged at the extremes of existence; between the one who – propelled by his own great talent and quest for recognition – was forced to leave behind the people and the places dear to him and thus compelled by a need to make restitution for his 'betrayal' in the manner of Rousseau, and the other who detested his childhood, who rebelled against his bourgeois background, against the 'salauds,' against those of 'bonne conscience' and bad faith, one who finally in *Words* turned against the lettered man that his distorted past had made him? How in all these matters could it be possible to avoid the psychological elements, not as extracts but rather as representing the intrinsic motive and meaning of their separate and yet conjoined journeys? Circumstances brought them together but it was more than circumstance that tore them apart.

As with the other dualisms of this study, so their long itinerary of encounter culminated in a very public and publicized dispute. There had been prior ruptures and strains in their relationship. In 1947 Camus vehemently denounced Merlau-Ponty's *Humanism and Terror* and stormed out of the room, slamming the door behind him, when Sartre seemed to come to the author's defence. This break was patched up after six months but it placed a strain on their relationship that begins to show in Simone de Beauvoir's more critical description of Camus (*La force des choses* 125–7).

The actual debate in the pages of *Les temps modernes* was not a chance event. One could of course ask whether it could have been otherwise, or whether it should have been otherwise. Sartre could have written the review himself, avoiding the flagrant insults and limiting himself to the brilliant second part of his response. Camus could have addressed Francis Jeanson by name and perhaps adopted more of a Voltairean wit in his response. But this is to fall into the trap of rewriting history according to a benign consensus of committee. What we do know and can accept is that, like the other dualisms of this study, it was in Bornkamm's word 'unavoidable.' And to respond to whether it should have been avoided, we can think back to Voltaire's embarrassed stance before David Hume at his entanglement with Rousseau, and his wish to consign the dispute to its deserved oblivion, but as we also know, David Hume would have none of this, rightly seeing the summary value in the antagonism between two such gladiators, between the titans and the gods. So Sartre, in his concluding words, wishes the polemic to be forgotten. But history did not comply, and in 2003–4, three books in English alone appeared devoted to the Camus-Sartre debate. Polemics lead to clarification, as Dostoevsky reminded us, and this debate and the grounds upon which it rests will continue to intrigue us, as the other not-to-be-forgotten dualisms continue to do, because of what they reveal about the history of their times, but also as perennial reminders of the tensions of our culture in which we continue to live. It is so deeply revealing that one could hardly wish it to have been otherwise.

Between the publication of *L'homme révolté* in November 1951 and Jeanson's review-essay of May 1952, Sartre had occasion to intimate to Camus that the coming review might not be all that favourable. But this did little to allay the uproar. If anything, the delay and the expectations heightened the tensions and rendered the ensuing storm even more electric. Much was made of Camus's addressing his response to 'Monsieur le directeur,' thus overstepping Jeanson himself, and in Sartre's mind treating him as a non-person. But this is something of an exaggeration. From the heart of a true dualism Camus knew where to strike home (moreover, as on other occasions, he observed the protocol of addressing his letter to the responsible party, the director of the journal). Perhaps Sartre was more right in objecting to the formality of the address, as they had been friends for ten years. But Camus was hurt to the quick and levelled the true charge of 'lack of generosity and loyalty' where it could only be borne and that was by Sartre himself (*Essais* 764). For a man who founded his philosophy on codes of conduct, this smacked of betrayal. Some of Jeanson's arguments were 'frivole[s]' but others, the more involving, were 'inimicale[s]' (773).

Camus was intuitively right in addressing his response to the source of the antagonism, thereby drawing out the full implications of the dualisms. Jeanson did write *La morale et la pensée de Sartre* and employs Sartrean language throughout, so why not go to the source? This point is clear in the explosion it produced, in the clamorous following it provoked. Sartre well admitted it when he declared that if their friendship should end it was Camus who had ended it. He realized the implications of Camus's response. Camus drew the battle lines clearly and Sartre rushed in, filling his rebuttal with personal insult, Camus's faults of character, and the differences between a true philosopher and a dabbler in second-hand texts. Camus had struck home and aroused animosity, and in animus there is clarification. The breaking up of friends is tragic, as one has misgivings about what might have been; the arousal of a true dualism is more like tragedy, one that exposes basic truths, that depends upon genuine revelation, a breaking out into the open of what was rankling with all of its unavoidability and finality, of something that was bound to happen because its basis for occurring was always there, in their temperaments, in their privately held opinion and in their growing ideological differences. Such clarification also brings a sense of liberation as when finally Rousseau was able to declare his hatred for Voltaire.

The rightness of Camus's address to Sartre is also evident in that it eliminated any intermediary. Dualisms are dyadic and not triadic. Its poles are what Hamlet called 'mighty opposites.' The young prince who is growing into kingly stature shows no regret for the deaths of Rosencrantz and Guildenstern:

'Tis dangerous when the baser nature comes
Between the pass and fell incensed points
Of mighty opposites. (5.2.61–3)

It is of course lurid to compare Francis Jeanson to the king's abject and willing cat's paws; he was in every respect, as Sartre described him to be, a just, ethical, and honourable person. But the fact remains that, except for some egregious errors, he remains a supernumerary to the dispute. Who is much concerned about his role in the drama, and moreover who pays much attention to his quite intelligent rebuttal also printed in the August issue? The mighty opposition that Camus's address to Sartre draws out is clearly between the two of them.

While Camus' response has been subject to much criticism, it is hard to see where he falters. At worse, it can be said, for those interested in academic score-keeping, it was a draw. Turning to specifics, it is clear that the criticisms based upon style and being praised by the wrong people were indeed unworthy. On top of this, Jeanson makes the gaffe of misreading *The Plague* and not comprehending that Dr Rieux is himself the narrator. In his rebuttal letter he rather weakly argues that he never *denied* that Dr Rieux was the narrator of the chronicle. Moreover, Jeanson pays only lip-service to Camus's cautions (about Rousseau and Hegel) and does not confront the premise of the work, which he could then have followed with his stringent criticisms of its omissions. While Camus did not say this outright, it can be said for him that his unquestionable masterpiece was not treated with the respect it deserved. Simone de Beauvoir reports that she and Sartre thought Jeanson would write a more tempered review but that he got carried away ('il se laissa emporter') (*La force des choses* 279). *The Rebel* was maltreated for what it supposedly did not do, and that was to show the way the injustices of the political and economic infrastructures contributed to the development of the revolutionary movements. Camus's work accordingly amounted to a 'refusal of history.' But such argument does injustice to Camus's own political-historical interests, his reportage on the Kabyles, his lifelong opposition to the death penalty (particularly as epitomized by the guillotine), his firm opposition to the formal virtues of bourgeois society (that neglected material injustices), his favour of the syndicalist movement (not only among the Scandinavian countries but in Britain as well – which went a long way toward the creation of the modern welfare state). But mainly the review ignores the validity of Camus's moral, literary, and philosophical imagination. Already in *The Myth of Sisyphus* he took as his main proposition the fundamental question of the day, whether in an absurdist universe the only way out was suicide. So in *The Rebel* he takes as his task the fundamental question of his time and that is whether murder, mass murder, can be legitimized by recourse to a rationale of history. As Tony Judt quite accurately remarks, none of the criticisms, particularly those accusing Camus of being anti-historical, or even ahistorical, 'weakens the central force of Camus' insight – that the problem of totalitarian violence was *the* moral and political dilemma of our age, and that the USSR and its satellites were not only admired by *philosophes*, they were governed by them – the heirs and fulfillment *ad absurdum* of the Western philosophical dream' (94–6).

Anticipating a wish that Sartre would espouse, Jeanson concludes by calling back the earlier Camus, the Camus they had once admired. They repeat the classic error in dealing with defection: they had not read the signs. They ignored in *The Stranger* and all his subsequent works the role of simple human sympathy. They had forgotten from *The Myth* and *Just Assassins* Camus's adherence to a code of conduct, one bound to honour, to the rules of the game, where one must be willing to pay the price for one's actions. They only observed without registering that Camus was always a man of the Left, and as a consequence from *The Stranger* onward keenly aware of the injustices condoned by bourgeois society. But perhaps most importantly, they refused to recognize the restrained writer of consciousness who was willing and able to live in the midst of contradiction, to be a rebel-reformer without being a revolutionary, and who knew where to draw the line.

Sartre accepts the challenge of this dualism into which he has been entered and lashes out at Camus the man, his incompetence in technical philosophy, and his abstention, as he sees it, from history itself and its necessities of choice. The personal assault is devastating, and yet it is Sartre who feels obliged to assume the responsibility for informing Camus of his deficiencies without the 'delicate handling' (the 'ménagements') that his mixture of 'suffisance sombre' et 'vulnérabilité' seemed to require. That no one has done this before has left Camus prey to the 'morne démesure,' which only conceals his interior difficulties and which Camus is pleased, 'je [Sartre] crois' to name Mediterranean measure (Sartre, *La réponse* 334).[29] Throughout Sartre will poke gibes at Camus's praise of the pagan Mediterranean sense of 'measure' or finitism. Camus, the 'belle âme,' insists on giving moralistic instructions from his own portable pedestal. These are not comments made at random, but rather impressions that had been long suppressed and now brutally expressed.

Equally long-standing is the disqualification of Camus as a philosopher. What if, Sartre disingenuously inquires, *The Rebel* only evidenced Camus's philosophical incompetence? He argues rhetorically that he does not say this is so, but what if it were (340)? Would his book not be open to criticism? This coyness is shed a few pages later when he quips that he and Hegel have one thing in common: Camus does not seem to have read either (344). He does add that Camus might find the reading of *Being and Nothingness* a bit too arduous, and then proceeds to give an explanation of why it is impossible to place a brake on freedom that an undergraduate philosophy major would have no trouble in comprehending (344).

Sartre's major argument is that history does not have a determined direction, but that man in his freedom of choice makes history. This evidently shoots down Camus's objection that Jeanson and Sartre labour in the grips of Marxist prophetic determinism, that they are the slaves of historicism. But one can ask whether Sartre does indeed answer Camus's objections. If by one's free choice within the necessities of the situation one chooses to ally one's interest with that of the proletariat, each working toward the establishment of a classless society, and if one is obliged to side, with whatever difficulty, with the sole country that seems to represent those causes, what does it matter if the choice is predetermined or is free? The outcome is the same, and one is obliged to speak more of the outrages of bourgeois capitalism, of racism, and of colonialism, than of the inherent ideological and practical difficulties of Marxist-Leninist theories and their despotic tendencies. Despite the lessons in philosophy – and here Sartre is more of the pedagogue than he accuses Camus of being – the outcome is the same.

Intertwined, the personal and the ideological emerge in this exchange of letters to produce a classic dualism. In perhaps the most important paragraph of his letter, the penultimate one, Camus cites this contradiction at the heart of Sartre's dilemma, the incapacity to reconcile 'la relative liberté et la nécessité de l'histoire.' They think in the direction of freedom, while their voting feet move in the direction of necessity (*Essais* 772). Such freedom is only a philosophical given, a matter for scholastic debate, while their actions drive to the point of historical necessity. One can wonder here who is the better philosopher.

Camus, for his part, knows how to strike where it hurts. In the same paragraph, one to which Sartre frequently refers, Camus admits to some fatigue at being given lectures on effectiveness by such armchair philosophers (a reference to the notorious episode where he found Sartre on the day of the Liberation asleep in a chair at the theatre, where he was supposedly a lookout).

They knew one another quite well, and in their exchanges 'interresponsiveness' as well as keen attentiveness thrived. That is why this debate, if it can be termed a draw, was not a standstill. It may have reduced each to silence, as Aronson argues, but eventually in their creative ways it was put to use. Near the end of his response, Sartre advances something of an apology. If Camus thinks his description cruel, he has not to fear, because soon Sartre will speak of himself in the same tone ('je parlerai de moi bientôt et sur le même ton' (351). He would soon begin writing *Words*.

12. Final Words: *The Fall* and *Words*

As for Camus, if he was stymied, he was far from stifled. One can well imagine the hurt inflicted by the controversy (he raged around the room like a stuck bull, his wife informs us), but that did not deter him from attempting to comprehend the reasons for the antagonism. This he did in an unpublished small 'défense' of *The Rebel* (now made available by the editors of the Pléaide edition of Camus's *Essais* and reproduced in translation by Sprintzen and van den Haven). Although brief, it is a major accounting of his thought, bearing all of its hallmarks, and should be published as an appendix to every new edition of *The Rebel*. It is an obvious response to the debate and to the criticisms of the work in which he took the greatest pleasure, allowing him to refine his arguments. It exhibits Camus's tendencies to recapitulate the development of his thought, and to reveal the overlapping qualities of all his works, as if he were in need to overcome the obvious breaches in his personal life, and provide a continuum. It shows even further his willingness to live in a state of contradiction, to confront the tensions of existence, and to encapsulate the urgencies of the historical moment. Lastly, if there is a constant need to resume his past thought, there is also the corollary presence of anticipation, as the sprouts of *The Fall* are quite in evidence.

The 'Défense' goes far in expanding on the arguments of *The Rebel*. In the early 1940s Camus was able to oppose the lies of the Nazis by an instinct for living rather than by any reasoned thought. His task, the modern task, was to formulate a reasoned theory, provide a code of conduct, that while repudiating nihilism did not renege on his own historical origins ('Défense' 1704–5; Sprintzen and Van den Hoven 207–8). The same procedure by which he was able to expose Nazism he applied to the Soviet system of state-sponsored murder. This he accomplished by developing the concept of revolt, transforming the Cartesian edict into his own: 'I revolt therefore we exist.' But even more importantly he refines his conception of 'limit' and 'measure' (1709; 211). They imply a tension within existence itself and within Camus. The revolt of consciousness by itself can lead to simple solitude, but revolution by itself leads to systematic murder (1706–7; 210). Both held together in balance, in a 'just equilibrium,' each can impose a limit on the excesses of the other. Goethe brought together Faust and Helen to produce Eurphorion. Modern thought, European thought, that of those who misunderstand his work would ignore Helen, the sense of beauty in nature. He would hold them together: 'Ni Faust sans Hélène; ni Hélène sans Faust, voila ce que je crois' (Neither Faust without Helen, nor Helen without Faust, that's what I believe) (1711; 214). This conjunction of North and South, of Germanic philosophy and Mediterranean sense of the bountifulness of existence is an obvious correction of the ridicule to which both Sartre and Jeanson had subjected his 'mediterraneanism.'

He further corrects the charge that he would be content to live outside of history, that his 'revolt' is merely supine. Again he turns to the necessary conjunction of supposed opposites as providing a sense of limits. Pure individualism, just as pure historicism, leads to the same conclusion: nihilism (1712; 215). The one enjoys the contentments of personal life, with no better purpose in view; the other submits to the iron laws of a historicism that results in a kind of necessity, or servitude. His entire work, Camus writes, has been an assertion of the just claims of each, the individual within the history of his times, addressing its major issues and yet retaining a residual part of himself, even a solitude, where he is free to criticize any false direction attributed to history, or historicism. Revolt breeds a sense of liberation, not only practical but material as well, and always includes the worker and the fuller benefits he deserves on the part of the society for which he labours.

The essay is quite positive, even optimistic in its belief that an intellectual advance has been made, the lessons of history have been learned. 'Malgré les apparences nous sommes plus riches aujourd'hui, et mieux armées que nous ne l'étions entre les deux guerres. Nous savons, et nous ne savions pas alors. La renaissance sans doute n'est pas pour demain, mais le nihilisme déjà appartient au passé' (In spite of appearances we are richer and better armed than we were before the two wars. Now we know and then we didn't. No doubt the renaissance is not for tomorrow, but nihilism is already a thing of the past) (1714–15; 218).

Summarizing, encapsulating, recuperating, seeking a continuum while in the midst of contradiction, Camus throughout his work also anticipates. Thus extracts from this 'Défense' may be seen as actual preludes to *The Fall*. Clearly his defence engages in an auto-critique that is so present in the later work. 'Il est bien clair d'abord que je n'ai fait le procès de personne sans faire en même temps le procès de ce que j'ai cru. J'ai décrit un mal dont je ne m'exclus pas. Loin de vouloir rien innocenter j'ai voulu comprendre la sorte de culpabilité où nous étions' (It is very clear from the outset that I did not put anyone on trial without at the same time putting on trial what I had believed. I have described an evil from which I don't exclude myself. Far from wishing to [whitewash] anything I wanted to understand the kind of guilt in which we were all involved) (1705; 208). This is the situation for which he is seeking a remedy in a sense of limits. But the dramaturgical tools are present that Jean-Baptiste Clamence will put to entirely different purposes. This becomes even clearer when Camus discriminates between those who do not seek to arise out of the very contradictions of the times. There are those who reside in the innocence of doctrinal unawareness and others, more to the point, 'jansenistes sans dieu qui restaurent le péché généralisé sans le compenser par la grâce, et qui, dans l'excès d'une pénitence sans charité, se mortifient dans le consentement à ce que les nie' (Jansenists without God – who restore universal sin without the compensation of grace, and, in an excess of penitence without charity, mortify themselves by consenting to that which denies them) (1714; 217). These same people 'démontrent que tous les hommes sont responsables du tout et du crime lui-même, et que ce tort universel et incessant fait le meilleur de leur: ils veulent sauver l'homme et ne peuvent, pour finir, qu'essayer de l'insulter et de le dégrader au jour le jour, en eux-mêmes et chez les autres' (demonstrate that all men are responsible for everything, including crime itself, and that this universal and unending error is their best justification. They wish to save mankind and, finally, from one day to the next, are only capable of trying to insult and degrade it, in themselves and in others) (1714; 217). The same phrases will be used by Clamence with nearly the same intent, and that is the diabolic logic of using universal guilt for purposes of personal exculpability.

The Fall very quickly outgrew its intended origins. It was first to be one of a group of short stories that eventually became *L'exil et le royaume* (*Exile and the Kingdom*). But Camus, in unwonted fashion, allowed himself to be carried away, swept up by the issues that presented themselves. Todd writes that it almost went beyond the will of the writer, quoting Camus to the same effect: 'J'ai besoin parfois d'écrire des choses qui m'échappent, mais qui précisément font la preuve que ce qui est en moi est plus fort que moi' (I have at times the need to write things that go beyond me, but precisely because of that are proof of something in me that is stronger than I – 636). Indeed, unlike *The Stranger* or *The Plague*, having emerged from its set, it stands alone and is not part of any advancing trilogy of concerns. When it was published in May 1956, it was an instant success. It surpasses the other stories for whose company it was originally intended because it is at once an auto-critique, a recapitulation or bridge to his other works, and because it encapsulates its time – that is, it bears all the marks of Camus's greatest efforts. But even exceeding these, it is impelled by the need to make response and to understand the at times incomprehensible hurt inflicted by the debate from which he had just emerged.

Sartre himself regarded it as a badly understood masterpiece in the ways Camus partially reveals and partially conceals himself (Todd 638). Indeed, *The Fall* is an encounter with himself in several ways: as a revelation of his defects, as a travesty of the criticisms to which he was subjected (particularly in the great debate), as an experience of a profound sense of rejection and defeat, and as an expression of remorse for some of his real failures, particularly in his relations with his wife, Francine. But always such encounters are transformed by his dedication to the strenuous demands of art.

The story is deliberately set in the far north, far from his own birthing (and that of his narrator) and far from the Eden of golden expectations. The innermost circle of Amsterdam suggests the last circle of hell, where crimes of the rational intellect are punished, crimes of deception and betrayal. Jean-Baptiste Clamence shares many of Camus's characteristics, both real and attributed. He loves to dance, is something of a ladies' man, and loves nothing better than theatre and sporting events. From his enemies' charges he seems to be in love with his own virtue (Simone de Beauvoir's faulty 'flawless' character), carries his pedestal with him (as Sartre charged), and seems possessed of the 'belle âme' that elevates him 'above' events. But these just and unjust accusations, largely accruing in the first parts of the story, serve a larger purpose, that of providing an emblem for his time.

Jean-Baptiste Clamence experiences three events that shatter his self-composure – indeed, the exposure of his own vulnerabilities owes its debt most to the rending experience of attack and enmity provoked by the debate with Sartre. But this is a larger experience as well. It is like that of Kurtz in *Heart of Darkness*, where the jungle found him out, where his so-called idealism was not met by the response of cheering and admiring crowds but instead by the stilled echo of his own voice; his idealism proved to be hollow. Jean-Baptiste follows the same path of undoing. Crossing over the Pont des arts, he seems to hear an unaccountable laughter, a laughter that lingers and exposes the selfishness of his own virtues. It is the laughter of the gods at his pretensions, at his duplicities and self-deceptions. Then there is the episode of the stalled motorcyclist, the ensuing argument, and the sidewinder punch that knocks him down, with the crowd's epithet 'poor dope' (pauvre type) ringing in his ears. The episode is told in a droll Parisian street language that in translation is difficult to emulate. What is important is not the episode itself, not the insult, but rather his inability to forget about it, to surmount it. In his need for a perfect virtue – that is, his egoism – this is a tarnish he cannot accept. The memory is like a thorn that only sinks deeper the more it is teased. It was an episode he could not get over – perhaps some symbolic presentation of the 'thrashing' Camus was supposed to have received in the debate. It was something he had to chew on and that incessantly chewed at him and his own self-esteem, leading to the conclusion, 'Si j'avais été l'ami de la vérité et de l'intelligence que je prétendais être, que m'eût fait cette aventure déjà oubliée de ceux qui en avaient été les spectateurs' (Had I been the friend of truth and intelligence I claimed to be, what would the episode have mattered to me? It was already forgotten by those who had witnessed it) (*TRN* 1503; *The Fall* 55). And the ghosts from Dostoevsky's *The Double* and *Notes from Underground* are obviously stirring here. His self-regarding need to be a man of virtue, his own doubleness prevent him from letting go of an event of little importance.

The third and final episode of his undoing occurs when he fails to come to the rescue of a young woman who commits suicide by leaping into the Seine. This is the severest moment in Camus's self-criticism, as his wife Francine, out of despair at his neglect and notorious affairs, did attempt suicide (Todd 638). She had accused her husband of always attending to the cries of others, but failing to hear the cries for help that were his own responsibilities. Francine recognized in *The Fall* the apology that was owed her. But with other women it was different. Sartre declared that by absenting himself from the necessities of historical choice, from his own situation, Camus had best live on a deserted island. Jean-Baptiste rejects the society of men, but does not flee to some island. Rather, he finds refuge in the company of women, opening various spellings of the footloose traveller. The extended pages devoted to his experiences with women are the most cynical, searing, compromising of the book. Don Juan becomes Don Juanism, and with one bitter aphoristic maxim after another, the narrator exposes the roles of ego, the human mechanisms that seem to dominate the relationships of the sexes, in fact, the need for domination itself, which once achieved, leaves open the way for abandonment.

But auto-critique, however literally or symbolically represented, soon turns to the *récit*'s higher purpose, and that is to present the portrait of the hero of his time. If he shows the effects of his own character, maligned or travestied, he subordinates them to the psychological and philosophical assumptions of the intellectual heroes of the age. Here the turnaround is derived from what Camus regards as one of the great characteristics of our time: the omnipresent contemporary need to escape judgment. One can reflect on how profound and far-reaching is Camus's insight: American education of the past twenty years has largely suffered under the duress of this particularly modern motivation – the need to avoid being judged. But in *The Fall* the tenants of this citadel of defensiveness are primarily 'nos philosophes' – an identifying epithet that was elided in the final version. If in the moment of auto-critique Camus addressed his own personal failings and even the impact of the debate on his need for pure virtue, here he turns the tables and returns to the accusations against Sartre and his existential confederates described in *The Rebel*, in the Letter to the Director, in the 'Défense' and in other responses as well. They – 'nos philosophes' – begin with freedom and they end with slavery, resuming the argument of Shigalyovism. But here in *The Fall*, the psychological explorations are more intricate, the slight-of-hand more subtle. Clamence is a 'juge-pénitent' – that is, by being penitent, by being confessional, he re-establishes himself as a judge, and retains the innocence, the freedom from being judged that is his primary endeavour. By professing guilt he becomes saviour, that is saviour of himself. If he is guilty, than everyone is guilty, should they share in his honesty – which is a dishonest honesty. 'Plus je m'accuse et plus j'ai le droit de vous juger' (The more I accuse myself the more I have a right to judge you) (1548; 140). Jean-Baptiste becomes the epitome of another lost generation, a generation over-eager to address faults in themselves and others, and by this manoeuvre to establish a zone of safety where they are exempt from judgment. Camus's constant purpose is to address this (his) generation and to define and to give it an aesthetic form. Some may have thought that Camus caught the worst of the great debate, but if that is the case, in *The Fall*, in his own merciless self-exposure, in his admissions and unmaskings, but also in his staunchly consistent views of the errors of the advanced consciousness of his time he has brought about his own vindication.

As with his other works, *The Fall* engages in the practice of recapitulation. (Todd sees a bridge between Meursault and Clamence, indeed one that passes over *The Plague*, whose characters, good and bad, he judges to be 'linear.') Such recapitulation is more than an aesthetic device; it is a psychological need. Camus seems drawn to re-establish connections between his works, to mark continuities, even to make reparations, and to overcome the breaks that have of necessity occurred in his ascension to world fame. He does not wish to disown that world that he had to abandon. This urge to continuity – in historical understanding and in personal life – we can signal as one of the abiding traits of the writer of consciousness.

On the other hand, with Sartre in *Words*, his final word that is not his last word, the need is quite contrary: he understands his past in order to disown it (*Les mots*). This is not a Proustian *Recherche du temps perdu*, let alone *Le temps retrouvé*, but rather an attempt to liberate himself from his past, which he feels has disfigured him. Consequently his work is not marked by a need to establish continuities but rather by breaks and ruptures. *Being and Nothingness* confirms this. The past is inert until reinterpreted by the future project. The 'pour-soi' is by its very nature free. Hence one is in a constant process of *remaking* oneself. Sartre underwent several conversions in this process of reformulation. Embedded in these stages of development is the sense of a 'new man' who is different from the old man, and who as a consequence must write from the moment where he is.

But even these considerations, accurate as far as they go – and that is quite far – do not go far enough. *Words* must of necessity be conjoined with *The Fall.* At the end of his response to Camus's letter, Sartre promises to write of himself – soon – as cruelly as he did of Camus. And in *Words* he does so; here is Sartre at his best, not writing an autobiography so much as an auto-critique, a meditative palinode, one where he attempts to revoke all that his past, the ideals of the nineteenth-century bourgeois writer, his own childhood had made of him, a bourgeois writer committed to words rather than to things, confined to that 'sedentary trade,' consumed by the desire for a posthumous glory. Never has recantation been so well written, so thoughtfully explained and explored. This is his 'confession,' but one that is not concerned with self-justification as it is with a rendering of accounts, the costs, the debits, but also with the necessities of who he is and what he has had to be. He finally realizes that the hold of childhood and the past is so firm that, try as one might, one cannot dislodge its fingers because they have entered into the making of who he is.

This mood of meditative introspection was not confined to *Words* but extended to three elegiac essays that form a suite in *Situations IV.* The first of these essays was written a few days after the death of Camus (January 1961), the second revived Sartre's friendship with the long-dead Paul Nizan, and the third, the longest, appeared in a special issues of *Les temps modernes* (October 1961) after the sudden death of Merleau-Ponty. Written separately, they are bound together as monodies on death and friendship. They are personal, reminiscent, lucidly and unsparingly analytical, biographical and auto-biographical, yet cast upon the larger screen of intellectual and political history from the 1930s to the 1960s. He admits his break with Camus and that they never saw one another again, but that he, like others, always wished to know what Camus was thinking in his sullen and silent withdrawal. He continues to place Camus in that most honourable of French traditions, amidst the *moralistes* of the eighteenth century. Such early and unexpected death is a scandal, but that does not deplete the cycle of his work or leave it unfinished, but only underlines its constant purpose, which was to express humanity's protest against the inhumanity of death.

Paul Nizan endured 'le vide' of the bourgeois life, the suicidal impulse toward which his father almost succumbed in facing the sameness of his schedule of life extending through the years to his death. Against such monotony Nizan protested with hatred and anger, and despite the calumnious efforts of the Communist Party to tarnish him as a paid informer, was thirty years ahead of Sartre in his current appeal that Sartre, in urging the publication of his forgotten works, did much to abet.

Yet he too is long gone in the shrouds of death, but not his memory or his current appeal to anger.

The fullest and most sustained essay is that on Merleau-Ponty, because it was marked by the dissolution and the partial re-establishment of a friendship that had endured a long time, and that was prevented from overcoming a lingering awkwardness by Merleau-Ponty's sudden death by heart failure. In *Being and Nothingness* Sartre can dismiss death as a nullity, totally alien to the human capacity for projection. Death, where is thy dominion; death, where is thy sting? In these essays, certainly influenced by the mood change attending the recantation of *Words*, death has extended its dominion and sharpened its sting, penetrating to the very fibre of these meditative essays, which nevertheless preserve some form of the human being, if only by their enunciation of bitter truths.

The same impetus motivates *Words*. Sartre was raised by a doting mother and grandparents who cosseted and closeted him. He lived for them and to show his virtues as a child genius. He lived in an imaginary world of bookish adventure, like Rousseau, filling his mind with the exploits of what he read. Hence, like Rousseau – and not the only point in which they can be brought together – he was later overtaken by an abhorrence of imaginative consciousness, the Quixotes and Tom Sawyers of aspiration. Put simply, his childhood limitations and deprivations contributed to the fashioning of an imaginary wishfulness that fell victim to the need for high-sounding resolutions. Thus also like Rousseau he would envy the more direct and simpler souls. But this punishing dichotomy also reveals the more positive appeal that each of them possesses and that is at the source of their powers – the capacity to identify fully with what they read, and the corollary necessity to identify fully with what they wrote.

As could be expected, Sartre, the master surveyor of French literary culture, is at his best when describing the ideals and the goals of the nineteenth-century bourgeoisie, which his grandfather, Charles Schweitzer, a noted pedagogue, represented. His family belonged to that branch of liberal protestantism that, under the influence of Voltaire, was dechristianizing itself (82). They were Christians of form, for special events. They abhorred any atheist, whom Sartre describes as the only one who spoke of God (even if to deny such presence). 'Bref, un monsieur qui avait des convictions religieuses.' Sartre would always avow that he was an atheist by 'conviction' (*Les écrits* 240). On the other hand, 'la bonne société croyait en Dieu pour ne pas parler de Lui' (good society believed in God in order not to speak of Him). These new Lutherans converted the Holy Spirit into a manifestation of the sublime and spiritual faith into 'bonne conscience.' Charles Schweitzer's most memorable line of self-satisfaction – one indeed that does an injustice to the more enduring virtues of the man – was delivered frequently at table, when he would conclude, 'Mes enfants, comme il est bon de ne rien avoir à se reprocher' (My children, how nice it is when there is nothing for which one can reproach oneself) (*Les mots* 53). It was the memory of such smugness that entered into the portraits of the leaders of Bouville in *Nausea*. It was Charles who sensed the works of the Holy Spirit in all things sublime, where indeed the Good, the True, and the Beautiful all came together, thus embracing the nineteenth-century bourgeois ideal of fusion and coherence (51). But he did make sure that his grandson knew his authors from Hesiod to Hugo, a bequest that meant that later Sartre could write of literature as being himself one of the chosen, with authority. This was a gift, indeed one that he could later ignore or be unconscious of, but which itself meant it was a dispensation.

Sartre himself provides the dating of his own itinerary. The work was begun soon after the response to Camus. He is correcting manuscript on 22 April 1963 (52), his literary blindness due to the haze of his childhood and its captivation by the ideals of the nineteenth-century bourgeois writer, devoted to solitude and posthumous glory, continued for some thirty years, which would be some time in the early 1950s; now, as he writes, some ten years later in his own fifties, he admits to the errors of his ways. Even his works that brought him fame were products of his own mystifications. In them he was still a believer in the medieval manner: he still thought words were tantamount to things ('je confondis les choses avec leurs noms' – 203). The basis of his new attitude toward *Nausea* is doubly remarkable. His argument that existence was 'injustifiée' was sincerely held; nevertheless it placed him, the analyst, outside contestation: 'Je me tins pour tiré d'affaires.' He was as philosophically 'berlue' or dim-sighted as he was physically. The existence of his cohorts was briny, while his was 'hors de cause.' Is he not here repeating Camus's arguments as being the 'juge-pénitent,' the condemning judge who escapes judgment? The same with *Being and Nothingness*, which he does not name: 'mystifié, j'écrivais joyeusement sur notre malheureuse condition. Dogmatique je doutais de tout sauf d'être l'élu de doute ... j'étais heureux' (mystified myself, I wrote joyfully of our unhappy condition. I dogmatically doubted everything except for myself being the elector of doubt ... I was happy) (204). The spirit above the dust, the elector of doubt, was happy in the country of despair. The metabolism of pleasure contradicted the message of anguish – a contradiction at the basis of this philosophy that Camus had repeatedly made, most pointedly in *The Fall.* Sartre himself courageously, with that fabled lucidity, admits to the same charge. The true feeling of religious doubt, the anguish of Luther, the dark night of the soul was not for his constant 'légèreté:' he fulfilled himself too much, he enjoyed himself too much in writing and speaking of anguish, forlornness, and despair. For ten years now (204), he has been a man as if awakened; the non-religious soul, the atheist, but one who must speak seriously of ultimate things, the one who rejected the cosy Lutheranism of his family, once again has experienced a sobering conversion. But what is to be done? He has lost his investiture but he has not been defrocked. The building is in ruins. He has come face-to-face with 'notre impuissance.' The tone of humility as well as humiliation is unmistakable. The tower has tumbled, resulting in that astonishing realization that overtakes all religious souls: 'La culture ne sauve rien ni personne, elle ne justifie pas' (Culture saves nobody and nothing; it cannot justify) (205). Are we not here back in the midst of Luther, Rousseau, and Dostoevsky, that is, among those in search of justification, and who then must endure such moments of abasement and renunciation? But of course Sartre can renounce his attitude toward his work but he cannot renounce himself. He is a writer born and bred. Least of all can he renounce his own childhood, and so here he is, more than in the middle of the way, as a fifty-year-old man, still harbouring all the traits of the long-ago imaginatively serious boy that he was.

Words (how preferable as an English title would be Hamlet's response, 'Words, words, words') is a work of terrible unmasking. The prince of letters in his day regards himself as a fraud. In a last gesture of renunciation the intellectual will find rejuvenation, a just cause, by providing a protective shield for the confiscated Maoist *La cause du peuple*, agreeing to serve as its editor-in-chief. Yet, indicating the continuing antinomy of his life, he spends his real moments up until the time of his total blindness in 1973 writing the massive and unfinished 'life' of Flaubert, where he was able to delineate once again as he had done in *Words* the failures of the nineteenth-century writer and his symbolic representation in the history of his times.

These were not his last words, but certainly his final words – despite his later publications. As Bernard-Henri Lévy has so adroitly turned the phrase, '[Sartre] is not the last of the intellectuals, but the first to cease being so' (713). *Words* announced the fall of the man of letters, the last of the public intellectuals, the last Dreyfusard, the death of literature, alternately using and being used by the new young radicals, envying their thoughts, as accomplishing in five years what it took him thirty to perceive. Some have praised this new lease on activism, praising not his works but his life. As Coleridge said of Luther, his whole life was a poem, and the same could be said of the other daemonic writers who underwent such turbulent change in the course of their careers. Others have deplored it, believing that his abdication opened the ways not only for the post-Sartrean *modernes philosophes*, whom Sartre would accuse in lump-sum fashion of the 'refusal of history' (*Les écrits* 434), but also for those who despised literature, the new nihilists of the boulevard, for whom a cobbler's work equalled that of Raphael, a cry in the street was deemed of more value than the achievement of an enduring work of art. Sartre himself questioned the value of *Nausea* when brought into balance with the death of an enfant.[30] But we know that only in moments of spiritual crisis do such false dichotomies acquire argumentative appeal. In their alignments they are colossally disproportionate. What possible parallelism could be drawn between them? Would any infant have been spared had he not written *Nausea*? By taking to the streets, did he save any infant? Did those whose absenteeism or actions might have been responsible for the death of children read *Nausea*? Or did those engaged in thoughtful efforts of redress not read *Nausea*? Of course one can never know, and that is why the imbalance of the proposition is to the point. Moreover, what would or does compensate for the death of a child? Why should a work of creative intelligence be placed in the balance? Certainly many other complex factors are at work here, for which he needed a Voltaire, the Voltaire of the letter to Rousseau, to right the balance, to disengage the issues.

Perhaps it is only a religious spirit seeking justification who is brought to such dire choices. Sartre, the ardent protestant in spirit, had already denounced culture, which does not justify, but in this moment of spiritual crisis Sartre unaccountably and uncustomarily lapses into a kind of blindness, the direct opposite of those who made the leap of faith, but with the same unsubsiding kinetic fervour. The spiritual crisis that beset the Russian intellectuals of the 1860s – fallen-away seminarians – submerged Sartre's mind. The new activists with whom Sartre allied himself denigrated the value of literary study and the validity of the literary imagination. Without knowing it, they contributed to the new age of non-attention that Simone de Beauvoir's Koestler-like character so accurately predicted. The king has become a commoner, which is what Sartre in his need for acceptance always wanted to be. What he found in the strange career change, hawking Leftist sheets in the street, haranguing workers coming from their plants with Marxist jargon (to which they remained quite impassive), was the fullness of life he always desired, the activity among brothers, a life of comradely transparency without hierarchies of class or privilege, of priority or position. What he sought was the plenitude of direct contact – all those things of which his childhood had deprived him – and more importantly what he offered was the greatest gift of his generation, democratic openness.

Allied with this larger recantation is the essential question of why he renounced his career as a novelist.[31] *La dernière chance*, the announced title of the fourth instalment of the work, needed to be written and yet could not be written. It would have brought together in a conclusive synthesis the truncated halves of *Troubled Sleep*, the first part of which traces the continuing development of Mathieu and the second the activities of Brunet in the camp of prisoners. As it now stands, the novel is a failure, despite the expressed preference for it of both Sartre and Simone de Beauvoir. As usual, Gaston Gallimard was correct in his understanding as to why the novel did not enjoy a popular success – it was a sequel that had no end (de Beauvoir, *La force des choses* 212).The fourth volume was to be the completion and synthesis. In it Mathieu becomes an active member of the Resistance, discovering his historical objectivity and meeting a heroic death by torture, the prime example through his complex development of the person who *makes* himself a hero. Brunet, in his turn, going beyond 'l'esprit de sérieux,' from solitude and doubt, discovers his 'subjectivity.' The novel thus turns out to be a romantic tragedy, with a reconciliation of opposites, and with all the characters (including Daniel) achieving their operatic redemption in death. It is not difficult to see why Sartre could not finish the novel. For one, it went against his essential conception of tragic conflict as represented in the essay on Georges Bataille. Further, following the critical year 1952, the year of his rupture with both Camus and Merleau-Ponty, the story of the Resistance and the great hopes for creative syntheses in private and public interests that the early years of Liberation promised no longer held true in the turbulent divisions of French intellectual life. Moreover, Sartre himself has changed and he could no longer commit his energies to complete an anachronistic work that did not represent the fullness of his current situation.

But to follow the Sartre of his later development is the way of the biographer, whose task is to trace the journey of a life. It is not the way of the critical reader. While Sartre may have given a new meaning to praxis, which in its later application came to mean action in the streets as well as his laudable striving for direct democracy, still his works remain. Sartre may have renounced his works, but we as readers do not have to do the same. Palinodes are always harsh, such acts of renunciation severe. If we allowed all recantations, we would not have the *Aeneid*, Petrarch's lyrics (his 'giovenile errore'), not even Chaucer's *Canterbury Tales*. The palinode must be recognized for what it is, a last stage of depletion, of 'impuissance' pushed to the limits, in extremis. The last is not always the best. That it is final and filled with renouncement does not privilege it. It might represent a betrayal of what was earlier and more appealing. We as readers are free to pick and choose. I prefer the Sartre of the antinomies, the Sartre of *Nausea* and the great novelistic trilogy joined with the brazen philosophical daring and hubris of *Being and Nothingness*, and the masterly surveyor of French literary culture in company with the beauty of his meditative essays on Merleau-Ponty, Nizan, and yes, on Camus. These are works of high literary culture to which we can turn and return, works of redemption and lucid uncompromising insight.

We can revisit the notion of two Sartres, but here meant in a different sense. There is the Sartre of anger and accusation, the Sartre who marches in the street, who signs petitions, and who writes manifestos, and the Sartre of meditative analysis and historical understanding. 1952 was indeed a critical year, what with the open debate with Camus and the publication of *Les communistes et la paix*. The first, virulent, resulted in the permanent breach with Camus, the second, with Merleau-Ponty. The latter work is practically unreadable, leaden, as even his loyal (but not uncritical) editors Contat and Rybalka are obliged to admit (*Les écrits* 275). But better examples may be garnered from two *inédits* retrieved in *Les écrits*. The first, '*Les animaux malades de la rage*,' is vitiated by a visceral anti-Americanism following the execution of the Rosenbergs in 1953. While his anti-Americanism is not a virtue, it is the least of the faults of this article, punctuated by extraordinary leaps of rage, from the Rosenbergs, to witch-hunts, to the 'inevitable' connection between their executions and America's launching of nuclear warfare. It is an understatement to say it was written without full comprehension. This article contrasts notably with Sartre's interview in 1959 with Francis Jeanson, where he details with brilliant analysis and historical understanding the germs of self-defeat, the nemesis inherent in colonialism. Two Sartres do exist, but not meant chronologically, as early and late, or pre- and post-conversion, but rather qualitatively and left to the judgment of the critical reader.

More than one circle is completed here, as the lively and hostile public debate between Sartre and Camus finds something of a denouement in their final words, not final chronologically of course, but final spiritually, as now there was no more to be said. Not final, also as being the last words, because their debate, which preceded them, will also continue long after them. The Thirty Golden Years of the French intellectual may have come to an end, what with the intervention of television, the cinema, and the Internet all bringing in a new type of celebrity, sounding loudly the tocsin for the seriously meditative champions of the word. The loss that Simone de Beauvoir predicted did not come about by total illiteracy but rather by superficial literacy, adapted to a mass technological society given to speed, sex, sport, and leisure. The role of the intellectuals, whose careers began with the Dreyfusards at the end of the nineteenth century, was rekindled by the animosities of the 1930s, and reached its intellectual dominance (one-sided) in the postwar years, may have suffered an interruption. But the recurrence of dualisms and the record of the 1990s would argue against a complete cessation. Both Sartre and Camus returned in full force, answering the needs of a society for intellectuals whose presence is total, that is totally given to the integrity of their thought as well as addressing the larger engulfing problems of a society.

13. Hybridity Prevails

Chronological arrangement and its corollary strategy of 'deep background' show that the dominant opposition of Sartre and Camus was historically positioned. They were twentieth-century second-generation modernists, with new intellectual starting points and baselines. Rejecting the nineteenth-century idealism of their forebears and the coherence theory they fostered, they began their intellectual maturity with a sense of the absurd, which they found in their existential predecessors. Their common task was to search out some basis for meaning in an increasingly meaningless universe and to address the issues of the times from a starting point of the absurd. And just as certainly the origins of the absurd differed for each of them, so with equal certainty here their paths diverged, as Sartre's own political activism, his need to be a man among men, would take precedence over his sense of the high values of literary commitment. Moreover, to address their large mental pictures, while Sartre sought out a 'plenum' of existence, he did so by disowning his past, by seeking separation from the dead hand that threatened to keep him from the living present. Camus, for his part, required a 'contin-

uum,' a reconnection with the past from which he had felt himself alienated. For him, to recover the past was an act of revitalization, of himself
and of those whom he had abandoned. Writing, for him, was an act of
reimbursement, a search for forgiveness, a way of transcending the
orphanhood in time, the isolation from both his homeland and the new
worlds he had conquered.

The complexities of twentieth-century thought brought about other
changes as well. This is the time where 'the centre does not hold,' where
intellects are beset by 'vacillations.' Almost naturally the normal alignments should waver and 'crossings' occur. Hybridity prevails. *Words* may
have consigned the public intellectual to a death sentence, and Sartre as
being the last of the Dreyfusards, but among the copious *éloges* printed in
Le monde after his death, that of the Frankfurter *Rundschau* declared with
greater historical perceptiveness that the epoch of Voltaire was finished.
As a man who championed causes and who found in the *philosophes*
themselves (and in particular in the *Dictionnaire philosophique*) the prototypes to emulate, Sartre was Voltairean. Like Voltaire, Sartre wrote to
change the world, and his method was also *écraser* because infamy – the
vilified dogs of anti-communism – abounded. Like Voltaire against a
background of destruction ('Nature is the empire of destruction') he
sought to retrieve some genuine human value. But equally like Voltaire
he was a man of *légèreté*; this does not mean simply humorous amusement
or a kind of spirited volatility, but rather a capacity to move on, not to get
stuck. Thus his 'conversions' represent changes to be sure, but changes
of choice and decision, not changes that overpower one, where one is in
the grips of some powerful force that compels the will, where one finds
some authentic being. Such movement and moments are alien to Sartre
as they were to Voltaire.

In the same voluminous memorial commentary with which *Le monde*
extolled the achievements of Sartre (only Raymond Aron abstained,
declaring that, as they did Sartre, such traditional *éloges* filled him with
horror), Louis Althusser issued his famous comparison with Rousseau.
Quoting Marx, as he says, from memory, he declares Sartre to be 'our'
Rousseau, because he was basically an intransigent who refused even the
least compromise with established authority. Whether this is totally accurate in regard to Rousseau might be open to dispute (again see *The Social
Contract*), nevertheless in their private lives, in the ways they each sought
to make their thought and actions to be at one, in their refusals to be
beholden, they were both uncompromising and the comparison holds
and is instructive. But again, he was 'our' Rousseau in more ways than

one, more than in his refusal to be beholden (as in his refusal to accept the Nobel Prize for literature – the Académie française he had already placed out of the question – just as Rousseau failed to show for the king's pension). He was like Rousseau in his adherence to the radical protestantism abandoned by the Lutherans of the nineteenth century, his sense of the terrible individual freedom, that one can find justification only by oneself, not through intermediaries, whether it be the Party or the church, that one must read the book of life directly, and that culture, above all culture, cannot save or justify. Like Luther and like Rousseau, he was in need of justification and thus underwent several modified 'conversions.' And yet he had to confront the fact that this 'élu de doute' was blessed with a 'légèreté' of spirit, one that belied the philosophy of angst. He was not an outsider but an insider, and despite his own need to escape from their limitations, to the manor and the manner born. Yet he did buck against the limitations of bourgeois life and sought out fullness of being, the plenitude that encompasses both high and low, although in his case it frequently veered in the direction of the low. Like Rousseau, he was a visionary, with a utopian vision of a classless society (about which his own doubts were very much in evidence). Indeed, his most attractive thoughts and yearnings embraced the spirit of festival, were carnivalesque. But unlike Rousseau, he had a penchant for violence – but in this too he was a child of his century. Also unlike Rousseau, he was, as Raymond Aron referred to him, in basic temperament a rebel. Or as Bernard-Henri Lévy calls him, a man of perpetual refusal. This is far from the Rousseau who only sought integration, within himself, with Nature, and with society, however much his efforts may have misplayed. For Rousseau, 'Le tout est bien,' and humankind in emulation of Plutarch's heroes must be willing to sacrifice themselves for the sake of a higher virtue.

In the century's extensive cross-breeding, Camus shares the divided parentage. Each was both Voltaire and Rousseau and neither at the same time. While there is ample sufficiency for comparing Camus in his many qualities with other writers of consciousness, whether it be the middling position of Erasmus or the restrained style of Voltaire, still it was he who underwent the misfortunes of Rousseau, of being misunderstood. It was with him that rebellion changed camps, and it was he who was treated as a defector and as a renegade from the ascendancy of the *philosophes* of his time, a heretic in the midst of the new orthodoxy. It was he who was another provincial come to the metropolitan city (how tantalizing is the notation added to *The First Man*, 'What they did not like in him was the

Algerian' – 317), which uprooting separated him from himself, his origins, and the ways he knew and loved, who felt the need to overcome the rupture with his past, to reconstitute his past, to seek forgiveness for betrayal, imagined or real.

Whole centuries went into the making of this most remarkable dualism of our time. Yet in the verve and fervour of their own accomplishments, in the engagements with themselves and with the urgent questions of their times, they had their unique qualities of attraction. Dualisms are replicative but non-imitative. They arise spontaneously, like wildfire, but still over recognizable historically conditioned terrain. By the curious path of recirculation, that Joyce made into the motif of his grandest work, it is by virtue of their very particularities and shared differences that they too embody the perennial tensions of our modern Western culture, and its two intellectual nations.

Epilogue

'Only the flash of recognition brings delight.'
– Stanley Kunitz, 'Tristia'

Dualisms and the Humanities

One can terminate but not bring to completion a work such as *Dualisms*, whose theme is so expansive and still expanding (even as I write, multiple additions could still be made to the preface's first endnote). Across a wide spectrum of interests the theme continues its advance. The preface also indicated other dualisms that could have been included. While as a scholar-critic I have been drawn to those figures who affirm the validity of the literary imagination and the value of literary studies, dualisms' extensive field of concepts and methods can provide transformative centres applicable to the sister arts, to other disciplines (e.g., anthropology, economics, religion, philosophy, history) and other dominant characters. In American political history, from Adams and Jefferson to Ike (Eisenhower) and Douglas (MacArthur), dualisms can help clarify the ways of seeing, the long-lasting disputes, and the openings to comprehension that such contention reveals.

Dualisms probes the deepest, most far-reaching and abiding tensions of our culture. It can provide the better pathways for understanding the nature and the appeal of the humanities, now in a state of crisis, threatened by dissolution from within and belittlement and disregard from without. Unlike some conferences on the humanities, or the programs of foundations to rescue the humanities by means of easy access and databases, reflections upon the crucial complexities of dualisms affirm the historical and still-continuing vitality of humankind's ability to encounter difference, to create it, and by enduring it to live more fully through it. My book maintains that it was their very differences that confirmed these figures as truth-seekers and that their truths did not come easily but were made out of contest with others, with themselves, with authorities, and with the past.

The first affirmation for the humanities that can be derived from *Dualisms* is the presence of the past. 'The past is never dead,' one of Faulkner's characters declares, 'it's not even past.'[1] While the faces and terminology change, there persists a constancy in debate, a contested opposition that lives through the centuries, as the same or similar questions are posed in different intellectual climates. Are the levels of existence congruent and do things conform to our words for them, or are they separate and alien (the Scholastics of the thirteenth century)? Is the burden of the Christian message ethical, deriving from some sense of convergence between the divine and the human, or is it metaphysical, obliging individuals to square existence with the dimensions of their souls (Erasmus and Luther in the sixteenth century)? Does one adhere to the testimony of one's senses, the evidence of an objective world, or does one follow the dictates of the Spirit, that *voix intérieure* (Voltaire and Rousseau in the eighteenth century)? Can one abide within limits, accepting contradictions and an ameliorist position that is gradual, advancing by slow steps, or is one's world antithetical, apocalyptic, with individuals moved by the urgency of the moment to follow the directives of history (the post-revolutionary choices of the nineteenth and twentieth centuries)? These are the many frontal positions on the compass of moral choice and of profound significance for the future of religion, philosophy, art, history, and culture. It is from and within such questions that the humanities take their form and substance.

But there is another reason for dualisms' abiding usefulness. They inspire the recognitions that Coleridge (and we like him) found so appealing. Dualisms comprise totems of resemblance, myths where the lines of opposing heroes have similar faces, pushing outward from the known into the unknown. Through them we both add to and recognize the gravitational centre, the densities of our culture. They are co-signers of another declaration of independence. We are their continuators. Not fossilized for museum spectacle, they are ever-present and recurrent, still active by the debate that inspired them, marked by signposts and warning signals, flashes lending light in the dusk, spectral illuminations of some inheritance that tell us where we have been and where sadly we are.

The second affirmation that should participate in any discussion of the humanities has been called *la présence totale*, the total presence of authors, artists, thinkers in the full engagement of their works. For Luther this meant the discovery of faith, for Rousseau, a positive sentiment adhering to that *sentiment intérieur,* for Dostoevsky, an active love expanding beyond the restrictive Slavophilism into a more universal pan-humanism, for Camus a belief that retrieves moral truths from the wreckage of a shattering absurdity. Such commitments do not describe a work ethic, but rather a sustaining endorsement of the arguments of one's being. Yet all, those of consciousness or the daemonic, were prone to moments of doubt, to bouts of depressive worthlessness, to Rousseau's emptiness ('le vuide'), of being pushed aside, *de trop,* forlorn. All great imaginations, including Shakespeare and Tolstoy, were beset by the laughter of the gods: 'We are such stuff as dreams are made on.' There is creative potential in this devastating perspective, yet where in the lexicon of the new discussants of the humanities is there place for the spiritual language of worthlessness?

It belongs to our situation that opposing voices should question the springs of belief, as they did Socrates' *daimon.* Against fervent conviction may be set the derision of scepticism, or the culture of mundanity. The ally of these counter forces is time, their tonic reduced expectations, a capacity to abide within the limits of human existence, including an acute sense of the progressive frittering away of all things, of high expectations and great moments, which means that nothing stands for long, that enthusiasms are ephemeral and ghostly fugitive. More positively, these more modest sceptics are convinced that when the dust settles a consolidation will take place and in the length of historical time reasonableness will enjoy its own restoration.

But such moments of resolution, providing new intellectual plateaus, will also find themselves in the grips of a new dualism. Debate is recurrent. Total presence does not lead to consensus but rather to contestation – the third affirmation that *Dualisms* affords the humanities. The conquests of truth-seekers are gained through contest. Full engagement moves each toward greater clarification, and this impetus separates a genuine dualism from what finally becomes nothing more than the matter of a quarrel. What the humanities require at this moment are not instruments of access but breakers of thought, public intellectuals consumed by their quest of a goal outside themselves and a driving faith from within. The absence of such figures is one of the disheartening and perplexing problems of our time. Internally, the absence of rational debate originates in this refusal of commitment; externally, we are silenced by what Camus called 'the technique of fear.'

Not only do dualisms generate change, they come together in debate over how to respond to change, certainly the essential question for humanistic thought. The beauty of genuine dualisms is that each of the contestants is in search of renewal, each has turned his face toward the future. Their differences lie in the ways one gets there. Writers of consciousness speak on behalf of the slow accumulation of reasoned thought, the gradual benefits of education, tolerance, and freedom, of knowing where to draw the line, of applying a 'brake.' But they also run the risk of recoiling from the radical change that is justified by being grounded in the legitimate principles that undergird a culture, when appeal is made to genuine values that have been ignored or abused. Debate and contestation arouse scrutiny over the justness of the various claims, and it is most crucially here that the humanities emerge as arbiters of moral choice.

Wars of discourse enlist their own means of response. Daemonic rhetoric introduces the particular problem of how one responds to radical persuasion. By virtue of the energy of accusation it places the writer of consciousness at a distinct disadvantage. Measuring reality against some ideal, all societies and social structures fall short. Accusing the Pharisee within, radical discourse brings discomfort to the individual as well. It is easy pickings. Under the duress of the urgency of the moment, its alternatives are dire and its argumentation lopsided, calling for a radical activism and invoking an iconoclastic suspicion of culture and civilization. It asks, as Sartre did, what is the value of *Nausea* in the balance with the death of a child? While apparently unanswerable and overwhelming, the question is logically nonsensical, caused by a disproportion in the terms. Does *Nausea* mean to stand for all the accomplishments of culture and civilization? While Sartre's dire choice is extreme, it does represent an undercurrent, and one might add a harmful contradiction, in the writers of daemonic force. Must their conversion experiences rely so heavily on a blast against culture or civilization? 'La culture ne suave rien ni personne, elle ne justifie pas' (Culture saves nobody and nothing; it cannot justify) (ch. 5, Sartre, *Les mots* 569). Or, a not dissimilar question from an earlier time: of what value is Aristotle in relation to Christ? Rousseau would prefer that his pupil be a shoemaker rather than a poet and that the theatre not be introduced into a small region; his argument would thus disband the regional troupes by which actors hone their talents and plays are improved. How does one ignore the totalitarian impulse present in the daemonic? How does one respond to such accusation? Erasmus's response to Dorp is exemplary, as is that of Voltaire to Rousseau, particularly with its blending of down-to-earth humour, the 'yes/but' trope, and a simple but passionate defence of the true qualities of simple reading, of art and culture. However subject to abuses, they rectify, bring solace, and console. Harold Bloom intensifies the defence of great literature when he writes of its aesthetic splendour, intellectual power, and wisdom (*Where Shall Wisdom Be Found?* 1).

Whatever their differences, the figures of a dualism represent the lived reality of mutual involvement. They represent in practice the intersubjectivity for which philosophers have sought to provide an intellectual foundation. And more than that, whether expatriates and cosmopolitan or repatriates and nativist, they all were determined to find the means to live their lives anew. In their entanglements they all espoused various versions of freedom. This is why they were at the forefront of debate in their times, and why, in our time, those whom we call daemonic may be distinguished at their base from fascism or any radical fanaticism.

This should remind us that above all what we find in genuine dualisms is a noble engagement, one that originally separates them from a simple quarrel or the breaking-up of friends. They are the guardians of culture or diagnosticians of its discontents, but across their squared-off antagonism a parity is achieved by means of difference as well as an uncommon clarification of what it is that divides them. By upholding their different manners of thinking true, in-depth and honest public debate takes place. Rational discussion is elevated by means of their intense and highly personalized grappling. This is surely the lesson *Dualisms* bears for our time.

Notes

Preface

1 An added instance is Edmonds and Eidinow's third instalment along the road of twosomes, *Rousseau's Dog*. However, this work, despite its billing as the story of 'two great thinkers at war in the age of the Enlightenment,' is more a high-gossip travelogue than a dialogue. For Rousseau and Hume, despite the two dozen or more letters exchanged between them, 'There is no dialogue or engagement about ideas' (Edmonds and Eidinow 141). This remains the story of a spat, an unfortunate one, an 'infernal' one, but still the small history of a quarrel. See chap. 3, n74. Showing the pertinence of the topic, this ever-expanding list now includes Richard Lingeman's *Double Lives: American Writers' Friendships*, which, with welcomed attention to American writers, describes some of their collaborative efforts, and despite all the tensions, breaches, and silences, the enduring sense of a friendship, if only remembered.

2 This dual emphasis indicates how this study differs from two works that I admire very much for their well-argued and elaborately sustained theses: Frank Sulloway's *Born to Rebel* and Randall Collins's *Sociology of Philosophies*. Sulloway's work, with its intriguing arguments and wealth of statistical data, keeps to the domain of family dynamics and maintains that the first-born in the family tend to be more conservative while the later-born sibling is more creative, hence 'born to rebel.' This account remains within the family birth order and thus avoids the changes that are brought about by extra-familial encounters, such as might be occasioned by dualisms. Collins's work produces a different problem. Where Sulloway emphasizes familial dynamics, Collins looks to the larger social structures. Where the one (Sulloway) scants the other, the other (Collins) discounts the one. We can readily accept his

premise that 'intellectual life is first of all conflict and disagreement,' and we agree when he locates individuals and their ideas in 'intellectual groups – such as coteries, or circles – in master-pupil chains and in contemporary rivalries' (Collins 6–7). But there is one crucial difference between his socio-logical structures and the nature of dualisms, and that concerns the roles of individuals. Collins argues against the notion that individuals *beget* ideas, sug-gesting that our reliance on individuals is a kind of shorthand fetishism born of the need to worship heroes. But it is also relying on straw figures to believe that supporting the role of individuals is also to believe that we act in a structural or historical vacuum. The whole point of a dualism belies this argument. The very affinities between the figures of a dualism argue for a cohortship of ideas, a mutuality in association. Dualisms do not dissolve any of the three kinds of groupings listed here; in fact, they employ them, but the simple history of groups does not do away with the role of individuals in conflict. In *Dualisms* intersubjectivity and individual assertion are conjoined.

3 See Ricardo J. Quinones, *The Changes of Cain*, and Alastair Reid, 'Neruda and Borges.' For Paz and Fuentes, see Steve Fainaru, 'Poisoned Pens'; for Rich-ardson and Fielding, see Michael McKeon, *The Origins of the English Novel, 1600–1740*. For Wordsworth and Coleridge, see Thomas P. McFarland, *Romanticism and the Forms of Ruin*. For Wordsworth and Byron, see Jerome McGann, *Byron and Wordsworth*. For Carlyle and Mill, see Rachel Cohen, 'Can You Forgive Him?' For Goethe and Schiller, see introduction by J.A. Elias to Friedrich von Schiller's *Naïve and Sentimental Poetry* and *On the Sublime*. For Burckhardt and Nietzsche, see introduction by Oswyn Murray to Jacob Burckhardt's *Greeks and Greek Civilization*, where Burckhardt's conception of the agon as a noble competition, one essential to the health of a society, was first made available to the modern reader.

Introduction

1 Several works of French criticism have already alerted us to the dangers of simple comparisons. Henri Gouhier avoids the classical comparisons marked by a series of 'parallel antitheses' that are representative of the French spirit. He then adds to the list of typical rivalries: Voltaire and Rousseau coming after Descartes and Pascal, Corneille and Racine, Bossuet and Fénelon, and preceding Paul Claudel and Paul Valéry. His aim is to produce a work that is 'strictly historical,' showing the changing images of Voltaire and Rousseau in successive mirror reflections (*Rousseau et Voltaire* 1). Jean Fabre disavows any attempt to simulate the classical 'parallel lives,' made for the schoolroom that would reduce the relationship to an ideal schema (155). Each then pur-sues what I have called an itinerary of encounter. In fact the same phrase is

used by Jean-Francois Sirinelli in his *Sartre et Aron*. By tracing their *itinéraire*,
Sirinelli is able to map the trajectory of the intellectual in the twentieth century. All three works represent a movement towards detailed histories of the
interchanges between their respective pairs, and the last in particular shows
their significance for the history of the century itself or rather the life of the
intellectual in the century.

2   Hegel's subtle psychological insights confront notable facts – the decline of
the Catholic South and the growth of the Protestant North – that would continue to attract and bedazzle commentators, mainly because of the abundance of very plausible causes. Although far from an 'idealistic"
interpretation, the one work that confronts the same objective picture as
does Hegel's is Max Weber's *The Protestant Ethic and the Spirit of Capitalism.*
This work first appeared in two parts in 1904–5, and was then revised for its
place in Weber's much larger interests in the sociology of world religions.
The very first sentence in ch. 1 confronts the elementary fact 'that the business leaders and owners of capital [he is writing of Germany] ... the higher
grades of skilled labor, and even more the higher technically and commer-
cially trained personnel of modern enterprises, are overwhelmingly Protestant' (35). His study carries him into the background of ideas (75) that
account for this phenomenon, thus it is the *Geist* that he seeks to explore. It
derives from two principles of Protestantism: the idea of a 'calling,' whereby
one's lay station in life is in God's eyes as valid as that of a cleric, and an inheritance of asceticism, which results in the exercise of frugality and the avoidance of ostentation. These factors effect an enormous transformation – what
would traditionally have been termed greed now receives its own justification. The great example of this transfer is Benjamin Franklin – paradoxically,
the son of the Enlightenment becomes the spiritual grandson of Calvin. Critics, of which there have been many, have missed the 'battery of qualifications'
(Anthony Giddens, introduction, added 1976), that attend Weber's thesis.
Still it remains a classic in the examination of the social effects of religious
ideas, and not inadvertently after Tocqueville's *Democracy in America,* the best
commentary on the fundaments of American life, and in this regard comparable (through different methodologies) to William James's *The Varieties of
Religious Experience.* Worlds that had formerly been divided are now conjoined: one can have success in this world and salvation in the next. Such
notable instances of *bonne conscience* do not draw Weber's total approval. The
work does deserve criticisms; it underestimates two important parts of this
study: the adherence to the notion of Christian liberty by both Erasmus and
Luther, and its subsequent transformation in the Enlightenment into political liberty. Voltaire, certainly not imbued with any sense of asceticism, valued
commerce as contributing to the wealth of a nation. This depended upon the

spirit of industry thriving under the aegis of political and religious freedom. Voltaire stresses the access of parvenus to riches and the extraordinary development of Pennsylvania, under the legacy of religious toleration advocated by William Penn. Like all such works, Weber's has had its historical moment and its thesis has been made a shambles by the late-twentieth-century's globalized technology: Catholic Dublin, Spain, and Chile are driving centres of modern technology. Still, for its concern with the impact of radical Protestantism – and the transformations brought about and undergone – it remains a classic.

3 For Hegel, from the same *Philosophy of History,* see 'Thus does the Spirit of the Catholic world in general sink behind the Spirit of an Age,' 419.

4 In a similar defence of the publication of the complete works of Voltaire and Rousseau against another *mandement* by the bishop of Troyes, Jean-Baptiste Touquet (1821) chooses this quotation from Rousseau as epigraph, and then proceeds to demonstrate the ill effects of censorship – quite counterproductive, for such *mandements* only provoke curiosity and promote book sales. See chap. 3, n1. Rousseau's letter to Christophe de Beaumont serves as a kind of palimpsest for Touquet's. For an excellent discussion of how Voltaire figures in the post-revolutionary cultural wars of the time, see Raymond Trousson's *Visages de Voltaire,* especially 141–8. At this time Touquet published four separate editions of Voltaire's works.

5 In *Genius* Bloom does write of the 'genius of appreciation.' Genius can transmit a transcendent sense of awe and admiration (7). He does this without relinquishing the importance of 'misunderstanding.' In his most recent work, *Where Shall Wisdom Be Found?* he still maintains, 'Plato's shrewdness is that of strong poets throughout the ages: clearly misinterpret the dominant poetic forerunner, in order to clear imaginative space for yourself' (62). This last-named work is much concerned with great oppositions, agons, between Homer and Plato, literature and philosophy, and ultimately Athens and Jerusalem. It includes many individual pairings, such as Cervantes and Shakespeare, Montaigne and Bacon, Emerson and Nietzsche, and others, thus lending support to the contention of the beginning of the preface here that the interest in eminent figures in association is growing.

6 See chap. 3, 199–200.

Chapter 1: Erasmus and Voltaire

1 Works that, among others, I have found to be particularly useful are Cornelis Augustijn, *Erasmus: Der Humanist als Theologe und Kirchenreformer* and *Erasmus: His Life, Works, and Influence,* Heinrich Bornkamm, 'Erasmus und Luther'

and *Luther in Mid-Career*; Georges Chantraine, *Érasme et Luther*; Jacques Chomarat, *Grammaire et rhétorique chez Érasme*; E.W. Kohls, *Luther oder Erasmus*; Robert H. Murray, *Erasmus and Luther*; E. Gordon Rupp and Philip S. Watson, eds., *Luther and Erasmus*; Heiko O. Oberman, *Luther: Man between God and the Devil*; among her many useful works, Erika Rummel's *Erasmus and His Catholic Critics*, and her brief but scintillating *Erasmus*, especially 90–105; and the classic work by Fiorella de Michelis Pintacuda, *Tra Erasmo e Lutero*. John W. O'Malley anticipates some of the directions of this study when he exposes the 'underlying pattern,' 'a radical heuristic framework which imposed on them a response-pattern to practically every major question they addressed' (48). Erasmus was committed to a world of continuity, while Luther's responses were prompted by his sense of discontinuity.

2 See my *Dante Alighieri* 41–6.

3 MacCulloch estimates 'that there are 390 editions of various Luther's writings published in Germany in 1523 alone' (152).

4 See chapter 3, 200.

5 See Charles Trinkaus, 'Petrarch' 3–56, where Trinkaus not only emphasizes the Italian origins of humanistic culture, but also of Italian Christian humanism.

6 See the brief bibliographical sketches in Bietenholz and Deutscher, *Contemporaries of Erasmus*.

7 See Brecht 1: 43. Surprisingly enough, in his great debate with Erasmus, Luther resorted to classical illusions more frequently than did his adversary. See introductory note by A.N. Marlow and B. Drewery in Rupp and Watson 30–1.

8 In his freewheeling but perceptive introduction, E. Gordon Rupp is obviously wrong-headed when he denies that this was 'a very great debate,' elevating others because they 'stuck more closely to their subject' (1). While not ignoring the doctrinal fine points, in this study I call attention to the far more momentous personal issues involved in the clash.

9 Johan Huizinga, *Erasmus and the Age of Reformation*; Lewis Spitz, *The Protestant Reformation*, 106; Augustijn, *Erasmus: His Life, Works, and Influence*; R.J. Schoeck, *Erasmus of Europe*. For Augustijn see, however, the crucial exposition, in n36 below.

10 Jacques Chomarat's defence of Erasmus on this point is luminous. Ever conscious of Erasmus's rooting of his rhetoric in Christian charity, he rightly denies *lâcheté*, or cowardly fear as the cause of Erasmus's reluctance to get involved, his wish to remain a spectator. His refusal to become member of a party is the consequence of his desire to remain an 'individual, a Christian.' But despite the denial of 'cowardice,' Chomarat is well aware of the many

complexities of Erasmus's thought and character. An inevitable perplexity intervenes even in Erasmus's defence, when he speculates that Erasmus would not have acted as did Thomas More in conflict with Henry VIII, considering such intransigence to be in vain. But Chomarat adds the important qualification, 'peut-être a tort.' See *Grammaire et rhetorique* 2: 1166.

11 See the judicious searching of this vexed problem in Schoeck, *Erasmus of Europe* 1: 26–41. The different effects of the two fathers is given admirable interpretive force in Chomarat. Erasmus is a secretive person, he writes, a man who steals away. Even his irony is a way of keeping at a distance. Chomarat attributes it to the absence of his father: Erasmus's theology rests more upon the 'abandoned son' than the all-powerful God of the Hebrew Bible. 'Erasmus has not interiorized the role of the father.' From this derives Erasmus's refusal to accept leadership. This is most unlike Luther, who certainly became the man his father wanted him to be – although the routing was circuitous – and became the head of a church, the leader of a people. Erasmus, for his part, was always content to remain on the margins of society, content with a circle of friends. See Chomarat 1165–6. Unlike other Reformation scholars, Chomarat was not unwilling to absorb Erik Erikson's *Young Man Luther.*

12 See *CWE*: 31. As Erasmus himself quotes approvingly, 'A proverb is a saying in popular use, remarkable for some shrewd and novel turn' (31: 4).

13 This edition of *Enchiridion* includes the all-important prefatory letter of defence addressed to Paul Volz that first appeared in the republication of 1518. The letter connects the earlier work with the later climate of opinion, even containing an oblique defence of Luther's efforts (*CWE* 66: 13). In his introductory remarks, O'Malley refers to Erasmus as being comprehensive (in his cultural references), corrective (mainly toward the scholastics, the monks, and the friars), and accommodating. The letter emphasizes two essential Erasmian arguments: the need for forbearance toward human weaknesses and the need for constant struggle and striving toward spiritual betterment. The letter is famous for its presentation of the four circles of Christian life, with Christ at the centre. Politically, while negating any 'divine right,' Erasmus does urge acquiescence to the authorities because they are necessary to the 'ordering of the state'; they handle the hard parts of social actions – those having no touch of 'Christian purity' – and thus they should not be criticized as their actions are 'necessary for the conservation of society' (66: 14–15).

14 O'Malley argues that the metaphor of a soldier in combat obfuscates the issues of grace and free will. He does acknowledge a strong 'moralizing' or ethical strain in Erasmus, but defends him against charges of Pelagianism. 'The Christian was saved in and through the grace that Christ brought to

earth and in no other way' (*CWE* 66: xxiii). Luther would obviously have a different view of Erasmus's position. Whatever their later differences, the suspicion exists that in the letter to Volz, Erasmus inserted an early defence of Luther against the 'Philistines,' who clog the divine springs of true religion, preaching 'human things and not divine – those things ... which tend not to Christ's glory but to the profit of those who traffic in indulgences' (*CWE* 66: 13).

15 The arguments of O. Schottenloher have been widely accepted. Poppen-ruyter is the 'uneducated private friend' (Letter to Volz, *CWE* 66: 8), the 'friend at court' (*CWE* 66: 24) for whom the handbook was intended and upon whom it produced no beneficial effect. Should this have been surprising, what with the platonising spiritualization of the *Enchiridion*, its demotion of the corporeal, carnal things of the world? Despite its attempts to reach out to the laity, and its wide popularity, Erasmus was preaching to the choir, to those prepared to accept his spirituality. He came to realize in the conclusion of the *Praise of Folly* that the gap between the two was wider than he thought.

16 Craig R. Thompson's admirable *Colloquies of Erasmus* has been incorporated and supplemented in the new edition of the *CWE*, vols. 39, 40. While making use of the splendid apparatus of the latter, my references in the text are to the earlier work.

17 Mme de Staël understood this principle perfectly when she contrasted Voltaire with Rousseau (see chap. 3, n1, in this volume). She writes that all the works that derive some merit from the circumstances of the moment do not retain an undying glory. This is true of Voltaire, where one admires the turn of phrase but soon tires of the subject (272–3).

18 One can see how far Erasmus's political thought varies from that of Shakespeare, who, in *Richard II* and the ensuing tetralogy, dramatizes this very principle, and seems, despite the many complexities, to justify Richard's deposition. While Luther bound people by a strict obedience to their magistrate – such was his awareness of the violent propensities of the masses (and perhaps his own indebtedness to the protection of the Elector Frederick) – one can see that within his very bold adherence to the doctrine of Christian liberty, there were contained the seeds of a political liberty as well. This tendency can be gleaned from a passage in *The Babylonian Captivity*: 'Therefore I declare that neither pope, nor bishop, nor anyone else, has the right to impose a single syllable of obligation upon a Christian man without his own consent' (304). Clearly the liberty referred to is a Christian liberty in matters of spiritual life and practical ordinances, but the categorical nature of the statement, the build-up of negatives, 'necque,' culminating in 'necque ullus hominum' ('nor anyone else,' or, 'nor any man whatsoever'), certainly car-

ries an explosive charge, the right of refusal, which future history would not ignore. The same phrasing is repeated several paragraphs later, as reprinted in *Martin Luther: Selections* and called quite eccentrically 'The Pagan Servitude of the Church.'

19 I quote from the charming translation of John Wilson, 42–3. See, however, *CWE* 46 for a full apparatus. While the Wilson translation is attractive, the Latin phrase below is actually *dissensio* of opinion rather than 'contrarity,' but Erasmus does use the phrase 'irreconciliabile bellum' (irreconcilable warfare) to indicate the loggerheads at which the worldly wise and the spiritually gifted find themselves (*Praise of Folly* 144–7).

20 Understandably enough, Dorp, who was completing his doctorate in theology, was not inclined to resist his lead professors. Erasmus was aware of the weaknesses of Dorp's character: 'Face to face he is all smiles, and uses his teeth behind my back.' Quoted by J.K. Sowards in his introduction, *CWE* 71: xvii. Dorp did manage to redeem himself later when he delivered an oration in defence of humane letters and even knowledge of Greek, thus showing himself finally to be a supporter of Erasmus and earning his mentor's praise: 'Oh blessings on your brave spirit.' See Soward, *CWE* 71: xviii–xix. I have benefited from Erika Rummel's meticulous study, *Erasmus and His Catholic Critics*. See also her arguments about the complementary nature of the work of Italian humanists and Erasmus with that of Jerome 1: 32–3.

21 See n11 above.

22 See the brilliant but neglected work of Guy Doneux, *Luther et Rousseau* 209.

23 Letter to Pope Leo X (1518), *Works* 2: 46–7.

24 See Brecht, *Luther* 1: 330; Luther, *Martin Luther: Selections* 153, 458–9; Rupp and Watson 157.

25 His sword is the 'sword of the spirit' (gladium spiritus) one that leads to greater piety.

26 Erasmus's intricate path of manoeuvre has been well followed by many scholars. Perhaps the most detailed analysis is provided by Charles Trinkaus in his lengthy introduction to vols. 76–7 of the *Collected Works of Erasmus*, containing translations of the *De Libero arbitrio* and the *Hyperaspistes* 1 and 2 (1999). Trinkaus follows step by step, letter by letter the growth of the animosity, or rather the uncovering of the differences that were always there but latent. He fully understands the complexities of the technical vocabulary involved but does not let them throw him off the essential nature of the confrontation, and with sterling simplicity he presents the core of Erasmus's beliefs (76: xcviii–civ). His essay is marred only by his reference to Luther as the 'antagonist of our story' (76: xxiii).

27 The letter to Botzheim is invaluable for its recounting of Erasmus's literary

career, particularly his youthful efforts. But it soon becomes entangled in his preoccupation with Luther.

28 Von Hutten did set in motion another type of dilemma in Erasmian criticism, that between the mind and the character of Erasmus. Most have been willing to credit the mental capacities of Erasmus, even his genius, but frequently the same have called into question his character. Huizinga has perhaps most prominently advanced this dichotomy. While arguing that the power of Erasmus's mind had a lasting influence, he adds 'that his character was not on a level with the elevation with his mind' (107). Some of the most interesting of modern criticism is devoted to bridging this gap, to showing the unity of the mind and its responses. Chomarat argues for the substantial prominence of grammar and rhetoric as a large habit of mind in Erasmus's approaches to issues; Erika Rummel writes effectively of his Christian scepticism and the legitimate role of 'expediency' in his Christian formulations; Charles Trinkaus also defends his middling position, his moderation as an inescapable part of his intellectual endeavour that naturally disinclined him to take assertive stands; and Pintacuda explores even more fully the close parallel between his ideas and his actions.

29 See n36.

30 See nn10–11.

31 Erasmus explicitly mentions Luther's 'assertion' defending his denunciation of free will against the papal bull. The important article 36 is reproduced in English translation *CWE* 76: 299–309. The first sentence of this article returns us to the Heidelberg disputation, particularly thesis 13, where Luther maintains that after the Fall, free will exists in name only.

32 If earlier, as in the exchange with Dorp, differences tended to concentrate on philological questions, once Luther appeared on the scene, Erasmus's Catholic critics thought him weak on theological questions, espying in his early writings as well as in the *Colloquies* signs of a proto-Lutheranism, or a Lutheranism clear cut. As Erika Rummel summarizes, 'Early polemics focused on philological points, later controversies are more concerned with doctrine' (*Erasmus and His Catholic Critics* 2: 152). The intervention of Luther thus changed not only Erasmus but also the nature of the charges brought against him; but Erasmus was not fooled: he detected in the differing responses the same attack on humane letters.

33 See Rupp, *Luther and Erasmus* 2, who attributes it to his nature as a satirist.

34 His editors rightly refer us to Rummel's classic study, where in his controversy with Catholic critics, Erasmus gave full demonstration to his skill at invective; but then, as I have argued, the quarrel with Luther compelled Erasmus to confront different aspects of his personality (*CWE* 76n10).

35 See Martin Brecht for this reopened controversy in *Martin Luther* 3: 78–84.

36 Cornelis Augustijn is quite right in stressing the continuities and discontinu-
ities in Erasmus's thought. In a paper first delivered at the all-important conference at Tours in 1969 and then reprinted (in German) in a collection of
his essays *Erasmus: Der Humanist als Theolgie und Kirchenreformer,* he advises
caution in separating the younger from the older Erasmus, particularly when
each placed Christ at the centre of his theology. But he then proceeds to
note the great difference, a 'shift' (Verschiebung) in his thought in the
Hyperaspistes 1. Now it is the consensus of the church and its tutorship
through the centuries that warrants the truths of interpretation. 'This stands
in stark opposition to Luther's understanding,' which represents 'pure sub-
jectivism.' The position of Erasmus is that the individual does not have the
right to separate from centuries of tradition. This is the 'tragic moment' in
his development: 'the liberty – so dear to Erasmus – is here strongly reduced'
(274–6). And with these words, a pre-eminent Erasmian scholar of our day
confirms Luther's criticisms. Or, giving the concluding words of regret to
Erasmus himself, 'Would that I could redo everything all over again, starting
from the beginning' (quoted by Rummel, *Erasmus and His Catholic Critics* 2:
154).

37 See the easily available John C. Olin, ed., *Desiderius Erasmus* 92–106.

Chapter 2: Voltaire and Rousseau

1 Three classical studies of historical importance are Charles Barthélémy, *Voltaire et Rousseau;* Gaston Maugras, *Voltaire et J.J. Rousseau;* and Henri Gouhier,
Rousseau et Voltaire. Barthélèmy, writing in the wake of five revolutions, places
a pox on both their houses. Maugras militates against Rousseau's presumed
antipathy for Voltaire, to whose rivalry Gouhier restores some intellectual
calm and order. His is a detailed magisterial study of historical depth.

2 For a full accounting of Rousseau's letter to Voltaire of 17 June 1760, see
Gouhier, *Rousseau et Voltaire* 127–50.

3 Gouhier quotes the letter to Madame de Warens for Rousseau's response to
Alzire (*Rousseau et Voltaire* 22). Voltaire's *Lettres* themselves had a remarkable
publishing history, with an English edition, *Letters Concerning the English
Nation,* appearing first, followed by *Lettres anglaises,* printed in London, and
Lettres philosophiques (1734), allegedly printed in Amsterdam but actually in
Rouen. The *Lettres* were condemned by the parlement de Paris and consigned to be burned. The entire episode reveals several things: the still-heavy
hand of the authorities guarding publication; the ruses, frequently with compliance, that authors had to employ in order to avoid detection; the growth

of Voltaire's philosophical interests that the final change in title attests, and – in what were ostensibly *Letters Concerning the English Nation* – Voltaire's inclusion of the concluding sections on Pascal and Jansenism. René Pomeau, who traces all the subterfuges and manoeuvres of Voltaire to have his works published, cautions that the volume did not have a relatively large readership, confined to a narrow elite of the 1730s. But the question is not how many, but who. Its impact on Rousseau was enormous. See René Pomeau, *D'Arouet à Voltaire* 321–32.

4 See Introduction 16.

5 See Henri Gouhier, 'Ce que le vicaire doit à Descartes.'

6 In Voltaire's *Discours en vers sur l'homme*, part 5, Calvin remains 'ce fou sombre et sévère.' Yet despite this personal aversion, the lineage is confirmed in René Pomeau's enormous study, *La religion de Voltaire*. Voltaire 'sera lui-même l'apôtre des temps modernes, le successeur de Luther et Calvin' (465); this successor to the early reformers, 'dans l'ordre de l'action ... , ose inscrire son nom à la suite des noms de Luther et de Calvin' (482). When it comes to action (a Sartrean recollection, intimated by 'temps modernes?') Voltaire, the *philosophe*, had his forerunners in the men of the Reformation.

7 The evidence is contradictory; Pomeau doubts that Voltaire was ever formally a member of any lodge, quoting quite convincingly Voltaire's secretary Jean-Louis Wagnière that Voltaire was never a Mason (*D'Arouet à Voltaire* 240–1). See n3 earlier in this chapter. However, among the many *éloges* dedicated to Voltaire upon his death is one by a M. de la Dixmerie, which was given in the Lodge of the *Neuf soeurs*, 'dont il [Voltaire] avait été membre.' See Vercruysse, *Les Voltairiens*, vol. 1.

8 One would be hard-pressed to affirm the same sense of lineage in the pages covering the Reformation in Voltaire's *Essai sur les moeurs et l'esprit des nations* 2: 217–47. For one, he describes the Lutheran revolt as being in its origins a simple dispute between Franciscans and Augustinians. But more importantly, the purpose of this massive study is to show the ways that the dawning enlightenment has *overcome* the dogmatic frenzy of those troubled times.

9 For added substance to these arguments, see Pomeau, *La religion de Voltaire*, 465, 467, 470, 475, 479, 481. At its origins, Voltaire insists, no religion was founded as an invitation to crime (*Essai sur les moeurs* 2: 809). Pernicious effects of religion occur only when it is exploited by politics, or when it is subjected to dogmatic frenzy.

10 For the complex interactions of Voltaire and Rousseau at this time, see Gouhier, *Rousseau et Voltaire*, ch. 6.

11 'Quel moment plus heureux pour établir solidement la paix universelle, que

celui où l'animosité des partis suspendue, laissait tout le monde en état d'écouter la raison?' (3: 802).

12 In her remarkable book, *Le citoyen de Genève et la république des lettres*, Ourida Mostefai makes of this simple fact of 'naming' and the need for identity that it implies an indicator of the larger controversy between Rousseau and Voltaire.

13 See the superb article by Jean Starobinski, entitled 'The Accuser and the Accused.'

14 Since Cassirer's foundation work, scholars have sought to register the divisions within Rousseau's thought accompanied always with a search for its unity. One need look no further than Rousseau's own ill-fated *Rousseau juge de Jean-Jacques, Dialogues* to see that Rousseau was the first to recognize the need to discover the 'true Rousseau.' But the same pattern of division in search of unity persists in modern criticism, whether it be devoted to the stylistic, moral, or philosophical aspects of his work. See Jean-Francois Perrin, 'Écrire doublement'; Marcel Raymond, 'J.-J. Rousseau'; and Jean Wahl, 'La bipolarité de Rousseau.' There is the active Rousseau and the passive Rousseau, the Rousseau of historical development and the Rousseau of 'spatial form,' and finally the Rousseau whose need for community leads him to the systematic thought of the *Social Contract* (with some adverse consequences) against the Rousseau of individual liberty. It is this last disjunction that Bénichou addresses, finding that the two positions are in opposition, but that the 'intention and the goal in view do not change ... the same themes of simplicity, fidelity to oneself, rectitude, human dignity, and the criticisms of the courtesan and of the *honnête homme* who live according to the ways of the world are found throughout his works' (145). Jean Guéhenno contributes excellent pages when he writes that the unity of Rousseau's life lies in his works (*Jean-Jacques* 262–70).

15 Benoit Mély's very valuable *Jean-Jacques Rousseau* is a study of the intellectual as member of a class. Taking his arguments beyond the purely philosophical or moral arrangements of thought, he locates the intellectual in rapport with his society and patronage. This was another source of contradiction in Rousseau's life. 'The rupture of Rousseau with the high society of his time was not and could not have been a definitive act once and done, but part of a living and contradictory process.' See particularly ch. 4, 'Rousseau et Diderot: un rupture irrevocable' (88–96), where he shows the contrasting ways of Diderot and of Rousseau, differences, to be sure, over money and over Thérèse Levasseur, but mainly over Diderot's willingness to make his way in the world and Rousseau's counter-tendency to rely on any dependence. One should also consult the brilliant pages in Herbert Lüthy's

From Calvin to Rousseau. 'Rousseau was both, the mentally sick and the prophet ... Even if we read his writings as the history of an alienation, they would not have acted on generations present and those to come ... if this alienation had been only his own, and if he had not touched the heart of his age' (258). 'Neither the apostasies nor the apparent confessional indifference could hide the almost frenzied Protestantism of this soul obsessed with the need to plumb its own depths and to justify itself' (265). Rousseau's revolt was that of a 'Genevan atavism' against the spirit of the age; the old Geneva was long gone, but Rousseau's Geneva, that of memory, was all the stronger, so 'Rousseau's triumph in France, and over France in a strange way was the vengeance of the republic of Geneva over its corruptors' (269).

16 Jean Starobinksi suggests another cogent reason for Rousseau's 'lastingness,' perhaps summarizable by a Falstaffian paraphrase that not only is he uneasy in himself, but he is the cause of unease in others. That is, Rousseau fits into the modern culture of accusation. By 'resacralizing' the secular he imports the language of religious reformation into the world of politics and culture. He issues the challenge of an inner renewal. This is why the worlds created by Rousseau exert such an attraction: 'they appear to offer a better life on earth for those who have the audacity to reject convention and servitude' (49). But he fits Rousseau even more deeply into one development of modern thought: 'to accuse evil and to exempt oneself from it.' Thus the accuser as well as the accused 'arrogate to themselves a privilege role – they are in position of light and transparency, whereas everything around them remains in darkness' (55). Such insight will be met again in the pages of Camus. But see Raymond Trousson's *Visages de Voltaire* for the continuing intellectual appeal of Voltaire.

17 English translation from Gourevitch 19–20. 'Dites-nous, célébre Arouet, combien vous avez sacrifié les beautés mâles et fortes à nôtre fausse délicatesse, et combien l'esprit de la galanterie si fertile en petites choses vous en a coûté de grandes?' in Rousseau, *Œuvres complètes* 3: 21.

18 *Les œuvres complètes de Voltaire* 8: 251–2. For instance, while in his *Oedipe*, produced in 1718, but worked on laboriously for several years before that, Voltaire is enthralled by the horror, but he spares the audience sight of the actual blinding, alluding to it only in a couplet.

19 In the same letter, see also Rousseau's discussion of Voltaire's *Mahomet*, 86–8, where he complains that most people will come away impressed with the grandeur of Mahomet rather than with his 'crimes.'

20 See also the excellent pages of René Pomeau, *D'Arouet à Voltaire* 203–9, where beyond matters of class Voltaire is found guilty of being a poet; in

addition, his own acerbic tongue and anti-clericalism made him a shunned figure, one getting his just desserts.

21 This is true on the macroplane as well. He was the first to introduce Shakespeare to the French, and was in his *Lettres philosophiques* a strong but not uncritical advocate of English culture and politics. Thus he countered the prevalent anglophobia. But later in life he righted the balance when anglomania became dominant. See Besterman's excellent discussion, 'Shakespeare and the Drama, 1726–1776,' 131–58. As an indication of the state of awareness, Pomeau reminds us that prior to Voltaire's two-year stay in England he had never heard of Shakespeare!

22 'Vouloir de l'amour dans toutes les tragédies me paraît un goût efféminé; l'en proscrire toujours est une mauvaise humeur bien déraisonnable.' *Les œuvres complètes de Voltaire* 5: 179.

23 See also Voltaire, *Mélanges* xii.

24 For a full discussion of the various facets of the name change, see the indispensable *D'Arouet à Voltaire*, by Pomeau. To be sure, the name change avoids the undesirable homophonic association with 'à rouer,' but the greater change at the time of his theatrical success is prompted by the need for his name to match his vivacity, or sprightliness (117–18).

25 Similarly, in his discussion of *Oedipe*, Pomeau in *D'Arouet à Voltaire* argues that the real theme is not parricide but rather the choice of a hero, Philocète, and the theme of friendship: 'L'amitié est élue par lui [Voltaire] comme une forme supérieure, épurée, de la relation affective' (129). While the lyrics declaim against the savage destiny imposed by the malignity of the gods, the music itself inclines toward human non-culpability and the possibilities of human freedom. Oedipus is a wise and just king. Jocaste and Philocète behave honourably, despite their passion for each other. The pagans were Jansenists, and Voltaire decidedly is not. That is, as Pomeau wisely asserts, in the choice of directions proposed by the rival theologies of the day, Voltaire sided with the Jesuits, 'les anciens maistres du poète débutant' (128–9). However, see n28 in this chapter. *Oedipe* is a work of audacity fitting youthful genius, in the manner of Dante or James Joyce. Begun probably in 1713–14 and not performed until late 1718, with this tragedy Voltaire enters into the lists with Corneille and Sophocles. And he did not fare badly. This audacity was topped by his *Lettres sur Oedipe* written in criticism of Sophocles, Corneille, and his own version of the theme. Adhering to the doctrine of *vraisemblance*, what we might call logical common sense, he succeeds in exposing some of the gaps in Sophocles' play (see the still-instructive Third Letter). In his own criticism he admits that the introduction of the Philocète-Jocaste love theme turned one play into two: the double theme serves no

purpose. However, there is a better reason for presenting the heroic, honour-bound Philocète, who rises above vile calumny and the judgments of the mob, who even resents being questioned as a possible suspect. Rather than Pomeau's interpretation of friendship, Philocète relies on his own sense of honour and glory. By making the Corneillean choice of honour he opens the way to his future 'gloire.' The reasons for this dramatically dubious insertion are not far to seek. It represents Voltaire's own situation, and is something of an auto-portrait. Just as Philocète rises above calumny, so Voltaire in showing himself a man of honour and a true poet, elevates himself above the charges of the scurrilous verse that brought him his first exile in 1716 and later not to be outdone landed him for the first time in the Bastille. This he makes clear in the first of the *Lettres*. *Oedipe* is his own fullest justification and the opening of his own way to '*gloire*.' For all this, see the excellent notes by David Jory in the *Œuvres complètes*, vol. 1A (Oxford: Voltaire Foundation, 2001). Voltaire's later prudence was hard-earned, but it is also indicative of his character and milieu that his harsh treatment was met by Voltaire with a light-hearted acceptance and some wit.

26   In a different study, much more would be made of this remarkable poem. At a very young age, Voltaire because of *Oedipe* became known as the heir of Corneille and Racine and with the publication of *La Henriade* – first by subscription in England in 1728, and only later upon his return to France – he was the French Virgil. The poem, set around the siege of Paris occupied by the Ligue and its foreign mercenaries, is more condemned than read. Even Besterman calls it a failure; oddly enough he repeats criticism that Voltaire's genius was epigrammatic, and thus not suited to the epic. See 102–3. I simply refer interested readers to the tenth 'chant,' or canto, to gain some sense of the poetic merit of the work. In a city under siege, and beset by famine, the inhabitants are compelled to dig out the marrow from the bones of their dead relatives in order to survive another few days. Foreign mercenaries turned marauders within the city suggest another Holocaust. One mother, rather than enduring their ravages, kills her son and then stabs herself, to the astonishment of her attackers. Voltaire shows her as making the right Sophie's choice. Henri shows his magnanimity in bringing stores to the starving city held by his enemies, and then restoring peace by becoming Catholic (*Les œuvres complètes* vol. 2). If it is true that a great historian must be a great tragedian, then we can see why the pages treating the emergence and the murder of 'bon Henri,' 'le grand Henri' are the finest and most heart-rending in Voltaire's *Essai sur les moeurs* 529–58. Just as there are great epochs, so there are superior individuals who seem to rise above their time. Henri IV was one such individual meriting inclusion in Voltaire's pantheon for his bravery, his clemency, his frankness, his

probity, and his politically flexible realism. See 2: 543–4 for one of Henri's speeches, which, Voltaire concludes, by the eloquence from the heart of a true hero surpasses all the harangues of antiquity.

27 René Pomeau, 'Voltaire et Rousseau devant l'affaire Calas,' 61–75. See also *Mélanges*, 'Traité sur la tolérance à l'occasion de la mort de Jean Calas,' 563–650.

28 In fact, turn almost at random to pages in the *Mélanges* and one will find anti-Jansenism, their insistence on controlling thought and satisfaction in knowing their opponents – the non-elect that are consigned to hell. See 'Entretien d'Ariste et d'Acrotal' and 'Anecdotes sur Bélisaire' (438, 921). However, he did not spare the Jesuits. In the Age of the Assassins, the Jesuits wrote in defence of regicide, thus enflaming the susceptible minds of young fanatics such as Jacques Clement and Ravaillac (549–57).

29 But the success was not continuous, nor did it occur overnight – there was an intervening period of great difficulty, of refusal on the part of the actors and various run-ins with the authorities. He did not enjoy a success similar to *Oedipe* until the *Zaire* of 1732. In fact, in the interval he had been advised to give up the theatre.

30 My prose version is based upon the translation of William F. Fleming, 'The Worldling,' 84–8.

31 See n30, 'The Man of the World,' 171–2.

32 See Venturi, 'The European Enlightenment' 1–32; Jonathan I. Israel, *The Radical Enlightenment* 20–1.

33 This 'literary republic' is constantly invoked by Voltaire. It represents a cohort-group of dedicated scholars, scientists, and intellectuals who independently (the meaning of *insensiblement*) work on common problems and come up with similar solutions. Their exchanges of information, through the medium of academies, contribute by slow steps to the advancement of science, culture, and not coincidentally to human freedom. See the conclusion to Groos, ch. 24, 2: 146.

34 See the learned and sensitive essay by Marc Fumaroli, 'Le genre des genres littéraires français.'

35 One can savour the taste of the more satiric Voltaire in his description of the flattering but empty pronouncements made by new members of the Académie in his *Lettres philosophiques*, 'Sur les académies' 24: 100–4; but some of his noted acerbity is not lacking in later additions, those of 1748 and 1752, see notes 1395–6. The very astute P-H. Azaïs in his essay of 1817 singles out this address as most typical of Voltaire's work, combining all of his talents and faults. One cannot write, he concludes, with greater simplicity, reason, and abundance about an important question of literature while at the same

time inserting the 'ridiculous' praises of Louis XV. See ch. 3, n1, in this volume, *Les Voltairiens* 7: 57.

36 This collusion existed in Voltaire's mind, despite his knowledge and deep resentment, that Richelieu was a determined opponent of *Le Cid*.

37 *Discours, qui a remporté le prix à l'Académie de Dijon,* thus the title of the original French goes on, without having yet reached the question (Rousseau, *Œuvres complètes* 3: 1; Gourevitch, *Rousseau* 1). Page references in the text indicate these two editions. For obvious reasons of convenience, this work shall be simply referred to as 'the first *Discours.*'

38 'On commença à sentir le principal avantage du commerce des muses, celui de rendre les hommes plus sociables en leur inspirant le désir de se plaire les uns aux autres par les ouvrages dignes de leur approbation mutuelle.'

39 'C'est par elle ... que notre siècle et notre Nation l'emporteront sur tous les tems et sur tous les Peuples.'

40 'Il règne dans nos moeurs une vile et trompeuse uniformité, et tous les esprits semblent avoir été jetés dans un même moule; sans cesse la politesse exige, la bienséance ordonne; sans cesse on suit des usages jamais son propre génie.'

41 All English translations are from *The Confessions of Jean-Jacques Rousseau.*

42 'A quoi bon chercher nôtre bonheur dans l'opinion d'autrui si nous pouvons le trouver en nous-mêmes?'

43 'Tes principes ne sont-ils pas gravés dans tous les coeurs, et ne suffit-il pas pour apprendre tes Lois de rentrer en soi-même et d'écouter la voix de sa conscience dans le silence des passions?'

44 All quotations are from Voltaire, *Correspondence* 16: 259–62. See first sentence of Commentary, 262. My English translations. When writing this so-called letter to Rousseau, Voltaire had evidently already intended it for publication in the same printing of his very successful stage play *L'Orphelin de la Chine,* through some manoeuvring he wanted Rousseau's reply of 7 Sept. 1755 also to be printed. But without the latter's permission, the printer declined. For all the complicated intricacies, consult Gouhier's excellent ch. 4 of *Rousseau et Voltaire,* where he also renders an accounting of Voltaire's letter (which the countess of Saxe-Goths called 'polie, spirituelle, et ingénieuse') as well as of Rousseau's remarkable response. In his defence Rousseau argues that his antagonism is not against knowledge but rather its 'massification'; not against scientists such as the great ones he mentions, but rather against what now might be called the 'rebellion of the masses.' In addition, he responds to Voltaire's general attack on the first *Discours* by invoking the arguments of the second. In a state of ignorance humankind has fewer means to commit evil. See Voltaire, *Correspondence* 16: 278.

45 Arthur M. Melzer makes the argument of 'the dialectical over-coming' –
    about the only point with which I disagree in his brilliant essay, 'The Origin
    of the Counter-Enlightenment.' Starobinski also denies utopian presence in
    Rousseau's thought, 'The Accuser and the Accused,' 45, 49. Pierre Burgelin,
    La philosophie de l'existence de J.-J. Rousseau, effectively shows the coincidence
    of Rousseau's personal quest with his inquiry into the structures of society.

46 'Je crois voir le peuple se multiplier, les champs se fertiliser, la terre prendre
    une nouvelle parure, la multitude et l'abondance transformer les travaux en
    fêtes, les cris de joie et les bénédictions s'élever du milieu des jeux autour du
    couple aimable qui les a ranimés. On traite l'age d'or de chimère, et c'en
    sera toujours une pour équivoque a la cœur et le goût gâtés. Il n'est pas
    même vrai qu'on le regrette, puisque ces regrets sont toujours vains. Que
    faudrait-il donc pour le faire renaître? Une seule chose mais impossible; ce
    serait de l'aimer' (*Œuvres complètes* 4: 859).

47 *Œuvre complètes* 1: 1014.

48 An intermediate work, the very brief but crucial *conte, Memon, ou la sagesse
    humaine* (1748–9), fulfils the same purpose. Applying the principles of a
    moral rigidity, Memon resolves to be happy by abstaining from women, wine,
    social pleasures, and the pursuit of advancement at the court. His normal
    human passions waylay his determinations, and he meets with disaster on all
    accounts. The fault lies not in the corruption he encounters but in his prior
    philosophy of abstention, which – now blind in one eye – he sees. The Leib-
    nizean personal genius describes for him an impossible 'other world,' where
    no disaster can occur; because it is angelic it has none of the earthly means
    for straying. While deeply personal, portraying the defeats both he and Mme
    du Châtelet experienced in their designs to follow a quasi-Stoic philosophy,
    the *conte* finally makes the Voltairean point of immersion in life, in accepting
    the liabilities and the pleasures that the passions provide. Human sentiment
    still reigns over the affectations that any program of distance can promote.

49 The chain of being has historically reputable parentage, growing out of the
    Thomistic view that grace completes nature, as well as Erasmus's view that
    there is a 'congruence' between human effort and the divine will.

50 See my *Changes of Cain* 87–108. Thus Susan Neiman, in her admirable study,
    Evil in Modern Thought, can draw her own historical alignments, which, based
    upon their attitudes toward evil, are valid enough. In the line of Voltaire,
    those who deny the reality of 'anything beyond brute appearance,' she
    includes Bayle, Hume, Sade, and Schopenhauer; while with Rousseau,
    among those who find an order in existence beyond 'the miserable one pre-
    sented by experience,' she includes Leibniz, Pope, Kant, Hegel, and Marx
    (11). At times these are strange bedfellows, but Professor Neiman's work has

the merit of emphasizing the full importance of Voltaire's Lisbon poem and Rousseau's reaction.

51 In the extraordinary poem 'La mort de Mademoiselle LeCouvreur, fameuse actrice,' following her death in 1730, Voltaire has cause to contrast her dismal funeral rites with the burial in Westminster Abbey of the English actress Anne (Nance) Oldfield, who rests with Newton and other 'beaux-esprits,' prompting the final question why France is no longer the native land 'et de la gloire et des talents.' See 'Poésies,' *Complete Works* 557–61, 607.

52 'Lettre de J.J. Rousseau à M. de Voltaire,' *Œuvres completes* 4: 1059. English translation in Gourevitch, *Rousseau* 232–46.

53 Gouhier argues for the coherence of Rousseau's thought, and points out that the letter was in fact private and not published until 1760. Gouhier writes in constant antithesis with Maugras's work, dating from 1889, and argues against Maugras's more personalized accounting for the origin of the *Letter to M. d'Alembert*. While Gouhier's study is masterful in its scholarship, and a constantly reliable resource, and while Maugras is positing a contrafactual condition, still it seems that Maugras's point is well taken, and that Rousseau was deeply sensitive to the possibility that Voltaire was corrupting the ways of the Genevans.

54 Showing the build-up necessary to the breakthrough of 1749–50, Rousseau was already at some odds with Pope's poem as early as 1742.

55 See p. 1071.

56 Taking issue with Voltaire's attribution of an 'atrocious soul' to Calvin, a Genevan by the name of David Rival issued a poetic challenge to Voltaire, quoting almost verbatim in its last strophe these words of Rousseau. See Besterman, *Voltaire* 654.

57 *Émile, Œuvres completes* 4: 565–635; *Émile*, trans. Alan Bloom, 266–313.

58 'Conscience, conscience! Instinct divin, immortelle et céleste voix, guide assuré d'un être ignorant et borné, mais intelligent et libre; juge infaillible du bien et du mal, qui rends l'homme semblable à Dieu; c'est toi qui fais l'excellence de sa nature et la mortalité de ses actions; sans toi je ne sens rien en moi qui m'élève au dessus des bêtes, que le triste privilège de m'égarer d'erreurs en erreurs à l'aide d'un entendement sans règle, et d'une raison sans principe' (290; 4: 600–1).

59 'Triomphant quand ils attaquent, ils sont sans vigueur en se défendant' (268; 4: 568).

60 Villemain, *Tableau de la littérature au dix-huitième siècle* (1838).

61 Naves's *Voltaire* is admirable for its succinct summary and compact brilliance of understanding and formulation. Rather than demonstrating the 'historical' importance of Voltaire, Naves argues for the enduring quality of Vol-

taire's philosophy and of his sensibility, capable of existing in contradiction and contrast, such that makes his dualism with Rousseau so engaging and perennial.

62 Despite appearing under a pseudonym, the slender volume sold 20,000 copies its first year.

63 Voltaire shows his fuller understanding of Milton's power in a dual essay written in English ('An Essay on Epic Poetry') and in French, with some alteration. He naturally praises the lovemaking of Adam and Eve; the prologues of self-address he absolves from criticism; yet he remains critical of the union between Sin and Death. But most important are his reasons why England has produced such an epic with suitable language while France seems incapable of the same (this by the author of the work in progress, *La Henriade*). The reason is simply the presence in English of valuable translations of the Bible, familiarity with which enhances the sublimity of the language. See *The English Essays of 1727*, 371–94, 555–73.

64 *Politics and the Arts; Lettre à M. D'Alembert sur son article Genève*. See Patrick Coleman's groundbreaking work on the *Lettre, Rousseau's Political Imagination*. The letter made its belated appearance only in vol. 5 of the Pléiade edition of the *Œuvres complètes* in 1995.

65 'Ce Philinte est le sage de la pièce: un de ces honnêtes gens du grand monde, dont les maximes ressemblent beaucoup à celles des fripons; de ces gens si doux, si modérés, qui trouvent toujours que tout va bien, parce que ils ont intérêt que rien n'aille mieux, qui sont toujours content de tout le monde, parce qu'ils ne se soucient de personne, qui autour d'une bonne table, soutiennent qu'il n'est pas vrai que le peuple ait faim; qui le gousset bien garni, trouvent fort mauvais qu'on déclame en faveur des pauvres' (100; 39). Ourida Mostefai correctly identifies this Philinte with Voltaire.

66 For extracts of their thoughts, see Corrigan's valuable anthology, *Comedy: Meaning and Form* 448–77.

67 'On était plus grossier de mon temps. Les enfants rustiquement élevés n'avaient point de teint a conserver, et ne craignaient point les injures de l'air aux quelles ils s'étaient aguerris de bonne heure' (112; 213).

68 All quotations refer to *Œuvres complètes*, vol. 4, and *Émile or On Education*.

69 To his list of names could be added that of John Dewey.

70 'Vous vous fiez à l'ordre actuel de la société, sans songer que cet ordre est sujet à des révolutions inévitable, et qu'il vous est impossible de prévoir ni de prévenir celle qui peut regarder vos enfants. Le Grand devient petit, le riche devient pauvre, le monarque devient sujet: les coups du sort sont-ils si rares que vous puissiez compter d'en être exempt? Nous approchons de l'état de crise et du siècle des révolutions.' 'Je tiens pour impossible, que les grandes

monarchies de l'Europe aient encore long tems à durer ... J'ai de mon opinion des raisons plus particulières que cette maxime; mais il n'est pas à propos de les dire, et chacun ne les voit que trop' (194; 468). See René Pomeau, 'Était-ce "la faute à Voltaire, la faute à Rousseau"?' 415–25.

71 See my *Renaissance Discovery of Time* 187–203.

72 For the role of memory in Rousseau (primarily in *The Confessions*) see Suzanne Nalbantian, *Memory in Literature: From Rousseau to Neuroscience*. She quite accurately makes the point that Rousseau 'arrived at his social philosophy' from episodes of remembrance (33).

73 See Gouhier, 'Voltaire en colère,' *Rousseau et Voltaire*. In addition, see the entry 'Jean-Jacques Rousseau' in *Dictionnaire Voltaire*, where Trousson indicates other works as expressions of Voltaire's anger (204), and explains it by the hostilities provoked by the *Lettre à d'Alembert* and by Rousseau's outing Voltaire as the author of *Sermon des cinquante* (205).

74 This work also marks the entrance of Voltaire into the 'infernal affair' between Rousseau and David Hume. While Edmonds and Eidinow declare it 'in fact' to be 'contrived' by 'a Bordes,' Charles Bordes vehemently denied any hand in it. Van den Heuvel includes it in the *Mélanges*, and both he and Trousson accept it as Voltaire's in *Dictionnaire Voltaire* (112, 204–5), but there is no separate entry. Besterman credits Voltaire (500), but with a 'pointless perspicacity' in so demolishing Rousseau. The story is a tangled one and is well told by Edmonds and Eidinow, where none of the participants is shown to advantage. Rousseau was injured to the quick by the fabricated note from the king of Prussia, which made a fool of Rousseau's manias, subjecting him to the most intolerable of taunts, mockery, and ridicule. If enmity is preferable to betrayal, then each is more acceptable than mockery, which reduces one to a childlike helplessness. At his myopic best, Rousseau believed the fake letter (which duly circulated between the capitals of Paris and London) to have been written by d'Alembert. Since Hume may have contributed one line of witticism to the letter, it was an easy task for Rousseau to connect the dots between Voltaire, d'Alembert, and other French enemies, and Hume. But given his state of mind, such lines of connection became deep trenches of conspiracy and warfare. Suggestion became certainty, and hypothesis fact. Let us not forget that this was a Rousseau who was chased from Paris, Motiers, and Berne, an outlawed figure, finding refuge in England, where he did not know the language and had no particular fondness for the people. This was also the Rousseau who just a few years earlier stood at the summit of his hard-won success, only to experience a mysterious fall from grace. From being a character out of Dostoevsky he became one out of Kafka, buffeted by strange, incomprehensible powers. In his proud independence, and defence

of his accomplishments and stature, his insecure susceptibility to imagined injuries and insults, the tumult with which his life had been turned over, certainly he deserved better. But the mocking fake letter, and then Voltaire's entrance into the fray with an English and French version of the letter to Jean-Jacques, followed by a letter to David Hume only confirmed Rousseau's suspicion (confirmation never lagged far behind suspicion) that his erstwhile benefactor was part of an Anglo-French conspiracy to blacken his name in his country of refuge. With his typical benevolent imagination and exhaustive scope of inquiry, Gouhier in chapters 14, 15, and 16 traces the ins and outs of this fracas. Guéhenno is impartial and sympathetic (161–202). Both justly remind us of Rousseau's enforced uprooting and his travails, in addition his proud sense of his own accomplishments, and more importantly that his reputation be preserved intact for posterity. In all of this Hume was relatively (but not totally) innocent. His involvement with Rousseau is not a major battle in the registers of the Enlightenment, perhaps a minor skirmish, not even a falling out of friends (they had known one another over a period of only four months), and certainly not a defining dualism. Good only to be forgotten, as Voltaire counsels him in an adjoining letter, it was unlike the more basic engagement between Voltaire and Rousseau, one proof of which is that we soon weary of a quarrel, but a true dualism is expansive and generative. If there was no itinerary of encounter between Hume and Rousseau, let alone any sustained friendship, this did not prevent others from making their separate lives into a larger representative clash. See Fordham, 'Allan Ramsey's Enlightenment,' 508–24.

75 In fact, in excised portions of *The Confessions* Rousseau explicitly sees the troubles with Hume as punishments for what he had done to 'poor Marion.' See Guéhenno 2: 190.

76 For a brief but acute account of these readings, see Guéhenno, 2: 246–47.

Chapter 3: Passages of History

1 I discuss this essay in full, despite the fact that at the time of its publication there was little novelty for the French in addressing the differences and still combined fortunes of Voltaire and Rousseau. Already in 1778, they are described as meeting after their passage over the river Styx; in another description they come together as joint heralds of the Napoleonic conquests (!), and still later they are joined when a defence is necessary for the publication of their complete works (1821), and soon thereafter they come together again when a subscription is underway for the erection of a suitable monument for each. Their roles as the pre-eminent figures – for good or for

ill – of the preceding century goes uncontested. Throughout, their differences are well noted. Together as they parade down the Champs-Elysées on 14 July, Voltaire has a different tack: he has enlightened his fellow citizens, he has floored [terrassés] fanaticism, broken the censor, and shaken the foundations of the throne (these activities in the causes of enlightenment are actually borrowed from a poem by Voltaire, *Les Torts* – see Besterman, 656); Rousseau as the sincere friend of children has called their mothers back to nature and has shaped men for virtue. J-B Touquet's letter of 1821 – itself a classic in irony and defence of letters against censorship – was referred to above, introduction n4. His following letter proposing monuments to such 'great men' is quite memorable for its reflections on where France and public opinion had been fifty years prior and where they were now because of Voltaire and Rousseau (the tone is quite Voltairean in its emphasis on the steps of progress). By far the most interesting comparison between the two indicates the same philosophical understanding of their achievements: Pierre-Hyacinthe Azaïs's *Jugement philosophique sur J.-J. Rousseau et sur Voltaire* appeared one year later than Valsecchi's great essay. It elaborates a fundamental distinction made in its epigraph, 'La recherche du vrai et la pratique du bien sont les deux objects de la philosophie.' We shall hear more about the search for the true and the practice of the good in the course of this study. For all these comparisons and more see, *Les Voltairians*, compiled by Jeroom Vercruysse, particularly vols. 1, 3, 6, 7, and 8, as well as Trousson's *Visages de Voltaire*. In these accounts I am choosing essays where the explicit subject is Voltaire and Rousseau. A landmark work of much broader scope is Mme de Staël (-Holstein)'s *De la littérature, considérée par ses rapports avec les institutions sociales* (1800), where Voltaire is the author of 'pleasantries' that mock the institutions to which he nevertheless adheres. He is not an instrument of change by himself. Rousseau, on the other hand, out of misfortune and some primitive passions, was able to 'shake' the government at its very bases. 'He discovered nothing; but he inflamed everything.' Nevertheless, the two, along with Montesquieu, represented the three giant steps that contributed to the developing philosophy of liberty (271–4).

2 Voltaire's own estimation of Saint-Évremond is of interest. In his *Lettres sur les français* he includes a brief synopsis and judgment of Saint-Évremond's 'caractère.' 'C'était un esprit agréable et assez juste; mais il avait peu de science, nul génie, et son goût était peu sur ... On peut le mettre au rang des hommes aimables et pleins d'esprit qui ont fleuri dans le temps brillant de Louis XIV, mais non pas au rang des hommes supérieurs' (*Mélanges* 1247). Accordingly Voltaire does afford Saint-Évremond a modest place in his *Temple du*

goût, as having in his day been among the 'first ranks' but was superseded by those who followed with superior taste (147). But Dacier, who is *only* a scholar, he ejects completely. His back is bent over a 'pile' of Greek authors; he 'coughs in ink' or is rather 'covered in ink,' and when asked to enter the Temple of Good Taste, he, with others, replies that their job is to re-edit at length from point to minute point what others have thought, 'mais nous ne pensons pas.' He does not present his own thoughts (*Mélanges* 136–7). One is reminded of Yeats's great short poem, 'The Scholars.'

3 For Arnold, see introduction 5; Nietzsche, *The Birth of Tragedy; Friedrich Nietzsche: Werke* 1; Turgenev, 'Hamlet and Don Quixote,' see below 229–35; James, 'The Present Dilemma in Philosophy'; Jung, 'The Problem of the Attitude-Type; Berlin, 'The Hedgehog and the Fox,' in *The Proper Study of Mankind*; Rahv, 'Paleface and Redskin.'

4 It is noteworthy that Valsecchi's remarkable essay was written prior to that of Schiller, yet it already begins to register the shifting weights in the balance between Rousseau and Voltaire. P.-H. Azaïs's essay (see above, n1) brings this change to completion and discerns the enduring lineaments of Rousseau and Voltaire in formation. He writes that as in Nature, after a storm a period of calm intercedes, so after the terrors of the revolution a time of 'conservation et équilibre' takes over. Now is the time to judge the historical and philosophical importance of Voltaire and Rousseau, not excluding either homage or censure. Rousseau has genius, but it is a troubled genius. His major works for Azaïs are consequently *The Confessions* and the *Dialoques*. He is not the 'ragionatore' of Valsecchi but rather the soul of misfortune, whose own agonies and grandeur we must appreciate. In the opposing scales, Rousseau has 'genius,' the capacity to follow a thought through in all its depth. In the exaltation of his spirit he fails to place things in their historical context, does not register the causes, and rather than stifling his opponents only exasperates them (*Les Voltairiens* 7: 24, 26). But the great change in historical estimation occurs in the description of Voltaire. In the numerous *éloges* written soon after his death, Voltaire is the rival of Corneille and of Sophocles in the grandeur of his tragedies; the rival of Virgil in his *Henriade. Candide* is never mentioned! Such an omission fails to register the split consciousness of the time: as Sylvain Menant reminds us in *Dictionnaire Voltaire*, 20,000 copies of *Candide* were sold in its first year of publication. But in Valsecchi, and more importantly in Azaïs's essay, Voltaire has become solely the writer of 'esprit,' that is of witty intelligence, who has facility, critical judgment, reason, and wit, but not the sustaining powers of creative genius. While an ardent defender of reason and foe of fanaticism, Voltaire has nevertheless debased his talents in favour of lightness and grace. Have the criticisms of

Rousseau taken hold? In any event, except for the quite similar case of Erasmus, never has a reputation undergone such extreme transformation (one can think, of course, how far that of Hemingway had plummeted in the course of the twentieth century). In essence, the renewed criticism returns Voltaire to the limitations of the culture of mundanity from which his own aspirations and sense of proportionate values had thought to escape. Once again to refer to Mme de Staël (see n1 above), while attributing to Voltaire the qualities of a witty mocker, she does not scant his plays, in particular the natural passions he represents in *Tancrède* (275–6).

5 Coleridge's articles have been called a 'brilliantly original series of paired portraits' by Coleridge's biographer, Richard Holmes, in *Coleridge: Darker Reflections*. This valuable study reaches questionable propositions when it claims that, in the portrait of Luther, Coleridge intended to show 'the fanatical personality of the revolutionary spirit' (167). Such a contention goes against the admiration expressed for Luther, his anchor in the Bible, and the development of the 'first vernal influences of true knowledge' that accounted for the Renaissance and Reformation. See introduction above. A needed corrective is provided by Bruce Mansfield, *Man on His Own*, where he shows Coleridge's even-handed treatment of both Erasmus and Luther, joining them together and even, in Erasmus's case, transcending the 'confessional' interpretations. They become joint heroes in an epoch of critical change. He also quotes Coleridge's rueful statement, summarizing the nature of all true dualisms, 'Such utter unlikes cannot but end in dislikes.' See 87–95. In *Table Talk* there is no doubt as to Coleridge's preference or his appreciation for Luther's genius: 'Erasmus's paraphrase of the New Testament is very explanatory and clear, but you cannot expect anything very deep from Erasmus. The only fit commentator on Paul was Luther, not by any means such a gentleman as the Apostle, but almost as great a Genius' (*The Collected Works of Samuel Taylor Coleridge* 389). For a brilliant, concise examination and explanation of Coleridge's critical genius, see Walter Jackson Bate, *Coleridge* 143–69, ending with the, for us, pertinent quotation, 'to *know* is to *resemble.*'

6 Carducci represents the liberal interpretations begun in the Enlightenment of a progressive development. In fact, the threefold association of Petrarch, Erasmus, and Voltaire was available: the Dutch historian C.B. Huet (1826–86) wrote 'that only three times did a single name so dominate European intellectual life: the times of Petrarch, Erasmus and Voltaire' (Mansfield, *Man on His Own* 306). Carducci's essay retains its value because it shows the *impact* of one figure upon the other and because it represents an Italian interest in these subjects (notably ignored, even by Mansfield).

Chapter 4: Turgenev and Dostoevsky

1 See Joseph Frank, *Dostoevsky* 1: 172–98.
2 One should also consult the more recent *A Writer's Diary*, which is valuable for a lengthy introductory essay by Gary Saul Morson.
3 For a sophisticated comparison of the two 'temporalities' of the works of Tolstoy and Dostoevsky, see Gary Saul Morson's introduction to *A Writer's Diary* 77–8, 101–2.
4 Quoted in Jackson, *Dostoevsky: New Perspectives* 2–3. The same recognition is provided by D.S. Mirsky, *A History of Russian Literature*. Locating Turgenev among the Victorians, Mirsky goes on to write, 'But for most lovers of Russian, he has been replaced by spicier food' (207).
5 For very insightful pages on Rousseau, Dostoevsky, and Camus, see Peter Brooks, *Troubling Confessions* 46–52, 163–6
6 See Frank 1: 155.
7 In his annual review of 1847, Belinsky praised *Khor and Kalinych*, the success of which induced Turgenev to continue with his sportsman's sketches. Belinsky, however, limited Turgenev's gift to the 'sketch,' denying him the power to create the kind of characters and their relationships necessary for the novel (472–3)! V.G. Belinsky, *Selected Philosophical Works* 472–3.
8 Richard Freeborn, introduction to Turgenev's *Sketches from a Hunter's Album*, 4
9 See my *Mapping Literary Modernism* 8.
10 See my *Changes of Cain* 201–5.
11 See my *Mapping Literary Modernism* 53–4, 141–8.
12 See my *Changes of Cain* 62–83, and *Foundation Sacrifice in Dante's 'Commedia'* 11–46.
13 Completing the linkage between *Fathers and Children* and the essays of Pisarev and Strakhov, Joseph Frank in finely tuned comments regards Raskolnikov's failed adoption of the 'great man' theory as an obvious response to and repudiation of Pisarev's own notions (4: 72–5, 126).
14 See Stephane Courtois et al., *Le livre noir du communisme*, and Martin Malia's review essay in *TLS*.
15 See chapter 3, 198–202.
16 See my *Changes of Cain* 196–200.
17 Ever mindful of Dostoevsky's dislike of contemporary Lutheranism and the risks they pose for leading the people astray (*DW* 564).
18 The speech is happily translated in Ceresh Allen 839–49.
19 The speech is reprinted in *Diary of a Writer* 967–80, with important adjoining material, such as his classic response to Gradovsky.

20 Yet with all these stabs at what might pass for concluding remarks, in none of
the other three pairs of this study do I have the same sense of shortsighted-
ness as I do when I consider Turgenev and Dostoevsky. Certainly justice has
been done to the synoptic powers of Dostoevsky, the accumulating powers of
his dominant ideas. It is Turgenev's growth, particularly in his later career,
that is missing. Abundant credit has been given to his skill as a novelist, even
suggesting a re-evaluation that would elevate in aesthetic pleasure and social
importance *On the Eve* and *Smoke* to the level of *Fathers and Children*. Nor have
I neglected 'A Propos of *Fathers and Children*,' with its sterling defence of creative freedom, or 'Hamlet and Quixote,' that most influential essay summarizing the bipolar principles of Russian culture, nor the artful speech at the
Pushkin festivities. Yet in all of these Turgenev still seemed to suffer under
the domination of Dostoevsky, and his due praise is of the sort that Carducci
allotted to Petrarch, Erasmus, and Voltaire for their bravery in defending
themselves with dignity and nobility. While not exactly backhanded, such
praise is not fulsome either. What is missing are the later efforts of Turgenev,
which seem so different. We must recall that he continued to write and
sketch out plots for projects up to his final days. This last phase has been
touched by the so-called supernatural influences of Poe and Hoffman. But
rather than supernatural I would prefer psychic, subconscious, as if in *The
Dream* 'this least self-analytical of men' finally was confronting some of the
basic issues of his life. The narrator is an only child, raised by his mother –
his father having died when he was seven. He acknowledges that this situation is not healthy, and that a certain reserve, if not awkwardness, exists
between him and his mother. He dreams of another man, a powerful, dangerous, and perhaps malevolent male, one with a notable scar across his
forehead. It soon becomes apparent that this man did most secretively enter
his mother's bed and is his actual father. His mother refuses to acknowledge
whether she submitted or succumbed to his presence, insisting only that her
mind went blank. The narrator is the product of this union. After a terrible
storm he finds the body of his real father washed up on the beach and
retrieves from his hand his mother's wedding ring, which the infiltrator had
removed at the time of his mysterious encounter. He returns the ring to his
mother, with the acknowledgment that in so doing he is bringing her
together with her true husband and his father. But an awkwardness persists
between them. The feminine principle of Nature – she is a Mother – is coun-
termanded by the dangerous male principle of superior seductive powers, of
eternal tension between male and female. Hence the son recoils in horror as
he recognizes this same principle in himself (*Essential Turgenev* 819).
    This piece is far from a coda, as it was part of a new burst of energy on Tur-

genev's part in his last years. But it shows that there was more to Turgenev and more that would have been shown had he been able to develop fully that last new area of creativity, represented by such works as *The Song of Triumphant Love, Clara Milic*, and his *Prose Poems*, chief among which are 'Threshold' and the already quoted 'Nature.' In the first-named *Song* another saintly woman is seduced by a returned friend. Schapiro refers to this encounter as being the 'intrusion of animal, sexual passion' (312), and indeed her husband does encounter her sobbing under a marble satyr. But there is more here like a mysterious sexual passion, a greater force and power to which the woman is vulnerable. And while she seems to return to the formerly happy life with her husband, inside her womb is throbbing with new life. In these later works Turgenev is portraying a passion and fulfilment by means of a dominant exotic male and an overwhelmed, susceptible woman – woman and her demon lover – such as he had never been able to achieve in his own life. While he may have adumbrated such a theme in earlier works (Schapiro 313), here the record is clearer, more violent, even with a touch of malevolence. Turgenev seems to be searching out a profounder part of his own psyche – in itself daemonic – and in so doing he engages the reader in ways he had heretofore not done.

Chapter 5: Sartre and Camus

1 For Sartre, the essential original texts will be found in *Œuvres romanesques; Théâtre complet; Les écrits de Sartre;* Anne Cohen-Solal, *Sartre: A Life;* and John Gerassi, *Jean-Paul Sartre: Hated Conscience of His Century.* English translations of the essential Sartrean texts will be given in their proper places in the course of this study. For Camus, the essential texts are *Théâtre, récits, nouvelles; Essais;* and Olivier Todd, *Albert Camus: une vie.* Reference may also be made to Todd's unfortunately abridged *Albert Camus: A Life.* The major study by Ronald Aronson, *Camus and Sartre,* has already been cited in the preface.

2 See Aronson, *Camus and Sartre* 50.

3 See preface, n3.

4 See the large vision brought to these matters by Jean-François Sirinelli, *Sartre et Aron, deux intellectuels dans le siècle.*

5 Of course in a friendship misunderstandings occur. Lunching at the Café Procope, Merleau-Ponty blatantly misread Sartre's demeanour and facial expressions, remarking on his 'glacial' tone and ironical responses. In a letter of defence, Sartre not only dismisses these interpretations but apologizes for his trait of being unable to congratulate the person in front of him (Stewart 351). *The Debate between Sartre and Merleau-Ponty* is a valuable compilation

of works by Sartre, de Beauvoir, and Merleau-Ponty himself, along with important critical essays. Professor Stewart's introduction is admirable.

6 See Stewart 448–91, 93, 112. Interestingly enough, many of the critical essays do suggest a kind of rapprochement between the thought of Sartre and Merleau-Ponty. 'The Philosophy of Existence,' a colloquium given by Merleau-Ponty, certainly explains his own interest in existentialism and Sartre's prodigious importance, even if by 1960 the philosophy is 'no longer our own.' He does speak of the 'friendship which continues to bind them together' (502–3). One section, 'Interrogation and Dialectic,' taken from the posthumous *The Visible and the Invisible,* sharply dismisses the concept of consciousness, the for-itself, as nothingness. He accuses Sartre of establishing an 'abstract dichotomy' between being and nothingness, when they are complementary (551). Oddly enough, de Beauvoir's attack against Merleau-Ponty's *réformisme,* his desire to bring about effective change from within the system, only supports the rightness of his position that later history would amply confirm in the vast improvements gained by the native industrialized workers of the West.

7 *TRN,* 1168. Trans., with small alterations by Stuart Gilbert (New York: Vintage, 1954), 76.

8 Coleridge's speculations about Shakespeare's full reception first among foreigners (Germans) are very appropriate here. The English mind devoted to defeating Napoleon ('the evil genius of the planet') required action and the recall of traditional values. But the German mind had been driven toward inner speculation and reordering of traditional thought. 'Incapable of acting outwardly, they have acted internally.' Thus, two of the dominant philosophies of the past several centuries emerged from the shadows of political defeat. See R.A. Foakes, *Coleridge on Shakespeare* 103–4. See also Richard Holmes, *Coleridge: Darker Reflections* 278. Place America in the position of England and France in the position of Germany and one can see a parallel situation, with French thought being more adventurous and American thought more 'rallying.' Mme de Staël concurs when she writes that the Germans, lacking a political country ('une patrie politique'), have nevertheless made 'une patrie littéraire et philosophique,' to their honour and glory (250).

9 See the sampling of the many reviews – mostly favourable – in *Œuvres romanesques* 1701–11.

10 See Quinones, *Mapping Literary Modernism* 148–63.

11 See ibid. 134–8.

12 Two additional points should be made here. The first, which accounts for his devoted following, is his flair as a lecturer. One has only to consult the inter-

views reprinted in *Situations IX* (the first section entitled 'Sur moi-même') to recognize his genius speaking extempore.

But of course these are not off-the-cuff remarks but rather moulded from the density of constant preoccupation with thought. And, as with Luther, Sartre, particularly after *Words*, has desacralized a calling – that of the writer. Now writing has become a professional job, which is of as much value as any other ('en tant que métier, une activité qui en vaut une autre' – *Situations IX* 39).

13 For Sartre's comments, see *Théâtre complet* 1180.

14 See her excellent summary, 333–5, which however regards the relationship as 'doomed from the start.'

15 Among a number of excellent interpretations in English of *Being and Nothingness* see Joseph S. Catalano, *A Commentary on Jean-Paul's 'Being and Nothingness,'* and *Jean-Paul Sartre: Basic Writings*, ed. Stephen Priest.

16 The always-engaging Harold Bloom totally discounts Sartre as a novelist: 'Sartre always knows too well what he thinks he is doing, and his characters never break away from him' (*Modern Critical Views: Jean-Paul Sartre* 1). The following pages and Camus himself (see Copleston 458) dispute that particular reading of Sartre's novelistic qualities. Bloom goes on, 'A few pages of Proust, read almost at random, suffice to obliterate the ideograms that Camus and Sartre vainly wish to establish as persons' (2). While his remarks may be accurate as regards *The Plague*, neither Meursault nor Clamence can be regarded as mere ideograms. And cannot a firm comparison be made between the Baron de Charlus and Daniel?

17 See *Œuvres romanesques*, interview with Christian Grisoli, 1912–17.

18 See Quinones, *Mapping Literary Modernism*, 114–19.

19 Sartre will later express horror that he might have entertained such a thought. 'What, he exclaims, I actually thought that!' Rather, he now believes humankind is 'totalement' conditioned by their situation (*Situations IX* 100). One can still wonder if the difference is as great as he later supposes. See nn21, 31 below.

20 See the translation in *Œuvres romanesques*, 1917–21.

21 As usual, the judiciously sympathetic Frederick Copleston identifies the disjuncture: 'The validity of the contention that in choosing a value one chooses ideally for all men is not so clear as Sartre thinks it is' (9: 366). His excellent discussion of Sartre – early and late, that is, *Being and Nothingness* and *Critique of Dialectical Reason,* where he suggests that they are not as far apart as might seem (383) – is admirably followed by some pages on Camus where he validates that writer's position as an insightful moralist.

22 Reprinted in *Situations II* 9–35.

23 Not too surprisingly a similar understanding is provided by Mme de Staël

when she observes that only within a circle of a small number of people, superior either by merit or education, are the rules and the taste of style maintained. Style is a form of address (265–6). Differences are just as notable: for her, literature reflects social institutions; for Sartre it is the expressive mode of a society. Sartre also might appear to have little sympathy with her notion of 'la perfectibilité.'

24 See Simon Schama, *Citizens*: 'The vanguard of the liberal nobility had long professed to want to exchange their titular status and feudal "superstitions" for the new aristocratic dignity of "citizen"' (438).

25 The sexual overtones of this passage are supported by pages from *Being and Nothingness*. By squeezing into a hole, by 'plugging' it up, 'I shall contribute to making a fullness of being exist in the world' (781). In his remarkable meditation on Paul Nizan, he contrasts the 'vide' or emptiness and the monotonous similarity of bourgeois daily existence with the fullness of life toward which he aspired. But the sense of the void or emptiness could not be confined to bourgeois life, as it was also keenly experienced by Turgenev and Rousseau. Sartre's class-determinism is somewhat short-sighted.

26 The stage reviewer for *Le Figaro* quite early used the same analogy *Théâtre complet* (1387), as did Sartre himself in a later interview (1948) with Paolo Caruso (*Les écrits* 182–4).

27 Even going beyond this exchange, Sandra Teroni establishes an interesting 'jeu intertextuel' between *The Just Assassins* and *Dirty Hands*, where Sartre is evidently replying to Camus's play by removing the 'halo' from the assassination, and instead establishes a true dialectic between the need for 'purity' and political realism. Her entire discussion is excellent (*Théâtre complet* 1377–8).

28 For the most recent and full discussion of all of Sartre's drama, original and adaptations, see Benedict O'Donohoe's *Sartre's Theatre: Dramas for Life*. This work quite valuably provides the intellectual and social context that enters into the plays.

29 I quote from the original as it appeared in *Les temps modernes*, August 1952, 334. A recent translation is in *Sartre and Camus: A Historical Confrontation*, eds. Sprintzen and Van den Hoven, 131–58.

30 This notorious phrase was quoted in an interview for *Le monde*, April 1964. Do you think, he asks, that I would be able to read Robbe-Grillet in an under-developed country? And then he adds, 'En face d'un enfant qui meurt, *La nausée* ne fait pas le poids.' The phrase created something of a scandal, and Sartre in another interview explained himself by saying that he did not even think of putting in the same scale of values the death of a child and a work of fiction. The question that interests him is of what value is literature in a world of hunger. He does not disallow the discrepancy; he simply intensifies it (*Les écrits* 398–9).

31 As late as in an interview of 1970, Sartre continued to praise the mythic qualities of the theatre and, despite his positive response to the question as to
whether he continued to write for the stage, this did not prevent *Les séquestrés
d'Altona* (1959) from being his last created play. (*Les Troyennes*, however successful and creditable as a political allegory, was in very large part an adaptation.) Its writing and constant rewriting and production difficulties literally
cost him blood and anguish. To his relief and that of Simone de Beauvoir,
the play was well received. Cohen-Solal (381–4) continues to regard it as
'undoubtedly his most poignant, imaginative and powerful play,' remaining
among his oeuvre 'unsurpassed.' In *Les écrits* (323–2), Contat and Rybalka
are more sensitive to its difficulties, its heaviness, obscurities, but end up by
affirming its place among the three best of the nine plays by Sartre (along
with *No Exit* and *The Devil and the Good Lord*). They further rightly associate it
with the contemporaneous *Critique de la raison dialectique* as being the most
sombre and pessimistic of all Sartre's works. This has something to do with
his passage from *Being and Nothingness* to the *Critique*, from a work of individual freedom of consciousness to one where humankind is 'totalement' conditioned by its situation. This is certainly the situation of *Les séquestrés*, where
the guilt of the Nazi past hangs over all, where all are guilty or complicitous,
and while depicting the drama of a German family with its skeletons, reaches
mythic proportions, when its true intent, as Sartre informs us (*Les écrits* 367)
is to describe the plight of Europe after the war, from the Russian concentration camps to the war (and revelations of torture) in Algeria. On another
plane, Contat and Rybalka touch the essential question when they ask
whether there is a true epistemological break between *Being and Nothingness*
and the *Critique* (*Les écrits* 338). See n21 above. These connections and developments should not blind us to the plain fact that by 1960, for whatever reasons, *all* creative endeavour went beyond Sartre's powers and interests; his
energies were flagging and he preferred plots that were laid out for him, as
in *Les Troyennes*, or where the information was voluminous, as in his massive
meditation on Flaubert, a work in which he thought he invented his personage, and one he considered the continuation of his novelistic ambitions.

Epilogue

1 Gavin Stevens in *Requiem for a Nun*. New York: Random House, 1950, 92.

Works Cited

Althusser, Louis. Sartre's importance. *Le monde*, 16 April 1980.

Arnold, Matthew. *Culture and Anarchy: An Essay in Political and Social Criticism*. Ed. J. Dover Wilson. Cambridge: Cambridge UP, 1961.

Aronson, Ronald. *Camus and Sartre: The Story of a Friendship and the Quarrel That Ended It*. Chicago: U Chicago P, 2004.

– 'Camus vs. Sartre: How the Cold War Destroyed a Friendship.' *TLS*, 22 September 2002.

Auden, W.H. 'September 1, 1939.' *The Collected Poetry of W.H. Auden*. New York: Random House, 1945.

Augustijn, Cornelis. *Erasmus: Der Humanist als Theologe und Kirchenreformer.* Leiden: Brill, 1996.

– *Erasmus: His Life, Works, and Influence*. Trans. J.C. Grayson. Toronto: U Toronto P, 1991.

Azaïs, Pierre-Hyacinthe. 'Jugement philosophique sur J.-J. Rousseau et sur Voltaire.' *Les Voltairiens*. Ed. Jeroom Vercruysee. Vol. 7. Nendeln: KTO, 1978. 11–65.

Barrett, William. *Irrational Man: A Study in Existential Philosophy.* Garden City: Double Day Anchor, 1962.

Barth, Karl. *Protestant Theology in the Nineteenth Century.* Trans. Brian Cozens and John Bowden. London: SCM, 2001.

Barthélèmy, Charles. *Voltaire et Rousseau: Jugés l'un par l'autre*. Paris: Blériot Frères, 1878.

Bate, Walter Jackson. *Coleridge*. New York: Macmillan, 1968.

Belinsky, V.G. *Selected Philosophical Works*. Moscow: Foreign Languages, 1948.

Bénichou, Paul. 'L'idée de nature chez Rousseau.' *Pensée de Rousseau*. Eds. Gérard Genette and Tzvetan Todorov. Paris: Seuil, 1984. 125–45.

Berdyaev, Nicolas. *The Origin of Russian Communism*. Trans. R.M. French. Ann Arbor: U Michigan P, 1960.

Berlin, Isaiah. 'The Hedgehog and the Fox.' *The Proper Study of Mankind.* New York: Farrar, Straus, and Giroux, 1998. 436–99.

– 'The Counter-Enlightenment.' *The Proper Study of Mankind.* New York: Farrar, Straus, and Girou, 1998. 243–68.

Besterman, Theodore, ed. *Voltaire.* 3rd ed. Chicago: Chicago UP, 1976.

Bietenholz, P.G., and T.B. Deutscher, eds. *Contemporaries of Erasmus: A Biographical Register of the Renaissance and Reformation.* Toronto: U Toronto P, 1985–7.

Bloom, Harold. *The Anxiety of Influence: A Theory of Poetry.* London: Oxford UP, 1973.

– *Genius.* New York: Warner, 2002.

– ed. *Modern Critical Views: Jean-Paul Sartre.* Philadelphia: Chelsea House, 2001.

– *Where Shall Wisdom Be Found?* New York: Riverhead, 2004.

Bloomfield, Morton W. 'The Two Cognitive Dimensions of the Humanities,' *Daedalus* (Spring 1970): 256–67.

Bois, Yve-Alain. *Matisse and Picasso.* Paris: Flammarion, 2001.

Bornkamm, Heinrich. 'Erasmus und Luther.' *Das Jahrhundert der Reformation.* 2nd ed. Gottingen: Vandenhoeck & Ruprecht, 1966.

– *Luther in Mid-Career.* Trans. E. Theodore Bachmann. Philadelphia: Fortress, 1983.

Brecht, Martin. *Martin Luther.* Vol. 1. *The Road to Reformation, 1483–1521.* Trans. James L. Schaaf. Minneapolis: Fortress, 1985.

– *Martin Luther.* Vol. 2. *Shaping and Defining the Reformation, 1521–1532.* Trans. James L. Schaaf. Minneapolis: Fortress, 1990.

– *Martin Luther.* Vol. 3. *The Preservation of the Church, 1532–1546.* Trans. James L. Schaaf. Minneapolis: Fortress, 1999.

Brée, Germaine. *Camus and Sartre: Crisis and Commitment.* New York: Delta, 1972.

Breger, Louise. *Dostoevsky: The Author as Psychoanalyst.* New York: New York UP, 1989.

Brooks, Peter. *Troubling Confessions.* Chicago: U Chicago P, 2000.

Budanova, N.F. *Dostoevsky i Turgenev: Tvorchesky Dialog.* Leningrad: Nauka, 1987.

Burckhardt, Jacob. *The Greeks and Greek Civilization.* Intro. Oswyn Murray. New York: St Martin's Griffin, 1998.

Burgelin, Pierre. *La philosophie de l'existence de J.-J. Rousseau.* Paris: Presses Universitaires de France, 1952.

Camus, Albert. *Essais.* Ed. Roger Quilliot. Paris: Gallimard Pléiade, 1965.

– *The Fall.* Trans. Justin O'Brien. New York: Vintage, 1956.

– *The First Man.* Trans. David Hapgood. New York: Vintage, 1995.

– *The Rebel.* Trans. Anthony Bower. New York: Vintage, 1956.

– *Théâtre, récits, nouvelles.* Ed. Roger Quilliot. Paris: Gallimard Pléiade, 1962.

Carducci, Giosue. *Studi litterari.* 2nd ed. Bologna: Zanichelli, 1907.

Cassirer, Ernst. *The Question of Jean-Jacques Rousseau.* Ed. Peter Gay. New York: Columbia UP, 1954.

Catalano, Joseph S. *A Commentary on Jean-Paul's 'Being and Nothingness.'* Chicago: U Chicago P, 1980.

Chantraine, Georges. *Érasme et Luther, libre et serf arbitre.* Namur: Presses Universitaires de Namur, 1981.

Chernyshevsky, Nikolai. *What Is To Be Done?* Trans. Michael B. Katz. Ithaca: Cornell UP, 1989.

Chomarat, Jacques. *Grammaire et rhetorique chez Érasme.* 2 vols. Paris: Société d'édition Les belles lettres, 1985.

Cohen, Rachel. 'Can You Forgive Him?' *New Yorker* 8 November 2004: 48–65.

– *A Chance Meeting: Intertwined Lives of American Writers and Artists, 1854–1967.* New York: Random House, 2004.

Cohen-Solal, Anne. *Sartre: A Life.* Trans. Anna Cancogni. New York: Pantheon, 1987.

Coleman, Patrick. *Rousseau's Political Imagination: Rule and Representation in the Lettre à D'Alembert.* Geneva: Droz, 1984.

Coleridge, Samuel Taylor. *The Collected Works of Samuel Taylor Coleridge.* Ed. Carl Woodring. Bollingen 75. Princeton: Princeton UP, 1990.

– *The Friend.* Ed. Barbara E. Rooke. Vol. 4 of *Collected Works.* Ed. Kathleen Coburn. Princeton: Princeton UP, 1969.

– *Literary Remains.* Ed. H.N. Coleridge. 4 vols. London: Pickering, 1836–9.

Collins, Randall. *The Sociology of Philosophies: A Global Theory of Intellectual Change.* Cambridge: Harvard Belknap, 1998.

Copleston, Frederick. *A History of Philosophy.* New York: Doubleday, 1974.

Corrigan, Robert, ed. *Comedy: Meaning and Form.* San Francisco: Chandler, 1965.

Courtois, Stephane, et al. *Le livre noir du communisme.* Paris: Laffont, 1998.

Cranston, Maurice. *Sartre.* Edinburgh: Oliver and Boyd, 1965.

Dante, Alighieri. *Dante's Purgatorio.* Trans. John D. Sinclair. New York: Oxford UP, 1972.

Davison, Ray. *Camus: The Challenge of Dostoevsky.* Exeter: U Exeter P, 1997.

de Beauvoir, Simone. *La force des choses.* Paris: Gallimard, 1963.

– *Les mandarins.* Paris: Gallimard, 1954. Trans. Leonard M. Friedman. New York: Norton, 1991.

Dictionnaire Voltaire. Dir. Jacques Lemaire, Raymond Trousson, and Jeroom Vercruysee. Brussels: Hachette, 1994.

Dobrolyubov, Nikolai. 'When Will the Real Day Come?' *Belinsky, Chernyshevsky, and Dobrolyubov: Selected Criticism.* Ed. Ralph E. Matlaw. Bloomington: Indiana UP, 1962. 176–226.

Doneux, Guy. *Luther et Rousseau.* Brussels: Houyoux, 1965.

Dostoevsky, Fyodor. *The Brothers Karamazov.* Ed. with revised trans. Richard Mat-
law. New York: Norton Critical Edition, 1976.
– *Crime and Punishment.* Trans. Jessie Coulson. Oxford: Oxford UP World's Clas-
sics, 1990.
– *Demons.* Trans. Richard Pevear and Larissa Volokhonsky. New York: Knopf,
1994.
– *The Diary of a Writer.* Trans. Boris Brasol. Haselmere: Ianmead, 1984.
– 'The Double.' Trans. George Bird. *Great Short Works of Fyodor Dostoevsky.* New
York: Harper & Row, 1968.
– *Great Short Works of Fyodor Dostoevsky.* New York: Harper & Row, 1968.
– *The House of the Dead.* Trans. David McDuff. Hammondsworth: Penguin,
1985.
– *The Idiot.* Trans. David Magarshack. Harmondsworth: Penguin Classics, 1958.
– *Notes from Underground.* Trans. Michael Katz. New York: Norton, 1989.
– *Poor Folk and Other Stories.* Trans. David McDuff. London: Penguin, 1988.
– *A Writer's Diary.* Trans. Kenneth Lantz. Evanston: Northwestern UP, 1994.
Edmonds, David, and John Eidinow. *Rousseau's Dog.* New York: HarperCollins,
2006.
– *Wittgenstein's Poker: The Story of a Ten-Minute Argument between Two Great Philoso-
phers.* New York: HarperCollins, 2001.
Edwards Jr, Mark. *Luther and the False Brethren.* Stanford: Stanford UP, 1975.
Erasmus, Desiderius. *Adages.* Vol. 31 of *The Collected Works of Erasmus.* Trans. Mar-
garet Mann Philips. Toronto: U Toronto P, 1988.
– *The Collected Works of Erasmus.* Toronto: U Toronto P, 1976–.
– *The Colloquies of Erasmus.* Trans. Craig R. Thompson. Chicago: U Chicago P,
1965.
– *The Correspondence of Erasmus.* Vol. 3 of *The Collected Works of Erasmus.* Intro.
John W. O'Malley. Trans. Charles Fantazzi. Toronto: U Toronto P, 1988.
– *Enchiridion.* Vol. 66 of *The Collected Works of Erasmus.* Ed. and Intro. John W.
O'Malley. Trans. Charles Fantazzi. Toronto: U Toronto P, 1988.
– *Erasmus and His Age: Selected Letters of Desiderius Erasmus.* Ed. Hans J. Hiller-
brand. New York: Harper Torch, 1970.
– *The Polemics of Erasmus of Rotterdam and Ulrich von Hutten.* Trans. Randolph J.
Klawiter. Notre Dame: U Notre Dame P, 1977.
– *The Praise of Folly.* Trans. John Wilson. 1668; repr., Ann Arbor: U Michigan P,
1958.
Erikson, Erik. *Young Man Luther.* New York: Norton, 1958.
Fabre, Jean. 'Deux frères ennemis: Diderot et Jean-Jacques.' *Diderot Studies* 3
(1963): 155–213.
Fainaru, Steve. 'Poisoned Pens.' *Boston Globe* 4 November 1997.

Faulkner, William. *Requiem for a Nun*. New York: Random House, 1950.

Flam, Jack. *Matisse and Picasso: The Story of Their Rivalry and Friendship*. Cambridge: Westview, 2003.

Fleming, William F. 'The Worldling.' *Works*. Vol. 36. Paris: DuMont, 1901, 36–41, 87–91.

Foakes, R.A. *Coleridge on Shakespeare*. London: Routledge and Kegan Paul, 1971.

Fordham, Douglas. 'Allan Ramsey's Enlightenment; Or, Hume and the Patronizing Portrait.' *Art Bulletin* 88 (2006): 508–24.

Frank, Joseph. *Dostoevsky*. Vol. 1. *The Seeds of Revolt, 1829–1849*. Princeton: Princeton UP, 1976.

– *Dostoevsky*. Vol. 2. *The Years of Ordeal, 1850–1859*. Princeton: Princeton UP, 1983.

– *Dostoevsky*. Vol. 3. *The Stir of Liberation, 1860–1865*. Princeton: Princeton UP, 1986.

– *Dostoevsky*. Vol. 4. *The Miraculous Years, 1865–1871*. Princeton: Princeton UP, 1995.

– *Dostoevsky*. Vol. 5. *The Mantle of the Prophet, 1871–1881*. Princeton: Princeton UP, 2002.

Fumaroli, Marc. 'Le genre des genres littéraires français: la conversation.' *The Zakaroff Lectures*. Oxford: Clarendon, 1992.

Gerassi, John. *Jean-Paul Sartre: Hated Conscience of His Century*. Chicago: U Chicago P, 1989.

Girard, René. *Resurrection from Underground: Feodor Dostoevsky*. Ed. and trans. James G. Wilson. New York: Crossroad, 1997.

Goffen, Rona. *Renaissance Rivals*. New Haven: Yale UP, 2002.

Gouhier, Henri. 'Ce que le vicaire doit à Descartes.' *Annales de la Société J.J. Rousseau* 35 (1959–62): 139–60.

– *Rousseau et Voltaire: portraits dans deux miroirs*. Paris: Vrin, 1983.

Gourevitch, Victor. *Rousseau: The Discourses and Other Early Political Writings*. Cambridge: Cambridge UP, 1997.

Grenier, Roger. *Albert Camus, soleil et ombre*. Paris: Gallimard, 1987.

Groos, René. *Le siècle de Louis XIV*. 2 vols. Paris: Garnier, 1947.

Guéhenno, Jean. *Jean-Jacques: Grandeurs et misères d'une vie*. 2 vols. Paris: Gallimard, 1962.

Hadot, Jean. 'La critique textuelle dans l'édition du Nouveau Testament d'Érasme.' *Le Christianisme d'Érasme: Sources, modalités, controverses, influences*, Colloquia Erasmiana Turonensia. Tours: Stage internationale d'études humaniste, 1969. 749–60.

Halpern, Sue. 'Rev. of *Raising America* by Ann Hulbert.' *New York Review of Books*, 29 May 2003.

Hegel, Georg Wilhelm Friedrich. *The Philosophy of History.* Trans. J. Sibree. Amherst: Prometheus, 1991.

Holmes, Richard. *Coleridge: Darker Reflections, 1804–1834.* New York: Pantheon, 1998.

Huizinga, Johan. *Erasmus and the Age of Reformation.* New York: Harper & Row, 1957.

Hulbert, Ann. *Raising America: Experts, Parents, and a Century of Advice about Children.* New York: Knopf, 2003.

Israel, Jonathan I. *The Radical Enlightenment: Philosophy and the Making of Modernity, 1650–1750.* Oxford: Oxford UP, 2001.

Jackson, Robert Louis, ed. *Dostoevsky: New Perspectives.* Englewood Cliffs: Prentice-Hall, 1984.

– 'Freedom in *Notes from Underground.*' Dostoevsky, *Notes from Underground* 179–88.

– 'The Root and the Flower: Dostoevsky and Turgenev; A Comparative Aesthetic.' *Dialogues with Dostoevsky.* Stanford: Stanford UP, 1993. 162–81.

Jacob, Margaret C. *The Radical Enlightenment: Pantheists, Freemasons and Republicans.* Rev. 2nd ed. Morristown, NJ: Temple, 2003.

James, William. 'The Present Dilemma in Philosophy.' *Pragmatism.* New York: Meridian Books, 1955. 17–37.

– *The Varieties of Religious Experience.* New York: Modern Library, 1936.

Jeanson, Francis. *Le problème morale et la pensée de Sartre.* Paris: L'édition du Myrte, 1947.

Judt, Tony. *The Burden of Responsibility: Blum, Camus, Aron and the French Twentieth Century.* Chicago: U Chicago P, 1998.

Jung, Carl. 'The Problem of the Attitude-Type.' 1942. *Two Essays on Analytical Psychology.* New York: Meridian, 1956. 51–73.

Klawiter, Randolph J. *The Polemics of Erasmus and Ulrich von Hutten.* Notre Dame: U Notre Dame P, 1977.

Kohls, E-W. 'Érasme et la réforme.' *Le Christianisme d'Érasme: Sources, modalités, controverses, influences.* Colloquia Erasmiana Turonensia. Tours: Stage Internationale d'études humaniste, 1969. 837–47.

– *Luther oder Erasmus: Luthers Theolgie in der Auseinandersetzung mit Erasmus.* Basel: Friedrich Reinhardt, 1972–8. 2 vols.

Lévy, Bernard-Henri. *Le siècle de Sartre.* Paris: Grasset, 2000.

Lingeman, Richard. *Double Lives: American Writers' Friendships.* New York: Random House, 2006.

Lovejoy, A.O. *The Revolt against Dualism.* La Salle, IL: Open Court, 1960.

Luther, Martin. *Martin Luther: Selections from His Writings.* Ed. John Dillenberger. New York: Double Day Anchor, 1962.

– *Works of Martin Luther.* 4 vols. Philadelphia: Mühlenberg, 1943.

Lüthy, Herbert. *From Calvin to Rousseau.* Trans. Salvator Attanasio. New York: Basic, 1970.

MacCulloch, Diarmaid. *The Reformation: A History.* New York: Penguin, 2004.

Malia, Martin. 'The Lesser Evil?' *Times Literary Supplement* 27 March 1998.

Mansfield, Bruce. *Man on His Own: Interpretations of Erasmus, c1750–1920.* Toronto: U Toronto P, 1992.

– *Phoenix of His Age: Interpretations of Erasmus c. 1550–1750.* Toronto: U Toronto P, 1979.

Matlaw, Ralph E., ed. *Selected Criticism: Belinsky, Chernyshevsky, and Dobrolyubov.* Bloomington: Indiana UP, 1962.

Maugras, Gaston. *Voltaire et J.-J. Rousseau.* Paris: Calman Lévy, 1886.

McFarland, Thomas P. *Romanticism and the Forms of Ruin: Wordsworth, Coleridge, and the Modalities of Fragmentation.* Princeton: Princeton UP, 1981.

– *Romanticism and the Heritage of Rousseau.* Oxford: Clarendon, 1995

McGann, Jerome. *Byron and Wordsworth.* School of English Studies. Nottingham: U Nottingham P, 1999.

McKeon, Michael. *The Origins of the English Novel, 1600–1740.* Baltimore: Johns Hopkins UP, 1987.

Mély, Benoit. *Jean-Jacques Rousseau: un intellectuel en rupture.* Paris: Minerva, 1985.

Melzer, Arthur M. 'The Origin of the Counter-Enlightenment: Rousseau and the New Religion of Sincerity.' *American Political Science Review* 90 (June 1996): 344–60.

Merleau-Ponty, Maurice. 'The Philosophy of Existence.' Trans. Allen S. Weiss. Stewart 492–503.

– 'The Visible and the Invisible.' Trans. Alphonso Lingis. Stewart 518–64.

Miller, Robin F. 'Dostoevsky and Rousseau: The Morality of Confession Reconsidered.' *Western Philosophical Systems in Russian Literature.* Ed. Anthony Mlikotin. Los Angeles: USC Press, n.d. 89–101.

Mirsky, D.S. *A History of Russian Literature.* Ed. Francis J. Whitfield. New York: Random House, 1958.

Mochulsky, Konstantin. *Dostoevsky,* Trans. Michael A Minihan. Princeton: Princeton UP, 1967.

More, Thomas. *The Complete Works of St Thomas More.* Ed. Daniel Kinney. New Haven: Yale UP, 1986.

Mostefai, Ourida. *Le citoyen de Genève et la république des lettres.* New York: Lang, 2003.

Murray, Robert H. *Erasmus and Luther: Their Attitude to Toleration.* New York: Franklin, 1920.

Nalbantian, Suzanne. *Memory in Literature: From Rousseau to Neuroscience.* New York: Palgrave Macmillan, 2003.

Naves, Raymond. *Voltaire*. 8th ed. Paris: Hatier, 1972.

Neiman, Susan. *Evil in Modern Thought*. Princeton: Princeton UP, 2002.

Nietzsche, Friedrich. *The Birth of Tragedy*. Trans. Francis Golfing. Garden City, NY: Doubleday, 1956.

– *Friedrich Nietzsche: Werke*. Munich: Hanser, 1956.

Nikolsky, Yuri. *Turgenev i Dostoevsky: Istoria odnoy vrazhdy*. Sofia: 1921.

O'Brien, Conor Cruise. *Albert Camus of Africa and Europe*. New York: Viking, 1970.

O'Donohoe, Benedict. *Sartre's Theatre: Dramas for Life*. Oxford: Lang, 2005.

O'Malley, John W. 'Erasmus and Luther: Continuity and Discontinuity as Key to Their Conflict.' *Sixteenth Century Journal* 5 (October 1974): 47–65.

Oberman, Heiko O. *Luther: Man between God and the Devil*. Trans. Eileen Walliser-Schwarzbart. New York: Doubleday, 1992.

Olin, John C., ed. *Desiderius Erasmus: Christian Humanism and the Reformation*. New York: Harper Torch Books, 1965.

Perrin, Jean-François. 'Écrire doublement.' *Magazine littéraire* 357 (1997): 26–9.

Picon, Gaëton. 'Notes on *The Plague*.' *Camus: A Collection of Critical Essays*. Ed. Germaine Brée. Englewood Cliffs: Prentice-Hall, 1962. 150–6.

Pintacuda, Fiorella de Michelis. *Tra Erasmo e Lutero*. Rome: Istituto Nazionale di Studii sul Rinascimento, 2001.

Podhoretz, Norman. *Ex-Friends: Falling Out with Allen Ginsberg and Diana Trilling, Lillian Hellman, Hannah Arendt, and Norman Mailer*. New York: Free Press, 1999.

Pomeau, René. *D'Arouet à Voltaire*. Oxford: Voltaire Foundation, 1985.

– 'Était-ce "la faute à Voltaire, la faute à Rousseau"?' *Voltaire and His World: Essays Presented to W.H. Barber*. Ed. W.H. Barber and R.J. Howells. Oxford: Voltaire Foundation, 1985.

– *La religion de Voltaire*. Updated. Paris: Nizet, 1969.

– 'Voltaire et Rousseau devant l'affaire Calas.' *Voltaire-Rousseau et la tolerance*. Actes du colloque franco-néerlandais. Amsterdam: Descartes, 1979. 59–75.

Porter, Dennis. *Rousseau's Legacy: Emergence and Eclipse of the Writer in France*. New York: Oxford UP, 1995.

Poulet, Georges. *Studies in Human Time*. Trans. Elliott Coleman. Baltimore: Johns Hopkins UP, 1956.

Quinones, Ricardo J. *The Changes of Cain*. Princeton: Princeton UP, 1991.

– *Dante Alighieri*. Updated. New York: Twayne, 1997.

– *Foundation Sacrifice in Dante's 'Commedia.'* University Park: Pennsylvania State UP, 1994.

– *Mapping Literary Modernism: Time and Development*. Princeton: Princeton UP, 1985.

‒ *Renaissance Discovery of Time.* Cambridge: Harvard UP, 1972.

Rahv, Philip. 'Paleface and Redskin.' *Literature and the Sixth Sense.* Boston: Houghton Mifflin, 1970. 1–6.

Raymond, Marcel. 'J.-J. Rousseau: Deux aspects de sa vie intérieure.' *Annales de la société J.-J. Rousseau* 29 (1941–2): 9–56.

Reid, Alastair. 'Neruda and Borges.' *New Yorker* 24 June 1996, 53–72.

Richards, I.A., ed. *The Portable Coleridge.* New York: Viking, 1950.

Rousseau, Jean-Jacques. *Les confessions.* Vol. 1 of *Œuvres complètes.* Paris: Gallimard, 1959.

‒ *The Confessions of Jean-Jacques Rousseau.* Trans. J.M. Cohen. 1953; repr., Baltimore: Penguin, 1960.

‒ *Du contrat social.* Vol. 3 of *Œuvres complètes.* Paris: Gallimard, 1964.

‒ *Émile or On Education.* Trans. Allan Bloom. New York: Basic, 1979.

‒ 'The first *Discours.*' Vol. 3 of *Œuvres complètes.* Paris: Gallimard, 1964.

‒ 'The second *Discours.*' Vol. 3 of *Œuvres complètes.* Paris: Gallimard, 1964.

‒ *Lettre à M. D'Alembert sur son article Genève.* Ed. Michel Launay. Paris: Garnier, 1967.

‒ *La nouvelle Heloise.* Vol. 2 of *Œuvres complètes.* Paris: Gallimard, 1964.

‒ *Œuvres complètes.* Paris: Galllimard, 1964–.

‒ *Politics and the Arts: Letter to M. D'Alembert on the Theater.* Trans. Allan Bloom. Ithaca: Cornell UP, 1960.

‒ *Rousseau: The Discourses and Other Early Political Writings.* Ed. Victor Gourevitch. Cambridge: Cambridge UP, 1997.

Rummel, Erika. *Erasmus.* New York: Continuum, 2004.

‒ *Erasmus and His Catholic Critics.* Nieuwkoop: De Graaf, 1989. 2 vols.

‒ 'Voices of Reform from Hus to Erasmus.' *Handbook of European History, 1400–1600.* Ed. Thomas A. Brady et al. Leiden: Brill, 1995. 62–81.

Rupp, E. Gordon, and Philip S. Watson, eds. *Luther and Erasmus: Free Will and Salvation.* Library of Christian Classics, 17. London: SCM, 1969.

Russell, John. 'The Return of Meyerhold.' *New York Review of Books* 15 July 1982.

Saint-Évremond. *Œuvres en prose.* Ed. René Ternois. Paris: Didier, 1962.

Santoni, Ronald E. *Sartre on Violence: Curiously Ambivalent.* University Park: Pennsylvania State UP, 2003.

Sartre, Jean-Paul. *The Age of Reason.* Trans. Eric Sutton. New York: Vintage, 1947.

‒ *Being and Nothingness.* Trans. Hazel E. Barnes. New York: Philosophical Library, 1956.

‒ *Les écrits de Sartre.* Ed. Michel Contat and Michel Rybalka. Paris: Gallimard, 1970.

‒ *Jean-Paul Sartre: Basic Writings.* Ed. Stephen Priest. London: Routledge, 2001.

‒ *Les mots.* Paris: Gallimard, 1964.

– *Nausea.* Trans. Lloyd Alexander. New York: New Directions, 1964.
– *Œuvres romanesques.* Ed. Michel Contat and Michel Rybalka, with Geneviève Idt and George H. Bauer. Paris: Gallimard Pléiade, 1981.
– 'Qu'est-ce que la littérature?' *Situations II.* Paris: Gallimard, 1948. 55–315.
– *The Reprieve.* Trans. Eric Sutton. New York: Vintage, 1947.
– *Situations I.* Paris: Gallimard, 1947.
– *Situations IX.* Paris: Gallimard, 1972.
– *Théâtre complet.* Ed. Michel Contat et al. Paris: Gallimard Pléiade, 2005.
Schama, Simon. *Citizens: A Chronicle of the French Revolution.* New York: Vintage, 1990.
Schapiro, Leonard. *Turgenev: His Life and Times.* Cambridge: Harvard UP, 1978.
Schiller, Friedrich. *Naïve and Sentimental Poetry* and *On the Sublime.* Trans. and intro. J.A. Elias. New York: Ungar, 1966.
– *Schriften.* Intro. Hans Meyer. Frankfurt: Insel Verlag, 1966.
Schoeck, R.J. *Erasmus of Europe.* 2 vols. Edinburgh: Edinburgh UP, 1990, 1993.
Schottenloher, O. 'Erasmus, Johann Popenruyter und die Entstehung des Enchiridion militis cristiani.' *Archiv fur Reformationsgeschichte* 45 (1954): 109–16.
Shakespeare, William. 'Henry IV, Part 2.' *The Riverside Shakespeare.* Boston: Houghton Mifflin, 1974.
Sirinelli, Jean-François. *Sartre et Aron, deux intellectuels dans le siècle.* Paris: Hachette, 1995.
Sisman, Adam. *The Friendship: Wordsworth and Coleridge.* New York: Viking, 2007.
Spitz, Lewis. *The Protestant Reformation, 1517–1559.* New York: Harper & Row, 1985.
Sprintzen, David, and Adrian Van den Hoven, eds. *Sartre and Camus: A Historical Confrontation.* Evanston: Northwestern UP, 2004.
Staël, Mme de (-Holstein). *De la littérature, considérée par ses rapports avec les institutions socials.* Paris: Charpentier, 1842.
Starobinski, Jean. 'The Accuser and the Accused.'. *Daedalus* (Spring 1978): 41–57.
Stewart, Jon, ed. *The Debate between Sartre and Merleau-Ponty.* Evanston: Northwestern UP, 1998.
Strakhov, N.N. 'Fathers and Sons.' Repr. in Ivan Turgenev. *Fathers and Sons.* Ed. Ralph E. Matlaw. New York: Norton Critical Edition, 1966. 218–29.
Sulloway, Frank. *Born to Rebel: Birth Order, Family Dynamics and Creative Lives.* New York: Pantheon, 1996.
Terras, Victor. *A Karamazov Companion.* Madison: U Wisconsin P, 1981.
Thody, Philip. *Sartre: A Biographical Introduction.* New York: Scribner's, 1971.
Tocqueville, Alexis de. *Democracy in America.* Ed. J.P. Mayer. Trans. George Lawrence. New York: Harper and Row, 1966.
Todd, Oliver. *Albert Camus: A Life.* Trans. Benjamin Ivry. New York: Knopf, 1997.

– *Albert Camus: une vie*. Paris: Gallimard, 1996.

Trinkaus, Charles. 'Petrarch: Man between Despair and Grace.' *In Our Image and Likeness*. London: Constable, 1970. 3–56.

Trousson, Raymond. *Jean-Jacques Rousseau*. Paris: Hachette, 1993.

– *Rousseau et sa fortune littéraire*. Bordeaux: Ducros, 1971.

– *Visages de Voltaire*. Paris: Champion, 2001.

Turgenev, Ivan. *The Essential Turgenev*. Ed. Elizabeth Cheresh Allen. Evanston: Northwestern UP, 1994.

– *On the Eve*. Trans. Gilbert Gardiner. Hammondsworth: Penguin, 1950.

– *Fathers and Sons (Children)*. Ed. Ralph E. Matlaw. New York: Norton Critical Edition, 1966.

– 'Hamlet and Don Quixote.' *The Essential Turgenev*. Ed. Elizabeth Cheresh Allen. Evanston: Northwestern UP, 1994. 547–84.

– *Sketches from a Sportsman's Album*. Trans. Richard Freeborn. London: Penguin, 1990.

– *Smoke*. Trans. Constance Garnett. Turtle Point, rpt. 1995.

– *Turgenev: Literary Reminiscences and Autobiographical Fragments*. Ed. David Magarshack. New York: Farrar, Straus, and Cudahy, 1958.

– *Turgenev's Letters*. Ed. A.V. Knowles. London: Athlone, 1983.

– *Winter Notes on Summer Impressions*. Trans. David Patterson. Evanston: Northwestern UP, 1997.

Valsecchi, Antonino. *Ritratti o Vite letterarie e paralleli di G.J. Rousseau e il Sig. di Voltaire, di Obbes e di Spinoza e Vita di Pietro Bayle*. Venice: Pasquali e Curti, 1816.

Venturi, Franco. 'The European Enlightenment.' *Italy and the Enlightenment*. Ed. Stuart Woolf. New York: New York UP, 1972. 1–32.

– *Italy and the Enlightenment*. Ed. Stuart Woolf. New York: New York UP, 1972.

Vercruysse, Jeroom, comp. *Les Voltairians*. 7 vols. Nendeln: KTO, 1978.

Villemain, Abel-François. *Tableau de la literature*. Paris: Didier, 1864.

Voltaire. *Candide*. Trans. Robert M. Adams. 2nd ed. New York: Norton, 1991.

– *The Complete Works: The English Essays of 1727*. Vol. 3B. Ed. David Williams. Oxford: Voltaire Foundation, 1996.

– *Correspondence*. Ed. Theodore Besterman. Banbury: Voltaire Foundation, 1971.

– *Dictionnaire philosophique*. Ed. Raymong Naves. Paris: Garnier, 1967.

– *Essai sur les moeurs et l'esprit des nations*. 2 vols. Ed. René Pomeau. Paris: Garnier, 1963.

– *La Henriade*. Ed. O.R. Taylor. 2nd ed. Geneva: Institut et musée Voltaire, 1970.

– *Letters on England*. Trans. Leonard Tancock. London: Penguin, 1980.

– *Mélanges*. Ed. Jacques van den Heuvel. Paris: Gallimard, 1961.

– *Les œuvres complètes*. Vol. 2. 2nd ed. Ed. O.R. Taylor. Geneva: Institut et musée Voltaire, 1970.

– *Les œuvres complètes: Brutus, tragédie.* Vol. 5. Ed. John Renwick. Oxford: Voltaire Foundation, 1998.
– *Les oeuvres complètes: Candide.* Vol. 48. Ed. René Pomeau. Oxford: Voltaire Foundation, 1968.
– *Les oeuvres complètes: Discours de M. de Voltaire à sa reception à l'Académie française.* Ed. Karlis Racevskis. Oxford: Voltaire Foundation, 2003.
– *Les oeuvres complètes: Mahomet.* Vol. 20B. Ed. Christopher Todd. Oxford: Voltaire Foundation, 2002.
– *Les œuvres complètes: La mort de César.* Vol. 8. Ed. D.J. Fletcher. Oxford: Voltaire Foundation, 1988.
– *Les œuvres complètes: Œdipe.* Vol. 1A. Ed. David Jory. Oxford: Voltaire Foundation, 2001.
– *Philosophical Dictionary.* 2 vols. London: W.W. Dugdale, 1843.
– *Philosophical Dictionary.* Trans. Theodore Besterman. New York: Penguin, 1979.
– *Romans et contes.* Ed. Frédéric Deloffre and Jacques van den Heuvel. Paris: Gallimard, 1979.
Wahl, Jean. 'La bipolarité de Rousseau.' *Annales de la société J.-J. Rousseau* 33 (1953–5): 49–55.
Weber, Max. *The Protestant Ethic and the Spirit of Capitalism.* Trans. Talcott Parsons. New York: Scribner's, 1958.
Weisberg, Richard H. 'The Formalistic Model.' *Notes from Underground.* Trans. Michael Katz. New York: Norton, 1989. 190–202.
Ziolkowski, Eric J. *The Sanctification of Don Quixote.* University Park: Pennsylvania State UP, 1996.

Index